Lecture Notes in Computer Science 14144

Founding Editors

Gerhard Goos
Juris Hartmanis

The series Lecture Notes in Computer Science (LNCS), including its subseries Lecture Notes in Artificial Intelligence (LNAI) and Lecture Notes in Bioinformatics (LNBI), has established itself as a medium for the publication of new developments in computer science and information technology research, teaching, and education.

LNCS enjoys close cooperation with the computer science R & D community, the series counts many renowned academics among its volume editors and paper authors, and collaborates with prestigious societies. Its mission is to serve this international community by providing an invaluable service, mainly focused on the publication of conference and workshop proceedings and postproceedings. LNCS commenced publication in 1973.

José Abdelnour Nocera ·
Marta Kristín Lárusdóttir · Helen Petrie ·
Antonio Piccinno · Marco Winckler
Editors

Human-Computer Interaction – INTERACT 2023

19th IFIP TC13 International Conference
York, UK, August 28 – September 1, 2023
Proceedings, Part III

 Springer

Editors
José Abdelnour Nocera 🆔
University of West London
London, UK

Helen Petrie 🆔
University of York
York, UK

Marco Winckler 🆔
Université Côte d'Azur
Sophia Antipolis Cedex, France

Marta Kristín Lárusdóttir 🆔
Reykjavik University
Reykjavik, Iceland

Antonio Piccinno 🆔
University of Bari Aldo Moro
Bari, Italy

ISSN 0302-9743   ISSN 1611-3349 (electronic)
Lecture Notes in Computer Science
ISBN 978-3-031-42285-0   ISBN 978-3-031-42286-7 (eBook)
https://doi.org/10.1007/978-3-031-42286-7

This Springer imprint is published by the registered company Springer Nature Switzerland AG
The registered company address is: Gewerbestrasse 11, 6330 Cham, Switzerland

Foreword

INTERACT 2023 is the 19th International Conference of Technical Committee 13 (Human-Computer Interaction) of IFIP (International Federation for Information Processing). IFIP was created in 1960 under the auspices of UNESCO. The IFIP Technical Committee 13 (TC13) aims at developing the science and technology of human-computer interaction (HCI). TC13 started the series of INTERACT conferences in 1984. These conferences have been an important showcase for researchers and practitioners in the field of HCI. Situated under the open, inclusive umbrella of IFIP, INTERACT has been truly international in its spirit and has attracted researchers from several countries and cultures. The venues of the INTERACT conferences over the years bear testimony to this inclusiveness.

INTERACT 2023 was held from August 28th to September 1st 2023 at the University of York, York, United Kingdom. The INTERACT Conference is held every two years, and is one of the longest-running conferences on Human-Computer Interaction. The INTERACT 2023 Conference was held both in-person and online. It was collocated with the British Computer Society HCI 2023 Conference.

The theme of the 19th conference was "Design for Equality and Justice". Increasingly computer science as a discipline is becoming concerned about issues of justice and equality – from fake news to rights for robots, from the ethics of driverless vehicles to the Gamergate controversy. The HCI community is surely well placed to be at the leading edge of such discussions within the wider computer science community and in the dialogue between computer science and the broader society. Justice and equality are particularly important concepts both for the City of York and for the University of York. The City of York has a long history of working for justice and equality, from the Quakers and their philanthropic chocolate companies, to current initiatives. The City of York is the UK's first Human Rights City, encouraging organizations and citizens to "increasingly think about human rights, talk about human rights issues and stand up for rights whether that's at work, school or home". The City of York has also launched "One Planet York", a network of organizations working towards a more sustainable, resilient and collaborative "one planet" future. York is now working to become the first "Zero emissions" city centre, with much of the medieval centre already car free.

Finally, great research is the heart of a good conference. Like its predecessors, INTERACT 2023 aimed to bring together high-quality research. As a multidisciplinary field, HCI requires interaction and discussion among diverse people with different interests and background. We thank all the authors who chose INTERACT 2023 as the venue to publish their research.

We received a total of 375 submissions distributed in 2 peer-reviewed tracks, 4 curated tracks, and 3 juried tracks. Of these, the following contributions were accepted:

- 71 Full Papers (peer reviewed)
- 58 Short Papers (peer reviewed)
- 6 Courses (curated)

- 2 Industrial Experience papers (curated)
- 10 Interactive Demonstrations (curated)
- 44 Interactive Posters (juried)
- 2 Panels (curated)
- 16 Workshops (juried)
- 15 Doctoral Consortium (juried)

The acceptance rate for contributions received in the peer-reviewed tracks was 32% for full papers and 31% for short papers. In addition to full papers and short papers, the present proceedings feature contributions accepted in the form of industrial experiences, courses, interactive demonstrations, interactive posters, panels, invited keynote papers, and descriptions of accepted workshops. The contributions submitted to workshops were published as an independent post-proceedings volume.

The reviewing process was primary carried out by a panel of international experts organized in subcommittees. Each subcommittee had a chair and a set of associated chairs, who were in charge of coordinating a double-blind reviewing process. Each paper received at least 2 reviews of associated chairs and two reviews from external experts in the HCI field. Hereafter we list the twelve subcommittees of INTERACT 2023:

- Accessibility and assistive technologies
- Design for business and safety/critical interactive systems
- Design of interactive entertainment systems
- HCI Education and Curriculum
- HCI for Justice and Equality
- Human-AI interaction
- Information visualization
- Interaction design for culture and development
- Interactive systems technologies and engineering
- Methodologies for HCI
- Social and ubiquitous Interaction
- Understanding users and human behaviour

The final decision on acceptance or rejection of full papers was taken in a Programme Committee meeting held in London, United Kingdom in March 2023. The full papers chairs, the subcommittee chairs, and the associate chairs participated in this meeting. The meeting discussed a consistent set of criteria to deal with inevitable differences among the large number of reviewers. The final decisions on other tracks were made by the corresponding track chairs and reviewers, often after electronic meetings and discussions.

INTERACT 2023 was made possible by the persistent efforts across several months by 12 subcommittee chairs, 86 associated chairs, 28 track chairs, and 407 reviewers. We thank them all.

September 2023

José Abdelnour Nocera
Helen Petrie
Marco Winckler

IFIP TC13 – http://ifip-tc13.org/

Established in 1989, the International Federation for Information Processing Technical Committee on Human–Computer Interaction (IFIP TC13) is an international committee of 37 IFIP Member national societies and 10 Working Groups, representing specialists of the various disciplines contributing to the field of human-computer interaction (HCI). This field includes, among others, human factors, ergonomics, cognitive science, computer science and design. INTERACT is the flagship conference of IFIP TC13, staged biennially in different countries in the world. The first INTERACT conference was held in 1984, at first running triennially and becoming a biennial event in 1993.

IFIP TC13 aims to develop the science, technology and societal aspects of HCI by encouraging empirical research promoting the use of knowledge and methods from the human sciences in design and evaluation of computing technology systems; promoting better understanding of the relation between formal design methods and system usability and acceptability; developing guidelines, models and methods by which designers may provide better human-oriented computing technology systems; and, cooperating with other groups, inside and outside IFIP, to promote user-orientation and humanization in system design. Thus, TC13 seeks to improve interactions between people and computing technology, to encourage the growth of HCI research and its practice in industry and to disseminate these benefits worldwide.

The main orientation is to place the users at the centre of the development process. Areas of study include: the problems people face when interacting with computing technology; the impact of technology deployment on people in individual and organisational contexts; the determinants of utility, usability, acceptability and user experience; the appropriate allocation of tasks between computing technology and users, especially in the case of autonomous and closed-loop systems; modelling the user, their tasks and the interactive system to aid better system design; and harmonizing the computing technology to user characteristics and needs.

While the scope is thus set wide, with a tendency toward general principles rather than particular systems, it is recognised that progress will only be achieved through both general studies to advance theoretical understanding and specific studies on practical issues (e.g., interface design standards, software system resilience, documentation, training material, appropriateness of alternative interaction technologies, guidelines, the problems of integrating multimedia systems to match system needs and organisational practices, etc.).

IFIP TC13 also stimulates working events and activities through its Working Groups (WGs). The WGs consist of HCI experts from around the world, who seek to expand knowledge and find solutions to HCI issues and concerns within their domains. The list of current TC13 WGs and their area of interest is given below:

- WG 13.1 (Education in HCI and HCI Curricula) aims to improve HCI education at all levels of higher education, coordinate and unite efforts to develop HCI curricula and promote HCI teaching.

- WG 13.2 (Methodology for User-Centred System Design) aims to foster research, dissemination of information and good practice in the methodical application of HCI to software engineering.
- WG 13.3 (Human Computer Interaction, Disability and Aging) aims to make HCI designers aware of the needs of people with disabilities and older people and encourage development of information systems and tools permitting adaptation of interfaces to specific users.
- WG 13.4/WG2.7 (User Interface Engineering) investigates the nature, concepts and construction of user interfaces for software systems, using a framework for reasoning about interactive systems and an engineering model for developing user interfaces.
- WG 13.5 (Resilience, Reliability, Safety and Human Error in System Development) seeks a framework for studying human factors relating to systems failure, develops leading-edge techniques in hazard analysis and safety engineering of computer-based systems, and guides international accreditation activities for safety-critical systems.
- WG 13.6 (Human-Work Interaction Design) aims at establishing relationships between extensive empirical work-domain studies and HCI design. It will promote the use of knowledge, concepts, methods and techniques that enable user studies to procure a better apprehension of the complex interplay between individual, social and organisational contexts and thereby a better understanding of how and why people work in the ways that they do.
- WG 13.7 (Human–Computer Interaction and Visualization) aims to establish a study and research program that will combine both scientific work and practical applications in the fields of Human–Computer Interaction and Visualization. It will integrate several additional aspects of further research areas, such as scientific visualization, data mining, information design, computer graphics, cognition sciences, perception theory, or psychology into this approach.
- WG 13.8 (Interaction Design and International Development) aims to support and develop the research, practice and education capabilities of HCI in institutions and organisations based around the world taking into account their diverse local needs and cultural perspectives.
- WG 13.9 (Interaction Design and Children) aims to support practitioners, regulators and researchers to develop the study of interaction design and children across international contexts.
- WG 13.10 (Human-Centred Technology for Sustainability) aims to promote research, design, development, evaluation, and deployment of human-centred technology to encourage sustainable use of resources in various domains.

IFIP TC13 recognises contributions to HCI through both its Pioneer in HCI Award and various paper awards associated with each INTERACT conference. Since the processes to decide the various awards take place after papers are sent to the publisher for publication, the recipients of the awards are not identified in the proceedings.

The IFIP TC13 Pioneer in Human-Computer Interaction Award recognises the contributions and achievements of pioneers in HCI. An IFIP TC13 Pioneer is one who, through active participation in IFIP Technical Committees or related IFIP groups, has made outstanding contributions to the educational, theoretical, technical, commercial, or professional aspects of analysis, design, construction, evaluation, and use of interactive systems. The IFIP TC13 Pioneer Awards are presented during an awards ceremony at each INTERACT conference.

In 1999, TC13 initiated a special IFIP Award, the Brian Shackel Award, for the most outstanding contribution in the form of a refereed paper submitted to and delivered at each INTERACT Conference, which draws attention to the need for a comprehensive human-centred approach in the design and use of information technology in which the human and social implications have been considered. The IFIP TC13 Accessibility Award, launched in 2007 by IFIP WG 13.3, recognises the most outstanding contribution with international impact in the field of ageing, disability, and inclusive design in the form of a refereed paper submitted to and delivered at the INTERACT Conference. The IFIP TC13 Interaction Design for International Development Award, launched in 2013 by IFIP WG 13.8, recognises the most outstanding contribution to the application of interactive systems for social and economic development of people around the world taking into account their diverse local needs and cultural perspectives. The IFIP TC13 Pioneers' Award for Best Doctoral Student Paper at INTERACT, first awarded in 2019, is selected by the past recipients of the IFIP TC13 Pioneer title. The award is made to the best research paper accepted to the INTERACT Conference which is based on the doctoral research of the student and authored and presented by the student.

In 2015, TC13 approved the creation of a steering committee for the INTERACT conference. The Steering Committee (SC) is currently chaired by Marco Winckler and is responsible for:

- Promoting and maintaining the INTERACT conference as the premiere venue for researchers and practitioners interested in the topics of the conference (this requires a refinement of the topics above).
- Ensuring the highest quality for the contents of the event.
- Setting up the bidding process to handle future INTERACT conferences. Decision is made up at TC13 level.
- Providing advice to the current and future chairs and organizers of the INTERACT conference.
- Providing data, tools, and documents about previous conferences to future conference organizers.
- Selecting the reviewing system to be used throughout the conference (as this impacts the entire set of reviewers).
- Resolving general issues involved with the INTERACT conference.
- Capitalizing on history (good and bad practices).

Further information is available at the IFIP TC13 website: http://ifip-tc13.org/.

IFIP TC13 Members

Officers

Chair

Paula Kotzé, South Africa

Vice-chair for Conferences

Marco Winckler, France

Vice-chair for Equity and Development

José Abdelnour-Nocera, UK

Vice-chair for Media and Communications

Helen Petrie, UK

Vice-chair for Membership and Collaboration

Philippe Palanque, France

Vice-chair for Working Groups

Simone D. J. Barbosa, Brazil

Vice-chair for Finance (Treasurer)

Regina Bernhaupt, The Netherlands

Secretary

Janet Wesson, South Africa

INTERACT Steering Committee Chair

Marco Winckler, France

Country Representatives

Australia

Henry B. L. Duh
Australian Computer Society

Austria

Christopher Frauenberger
Austrian Computer Society

Belgium

Bruno Dumas
IMEC – Interuniversity
Micro-Electronics Center

Brazil

André Freire
Simone D. J. Barbosa (section b)
Sociedade Brasileira de Computação
(SBC)

Bulgaria

Petia Koprinkova-Hristova
Bulgarian Academy of Sciences

Croatia

Andrina Granić
Croatian Information Technology
Association (CITA)

Cyprus

Panayiotis Zaphiris
Cyprus Computer Society

Czech Republic

Zdeněk Míkovec
Czech Society for Cybernetics and
Informatics

Denmark

Jan Stage
Danish Federation for Information
Processing (DANFIP)

Finland

Virpi Roto
Finnish Information Processing
Association

France

Philippe Palanque
Marco Winckler (section b)
Société informatique de France (SIF)

Germany

Tom Gross
Gesellschaft fur Informatik e.V.

Ireland

Liam J. Bannon
Irish Computer Society

Italy

Fabio Paternò
Associazione Italiana per l' Informatica ed
il Calcolo Automatico (AICA)

Japan

Yoshifumi Kitamura
Information Processing Society of Japan

Netherlands

Regina Bernhaupt
Koninklijke Nederlandse Vereniging
van Informatieprofessionals (KNVI)

New Zealand

Mark Apperley
Institute of IT Professionals New Zealand

Norway

Frode Eika Sandnes
Norwegian Computer Society

Poland

Marcin Sikorski
Polish Academy of Sciences (PAS)

Portugal

Pedro Filipe Pereira Campos
Associacão Portuguesa para o
Desenvolvimento da Sociedade da
Informação (APDSI)

Serbia

Aleksandar Jevremovic
Informatics Association of Serbia (IAS)

Singapore

Shengdong Zhao
Singapore Computer Society

Slovakia

Wanda Benešová
Slovak Society for Computer Science

Slovenia

Matjaž Kljun
Slovenian Computer Society
INFORMATIKA

South Africa

Janet L. Wesson
Paula Kotzé (section b)
Institute of Information Technology
Professionals South Africa (IITPSA)

Sri Lanka

Thilina Halloluwa
Computer Society of Sri Lanka (CSSL)

Sweden

Jan Gulliksen
Swedish Interdisciplinary Society for
Human-Computer Interaction
Dataföreningen i Sverige

Switzerland

Denis Lalanne
Schweizer Informatik Gesellschaft (SI)

United Kingdom

José Luis Abdelnour Nocera
Helen Petrie (section b)
British Computer Society (BCS),
Chartered Institute for IT

International Members at Large Representatives

ACM

Gerrit van der Veer
Association for Computing
Machinery

CLEI

César Collazos
Centro Latinoamericano de Estudios en
Informatica

Expert Members

Anirudha Joshi, India
Constantinos Coursaris, Canada
Carmelo Ardito, Italy
Daniel Orwa Ochieng, Kenya
David Lamas, Estonia
Dorian Gorgan, Romania
Eunice Sari, Australia/Indonesia
Fernando Loizides, UK/Cyprus
Geraldine Fitzpatrick, Austria

Ivan Burmistrov, Russia
Julio Abascal, Spain
Kaveh Bazargan, Iran
Marta Kristin Lárusdóttir, Iceland
Nikolaos Avouris, Greece
Peter Forbrig, Germany
Torkil Clemmensen, Denmark
Zhengjie Liu, China

Working Group Chairpersons

WG 13.1 (Education in HCI and HCI Curricula)

Konrad Baumann, Austria

WG 13.2 (Methodologies for User-Centered System Design)

Regina Bernhaupt, Netherlands

WG 13.3 (HCI, Disability and Aging)

Helen Petrie, UK

WG 13.4/2.7 (User Interface Engineering)

Davide Spano, Italy

WG 13.5 (Human Error, Resilience, Reliability, Safety and System Development)

Tilo Mentler, Germany

WG13.6 (Human-Work Interaction Design)

Barbara Rita Barricelli, Italy

WG13.7 (HCI and Visualization)

Gerrit van der Veer, Netherlands

WG 13.8 (Interaction Design and International Development)

José Adbelnour Nocera, UK

WG 13.9 (Interaction Design and Children)

Gavin Sim, UK

WG 13.10 (Human-Centred Technology for Sustainability)

Masood Masoodian, Finland

Organization

General Chairs

Helen Petrie   University of York, UK
Jose Abdelnour-Nocera   University of West London, UK and ITI/Larsys, Portugal

Technical Program Chair

Marco Winckler   Université Côte d'Azur, France

Full Papers Chairs

Antonio Piccinno   University of Bari Aldo Moro, Italy
Marta Kristin Lárusdóttir   Reykjavik University, Iceland

Short Papers Chairs

Marta Rey-Babarro   Zillow, USA
Frode Eika Sandnes   Oslo Metropolitan University, Norway
Grace Eden   University of York, UK

Poster Chairs

Alena Denisova   University of York, UK
Burak Merdenyan   University of York, UK

Workshops Chairs

Jan Stage   Aalborg University, Denmark
Anna Bramwell-Dicks   University of York, UK

Panels Chairs

Effie Lai-Chong Law   Durham University, UK
Massimo Zancanaro   University of Trento, Italy

Student Volunteers Chairs

Sanjit Samaddar   University of York, UK
Daniel Lock   University of York, UK

Interactive Demonstrations Chairs

Barbara Rita Barricelli   University of Brescia, Italy
Jainendra Shukla   Indraprastha Institute of Information Technology,
                             India

Courses Chairs

Nikos Avouris   University of Patras, Greece
André Freire   Federal University of Lavras, Brazil

Doctoral Consortium Chairs

David Lamas   Tallinn University, Estonia
Geraldine Fitzpatrick   TU Wien, Austria
Tariq Zaman   University of Technology Sarawak, Malaysia

Industrial Experiences Chairs

Helen Petrie   University of York, UK
Jose Abdelnour-Nocera   University of West London, UK and ITI/Larsys,
                             Portugal

Publicity Chairs

Delvin Varghese   Monash University, Australia
Lourdes Moreno   Universidad Carlos III de Madrid, Spain

Advisors

Marco Winckler	University of the Côte d'Azur, France
Fernando Loizides	Cardiff University, UK
Carmelo Ardito	LUM Giuseppe Degennaro University, Italy

Web Master

Edmund Wei	University of York, UK

INTERACT Subcommittee Chairs

Anirudha Joshi	Industrial Design Centre, IIT Bombay, India
Célia Martinie	IRIT, Université Toulouse III - Paul Sabatier, France
Fabio Paternò	CNR-ISTI, Pisa, Italy
Frank Steinicke	Universität Hamburg, Germany
Gerhard Weber	TU Dresden, Germany
Helen Petrie	University of York, UK
José Campos	University of Minho, Portugal
Nikolaos Avouris	University of Patras, Greece
Philippe Palanque	IRIT, Université Toulouse III - Paul Sabatier, France
Rosa Lanzilotti	University of Bari, Italy
Rosella Gennari	Free University of Bozen-Bolzano, Switzerland
Simone Barbosa	PUC-Rio, Brazil
Torkil Clemmensen	Copenhagen Business School, Denmark
Yngve Dahl	Norwegian University of Science and Technology, Norway

INTERACT Steering Committee

Anirudha Joshi	Industrial Design Centre, IIT Bombay, India
Antonio Piccinno	University of Bari, Italy
Carmelo Arditto	University of Bari, Italy
Fernando Loizides	University of Cardiff, UK
Frode Sandnes	Oslo Metropolitan University, Norway
Helen Petrie	University of York, UK
Janet Wesson	Nelson Mandela University, South Africa
Marco Winckler (Chair)	Université Côte d'Azur, France
Marta Lárusdóttir	Reykjavik University, Iceland

Paolo Buono	University of Bari, Italy
Paula Kotzé	University of Pretoria, South Africa
Philippe Palanque	IRIT, Université Toulouse III - Paul Sabatier, France
Raquel Oliveira Prates	Universidade Federal de Minas Gerais, Brazil
Tom Gross	University of Bamberg, Germany

Program Committee

Alan Chamberlain	University of Nottingham, UK
Alessandra Melonio	Ca' Foscari University of Venice, Italy
Alessandro Pagano	University of Bari, Italy
Andrea Marrella	Sapienza Università di Roma, Italy
Andrés Lucero	Aalto University, Finland
Anna Sigríður Islind	Reykjavik University, Iceland
Antonio Piccinno	University of Bari, Italy
Ashley Colley	University of Lapland, Finland
Aurora Constantin	University of Edinburgh, UK
Barbara Rita Barricelli	Università degli Studi di Brescia, Italy
Bridget Kane	Karlstad University Business School, Sweden
Bruno Dumas	University of Namur, Belgium
Carla Dal Sasso Freitas	Federal University of Rio Grande do Sul, Brazil
Célia Martinie	Université Toulouse III - Paul Sabatier, France
Chi Vi	University of Sussex, UK
Christopher Power	University of Prince Edward Island, Canada
Christopher Clarke	University of Bath, UK
Cristian Bogdan	KTH, EECS, HCT, Sweden
Cristina Gena	Università di Torino, Italy
Dan Fitton	University of Central Lancashire, UK
Daniela Fogli	University of Brescia, Italy
Daniela Trevisan	Universidade Federal Fluminense, Brazil
Denis Lalanne	University of Fribourg, Switzerland
Dipanjan Chakraborty	BITS Pilani, Hyderabad Campus, India
Fabio Buttussi	University of Udine, Italy
Federico Cabitza	University of Milano-Bicocca, Italy
Fernando Loizides	Cardiff University, UK
Frode Eika Sandnes	Oslo Metropolitan University, Norway
Gerd Bruder	University of Central Florida, USA
Gerhard Weber	TU Dresden, Germany
Giuliana Vitiello	Università di Salerno, Italy
Giuseppe Desolda	University of Bari Aldo Moro, Italy

Sumita Sharma	University of Oulu, Finland
Sven Mayer	LMU Munich, Germany
Tania Di Mascio	Università dell'Aquila, Italy
Theodoros Georgiou	Heriot-Watt University, UK
Thilina Halloluwa	University of Colombo, Sri Lanka
Tilo Mentler	Trier University of Applied Sciences, Germany
Timothy Merritt	Aalborg University, Denmark
Tom Gross	University of Bamberg, Germany
Valentin Schwind	Frankfurt University of Applied Sciences, Germany
Virpi Roto	Aalto University, Finland
Vita Santa Barletta	University of Bari Aldo Moro, Italy
Vivian Genaro Motti	George Mason University, USA
Wricha Mishra	MIT Institute of Design, India
Zdeněk Míkovec	Czech Technical University Prague, Czech Republic
Zeynep Yildiz	Koç University, Turkey

Additional Reviewers

Abhishek Shrivastava
Adalberto Simeone
Aditya Prakash Kulkarni
Adrien Chaffangeon Caillet
Adrien Coppens
Aekaterini Mavri
Ahmad Samer Wazan
Aidan Slingsby
Aimee Code
Aizal Yusrina Idris
Akihisa Shitara
Aku Visuri
Alberto Monge Roffarello
Alessandro Forgiarini
Alessio Malizia
Alex Binh Vinh Duc Nguyen
Alex Chen
Alexander Maedche
Alexander Meschtscherjakov
Alexander Wachtel
Alexandra Voit
Alexandre Canny
Ali Gheitasy

Aline Menin
Alisson Puska
Alma Cantu
Amy Melniczuk
An Jacobs
Ana Serrano
Anderson Maciel
André Freire
Andre Salgado
Andre Suslik Spritzer
Andrea Antonio Cantone
Andrea Bellucci
Andrea Esposito
Andreas Fender
Andreas Mallas
Andreas Sonderegger
Andres Santos-Torres
Ángel Cuevas
Angela Locoro
Angus Addlesee
Angus Marshall
Anicia Peters
Anirudh Nagraj

Ankica Barisic
Anna Spagnolli
Annika Schulz
Anthony Perritano
Antigoni Parmaxi
Antje Jacobs
Antonella Varesano
Antonio Bucchiarone
Antonio Piccinno
Anupriya Tuli
Argenis Ramirez Gomez
Arminda Lopes
Arnaud Blouin
Ashwin Singh
Ashwin T. S.
Asim Evren Yantac
Axel Carayon
Aykut Coşkun
Azra Ismail
Barsha Mitra
Basmah Almekhled
Beat Signer
Beenish Chaudhry
Behnaz Norouzi
Benjamin Schnitzer
Benjamin Tag
Benjamin Weyers
Berardina De Carolis
Bharatwaja Namatherdhala
Bhumika Walia
Biju Thankachan
Bram van Deurzen
Çağlar Genç
Canlin Zhang
Carolyn Holter
Céline Coutrix
Chameera De Silva
Charlotte Magnusson
Chiara Ceccarini
Chiara Natali
Chikodi Chima
Christian Frisson
Christophe Kolski
Christopher Frauenberger
Christos Katsanos

Christos Sintoris
Cléber Corrêa
Cleidson de Souza
Daisuke Sato
Damianos Dumi Sigalas
Damon Horowitz
Dan Fitton
Daniel Görlich
Daniel Zielasko
Danielle Langlois
Daphne Chang
Dario Bertero
David Gollasch
David Navarre
Davide D'Adamo
Davide Mulfari
Davide Spallazzo
Debjani Roy
Diana Korka
Diego Morra
Dilrukshi Gamage
Diogo Cabral
Dixie Ching
Domenico Gigante
Dominic Potts
Donald McMillan
Edwige Pissaloux
Edy Portmann
Effie Law
Eike Schneiders
Elisa Mekler
Elise Grevet
Elizabeth Buie
Elodie Bouzbib
Emanuele Pucci
Enes Yigitbas
Eric Barboni
Estela Peralta
Euan Freeman
Evangelia Chrysikou
Evelyn Eika
Fabiana Vernero
Fabio Cassano
Fabrizio Balducci
Fanny Vainionpää

Fausto Medola
Favour Aladesuru
Federica Cena
Federico Botella
Florian Gnadlinger
Francesco Cauteruccio
Francesco Chiossi
Francesco Ferrise
Francesco Greco
Francisco Iniesto
Francisco Maria Calisto
Frank Beruscha
Frank Fischer
Frank Nack
Frida Milella
Funmi Adebesin
Gavin Sim
George Adrian Stoica
George Raptis
Georgios Papadoulis
Gianluca Schiavo
Girish Dalvi
Grischa Liebel
Guanhua Zhang
Guilherme Schardong
Gustavo Rovelo Ruiz
Hanne Sørum
Heidi Hartikainen
Himanshu Verma
Holger Regenbrecht
Hsin-Jou Lin
Hui-Yin Wu
Ikram Ur Rehman
Isabela Gasparini
Ivo Malý
Jack Jamieson
James Simpson
Jan Leusmann
Jana Jost
Jannes Peeters
Jari Kangas
Jayden Khakurel
Jean Hallewell Haslwanter
Jemma König
Jermaine Marshall

Jeroen Ceyssens
Jesper Gaarsdal
Jessica Sehrt
Jiaying Liu
Job Timmermans
Joe Cutting
Jonas Moll
Jonathan Hook
Joni Salminen
Joongi Shin
Jorge Wagner
José Campos
Joseph O'Hagan
Judith Borghouts
Julia Hertel
Julio Reis
Kajetan Enge
Kasper Rodil
Kate Rogers
Katerina Cerna
Katherine Seyama
Kathia Oliveira
Kathrin Gerling
Khyati Priya
Konstantin Biriukov
Kostantinos Moustakas
Krishna Venkatasubramanian
Laden Husamaldin
Lars Lischke
Lars Oestreicher
Laura Helsby
Leena Ventä-Olkkonen
Lele Sha
Leonardo Sandoval
Lorena Riol-Blanco
Lorenzo Torrez
Louise Barkhuus
Luis Leiva
Luis Teran
M. Cristina Vannini
Maälis Lefebvre
Magdaléna Kejstová
Malay Dhamelia
Manik Gupta
Manuel J. Fonseca

Marco de Gemmis
Marco Manca
Marco Romano
Margarita Anastassova
Margault Sacré
Margherita Andrao
Mari Karhu
Maria Fernanda Antunes
María Óskarsdóttir
Marianna Di Gregorio
Marika Jonsson
Marios Constantinides
Mark Apperley
Mark Lochrie
Marko Tkalcic
Markus Löchtefeld
Markus Tatzgern
Marta Serafini
Martin Hedlund
Martin Kocur
Massimo Zancanaro
Mateusz Dubiel
Matthias Baldauf
Matthias Heintz
Max Birk
Maxime Savary-Leblanc
Maximiliano Jeanneret Medina
Mehdi Rizvi
Mengyu Chen
Michael Burch
Michael Rohs
Michalis Xenos
Mihail Terenti
Min Zhang
Mireia Ribera
Mirko De Vincentiis
Miroslav Macík
Mohd Kamal Othman
Monica Divitini
Monisha Pattanaik
Mrim Alnfiai
Murali Balusu
Nada Attar
Nadine Flegel
Nadine Vigouroux

Nadir Weibel
Nahal Norouzi
Najla Aldaraani
Nancy Alajarmeh
Nicholas Vanderschantz
Nicoletta Adamo
Niels van Berkel
Nikolaos Avouris
Nils Beese
Nivan Ferreira
Nurha Yingta
Ohoud Alharbi
Omar Al Hashimi
Pallabi Bhowmick
Pallavi Rao Gadahad
Panayiotis Koutsabasis
Paolo Massa
Parisa Saadati
Pascal Lessel
Patricia Arias-Cabarcos
Paula Alexandra Silva
Pavel Slavik
Peter Bago
Philippe Truillet
Pinar Simsek Caglar
Po-Ming Law
Prabodh Sakhardande
Pranjal Protim Borah
Quynh Nguyen
Radovan Madleňák
Ragad Allwihan
Rahat Jahangir Rony
Rajni Sachdeo
Razan Bamoallem
Rekha Sugandhi
Rishi Vanukuru
Rogério Bordini
Rohan Gaikwad
Romane Dubus
Rosella Gennari
Rui José
Sabrina Burtscher
Sabrina Lakhdhir
Sahar Mirhadi
Saif Hadj Sassi

Salvatore Andolina
Salvatore Sorce
Samangi Wadinambi Arachchi
Sanika Doolani
Sanjit Samaddar
Sara Capecchi
Sarah Hodge
Saumya Pareek
Scott MacKenzie
Scott Trent
Sebastian Feger
Sebastian Günther
Sebastian Weiß
Sébastien Scannella
Shah Rukh Humayoun
Shunyao Wu
Siddharth Gulati
Siiri Paananen
Silvia Espada
Silvia Gabrielli
Simon Ruffieux
Simon Voelker
Simone Barbosa
Siti Haris
Sónia Brito-Costa
Sophie Dupuy-Chessa
Sophie Lepreux
Soraia M. Alarcão
Srishti Gupta
Stefan Johansson
Stéphanie Fleck
Stine Johansen
Subrata Tikadar
Suzanna Schmeelk
Sybille Caffiau
Sylvain Malacria
Taejun Kim
Tahani Alahmadi
Tahani Albalawi
Takumi Yamamoto
Tariq Zaman
Tathagata Ray
Telmo Zarraonandia
Teresa Onorati
Tero Jokela
Theodoros Georgiou

Thomas Kosch
Tilman Dingler
Tom Veuskens
Tomas Alves
Tomáš Pagáč
Tomi Heimonen
Tommaso Turchi
Tong Wu
Tzu-Yang Wang
Valentino Artizzu
Vanessa Cesário
Vanessa Maike
Vania Neris
Vasiliki Mylonopoulou
Vera Memmesheimer
Vickie Nguyen
Victor Adriel de Jesus Oliveira
Vidushani Dhanawansa
Vikas Upadhyay
Vincent Zakka
Vincenzo Dentamaro
Vincenzo Gattulli
Vinitha Gadiraju
Vit Rusnak
Vittoria Frau
Vivek Kant
Way Kiat Bong
Weiqin Chen
Wenchen Guo
William Delamare
Xiying Wang
Yann Savoye
Yao Chen
Yaoli Mao
Yaxiong Lei
Yilin Liu
Ying Ma
Yingying Zhao
Yong-Joon Thoo
Yoselyn Walsh
Yosra Rekik
Yuan Chen
Yubo Kou
Zhiyuan Wang
Zi Wang

Sponsors and Partners

Sponsors

Partners

International Federation for Information Processing

In-cooperation with ACM

In-cooperation with SIGCHI

Contents – Part III

Recommendation Systems and AI Explainability

Social AI

Social and Ubiquitous Computing I and II

Social Media and Digital Learning

Understanding Users and Privacy Issues

User Movement and 3D Environments

Natural Language Processing and AI Explainability

Exploring Natural Language Processing Methods for Interactive Behaviour Modelling

Guanhua Zhang[1], Matteo Bortoletto[1], Zhiming Hu[1,2(✉)], Lei Shi[1],
Mihai Bâce[1], and Andreas Bulling[1]

[1] Institute for Visualisation and Interactive Systems, Stuttgart, Germany
{guanhua.zhang,matteo.bortoletto,zhiming.hu,lei.shi
mihai.bace,andreas.bulling}@vis.uni-stuttgart.de
[2] Institute for Modelling and Simulation of Biomechanical Systems,
University of Stuttgart, Stuttgart, Germany

Abstract. Analysing and modelling interactive behaviour is an important topic in human-computer interaction (HCI) and a key requirement for the development of intelligent interactive systems. Interactive behaviour has a sequential (actions happen one after another) and hierarchical (a sequence of actions forms an activity driven by interaction goals) structure, which may be similar to the structure of natural language. Designed based on such a structure, natural language processing (NLP) methods have achieved groundbreaking success in various downstream tasks. However, few works linked interactive behaviour with natural language. In this paper, we explore the similarity between interactive behaviour and natural language by applying an NLP method, byte pair encoding (BPE), to encode mouse and keyboard behaviour. We then analyse the vocabulary, i.e., the set of action sequences, learnt by BPE, as well as use the vocabulary to encode the input behaviour for interactive task recognition. An existing dataset collected in constrained lab settings and our novel out-of-the-lab dataset were used for evaluation. Results show that this natural language-inspired approach not only learns action sequences that reflect specific interaction goals, but also achieves higher F1 scores on task recognition than other methods. Our work reveals the similarity between interactive behaviour and natural language, and presents the potential of applying the new pack of methods that leverage insights from NLP to model interactive behaviour in HCI.

Keywords: Interactive Behaviour Modelling · Natural Language Processing · Mouse and Keyboard Input · Out-of-the-lab Dataset

1 Introduction

Computational modelling of interactive behaviour has emerged as a key component of intelligent user interfaces (IUIs) in human-computer interaction

J. Abdelnour Nocera et al. (Eds.): INTERACT 2023, LNCS 14144, pp. 3–26, 2023.
https://doi.org/10.1007/978-3-031-42286-7_1

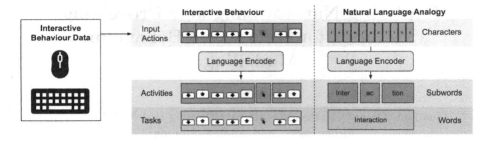

Fig. 1. Given that both interactive behaviour and natural language are sequential and hierarchical, we explored their similarity by applying an NLP method (a language encoder) to model mouse and keyboard behaviour.

(HCI) [2,3,14,66,70]. For example, understanding interactive behaviour helps HCI researchers and user experience (UX) designers analyse and improve interactive systems [7,51]. Mouse and keyboard input is particularly promising because it is readily available on a large number of devices and pervasively used in daily life [59,66]. Interactive behaviour consists of low-level, atomic input actions that cannot be further decomposed [41], which may resemble characters in natural language. Furthermore, a sequence of such actions (an activity) that can reflect higher-level interaction goals may resemble a (sub)word that is a sequence of characters with semantic meanings. As such, interactive behaviour has both a sequential (actions happen one after another) and a hierarchical structure (a sequence of actions forms an activity driven by specific interaction goals), and hence may be similar to natural language (see Fig. 1). On the other hand, NLP methods, leveraging the sequential and hierarchical structure of input data, have recently achieved groundbreaking success in various downstream tasks like machine translation and question-answering [32,34,36,45]. However, analysing the possible similarity and link between interactive behaviour and natural language remains under-explored in HCI. One notable exception is the work by Han et al. that encoded n consecutive actions (like mouse clicks) into tokens to learn action embeddings [21]. However, at its core, the method uses n-gram, which limits the length of action sequences to a fixed length n and requires a dedicated search for its optimal value. Moreover, the vocabulary size grows exponentially as n increases [57]. Due to such drawback, n-gram has been dropped in NLP in favour of more flexible methods such as byte pair encoding (BPE) [47,48]. BPE and its variants are used in a significant number of large language models (LLMs) to encode text as subwords, allowing rare or unseen words to be handled without introducing new tokens every time [53,54]. Additionally, subwords in the vocabulary generated by BPE can have various lengths, allowing a rich and flexible vocabulary. In this work, we explore the similarity between mouse and keyboard behaviour and natural language, by using BPE to learn a vocabulary, i.e., a set of activities, which is further used to encode the behaviour to perform interactive task recognition. Knowing which task the user is conducting is essential for adaptive interactive systems that aim to understand interactive behaviour and interaction goals [17,26,44].

Existing mouse and keyboard datasets were typically collected in controlled laboratory settings, although behaviour tends to be more natural in out-of-the-lab settings [40]. We evaluate the method on two datasets that cover both settings and offer both modalities. For the lab setting, we chose the Buffalo dataset collected by Sun et al. [59] as it is the largest available dataset [43]. For the out-of-the-lab setting, given a lack of suitable publicly available data, we collected a novel multimodal dataset named EMAKI (Everyday Mouse And Keyboard Interactions)[1] EMAKI was collected from 39 participants performing three interactive tasks: *text entry and editing*, *image editing* and *questionnaire completion*. These tasks can be found in a wide range of applications and UIs, and cover varying types of mouse and keyboard actions.

On the two datasets, vocabulary analysis shows that BPE could learn explainable activities, e.g., reflecting graphical user interface (GUI) layouts and indicating interaction goals such as performing mouse dragging or keyboard shortcuts. Results from interactive task recognition show that BPE outperformed other methods on both modalities and datasets. In summary, our contributions are three-fold: (1) We collect EMAKI, a novel 39-participant out-of-the-lab mouse and keyboard dataset. (2) We explore the potential similarity between natural language and mouse and keyboard behaviour by learning meaningful activities via a commonly used NLP method, BPE. (3) We show that encoding with BPE also improves the performance of interactive task recognition. As such, our work uncovers the similarity between natural language and interactive behaviour, showing the potential for applying the new pack of methodology, i.e., NLP methods, to computational interactive behaviour modelling in HCI.

2   Related Work

2.1   Modelling Interactive Behaviour in HCI

Classical HCI approaches include descriptive models, e.g., Fitts's Law [1], and predictive models, e.g., the keystroke-level model (KLM) [12]. However, they are limited in strict controls and modelling simple tasks like pointing to a target or routine tasks that have to be specified step by step [12]. Recent research used 1D convolutional neural networks (CNN) [25,28], long short-term memory (LSTM) [26] and gated recurrent unit (GRU) [26] to encode gaze and head behaviour, based on the sequential structure, while others focused on spatial analysis and modelling [28,29]. Specifically, Xu et al. modelled mouse and keyboard behaviour by accumulating cursor positions into binary attention maps [66]. Other researchers modelled interactive behaviour from a statistical perspective. For example, Borji et al. used Hidden Markov Models (HMM) to encode motor actions including mouse clicks, mouse positions, and joystick

---

[1] The dataset and code are available here: https://git.hcics.simtech.uni-stuttgart.de/public-projects/EMAKI.

positions in video games [8], while Sun et al. applied Gaussian mixture models (GMM) on keystrokes in text editing tasks [59]. Researchers also encoded eye movements [11] or gestures [55,63] into strings for activity recognition. Given that interactive behaviour has a sequential and hierarchical structure, which may resemble natural language, we explored modelling interactive behaviour from an NLP perspective.

2.2   Encoding Methods for Natural Language

Recent attractive success in NLP has been largely attributed to methods that efficiently encode characters [34], words [45] or sentences [50] into a vector representation. HCI researchers also followed this trend to model GUIs [38,61] or behavioural differences over time [21]. A key requirement for such methods is to encode or tokenise the input to generate a usable vocabulary of concepts. Due to the clear structure of natural language, NLP methods encode at the character, subword or word level. One popular approach is n-gram, which uses n words in a sequence to determine the context where commonly $n \leq 5$ [21,30,31,49]. However, such a method is limited by the choice of n, and the exponential increase of vocabulary size along n. More promising approaches learn a vocabulary of subwords, among which BPE has been widely used given that it allows rich and flexible vocabulary and understanding rare or unseen words [35,47,48,62]. Consequently, we employ BPE as the NLP method to create a vocabulary for interactive behaviour.

2.3   Analysis and Modelling of Mouse and Keyboard Behaviour

The mouse and keyboard are among the most widely used input modalities in daily interactions with computers [59,66]. Some researchers only focused on one modality, i.e., mouse or keyboard. Arapakis et al. explored different representations of mouse movements in web search tasks, including time series, heatmaps, and trajectory-based images [5], while Antal et al. employed 1D CNN to encode mouse actions including click and drag [3]. Dhakal et al. analysed keystroke patterns in a transcription typing task by correlation analysis [14], while Acien et al. employed LSTM to encode keystroke sequences in free text typing [2]. In contrast, Sun et al. explored both mouse and keyboard actions in two typing tasks, yet the work was limited to fully controlled laboratory settings [59].

3   Datasets for Evaluation

Although interactive behaviour, and specifically mouse and keyboard data, has been widely studied in HCI [59,66], most existing datasets have been collected in strictly controlled laboratory settings. Laboratory settings have the advantages of control and internal validity, but their ecological validity is highly limited [4]. Our out-of-the-lab data collection did not control where, when, how long and via which laptop or desktop participants could join, allowing more natural behaviour [40,46]. In addition, most datasets only include either mouse or keyboard data, while we opted for evaluations on both modalities. As such, we analysed mouse and keyboard behaviour from the in-the-lab Buffalo dataset [59] and EMAKI, a novel multimodal out-of-the-lab dataset that we collected specifically for this purpose, given lacking suitable publicly available data. To evaluate constraints in data collection from a time perspective, *task* and *study* completion times were calculated. The former only counts the time spent on tasks, while the latter refers to finishing the entire study, including pauses.

3.1   The Buffalo Dataset

To the best of our knowledge, Buffalo [59] is the largest publicly available in-the-lab dataset containing both mouse and keyboard interactions. The dataset was collected with standalone keyboards over three sessions. 148 participants performed two typing tasks: transcribing a pre-defined text and typical office activities, such as answering predefined questions and sending emails. The average number of mouse actions and keystrokes per participant exceeded 19 K and 17 K, respectively. 75 participants completed both tasks with the same keyboard, while the remaining used three keyboards across sessions. Data from the former 75 participants were used in this work for a more controlled condition, following [65]. The average *task* completion time was 41.71 mins (SD = 6.34), while the average *study* completion time was slightly longer, 41.81 mins (SD = 6.27), indicating that participants barely took breaks in this constrained setting.

3.2   The EMAKI Dataset

We opted for an online study including three tasks: text entry and editing, image editing, and questionnaire completion. These tasks can be found in a wide range of interactive applications and UIs, and cover varying types of mouse and keyboard actions [59,66]. Furthermore, the tasks are neither limited to a particular real-world application [9,13] nor too controlled or artificial [14,70,71], different from the typing-focused tasks in Buffalo. Two short assessments were designed to analyse if participants show different proficiencies in using mouse and keyboard.

The study was implemented as a web application and hosted on our university server. The link to the study was sent directly to the participants. The frontend was implemented in JavaScript, while the backend consisted of a Node.js server and an SQLite database. We recorded clicks and key presses with separate events for press and release, mouse movements and their associated timestamps.

Participants. We recruited 52 participants through university mailing lists and social networks. 12 participants who did not finish the study and one teenage participant were filtered out, leading to 39 participants in the end (18 female, 18 male and 3 "other gender"). Their ages ranged between 18 and 54 years (M = 25.05, SD = 6.51). Participants completed the study from 16 countries. On average, they reported having used mouse and keyboard for 13.64 years

Fig. 2. Screenshots of the three interactive tasks in our online study: (a) text entry and editing, (b) image editing, and (c) questionnaire completion.

(SD = 6.80). 15 participants used laptop touchpads, while the others used traditional mice. 28 participants used laptop keyboards and the rest used standalone keyboards.

Interactive Tasks. In task *text entry and editing*, participants wrote a piece of text in English in a text editor[2] for one trial (Fig. 2a). We did not specify the topic but offered suggestions, such as "summarise a movie/TV series/documentary that you recently watched" or "describe your pet". We asked participants to write ≥200 words and apply ≥15 formatting rules, e.g. change font size or alignment. We allowed any operation provided by the editor, such as copy-paste and undo. Two counters in the top left showed the number of words they already typed and formatting operations they applied. These counters were initially red and turned green once the minimum thresholds were reached.

In task *image editing*, participants were presented with two images shown side-by-side in an image editor[3] (Fig. 2b). The image on the left was a real photograph, whereas the image on the right was a sketch. On either or both sides, participants performed operations provided by the editor in any order they wanted. Candidate operations are drawing, cropping, flipping, rotating, adding icons and adding filters. To proceed to the next task, they had to perform at least 100 editing operations. In addition, we asked them to add at least one text box that contained a minimum of 10 characters. Similarly to the previous task, counters showed the task progress.

Questionnaire completion involved participants in completing four questionnaires[4], leading to four trials (Fig. 2c). These questionnaires served a dual purpose: providing information about participants, which can serve as metadata for future work on the dataset, while at the same time allowing us to record naturalistic mouse and keyboard data. The first questionnaire focused on demographics and included questions on gender, age, country of origin, country of residence, experience in using mouse and keyboard, and whether participants had any visual impairments. Afterwards were three widely-used personality question-

---

[2] https://github.com/tinymce/tinymce.
[3] https://github.com/nhn/tui.image-editor.
[4] https://github.com/surveyjs/survey-library.

naires: BFI-44 (Big Five)[5], BIS-11 (Barratt Impulsiveness Scale)[6] and BIS-BAS (the Behavioural Inhibition and Approach System)[7].

Procedure. Before starting with the tasks, participants were asked to carefully read the study goals and task descriptions. They were then asked whether they were using a mouse or touchpad, and a laptop or standalone keyboard. To start the study, participants had to click two checkboxes to confirm that (1) they had read and understood the goals of the study, and (2) their data may be published and analysed for research purposes. Afterwards, participants performed tasks in fullscreen. If they left the fullscreen mode during a task, the task was restarted. We opted for the design to discourage participants from multitasking. To reduce potential effects of task order, half of the initial 52 participants performed the text entry and editing task first, followed by the image editing task, while the other half performed in the inverse order. After data filtering, 24 participants did the text task and then image task, while the other 15 in the inverse order. We always showed questionnaires at the end, following studies that also collected personality questionnaires [24,42]. Detailed guidelines for tasks were available to participants throughout the study. Participants could contact us whenever they had questions, felt uncomfortable or unsure of any task or wanted to withdraw. Upon completion of the study, participants were shown their results of personality questionnaires as compensation. No monetary compensation was made.

Dataset Statistics. The average task completion time was 37.40 mins (SD = 13.91), in which 16.60 mins (SD = 8.51) were spent on text entry and editing, 6.15 mins (SD = 3.60) on image editing, and 9.84 mins (SD = 4.48) on questionnaires. The average study completion time was significantly longer, 55.33 mins (SD = 29.32). In total, we collected 1.14 M mouse actions and 205 K keyboard actions. 38% of mouse actions were generated from the image editing task, 43% from questionnaire completion, while only 19% came from the text entry and editing task. Text entry and editing contributed 92% of the keyboard actions, while only 8% were from the other two tasks (image editing: 3%, questionnaire completion: 5%).

Assessments of Proficiency. Before interactive tasks, our study also included two short assessments to analyse if participants who used different types of input devices showed different proficiencies in using mouse and keyboard. The two assessments were *text typing* for keyboard proficiency and *move and click* for mouse proficiency, shown in Fig. 3. *Text typing* involved copying a short piece of text (∼100 words, Fig. 3a) as quickly as possible [19]. The average duration of key presses and the number of keys pressed per minute were calculated as keyboard metrics [19]. *Move and click* was inspired by a Fitts's Law task [56], where participants clicked an orange dot that randomly appeared at a predefined location as quickly as possible over multiple rounds. Once clicked, the orange

---

[5] https://www.ocf.berkeley.edu/~johnlab/bfi.php.
[6] http://www.impulsivity.org/measurement/bis11.
[7] https://local.psy.miami.edu/people/faculty/ccarver/availbale-self-report-instruments/bisbas-scales/.

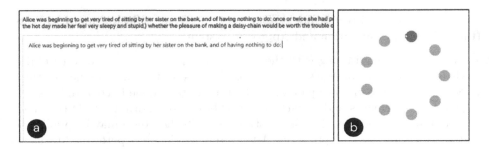

Fig. 3. Two proficiency assessments: (a) text typing and (b) move and click.

dot turned grey and another random dot turned orange (Fig. 3b). Fitts's law [15] models movement time as $MT = a + b\log_2\left(\frac{2d}{w}\right)$, where d is the distance between the centre of the target and the starting point; w is the width of the target; a and b are constants that can be interpreted as the delay and the acceleration. Based on d, w and MT recorded in *move and click*, we computed a and b via linear regression and used them as metrics of mouse proficiency.

Based on the type of mouse (touchpad vs. traditional mouse), we split participants into two groups and then calculated mouse metrics from data collected in the mouse assessment. A Mann-Whitney U test showed that both metrics were significantly different between the two groups. One reason is that touchpad and traditional mouse lead to different pointing speeds and accuracies [23]. Then, we split participants into two groups based on using a laptop or standalone keyboard. No significant difference was found in keyboard metrics calculated from the keyboard assessment.

4   Modelling Interactive Behaviour with an NLP Method

As Fig. 4 shows, the raw data (mouse and keyboard action sequences) are first segmented into subsequences. Core to our approach is BPE learning a vocabulary of subwords, i.e. a set of meaningful mouse and keyboard activities, and then encoding the behaviour based on the vocabulary. As BPE requires discrete inputs, mouse data are preprocessed additionally using the dispersion-threshold identification (I-DT) algorithm, that converts continuous-valued mouse coordinates into discrete tokens. The encodings generated by BPE are then evaluated in two ways to explore if a natural language-like structure exists in mouse and keyboard behaviour that can be captured by this widely used NLP method: (1) analyse the semantic meaning of the vocabulary, i.e., interaction goals underlying learnt activities, and (2) as input to train a Transformer-based classifier for task recognition. The two evaluations are demonstrated in Sect. 5.

4.1   Data Preprocessing

Different from natural language where words and sentences are separated by spaces and punctuations, modelling interactive behaviour first requires splitting

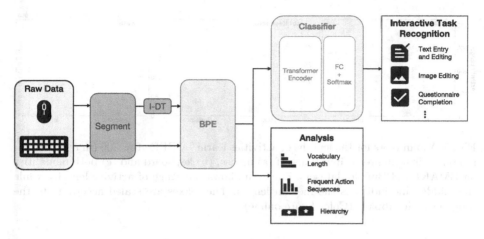

Fig. 4. Overview of our pipeline of exploring modelling interactive behaviour from an NLP perspective.

data into smaller units. Thus, a sliding non-overlapping window was used to segment the long raw data. On the keyboard actions, the window lengths L_{win} were empirically set to 10, 50, and 100. The window lengths L_{win} for the mouse actions were set to 20, 100 and 200, as we observed on both datasets that, the number of generated mouse actions for a fixed time window is roughly twice as many as the keyboard actions. When using both modalities jointly, the window lengths were set to the mean value of those for single modalities, i.e. $L_{win} = 15$, 75 and 150. For keyboard actions, the action type and the key value were concatenated as a token, e.g., *KeyDown_a* (a↓) or *KeyUp_Shift* (Shift↑). Buffalo recorded 91 key values, while EMAKI had 137 values, yielding 182 and 274 atomic actions forming the starting vocabulary, respectively. With more types of keys, EMAKI can potentially reflect more behaviour varieties.

Participants completed our study on their own computers with different screen resolutions, so we first re-scaled the mouse coordinates to $[0, 1]$. For consistency, we re-scaled Buffalo mouse data to the same range. We observed two categories of mouse behaviour: *pinpoint*, i.e. interacting with the target UI element in a small area, where moves are shorter, slower and more concentrated, resembling gaze fixations; and *re-direction* between targets, resembling fast saccadic eye movements between fixations [52]. Inspired by gaze fixation detection, we used I-DT [52] to preprocess mouse data (see Appendix). Then we divided the screen equally into four areas (0: top-left, 1: top-right, 2: bottom-left, 3: bottom-right). The action type (move or click), mouse behaviour category (pinpoint or re-direction), and the screen area were concatenated as a token, e.g., *Move_Redirection_Area0* or *Click_Pinpoint_Area3*. When representing clicks, Buffalo only recorded a *Click*, while we recorded both *Down* (press) and *Up* (release) events. Therefore, Buffalo has $2 \times 2 \times 4 = 16$ atomic actions and EMAKI has $3 \times 2 \times 4 = 24$.

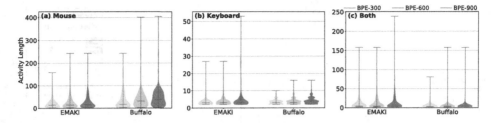

Fig. 5. Violin plots for the lengths of activities learnt by BPE after 300 (in red), 600 (in blue) and 900 (in green) iterations, of (a) mouse, (b) keyboard and (c) both modalities on EMAKI and Buffalo datasets. Each bar shows the range of activity lengths, while the middle line indicates the median length. The y-axes are scaled according to the range in each subplot. (Color figure online)

4.2   Encoding Mouse and Keyboard Behaviour with BPE

We employed BPE (see Appendix for its algorithm) to learn a vocabulary of subwords, i.e., activities that consist of various numbers of consecutive actions. Starting from the action sequence set D, the vocabulary V is built after k iterations. In each iteration, the most frequent pair of actions or activities form a new activity, which is added into V and used to update D. We consider each action as a character, given it is an inseparable, atomic unit. The initial vocabulary is composed of actions and one extra token representing the end of the action sequence from one task trial. Thus, the initial vocabulary sizes are $|V|_{mouse} = 17$ and $|V|_{key} = 183$ in Buffalo, and $|V|_{mouse} = 25$, $|V|_{key} = 275$ in EMAKI. We set k to 300, 600 and 900 empirically.

5   Evaluations of the NLP Method

As mentioned at the beginning of Sect. 4, BPE was evaluated in two ways: (1) we analysed its vocabulary to examine if the way of learning semantic subwords from characters could learn meaningful activities from interactive actions; and (2) we tested if encoding interactive behaviour in this NLP fashion benefited a downstream task, interactive task recognition, using a Transformer-based classifier.

5.1   Analysis of the Learnt Vocabulary

We first examined statistics of the vocabulary including its size and activity lengths. Then we analysed semantic meanings of the most frequent and long activities. Frequent activities are short, low-level and pervasively exist in various activities, while long activities reflect high-level and complex goals.

Table 1. Vocabulary sizes generated using BPE after 300, 600 and 900 iterations, on EMAKI and Buffalo datasets.

Dataset	EMAKI			Buffalo		
Method	BPE-300	BPE-600	BPE-900	BPE-300	BPE-600	BPE-900
Mouse	322	622	921	310	609	909
Keyboard	513	808	1103	473	770	1067
Both	569	864	1163	496	790	1084

Table 2. The ten most frequent keyboard activities found by BPE. The ⊔ symbol represents Space. The ⇐ symbol means Backspace. The down arrow ↓ and up arrow ↑ denote *KeyDown* and *KeyUp*, respectively.

Rank	1	2	3	4	5	6	7	8	9	10
EMAKI	⊔↓, ⊔↑	⇐↓,⇐↑	e↓, e↑	t↓, t↑	a↓, a↑	o↓, o↑	⇐↓,⇐↑,⇐↓,⇐↑	i↓, i↑	s↓, s↑	n↓, n↑
Buffalo	⊔↓, ⊔↑	⇐↓,⇐↑	e↓, e↑	t↓, t↑	o↓, o↑	i↓, i↑	a↓, a↑	s↓, s↑	n↓, n↑	l↓, l↑

Vocabulary Statistics. As Fig. 5a shows, in EMAKI the maximum length of mouse activities reached 243 actions (BPE-900), while the median length was 16. The longest keyboard activity had 53 actions, while the median length was 3 (Fig. 5b). When using both modalities jointly, the maximum activity length was 239 after 900 iterations, while the median length was 4 (Fig. 5c). In Buffalo, the lengths of activities had a maximum of 405 and a median of 39 from mouse behaviour (Fig. 5a); a maximum of 16 and a median of 4 from keyboard behaviour (Fig. 5b); and a maximum of 158 and a median of 4 from joint modalities (Fig. 5c). Mouse activities were longer than keyboard activities, indicating that the preprocessed mouse data were more similar compared to preprocessed keyboard data. Comparisons between datasets show that mouse activities in EMAKI were more diverse, while Buffalo contained more diverse keyboard activities.

Table 1 shows the vocabulary sizes generated by BPE on the two datasets. Note that starting from BPE-k and running the algorithm for k more iterations, the vocabulary size increases by approximately k elements – showing that BPE overcomes the issue of exponential growth of vocabulary size in n-gram.

Frequent Activities. The three BPE iterations learnt the same top-10 frequent keyboard action sequences as shown in Table 2. Eight out of ten action sequences are the same on the two datasets, although they were collected from different participants in different experimental settings, indicating that generalised patterns underlie keyboard behaviour. The interaction goal behind the most frequent activity is to press the spacebar, which is in line with the observation that spaces occur often when typing in various languages. The second frequent activity reflects an intention of pressing Backspace which is frequently and widely used to correct what has been typed. Most frequent activities correspond to character keystrokes, and reflect the top-7 most frequent English letters: "e" (12.15%), "a" (8.67%), "t" (8.60%), "i" (7.53%), "o" (7.38%), "n" (7.34%) and "s" (6.63%) [20]. The difference in their order may be due to that the datasets are limited to specific typing scenarios and not representative of the entire English language. We also noticed that the left and right arrows, for redirecting typing locations, were also frequent on both datasets.

The most frequent ten mouse action sequences learnt by BPE were also the same on the two datasets. All of them are mouse moves of pinpoint, implying that participants follow similar ways to interact with UI targets even in different tasks and settings. These pinpointing regions were primarily in the top-left and bottom-left areas, while fewer pinpoints fell on the right side. This matches the layouts of not only general GUIs but also those used in our user study. For example, menu bars and sidebars are commonly at the top and to the left of interactive windows, respectively. Also, our text formatting tools were at the top of the text editor. The image editing tools were in the leftmost of the image editor. Additionally, our questionnaires were left-aligned, so the choices for participants to click lay to the left.

Interaction Goals Behind Activities. We also analysed long activities to examine if BPE learnt a hierarchy, i.e., if atomic actions form meaningful activities driven by complex goals. An example is "Dot↓, Dot↑, Space↓, Space↑, Shift↓, i↓, i↑, Shift↑, Space↓, Space↑". The goal behind the whole sequence is to start a sentence with the word "I", in line with the common texting or typing scenario of writing about oneself. It consisted of the low-level goal of pressing each aforementioned key, which was further composed of atomic actions *KeyDown* and *KeyUp*. BPE also learnt "Space↓, Space↑, Backspace↓, Backspace↑" from EMAKI, suggesting that participants typed at a faster pace than their thought process. Another example is "Ctrl↓, s↓, s↑, Ctrl↑" from Buffalo, representing the shortcut for saving files. Looking at mouse behaviour, BPE captured drag behaviour, represented as a *MouseDown* action followed by multiple *MouseMove* actions and ending with a *MouseUp* action. Another learnt long activity had 37 actions with 35 moves and a click as pinpoint in area 0, reflecting the goal of adjusting the cursor to a target and then clicking.

5.2   Interactive Task Recognition

We also evaluated the practical effectiveness of our approach on interactive task recognition. Knowing which task a user is performing enables adaptive UIs to understand the interactive behaviour and goals [26,27]. We compared our approach with two baselines: an ablated version which bypasses encoding (noted as NoEncoding) and replacing BPE with an autoencoder (AE). Autoencoder, consisting of an encoder and a decoder, is trained in a self-supervised way to reconstruct the input with the lowest error. Therefore, it needs no annotations and has a high generalisability, also used on language data [37]. To control variables, i.e., restrict the comparison to the encoding, we set two rules: (1) to reduce the impact of sophisticated designs of the encoders, use vanilla AE and BPE; (2) use the same hyperparameter sets for the classifier.

We implemented an AE that includes four components: an embedding layer of dimension $d_e = 128$ to handle discrete tokens; an encoder component composed of one to three fully connected (FC) layers with hidden dimensions (64), (64, 32) and (64, 32, 16); a decoder component, which is symmetric to the encoder; and a reconstruction component consisting of an FC layer and a softmax layer. Dropout was added after FC layers to avoid overfitting. We denote the autoencoder that has one, two, or three FC layers in the encoder and decoder components as AE-1, AE-2 and AE-3. Cross entropy between the reconstructed sequences and the input was used as the loss function. After training, the encoder component was used to encode interactive behaviour.

Our task classifier is based on a Transformer [60], which is well known for its success in NLP and capability to handle long dependencies in temporal signals. The classifier is composed of $N = \{2, 4, 6\}$ Transformer encoder layers, then an FC and softmax layer. Each Transformer encoder layer had $h = 4$ attention heads, $d_{model} = \{16, 64\}$ expected features, $d_{ff} = 4d_{model}$ dimension in feedforward layers and uses the ReLU activation function. During training, we applied label smoothing with $\epsilon = 0.1$ [60]. We used AdamW optimizer with learning rate $lr = \{10^{-3}, 10^{-4}\}$ and $\beta = (0.9, 0.999)$ [10] and the cross entropy as loss function. The training was done on a Tesla V100 GPU with a batch size of 64 and a dropout rate of 0.5. The classifier was trained for 30 epochs, while the AE was trained for 10 epochs because of its faster convergence. Because activities in the flexible vocabulary learnt by BPE have different lengths, we padded short samples and applied padding masks.

EMAKI has three main interactive tasks, posing a three-class classification problem, while Buffalo has two tasks, posing a binary classification problem. The evaluation follows 5-fold participant-independent cross-validation, where data from 80% of participants form the training set and the remaining participants form the test set. This scheme can evaluate the performance of unseen users. Macro F1 score [24] was chosen as evaluation metric because of the imbalanced classes, e.g., most keyboard data were from the text task on EMAKI. For each model, we report the highest F1 score achieved among all the parameter sets. Results show that on both datasets methods using BPE encoding outperformed the others (see Fig. 6 and 7).

Results on EMAKI. On mouse data, BPE-300 consistently outperformed other methods (Fig. 6a). A one-way ANOVA test showed that differences between methods are significant ($p < .001$): $F = 9.697$ on $L_{win} = 200$, $F = 12.396$ on $L_{win} = 100$ and $F = 7.194$ on $L_{win} = 20$. A post-hoc Tukey HSD test further confirmed that BPE-300 significantly outperformed the other methods on $L_{win} = 200$, $L_{win} = 100$ ($p < .001$ for AE and $p < .05$ for NoEncoding) and $L_{win} = 20$ ($p < .01$ for both AE and NoEncoding). Figure 6b shows that BPE-600 achieved the best results for $L_{win} = 100$ and $L_{win} = 50$, whereas when $L_{win} = 10$ the best was BPE-300. Differences between methods are significant ($F = 13.044$, $p < .001$ for $L_{win} = 100$, $F = 4.620$, $p < .01$ for $L_{win} = 50$ and

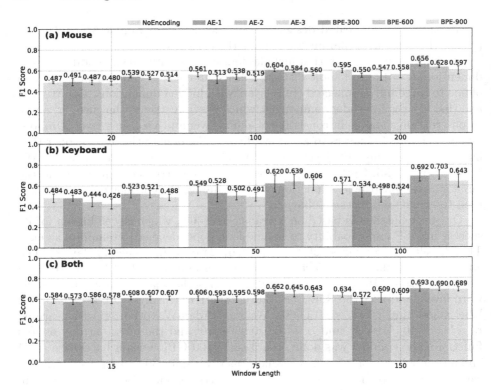

Fig. 6. F1 scores of recognising three interactive tasks on EMAKI from (a) mouse, (b) keyboard and (c) both modalities, segmented by different windows. Error bars represent the standard deviation from a 5-fold cross-validation.

$F = 4.220$, $p < .01$ for $L_{win} = 10$). Post-hoc Tukey HSD tests confirmed that BPE-600 significantly outperformed NoEncoding ($p < .01$) and AE-1 ($p < .001$) for $L_{win} = 100$. On joint modalities, BPE-300 performed the best, with the highest F1 score of 0.693 (Fig. 6c). Differences between methods were again significant with $F = 13.996$, $p < .001$ on $L_{win} = 150$, $F = 5.678$, $p < .001$ on $L_{win} = 75$ and $F = 2.665$, $p < .05$ on $L_{win} = 15$. Tukey HSD test indicated that BPE-300 significantly outperformed AE ($p < .01$) and NoEncoding ($p < .05$) on $L_{win} = 150$ and both of them at $p < .05$ when $L_{win} = 75$.

In Sect. 3.2, we report that participants using touchpads and traditional mice show different proficiencies. Therefore, we analysed if such differences affected task recognition. We separately performed 5-fold cross-validation based on the two groups. Since 24 participants used traditional mice while only 15 used touchpads, we randomly selected 15 traditional mouse users to reduce the influence of data amount on performance. Because BPE-300 on the longest window achieved the best results on mouse data (Fig. 6a), we used the same setting and did a Mann-Whitney U test on F1 scores achieved from two groups. To mitigate the randomisation introduced by participant selection, we repeated the above

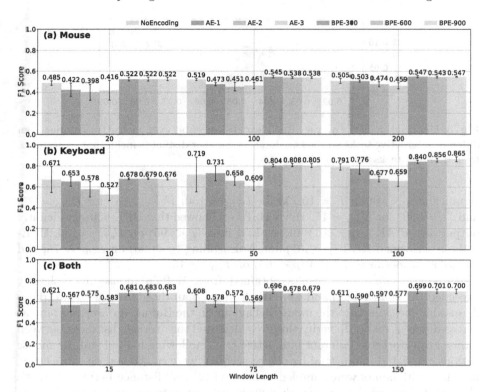

Fig. 7. F1 scores of recognising two interactive tasks on Buffalo from (a) mouse, (b) keyboard and (c) both modalities, segmented by different windows. Error bars represent the standard deviation from a 5-fold cross-validation.

procedure five times. None of the five tests found a significant difference in performance. The reason may be that our method does not explicitly encode time information, thus ignoring the speed difference in moving the cursor [23].

Results on Buffalo. On mouse data (Fig. 7a), BPE-300 performed the best and got the highest F1 score of 0.547. One-way ANOVA showed that differences between methods were significant ($p < .001$) with $F = 20.345$ for $L_{win} = 200$, $F = 18.609$ for $L_{win} = 100$ and $F = 5.589$ for $L_{win} = 20$). Post-hoc Tukey HSD tests showed that BPE-300 significantly outperformed NoEncoding ($p < .05$) and AE-1 ($p < .001$) when $L_{win} = 200$. On keyboard data (Fig. 7b), BPE-900 and BPE-600 outperformed other methods. Differences between methods are significant with $F = 30.218$ for $L_{win} = 100$, $F = 5.884$ for $L_{win} = 50$ (both $p < .001$) and $F = 4.791$, $p < .01$ for $L_{win} = 10$. According to post-hoc Tukey HSD tests, BPE-900 significantly outperformed AE-1 ($p < .01$) and NoEncoding ($p < .05$) when $L_{win} = 100$, and BPE-600 significantly outperformed AE-1 ($p < .001$) when $L_{win} = 50$. On joint modalities (Fig. 7c), BPE resulted in similar yet higher F1 scores than baselines. The best result was achieved by BPE-600 on the longest window of 0.701. Differences between methods were again

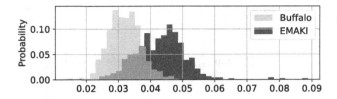

Fig. 8. Distribution of the average Euclidean distances between mouse trajectories from different interactive tasks on the two datasets. Smaller distances mean that trajectories from different tasks are more similar.

significant $(p < .001)$: $F = 10.733$ for $L_{win} = 150$; $F = 11.151$ for $L_{win} = 75$; and $F = 7.397$ for $L_{win} = 15$. Tukey HSD test showed that BPE-600 significantly outperformed AE-2 $(p < .01)$ and NoEncoding $(p < .05)$ on $L_{win} = 150$; BPE-300 outperformed AE-1 $(p < .01)$ and NoEncoding $(p < .05)$ on $L_{win} = 75$; and BPE-600 outperformed AE-3 $(p < .05)$ on $L_{win} = 15$.

It is noticeable that results obtained from Buffalo mouse data slightly exceeded the chance level and were much worse than those from keyboard data. A possible reason is that the mouse behaviour on the Buffalo dataset was similar across different tasks. To verify this, we calculated the average distances between mouse trajectories in different interactive tasks, following [64]: (1) all the mouse actions generated in one trial by one participant were considered one trajectory, on which 101 points were sampled uniformly; (2) the distance between two trials was defined as the average Euclidean distance between each pair of points on two trajectories; (3) the distance between two tasks was computed as the average distance between each trial from task 1 and each from task 2. Figure 8 shows that the distance between tasks from Buffalo is smaller than EMAKI, suggesting that mouse behaviour generated from the two tasks from Buffalo is similar, consistent with the statistics of BPE vocabulary (Sect. 5.1). Therefore, it is more difficult to classify tasks based on Buffalo mouse data.

6 Discussion

6.1 Modelling Interactive Behaviour from a Natural Language Perspective

Our work is among the first to explore the similarity between interactive behaviour and natural language, given that both have a sequential and hierarchical structure. Towards this goal, we applied BPE, which has been commonly used in state-of-the-art large language models to encode mouse and keyboard behaviour. At the lowest level, input actions were considered as characters since they are atomic and inseparable. For higher levels, BPE learned "subwords" from interactive behaviour, which were interactive activities, i.e., action sequences driven by underlying interaction goals. The analysis of the learnt vocabulary showed that following the same way of learning the semantic hierarchy of language, BPE was able to capture meaningful activities such as mouse drags, keyboard shortcuts and precisely adjusting the mouse to click on a UI element (Sect. 5.1). Despite representing just a first exploration, the insights from our analysis underline the similarity between interactive behaviour and natural language, and indicate the possibility of applying more powerful NLP methods like BERT [32,39] to encode interactive behaviour. Besides the state-of-the-art performances achieved, such LLMs also have noticeable advantages of generalisability and reusability. They can be pretrained on one dataset and re-used to encode other datasets to solve various downstream tasks with fine-tuning, which is more cost-effective than dedicating a specific large model towards each dataset or task [58]. Future HCI research can follow such NLP methods to build reusable pretrained interactive behaviour models for better generalisability and cost-effectiveness.

6.2   NLP Encoding for Interactive Task Recognition

Interactive task recognition is one of the key requirements of intelligent interactive systems to understand and adapt to interactive behaviour and interaction goals [17,18,33,44]. On this recognition task, encoding with BPE significantly outperformed baselines on both datasets, all the modalities and windows. Specifically, on our out-of-the-lab, newly collected EMAKI dataset, encoding with BPE obtained the highest F1 score of 0.703 recognising three tasks (Fig. 6). On average, BPE improved the F1 score by 0.087 on keyboard data, 0.051 on mouse, and 0.044 on the joint modalities. On the Buffalo dataset, BPE achieved the highest F1 score of 0.865 (Fig. 7) recognising two tasks. On average, BPE improved the F1 score by 0.080 on joint modalities, 0.053 on keyboard data and 0.035 on mouse data. These results, from a practical perspective, further reveal the promising effectiveness of modelling interactive behaviour as natural language.

We observed that methods generally achieved better results on longer windows, which may be due to that more actions may uncover richer characteristics of the tasks. However, increasing the window size yields fewer training samples and makes the recognition model wait longer for a complete window of actions to provide a prediction. In our experiments, windows that led to the best performance on mouse, keyboard and joint modalities had 200, 100 and 150 actions, respectively. These values can be a reference for future mouse and keyboard behaviour modelling methods.

In addition, on both datasets, using BPE on keyboard behaviour improved the F1 score more than on mouse behaviour, indicating its better ability of handling keyboard than mouse behaviour. This finding is expected, as typing on a keyboard is directly linked to expressing natural language. A second reason might be that discretising mouse data caused a loss of information [67,68]. On the joint modalities, we observed a general performance improvement from individual modalities on EMAKI, but not on Buffalo. As shown in Sect. 5.2, Buffalo lacks the diversity in mouse behaviour and thus performance achieved by combining mouse and keyboard is in-between that of individual modality.

6.3   EMAKI Dataset

Most publicly available mouse and keyboard datasets were collected in constrained laboratory settings, such as the Buffalo dataset. In contrast, our EMAKI is a step towards fully unconstrained settings to allow more natural interactive behaviour. Our study did not control where, when, or how long participants joined the study. In addition, participants used their own devices, which contributes to ecological validity. Consequently, our participant pool is more diverse given that participants are from different countries, and used different input devices and screen resolutions. All of Buffalo's participants were university students between 20–30 years old, while ours were between 18–54 and covered non-student participants. Moreover, our participants spent various time on tasks as they were freer to pause and resume (as shown in Sect. 3.1 and 3.2). Buffalo primarily uses typing-focused tasks, while EMAKI has complementary characteristics and tasks – like image editing and questionnaires – encouraging diverse mouse behaviour, as confirmed by our analysis in Sect. 5.1. Furthermore, higher diversity in behaviour can lead to better task recognition performance (Sect. 5.2). We also verified that the amount of data in EMAKI is sufficient for training the method for task recognition (see Appendix). Besides serving as a benchmark for task recognition, the questionnaires included in EMAKI also encourage future research on the interplay between multimodal behaviour and personality traits [71].

6.4   Limitations and Future Work

Our user study covered diverse but predefined tasks and did not allow multitasking. In the future, we will move towards fully uncontrolled settings. Time information may further improve behaviour modelling [6,16] and will be explicitly encoded in future work. We chose BPE over N-gram due to its flexibility, yet for systems where activities have similar lengths, N-gram might be efficient enough. An interesting future work is to explore the boundary of where the methods lead over the other. Also, even used on both modalities jointly, BPE learned activities composed of single modalities. A possible reason is that the behaviour of switching between mouse and keyboard is diverse, which BPE could not capture. Future work can explore the use of other NLP methods to better learn the interplay between mouse and keyboard behaviour [39,47,48]. Automatic interpreters can be studied to identify meaningful and interesting insights into behaviour from the BPE vocabulary, instead of human interpretation. Moreover, we intend to study other interactive modalities, such as screen touch and mid-air gesture, as well as other HCI downstream tasks like personality recognition.

7   Conclusion

We explored the similarity between interactive behaviour and natural language, given that both of them have a sequential and hierarchical structure. Towards the goal, we applied a widely used NLP method, BPE, to encode mouse and keyboard behaviour by learning its subwords, i.e., activities. Results on an existing controlled dataset and a novel out-of-the-lab dataset showed that the method can capture meaningful activities. Moreover, encoding with BPE significantly improved interactive task recognition, which is commonly required in intelligent interactive systems. Taken together, our exploratory work links interactive behaviour with natural language and provides a promising NLP perspective for modelling interactive behaviour, which has the potential to improve the generalisability of computational interactive behaviour models (Sect. 6.1) and also performances of interactive behaviour-based HCI tasks.

Acknowledgement. The authors thank the International Max Planck Research School for Intelligent Systems (IMPRS-IS) for supporting G. Zhang. M. Bortoletto and A. Bulling were funded by the European Research Council (ERC; grant agreement 801708). Z. Hu and L. Shi were funded by the Deutsche Forschungsgemeinschaft (DFG, German Research Foundation) under Germany's Excellence Strategy - EXC 2075 - 390740016. M. Bâce was funded by a Swiss National Science Foundation (SNSF) Postdoc.Mobility Fellowship (grant number 214434). We acknowledge the support by the Stuttgart Center for Simulation Science (SimTech). We would like to thank Yuanfan Ying and Dominike Thomas for their helpful suggestions. Lastly, we would like to thank the anonymous reviewers for their useful feedback.

A   Preprocessing Mouse Data with I-DT

As written in Sect. 4.1, the Dispersion-threshold identification (I-DT) algorithm [52] was used to categorise mouse behaviour to *pinpointing* a target (resembling gaze fixations) and *re-direction* between targets. I-DT operates on a window of duration-threshold consecutive samples. On this window, it calculates the dispersion value as $Dispersion = [max(x) - min(x)] + [max(y) - min(y)]$. If the dispersion value exceeds the dispersion threshold, samples inside the window are not considered to belong to a pinpoint and the window is slid forward by one sample. If the value is below the threshold, the samples within the window are considered to belong to a pinpoint. The window then expands to incorporate new samples until the dispersion value is above the threshold again. We empirically set the duration threshold to 100 ms and the dispersion threshold to 0.1.

B   The Algorithm of Byte Pair Encoding

Algorithm 1 shows how byte pair encoding (BPE) constructs the vocabulary V, as introduced in Sect. 4.2.

C   Analysis of EMAKI Data Amount for Interactive Task Recognition

As written in Sect. 6.3, we evaluated if the size of EMAKI allows our data-driven method to recognise interactive tasks. We used different percentages of

---

Algorithm 1 Byte pair encoding (BPE) [22,69]

Input: action sequence set D, the number of iterations k
procedure BPE(D, k)
   $V \leftarrow$ all unique actions in D
   for $i \leftarrow 1$ to k **do**
      $t_L, t_R \leftarrow$ Most frequent two consecutive units (actions or activities) in D
      $t_{new} \leftarrow t_L + t_R$ ▷ Merge to form a new activity
      $V \leftarrow V + [t_{new}]$
      Replace each occurrence of t_L, t_R with t_{new} in D
   end for
   return V
end procedure

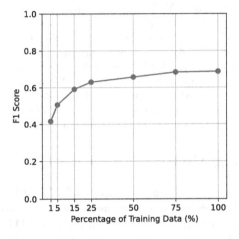

Fig. 9. F1 scores of interactive task recognition achieved by BPE, trained on different percentages of the training set.

the training set to train the method and examined their performances. According to Fig. 6c, the best results were achieved by BPE-300 when windows have 150 actions. Therefore, we followed the above setting. Figure 9 shows the results of interactive task recognition by training the model with 1%, 5%, 15%, 25%, 50%, 75% of randomly selected training instances, as well as with the entire training set (100%). It can be seen that as the percentage increases, the F1 score first increases fast (before 25%) but then slowly (25% to 75%). The increase in F1 score from using 75% of training data and the entire training set was subtle (only 0.004). Taken together, the amount of data in our dataset is sufficient to perform interactive task recognition.

References

1. Accot, J., Zhai, S.: Beyond fitts' law: models for trajectory-based HCI tasks. In: Proceedings of the ACM SIGCHI Conference on Human Factors in Computing Systems, pp. 295–302 (1997)
2. Acien, A., Morales, A., Vera-Rodriguez, R., Fierrez, J., Monaco, J.V.: Typenet: scaling up keystroke biometrics. In: Proceedings of the 2020 IEEE International Joint Conference on Biometrics, pp. 1–7. IEEE (2020)
3. Antal, M., Fejér, N., Buza, K.: Sapimouse: mouse dynamics-based user authentication using deep feature learning. In: Proceedings of the 2021 IEEE International Symposium on Applied Computational Intelligence and Informatics, pp. 61–66. IEEE (2021)
4. Apaolaza, A., Harper, S., Jay, C.: Understanding users in the wild. In: Proceedings of the 10th international cross-disciplinary conference on web accessibility. pp. 1–4 (2013)
5. Arapakis, I., Leiva, L.A.: Learning Efficient Representations of Mouse Movements to Predict User Attention, pp. 1309–1318. Association for Computing Machinery, New York (2020)
6. Azcarraga, J.J., Ibañez, J.F., Lim, I.R., Lumanas Jr, N.: Use of personality profile in predicting academic emotion based on brainwaves signals and mouse behavior. In: 2011 Third International Conference on Knowledge and Systems Engineering, pp. 239–244. IEEE (2011)
7. Bi, X., Smith, B.A., Zhai, S.: Multilingual touchscreen keyboard design and optimization. Hum.-Comput. Interact. **27**(4), 352–382 (2012)
8. Borji, A., Sihite, D.N., Itti, L.: Probabilistic learning of task-specific visual attention. In: Proceedings of the 2012 IEEE Conference on Computer Vision and Pattern Recognition, pp. 470–477. IEEE (2012)
9. Brown, E.T., Ottley, A., Zhao, H., Lin, Q., Souvenir, R., Endert, A., Chang, R.: Finding waldo: learning about users from their interactions. IEEE Trans. Visual Comput. Graphics **20**(12), 1663–1672 (2014)
10. Brückner, L., Leiva, L.A., Oulasvirta, A.: Learning GUI completions with user-defined constraints. ACM Trans. Interact. Intell. Syst. (TiiS) **12**(1), 1–40 (2022)
11. Bulling, A., Ward, J.A., Gellersen, H., Tröster, G.: Robust recognition of reading activity in transit using wearable electrooculography. In: Proceedings of International Conference on Pervasive Computing (Pervasive), pp. 19–37 (2008). https://doi.org/10.1007/978-3-540-79576-6_2
12. Card, S.K., Moran, T.P., Newell, A.: The keystroke-level model for user performance time with interactive systems. Commun. ACM **23**(7), 396–410 (1980)
13. Chudá, D., Krátky, P.: Usage of computer mouse characteristics for identification in web browsing. In: Proceedings of the 15th International Conference on Computer Systems and Technologies, pp. 218–225 (2014)
14. Dhakal, V., Feit, A.M., Kristensson, P.O., Oulasvirta, A.: Observations on typing from 136 million keystrokes. In: Proceedings of the 2018 CHI Conference on Human Factors in Computing Systems, CHI 2018, pp. 1–12. Association for Computing Machinery, New York (2018). https://doi.org/10.1145/3173574.3174220
15. Fitts, P.M.: The information capacity of the human motor system in controlling the amplitude of movement. J. Exp. Psychol. **47**(6), 381 (1954)
16. Freihaut, P., Göritz, A.S.: Does peoples' keyboard typing reflect their stress level? an exploratory study. Zeitschrift für Psychologie **229**(4), 245 (2021)

17. Fu, E.Y., Kwok, T.C., Wu, E.Y., Leong, H.V., Ngai, G., Chan, S.C.: Your mouse reveals your next activity: towards predicting user intention from mouse interaction. In: 2017 IEEE 41st Annual Computer Software and Applications Conference (COMPSAC), vol. 1, pp. 869–874. IEEE (2017)

18. Gajos, K., Weld, D.S.: Supple: automatically generating user interfaces. In: Proceedings of the 9th International Conference on Intelligent User Interfaces, pp. 93–100 (2004)

19. Grabowski, J.: The internal structure of university student's keyboard skills. J. Writing Res. **1**(1), 27–52 (2008)

20. Grigas, G., Juškevičienė, A.: Letter frequency analysis of languages using latin alphabet. Int. Linguistics Res. **1**(1), p18–p18 (2018)

21. Han, L., Checco, A., Difallah, D., Demartini, G., Sadiq, S.: Modelling user behavior dynamics with embeddings. In: Proceedings of the 29th ACM International Conference on Information & Knowledge Management, pp. 445–454 (2020)

22. Heinzerling, B., Strube, M.: Bpemb: tokenization-free pre-trained subword embeddings in 275 languages. arXiv preprint arXiv:1710.02187 (2017)

23. Hertzum, M., Hornbæk, K.: The effect of target precuing on pointing with mouse and touchpad. Int. J. Hum.-Comput. Interact. **29**(5), 338–350 (2013)

24. Hoppe, S., Loetscher, T., Morey, S.A., Bulling, A.: Eye movements during everyday behavior predict personality traits. Frontiers in human neuroscience p. 105 (2018)

25. Hu, Z., Bulling, A., Li, S., Wang, G.: Fixationnet: forecasting eye fixations in task-oriented virtual environments. IEEE Trans. Visual Comput. Graphics **27**(5), 2681–2690 (2021)

26. Hu, Z., Bulling, A., Li, S., Wang, G.: Ehtask: recognizing user tasks from eye and head movements in immersive virtual reality. IEEE Trans. Vis. Comput. Graph. **29**, 1992–2004 (2022)

27. Hu, Z., Li, S., Gai, M.: Research progress of user task prediction and algorithm analysis. J. Graph. **42**(3), 367–375 (2021). http://www.txxb.com.cn/CN/10.11996/JG.j.2095-302X.2021030367

28. Hu, Z., Li, S., Zhang, C., Yi, K., Wang, G., Manocha, D.: Dgaze: CNN-based gaze prediction in dynamic scenes. IEEE Trans. Visual Comput. Graphics **26**(5), 1902–1911 (2020)

29. Hu, Z., Zhang, C., Li, S., Wang, G., Manocha, D.: Sgaze: a data-driven eye-head coordination model for realtime gaze prediction. IEEE Trans. Visual Comput. Graphics **25**(5), 2002–2010 (2019)

30. Inoue, H., et al.: A classification method of cooking operations based on eye movement patterns. In: Proceedings of the Ninth Biennial ACM Symposium on Eye Tracking Research & Applications, pp. 205–208 (2016)

31. Jansen, B.J., Jung, S.G., Robillos, D.R., Salminen, J.: Next likely behavior: predicting individual actions from aggregate user behaviors. In: 2021 Second International Conference on Intelligent Data Science Technologies and Applications (IDSTA), pp. 11–15. IEEE (2021)

32. Jawahar, G., Sagot, B., Seddah, D.: What does bert learn about the structure of language? In: ACL 2019–57th Annual Meeting of the Association for Computational Linguistics (2019)

33. Joachims, T.: Optimizing search engines using clickthrough data. In: Proceedings of the Eighth ACM SIGKDD International Conference on Knowledge Discovery and Data Mining, pp. 133–142 (2002)

34. Kim, Y., Jernite, Y., Sontag, D., Rush, A.M.: Character-aware neural language models. In: Thirtieth AAAI Conference on Artificial Intelligence (2016)

35. Kudo, T.: Subword regularization: Improving neural network translation models with multiple subword candidates. arXiv preprint arXiv:1804.10959 (2018)
36. Kunchukuttan, A., Bhattacharyya, P.: Learning variable length units for SMT between related languages via byte pair encoding. arXiv preprint arXiv:1610.06510 (2016)
37. Li, J., Luong, M.T., Jurafsky, D.: A hierarchical neural autoencoder for paragraphs and documents. arXiv preprint arXiv:1506.01057 (2015)
38. Li, T.J.J., Popowski, L., Mitchell, T.M., Myers, B.A.: Screen2vec: semantic embedding of GUI screens and GUI components. Proceedings of the 2021 CHI Conference on Human Factors in Computing Systems (2021)
39. Liu, Y., et al.: Roberta: a robustly optimized bert pretraining approach. arXiv preprint arXiv:1907.11692 (2019)
40. Mazilu, S., et al.: A wearable assistant for gait training for parkinson's disease with freezing of gait in out-of-the-lab environments. ACM Trans. Interact. Intell. Syst.(TiiS) 5(1), 1–31 (2015)
41. Motwani, A., Jain, R., Sondhi, J.: A multimodal behavioral biometric technique for user identification using mouse and keystroke dynamics. Int. J. Comput. Appl. 111(8), 15–20 (2015)
42. Müller, P., Huang, M.X., Bulling, A.: Detecting low rapport during natural interactions in small groups from non-verbal behaviour. In: 23rd International Conference on Intelligent User Interfaces, pp. 153–164 (2018)
43. Murphy, C., Huang, J., Hou, D., Schuckers, S.: Shared dataset on natural human-computer interaction to support continuous authentication research. In: 2017 IEEE International Joint Conference on Biometrics (IJCB), pp. 525–530. IEEE (2017)
44. Pasqual, P.T., Wobbrock, J.O.: Mouse pointing endpoint prediction using kinematic template matching. In: Proceedings of the SIGCHI Conference on Human Factors in Computing Systems, pp. 743–752 (2014)
45. Pennington, J., Socher, R., Manning, C.D.: Glove: Global vectors for word representation. In: EMNLP (2014)
46. Petersen, G.B., Mottelson, A., Makransky, G.: Pedagogical agents in educational VR: an in the wild study. In: Proceedings of the 2021 CHI Conference on Human Factors in Computing Systems, pp. 1–12 (2021)
47. Radford, A., Wu, J., Child, R., Luan, D., Amodei, D., Sutskever, I., et al.: Language models are unsupervised multitask learners. OpenAI blog 1(8), 9 (2019)
48. Raffel, C., et al.: Exploring the limits of transfer learning with a unified text-to-text transformer. J. Mach. Learn. Res. 21(140), 1–67 (2020)
49. Reani, M., Peek, N., Jay, C.: An investigation of the effects of n-gram length in scanpath analysis for eye-tracking research. In: Proceedings of the 2018 ACM Symposium on Eye Tracking Research & Applications, pp. 1–8 (2018)
50. Reimers, N., Gurevych, I.: Sentence-bert: Sentence embeddings using siamese bert-networks. ArXiv abs/1908.10084 (2019)
51. Salmeron-Majadas, S., Santos, O.C., Boticario, J.G.: An evaluation of mouse and keyboard interaction indicators towards non-intrusive and low cost affective modeling in an educational context. Procedia Comput. Sci. 35, 691–700 (2014)
52. Salvucci, D.D., Goldberg, J.H.: Identifying fixations and saccades in eye-tracking protocols. In: Proceedings of the 2000 Symposium on Eye Tracking Research & Applications, pp. 71–78 (2000)
53. Schuster, M., Nakajima, K.: Japanese and korean voice search. In: 2012 IEEE International Conference on Acoustics, Speech and Signal Processing (ICASSP), pp. 5149–5152. IEEE (2012)

54. Sennrich, R., Haddow, B., Birch, A.: Neural machine translation of rare words with subword units. arXiv preprint arXiv:1508.07909 (2015)
55. Shirahama, K., Grzegorzek, M.: On the generality of codebook approach for sensor-based human activity recognition. Electronics **6**(2), 44 (2017)
56. Soukoreff, R.W., MacKenzie, I.S.: Towards a standard for pointing device evaluation, perspectives on 27 years of fitts' law research in HCI. Int. J. Hum Comput Stud. **61**(6), 751–789 (2004)
57. Subba, B., Biswas, S., Karmakar, S.: Host based intrusion detection system using frequency analysis of n-gram terms. In: TENCON 2017–2017 IEEE Region 10 Conference, pp. 2006–2011. IEEE (2017)
58. Sun, C., Qiu, X., Xu, Y., Huang, X.: How to fine-tune BERT for text classification? In: Sun, M., Huang, X., Ji, H., Liu, Z., Liu, Y. (eds.) CCL 2019. LNCS (LNAI), vol. 11856, pp. 194–206. Springer, Cham (2019). https://doi.org/10.1007/978-3-030-32381-3_16
59. Sun, Y., Ceker, H., Upadhyaya, S.: Shared keystroke dataset for continuous authentication. In: 2016 IEEE International Workshop on Information Forensics and Security (WIFS), pp. 1–6. IEEE (2016)
60. Vaswani, A., et al.: Attention is All you Need. In: Guyon, I., Luxburg, U.V., Bengio, S., Wallach, H., Fergus, R., Vishwanathan, S., Garnett, R. (eds.) Advances in Neural Information Processing Systems, vol. 30. Curran Associates, Inc. (2017)
61. Wang, B., Li, G., Zhou, X., Chen, Z., Grossman, T., Li, Y.: Screen2words: automatic mobile UI summarization with multimodal learning. In: The 34th Annual ACM Symposium on User Interface Software and Technology (2021)
62. Wang, C., Cho, K., Gu, J.: Neural machine translation with byte-level subwords. In: AAAI (2020)
63. Wang, Z., Li, B.: Human activity encoding and recognition using low-level visual features. In: Twenty-First International Joint Conference on Artificial Intelligence. Citeseer (2009)
64. Wulff, D.U., Haslbeck, J.M., Kieslich, P.J., Henninger, F., Schulte-Mecklenbeck, M.: Mouse-tracking: detecting types in movement trajectories. In: A Handbook of process tracing methods, pp. 131–145. Routledge (2019)
65. Xiaofeng, L., Shengfei, Z., Shengwei, Y.: Continuous authentication by free-text keystroke based on CNN plus RNN. Procedia Comput. Sci. **147**, 314–318 (2019)
66. Xu, P., Sugano, Y., Bulling, A.: Spatio-temporal modeling and prediction of visual attention in graphical user interfaces. In: Proceedings of the 2016 CHI Conference on Human Factors in Computing Systems, pp. 3299–3310 (2016)
67. Yue, Z., Wang, Y., Duan, J., Yang, T., Huang, C., Tong, Y., Xu, B.: Ts2vec: towards universal representation of time series. In: Proceedings of the AAAI Conference on Artificial Intelligence, vol. 36, pp. 8980–8987 (2022)
68. Zerveas, G., Jayaraman, S., Patel, D., Bhamidipaty, A., Eickhoff, C.: A transformer-based framework for multivariate time series representation learning. In: Proceedings of the 27th ACM SIGKDD Conference on Knowledge Discovery & Data Mining, pp. 2114–2124 (2021)
69. Zhan, J., et al.: An effective feature representation of web log data by leveraging byte pair encoding and TF-IDF. In: Proceedings of the ACM Turing Celebration Conference-China, pp. 1–6 (2019)
70. Zhang, G., et al.: Predicting next actions and latent intents during text formatting (2022)
71. Zhao, Y., Miao, D., Cai, Z.: Reading personality preferences from motion patterns in computer mouse operations. IEEE Trans. Affective Comput. (2020)

"Garbage In, Garbage Out": Mitigating Human Biases in Data Entry by Means of Artificial Intelligence

Sven Eckhardt[1]([✉]) [iD], Merlin Knaeble[2] [iD], Andreas Bucher[1] [iD], Dario Staehelin[1] [iD], Mateusz Dolata[1] [iD], Doris Agotai[3] [iD], and Gerhard Schwabe[1] [iD]

[1] University of Zurich, Zurich, Switzerland
{eckhardt,bucher,staehelin,dolata,schwabe}@ifi.uzh.ch
[2] Karlsruhe Institute of Technology, Karlsruhe, Germany
merlin.knaeble@kit.edu
[3] University of Applied Sciences and Arts Northwestern Switzerland, Windisch, Switzerland
doris.agotai@fhnw.ch

Abstract. Current HCI research often focuses on mitigating algorithmic biases. While such algorithmic fairness during model training is worthwhile, we see fit to mitigate human cognitive biases earlier, namely during data entry. We developed a conversational agent with voice-based data entry and visualization to support financial consultations, which are human-human settings with information asymmetries. In a pre-study, we reveal data-entry biases in advisors by a quantitative analysis of 5 advisors consulting 15 clients in total. Our main study evaluates the conversational agent with 12 advisors and 24 clients. A thematic analysis of interviews shows that advisors introduce biases by "feeling" and "forgetting" data. Additionally, the conversational agent makes financial consultations more transparent and automates data entry. These findings may be transferred to various dyads, such as doctor visits. Finally, we stress that AI not only poses a risk of becoming a mirror of human biases but also has the potential to intervene in the early stages of data entry.

Keywords: Data Entry · Cognitive Bias · Conversational Agent · Reliance · Trust

1 Introduction

The term bias can be seen in two contexts. For one, in psychological research and everyday life, "bias usually implies a prejudgment or prejudice" [1] against individuals. For example, bias can be induced based on "gender, race/ethnicity, and age" [1]. These so-called cognitive biases stem from systematic errors in processing and interpreting information and human decisions or judgments [2, 3]. At the same time, bias in statistics and adjacent disciplines refers to a value-neutral systematic skew in data, for instance, due to sampling errors. In AI research, however, these two conceptualizations co-occur when automated systems reproduce human prejudice due to malignant data [4]. No AI system can make reliable (nor ethical) predictions based on flawed data.

© The Author(s), under exclusive license to Springer Nature Switzerland AG 2023
J. Abdelnour Nocera et al. (Eds.): INTERACT 2023, LNCS 14144, pp. 27–48, 2023.
https://doi.org/10.1007/978-3-031-42286-7_2

In response to such issues, current HCI research often focuses on mitigating AI biases and making AI systems more ethical, denoted as "Algorithmic Bias Mitigation" in Fig. 1. This often is done by introducing algorithmic fairness in the model training [5]. Algorithmic fairness research has already identified the first ideas to mitigate the transfer of biases from data to models [6–8]. Despite this growing concern, we see AI not only as being at risk of mirroring human biases but also as a powerful tool to intervene in the early stages of potentially biased data creation. In this study, we aim to intervene in the data entry, denoted as "Human Bias Mitigation" in Fig. 1.

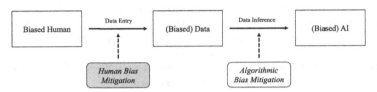

Fig. 1. The positioning of our study (own representation)

HCI research has recently introduced ideas on supporting humans in data entry and decision-making tasks with AI-based systems to overcome cognitive biases [9]. Such solutions are often limited to single-user interactions with a system. Real-life scenarios, however, often involve situations with multiple parties. Such interactions include, for example, doctor-patient encounters [10] or used car price negotiations [11]. Research continuously shows the presence of bias in such social interactions. For instance, black individuals regularly receive less pain medication due to an unfounded belief that their pain tolerance may be higher [12]. Other important examples of such dyads are financial consultations. The right or wrong investment decisions can drastically influence one's life. However, dyadic settings need specialized system designs instead of more traditional single-user systems, e.g., by introducing a conversational agent [13].

To address this, we have developed a tool supporting financial consultations. We call the tool MO (pronounced as /moʊ/). MO can take on many tasks. In this study, we focus on the tasks concerning data entry processes. Following recent findings by Zheng et al. [13], for these situations, we designed MO as a passive conversational agent, meaning it can understand user input and gives a limited amount of output, mostly staying in the background. However, MO does record all key aspects of the consultation. Additionally, MO has a tabletop projection to present the key aspects visually. Informed by the literature and supported by our findings, tabletop projections have several advantages over screens or tablets [14–17]. The goals of MO can be summarized as (1) to mitigate the bias of the financial advisor, (2) to improve data entry quality, and (3) to increase the trust of clients in the data entry process of financial consultation.

We take a two-study approach. In a pre-study, we point out issues in the data entry process with 5 real-world financial advisors and 15 clients. With this pre-study, we lay the groundwork for better awareness of the problem of biases in human-human dyads. We compare reports written by the advisors with the actual content of the prior consultation. In the main study, we evaluate MO with 24 clients in an experimental setting, testing at a bank's office with 12 real-world advisors. We use interviews after the consultations to gain insight into the perceptions of advisors and clients alike.

2 Background and Related Work

2.1 Algorithmic Bias Mitigation

AI regularly exceeds human capabilities on various tasks. However, in practical settings, humans often still need to implement the AI output. Therefore, users need to trust these AI systems [18]. Ways to achieve trust include transparency and explainability [19, 20]. However, in practical settings, trust is not always enough. While trust is an attitude, reliance is a behavior [21]. Only if humans rely on the AI output AI can unfold its full potential [22]. Research on reliance on AI aims to design for appropriate reliance [23]. For that, the users must distinguish between correct and incorrect recommendations made by the system [24] and not follow incorrect advice [25].

Reliance on AI can be achieved by tackling the biases of these AI systems. Therefore, in the past years, HCI research has often focused on the issue of biases in AI. For instance, Amershi et al. [26] propose a guideline to "mitigate social biases". Researchers successfully argue that eliminating such biases is not only a worthwhile cause but has benefits beyond supporting marginalized groups. For example, Woodruff et al. [6] argue that businesses promoting fairness, e.g., in the housing market, could increase user trust and, thus, profitability. Regarding the financial context, it has been shown that models taking over routine decisions, such as loan approvals, frequently repeat existing biases learned from existing data initially created by humans [27]. Since biases can lead to unfairness, toolkits recently emerged to bring fair AI into practice [6–8].

Overall, a wide array of algorithmic bias mitigation research focuses on identifying biased data and preventing AI from following such biases. However, as indicated in Fig. 1, there is another way to prevent biases in AI systems: targeting human data entry as a root cause of biases in data. Such a sociotechnical view on bias mitigation provides a more comprehensive approach to AI fairness [28].

2.2 Human Bias Mitigation

Human behavior and thinking are prone to cognitive bias. Cognitive biases are systematic errors in processing and interpreting information and decisions or judgments [2, 3]. They are extensively studied in psychology and behavioral economics as a predictable propensity of humans towards irrationality caused by the limits of the mind's attention or application of defaults or heuristics acting as mental shortcuts, i.e., bounded rationality [29]. These biases–implicitly or explicitly–affect everyone's life.

Subsequently, frontline employees, like financial advisors, are subject to cognitive biases equally. Retail employees are shown to engage in sympathetic behavior in a discriminatory manner based on gender, age, race, and outfit [30]. Government officials frequently engage in biased decisions due to the considerable decision discretion and the pressure to adhere to organizational policies [31]. Medical personnel adapt their decisions based on their first impressions of patients resulting in a confirmation bias [32,

33]. For instance, they ask questions and provide answers in a way consistent with their initial assumptions about the patient [32]. This behavior is associated with the risk of medical errors [33] and shows the drastic effects of biases in frontline employees.

Even though dedicated and extensive studies of bias in financial advisors are still missing, existing evidence suggests that they—like the professionals in other frontline settings—also engage in biased behaviors and discriminate according to race or wealth in how they communicate, the advice they give, or the information they provide [34, 35]. Information or assumptions about the client's social class and race influence their behavior [35]. Some biases become apparent only when such frontline employees reflect on their decisions and must explain their reasoning, while others remain implicit even then [34]. When a financial advisor can make decisions on behalf of clients, new incentives arise. Given the organizational benefits, financial advisors are encouraged to sell more expensive and higher-risk products generating more revenue for the organization and bonus payments for the advisor [36, 37]. This is known as the principal-agent problem [38], where the financial advisor serves as an agent to the client.

Current HCI literature already deals with overcoming biases in various settings [3, 39–41]. Most notably, research offers design suggestions for human-AI collaboration in specific scenarios. For instance, in the medical field, searching for visually comparable biopsy imagery from previous medical patients may help create unbiased diagnoses [42]. Further, AI can support radiologists for chest image classification [43], e.g., with the help of human-centric AI assistants [44], AI can support text entry in the medical field [45], or help in medical diagnosis [46]. In other fields, sexism manifests in the mistreatment of women on gig platforms [47]. Algorithmic management institutionalizes the human-caused discrimination women may have faced under human supervision and normalizes this state by being distant from individual cases. Wang et al. [48] identify how explainable AI can mitigate common cognitive biases. Also, Echterhoff et al. [9] show how to mitigate anchoring biases in sequential decision tasks. Introducing AI support into a sequential decision-making process could decrease biases and increase agreement [9]. Their approach aligns with our intention to use AI support to mitigate human biases during data entry. However, current research rarely attends to collaborative encounters in professional settings. We aim to explore how collaborative technology can help overcome biases in dyadic settings, for the case of financial consultations.

2.3 Support for Dyadic Settings

Dyadic human-human settings supported by AI require a different systems design than human-AI interaction. It is not straightforward what kind of technology, media, or interaction pattern is needed for such settings. Only recently, Zheng et al. [13] conducted a literature review to consider settings other than the classical human-AI interaction and analyzed the human-human setting supported by a conversational agent. Other research shows how embodied conversational agents such as a virtual health counselor, digital prayer walls, and physical and spiritual activity logging support well-being in church communities [49]. Further, voice-based interfaces, primarily through smart speakers, e.g., Amazon Alexa, see ever-growing adoption rates in family households. Research has investigated issues regarding the impact on family dynamics, especially in dyadic settings complemented by the smart speaker [50], and the integration of such voice interfaces into everyday family conversations [51]. Beneficial effects of empowerment have been found in dyads of caretakers and older adults with mild cognitive impairments [52]. Such research highlights the importance of voice-based interactions in dyadic settings by being hands- and eyes-free, as in not taking away critical attention from the human-human interaction while providing unique benefits.

The focus of current systems lies often on informal dyads, such as parenting, caretaking, or churchgoing. Until now, there is comparably little research on support in institutionalized dyadic settings, where one party does not necessarily know the other beforehand or does not have an inherent trust. Research has shown that computer support in dyadic settings can also bring unintended consequences in financial consultations. For instance, the phenomenon of "coercion into completeness" [17] can occur, where digital guidelines on advisory topics are being treated as a checklist to be filled. Additionally, past research has introduced a tabletop setting [16] that has been shown to integrate well into seated dyadic settings by not distracting from the personal relationship. These tabletop settings were further developed into tabletop projections [14, 15]. Finally, financial consultations have been investigated for leveraging AI capabilities to support co-decision-making [53]. These results show that trust in automated decision support (much less decision-making) is low in financial consultation [53]. As AI-based dyadic support systems have shown promising results in informal settings, a similar investigation in institutionalized settings seems adamant.

3 Pre-Study: Problem Awareness

We conduct a pre-study observing the issues of financial advisors in an experimental setting to first point out the problem of biases in human-human dyadic settings.

3.1 Methodology

For the pre-study, we acquired 5 real-world financial advisors[1] through our partnering banks. The advisors advised 3 clients each. Clients were acquired using convenience sampling, which was open to the public. Invitations were distributed through various channels, such as online marketplaces, panels of already registered experiment participants, and social media amplified by the authors' personal and professional networks. On average, the consultations had a length of about 24 min (min = 13, max = 38, sd = 6.91). While the financial advisors are used to conducting training and evaluations like these as part of a normal working day, the clients received compensation of about (converted) $ 70 for taking part. We also held interviews with clients and advisors, that only play a secondary role in this pre-study.

The financial advisors created a report for the prior consultation after each conventional conversation. Creating such a report is common practice for advisors and is required by regulations. Senior advisors confirmed the key aspects considered in this study as being highly relevant and are commonly unknown to them before initial consultations. The advisors in this study were instructed to include the key aspects in their

---

[1] Originally, 6 advisors participated in the pre-study. Due to personal time constraints, one advisor could only complete two sessions. We consequently omitted their data from further analysis.

reports. The key aspects can be divided into four categories: (A) Personal Information (containing: Name, Age, Civil Status, Profession, Residence), (B) Financial Knowledge and Experience, (C) Financial Background and Investment interests (containing: Total Assets, Assets to be invested, Income, Saving Rate, Investment objectives, Investment horizon, Risk profile, Investment interests) and (D) Transactions done during the financial consultation. We compare the consultations' transcripts with the advisors' handwritten reports to gain insight into the problem. For this, we binary code the transcripts and reports using a qualitative analysis. This comparison focuses on the coverage of the key aspects of the consultation in the reports written by the advisors. For the results, we aggregate these key aspects into their respective categories.

3.2 Results

Table 1. Results of our pre-study. The coverage in the consultation transcripts gives the percentage of consultations where the information item has been talked about (averaged over all items in the class). The coverage in advisors' reports gives the same percentage for the manual reports written by the advisors. The relative coverage gives the percentage of reports containing the information item, where the information item has also been talked about in the consultation.

Information Item Class (number of items)		Coverage in consultation transcripts [%]	Coverage in advisors' reports [%]	Relative coverage of reports compared to transcripts [%]
(A)	Personal Information (5)	88.00	65.33	72.62
(B)	Financial Knowledge and Experience (1)	100.00	66.67	66.67
(C)	Financial Background and Investment Interests (8)	80.00	57.50	71.00
(D)	Transactions (1)	93.33	60.00	64.29
	Overall [%]	**84.89**	**60.89**	**70.80**

Table 1 gives an overview of the results. While the coverage of the key aspects is relatively high in the consultation transcripts, the coverage in the advisors' reports is noticeably lower. Directly after the consultations, our financial advisors generally only reconstruct about 70% of the discussed key aspects. Additionally, many advisors indicated in the interviews that these reports are regularly not done directly after the consultation but rather some time later. This was also stated by one of the advisors of this pre-test: *"The problem is when I don't write the report for a week [which] has happened to me [..., then after a few days I ask myself] what did they say?"*.

Additionally, the data is not only incomplete but also biased towards key aspects needed to make a successful deal with the client. While many advisors could remember the client's financial background and investment interests, fewer could remember the client's financial knowledge or experience. The focus on key aspects more important to the advisors' interests than the clients indicates a first problem of the advisors' biases. In addition, this bias reduces the data accuracy of the reports written by the advisors. The extent of this matter can be seen in the following statement by one of the advisors of the pre-test: *"[In the conventional consultation,] I have the feeling that I can get more information out of the client there, which could create a certain potential for the bank. The bank is primarily looking for where we can expand [author's remark: cross-selling opportunities] a client. Where does the client have potential."*

Overall, during data entry for financial consultations, we find problems in incomplete data and a bias towards certain data. We introduce a tool to support financial consultations in the subsequent main study. We analyze statements by advisors and clients to get insights into the design and functionalities of our tool.

4 System Design

This study is part of a larger research project involving two universities, two regional banks, and two technology partners in Switzerland. The overarching goal of the project is to explore and test the use of conversational agents in financial consultations. Based on our findings in the pre-study and the literature, we developed a tool to support financial consultations called MO. MO is a large system spanning many functionalities. Therefore, in this description, we focus on the parts that are relevant to this study. Following recent findings by Zheng et al. [13], for the data entry processes, we designed MO as a passive conversational agent. MO can understand user input and gives a limited amount of output, mostly staying in the background. However, MO does record all key aspects of the consultation. The goals of MO can be summarized as (1) to mitigate the bias of the financial advisor, (2) to improve data entry quality, and (3) to increase the trust of clients in the data entry process of financial consultation.

Fig. 2. The financial-consultation-supporting tool MO (reenacted from observed consultations).

MO consists of multiple parts. First, a vertical projector displays all relevant information on the table between the advisor and client. The visualization windows can be moved and rotated by a so-called "token", i.e., a tangible object on the table. Using such tokens has been shown to provide a visual aid to help understand complex processes [14, 15]. These tokens can also be seen in Fig. 2. These tokens get recognized by a Microsoft Azure Kinect camera [54], which films the table. A Microsoft Surface Dial is used for scrolling through the pages. The camera can also detect input by the user via hand movement, such as a "touch" on the table. Finally, a microphone detects auditive input that gets processed using a custom natural language processing (NLP) architecture. Some auditive output emulates a component like a conversational agent, such as Amazon's Alexa or Apple's Siri. The design was mainly informed by the prior findings of [14–17] for the domain of financial consultation. This research introduces a tabletop projection into the setting of financial consultations and shows how IT tools can hinder or enrich financial consultation. Additionally, the design of our conversational agents follows the recent guidelines of Zheng et al. [13] to be "visible" and "ignorable" at the same time. While there always was a visual representation of our agent, it remained in the background, both visually and auditive.

MO can support the financial consultation during the five common phases of a financial consultation. MO's design during these phases is presented in more detail in the following. Once the client enters the consultation room, they are greeted with the word *"Grüezi"* (eng. *"Welcome"*) on the table. This marks the **Welcome** phase. In this phase, the advisor introduces the system and the goal of the consultation. After explicit request, MO will introduce itself with a short auditive welcoming message. Along with this message, a figure with a facial expression is shown on the table. This figure visually represents MO and can be seen in Fig. 3.

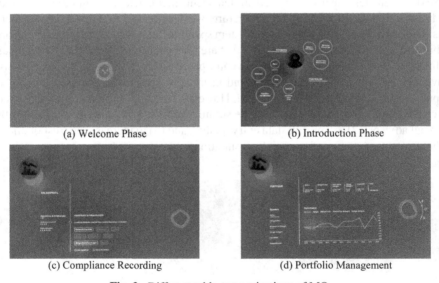

(a) Welcome Phase

(b) Introduction Phase

(c) Compliance Recording

(d) Portfolio Management

Fig. 3. Different table-top projections of MO.

In the **Introduction** phase, the personal information denoted by (A) in the pre-study is collected. The first "token", i.e., a 3d-printed figure, will be put on the table by the advisor. The camera recognizes this token, and the custom front-end will change the visualizations. In this phase, the advisor introduces themselves and also lets the client introduce themselves. During that phase, the system already collects some of the needed information, such as name, age, civil status, profession, and residence, but also includes some broader topics, such as hobbies. Advisors are instructed to only end this phase by removing the token if all the information is filled in. We are conducting our research in

Switzerland, a German-speaking country with a dialect of German called Swiss German. During testing, we noticed that the NLP system has difficulties dealing with localized words, such as names, places of residence, or employers. Hence, for those parts of the system responsible for recognizing personal matters, we included human input as a replacement for the NLP in the form of a Wizard of Oz testing. This approach ensures a more stable and pleasant experience for the clients and advisors. There are other situations where the wizard can intervene manually. However, this is the only situation not implemented by the NLP architecture.

In the **Compliance Recording** phase, the financial knowledge and background, denoted by (B) and (C) in the pre-study, are collected. Further, information required by law and regulations is recorded. For that, the old token is replaced by a new token and the visualizations change. The information is collected in a standardized way using multiple-choice answers. Questions can be answered either by using the touch functionality or (for some questions) using verbal commands that the NLP model understands. This phase only ends if all the information is filled in on the table.

Afterward, based on these answers, one of three standardized portfolios is shown, and the **Portfolio Management** phase begins. In this phase, the financial transactions, denoted by (D) in the pre-study, are collected. The client and advisor can change stocks by voice input. Commands can either be explicit (e.g., *"MO, buy ten apple stocks"*) or recognized from the context (e.g., *"...then we should buy ten stocks of apple"*).

Finally, after the portfolio has been managed and the client is content with the result, the **Farewell** phase begins. In this phase, MO farewells the client after an explicit request by the advisor. Additionally, the advisor ends the consultation by also farewelling the client. There is no change in visualization for that phase. However, MO's facial expressions will react to its spoken words.

Overall, the designs address the problems stressed by the pre-study and ensure a complete data entry. There is no way to circumvent the data needed for compliance reasons, and all transactions will be logged since they are managed by MO. This ensures full coverage of the required data points. This also makes an evaluation such as the one in the pre-study obsolete. Rather it is important to how the clients perceive this tool. Therefore, instead of comparing coverages in the main study, we conduct interviews to get insights into how the users use and perceive MO.

5 Main Study: User Evaluation

After pointing out the problem of biases in human-human dyads, we aim to get a deeper insight into biases in financial consultations and introduce our tool, MO, to support the consultation.

5.1 Methodology

For the evaluation of MO, we tested at a real bank office with real advisors that are regularly part of similar training and evaluations. For the main study, we acquired 12 real-world financial advisors through our partnering banks that advised 2 clients each over one day, leading to 24 clients. Clients were acquired analogously to the pre-study through convenience sampling open to the public over the same channels. The advisors (9 male and 3 female) had an average age of about 31 years (min = 18, max = 47, sd = 9.46). The clients (12 male and 12 female) had an average age of about 29 years (min = 20, max = 49, sd = 7.83). While the financial advisors are used to conducting training and evaluations like these as part of a normal working day, the clients received compensation of about (converted) \$ 100 for taking part.

Each client had two consultations in a balanced, randomized order: one conventional consultation and one with MO. The conventional consultations had an average length of about 32 min (min = 15, max = 44, sd = 7.42), and the supported consultations had an average length of 35 min (min = 23, max = 53, sd = 8.19).

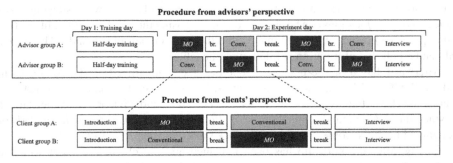

Fig. 4. Overview of the study design and procedure from the advisors' and clients' perspectives.

The whole evaluation procedure for the advisors and clients is shown in Fig. 4. The advisors were trained on a separate day shortly before the evaluation. Between consultations, the clients and advisors had a short break. After each session, the clients and advisors each had an interview. This leads to a total of 12 interviews with advisors (average length of 74 min, min = 51, max = 99, sd = 14.80) and 24 interviews with clients (average length of about 61 min, min = 43, max = 91, sd = 12.42).

The interviews were transcribed and analyzed using thematic analysis, according to Braun and Clark [55]. After initial coding, we had a total of 1985 coded statements for the clients and 880 coded statements for the advisors. Relevant statements were clustered and merged into six themes introduced in the subsequent chapter. The first author performed the initial coding and gradually refined and reviewed it in a series of workshops with the co-authors. The interviews follow the naming convention of I-C01... I-C24 for client interviews, and I-A01 ... I-A12 for advisor interviews.

5.2 Results

Based on the system design of MO, virtually full coverage of all relevant information items introduced in the pre-study in Sect 3 can be assumed. Our observations support this, as the design of MO enforces this effect. Therefore, a similar comparison as in the pre-study is of no valuable use here. Instead, we need to analyze how people perceive MO. During our analysis, we identified six emerging themes presented in Table 2. Themes 1 and 2 concern the data entry process and the occurring problems (A). Themes 3, 4, and 5 are concerned with introducing a dyad-supporting tool and potential solutions to the problems (B). Theme 6 is concerned with the overall trust in financial advice after introducing a dyad-supporting tool (C).

Table 2. Overview of the themes found using the thematic analysis of the interviews

Theme		Short Description
A	(1) "Forgetting" Data	Advisors tend to "forget" key aspects after the consultation, thus, leading to an incomplete data entry
	(2) "Feeling" Data	Advisors tend to have their own opinion about clients and try to "feel" certain key aspects of the client, which can lead to poor data accuracy
B	(3) Automating Data Entry	An automated data entry by voice input increases the data quality and the certainty of high completeness and quality data entry
	(4) Presenting Visual Feedback	Visual feedback increases transparency involves the client in the data entry process and leads to a multimodal interaction with the system
	(5) Allowing Manual Override	There are two possible sources of wrong data entry: an error made by the system and an error made by the users. For both, we need the possibility for the users to make changes to the recorded data
C	(6) Trust in Financial Advice	Clients tend to trust recommendations, statistics, and information from an automated system, thus, increasing trust in financial advice

"Forgetting" Data. Advisors are prone to *"forget"* (I-A03) certain aspects and cannot successfully note all the relevant key aspects during the consultation. Even when completing their notes directly after the consultation, they miss certain key aspects in their reports. One advisor mentioned that they only recalled real estate ownership in the form of *"a vacation home"* (I-A03) after *"running to the coffee machine"* (I-A03). If the inclusion or omission of such essential facts is subject to accidental remembrance, potential biases expand beyond traditional issues in data quality. Hence, we identified a problem in manually recording data due to a lack of completeness.

The problem of not remembering all key aspects is also in line with existing literature. Several biases can influence information retrievals, such as attentional biases or cherry-picking of seemingly relevant information. On the contrary, forgotten information is considered less critical [56]. At the same time, people are limited in memorizing a lot of different key aspects and are only able to mentally take note of at most seven (plus minus two) aspects [57]. Additionally, people can only recall a small fraction of things discussed during a conversation, even less after some time has passed [58]. Hence, it is expected that advisors cannot successfully create a report with all the relevant key aspects after the consultation. The traditional mitigation strategy of taking notes during the consultation is not always applicable either, as discussed in Theme 3. Putting the "forgetting bias" [56] together with the fact that people will forget certain aspects paints a clear picture of biased information in the present setting.

"The challenge is always not to forget" (I-A03), said one advisor and summarized an issue many of their colleagues shared with us during the interviews. They *"realize that there are still differences between what [they] wrote down and what [they] got out of the conversation without writing anything down"* (I-A10). Lastly, having a complete report is not only beneficial for clients and required by law, but also the advisors themselves see the need for complete reports. Especially if they need to remember what they talked about with the clients, as shown by one quote from the advisors, reiterating a story about an advisor that needed to show in court that they informed the client about certain risks: *"I think one could have been much more relaxed if one had said more precisely at the product closing that the client had been informed about the risk or the possible dangers of a title transfer."* (I-A01).

"Feeling" Data. Advisors tend to have their own opinion about the clients and try to *"feel"* (I-A12) certain key aspects about the client, which can lead to poor data accuracy. Therefore, the second source of potential biases lies in inaccurate und reliable data in the form of faulty notes. For example, when reconstructing the prior consultation, advisors could falsely assume the risk affinity of a client based on their job and income or their investment experience based on their age.

Open-ended inference is in our everyday life, meaning that when meeting new people, we automatically and subconsciously try to infer information about them based on previous experiences [59]. Doing a cognitive-intensive task, such as advising a client, and being prone to open-ended inference can lead to biased notetaking and documentation. For example, this is shown in the field of nursing [60], which may be transferred to financial consultation reports.

Many statements by our advisors pointed toward that problem. Examples include that the advisors rely on their feeling about the client: *"You always feel the risk with clients extremely quickly. You know what makes the client tick as early as the needs assessment stage"* (I-A12). To add to this, one advisor (while knowing to be on the record during the interview) talked about one client like the following: *"With him, I have had the feeling that the level, this is not to sound disparaging, but the [cognitive] level has been almost too low "*(I-A09) and further while talking about different clients used the term of a *"stupid guy"* (I-A09). If the advisors talk like this while being on the record, one can only imagine their biases that they are unwilling to share out loud.

Automating Data Entry. Automated data entry is often talked about by the clients. They stated that MO successfully noted what they said during the conversation, which was helpful for the overall consultation. Additionally, this has the advantage that the advisor does not have to take care of the notetaking but can advise the client. Imagine sitting across from someone *"just taking notes the whole time "* while you, as a client, need to take over the *"active"* (I-C18) role of the consultation. In the interviews, clients describe this situation as a *"steady distraction"* (I-C15). They pointed out that the *"communication suffered [from] writing down again and again"* (I-C22).

While notetaking could resolve the issues of "forgetting" and "feeling" data, it is a very cognitive-intensive task [61]. This cognitive effort is better spent on the main activity, i.e., consulting the client. In contrast, the manual data entry after the consultation is generally an error-prone activity [62, 63], further exacerbating the issues of Themes 1 and 2. With current state-of-the-art voice detection devices, this data entry can be automated. Such voice detection systems have become better at situational awareness and do not always have to be triggered by fixed keywords anymore [64].

Therefore, automated data entry solves the problem of your counterpart always taking notes. Also, our clients tend to trust MO to take notes, some even more than humans. They tend to perceive the automated *"data collection [as] more secure than when people write something on a piece of paper."* (I-C05) and *"trust a system more than a human being purely for data, data acquisition, or data processing because that is exactly what [... these systems] are for."* (I-C07).

Presenting Visual Feedback. An essential aspect of MO is visual feedback given via a tabletop projection. Tabletop projections can increase transparency in the overall financial consultation and the client's involvement. Furthermore, given that we have a voice-based data input, visual feedback increases the multimodality of the system.

Existing research for financial consultations has explored the possibility of manually filling a mind map visualization of important key facts [17]. However, automating the data entry into the tool does not suffice. The choice of visualization seems crucial as, for example, typical output modalities like displays can be equally distracting to the conversation as the notepads [16]. Instead, clients stated that *"thanks to the projection [the consultation] was like teamwork"* (I-C22), which is also in line with existing research that shows that desktop-embedded displays are supportive in dyadic settings [16]. While visual tools in financial consultations have the potential to "coerce into completeness" [17], MO does not seem to have this effect. Additionally, multimodality has shown to be good, e.g., for multitasking performance in a complex setting [65] like financial consultation, where the advisor has to think about a lot of things and the clients need to understand a lot of new concepts and make critical decisions.

Transparency is vital to trust in AI systems [66]. However, the transparency given by our visual feedback is different from typical explainable AI approaches. For instance, we do not make a decision boundary understandable but rather show the data collected by the system. This approach aligns with existing research demonstrating the necessity of process transparency for financial consultations [67]. Clients *"find it very important [to get] feedback"* (I-C22) to know if the system has entered the data *"correctly or wrongly"* (I-C22). *"If there was not [any feedback], [they] could not be sure if the right thing was really understood. But by seeing that it is filled in, [they] trust that that is the right thing to do"* (I-C19). One participant summarized this in the following quote: *"It is more trustworthy when you have the data in front of you."* (I-C15).

Allowing Manual Override. System errors create an unpleasant experience. There are two possible sources of wrong data entry in the human-human dyad. For one, MO could make an error, i.e., the NLP makes an error in language understanding. For the other, the users can state a wrong fact, i.e., make an error when stating information.

The key to giving control to the user is the option to override or correct entered data or information. For example, Putze et al. [68] use a "manual override" to correct system errors, which achieves a higher correction performance than any other error correction strategy. In our case, this is important to ensure correct data. Additionally, the option to manually override algorithms is whished by participants in several studies [7].

Our clients saw the importance of a manual override as a possible error-handling strategy. It is essential that clients *"must be able to change it if something is wrong"* (I-C18) or acknowledge that in the current system, *"if there had been mistakes, [they] could have changed them"* (I-C05). Also, they stated that *"it is more trustworthy when [they] have the data in front of [them ... because then they can] come forward and say [they] want to change something"* (I-C15). Finally, critical errors that cannot be undone need to be prevented because if *"something was completely misunderstood and could no longer be undone, then [the client] would no longer use the system."* (I-C23). However, even the best error-handling strategy would not work if the system were very error-prone: *"If it were one error or so, then it would be okay, but if you must [correct every statement] again anyway, then you can [input it yourself] right from the beginning, and then it would be rather annoying."* (I-C09).

Trust in Financial Advice. For financial advisors, trust is one of the most critical assets. Especially after the financial crisis of 2008, trust in financial consultations has significantly decreased [69]. Literature suggests replacing humans with artificial intelligence tools, for example, using robo-advisors [70]. Robo-advisors have advantages over financial advisors, such as lower fees and algorithm-based decision-making [71]. However, it also comes with several disadvantages, such as a conflict of interest or a lack of personal contact [70]. Especially the regulatory body, such as SEC and FINRA, warn against the risk assessment of automated investment tools without the support of a financial professional [72].

Clients *"expect personal contact"* (I-C14) and *"appreciate that they can still talk to a person"* (I-C19). While clients like personal contact, they would still like the advisor to be *"supported by tools"* (I-C19). Regarding the investment suggestions, clients will rely on the tool more than the advisor since it is based on clear logic and not flawed by personal opinions or emotions. This argument was summarized by one of our clients: *"I think [I would rely on the tool] even more than an advisor. Because I feel that there is a database behind it and an algorithmic approach independent of emotions. And I trust that more than a person who maybe has their own intentions and decides based on emotions, based on how the person just got to know me, or how I have given myself. And I feel that the system then works so completely neutrally."* (I-C19).

Furthermore, financial advice given by systems is often seen as inherently neutral and objective. Clients *"would trust [the systems] if [they] knew that the input of the model was captured correctly and then that there was some form of mathematical modeling going on"* (I-C05). Overall, clients appreciate that we need the three parts of the successfully supported financial consultation: (1) the advisor, (2) the system, and (3) the client themselves, which was summarized by one of our clients: *"If I have questions, I will ask the advisor in addition. But basics, information, suggestions [from the system], that is okay. But I have to see it for myself and then decide what to do."* (I-C24).

6 Discussion

This study aims to understand human bias in data entry in financial consultations as an example of human-human dyads. We identify six themes covering bias origins, solutions to mitigate biases, and effects on the consultation when introducing these solutions. While our study focuses on one form of dyadic settings, we propose that our findings are valuable for similar encounters. For example, doctor-patient encounters might face similar problems when doctors write their diagnosis on a patient's condition. In such settings, a system like MO could have similar positive effects. As introduced in Sect. 4, the first goal of MO is to mitigate the bias of the financial advisor. This is further discussed in Sect. 6.1. The second goal is to improve the data entry quality, which is further discussed in Sect. 6.2. Finally, the third goal of increasing the trust of clients in the data entry process of financial consultations is further discussed in Sect. 6.3. We end this Chapter with some limitations of our study and possible future work in Sect. 6.4.

6.1 Don't "Forget", but Don't "Feel" Either

In this study, we showed quantitatively (using the pre-study) and qualitatively (using the main study) that advisors have an inherent bias in writing consultation reports. We identified the two crucial and disjunct sources of biases: "forgetting" data and "feeling" data. In the former, advisors fail to reconstruct all key aspects and "forget" many aspects. Some advisors tend to remember different aspects than others. In the latter, they try to infer certain information based on "feeling" and only remember certain aspects. The captured data might potentially be compromised and biased. Both sources of biases occur in financial consultations and, thus, need to be addressed.

Both sources of biases can have different reasons. A lack of human capabilities can lead to forgetting and feeling data, such as bounded rationality [29]. While discrimination based on race or gender seems rather unlikely in our settings of financial consultations, a bias based on appearance is more likely, confirming Martin et al. [30]. Another likely source of bias in the setting of financial consultations is the principle-agent problem [38]. Financial advisors are inclined to give advice that suits their own and their organizational interests [36, 37]. For example, an advisor could sell stocks to a client regardless of their preferences to reach the goals imposed by the organization. From our observation, we conclude that advisors are biased towards organizational policies [31] and implicitly or explicitly "forget" or "feel" data in favor of their organization. Our design of MO can support an independent data entry process and assist the advisors to not "forget" and "feel" data.

Current HCI research often focuses on the single-user, human-AI interaction, where tools can help mitigate human biases [9, 48]. While these tools show potential in these settings, they are often unsuitable for human-human dyads. The introduced system, MO, is informed by previous literature on financial consultations and conversational agents alike [14–17, 64] and can seamlessly be integrated into human-human dyads.

Ensuring the completeness and accuracy of data entry also translates to current issues in machine learning. Concerning data completeness, modern AI models are still limited to the knowledge and data they have been trained on. An inherent bias in the data might be inconvenient to some people but might also be life-threatening to others. An example is the case of race and gender bias in modern medicine. White healthcare professionals *feel* that black people have a different pain perception [12]. This racial bias will influence AI training data in a modern AI-driven society. It will create bias in future AI systems, much like in our case, albeit even more dramatic.

To sum up, we point out criteria for evaluating information. For one, the advisors in our case tend to "forget" data, which leads to a lack of data completeness. Additionally, the advisors tend to "feel" data, which leads to poor data accuracy. Mitigating both aspects is needed to ensure an unbiased data entry. If unattended, these problems in incomplete and inaccurate data will translate to AI systems making biased decisions.

6.2 "Garbage In, Garbage Out"

"Garbage in, garbage out" (I-C17) is a quote from one of our clients but also a concept generally known in the field of computing. In computing and everyday life, we rely on complete and high-quality information to assess situations and make predictions. Without the correct information, i.e., "garbage", arriving at the correct conclusion of action is only a matter of luck. Most likely, we will also arrive at "garbage".

That is especially important in dyadic settings as they often have an information asymmetry. In our case, the advisor is the expert and knows more about the financial field than the client. However, only the client knows their personal information imposing a two-sided information asymmetry. Therefore, mutual trust is essential as both parties must rely on each other to make the correct decisions based on the available information. Since financial consultations are usually long-term relationships, adequate decision-making must be ensured for repeated decisions after months or years have passed, when the advisor must rely on notes and reports. Even more so if the client is assigned a new advisor who must rely on existing information. A new advisor can only know what is written down in the reports and needs to rely on this explicit knowledge.

Clients and advisors not only need to rely on each other but also on MO. MO builds on AI technology, such as NLP. Only if the clients and advisors rely on the system, it can show its full potential [22]. Without reliance on MO by both parties, the clients and advisors would have stuck to a more traditional form of financial consultation, i.e., pen-and-paper [14]. Then the system could have made no impact on the financial consultation. Several design decisions we undertook aimed toward this reliance. First, MO creates transparency by providing visual feedback. Further, users are not confronted with final decisions by the system but rather have the possibility to override decisions. Finally, users mostly interact voice-based with the system, fitting into the rituals and practices of financial consultations [15]. All these design decisions lead to a reliance of both parties on MO and, thus, an improved multi-party setting.

While bad decisions might not be life-threatening in the financial field, our findings can be transferred to a consultation with medical personnel, where they take notes and creates reports of your symptoms and problems. For example, Martin et al. [60] show that flawed reports in nursing can cause problems and serious harm if personnel changes. In the case of a change of advisor or nurse, another human takes over. This other human can adapt or change the information they got from the report. However, this is not the case if we use the gathered data as a base for AI systems. Feeding biased data into an AI system leads to biased predictions—again arriving at the topic of "garbage in, garbage out". While there are strategies to mitigate the biases of AI systems, such as algorithmic fairness [6–8], one should aim at removing biases earlier on in the pipeline. With this, we are not only considering mitigation biases in algorithmic decisions, i.e., concentrating on the "out" part. Instead, we aim at mitigating biases in the systems from the beginning, i.e., concentrating on the "in" part. This holistic and sociotechnical view [28] is essential to achieving the goal of creating ethical systems.

In conclusion, data is the base for most decisions. If this basis is flawed, the decisions might lead to wrong actions. This holds for human decision-making and AI systems alike. The consideration of both sides is the key to unbiased and ethical systems.

6.3 Trust Through Transparency

Advisors want their clients to be happy and rely on their decisions. In some dyadic settings, like parenting [50], churchgoing [49], or caretaking [52], the "clients" trust the "advisor" inherently. However, achieving trust is especially hard in institutionalized and potentially untrusted settings with much information asymmetry.

Our system proposes two levels of transparency. First, we have "positive" transparency, i.e., the clients know which data points are saved. Second, we also need to ensure "negative" transparency. With "negative" transparency, we refer to the fact that in seeing all attributes saved in the system, the clients also know that specific, sensitive attributes that are not needed for decision-making are not part of the system. For example, in our case, we do not input gender or ethnicity into the system, as this should never be part of an investment decision. However, we do enter age, which is required for fitting suggestions while having potential for discrimination. One would not suggest to an older person a very long-running investment product. We achieve this transparency by showing the data entered into the system while not "coercing into completeness" [17]. With this, we can potentially increase the trust in financial consultations and positively affect both sides of the dyad. The advisor has a more satisfied client and better data to base their advice on. The client can rely more on the advisor to make suitable suggestions and ensure they get a high-quality consultation.

In summary, transparency is of utmost importance to achieve trust and reliance. Especially in settings that have a much information asymmetry, this is of importance. If we increase transparency, the overall trust in the setting will also be increased.

6.4 Limitations and Outlook

This study comes with some limitations. For one, our tool was only tested in a specific design configuration; many more are imaginable. While this study is needed to have a starting point and benchmark, in future studies, many more designs of such a tool can be tested. Additionally, we only tested in one context—financial consultations. While they have important decisions at stake and fit the use case well, other dyadic settings are imaginable, such as a doctor visit or a government appointment. Finally, our study has a qualitative focus, which aims to investigate the advisors' and clients' perceptions. As a next step, the system should be developed further to also be able to reliably cope with localized words and not rely on a Wizard of Oz. After that, it would be beneficial to conduct a field study to see our effects translated into actual investment decisions.

It would also be interesting to accompany clients over several consultations for many years to fully get insights into the long-term implications of such a tool. Nonetheless, with this study, we show the feasibility and usefulness of MO.

7 Conclusion

This study introduces MO, a passive conversational agent supporting human-human dyads. We point out the importance of mitigating human biases in financial consultations. Our findings show that advisors tend to "feel" and "forget" data. MO helps build trust in the financial consultation, increases transparency, automates data entry, and provides the possibility of manually overriding the system. In this study, we stress that AI does not only have to be at risk of becoming a mirror of human biases but also as a powerful tool to intervene in the early stages of potentially biased. With modern AI systems, people are discriminated against because of biases in data and the systems themselves. Biases lead to people not trusting and not relying on the system. To conclude, there is a lot of research on biases in AI systems, and rightfully so. However, many forget that biases often originate from humans, e.g., during data labeling or entry processes. With this study, we want to remind and invite future HCI and AI researchers to consider the biases introduced during human data entry more often.

References

1. López, S.R.: Patient variable biases in clinical judgment: conceptual overview and methodological considerations. Psychol. Bull. **106**, 184–203 (1989)
2. Arnott, D.: Cognitive biases and decision support systems development: a design science approach. Inf. Syst. J. **16**, 55–78 (2006)
3. Zhang, Y., Bellamy, R.K.E., Kellogg, W.A.: Designing information for remediating cognitive biases in decision-making. In: Proceedings of the 33rd Annual ACM Conference on Human Factors in Computing Systems, pp. 2211–2220. ACM, New York, NY, USA (2015)
4. Buranyi, S.: Rise of the racist robots – how AI is learning all our worst impulses (2017). https://www.theguardian.com/inequality/2017/aug/08/rise-of-the-racist-robots-how-ai-is-learning-all-our-worst-impulses
5. Abdul, A., Vermeulen, J., Wang, D., Lim, B.Y., Kankanhalli, M.: Trends and trajectories for explainable, accountable and intelligible systems: an HCI research agenda. In: Proceedings of the 2018 CHI Conference on Human Factors in Computing Systems, pp. 1–18. ACM, Montreal QC Canada (2018)
6. Woodruff, A., Fox, S.E., Rousso-Schindler, S., Warshaw, J.: A qualitative exploration of perceptions of algorithmic fairness. In: Proceedings of the 2018 CHI Conference on Human Factors in Computing Systems, pp. 1–14. ACM, Montreal QC Canada (2018)
7. Lee, M.K., Kim, J.T., Lizarondo, L.: A human-centered approach to algorithmic services: considerations for fair and motivating smart community service management that allocates donations to non-profit organizations. In: Proceedings of the 2017 CHI Conference on Human Factors in Computing Systems, pp. 3365–3376. ACM, New York, NY, USA (2017)
8. Lee, M.K., Kusbit, D., Metsky, E., Dabbish, L.: Working with machines: the impact of algorithmic and data-driven management on human workers. In: Proceedings of the 33rd Annual ACM Conference on Human Factors in Computing Systems, pp. 1603–1612. ACM, New York, NY, USA (2015)

9. Echterhoff, J.M., Yarmand, M., McAuley, J.: AI-moderated decision-making: capturing and balancing anchoring bias in sequential decision tasks. In: CHI Conference on Human Factors in Computing Systems, pp. 1–9. ACM, New Orleans LA USA (2022)

10. Dennis, A., Newman, W.: Supporting doctor-patient interaction: using a surrogate application as a basis for evaluation. In: Conference Companion on Human Factors in Computing Systems, pp. 223–224. ACM, New York, NY, USA (1996)

11. Eckhardt, S., Sprenkamp, K., Zavolokina, L., Bauer, I., Schwabe, G.: Can artificial intelligence help used-car dealers survive in a data-driven used-car market? In: Drechsler, A., Gerber, A., Hevner, A. (eds.) The Transdisciplinary Reach of Design Science Research, pp. 115–127. Springer International Publishing, Cham (2022)

12. Hoffman, K.M., Trawalter, S., Axt, J.R., Oliver, M.N.: Racial bias in pain assessment and treatment recommendations, and false beliefs about biological differences between blacks and whites. Proc Natl Acad Sci U S A. **113**, 4296–4301 (2016)

13. Zheng, Q., Tang, Y., Liu, Y., Liu, W., Huang, Y.: UX research on conversational human-AI interaction: a literature review of the ACM digital library. In: Proceedings of the 2022 CHI Conference on Human Factors in Computing Systems, pp. 1–24. ACM, New York, NY, USA (2022)

14. Dolata, M., Agotai, D., Schubiger, S., Schwabe, G.: Pen-and-paper rituals in service interaction: combining high-touch and high-tech in financial advisory encounters. Proc. ACM Hum.-Comput. Interact. **3**, 224:1–224:24 (2019)

15. Dolata, M., Agotai, D., Schubiger, S., Schwabe, G.: Advisory service support that works: enhancing service quality with a mixed-reality system. Proc. ACM Hum.-Comput. Interact. **4**, 120:1–120:22 (2020)

16. Heinrich, P., Kilic, M., Aschoff, F.-R., Schwabe, G.: Enabling relationship building in tabletop-supported advisory settings. In: Proceedings of the 17th ACM Conference on Computer Supported Cooperative Work & Social Computing, pp. 171–183. ACM, Baltimore Maryland USA (2014)

17. Kilic, M., Heinrich, P., Schwabe, G.: Coercing into completeness in financial advisory service encounters. In: Proceedings of the 18th ACM Conference on Computer Supported Cooperative Work & Social Computing, pp. 1324–1335. ACM, Vancouver BC Canada (2015)

18. Jacovi, A., Marasović, A., Miller, T., Goldberg, Y.: Formalizing trust in artificial intelligence: prerequisites, causes and goals of human trust in AI. In: Proceedings of the 2021 ACM Conference on Fairness, Accountability, and Transparency, pp. 624–635. ACM, New York, NY, USA (2021)

19. Shin, D.: The effects of explainability and causability on perception, trust, and acceptance: implications for explainable AI. Int. J. Hum Comput Stud. **146**, 102551 (2021)

20. Eschenbach, W.J.: Transparency and the black box problem: why we do not trust aI. Philosophy & Technol. **34**(4), 1607–1622 (2021)

21. Lee, J.D., See, K.A.: Trust in Automation: Designing for Appropriate Reliance. Human Factors **31** (2004)

22. Lai, V., Chen, C., Liao, Q.V., Smith-Renner, A., Tan, C.: Towards a Science of Human-Ai Decision Making: a Survey of Empirical Studies. arXiv preprint arXiv:2112.11471 (2021)

23. Benda, N.C., Novak, L.L., Reale, C., Ancker, J.S.: Trust in AI: why we should be designing for appropriate reliance. J. Am. Med. Inform. Assoc. **29**, 207–212 (2021)

24. Schemmer, M., Kuehl, N., Benz, C., Bartos, A., Satzger, G.: Appropriate reliance on ai advice: conceptualization and the effect of explanations. In: Proceedings of the 28th International Conference on Intelligent User Interfaces, pp. 410–422. ACM, New York, NY, USA (2023)

25. Yang, F., Huang, Z., Scholtz, J., Arendt, D.L.: How do visual explanations foster end users' appropriate trust in machine learning? Presented at the Proceedings of the 25th International Conference on Intelligent User Interfaces (2020)

26. Amershi, S., et al.: Guidelines for human-AI interaction. In: Proceedings of the 2019 CHI Conference on Human Factors in Computing Systems, pp. 1–13. ACM, New York, NY, USA (2019)

27. Kallus, N., Zhou, A.: Residual unfairness in fair machine learning from prejudiced data. In: Proceedings of the 35th International Conference on Machine Learning, pp. 2439–2448. PMLR (2018)

28. Dolata, M., Feuerriegel, S., Schwabe, G.: A sociotechnical view of algorithmic fairness. Inf. Syst. J. **32**, 754–818 (2022)

29. Ariely, D.D.: Predictably Irrational, Revised and Expanded Edition: The Hidden Forces That Shape Our Decisions. Harper Perennial, New York, NY (2010)

30. Martin, C.L., Adams, S.: Behavioral biases in the service encounter: empowerment by default? Mark. Intell. Plan. **17**, 192–201 (1999)

31. Moseley, A., Thomann, E.: A behavioural model of heuristics and biases in frontline policy implementation. Policy Polit. **49**, 49–67 (2021)

32. Gibbons, L., Stoddart, K.: "Fast and frugal heuristics": clinical decision making in the emergency department. Int. Emerg. Nurs. **41**, 7–12 (2018)

33. Mendel, R., et al.: Confirmation bias: why psychiatrists stick to wrong preliminary diagnoses. Psychol. Med. **41**, 2651–2659 (2011)

34. Baker, H.K., Filbeck, G., Ricciardi, V.: How Behavioural Biases Affect Finance Professionals (2017). https://papers.ssrn.com/abstract=2899214

35. Friedline, T., Oh, S., Klemm, T., Kugiya, J.: Exclusion and Marginalization in Financial Services: Frontline Employees as Street-Level Bureaucrats (2020)

36. Golec, J.H.: Empirical tests of a principal-agent model of the investor-investment advisor relationship. J. Financial Quantitative Analysis **27**, 81–95 (1992)

37. Schwabe, G., Nussbaumer, P.: Why IT is not being used for financial advisory. Presented at the 17th European Conference on Information Systems (ECIS 2009) , Verona June 10 (2009)

38. Eisenhardt, K.M.: Agency theory: an assessment and review. Acad. Manag. Rev. **14**, 57–74 (1989)

39. Hayashi, Y., Wakabayashi, K.: Can AI become reliable source to support human decision making in a court scene? In: Companion of the 2017 ACM Conference on Computer Supported Cooperative Work and Social Computing, pp. 195–198. ACM, New York, NY, USA (2017)

40. Pinder, C., Fleck, R., Segundo Díaz, R.L., Beale, R., Hendley, R.J.: Accept the banana: exploring incidental cognitive bias modification techniques on smartphones. In: Proceedings of the 2016 CHI Conference Extended Abstracts on Human Factors in Computing Systems. pp. 2923–2931. ACM, New York, NY, USA (2016)

41. Pinder, C., Vermeulen, J., Cowan, B.R., Beale, R.: Digital behaviour change interventions to break and form habits. ACM Trans. Computer-Human Interaction (TOCHI). **25**, 1–66 (2018)

42. Cai, C.J., et al.: Human-centered tools for coping with imperfect algorithms during medical decision-making. In: Proceedings of the 2019 CHI Conference on Human Factors in Computing Systems, pp. 1–14. ACM, Glasgow Scotland Uk (2019)

43. Rädsch, T., Eckhardt, S., Leiser, F., Pandl, K.D., Thiebes, S., Sunyaev, A.: What Your Radiologist Might be Missing: Using Machine Learning to Identify Mislabeled Instances of X-ray Images (2021)

44. Calisto, F.M., Santiago, C., Nunes, N., Nascimento, J.C.: Introduction of human-centric AI assistant to aid radiologists for multimodal breast image classification. Int. J. Hum Comput Stud. **150**, 102607 (2021)

45. Wintersberger, P., et al.: Designing for continuous interaction with artificial intelligence systems. In: Extended Abstracts of the 2022 CHI Conference on Human Factors in Computing Systems, pp. 1–4. ACM, New York, NY, USA (2022)

46. Calisto, F.M., Nunes, N., Nascimento, J.C.: BreastScreening: on the use of multi-modality in medical imaging diagnosis. In: Proceedings of the International Conference on Advanced Visual Interfaces, pp. 1–5. ACM, New York, NY, USA (2020)

47. Ma, N.F., Rivera, V.A., Yao, Z., Yoon, D.: "Brush it off": how women workers manage and cope with bias and harassment in gender-agnostic gig platforms. In: CHI Conference on Human Factors in Computing Systems, pp. 1–13. ACM, New Orleans LA USA (2022)

48. Wang, D., Yang, Q., Abdul, A., Lim, B.Y.: Designing theory-driven user-centric explainable AI. In: Proceedings of the 2019 CHI Conference on Human Factors in Computing Systems, pp. 1–15. ACM, New York, NY, USA (2019)

49. O'Leary, T.K., Parmar, D., Olafsson, S., Paasche-Orlow, M., Bickmore, T., Parker, A.G.: Community dynamics in technospiritual interventions: lessons learned from a church-based mhealth pilot. In: CHI Conference on Human Factors in Computing Systems, pp. 1–23. ACM, New Orleans LA USA (2022)

50. Beneteau, E., Boone, A., Wu, Y., Kientz, J.A., Yip, J., Hiniker, A.: Parenting with alexa: exploring the introduction of smart speakers on family dynamics. In: Proceedings of the 2020 CHI Conference on Human Factors in Computing Systems, pp. 1–13. ACM, Honolulu HI USA (2020)

51. Porcheron, M., Fischer, J.E., Reeves, S., Sharples, S.: Voice interfaces in everyday life. In: Proceedings of the 2018 CHI Conference on Human Factors in Computing Systems, pp. 1–12. ACM, Montreal QC Canada (2018)

52. Zubatiy, T., Vickers, K.L., Mathur, N., Mynatt, E.D.: Empowering dyads of older adults with mild cognitive impairment and their care partners using conversational agents. In: Proceedings of the 2021 CHI Conference on Human Factors in Computing Systems, pp. 1–15. ACM, Yokohama Japan (2021)

53. Heyman, S., Artman, H.: Computer support for financial advisors and their clients: co-creating an investment plan. In: Proceedings of the 18th ACM Conference on Computer Supported Cooperative Work & Social Computing, pp. 1313–1323. ACM, New York, NY, USA (2015)

54. Azure Kinect DK – Develop AI Models | Microsoft Azure. https://azure.microsoft.com/en-us/services/kinect-dk/. Accessed 20 Aug 2022

55. Braun, V., Clarke, V.: Using thematic analysis in psychology. Qual. Res. Psychol. **3**, 77–101 (2006)

56. Castel, A.D., Rhodes, M.G., McCabe, D.P., Soderstrom, N.C., Loaiza, V.M.: Rapid communication: The fate of being forgotten: information that is initially forgotten is judged as less important. Quarterly J. Experimental Psychol. **65**, 2281–2287 (2012)

57. Miller, G.A.: The magical number seven, plus or minus two: some limits on our capacity for processing information. Psychol. Rev. **101**, 343–352 (1994)

58. Stafford, L., Burggraf, C.S., Sharkey, W.F.: Conversational memory the effects of time, recall, mode, and memory expectancies on remembrances of natural conversations. Human Comm Res. **14**, 203–229 (1987)

59. Rubio-Fernández, P., Mollica, F., Ali, M.O., Gibson, E.: How do you know that? automatic belief inferences in passing conversation. Cognition **193**, 104011 (2019)

60. Martin, K., Bickle, K., Lok, J.: Investigating the impact of cognitive bias in nursing documentation on decision-making and judgement. Int J Mental Health Nurs. **31**, 897–907 (2022)

61. Piolat, A., Olive, T., Kellogg, R.T.: Cognitive effort during note taking. Appl. Cognit. Psychol. **19**, 291–312 (2005)

62. Nadj, M., Knaeble, M., Li, M.X., Maedche, A.: Power to the oracle? design principles for interactive labeling systems in machine learning. Künstl Intell. **34**, 131–142 (2020)

63. Knaeble, M., Nadj, M., Germann, L., Maedche, A.: Tools of Trade of the Next Blue-Collar Job? Antecedents, Design Features, and Outcomes of Interactive Labeling Systems. ECIS 2023 Research Papers (2023)

64. Zhang, X., Su, Z., Rekimoto, J.: Aware: intuitive device activation using prosody for natural voice interactions. In: Proceedings of the 2022 CHI Conference on Human Factors in Computing Systems, pp. 1–16. ACM, New York, NY, USA (2022)

65. Kim, G., Kim, H.C.: Designing of multimodal feedback for enhanced multitasking performance. In: Proceedings of the SIGCHI Conference on Human Factors in Computing Systems, pp. 3113–3122. ACM, New York, NY, USA (2011)

66. Ehsan, U., Liao, Q.V., Muller, M., Riedl, M.O., Weisz, J.D.: Expanding explainability: towards social transparency in AI systems. In: Proceedings of the 2021 CHI Conference on Human Factors in Computing Systems, pp. 1–19. ACM, New York, NY, USA (2021)

67. Nussbaumer, P., Matter, I., Schwabe, G.: "Enforced" vs. "casual" transparency -- findings from IT-supported financial advisory encounters. ACM Trans. Manage. Inf. Syst. **3**, 11:1–11:19 (2012)

68. Putze, F., Amma, C., Schultz, T.: Design and evaluation of a self-correcting gesture interface based on error potentials from EEG. In: Proceedings of the 33rd Annual ACM Conference on Human Factors in Computing Systems, pp. 3375–3384. ACM, Seoul Republic of Korea (2015)

69. Roth, F.: The effect of the financial crisis on systemic trust. Intereconomics **44**, 203–208 (2009)

70. Fein, M.L.: Robo-Advisors: A Closer Look (2015). https://papers.ssrn.com/abstract=2658701

71. Park, J.Y., Ryu, J.P., Shin, H.J.: Robo advisors for portfolio management. Advanced Science and Technology Lett. **141**, 104–108 (2016)

72. SEC.gov | Investor Alert: Automated Investment Tools. https://www.sec.gov/investment/investor-alerts-and-bulletins/autolistingtoolshtm. Accessed 21 Aug 2022

Is Overreliance on AI Provoked by Study Design?

Zelun Tony Zhang[1,2]([⊠]) [iD], Sven Tong[2], Yuanting Liu[1][iD], and Andreas Butz[2][iD]

[1] fortiss GmbH, Research Institute of the Free State of Bavaria, Munich, Germany
{zhang,liu}@fortiss.org
[2] LMU Munich, Munich, Germany
sven.tong@campus.lmu.de, butz@ifi.lmu.de

Abstract. Recent studies found that humans tend to overrely on AI when making decisions with AI support. AI explanations were often insufficient as mitigation, and sometimes even increased overreliance. However, typical AI-assisted decision-making studies consist of long series of decision tasks, potentially causing complacent behavior, and not properly reflecting many real-life scenarios. We therefore raise the question whether these findings might be favored by the design of these studies. In a first step to answer this question, we compared different study designs in an experiment and found indications that observations of overreliance might indeed be favored by common study designs. Further research is needed to clarify to what extent overreliance can be attributed to study designs rather than more fundamental human-AI interaction issues.

Keywords: human-AI interaction · AI-assisted decision-making · explainable AI · overreliance

1 Introduction

Artificial intelligence (AI) is increasingly used to support human decisions, often in high-stakes domains such as healthcare, finance, or criminal justice (e.g. [2,6,18]). The hope is that AI complements human decision-making, given the supposedly complementary strengths and weaknesses of humans and machines [7,9]. However, recent studies repeatedly demonstrate that humans are prone to overrely on AI, i.e. they adopt AI outputs, even when they are flawed [1–3,6,8]. To address this issue, a common approach is to provide explanations of AI outputs. The reasoning is that by explaining how the AI comes to a result, humans should be able to better calibrate their reliance on the AI [17]. However, several studies show that in many cases, AI explanations may even increase blind trust in AI, rather than improve calibration [1,2,8,13]. Two recent studies [3,5] indicate that the reason for this effect is that people do not engage analytically with AI decision support, instead relying on fast but error-prone heuristic thinking [10].

J. Abdelnour Nocera et al. (Eds.): INTERACT 2023, LNCS 14144, pp. 49–58, 2023.
https://doi.org/10.1007/978-3-031-42286-7_3

Studies of AI-assisted decision-making typically involve a series of tasks which participants have to solve with the support of an AI model. Typically, these series are quite long, with up to 50 tasks being common, as shown in Table 1. With such tiring task series lengths, one can reasonably suspect that participants become complacent over time, reducing their analytic engagement with the AI, and therefore increasing overreliance. At the same time, these long, intensive task series do not reflect well many real-world scenarios of AI-assisted decision-making. This raises the following question:

RQ: Is overreliance indeed a fundamental issue of AI-assisted decision-making and explainable AI, or are the observations of overreliance in recent studies rather provoked by their long task series?

Table 1. Examples of studies that found overreliance in AI-assisted decision-making, along with the type and number of tasks participants had to solve.

Publication	Study task	# Tasks
Bansal et al. [1]	Sentiment classification	50
	Law School Admission Test	20
Buçinca et al. [3]	Nutrition assessment	26
Green and Chen [6]	Recidivism risk assessment	40
	Loan risk assessment	40
Lai and Tan [11]	Deception detection	20
Liu et al. [12]	Recidivism prediction	20
	Profession classification	20
Schmidt and Biessmann [15]	Sentiment classification	50
Wang and Yin [17]	Recidivism prediction	32
	Forest cover prediction	32

In this paper, we present a first attempt at answering this question. In particular, we approached the question through two novel study elements. If long task series indeed contribute to overreliance, the tendency to overrely should . . .

1. . . . increase with the progression of the task session. We therefore employed a study design which allows us to measure how the tendency to overrely develops over the course of the task series (Sect. 2.2).
2. . . . be less pronounced in shorter series. We therefore compare the common study design of a single, long task session to a design where participants solve the tasks in multiple short sessions, either with or without AI explanations (Sect. 2.3).

2   Experimental Setup

2.1   Study Task, Apparatus and Procedure

We followed Liu et al. [12] in choosing profession classification as the study task, since it does not require participants to have special knowledge or skills. The task also bears some resemblance to AI applications in human resources, a domain where the stakes for the outcome of AI-assisted decision-making are high.

The task was based on a dataset by De-Arteaga et al. [4], consisting of short biographies scraped from the internet and each labeled with one of 29 occupations. The participants' task was to read a series of 50 biographies and to determine the occupations of the described persons, as shown in Fig. 1. To keep the task manageable, we limited the choice of occupations to the same five as in Liu et al. [12]. Above each biography, participants saw the prediction of a logistic regression model. Depending on the study condition (Sect. 2.3), participants also saw explanations for the predictions, generated with LIME [14] and visualized through color-coded text highlights, similar to Liu et al. [12].

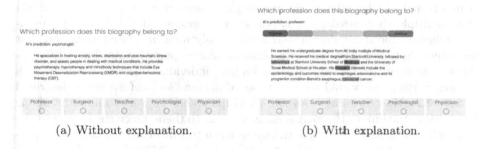

(a) Without explanation.   (b) With explanation.

Fig. 1. Examples of the occupation classification task presented to participants.

The study was set up as an online survey, distributed via university mailing lists and the online research platform SurveyCircle [16]. It started with a demographic questionnaire and an introduction to the task. After completing all tasks, participants answered an exit survey in which they could provide free text feedback. In addition to the 50 study tasks, we included two attention checks. Completing the study took 22.54 min on average. Each participant received a 10€ Amazon voucher as compensation. As an incentive to perform accurately, the most accurate participants could win an additional 5€ Amazon voucher.

2.2   Measures

We measured *agreement* with the AI and *overreliance* in two different ways: *per participant* and *per task*, i.e. as development over the course of the task series. Agreement per participant was measured as the share of all tasks in which a participant's answer was the same as the AI prediction. Overreliance was measured as the share of tasks in which a participant agreed with a wrong AI prediction. This conforms to measures commonly used in related work (e.g. [1, 3, 11, 12, 15, 17]).

To measure the development throughout the task series, we divided the 50 tasks into ten blocks with five tasks each. Each block contained exactly one wrong AI prediction. This means that participants experienced an AI accuracy of 80%, which corresponds to the 86% test set accuracy of our logistic regression model. The order of the blocks and the order of the questions within the blocks were both randomized. This yielded one measurement point for overreliance for each block of five tasks. For each block, we measured overreliance as the share of participants who agreed with the wrong AI prediction in that block. The agreement for each task was measured similarly as the share of participants whose answer was the same as the AI prediction. Lastly, we also recorded the *time* participants took for each task.

2.3   Study Design and Conditions

We employed a 2×2 between-subject design. The first factor was whether participants had to solve all 50 tasks in a single session (*single session group*—SSG) or in multiple short sessions (*multiple sessions group*—MSG). The SSG condition reflected the study design that is commonly used in related work and that we suspected to induce complacent behavior among participants. The MSG condition was meant to be less tiring by keeping individual sessions short. In each session, participants would solve only one of the ten blocks of five tasks described in Sect. 2.2. After finishing a session, participants had to wait a minimum of one hour before the link to the next session was sent to them. Once they received the new link, participants were free to choose when to solve the task block. If a participant did not submit the current task block within 24 h, they would receive a reminder message. To make participation more convenient, we sent session links and reminders to participants' smartphones via WhatsApp.

Previous studies showed that explanations sometimes increase participants' overreliance. We wanted to investigate whether this applied to participants in the MSG condition as well. If participants in the MSG condition were less complacent, they might engage with explanations more analytically, possibly leading to improved trust calibration. The second factor was therefore whether participants would see explanations for model outputs or not (see Fig. 1).

3   Results

After filtering out drop-outs, submissions that failed the attention checks, and other invalid submissions, the number of participants was 47 (average age: 30.1 years, 20 female, 27 male). On average, participants' self-assessed English level was moderately high (3.78 on a five-point Likert scale with 1=basic, 5=native speaker). Participants' average self-assessed AI expertise was moderate (2.91 on a five-point Likert scale with 1=no expertise, 5=expert).

Figure 2 shows the *agreement* with AI and *overreliance* in all four conditions per participant. While *agreement* was slightly higher with explanations, the main effect of explanations was not significant according to a two-way ANOVA test, $F(1, 43) = 1.547, p = 0.220$. Both the main effect of the factor *session*, $F(1, 43) = 0.150, p = 0.701$, as well as the interaction effect between *explanation* and *session*, $F(1, 43) = 0.253, p = 0.618$, were also not significant. For *overreliance*, there appeared to be a more pronounced interaction effect between the factors *explanation* and *session*: Overreliance did not differ between the two SSG conditions, but was higher with explanations than without in the MSG conditions, which was against our expectation. However, this interaction effect was not significant according to a two-way ANOVA test, $F(1, 43) = 0.905, p = 0.347$. The main effects of *explanation*, $F(1, 43) = 0.498, p = 0.484$, and *session*, $F(1, 43) = 1.636, p = 0.208$, were also not significant.

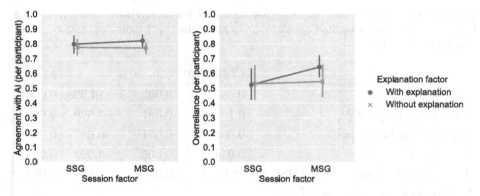

Fig. 2. Participants' agreement with AI predictions (left) and their overreliance (right) per participant. Error bars represent 95% confidence intervals.

Figures 3–5 show how participants' *overreliance*, their *agreement* with AI, and the *time* they took on average for a task developed throughout the task series in each of the four conditions. We analyzed these results using linear regression, as shown in Tables 2–4. We included the position of a task (or task block for overreliance), the session factor, and the explanation factor as main effects in each model. We further included interaction effects into the models where the data suggested the possible presence of interactions. While we performed linear regression with ordinary least squares for *agreement* and *time*, we resorted to robust linear regression using iterated re-weighted least squares (IRLS) and Huber's T norm for *overreliance* due to the inherently smaller number of measurement points and the resulting larger impact of outliers.

The most prominent observation is that in general, both *overreliance* and *agreement* significantly increased throughout the task series, while the *time to solve a task* decreased significantly. This suggests that participants indeed spent less effort on the tasks as the series progressed, as we expected. However, differently than expected, this observation applies to both the SSG and the MSG con-

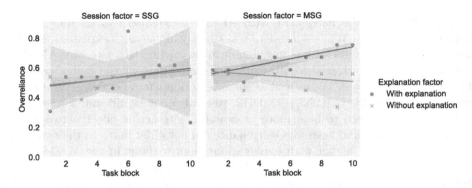

Fig. 3. Participants' overreliance over each task block. The lines represent linear regressions for each condition, the translucent bands around the lines represent 95% confidence intervals.

Table 2. Output of robust linear regression model for *overreliance*, using IRLS and Huber's T norm with median absolute deviation scaling. (*) indicates statistical significance at $\alpha = 0.05$.

	Coefficient	Std. error	z	p
(Intercept)	0.4537	0.032	14.328	0.000
Session factor [MSG]	0.1078	0.031	3.529	0.000*
Explanation factor [with]	0.0026	0.031	0.087	0.931
Task block	0.0147	0.005	3.208	0.001*
Task block * Session factor [MSG] * Explanation factor [without]	−0.0194	0.007	−2.931	0.003*

ditions. One notable exception is that *overreliance* (Fig. 3 and Table 2) slightly decreased throughout the task series in the MSG condition without explanations, while it significantly increased with explanations. While this interaction effect was significant, it has to be interpreted with caution due to the small number of participants and the resulting noise in the data. Also in contrast to our expectation, participants in the MSG conditions were on average significantly more overreliant than in the SSG conditions.

Some more subtle effects could be observed for the *agreement* with AI (Fig. 4 and Table 3). Explanations appeared to induce higher agreement with the AI for both SSG and MSG; however, the effect was not significant. There was also no statistically significant difference between SSG and MSG in terms of agreement with AI. The slight interaction between the explanation factor and task position in the SSG conditions visible in Fig. 4 was not significant either.

As for the *time to solve a task* (Fig. 5 and Table 4), MSG and SSG conditions differed significantly, with MSG participants taking significantly more time. The time participants took also decreased significantly faster in the MSG conditions.

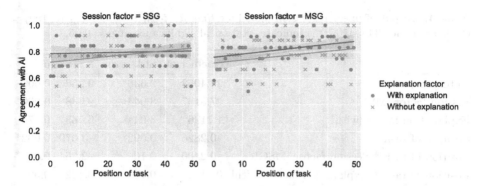

Fig. 4. Participants' agreement with AI predictions over each task. The lines represent linear regressions for each condition, the translucent bands around the lines represent 95% confidence intervals.

Table 3. Output of linear regression model for *agreement with AI*, $R^2 = 0.076$, $F(4, 195) = 4.033, p = 0.004 < 0.05$. (*) indicates statistical significance at $\alpha = 0.05$.

	Coefficient	Std. error	t	p
(Intercept)	0.7138	0.024	29.652	0.000
Session factor [MSG]	0.0094	0.016	0.578	0.564
Explanation factor [with]	0.0547	0.032	1.706	0.090
Position of task	0.0022	0.001	2.802	0.006*
Position of task * Explanation factor [with]	−0.0008	0.001	−0.705	0.482

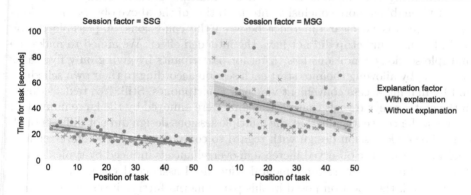

Fig. 5. Average time participants took to solve each task. The lines represent linear regressions for each condition, the translucent bands around the lines represent 95% confidence intervals.

The reason for these differences is not clear, although we suspect that they might be the result of MSG participants using their smaller smartphone screens. The explanation factor had no significant effect on the time participants took, neither as a main effect, nor in interaction with the task position.

Table 4. Output of linear regression model for *time for task*, $R^2 = 0.586, F(5, 190) = 53.78, p = 1.34\mathrm{e}{-34} < 0.05$. (*) indicates statistical significance at $\alpha = 0.05$.

	Coefficient	Std. error	t	p
(Intercept)	24.4063	2.636	9.258	0.000
Session factor [MSG]	27.5137	3.044	9.038	0.000*
Explanation factor [with]	1.7126	3.044	0.563	0.574
Position of task	−0.2826	0.092	−3.079	0.002*
Position of task * Session factor [MSG]	−0.2400	0.106	−2.264	0.025*
Position of task * Explanation factor [with]	0.0129	0.106	0.122	0.903

4 Discussion and Outlook

Our results suggest that participants indeed spend significantly less effort as they progress through the task series of a typical AI-assisted decision-making study: Both participants' agreement with the AI and their overreliance increase throughout the task series, while the time they spend on a task decreases. Yet, by itself, this observation is not enough to conclude that overreliance in prior work was induced by the long task series in those studies. An alternative explanation could be, for instance, that people generally gain (potentially unjustified) trust into AI over time, irrespective of how tasks are presented to them. This would be a more fundamental issue for AI-assisted decision-making.

Comparing the single session with the multiple sessions study design was meant to enable a more conclusive interpretation of the above observation. However, there was no clear difference between the conditions. A possible reason could be that our setup did not have the intended effect. We aimed to make the multiple sessions conditions less tiring for participants by giving only five tasks at a time, by allowing them to start each session according to their own schedule, and by making access convenient via their smartphones. Still, free text feedback in the exit surveys reveals that participants were annoyed by the large number of sessions. Hence, we assume that the multiple sessions design did not differ enough from the single session design with regard to complacency. It therefore remains unclear whether the observed increase in overreliance is induced by typical study designs, or if it is a more fundamental issue of AI-assisted decision-making.

We think the question posed in this paper merits further investigation, since the answer would be crucial for the interpretation of prior results and the design of future studies. We presented a first attempt with a small number of participants. Apart from recruiting more participants, a future follow-up study needs to find a better way to administer tasks in a less tiring way. Other task domains, subjective measures (e.g. self-rated trust), or qualitative evaluations might also be of interest. On the other hand, our task-block-based setup is a promising direction for future work, enabling the measurement of overreliance over the course of the task series instead of merely aggregated over all tasks. This potentially provides more nuanced insights into how AI impacts human decision-making.

References

1. Bansal, G., et al.: Does the whole exceed its parts? The effect of AI explanations on complementary team performance. In: Proceedings of the 2021 CHI Conference on Human Factors in Computing Systems, pp. 81:1–81:16. CHI 2021, ACM, Yokohama, Japan (May 2021). https://doi.org/10.1145/3411764.3445717

2. Bussone, A., Stumpf, S., O'Sullivan, D.: The role of explanations on trust and reliance in clinical decision support systems. In: Proceedings of the 2015 International Conference on Healthcare Informatics, pp. 160–169. ICHI 2015, IEEE, Dallas, TX, USA (Oct 2015). https://doi.org/10.1109/ICHI.2015.26

3. Buçinca, Z., Malaya, M.B., Gajos, K.Z.: To trust or to think: cognitive forcing functions can reduce overreliance on AI in AI-assisted decision-making. Proc. ACM on Hum. Comput. Interact. 5, 188:1–188:21 (2021). https://doi.org/10.1145/3449287

4. De-Arteaga, M., et al.: Bias in bios: a case study of semantic representation bias in a high-stakes setting. In: Proceedings of the Conference on Fairness, Accountability, and Transparency, pp. 120–128. FAT* 2019, ACM, Atlanta, GA, USA (Jan 2019). https://doi.org/10.1145/3287560.3287572

5. Gajos, K.Z., Mamykina, L.: Do people engage cognitively with AI? Impact of AI assistance on incidental learning. In: 27th International Conference on Intelligent User Interfaces, pp. 794–806. IUI 2022, ACM, Helsinki, Finland (Mar 2022). https://doi.org/10.1145/3490099.3511138

6. Green, B., Chen, Y.: The principles and limits of algorithm-in-the-loop decision making. Proc. ACM Hum. Comput. Interact. 3, 50:1–50:24 (2019). https://doi.org/10.1145/3359152

7. Guszcza, J.: Smarter together: why artificial intelligence needs human-centered design. Deloitte Rev. 22, 36–45 (2018)

8. Jacobs, M., Pradier, M.F., McCoy, T.H., Perlis, R.H., Doshi-Velez, F., Gajos, K.Z.: How machine-learning recommendations influence clinician treatment selections: the example of antidepressant selection. Transl. Psychiatry 11(1), 108:1–108:9 (2021). https://doi.org/10.1038/s41398-021-01224-x

9. Jarrahi, M.H.: Artificial intelligence and the future of work: human-AI symbiosis in organizational decision making. Bus. Horiz. 61(4), 577–586 (2018). https://doi.org/10.1016/j.bushor.2018.03.007

10. Kahneman, D.: Thinking Fast Slow. Farrar, Straus and Giroux, New York (2011)

11. Lai, V., Tan, C.: On human predictions with explanations and predictions of machine learning models: a case study on deception detection. In: Proceedings of the Conference on Fairness, Accountability, and Transparency, pp. 29–38. FAT* 2019, ACM, Atlanta, GA, USA (Jan 2019). https://doi.org/10.1145/3287560.3287590

12. Liu, H., Lai, V., Tan, C.: Understanding the effect of out-of-distribution examples and interactive explanations on human-AI decision making. Proc. ACM Hum. Comput. Interact. 5, 408:1–408:45 (2021). https://doi.org/10.1145/3479552

13. Poursabzi-Sangdeh, F., Goldstein, D.G., Hofman, J.M., Vaughan, J.W., Wallach, H.: Manipulating and measuring model interpretability. In: Proceedings of the 2021 CHI Conference on Human Factors in Computing Systems, pp. 237:1–237:52. CHI 2021, ACM, Yokohama, Japan (May 2021). https://doi.org/10.1145/3411764.3445315

14. Ribeiro, M.T., Singh, S., Guestrin, C.: "Why should I trust you?": explaining the predictions of any classifier. In: Proceedings of the 22nd ACM SIGKDD International Conference on Knowledge Discovery and Data Mining, pp. 1135–1144. KDD 2016, ACM, San Francisco, CA, USA (Aug 2016). https://doi.org/10.1145/2939672.2939778

15. Schmidt, P., Biessmann, F.: Calibrating human-AI collaboration: impact of risk, ambiguity and transparency on algorithmic bias. In: Holzinger, A., Kieseberg, P., Tjoa, A.M., Weippl, E. (eds.) CD-MAKE 2020. LNCS, vol. 12279, pp. 431–449. Springer, Cham (2020). https://doi.org/10.1007/978-3-030-57321-8_24

16. SurveyCircle: Research website SurveyCircle. Published 2016. (2022). https://www.surveycircle.com

17. Wang, X., Yin, M.: Are explanations helpful? A comparative study of the effects of explanations in AI-assisted decision-making. In: Proceedings of the 26th International Conference on Intelligent User Interfaces, pp. 318–328. IUI 2021, ACM, College Station, TX, USA (Apr 2021). https://doi.org/10.1145/3397481.3450650

18. Yang, Q., Steinfeld, A., Zimmerman, J.: Unremarkable AI: fitting intelligent decision support into critical, clinical decision-making processes. In: Proceedings of the 2019 CHI Conference on Human Factors in Computing Systems, pp. 238:1–238:11. CHI 2019, ACM, Glasgow, Scotland, UK (May 2019). https://doi.org/10.1145/3290605.3300468

RePaLM: A Data-Driven AI Assistant for Making Stronger Pattern Choices

Christina Milousi[1], George E. Raptis[2(✉)], Christina Katsini[2],
and Christos Katsanos[1]

[1] Aristotle University of Thessaloniki, Thessaloniki, Greece
{cmilousi,ckatsanos}@csd.auth.gr
[2] Human Opsis, Patras, Greece
{graptis,ckatsini}@humanopsis.com

Abstract. Security mechanisms based on patterns, such as Pattern Lock, are commonly used to prevent unauthorized access. They introduce several benefits, such as ease of use, an additional layer of security, convenience, and versatility. However, many users tend to create simple and easily predictable patterns. To address this issue, we propose a data-driven real-time assistant approach called RePaLM. RePaLM is a neural network-based assistant that provides users with information about less commonly used pattern points, aiming to help users to make stronger, less predictable pattern choices. Our user study shows that RePaLM can effectively nudge users towards using less predictable patterns without compromising memorability. Overall, RePaLM is a promising solution for enhancing the security of pattern-based authentication systems.

Keywords: Usable security · User authentication · Artificial intelligence · Neural networks · Data-driven recommendation · Patterns · User study

1 Introduction

User authentication is crucial in mobile, embedded, and ubiquitous computing to secure and protect user data. However, limitations in the process can impact both security and usability [6]. A persistent issue is that users tend to make predictable choices [11], which may lead to negative outcomes for both users (e.g., leak of personal data) and service providers (e.g., harming reliability). Focusing on the Pattern Lock[1] mechanism, a widely used authentication scheme for smartphones, users tend to choose easily guessable patterns, thereby compromising their devices' security. For example, they create patterns starting from the top-left edge or simple shapes [17,25]. Aiming to address this challenge, we introduce RePaLM. RePaLM is a data-driven mechanism that attempts to nudge

---

[1] We use the term *"Pattern Lock"* to describe securing a device by creating a custom pattern in a 3×3 grid. In literature, similar terms are *"unlock pattern"*, *"unlock gesture"*, *"Android password pattern"* and *"Android unlock pattern"*.

© The Author(s), under exclusive license to Springer Nature Switzerland AG 2023
J. Abdelnour Nocera et al. (Eds.): INTERACT 2023, LNCS 14144, pp. 59–69, 2023.
https://doi.org/10.1007/978-3-031-42286-7_4

people to make better choices when creating patterns. It is based on real-time neural network analysis, allowing the system to learn from and make predictions based on existing data. It analyzes patterns that users have selected and uses this information to provide real-time accurate and personalized recommendations for creating stronger patterns. The following sections discuss related works, motivation, and research question, present RePaLM and report its evaluation study, and discuss the findings, implications, limitations and future work.

2   Related Work, Motivation, and Research Question

Research on safeguarding user security in Pattern Lock schemes has focused on enhancing the resilience of Pattern Lock systems by developing mechanisms to counteract specific types of attacks, including thermal attacks [1,2], shoulder surfing attacks [9,14], and smudge attacks [8,21]. However, these mechanisms prioritize the login process rather than the pattern creation process, resulting in users choosing simple and similar patterns [26], making the patterns more predictable and thus more vulnerable to guessing attacks.

Previous works to solve the predictability of the authentication patterns have explored solutions for nudging or forcing people towards more secure choices. Such solutions include the use of blocklists to deter users from creating certain patterns [19], the adoption of dynamic user interfaces with symbols that mutate every time a user swipes the screen of the Pattern Lock scheme [4], and the use of double patterns that are visually imposed on one another [10]. Although such methods can be effective regarding security, they introduce other issues like limited flexibility, lack of personalization, added complexity for users in having to remember and navigate a dynamic grid, increased frustration and difficulty in inputting the password correctly, or they might be viewed as restrictive by users and discourage them from using the system, leading to low adoption rates.

Other user authentication schemes (e.g., graphical passwords and patterns) have employed similar techniques to increase security, such as limiting available user choices [3], incorporating gameful elements [15,20], and providing recommendations and feedback [22,23]. However, these methods may only sometimes provide accurate or personalized feedback or directions. They may introduce further vulnerabilities because they are often based on static data (e.g., salient points of images, static pattern datasets) and do not adapt over time. These solutions only shift user choices towards new predictable ones. To address these limitations, we could use data-driven approaches, which utilize large datasets to provide more accurate feedback, ultimately improving the system's overall security and providing a more seamless user experience.

Considering that data-driven approaches successfully applied to alphanumeric passwords [18,24], we anticipate they could also be applied to Pattern Lock schemes. Motivated by the need to address the challenge of creating secure authentication patterns in the context of Pattern Lock schemes, we aim to answer the following question: *"Can we build a data-driven mechanism that could nudge people into making stronger pattern choices?"* To answer our research question, we designed RePaLM and performed a comparative evaluation study.

3   RePaLM

RePaLM aims to introduce a recommendation layer on Pattern Lock mechanisms. Pattern Lock is a graphical password authentication mechanism incorporating a 3×3 grid of small dots as its basic user interface on the touchscreen. The users are required to draw memorized graphical patterns on the grid. The streaks the users draw must be a one-way path connecting four or more dots on the grid. That is a specific form of a directed graph with nine vertices at maximum and distinct starting and ending points.

RePaLM implements a recommendation engine to nudge users making less predictable pattern choices (Fig. 1). As the user selects each pattern point, a long short-term memory (LSTM) component analyzes the pattern the user has created (so far) and the patterns available in a pattern repository. Based on them, it provides real-time recommendations for the less frequent point(s). LSTM is well-suited for sequence prediction problems as it can effectively retain information, dependencies, and sequential data from previous (time) steps. Therefore, it is a good fit for predicting the next step in a Pattern Lock creation process. The pattern repository contains pattern datasets [7,25] and dynamically updates with new ones. The recommendations are based on the real-time prediction analysis of the data provided and aim to guide the users to create less predictable patterns. After pattern creation, RePaLM continues to learn and improve over time by analyzing more patterns. From a technical side, we deployed RePaLM as a web application based on `Flask` and `Python`. We used `TensorFlow` and `NumPy` to deliver the LSTM recommendation model. The parameters of the final model are: `activation=softmax, loss=categorical_crossentropy, optimizer=adam, activation=softmax, units=64, dropout=0.2`.

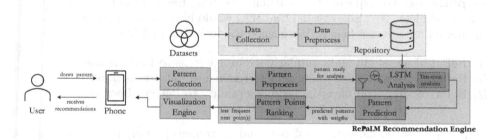

Fig. 1. The conceptual architecture of RePaLM.

We created two alternative versions of RePaLM: RePaLM R1 recommends the least frequent next point, while RePaLM R3 recommends the three less frequent next points. We opened up the range of the next points to provide users with more options, not bias them into a single point, and increase the chances of finding a pattern that is both secure and memorable. To visualize the recommendations (Fig. 2), we colored the recommended point(s) with a semi-transparent shade (blue color), aiming to provide a visual cue that helps users to identify the recommended points. This coloring scheme allows them to stand out from the background without overwhelming the user's attention. We performed a between-subjects comparison study to investigate whether RePaLM would nudge people to make better pattern choices compared to the original scheme.

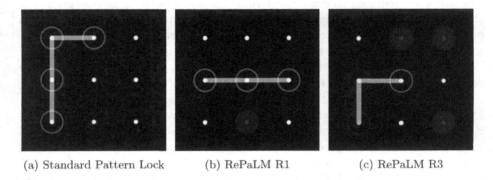

(a) Standard Pattern Lock   (b) RePaLM R1   (c) RePaLM R3

Fig. 2. The standard Pattern Lock Mechanism and RePaLM. In RePaLM R1(b), point 8 is the less frequent point of a 4-5-6 pattern; in RePaLM R3(c) points 2, 3, and 9 are the less frequent points of a 7-4-5 pattern. **Note**: Numbering starts from the top-left point and continues from left to right and from top to bottom.

4   Study

4.1   Methodology

Hypotheses. We expected that participants using RePaLM would make better pattern choices. We also expected that they would have similar performance and memorability across schemes. We formed the following null hypotheses:

H_1 RePaLM users will make similarly secure patterns to Pattern Lock users.
H_2 RePaLM users will have similar performance to Pattern Lock users.
H_3 RePaLM users will have similar memorability to Pattern Lock users.

Participants. 64 individuals (32 men and 32 women) participated in the study. Their age range was between 19 and 52 ($M = 32$, $SD = 7$). The vast majority mentioned that are familiar with and have used Pattern Lock mechanisms (86%).

Instruments and Metrics. To assess the participants' pattern choices (H_1), we used the *pattern strength score (M_p)* [22]. M_p is a validated strength score function based on both heuristics and attack-related findings (e.g., shoulder surfing attacks). It uses three dimensions: pattern length (L_p), ratio of non-repeated segments (N_p), and number of intersecting points (I_p). The higher the M_p score (Eq. 1; $w_L = .81$, $w_N = .04$, and $w_I = .15$ [22]), the stronger the pattern is.

$$M_p = w_L \times \frac{L_p}{15} + w_N \times N_p + w_I \times \frac{min(I_p, 5)}{5} \in [0, 1] \qquad (1)$$

To evaluate participants' performance (H_2), we used metrics commonly found in the literature: i) *pattern selection time (T_s)*, as in [17,19], ii) *authentication time (T_a)*, as in [9,13,14,19], and iii) *basic error rate (E_b)* (i.e., authentication was successful overall, but took the participant two or three times to correctly authenticate), as in [9,13]. To assess participants' memorability (H_3), we also used metrics found in the literature: i) number of *recall attempts (N_a)*, as in [19], ii) *successful logins (L_s)*, as in [14,19], and iii) number of *resets (N_r)*, as in [20].

To assess participants' *perceived security and experience*, we used a questionnaire consisting of statements the participants had to declare whether they disagreed or agreed (5-point Likert scale). The statements were, for RePaLM: i) It helped me create a strong pattern; ii) It helped me create a stronger pattern than what I would create if I had used the typical pattern lock mechanism; iii) It helped me create a memorable pattern; iv) I chose points based on what was recommended; v) I considered recommendations; vi) The recommendation mechanism was easy to understand; vii) The recommendations were useful — for the Pattern Lock scheme: i) I created a strong, hardly be guessed, pattern; ii) I created a memorable pattern; iii) If I knew the points that are less likely to be used, I would have created a stronger pattern; iv) If I knew the points that are most likely to be used, I would have created a stronger pattern. We encouraged participants to provide any further comments they wished to share.

To collect *demographic information*, we asked the participants i) about general information (gender, age) and ii) experience with pattern lock mechanisms. During the second section, the participants stated: i) if they had used pattern lock mechanisms in the past; ii) if so, in what cases, iii) if they had used mechanisms that recommend them the next movement, do not let them choose specific points, show them the pattern strength in real-time; iv) if they use pattern lock mechanisms in their everyday life; v) if they consider pattern lock mechanisms secure; vi) if they consider pattern lock mechanisms usable.

Experimental Procedure. First, we performed the recruitment process by communicating the study through social media and personal acquaintances. We recruited 64 participants; the participation was remote, voluntary, and with no compensation. We provided them with a link to the study website for details about the procedure; they provided their consent for participation, data collection, and data manipulation. Following a between-subjects design, each participant was allocated with a Pattern Lock mechanism sequentially (i.e., the first participant with the standard Pattern Lock, the second with RePaLM R1, the third with RePaLM R3, and so on); sample sizes per condition were: Pattern Lock = 22, RePaLM R1 = 21, and RePaLM R3 = 21. They received textual and visual instructions (video demonstration) on how the assigned mechanism works. Next, participants created their patterns on the assigned mechanisms.

Then, they had to re-draw their pattern to confirm and store it. Next, the participants answered the perceived security and experience and demographics questionnaires. A login session followed; there were no hints or other assistance. If they could not recall their pattern, they could reset it by creating and confirming a new one. Following a three-weeks period protocol [14], we asked participants to log in frequently to the system, mimicking smartphone use. We encouraged them to use any mobile device they wanted to create their patterns (and then log in), aiming to make them more comfortable (e.g., use the mechanisms as they would normally do), and thus, increase the study's ecological validity. Finally, we collected and analyzed the study data using quantitative and qualitative methods.

4.2   Results

We conducted ANOVA tests to assess our hypotheses, with the independent between-subjects variable being the different scheme versions and the dependent variables being the metrics discussed in Sect. 4.1. We ensured that the tests satisfied the necessary assumptions unless specified otherwise in the following. Furthermore, we conducted post hoc analyses with appropriate Bonferroni adjustments (Table 1). Next, we discuss only the significant differences.

Pattern Strength. There was statistically significant difference in M_p ($F = 17.302$, $p < .001$, $\eta_p^2 = .200$). Post hoc analysis showed that the patterns created with RePaLM R1 and R3 had significantly better strength scores than those created with Pattern Lock ($p < .001$, 95% $C.I. = [.085, .249]$; $p < .001$, 95% $C.I. = [.107, .266]$). Following the quantization approach [12, 22], we divided M_p into three strength categories: weak ($.00$–$.40$), medium ($.41$–$.56$), and strong ($.57$–1.00). Most patterns created with the RePaLM versions are categorized as strong (RePaLM R1: 22% medium, 78% strong patterns; RePaLM R3: 4% weak, 19% medium, and 77% strong patterns). On the other hand, we observe a more balanced distribution for the patterns created with the Pattern Lock scheme: 35% weak, 40% medium, and 25% strong patterns. Focusing on the M_p dimensions, there was statistically significant difference in L_p ($F = 28.781$, $p < .001$, $\eta_p^2 = .294$) and I_p ($F = 3.297$, $p = .040$, $\eta_p^2 = .046$). Patterns created with RePaLM R1 and R3 were longer ($p < .001$, 95% $C.I. = [1.290, 2.849]$; $p < .001$, 95% $C.I. = [1.435, 3.009]$) and had more intersecting points than those created with Pattern Lock ($p = .044$, 95% $C.I. = [.012, 1.254]$).

Performance. There was statistically significant difference in T_s ($F = 4.577$, $p = .012$, $\eta_p^2 = .065$). Post hoc analysis showed that participants who used RePaLM R3 had longer selection times than those who used Pattern Lock ($p = .017$, 95% $C.I. = [.563, 7.702]$). This may be because participants adhered to the recommendations when using RePaLM, resulting in longer and more intricate patterns that required additional time to create. Participants had similar authentication times (T_a) and similar basic error rates (E_b) across the schemes, findings which are similar to the findings of other works [5, 13].

Memorability. There were no significant differences; participants made similar number of recall attempts (N_a) and resets (N_r) and had similar successful login ratios (L_s). The scores align with scores reported in other works [14,19,20].

Exploring Participants' Perceptions. The majority of the participants reported that RePaLM helped them create a strong pattern (80%), actively considered the recommendations when creating their pattern (72%), did not face any memorability issues (75%), and their patterns were stronger than the ones they would typically create with no assistance (79%). Moreover, most found RePaLM useful (80%) and easy to understand (86%). Regarding those who used the Pattern Lock, most agreed that knowing the most or least frequent points would help them create stronger patterns (64%). In general, study participants liked RePaLM and mentioned that they felt that they could create more secure patterns, compared to the ones they would create with a typical pattern lock mechanism (P14: "[RePaLM] *helped me to create a secure pattern*", P27: "*these patterns definitely are stronger than the normal ones*", P38: "*I liked it because you can create a pattern that can hardly be guessed*", P42: "*[recommendations] helped me create a pattern that is not easy to crack*"). They found it easy to use (P12: "[RePaLM] *is super helpful and easy to follow*") and fast (P42: "*recommendations were fast*"). They also stated that they would use it (P6: "*I'll use it for sure*"). Although most participants provided positive feedback, one was concerned that such recommenders may lead users to make biased choices. Some participants provided suggestions for improvements and future directions, such as including a strength meter or further enhancements to improve memorability.

Table 1. Results from comparison analysis for patterns created with Pattern Lock (PL), RePaLM R1 (R1), and RePaLM R3 (R3).

	Pattern Lock		RePaLM R1		RePaLM R3		PL vs R1	PL vs R3	R1 vs R3
	M	SD	M	SD	M	SD			
M_p	.525	.127	.692	.153	.709	.175	$p < .001$	$p < .001$	$p = 1.000$
L_p	5.191	1.816	7.260	1.536	7.408	1.645	$p < .001$	$p < .001$	$p = 1.000$
N_p	.585	.193	.512	.375	.467	.319	$p = .798$	$p = .217$	$p = 1.000$
I_p	.429	.991	.920	1.275	1.061	1.329	$p = .168$	$p = .044$	$p = 1.000$
T_s	6.536	3.975	8.862	5.162	10.669	4.573	$p = .061$	$p = .017$	$p = .517$
T_a	2.247	1.015	2.508	1.600	2.812	1.210	$p = .875$	$p = .240$	$p = .948$
E_b	.284	.453	.286	.456	.231	.430	$p = 1.000$	$p = 1.000$	$p = 1.000$
N_a	1.440	.626	1.411	.686	1.272	.533	$p = 1.000$	$p = .724$	$p = 1.000$
L_s	.970	.057	.954	.079	.980	.060	$p = .723$	$p = 1.000$	$p = .166$
N_r	.286	.636	.540	.930	.225	.715	$p = .362$	$p = 1.000$	$p = .137$

5   Discussion, Limitations, and Future Work

The user study showed that data-driven recommendations can nudge people to make better pattern choices and create stronger yet memorable patterns. The practical implications of RePaLM for usable security include improving the strength of authentication patterns, leading to increased security for users. Additionally, the real-time recommendations of RePaLM make it easier for users to create strong patterns without affecting memorability, thus reducing the likelihood of users forgetting or choosing weak patterns. The recommendations do not restrict user choices, as users are free to select patterns they can recall but are also aware of more secure options. From a theoretical perspective, using LSTM in RePaLM demonstrates the potential for employing AI and machine learning techniques to design usable security systems and inform future research.

RePaLM has potential implications for HCI by providing real-time and personalized recommendations to users when creating their patterns in authentication schemes like Android Pattern Lock. It can enhance the user experience by reducing the time and effort required to create a secure and memorable pattern. By providing recommendations immediately after each pattern point is selected, RePaLM can guide users in creating a strong pattern efficiently and intuitively. Machine learning techniques, such as LSTM, can provide a new direction for the design of usable security systems by introducing personalized and real-time recommendations, thus, increasing the acceptance and adoption of the security mechanism. Additionally, RePaLM can provide a valuable data source to evaluate and improve AI-based interactive systems, leading to a better understanding of how AI can enhance the usability and security of interactive systems.

Although we made efforts to ensure the study's validity (e.g., controlled comparison, hypotheses, and participants using their devices), some limitations remain, including: i) the sample size is small, ii) we evaluated the system over a short time, which may not accurately reflect the long-term effectiveness of RePaLM, and iii) focused on a single metric to evaluate security. Our next steps are: i) further testing with a larger sample size and diverse population for a longer time to validate the results and generalize the findings, ii) comparative studies to other pattern lock schemes (e.g., gesture-based authentication) to determine the relative strengths and weaknesses of each approach, iii) security evaluation to assess its resistance to various types of attacks (e.g., shoulder-surfing, guessing attacks) and further analysis (e.g., guessability analysis), iv) integration with other security systems (e.g., biometric authentication, gaze-based authentication [16]) to provide additional layers of security, v) development of personalized models that adapt to the user's behavior, preferences, and cognitive abilities to provide tailored recommendations and improve the overall user experience.

6   Conclusion

This paper presented RePaLM, a data-driven assistant that aims to improve the security of pattern-based authentication systems by nudging users into making stronger pattern choices. RePaLM implements an artificial neural network, specifically, a long short-term memory (LSTM) model, allowing for real-time recommendations. The LSTM model is trained on a dataset of patterns, allowing it to learn patterns that other users less frequently use. When a user attempts to create a new pattern, RePaLM suggests points on the pattern grid that are less commonly used, helping the user create a more secure and unique pattern. We conducted a user study to evaluate the proposed system, which shows that users who used RePaLM created patterns that were less predictable than those created with a typical pattern lock scheme. RePaLM is a promising solution for enhancing the security of pattern-based authentication systems by encouraging users to create secure patterns.

References

1. Abdelrahman, Y., Khamis, M., Schneegass, S., Alt, F.: Stay Cool! Understanding thermal attacks on mobile-based user authentication. In: Proceedings of the 2017 CHI Conference on Human Factors in Computing Systems, pp. 3751–3763. CHI 2017, Association for Computing Machinery, New York, USA (2017). https://doi.org/10.1145/3025453.3025461
2. Alotaibi, N., Williamson, J., Khamis, M.: ThermoSecure: investigating the effectiveness of AI-driven thermal attacks on commonly used computer keyboards. ACM Trans. Priv. Secur. (2022). https://doi.org/10.1145/3563693
3. Alt, F., Mikusz, M., Schneegass, S., Bulling, A.: Memorability of cued-recall graphical passwords with saliency masks. In: Proceedings of the 15th International Conference on Mobile and Ubiquitous Multimedia, pp. 191–200. MUM 2016, Association for Computing Machinery, New York, USA (2016). https://doi.org/10.1145/3012709.3012730
4. Andriotis, P., Kirby, M., Takasu, A.: Bu-Dash: a universal and dynamic graphical password scheme. Int. J. Inf. Secur. **22**, 1–21 (2022)
5. Anwar, M., Imran, A.: A comparative study of graphical and alphanumeric passwords for mobile device authentication. In: Modern Artificial Intelligence & Cognitive Science Conference (MAICS), pp. 13–18 (2015)
6. Arias-Cabarcos, P., Krupitzer, C., Becker, C.: A survey on adaptive authentication. ACM Comput. Surv. **52**(4), 1–30 (2019). https://doi.org/10.1145/3336117
7. Aviv, A.J., Dürmuth, M.: A survey of collection methods and cross-data set comparison of Android Unlock patterns. arXiv preprint arXiv:1811.10548 (2018)
8. Aviv, A.J., Gibson, K., Mossop, E., Blaze, M., Smith, J.M.: Smudge attacks on smartphone touch screens. In: 4th USENIX Workshop on Offensive Technologies (WOOT 10) (2010)
9. De Luca, A., et al.: Now you see me, now you don't: protecting smartphone authentication from shoulder surfers. In: Proceedings of the SIGCHI Conference on Human Factors in Computing Systems, pp. 2937–2946. CHI 2014, Association for Computing Machinery, New York, USA (2014). https://doi.org/10.1145/2556288.2557097
10. Forman, T.J., Roche, D.S., Aviv, A.J.: Twice as nice? A preliminary evaluation of double Android Unlock patterns. In: Extended Abstracts of the 2020 CHI Conference on Human Factors in Computing Systems, pp. 1–7. CHI EA 2020, Association for Computing Machinery, New York, USA (2020). https://doi.org/10.1145/3334480.3382922

11. Furnell, S.: Assessing website password practices - unchanged after fifteen years? Computers & Security (2022)
12. Golla, M., Rimkus, J., Aviv, A.J., Dürmuth, M.: On the in-accuracy and influence of Android pattern strength meters. In: Workshop on Usable Security, USEC. vol. 19 (2019)
13. Guerar, M., Merlo, A., Migliardi, M.: ClickPattern: a pattern lock system resilient to smudge and side-channel attacks. J. Wirel. Mob. Networks Ubiquitous Comput. Dependable Appl. **8**(2), 64–78 (2017)
14. Gugenheimer, J., De Luca, A., Hess, H., Karg, S., Wolf, D., Rukzio, E.: ColorSnakes: using colored decoys to secure authentication in sensitive contexts. In: Proceedings of the 17th International Conference on Human-Computer Interaction with Mobile Devices and Services, pp. 274–283. MobileHCI 2015, Association for Computing Machinery, New York, USA (2015). https://doi.org/10.1145/2785830.2785834
15. Hartwig, K., Englisch, A., Thomson, J.P., Reuter, C.: Finding secret treasure? Improving memorized secrets through gamification. In: Proceedings of the 2021 European Symposium on Usable Security, pp. 105–117. EuroUSEC 2021, Association for Computing Machinery, New York, USA (2021). https://doi.org/10.1145/3481357.3481509
16. Katsini, C., Abdrabou, Y., Raptis, G.E., Khamis, M., Alt, F.: The role of eye gaze in security and privacy applications: survey and future HCI research directions. In: Proceedings of the 2020 CHI Conference on Human Factors in Computing Systems, pp. 1–21. CHI 2020, Association for Computing Machinery, New York, USA (2020). https://doi.org/10.1145/3313831.3376840
17. Loge, M., Duermuth, M., Rostad, L.: On user choice for Android Unlock patterns. In: European Workshop on Usable Security, ser. EuroUSEC. vol. 16 (2016)
18. Melicher, W., et al.: Fast, lean, and accurate: Modeling password guess ability using neural networks. In: 25th USENIX Security Symposium (USENIX Security 16), pp. 175–191 (2016)
19. Munyendo, C.W., Grant, M., Markert, P., Forman, T.J., Aviv, A.J.: Using a blocklist to improve the security of user selection of Android patterns. In: Seventeenth Symposium on Usable Privacy and Security (SOUPS 2021), pp. 37–56 (2021)
20. Raptis, G.E., Katsini, C., Cen, A.J.l., Arachchilage, N.A.G., Nacke, L.E.: Better, funner, stronger: A gameful approach to nudge people into making less predictable graphical password choices. In: Proceedings of the 2021 CHI Conference on Human Factors in Computing Systems. CHI 2021, Association for Computing Machinery, New York, USA (2021). https://doi.org/10.1145/3411764.3445658
21. Schneegass, S., Steimle, F., Bulling, A., Alt, F., Schmidt, A.: SmudgeSafe: geometric image transformations for smudge-resistant user authentication. In: Proceedings of the 2014 ACM International Joint Conference on Pervasive and Ubiquitous Computing, pp. 775–786. UbiComp 2014, Association for Computing Machinery, New York, USA (2014). https://doi.org/10.1145/2632048.2636090
22. Song, Y., Cho, G., Oh, S., Kim, H., Huh, J.H.: On the effectiveness of pattern lock strength meters: measuring the strength of real world pattern locks. In: Proceedings of the 33rd Annual ACM Conference on Human Factors in Computing Systems, pp. 2343–2352. CHI 2015, Association for Computing Machinery, New York, USA (2015). https://doi.org/10.1145/2702123.2702365
23. Sun, C., Wang, Y., Zheng, J.: Dissecting pattern unlock: the effect of pattern strength meter on pattern selection. J. Inf. Secur. Appl. **19**(4–5), 308–320 (2014)

24. Ur, B., et al.: Design and evaluation of a data-driven password meter. In: Proceedings of the 2017 CHI Conference on Human Factors in Computing Systems, pp. 3775–3786. CHI 2017, Association for Computing Machinery, New York, USA (2017). https://doi.org/10.1145/3025453.3026050
25. Ye, G., et al.: Cracking Android Pattern Lock in five attempts. In: Proceedings of the 2017 Network and Distributed System Security Symposium 2017 (NDSS 17). Internet Society (2017)
26. von Zezschwitz, E., et al.: On quantifying the effective password space of grid-based unlock gestures. In: Proceedings of the 15th International Conference on Mobile and Ubiquitous Multimedia, pp. 201–212. MUM 2016, Association for Computing Machinery, New York, USA (2016). https://doi.org/10.1145/3012709.3012729

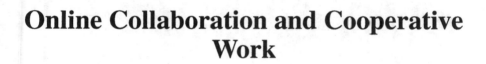

Online Collaboration and Cooperative Work

A Systematic Literature Review of Online Collaborative Story Writing

Stefano Montanelli[1]([⊠])[iD] and Martin Ruskov[2][iD]

[1] Department of Computer Science, Università degli Studi di Milano,
20133 Milan, Italy
stefano.montanelli@unimi.it
[2] Department of Languages, Literatures, Cultures and Mediations,
Università degli Studi di Milano, 20123 Milan, Italy
martin.ruskov@unimi.it

Abstract. Collaboratively writing a narrative is a challenging task. Further complications emerge when the involved contributors do not know each other, as it commonly occurs in online crowdsourcing. The paper presents a systematic literature review of online *collaborative story writing* with the aim of analysing what are the different forms of user involvement in such approaches and systems. To this end, we propose a reference definition based on essential features that characterise online collaborative story writing and we follow an exploratory approach based on a two-step method characterised by i) identification and selection of relevant publications, and ii) analysis of the selected literature. For the analysis, we consider relevant dimensions from the Taxonomy of Collaborative Writing [30] and we compare approaches according to *modes of work*, *writing roles*, and *writing activities*. As a summary of our results, about the modes of work, we focused on *synchronicity* and we observed that *synchronous* communications are mostly adopted by dialogue-based approaches, whereas *asynchronous* communications frequently characterise scene-based ones. On the writing roles, *writer*, *consultant*, and *reviewer* are commonly included in the writing process of the reviewed approaches. Furthermore, the roles of *editor* and *leader* are sometimes employed, while the *facilitator* role never appears in the considered approaches. As for the activities, collaborators are mostly involved in *drafting* tasks, but the tasks of *brainstorming*, *reviewing*, and *revising* are very common as well. On the opposite, activities like *converging*, *outlining*, and *copyediting* are rarely employed. In line with the results of our review, we propose four further research directions to study: *collaborator recruitment*, *collaborator awareness*, *creative guidance*, and *modalities of contribution*. This review should be helpful for researchers and practitioners interested in engaging contributors in effective online collaborative story writing.

Keywords: Crowdsourced story writing · Interactive narrative · Online collaborative writing

S. Montanelli—Idea and article editing
M. Ruskov—Literature review and analysis.

1   Introduction

Writing is a challenging creative task, arguably among the most complex ones due to the variety of styles and inclinations that humans can have when facing it. Using online technologies and intelligent systems for writing allows for rapid distribution of creative work and introduces the opportunity to work collaboratively, so that multiple writers can contribute with their own ideas to create a shared text (e.g., a story) as a result.

There are a range of approaches that support collaborative writing with a number of different goals and contexts, like entertainment [6], literary [49], educational [22,43], or documentary [26] purposes. Approaches are characterised by a very heterogeneous range of features and collaboration processes, especially in the forms of involvement, the kind of contributions being provided, and the level of awareness about the goals of the writing activity [15,19].

Feldman and McInnis conducted a survey to analyse approaches and systems where a multitude of workers is involved in writing tasks based on the crowd-sourcing paradigm (i.e., *crowd-writing*) [16]. Rettberg proposed a classification framework to analyse "human computation in electronic literature", in which different types of participation are identified [41]. A further survey is proposed by Zhang, Gibbons, and Li where computer-mediated collaborative writing in educational settings is analysed with focus on i) the kind of writing tasks, and ii) the metrics for measuring the produced texts [52]. However, the classification of collaborative writing approaches is still an open issue, and we believe that the claim of Lowry et al. is valid also nowadays: *"the lack of an interdisciplinary approach and common understanding of collaborative writing undermines the ability of researchers and practitioners to solve the core issues"* and *"collaborative writing researchers and practitioners do not even agree on a common term for collaborative writing"* [30].

In this paper, we study *online collaborative story writing*, by first providing a reference definition based on essential features that characterise it. Then, we review the relevant literature and analyse the different forms of collaborator involvement in online collaborative story writing. To this end, we follow an exploratory approach based on a two-step method characterised by i) harvesting of relevant publications according to a collection of selected keywords (*identification and selection*), and ii) classification of retrieved literature along specific dimensions of interest (*systematic literature review*). The keywords for literature harvesting are chosen by exploring existing surveys and by considering the different terminology used in various research contexts where a form of online collaboration in writing is somehow enforced [16,30,41]. The subsequent analysis of the harvested literature is based on the three dimensions taken from the Taxonomy of Collaborative Writing proposed by Lowry et al., namely *modes of work*, *writing roles*, and *writing activities* [30]. The modes of work consider literature according to synchronicity, i.e. whether collaborators are involved in synchronous or asynchronous tasks. The writing roles describe the variety of positions that collaborators in online writing can assume, which are writer, consultant, editor, reviewer, team leader, and facilitator. Finally, the writing activities describe the tasks in the writing process, namely brainstorming, converging on brainstorming, outlining, drafting, reviewing, revising, and copyediting.

We acknowledge that a relevant issue to consider in online collaborative story writing is the quality of the generated text. However, the definition of formal criteria and metrics to ensure the quality of a narrative is hard to define [2,19]. As such, the analysis of quality-related aspects in collaborative story writing is out of the scope of this review.

This paper is organised as follows. In Sect. 2, we provide our reference definitions and we describe the method we followed in our systematic literature review of online collaborative story writing. The results of our analysis are discussed with respect to three different dimensions, namely modes of work in Sect. 3, writing roles in Sect. 4, and writing activities in Sect. 5. Finally, we summarise the review results and we outline possible directions for future work in Sect. 6.

2   Survey Criteria and Method

In this section, we first define online collaborative story writing and the criteria used for the selection of relevant literature. Then, we describe the method we followed to retrieve the relevant publications to include in the review.

2.1   Definitions and Survey Criteria

To our knowledge, there is no shared and widely-accepted definition of online collaborative story writing. Useful formulations and discussions can be found in related surveys, such as [30] and [52]. This literature allowed us to propose a definition of online collaborative story writing, based on three distinctive features that capture what we consider the essential aspects of the issue.

We define *online collaborative story writing* as a creative activity characterised by:

- **Feature 1.** The activity is performed *online*, namely on a web platform without any assumed collocation of the collaborators.
- **Feature 2.** The activity involves a *group of collaborators* that are not assumed to know each other beforehand, as in crowdsourcing [16].
- **Feature 3.** The outcome of the activity is a *narrative*, namely a description of a sequence of events [19].

Lowry et al. propose a Taxonomy of Collaborative Writing that classifies approaches according to the following dimensions: writing strategies, document control modes, modes of work, writing roles, and writing activities [30]. Writing strategies and document control modes poorly contribute to capturing the complexity of the collaborative writing process, as it can be observed in the work of Kim et al [25–27]. However, we believe that the remaining three dimensions of the taxonomy are appropriate to capture the relevant aspects that characterise the approaches towards collaborative story writing. As such, in the following, we consider *modes of work*, *writing roles*, and *writing activities* as dimensions of analysis in our review.

Modes of Work. The modes of work are distinguished according to proximity and synchronicity [30]. Since we are interested in online approaches to collaborative story writing (see Feature 1 of our definition), the proximity aspects are not pertaining to our review, thus all the approaches we consider are assumed to have collaborators distributed in different places. In contrast, we are interested in synchronicity that distinguishes between i) approaches where the writing activities require that collaborators work synchronously, and ii) approaches where the activities allow collaborators to work asynchronously.

Writing Roles. A collaborator can play multiple roles in collaborative writing, and their roles can change during the writing process. The roles identified by Lowry et al. are the following:

- *Writer* – responsible for writing some portion of the text.
- *Consultant* – responsible for providing feedback about the content.
- *Editor* – owner of the overall text who can also make changes to it.
- *Reviewer* – responsible for providing comments and edit proposals to the text, but not allowed to apply these changes autonomously.
- *Team leader* – responsible of the overall group of collaborators in the story writing process; they can also participate in the writing tasks.
- *Facilitator* – responsible for providing organisational support without contributing to the content creation itself.

Writing Activities. For this dimension, Lowry et al. focus on the key activities that deal with the actual content production. The execution flow of these activities can be dynamic, meaning that these activities do not represent a pipeline and they can occur in any order in the various approaches. These key activities are:

- *Brainstorming* – developing preliminary ideas to be included in the story.
- *Converging* on brainstorming – selecting brainstormed ideas that are worthy of being further developed.
- *Outlining* – creating an overall frame and/or direction of the text to write.
- *Drafting* – actually putting down ideas into text.
- *Reviewing* – reading and annotating the document draft for content, grammar, and style improvements.
- *Revising* – including the application of suggested changes or rewriting snippets into the text.
- *Copyediting* – finalising the review of the overall text.

We are interested in approaches where the above writing activities are performed by online collaborators. However, it is also possible that some activities are executed by system designers or software agents with the support of AI techniques. In some cases, the results provided by AI agents generate further tasks that are subsequently assigned to collaborators. One example of this are the type of crowdsourcing systems where human workers are employed to validate and measure the effectiveness of AI agents [4,50]. In some other cases, tasks are performed by the system designers who implicitly assume the role of writer, editor or leader. This frequently occurs in the initial steps of story creation (i.e., brainstorming and outlining) that some approaches do not consider as part of their writing process [4,26,45]. Since the focus of our review is to analyse the roles of online human collaborators, we do not consider the writing activities performed by designers or software agents.

2.2   Survey Method

For our exploratory analysis, we first identify and select the relevant literature, and then we analyse it according to the dimensions presented above.

Identification and Screening. We first define the keywords to use for searching for the relevant literature to consider in our review. Then, we discuss how we use the selected keywords to harvest publications, and the process for screening and analysing the eligibility of the obtained results to finally determine the publications to include. The resulting PRISMA flow diagram [36] of our survey work is shown Fig. 1.

For our literature review, a number of research fields can provide relevant contributions, each one characterised by its own terminology. Some examples of such relevant research fields are *interactive narrative* [42], *multiuser dungeons (MUD)* [1], and *collaborative writing* [16]. We aim to explore all the potentially interesting fields and their corresponding terminologies. As a result, to specify the relevant keywords, we propose two distinct collections of terms for capturing the potential differences in terminology with respect to Feature 2 and Feature 3 of our definition of online collaborative story writing. For each keyword, we motivate our choice to include it in the collection.

The keywords that we identified regarding Feature 2 are the following:

- Crowdsourcing. This term has a wide meaning, but it is commonly used to refer to platforms involving a large pool of workers that do not know each other. One particular type of crowdsourcing task is crowd-writing [16].
- Collaborative. This term is used to indicate a group of people working towards a common goal. Lowry et al. use "collaborative writing" as the defining phrase in their reference taxonomy [30].
- Interactive. This terms refers to systems that involve users interactively, in a group or individually. The combination of a number of iterations – even if generated independently – can result in a collaborative product [42].
- Multiplayer. This term refers to a game (or some form of entertainment in general) where multiple users are involved [1].

As for Feature 3, we identified the following keywords:

- Narrative. A contemporary definition of the term narrative encompasses the combination of a fable and a discourse. The former highlights the events that

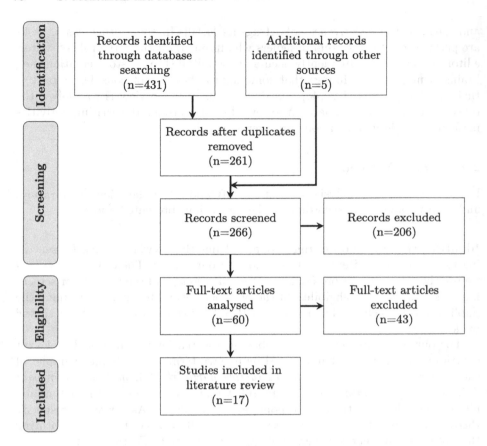

Fig. 1. A PRISMA flow diagram of our literature review [36].

are being narrated, and the latter focuses on the actual techniques used to narrate them [19]. The term narrative better denotes the final written text, and thus it is more appropriate in our search.

- Fiction. The term fiction is used to refer to a subset of the category of narrative where non-factual events are being narrated [19]. This is a very popular genre inspiring also contributions from amateurs.
- Dungeon. The term dungeon has been adopted in several genres of group narration. The name is inspired by the well-known table-top game Dungeons and Dragons [1].
- Writing. This is the most general term that can also capture non-narrative texts. However, it is often implicitly used to refer to narrative due to the diffusion of narrative in human culture and cognition [52].

The following keywords have been also considered, but they have been discarded due to their ambiguous meaning and/or absence of relevant results, namely group, pair, coauthor, shared as a descriptor of Feature 2, and authoring, novel, storytelling as a descriptor of Feature 3.

We used Google Scholar for retrieving publications according to the above collections of keywords, since it is shown to produce a more comprehensive set of results with respect to other repositories commonly considered for publication retrieval [21]. Moreover, Google Scholar roughly represents "essentially a superset of WoS [i.e., Web-of-Science] and Scopus" [34]. While we are aware of the discussion regarding the limitations of Google Scholar [21,38], we aimed to retrieve a large number of potentially interesting publications, by also including preprints, PhD theses, and workshop publications that are usually excluded by other publication repositories.

For searching, we paired the keywords of Feature 2 with the ones of Feature 3 to generate 16 keyword combinations. We limited our results to publications from 2012 and later. We started from 2012 since we found that the topic of online collaborative story writing is quite recent and we empirically observed that only marginal interesting results are available before.

When multiple publications are available about a given approach, we review them all and we cite the one that we considered most relevant to our subject definition, or – when undecided – the most recent one.

Eligibility. For research fields that are borderline to the topic of interest considered here, we used the following criteria to select which publications to consider in the review.

AI Training. AI is sometimes used for automatic story generation. This is done by relying on models that are trained on general-purpose datasets and on task-specific data. An example of the latter is the AI model of Shelley, which is trained on a dataset crowdsourced from an online community with a special interest in story writing [50]. In such cases – even if they are not aware of it – the approach involves people that generate this content as collaborators to the writing process.

Text Summarisation. The text summarisation systems are included in our review when there is an explicit narrative requirement for their final outcome. For instance, in Storia, crowdsourcing is employed to summarise social media contents and crowd workers are asked to provide a narrative structure to the summary they produce [26]. Similarly, crime-solving systems are included in our review when their outcome includes a narrative presentation, e.g. CrowdAI [29].

Interactive Narrative. The platforms for interactive narrative experiences work with a trade-off between the need to allow freedom of expression to their collaborators (i.e. players) and the need to ensure some narrative integrity to the final outcome. As a result, some approaches introduce constraints to the possible player actions, such as the use of a controlled language or predefined interaction templates to be chosen by players. In our review, we exclude approaches based on pre-authored branching stories similar to game books, where players can only choose among predefined paths [19]. On the contrary, we include approaches where the interaction among players allows new narratives to emerge, even if a constrained editing environment is adopted (see for example StoryMINE [45]).

Table 1. Overview of selected publications included in our review.

Authors & Reference	Year	Name	Self-Identification	Theoretic Model	Platform
Yanardag, Cebrian et al [50]	2021	Shelley	crowdsourced collaborative writing	N/A	Reddit, Twitter
Caniglia [6]	2020	Cast	collaborative storytelling	N/A	mobile app
Huang, Huang et al [24]	2020	Heteroglossia	crowdsourced story ideation	Six Thinking Hats [3]	GoogleDocs, MTurk
Wiethof, Tavanapour et al [49]	2020	N/A	collaborative story writing	Multimotive Information Systems Continuance Model [31]	web
Castano, Ferrara et al [8]	2019	Argo	creative story writing	N/A	web
Feng, Carstensdottir et al [17]	2019	Empirica	collection of social narrative	Active Analysis [7]	MTurk
Li, Luther et al [29]	2018	CrowdIA	mistery-solving	Sensemaking Process [40]	MTurk
Mandal, Agarwal et al [33]	2018	Image Chains	collective story writing	N/A	N/A
Spawforth, Gibbins et al [45]	2018	StoryMINE	interactive narrative	Quality-Based Narrative [44]	web
Borromeo, Laurent et al [4]	2017	CDeployer	crowdsourcing narrative writing	N/A	MTurk
Kim, Sterman et al [27]	2017	Mechanical Novel	story crowdsourcing	Cognitive Proccess Model [18]	MTurk
Kim & Monroy-Hernandez [26]	2016	Storia	event summarisation	Visual Narrative Structure [11]	Seen.co, MTurk
Sauro & Sundmark [43]	2016	N/A	fan fiction	Information Gap Tasks [39]	blog
Kim, Cheng et al [25]	2014	Ensemble	collaborative story writing	Online Leadership [32]	web
Verroios & Bernstein [48]	2014	Context Trees	text summarisation	N/A	MTurk
Hamid & Mansor [22]	2012	N/A	collaborative story writing	N/A	Wetpaint
Li, Lee-Urban et al [28]	2012	Scheherazade	interactive narrative	N/A	MTurk

Systematic Literature Review. As shown in Fig. 1, we identified 431 publications, we screened 261 of them, and we analysed the full-text of 60 papers. We note that online collaborative story writing is relevant to many research areas and fields that are only partially concerned with the research focus of our work. The survey criteria illustrated above allowed us to effectively filter the eligible publications. Finally, 17 papers are selected for the systematic literature review. We believe that these papers are appropriate and sufficient to cover all the relevant aspects to discuss with respect to our dimensions of analysis.

An overview of the 17 selected publications is provided in Table 1.

For each approach, we show the basic bibliographic information, such as authors, year, and name of the proposed approach or of its most distinctive feature (when present). Furthermore, we show further information about the context in which the paper has been published, such as self-identification of the approach, theoretical model (if any), and platform.

By *self-identification* we refer to a description as provided by the authors of the approach to describe the goal of what they propose, and the terminology and research field in which the research work is framed. The majority of the considered approaches explicitly deal with collaborative writing of narratives. Further goals emerge such as interactive narrative [28,45], information extraction [17,29], and summarisation [26,48].

The *theoretical model* represents the foundational framework the work refers to. It also provides a further indication about the considered research field and a rationale of what is proposed beyond the specific implementation details. Considering the publications based on a theoretical model, we can group them by narratological [17,26,45], organisation-scientific [24,25,49], cognitive [27,40], and educational [39]. However, we note that about half of the reviewed approaches do not rely on a theoretical model, and they are based on empirical experiments.

The *platform* is the software environment in which the approach proposed in the publication is put in action. In addition, the platform has an impact on how the collaborators are engaged, and thus it could play a role in the final outcome. On one hand, its affordances could include the criteria used to select workers, how they are motivated, and what understanding they develop about the intention and purpose of the activity. On the other hand, each platform has an inherent limitation on the types of supported interactions. The platform indirectly indicates how collaborators are motivated. For example, approaches that use paid crowdsourcing platforms (e.g., Mechanical Turk) view collaborators as business partners, in the sense that they are engaged to reach a target result in exchange for a fee. In other approaches, collaborators are engaged for entertainment [6,25,50], for professional practice [8,49], or for learning [22,43].

In the following sections, the selected publications are reviewed in light of the three different dimensions – modes of work, writing roles, and writing activities.

3   Review by Modes of Work

This dimension focuses on synchronous and asynchronous modalities adopted by contributors. In some cases, the modality is imposed by the adopted software platform. This is the case of Twitter [50], blogs [43], and wikis [22] that are asynchronous by definition. Platforms like Google Docs are designed to support synchronous collaboration [24]. On the other hand, the API interface of Mechanical Turk does not impose a constraint on the writing modality and it can support both synchronous and asynchronous interaction.

Beyond the limitations of the underlying platform, the mode of collaboration represents a design choice. Typically, dialogue-based systems, such as Cast [6] and Empirica [17] involve their collaborators in synchronous conversations thus taking advantage of real-time group dynamics during interaction. Such systems typically assign different character roles to different collaborators, thus engaging them in what is called *role-based storytelling* (not to be confused with writing roles) [9]. This allows for the rapid creation of a narrative, where collaborators are engaged in a natural conversation as actors that develop their individual perceptions of the situation, instead of authoring a carefully-designed plot where all the aspects of the narrative are coordinated. In [43], the authors propose to operate at higher level, by assigning the responsibility for an entire role-based narrative to individual collaborators, namely each collaborator provides a distinct story from the viewpoint of a specific character. Due to their relative independence, approaches of this kind adopt an asynchronous modality. The role-based approach is not adopted only for the tasks of story writing. For example, in Heteroglossia, a synchronous role-play mechanism is used for generating ideas about the stories to write (i.e., brainstorming) [24].

As an alternative to role-based approaches, the responsibility of different chronological snippets are assigned to collaborators (i.e. a scene-based approach), by giving them the complete control on that snippet. This is commonly realised in an asynchronous mode. As a way to maintain narrative consistency, such approaches tend to assign large snippets of the story (e.g., an entire scene [27, 28]) to collaborators. From the perspective of mode of work, this is similar to the assignment mechanism of entire narratives proposed by Sauro and Sundmark [43].

4   Review by Writing Roles

A summary view of the reviewed approaches by writing roles is provided in Table 2. We observe that the most frequently-used roles for involving collaborators are writer, consultant, editor, and reviewer. The leader role is not common in collaborative story writing and it is employed only by two approaches that focus their research on leadership in writing [24, 25]. Approaches related to learning are less structured and roles are not explicitly defined. In these cases, we did our best to deduce roles from the context [22, 43]. None of the reviewed approaches explicitly considers involving collaborators in the facilitator role.

In Mechanical Novel, all the common roles used in story writing (i.e., writer, consultant, editor, and reviewer) are employed [27]. Indeed, Mechanical Novel involves collaborators in a highly-structured and articulated writing process, and it provides an example of how to effectively combine different roles.

Most of the approaches directly involve collaborators in writing new textual content in one form or another. In the educational field, the approaches take a macro-management approach as simple as assigning to a single collaborator the responsibility for a distinct narrative in its entirety [22, 43]. These studies often take a more relaxed approach and they do not impose limits to what one collaborator can do. Such an approach allows for the study of how deep collaborators are willing to get engaged in the process.

Further approaches – typically coming from the field of crowdsourcing – adopt a structured approach, by strictly defining short involvements of collaborators. This can be explained by the fact that collaborators are commonly engaged by an external motivation (typically a remuneration). As a consequence, there is a real risk that they attempt to game the rules to their personal benefit [13, 14].

In contrast, approaches motivated by entertainment focus on providing a satisfying experience that matches the possible expectations of self-selected collaborators [6, 45]. However, such approaches inevitably risk that collaborators interrupt their involvement at the slightest whim of annoyance.

In other cases, collaborators are involved as consultants and they are asked to generate ideas [24, 49]. We also classify as consultants those collaborators that contribute with content that is not intended for the final text. Examples of this kind are those focused on training AI algorithms [50], those collecting content

Table 2. Reviewed approaches by collaborative writing role.

Authors	Writer	Consultant	Editor	Reviewer	Leader	Facilitator
Yanardag, Cebrian et al [50]	✓	✓		✓		
Caniglia [6]	✓					
Huang, Huang et al [24]		✓			✓	
Wiethof, Tavanapour et al [49]	✓	✓		✓		
Castano, Ferrara et al [8]	✓			✓		
Feng, Carstensdottir et al [17]	✓					
Li, Luther et al [29]	✓	✓		✓		
Mandal, Agarwal et al [33]	✓	✓				
Spawforth, Gibbins et al [45]		✓				
Borromeo, Laurent et al [4]	✓		✓	✓		
Kim, Sterman et al [27]	✓	✓	✓	✓		
Kim & Monroy-Hernandez [26]	✓	✓		✓		
Sauro & Sundmark [43]	✓					
Kim, Cheng et al [25]	✓	✓		✓	✓	
Verroios & Bernstein [48]			✓	✓		
Hamid & Mansor [22]	✓		✓			
Li, Lee-Urban et al [28]	✓					

(i.e., notes [29], images [33]) that would influence the subsequently-written narrative, and those collecting suggestions for possible narrative improvements [27].

This involvement of consultants is taken to an extreme in the StoryMINE system, where textual interactions are predefined through a controlled language of possible actions. Nevertheless, StoryMINE has narratives generated by collaborators, because it is a multiplayer platform and the interaction between different collaborators (players) results in the generation of different stories [45]. This is a key property of the underlying Quality-based Narrative approach [44] where possible relationships among events are defined by system designers through logical gatekeeping conditions.

Typically, summarisation systems start from preexisting content and involve collaborators in editing activities [48]. However, more complex systems also introduce specific interactions that might be viewed as mixed roles. For example, in CrowdIA [29], there are tasks that seem to be appropriate for the consultant role. An example is the extraction of preliminary information that would not find place in the final narrative. Further, voting for acceptable hypothesis – which would later contribute to what remains in the narrative – is a typical reviewer task. It is not an editor role, because even when the voting result is decisive for the final content, the collaborators do not decide how the results of the voting get transformed into the final textual outcome. Instead, the consequences of the voting process are defined beforehand by the system designers. Finally, there is a write-up step of the narrative, which is responsibility of the writer role.

Approaches that ask collaborators to vote for the preferred content are a typical case of involvement in the reviewer role. The content in question could be AI-generated [50] or collaborator-generated [8,49]. In some cases, the result of reviewing is filtering since it removes a part of the proposed content [8,26,50]. In others, the content is fully retained, but weighted by importance [48].

Role-based approaches typically limit the responsibility of individual collaborators to one specific character. Often, the idea behind this decision is that by limiting collaborators to specific narrative roles, they can better focus on writing, without the distractions of other narrative perspectives [6,17]. An exception is Heteroglossia where collaborators contribute as idea-generating consultants [24].

Some approaches are purposefully designed around a leader of the writing team, meaning the other collaborators contribute in assisting this leader. As an example, in [24,25], the leader is a leading writer who ultimately assumes the editor role.

We note that some approaches crowdsource work from collaborators without actually involving them. This means that collaborators are not aware about the goals of the writing activities. This absence of awareness takes such collaborators out of the considered list of possible roles. Examples of such approaches are cases where user-generated content is used as a dataset for training AI algorithms [28, 50]. Rettberg calls such collaborators unwitting participants [41]. In the general case, these contributions are not directly used in the final content, so we consider these collaborators to assume the consultant role. This choice is coherent with the Taxonomy of Collaborative Writing where a consultant is someone who provides feedback, but has not ownership or responsibility for content.

5 Review by Writing Activities

A summary of the reviewed approaches by writing activities is provided in Table 3. We note that drafting, brainstorming, and reviewing are widely used in the reviewed approaches, whereas converging, outlining, reviewing, and copy-editing are less frequently employed.

The authors of Shelley collect stories from Reddit as training data that is later fed into an AI model [50]. As a consequence, the collected stories are not presented in their original form. Instead, the AI model generates combinations from them. Due to this, we consider the human contribution to be a case of a brainstorming activity (and not e.g., drafting).

As mentioned in the previous section, Heteroglossia involves collaborators to generate ideas for the leading author, who is the principal user of the application [24]. Due to the overarching role of this leading contributor and the freedom granted by the interface of the platform (i.e., Google Docs), the leader activities are defined by the leader at their own discretion. Their role here resembles the role of the system designer in other approaches, e.g. in the Ensemble system [25].

Table 3. Reviewed approaches by collaborative writing activities.

Authors	Brainstorming	Converging	Outlining	Drafting	Reviewing	Revising	Copyediting
Yanardag, Cebrian et al [50]	✓			✓	✓		
Caniglia [6]				✓			
Huang, Huang et al [24]	✓						
Wiethof, Tavanapour et al [49]	✓			✓	✓		
Castano, Ferrara et al [8]	✓	✓		✓	✓		
Feng, Carstensdottir et al [17]	✓			✓		✓	
Li, Luther et al [29]		✓		✓	✓		✓
Mandal, Agarwal et al [33]	✓			✓			
Spawforth, Gibbins et al [45]				✓			
Borromeo, Laurent et al [4]				✓			✓
Kim, Sterman et al [27]		✓		✓	✓	✓	
Kim & Monroy-Hernandez [26]	✓			✓	✓		
Sauro & Sundmark [43]			✓	✓			
Kim, Cheng et al [25]				✓	✓		
Verroios & Bernstein [48]					✓	✓	
Hamid & Mansor [22]	✓			✓		✓	
Li, Lee-Urban et al [28]	✓						

As a consequence, we do not show the activities of these leading contributors in Table 3. Mandal et al. [33] ask collaborators to contribute with images in the process up to the final write up of the stories. Thus, this image collection is a brainstorming activity.

In our reference taxonomy, converging on brainstorming is a distinct activity from brainstorming itself. Once ideas are collected regardless of their merit, converging is used to select the contributions that are considered worthy to be further developed. As an example, in the fourth step of the crime-solving CrowdIA, collaborators select some available evidences to consider for creating hypotheses. Yet, the generated content takes the form of a narrative only in the fifth and final stage of the overall process [29]. For this reason, we consider the fourth step to be an example of converging on brainstorming activity.

On outlining, a possible approach – which could be called scene-based – is to define the overall dramatic arc of the story and the scenes that realise it. As this step requires an understanding of "the big picture", it is usually performed by system designers. For example, in Mechanical Novel, it is upfront decided that the result should contain exactly six distinct scenes [27]. However, in this example, system designers do not define constraints on characters, as it is typically done in role-based approaches, like in Empirica [17]. In Sauro and Sundmark's study of language learning, this role-based approach is also adopted when collaborators are considered as independent authors [43]. In this case, collaborators assume the responsibility of a role from the beginning to the end. As a consequence, they can choose how to organise themselves and how to do their implicit outlining.

In examples from interactive storytelling experiences, the creators of Cast and StoryMINE prepare the settings of the whole experience and they involve collaborators only in the actual writing [6,45]. We consider this to be drafting, despite the fact that the generated text remains final and revising or copyediting do not occur. More generally, we consider as drafting activities where collaborators contribute with individual new content that allow the story to unfold. This can happen at different levels. In role-based systems, collaborators assume an individual role and they typically focus on contributing one line at a time [17]. In Scheherazade, the authors use Mechanical Turk to perform drafting, with the aim to enable a subsequent step of editing by an AI system [28]. In summarisation [26,48] or problem-solving systems [29], this step can take the form of question answering. In Shelley, the authors engage Twitter users to write story bits that continue from a story start, provided by an AI algorithm [50]. We consider the final conversion of images to text in Image Chains as a typical example of drafting [33]. Same holds for the aforementioned fifth step of CrowdIA [29] where the collected content is organised in a narrative, and no further steps of revising or copyediting are enforced. Similarly, we consider it as an example of drafting whenever such a summarisation step is based on information that has not been structured as a narrative yet [26,33,50].

Asking collaborators to write summaries when some narrative is already present poses a different situation. When only part of the content is summarised (local summarisation), this is a typical revising task [48]. It is also a common for text summarisation tasks to involve crowdworkers in the reviewing phase, with the aim at validating the quality of the produced summaries [8,27,48,50].

When the overall content is summarised into a holistic narrative (global summarisation), this represents an example of copyediting. Typically, the copyediting activity is done at the end of the writing process. In cases where the overall text is short, like in the example of CDeployer [4], the final application of copyediting is equivalent to blending the copyediting and the revising activities.

When the objective of the writing activity is teaching, the main focus is on learning. The collaborators have the responsibility to manage the workflow and to write independent, but mutually-related texts [22,43]. As a result, collaborators are in charge of the resulting narrative, and this is somewhat similar to the situation where a leading author is assigned. In these approaches focused on learning, an explicit description of the writing activities is usually missing in the corresponding publications. Thus, we attempted to deduce the activities from the loose description of the process. As far as we understand, the specific activities to perform are decided by collaborators themselves.

The Cognitive Process Model is the theoretical framework used by the authors of Mechanical Novel. It is articulated in three steps [18], namely planning, translating (i.e., transforming ideas into text), and reviewing. It is interesting to note that the authors of Mechanical Novel consider the writing of a first draft (drafting activity in Lowry's terms) to be something that can be seen as in between brainstorming and drafting. On one hand, outlining takes place only after this step is completed. On the other, the text generated in this step is passed to reviewing and revising steps.

Crowdsourcing approaches typically dive directly into writing and collaborators are usually asked to vote for the text alternatives produced by the participating workers as for example in Argo [8]. The goal is to preserve the text contributions that receive high preferences, while discarding those that are poorly voted at the same time. As a result, we consider these kind of voting activities as something in between convergence and reviewing.

As a final example, Empirica builds on an improvisational theory and it does not directly consider any revising step. However, three different replays of the story are requested with the intention to create better, thought-through stories [17]. This can lead collaborators to converging, reviewing, and revising, but it is latent and not explicitly formalized as a requirement.

6   Discussion and Future Work

In this paper, we discuss a systematic literature review of online collaborative story writing with focus on the different forms of user involvement in such approaches. In particular, we propose a reference definition based on essential features that characterise collaborative story writing and we review a selection of the literature according to three different dimensions of analysis, that are modes of work, writing roles, and writing activities. In modes of work, we focused on synchronicity and we observed that synchronous communications are mostly adopted by dialogue-based approaches, whereas asynchronous communications frequently characterise scene-based ones. In writing roles, we found that collaborators were often involved in the tasks that require effort and/or creativity as writer, consultant, and reviewer. Less frequently, they were involved as editor or leader where they can have a relevant impact on the final written outcome. In none of the reviewed approaches collaborator were engaged to contribute in the role that Lowry et al. call facilitator. As for the activities, collaborators are mostly involved in drafting tasks where they typically contribute with the creation of the produced content. Other writing activities that we found to be widely used are brainstorming and reviewing that require critical attention to details by the collaborator, even if not commonly and directly contributing with the writing content. Less frequently collaborators were involved in revising, converging, outlining, and copyediting.

According to the results discussed above, we envisage some possible research directions to further expand the understanding on how system designers engage collaborators on tasks of online collaborative story writing.

Recruitment of Collaborators. Some of the most widely adopted activities like drafting and revising, as well as roles like writer and editor require that collaborators are aligned with the intentions behind the story writing process. Such alignment strongly depends on how collaborators are recruited to form the writing groups. In particular, how collaborators are motivated is a crucial aspect of the recruitment success. For example, consider the widespread approach – typically adopted by crowdsourcing platforms like Mechanical Turk – to pay crowd workers to perform their tasks. Such an extrinsic stimulus ensures a large availability of collaborators. However, the remuneration distorts their motivation down to getting most pay off from the task, rather than getting interested with the final quality of the overall product and "walking an extra mile" to achieve it [13,14]. Furthermore, ethical issues need to be kept into account when collaborators are paid for their effort, see for instance [10,14].

Awareness of Collaborators. Another potential step towards making sure that the goals of collaborators are aligned with those of system designers are possible preliminary activities (i.e. onboarding mechanisms) to develop a shared awareness of the task. However, collaborators are typically involved without any shared background knowledge of the approach and related organisational process. The degree of collaborator awareness can be seen as a platform-related issue. For example, paid crowdsourcing platforms like Mechanical Turk aim to provide the minimal necessary onboarding mechanism since the execution of atomic, independent tasks does not require a lot of background knowledge. In other words, onboarding is seen as a marginal aspect in such a kind of systems. Entertainment storytelling experiences work to persuade their users to get involved for a long period and to become contributory participants who not only put a genuine effort to understand the background of their work, but are also engaged in a continuously growing understanding of the working context. Rettberg's degree of awareness of collaborators (*conscious participation, contributory participation* and *unwitting participation*) can be a starting point for the specification of this dimension of analysis [41].

Creative Guidance. The actual form of collaborator involvement is only partially described by writing activities and modes of writing. In particular, the way the activities are introduced impacts the contributions and it represents a form of creative guidance. This aspect is related to the development of awareness among collaborators. While onboarding aims to give collaborators the necessary knowledge to effectively participate, guidance aims to predispose collaborators to unleash their creativity. An example of guidance can be seen in Mechanical Novel where collaborators are prompted with a story start to prime their input [27]. More generally, guidance can provide information about the story context [29,48] or previous events in the story [8,50]. Sometimes, guidance can provide constraints, such as assignment of roles [6] or definition of possible actions [45].

Modalities of Contribution. We call modalities of contribution the affordances offered to the collaborators for providing their contributions. In this respect, system designers could rely on many alternatives, such as to write a free text [8,27], to choose from a list of predefined choices [45], or to upload images [33]. The modality of contribution provides a trade-off between freedom of expression for collaborators and centralised control of the narrative. Moreover, it allows to enforce creative design decisions for aligning collaborators.

Further Research Directions. As mentioned in Sect. 1, narrative quality is a very important issue to consider, yet difficult to address. When the final text provided by collaborators lacks of consistency, revision and copyediting activities can barely take to a consistent story. To maintain narrative consistency throughout content creation, two possible strategies emerge from the literature, namely scene-based and role-based ones. In scene-based strategies, collaborators have the full control of writing and they are asked to provide the single-handed creation of an entire scene [27,28]. In role-based approaches (typically adopted in conversational systems), each character is assigned to an individual collaborator who has the responsibility of that character's integrity [17]. Moreover, measuring the quality of the produced narrative remains an open issue. On one hand, this is relevant for the intent of the produced narrative. On the other hand, it can be useful for the narrative's attractiveness [51]. In the field of crowdsourcing, a number of quality metrics have been proposed [12]. Some of these could be used to assess the quality of a story if combined with a quantitative evaluation. A number of quantitative measures have been proposed [20,37,46,47]. However, some of these measures are characterized by limitations, and sometimes they can result in a contradictory outcome when an unnatural narrative is considered [2]. This is why further investigation is needed.

A further research direction is to better understand how the decisions of systems designers are perceived by target users like collaborators and story readers. In this direction, collecting opinions from stakeholders would allow to compare and validate our findings against qualitative data to both clarify boundaries and to elicit potential conflicting requirements.

The possible use of AI models in collaborative story writing is a further direction of research. Examples of this kind already exist, like Shelley [50] that is also included in our literature review. Further examples are Dungeon [23], Spindle [5], and Dramatron [35] that have been considered in our work, but excluded (see Sect. 2). Contacting stakeholders would allow to expand this discussion to better understand whether and how AI-generated story contributions can be considered as part of collaborative writing.

Acknowledgements. ▨ This project has received funding from the European Union's Horizon 2020 research and innovation programme under grant agreement No 101004949. This document reflects only the author's view and the European Commission is not responsible for any use that may be made of the information it contains.

References

1. Acharya, D., Wardrip-Fruin, N.: Building worlds together: understanding collaborative co-creation of game worlds. In: Proceedings of the 14th International Conference on the Foundations of Digital Games, FDG 2019. Association for Computing Machinery, New York (2019). https://doi.org/10.1145/3337722.3337748
2. Alber, J., Heinze, R. (eds.): Unnatural Narratives - Unnatural Narratology. De Gruyter, Berlin, Boston (2011). https://doi.org/10.1515/9783110229042
3. de Bono, E.: Six Thinking Hats: the multi-million bestselling guide to running better meetings and making faster decisions. Penguin Books Limited (2017). https://www.penguin.co.uk/books/56270
4. Borromeo, R.M., Laurent, T., Toyama, M., Alsayasneh, M., Amer-Yahia, S., Leroy, V.: Deployment strategies for crowdsourcing text creation. Inf. Syst. **71**, 103–110 (2017). https://doi.org/10.1016/j.is.2017.06.007
5. Calderwood, A., Wardrip-Fruin, N., Mateas, M.: Spinning coherent interactive fiction through foundation model prompt. In: Proceedings of the 13th International Conference on Computational Creativity, pp. 44–53. Association for Computational Creativity, New York (2022). https://computationalcreativity.net/iccc22/wp-content/uploads/2022/06/ICCC-2022_2L_Calderwood-et-al..pdf
6. Caniglia, G.: Cast: A context-aware collaborative storytelling platform. In: Extended Abstracts of the 2020 CHI Conference on Human Factors in Computing Systems, CHI EA 2020, pp. 1–7. Association for Computing Machinery, New York (2020). https://doi.org/10.1145/3334480.3382966
7. Carnicke, S.M.: Stanislavsky in focus: An acting master for the twenty-first century. Routledge (2008). https://www.routledge.com/p/book/9780415774970
8. Castano, S., Ferrara, A., Montanelli, S.: Creative story writing through crowdsourcing empowerment (2019). https://dc2s2.github.io/2019/papers/dc2s2-castano.pdf, workshop on Designing Crowd-powered Creativity Support Systems
9. Cavazza, M., Pizzi, D.: Narratology for interactive storytelling: a critical introduction. In: Göbel, S., Malkewitz, R., Iurgel, I. (eds.) TIDSE 2006. LNCS, vol. 4326, pp. 72–83. Springer, Heidelberg (2006). https://doi.org/10.1007/11944577_7
10. Chan, A., Okolo, C.T., Terner, Z., Wang, A.: The limits of global inclusion in AI development. In: Fokoue, A., Agunwa, C., Lee, K., Quigley, L.T., Hobson, S. (eds.) Short Paper Proceedings of the Workshop on Reframing Diversity in AI: Representation, Inclusion and Power, pp. 9–16. No. 2812 in CEUR Workshop Proceedings, CEUR-WS, Aachen (2021). https://doi.org/10.48550/ARXIV.2102.01265. https://ceur-ws.org/Vol-2812/RDAI-2021_paper_5.pdf
11. Cohn, N.: Visual narrative structure. Cogn. Sci. **37**(3), 413–52 (2013). https://doi.org/10.1111/cogs.12016, copyright 2012 Cognitive Science Society, Inc
12. Daniel, F., Kucherbaev, P., Cappiello, C., Benatallah, B., Allahbakhsh, M.: Quality control in crowdsourcing: A survey of quality attributes, assessment techniques, and assurance actions. ACM Comput. Surv. **51**(1) (2018). https://doi.org/10.1145/3148148
13. Deci, E.L., Koestner, R., Ryan, R.M.: A meta-analytic review of experiments examining the effects of extrinsic rewards on intrinsic motivation. Psychol. Bull. **125**(6) (1999). https://doi.org/10.1037/0033-2909.125.6.627
14. d'Eon, G., Goh, J., Larson, K., Law, E.: Paying crowd workers for collaborative work. Proc. ACM Hum.-Comput. Interact. 3(CSCW) (2019). https://doi.org/10.1145/3359227

15. DiPardo, A.: Narrative knowers, expository knowledge: discourse as a dialectic. Writ. Commun. **7**(1), 59–95 (1990). https://doi.org/10.1177/0741088390007001003
16. Feldman, M.Q., McInnis, B.J.: How we write with crowds. Proc. ACM Hum.-Comput. Interact. 4(CSCW3) (2021). https://doi.org/10.1145/3432928
17. Feng, D., Carstensdottir, E., Seif El-Nasr, M., Marsella, S.: Exploring improvisational approaches to social knowledge acquisition. In: Proceedings of the 18th International Conference on Autonomous Agents and MultiAgent Systems, AAMAS 2019, pp. 1060–1068. International Foundation for Autonomous Agents and Multiagent Systems, Richland, SC (2019). https://dl.acm.org/doi/10.5555/3306127.3331804
18. Flower, L., Hayes, J.R.: A cognitive process theory of writing. Coll. Compos. Commun. **32**(4), 365–387 (1981). http://www.jstor.org/stable/356600
19. Fludernik, M.: An Introduction to Narratology. Routledge, 0 edn. (2009). https://doi.org/10.4324/9780203882887
20. Gomes, P., Paiva, A., Martinho, C., Jhala, A.: Metrics for character believability in interactive narrative. In: Koenitz, H., Sezen, T.I., Ferri, G., Haahr, M., Sezen, D., Çatak, G. (eds.) ICIDS 2013. LNCS, vol. 8230, pp. 223–228. Springer, Cham (2013). https://doi.org/10.1007/978-3-319-02756-2_27
21. Gusenbauer, M.: Search where you will find most: comparing the disciplinary coverage of 56 bibliographic databases. Scientometrics **127**(5), 2683–2745 (2022). https://doi.org/10.1007/s11192-022-04289-7
22. Hamid, S.K.S., Mansor, W.F.A.W.: Discovering the potential of wiki through collaborative story writing. Procedia Soc. Behav. Sci. **66**, 337–342 (2012). https://doi.org/10.1016/j.sbspro.2012.11.276, the 8th International Language for Specific Purposes (LSP) Seminar - Aligning Theoretical Knowledge with Professional Practice
23. Hua, M., Raley, R.: Playing with unicorns: AI dungeon and citizen NLP. Digit. Humanit. Q. **14**(4) (2020). https://www.proquest.com/scholarly-journals/playing-with-unicorns-ai-dungeon-citizen-nlp/docview/2553526112/se-2
24. Huang, C.Y., Huang, S.H., Huang, T.H.K.: Heteroglossia: in-situ story ideation with the crowd. In: Proceedings of the 2020 CHI Conference on Human Factors in Computing Systems, CHI 2020, pp. 1–12. Association for Computing Machinery, New York (2020). https://doi.org/10.1145/3313831.3376715
25. Kim, J., Cheng, J., Bernstein, M.S.: Ensemble: exploring complementary strengths of leaders and crowds in creative collaboration. In: Proceedings of the 17th ACM Conference on Computer Supported Cooperative Work and Social Computing, CSCW 2014, pp. 745–755. Association for Computing Machinery, New York (2014). https://doi.org/10.1145/2531602.2531638
26. Kim, J., Monroy-Hernandez, A.: Storia: summarizing social media content based on narrative theory using crowdsourcing. In: Proceedings of the 19th ACM Conference on Computer-Supported Cooperative Work and Social Computing, CSCW 2016, pp. 1018–1027. Association for Computing Machinery, New York (2016). https://doi.org/10.1145/2818048.2820072
27. Kim, J., Sterman, S., Cohen, A.A.B., Bernstein, M.S.: Mechanical novel: crowdsourcing complex work through reflection and revision. In: Proceedings of the 2017 ACM Conference on Computer Supported Cooperative Work and Social Computing, CSCW 2017, pp. 233–245. Association for Computing Machinery, New York (2017). https://doi.org/10.1145/2998181.2998196
28. Li, B., Lee-Urban, S., Appling, D.S., Riedl, M.O.: Crowdsourcing narrative intelligence. Adv. Congnitive Syst. **2**, 25–42 (2012). http://www.cogsys.org/journal/volume2/abstract-2-4.html

29. Li, T., Luther, K., North, C.: CrowdIA: solving mysteries with crowdsourced sense-making. Proc. ACM Hum.-Comput. Interact. 2(CSCW) (2018). https://doi.org/10.1145/3274374

30. Lowry, P.B., Curtis, A., Lowry, M.R.: Building a taxonomy and nomenclature of collaborative writing to improve interdisciplinary research and practice. J. Bus. Commun. (1973) 41(1), 66–99 (2004). https://doi.org/10.1177/0021943603259363

31. Lowry, P.B., Gaskin, J.E., Moody, G.D.: Proposing the multimotive information systems continuance model (misc) to better explain end-user system evaluations and continuance intentions. J. Assoc. Inf. Syst. 2–s2.0-84939128272 (2015). http://hdl.handle.net/10722/233856

32. Luther, K., Bruckman, A.: Leadership in online creative collaboration. In: Proceedings of the 2008 ACM Conference on Computer Supported Cooperative Work, CSCW 2008, pp. 343–352. Association for Computing Machinery, New York (2008). https://doi.org/10.1145/1460563.1460619

33. Mandal, A., Agarwal, M., Bhattacharyya, M.: Collective story writing through linking images. In: Proceedings of the HCOMP 2018 Works in Progress and Demonstration Papers Track of the Sixth AAAI Conference on Human Computation and Crowdsourcing (HCOMP 2018). No. 2173 in CEUR Workshop Proceedings, Aachen (2018). http://ceur-ws.org/Vol-2173/paper12.pdf

34. Martín-Martín, A., Orduna-Malea, E., Thelwall, M., Delgado López-Cózar, E.: Google scholar, web of science, and scopus: a systematic comparison of citations in 252 subject categories. J. Inform. 12(4), 1160–1177 (2018). https://doi.org/10.1016/j.joi.2018.09.002. https://www.sciencedirect.com/science/article/pii/S1751157718303249

35. Mirowski, P., Mathewson, K.W., Pittman, J., Evans, R.: Co-writing screenplays and theatre scripts with language models: evaluation by industry professionals. In: Proceedings of the 2023 CHI Conference on Human Factors in Computing Systems. CHI '23. Association for Computing Machinery, New York (2023). https://doi.org/10.1145/3544548.3581225

36. Moher, D., Liberati, A., Tetzlaff, J., Altman, D.G., Group, T.P.: Preferred reporting items for systematic reviews and meta-analyses: the prisma statement. PLoS Med. 6(7), 1–6 (2009). https://doi.org/10.1371/journal.pmed.1000097

37. Partlan, N., et al.: Exploratory automated analysis of structural features of interactive narrative. In: Proceedings of the AAAI Conference on Artificial Intelligence and Interactive Digital Entertainment 14(1), 88–94 (2018). https://doi.org/10.1609/aiide.v14i1.13019

38. Pastor-Ramón, E., Herrera-Peco, I., Agirre, O., García-Puente, M., Morán, J.M.: Improving the reliability of literature reviews: Detection of retracted articles through academic search engines. Europ. J. Invest. Health Psychol. Educ. 12(5), 458–464 (2022). https://doi.org/10.3390/ejihpe12050034

39. Pica, T., Kang, H.S., Sauro, S.: Information gap tasks: their multiple roles and contributions to interaction research methodology. Stud. Second. Lang. Acquis. 28(2), 301–338 (2006). https://doi.org/10.1017/S027226310606013X

40. Pirolli, P., Card, S.: The sensemaking process and leverage points for analyst technology as identified through cognitive task analysis. In: Proceedings of International Conference on Intelligence Analysis, pp. 2–4 (2005). https://analysis.mitre.org/proceedings/Final_Papers_Files/206_Camera_Ready_Paper.pdf

41. Rettberg, S.: Human computation in electronic literature. In: Michelucci, P. (ed.) Handbook of Human Computation, pp. 187–203. Springer, New York (2013). https://doi.org/10.1007/978-1-4614-8806-4_17

42. Riedl, M.O., Bulitko, V.: Interactive narrative: an intelligent systems approach. AI Mag. **34**(1), 67 (2012). https://doi.org/10.1609/aimag.v34i1.2449
43. Sauro, S., Sundmark, B.: Report from Middle-Earth: fan fiction tasks in the EFL classroom. ELT J. **70**(4), 414–423 (2016). https://doi.org/10.1093/elt/ccv075
44. Short, E.: Beyond branching: quality-based, salience-based, and waypoint narrative structures (2016). https://emshort.blog/2016/04/12/beyond-branching-quality-based-and-salience-based-narrative-structures/
45. Spawforth, C., Gibbins, N., Millard, D.E.: StoryMINE: a system for multiplayer interactive narrative experiences. In: Rouse, R., Koenitz, H., Haahr, M. (eds.) ICIDS 2018. LNCS, vol. 11318, pp. 534–543. Springer, Cham (2018). https://doi.org/10.1007/978-3-030-04028-4_62
46. Szilas, N., Ilea, I.: Objective metrics for interactive narrative. In: Mitchell, A., Fernández-Vara, C., Thue, D. (eds.) ICIDS 2014. LNCS, vol. 8832, pp. 91–102. Springer, Cham (2014). https://doi.org/10.1007/978-3-319-12337-0_9
47. Veloso, C., Prada, R.: Validating the plot of interactive narrative games. In: 2021 IEEE Conference on Games (CoG), pp. 01–08 (2021). https://doi.org/10.1109/CoG52621.2021.9618897
48. Verroios, V., Bernstein, M.: Context trees: Crowdsourcing global understanding from local views. In: Proceedings of the AAAI Conference on Human Computation and Crowdsourcing 2(1), pp. 210–219 (2014). https://doi.org/10.1609/hcomp.v2i1.13149
49. Wiethof, C., Tavanapour, N., Bittner, E.: Design and Evaluation of a Collaborative Writing Process with Gamification Elements. ECIS 2020 Research Papers (2020). https://aisel.aisnet.org/ecis2020_rp/43
50. Yanardag, P., Cebrian, M., Rahwan, I.: Shelley: a crowd-sourced collaborative horror writer. In: Creativity and Cognition, C&C '21. Association for Computing Machinery, New York (2021). https://doi.org/10.1145/3450741.3465251
51. Young, R.D., Monroe, M.C.: Some fundamentals of engaging stories. Environ. Educ. Res. **2**(2), 171–187 (1996). https://doi.org/10.1080/1350462960020204
52. Zhang, M., Gibbons, J., Li, M.: Computer-mediated collaborative writing in l2 classrooms: a systematic review. J. Second. Lang. Writ. **54**, 100854 (2021). https://doi.org/10.1016/j.jslw.2021.100854

Algorithmic Management for Community Health Worker in Sub-Saharan Africa: Curse or Blessing?

Dario Staehelin[1]([✉]) [ID], Mateusz Dolata[1] [ID], Nicolas Peyer[1] [ID], Felix Gerber[2,3] [ID], and Gerhard Schwabe[1] [ID]

[1] Department of Informatics, University of Zurich, Zürich, Switzerland
staehelin@ifi.uzh.ch
[2] Department of Clinical Research, University Hospital Basel, Basel, Switzerland
[3] University of Basel, Swiss Tropical and Public Health Institute, Basel, Switzerland

Abstract. Algorithmic management can potentially improve healthcare delivery, for example, in community-based healthcare in low-and middle-income countries. However, most research neglects the user perspective and focuses on health-related outcomes. Consequently, we know little about the effects of algorithmic management on the user: community health workers. This paper reports on a 12-week pilot study in ComBaCaL, a community-based healthcare project tackling the increasing burden of non-communicable diseases (NCDs). We evaluate the Community Health Toolkit (CHT), a digital tool designed to support CHWs in community-based NCD care. We find that CHT is generally suitable for this purpose and can help CHWs to assume broader responsibilities. However, its design creates a tension between control and autonomy when confronted with reality. This tension could lead to disempowerment and attrition among CHWs. We propose design adaptations for CHT's task scheduling, balancing the socio-technical system to resolve the tension between control and autonomy.

Keywords: Community Health Worker · Algorithmic Management · Digital Empowerment

1 Introduction

The potential benefits and challenges of algorithms in work contexts have generated broad interest in HCI and information systems. This emerging research stream of algorithmic management focuses on algorithms performing tasks usually executed by humans, such as data analysis or work allocation and scheduling to increase effectiveness and efficiency [27, 47, 53]. Algorithmic management has also found its way into the health system in the form of decision support tools [1] or to optimize scheduling [14]. Induced by a projected workforce shortage in healthcare of 10 Million by 2030 [57], the utilization of algorithm-centered digital tools for community health workers (CHWs) in low- and middle-income countries (LMICs) has been extensively studied in recent years [3, 20, 23, 24, 56, 59]. Such tools are ascribed the potential to increase the performance

J. Abdelnour Nocera et al. (Eds.): INTERACT 2023, LNCS 14144, pp. 94–114, 2023.
https://doi.org/10.1007/978-3-031-42286-7_6

and retention of CHWs [20] and empower them to assume more responsibilities, such as the treatment of NCDs, to counter the workforce shortage [44]. At first sight, digital tools appear to live up to the expectations of boosting performance and increasing retention of CHWs [1, 20, 59].

However, at second sight, most of these studies focus on the effect of digital tools on health-related outcomes. This emphasis leads to a neglect of CHWs' needs and preferences. Consequently, we lack an understanding of the impact of digital tools on their actual users: the CHWs. Prior work highlights the empowering effects of digital tools and the potential of CHWs as more active members of the health system without providing a conclusive answer on how to connect means and aims [21, 28, 52]. Consequently, we propose the following research question:

Is algorithmic management a curse or blessing for community health workers in non-communicable disease care?

We answer this research question by evaluating a 12-week pilot study in ComBaCaL (Community-Based Chronic Disease Care), a community-based NCD care project in Lesotho. First, we study the design of work planning in the Community Health Toolkit (CHT), the underlying objectives, and its understanding of the CHW role (Sect. 4). Second, we evaluate CHT's suitability for community-based NCD care focusing on system usability and CHW empowerment (Sect. 5). Finally, we discuss uncovered problems and a solution proposition (see Sect. 6). In this study, we aim to contribute to the neglected but emerging discourse on empowering CHWs to become active members of the healthcare systems [17, 21]. While we agree with the positive reputation of digital tools, we highlight algorithmic management as a double-edged sword that could amplify the challenges through excessive control.

2 Related Work

2.1 Community-Based Healthcare

The WHO projects a workforce shortage of 14 million health workers by 2030 [57]. As with NCD-related deaths, this shortage is also expected to affect LMICs disproportionately. LMICs often apply community-based healthcare approaches to counter the general workforce shortage and to address the rapid spread of NCDs [10]. For decades, community-based healthcare has been a well-established approach in LMICs to grant remote populations access to primary healthcare in an attempt to achieve health equity [8, 41]. Community-based approaches allow LMICs to recruit from a vast pool of resources: their citizens. CHWs are citizens without a formal medical education who seldom possess a higher education degree and often come from modest economic backgrounds [9, 38]. Besides their availability in large numbers, CHWs have the advantage that they usually live in or near the community they serve. This characteristic makes them a valuable link between health facilities and the rural population. CHWs receive training to provide basic health services such as general health promotion, disease screening, detecting danger signs and referring patients to clinics, and follow-up counseling after clinical care [30, 40, 48]. Overall, the literature describes CHWs as valuable sensors to the health system. Their vast number, relatively little cost, and connection with their community allow health systems to extend their reach beyond easily accessible urban centers.

Community-based health programs have attracted attention from research and practice. They have been implemented in maternal and child care [1, 3], tackling infectious diseases such as malaria and tuberculosis [13], and enrollment in HIV therapy [7] and many other fields. Against this background, community-based healthcare could play a central role in tackling the rising burden of NCDs in LMICs. However, literature on the feasibility and effects of community-based NCD care is scarce. Including first-line treatment in community-based NCD care would require more active CHWs to established use cases [44]. Nevertheless, community-based programs have difficulties sustaining and increasing CHW performance [42] and often suffer from high attrition rates [35]. These issues stem from a lack of organizational support and appreciation (e.g., by supervisors) [37, 42], inadequate training and learning opportunities [43], and inadequate monetary compensation [55]. The persisting issues and their root causes make the nationwide and sustainable rollout of community-based programs challenging.

Mobile health (mHealth) tools promise to address these challenges by increasing the effectiveness and efficiency of community-based healthcare and empowering CHWs to accept more responsibilities as needed for NCD care (e.g., first-line treatment)[20]. mHealth increases performance and reduces attrition rates through decision support systems [1, 3, 24, 59], performance dashboards [23, 56], and mobile learning approaches [31, 45]. Despite these efforts in supporting CHWs with digital tools, research predominantly focuses on patient-centered outcomes (e.g., diagnosis accuracy or treatment outcomes) evaluated through health outcome-centered approaches (i.e., randomized controlled clinical trials). While such studies provide invaluable insights into the benefits of digital tools for healthcare, they neglect the user of these tools and their experience. Therefore, more user- and human-centered approaches are needed to complement medical insights to leverage the empowering potential of digital tools [17].

Empowerment is a concept from organizational science and psychology concerned with the impact of structural work conditions (structural empowerment) on perceived control over one's work (psychological empowerment) [32, 34]. Empowerment has been shown to increase employee performance, staff retention, and to decrease job strain [26, 32, 49]. Structural empowerment focuses on organizational conditions assessed by access to *information* (e.g., medical history), *resources* (e.g., materials, means, time), *support* (e.g., guidance and feedback from a supervisor), and *opportunities* (e.g., for personal development within an organization) [22, 25]. Psychological empowerment – a product of structural empowerment – is a state of intrinsic motivation [4, 46, 50]. This cognitive state is a combination of perceived *meaning* (i.e., degree of accordance of work and one's beliefs), *competence* (i.e., belief in one's capabilities), *autonomy* (i.e., perception of being the locus of causality), and *impact* (i.e., perceived influence over task outcomes) [50]. CHW empowerment has been described as a central construct for leveraging CHWs' "potential as agents of social change, beyond their role as links between the community and the health system." [21].

Nevertheless, the literature on the digital empowerment of CHWs has not yet adopted this conceptualization [18, 58], while domains such as crisis response [28] and traditional healthcare approaches [52] are receiving increased attention. We know little about the empowering effect of digital tools and their capabilities for decision support and work organization for CHWs [51].

2.2 Algorithmic Management

Algorithms are central in the advances of digital tools in community-based health care. Widely used tools (e.g., CommCare by dimagi[1] and CHT by Medic[2]) center around medical algorithms for clinical decision support and task management to ensure patient safety and increase user performance. Medical algorithms facilitate community-based health care as they compensate for the lack of formal medical education for CHWs.

An increasing body of literature studies these human-algorithm interactions under the term algorithmic management. It is defined as shifting "power from a hierarchy of managers to larger cadres of professionals who master analytics, programming, and business. Management is no longer a human practice, but a process embedded in technology." [47]. In algorithmic management, algorithms perform tasks usually executed by humans [27]. Algorithms assume tasks such as performance tracking (managerial) or work allocation and scheduling (operational) [53]. Algorithmic scheduling has been shown to increase patient volume without increasing the perceived burden by doctors [14] or increasing perceived fairness in work allocation [2].

However, there are also potential downsides to algorithmic work. While not exclusively, the negative aspects often affect blue-collar workers, who are more vulnerable to exploitation. A recent study points to the potential increasing burden of algorithmic systems as it would require housekeepers to clean hotel rooms based on effectiveness (i.e., the arrival of guests) and not efficiency (i.e., shortest path). As a result, the algorithm made the housekeepers' work more physically demanding as they had to move their equipment across the hotel multiple times a day [39]. Further, algorithms have favored high-performing employees in work scheduling, leaving lower-performing employees with poorer schedules in restaurants [29]. Algorithmic scheduling can have a negative impact on employees and their environment. This is especially true for digital work settings where working hours are often not explicitly set [54]. These adverse effects are often accompanied by a (perceived) loss of autonomy.

Independent from the application area, these challenges typically stem from four characteristics of the algorithms that are often intentionally incorporated in the design [53]: (1) lack of transparency of computational logic, (2) lack of connection between tasks, (3) lack of holistic understanding of user's context, (4) incomplete or untimely information provision. These ambiguities and conflicts lead to three typical reactions from users. First, users perform the task as instructed by the algorithm. After executing the task, they could either experience a positive (e.g., attended patient at the correct time) or negative outcome (e.g., working at an unwanted time) [39, 53]. Second, users often work around the system if it limits their autonomy too much or does not provide a desired functionality [19, 53]. Third, users could engage in "gaming", ignoring the algorithm's instructions, if they believe they know better [27, 53]. Gaming refers to the anticipation to avoid the negative consequences of ignoring instructions [53].

However, despite our understanding of the benefits and potential challenges in algorithmic management, we know little about its application in resource- and know-how-limited settings such as community-based healthcare in LMICs. Recent studies have

---

[1] https://www.dimagi.com.

[2] https://medic.org.

demonstrated the potential benefits of algorithm-centric digital tools for healthcare systems [1, 3, 24, 59]. Yet, the role of algorithmic management in tackling challenges in the performance and attrition rate of CHWs is unclear. Does it contribute to resolving the persisting issues by empowering CHWs, or is it a double-edged sword that could amplify the challenges through excessive control?

3 Methodology and Data Collection

This study focuses on algorithmic task scheduling as a form of algorithmic management. To answer the research question, we evaluate the suitability of the Community Health Toolkit (CHT, a broadly accepted, open-source framework) in a 12-week evaluation of a pilot study in ComBaCaL with ten CHWs delivering community-based NCD care in Lesotho. Evaluating the software in a real-world environment is essential in answering our research question, as only artifacts-in-use can uncover unintended consequences [12]. Such (positive or negative) unintended consequences experienced by the users (i.e., CHWs) allow us to study the effects of algorithmic task scheduling.

3.1 ComBaCaL (Community-Based Chronic Disease Care Lesotho)

Our study reports on the pilot study in ComBaCaL, an implementation project for community-based NCD care in Lesotho. ComBaCaL aims to tackle the rapidly spreading NCD epidemic in Lesotho by capacitating CHWs to provide NCD care at the community level supported by a digital tool. The CHWs in ComBaCaL will screen and monitor NCDs, specifically type 2 diabetes and hypertension, guided through clinical algorithms instantiated in CHT running on a tablet. In addition to screening and monitoring services, they will provide a care package including prescription of first-line treatment for uncomplicated type 2 diabetes. This way, ComBaCaL aims to provide uncomplicated type 2 diabetes care in the community, reducing the need for travel and making care more accessible for people in remote areas without compromising patient safety and quality of care. ComBaCaL chose CHT due to the system's focus on the global south and community-based perspective, offline-first approach, and the options for flexible configuration of the medical algorithm to specific needs or diseases in focus. The interdisciplinary and multicultural project team gathered extensive requirements for the intended community-based approach with support from students in Lesotho and Switzerland. They adopted a human-centered design approach to allow the inclusion of all relevant stakeholders and their needs [6, 17]. Two characteristics distinguish ComBaCaL from the typical CHT use case: (1) The extension of the CHWs' responsibilities to provide NCD treatment in addition to screening and diagnosis; (2) the longitudinal aspect of NCD care requiring lifelong counseling.

3.2 Evaluation

Ten newly recruited CHWs were trained for two weeks at the beginning of the evaluation. CHWs were elected by the population of their village after pre-selection by the study team according to the Lesotho Ministry of Health criteria that define minimal educational standards, such as basic literacy in the local language, Sesotho and English. During the first week of training, the CHWs were educated on diabetes risk factors, pathophysiology, diagnosis, treatment approaches, and medical procedures, such as capillary blood glucose measurement. The second week focused on practice-oriented counseling to combine medical knowledge with CHT, including counseling techniques and tablet handling. The counseling techniques were codified in a recipe-like form consisting of social scripts, medical instructions, and examples of how to apply the techniques [11]. They were adjusted during the training to incorporate the social and cultural context. The training concluded with two days in a village where the CHWs practiced their newly gained knowledge and skills in a real-world setting. Finally, the CHWs participated in a focus group discussion (two groups per five CHWs) to discuss their training experience and expectations for their work after returning to their community. Further, each CHW filled out a questionnaire consisting of the system usability scale (SUS) [5], the conditions for work effectiveness questionnaire (structural empowerment) [26], and Spreitzer's measure for psychological empowerment [50].

After completing the training, the CHWs returned to their village, registering and screening their community and providing diabetes care for diagnosed patients. After approximately 12 weeks, the CHWs again filled out the same questionnaire. In addition, each CHW provided insights into their work planning practices in an individual interview. We followed the interview-to-the-double approach prompting the CHWs to explain their practices as if the interviewer would take over their work. This approach allowed "to capture and formalize experience and to enrich it through reflection" [36].

The combination of selected measures in the questionnaire and qualitative insights from the focus group discussions and individual interviews allowed us to evaluate the suitability of CHT for community-based NCD care as instantiated in ComBaCaL. We could study its effect on the CHWs' perceived structural and psychological empowerment. While the small sample size (n = 10) does not allow for in-depth statistical analysis, we could observe changes over time between the training and the end of the evaluation. We derived trends indicated in Table 2 and Table 3 with arrows pointing up (i.e., improvement) and down (i.e., deterioration), drawing on our understanding of the local context. Furthermore, we derived critical incidents from the interviews indicating breakdowns in the socio-technical system [15]. Through these breakdowns, we could formulate hypothetical explanations for the trends observed in the questionnaires. We discussed these hypotheses iteratively and under consideration of similar breakdowns reported by the CHWs. This analysis of two data types allowed us to triangulate specific design choices that lead to the tension between control and autonomy and the subsequent breakdowns in the socio-technical system.

4 Is CHT an Appropriate Solution for Community-Based NCD Care?

Effective community-based NCD care requires repeating screening activities and long-term counseling of clients for the prevention and treatment of NCDs. CHWs must be empowered to accept such broader responsibilities. Structural empowerment of health workers can be achieved through IT. This section discusses the Community Health

Toolkit (CHT), an open-source framework that aims to make digital health tools readily available to reach most rural areas. We review the underlying conceptualization of community-based healthcare and CHWs, goals, and requirements according to CHT to examine its suitability for community-based NCD care.

CHT is a progressive web app that follows an offline-first approach making it suitable for use in remote areas with no internet connection. It comprises a core framework and configuration code that facilitates rapid development and rollout of scalable digital health applications. The core framework provides measures for data security, APIs for extensions, and open-source NoSQL databases that run locally on the device (i.e., PouchDB) and a server (CouchDB) facilitating offline functionality. The configuration code allows developers to customize CHT through hierarchies, user roles, and workflows. Developers can define medical algorithms (so-called care guides) for decision support and task management to support CHWs in their work.

Typical responsibilities of CHWs are "registering new people and families, conducting guided health assessments, screening for and tracking of specific conditions, providing basic medicines and health supplies (e.g., pain medication), reporting danger signs and referring to the clinic, following up about clinic visits and care" [33]. In this role, CHWs serve as sensors linking the communities and health facilities. CHT supports the CHWs by tackling the knowledge gap as the central problem in community-based healthcare. CHT aims to solve this problem by organizing the CHWs' work. CHT does this by telling the CHWs WHO to counsel on WHAT and WHEN according to the configured workflows. CHWs must do this effectively (patient safety) and efficiently (e.g., timely). Figure 1 and the subsequent paragraph highlight how this is anchored in CHT's design.

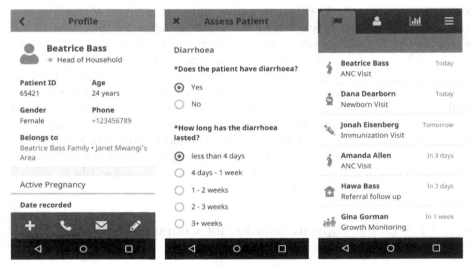

Fig. 1. Design of Client Profile (left), "Care Guide" (middle), and Task List (right) in CHT [33].

Who: CHWs are responsible for up to several hundred clients depending on the scope of their work. Regardless of the scope, CHWs need access to each client's electronic medical record. CHT offers the people tab that allows the allocation of individuals to places (e.g., households). Each person has a profile with relevant personal and medical information (see Fig. 1 left).

What: As CHWs do not have a formal medical education, CHT offers decision support to guide them through client interactions (see Fig. 1 middle). These "care guides allow CHWs to register new families and people, take a structured medical history, or document findings of clinical examinations. They can present different types of questions, skip logic, images, and videos." Furthermore, care guides can refer to previously entered data and can be configured to provide a summary with diagnoses and recommendations.

When: Independent from the scope and responsibilities, CHWs often have recurring consultations with their clients. For example, in maternal health, one of the primary use cases of CHT, CHWs accompany female clients over time by counseling them on family planning and antenatal and postnatal care. To support these activities, CHT schedules follow-up tasks based on the care guides to ensure the timely attendance of clients. Open tasks are displayed as a list in the task tab. "Tasks ensure that the right actions are taken for the right people at the right time. CHWs should strive to complete tasks before they are overdue. Many programs add targets to track task completion and timeliness." [33]. Each task in the list shows a due date that turns red if it is in the past (WHEN). Furthermore, tasks are specified with an icon and name (WHAT) and display the client's name (WHO) (see Fig. 1 right). The CHWs can open the care guide by clicking on the respective task.

Table 1. Overview of problems, solution objectives, and design requirements for CHW work organization by CHT.

Problem	Solution Objectives	Design Requirement
Large number of clients	CHWs must know WHO they are counseling	"a profile where you can see detailed information about that person or place"
Limited medical knowledge (procedural)	CHWs need guidance on WHAT they should counsel their clients on	"Care guides that take health workers through care protocols and provide decision support for their interactions with patients"
Limited medical knowledge (time management)	CHWs should receive instructions on WHEN to counsel their clients	"Tasks ensure that the right actions are taken for the right people at the right time."

Table 1 summarizes CHT's solution objectives and design requirements for the work organization of CHWs. Overall, CHT – like many other similar tools – anchors its design in assumptions about community-based health care and the role of CHWs based on the established literature (see Sect. 2.1). First, CHWs have a continuous need for guidance. It assumes a persistent level of competency requiring decision support from medical algorithms. Further, designers (e.g., medical professionals) choose how to adapt CHT to the specific context. Second, CHWs have the resources to accommodate the algorithm's instructions to attend to clients. Third, CHWs can organize their work independently, only working against due dates imposed by the algorithm. As a result, the role of CHWs as sensors is embedded in the design of CHT.

In summary, CHT might offer a solution for community-based NCD care. Yet, whether it is an appropriate solution depends on the validity of the assumptions behind its design. While intended consequences can often be assessed upfront, unintended consequences only emerge from using CHT in its specific context [12]. Hence, we study CHT in ComBaCaL to evaluate its suitability for community-based NCD care.

5   CHT Instantiated in ComBaCaL

This section outlines the results from a 12-week evaluation of the pilot study in ComBa-CaL. This evaluation aims to assess CHT's suitability for community-based NCD care programs with a similar scope as ComBaCaL, including first-line treatment services. For this, we gathered data in two points: After the initial training, before the CHWs started their work (T1), and after 12 weeks of field experience (T2).

The 12-week evaluation generally shows promising results regarding the empowerment of the CHWs (Table 2) and the system usability of CHT (Table 3). Overall, the CHWs feel empowered by CHT and the organizational structures in ComBaCaL to perform their work (Item K). The slight reduction might stem from the fading of the initial enthusiasm. Most core empowerment dimensions (Items A-F) slightly vary over the evaluation period. However, access to support and resources is less well perceived after the field experience (Items G & H). Furthermore, the CHWs rate their formal (job activities scale, Item I) and informal power (organizational relationship scale, Item J) considerably lower after the evaluation period than at the beginning.

When questioned about CHT's usability, the CHWs draw similar conclusions regarding their perceived empowerment. The CHW rate the usability of CHT with 74.25 after the training and slightly better with 76.5 after their field experience on the system usability scale (SUS). The scores indicate that CHT overall is a sound system with some room for improvement [5]. While the items' individual scores have no validity per se, they can provide qualitative insights that are noteworthy for this study (see Table 3). First, the CHWs like to use CHT frequently (Q1; 95), find it easy to use (Q3; 87.5), and are confident in using it (Q9; 92.5) even after working with CHT for 12 weeks. Second, the CHWs rank CHT lower in three items after 12 weeks: "I found the app unnecessarily complex" (Q2), "I found the various functions in this app were well integrated" (Q5), and "I thought there was too much inconsistency in this app" (Q6). From the empowerment measure and the SUS, it appears the CHWs begin to experience the boundaries set by CHT. The lower rating of Questions 2, 5, and 6 of the SUS hint at frustration with the general design idea of CHT. To make sense of the observed trends, we searched for critical incidents in the interviews with the CHWs after 12 weeks that highlight breakdowns in the socio-technical system.

Our analysis uncovered breakdowns in three areas: environment, organization, and context. We analyzed accounts of situations that forced the CHWs to deviate from the

Table 2. Results from the empowerment survey based on Spence-Laschinger et al. [49], T1 = after training, T2 = after 12 weeks, n = 10.

	Domain	T1	T2	Trend
A	Meaning	4.9	4.7	↓
B	Competence	4.6	4.5	↓
C	Autonomy	4.1	4.2	↑
D	Impact	3.8	4	↑
E	Access to opportunity	4.5	4.6	↑
F	Access to information	4.6	4.6	-
G	Access to support	4.3	4	↓
H	Access to resources	4.6	4.3	↓
I	Job activity scale	3.2	2.7	↓
J	Organizational relationship scale	4	3.3	↓
K	General Empowerment	4.9	4.8	↓

Table 3. Results from the system usability scale [5], T1 = after training, T2 = after 12 weeks, n = 10.

#	Domain	T1	T2	Trend
1	I think that I would like to use the app frequently	87.5	95	↑
2	I found the app unnecessarily complex	67.5	65	↓
3	I thought the app was easy to use	82.5	87.5	↑
4	I think that I would need the support of a technical person to be able to use this app	62.5	65	↑
5	I found the various functions in this app were well integrated	87.5	85	↓
6	I thought there was too much inconsistency in this app	75	65	↓
7	I would imagine that most people would learn to use this app very quickly	75	82.5	↑
8	I found the app very cumbersome (difficult) to use	82.5	85	↑
9	I felt very confident using the app	85	92.5	↑
10	I needed to learn a lot of things before I could get going with this app	37.5	42.5	↑
	Total SUS Score	**74.25**	**76.5**	↑

algorithm's instructions (i.e., ignore and engage in gaming and using workarounds) or surrender to the algorithm and execute instructions (i.e., involuntary execution) [53].

Environmental Breakdowns: We identified two critical incidents caused by the environment within the CHWs' work. First, a female CHW shared her discomfort when counseling a single male client in his home. While no incident has been reported, sexual violence is a serious danger [16]. Second, several CHWs report harsh weather conditions as a hazard, as heavy rain or snow can render paths and roads into streams of mud. Such conditions make traveling – usually on foot – challenging and dangerous. The CHWs are forced to decide on their response to CHT's instructions. They could either follow the instructions and complete the task – while exposed to a potential threat – or engage in gaming or find a workaround. For example, the female CHW counsels her single male client in fear of sexual violence or engages in gaming by entering false medical data to manipulate the algorithm, not to schedule follow-up tasks. A workaround for weather conditions could be marking a task complete (by entering dummy data) to avoid overdue tasks and completing it once traveling is safe again.

Organizational Breakdowns: Many CHWs report various formal and informal responsibilities besides their work as a CHW. Some engage in subsistence farming to produce food for their family or fix electronics such as radios or TVs to earn money. Others run small shops selling products such as salty and sugary snacks or vouchers for mobile data. One CHW describes her usual workday: *"In the morning, I wake up very early. The first thing I do is to go to the shop, clean, and then close it, then prepare myself and go to the work for CHW after finishing. I will go to the shop and sell."*

Some clients would take longer as they ask many questions or have difficulties understanding the causes and effects of diabetes. Others would grasp the situation quickly and take less time. Depending on the clients, she would open her shop earlier or later in the afternoon or ask her family member to help sell goods.

However, not all CHWs can rely on others to balance their workload, forcing them again to weigh their options in responding to the demands of the algorithm. Depending on their decision, they either neglect their other responsibilities or ignore the instructions by CHT. One common workaround is maintaining a separate agenda. One CHW explains she plans her work on a self-made timetable where she notes down all clients she wants to attend in a week as an effort to balance her workload.

Contextual Breakdowns: Two critical incidents highlight breakdowns due to the cultural context. First, clients are absent when the CHWs arrive at their homes. Second, clients might be home on the agreed day and time but are not ready for the consultation. For example, CHWs must take a fasted blood glucose measurement for the diagnosis or treatment monitoring of diabetes. For this, clients are not allowed to consume calories (i.e., eat or drink sugary beverages). Despite reminding the clients of this necessity, they sometimes do not adhere, as one CHW explains: *"What I don't like is that sometimes when I have to go to confirm [...] my plans. After telling them not to eat eight hours before, sometimes I've caught them eating, and I have to go [back to them] another day."* Again, the CHWs find workarounds to incorporate such unforeseen circumstances as they cannot strictly adhere to CHT's instructions.

Overall, CHT is suitable for community-based NCD care as applied in ComBaCaL and is well received by the CHWs. After 12 weeks of field experience, the system usability was still acceptable and had an empowering effect on the CHWs. However, critical incidents from the follow-up interviews uncover several breakdowns in the interaction between CHWs and algorithm. In the following, we discuss the implication of these breakdowns and propose a preliminary solution.

6 Discussion and Conclusions

This study addresses the research question of how algorithmic management contributes to resolving the persisting issues in community-based healthcare. We answer this question by analyzing CHT's understanding of community-based healthcare and CHWs, its solution objectives, and design requirements. We then evaluate CHT's suitability for community-based NCD care in a pilot study. This evaluation uncovers unintended consequences of CHT's design leading to the control vs. autonomy tension. This study makes a two-fold contribution: First, we unpack the blackbox "algorithmic management" and discuss the tension between control and autonomy. Second, we propose design requirements to balance control and autonomy in algorithmic scheduling.

6.1 Discussion of Design Problems

The evaluation demonstrates the value of algorithmic management in community-based healthcare. Besides the CHWs' generally positive resonance, the fact that the pilot study could run over 12 weeks and is still running is proof of its feasibility. CHT and the medical algorithm at its core empower ten CHWs to provide quality NCD care. Nevertheless, the breakdowns uncover a tension between control and autonomy in algorithmic management. This tension forces CHWs to either subordinate to the algorithm or insist on their autonomy in favor of themselves and their environment. This tension is evident in the breakdowns outlined in Sect. 5 and stems from three design choices:

(1) The algorithm *neglects the personal preferences* of the CHWs. Their work as a CHW is often embedded in a network of formal and informal responsibilities, and they express specific expectations towards their working hours (e.g., only in the morning). Instead of the algorithm balancing workload and incorporating preferences, the CHWs face a difficult decision. They either neglect their work in ComBaCaL (i.e., not completing all tasks) or surrender (part of) their autonomy (i.e., neglect other responsibilities) by adhering to the algorithm's schedule. Similar adverse effects of algorithmic scheduling have been reported in housekeeping, gastronomy, and industry [39, 54].

(2) The algorithm does *not consider external conditions* in task scheduling. Like the neglect of personal preferences, the context within which the CHWs work is not sufficiently reflected or, more bluntly, cropped out in the development of the medical algorithm. The CHWs again face a dilemma where they must factor in external conditions such as weather or the fear of sexual assault in their decision. This consideration goes beyond personal preferences and their direct effect (i.e., either overdue tasks or neglect of other responsibilities). As a result, CHWs could potentially engage in gaming, as observed in other application areas of algorithmic management [19, 53]. However, in contrast to Uber drivers, the stake in this context is the CHWs' and their clients' health.

(3) The algorithm unloads the *burden of autonomy* on the CHWs when scheduling tasks. Despite CHWs not explicitly raising this issue, it is visible in the design of CHT. It provides the CHWs with a task list indicating the due date, task type, and client name. While this information might be enough for professionals to organize their work, CHWs might find work planning challenging. Furthermore, as described above, they often only work part-time as CHWs making efficient work planning even more critical. Despite collecting information such as GPS coordinates of the household, CHT does not

consider it in task scheduling, for example, to minimize travel time by grouping tasks for a household or optimizing the route in which CHWs work through their open tasks. While a recent study on housekeeping in hotels argues for the negative impact of such algorithmic optimization as it deprives the user of their autonomy [39], the CHWs could benefit from more support.

6.2 Interpretation under Consideration of the Literature

Under consideration of the breakdowns resulting from the design choices outlined in Sect. 6.1, it becomes clear that the control vs. autonomy tension is the result of an imbalance in the socio-technical system. The technical system – CHT and medical algorithm – dominates the social system. This dominance originates from the historical understanding of CHWs as sensors and its underlying assumptions (see Table 1). In their role as sensors, CHWs are considered part of the technical system. For example, they screen and monitor NCDs with the guidance of a clinical decision support system [59]. In maternal health, CHWs use a decision support application to determine if a woman needs to be referred to a health facility [3]. In abstract terms, they monitor and alarm medical experts when they detect deviations from the norm. Some underlying assumptions are justified by the lack of formal medical education and to ensure patient safety. However, when exploring digital tools in healthcare, researchers and practitioners focus on the empowering potential of these tools without reconsidering the validity of pre-existing assumptions. Furthermore, they – implicitly or explicitly – assume the insights from empowerment research: digital tools facilitate structural empowerment, which leads to psychological empowerment and, consequently, to increased performance, better retention, and less job strain [32, 49, 52].

Indeed, algorithmic scheduling supports CHWs in their work planning by performing tasks where it is superior to human skills. For example, tracking the need for continuous counseling for an entire village is enormously laborious for humans compared to algorithms. However, this insight contradicts the assumption of a positive correlation between structural and psychological empowerment [32, 49]. This contradiction lead to the observation of an interesting effect: Work conditions that would be perceived as disempowering (i.e., restricted access to resources) lead to the perceived empowerment of CHWs. The CHWs willingly accept a restriction by algorithmic scheduling to allocate their resources. Even more so, the exerted algorithmic control leads to a feeling of empowerment among the CHWs, enabling them to do something they could not do otherwise (i.e., provide quality NCD care). This effect might stem from their non-professional background compared to the existing literature [26, 49].

While we do not question the positive correlation between structural and psychological empowerment per se, we argue that temporary disempowering work conditions (i.e., restriction through algorithms) can have empowering effects on laypeople. Specifically, algorithmic control can empower CHWs, and other lay people. It restricts their autonomy, which could be overwhelming due to a lack of professional knowledge (e.g., "where do I start?"). Overall, the emphasis on the technical system seems justified, despite the counterintuitive relation between structural and psychological empowerment. However, the perception of algorithmic control can change over time. This change is induced by breakdowns in the socio-technical system. While at first empowering, after some time, the control vs. autonomy tension leads to the disempowerment of CHWs. In some situations, the medical algorithm exerts too much control over the CHWs, resulting in a loss of autonomy. For example, the strict deadlines give the CHWs little flexibility to balance work and personal life. However, control does not always have to be disempowering. For example, CHT leaves detailed work planning entirely to the CHWs. It assumes they can plan their work based on the task list and due dates. This autonomy might lead to cognitive overload if they lack the professional knowledge to assess the urgency. More algorithmic control could be empowering in such cases, as it reduces planning efforts.

The CHWs are caught in this control vs. autonomy tension, trying to harmonize the demands from the technical system (i.e., medical algorithm) with the social subsystem (i.e., their needs and capabilities and the structure within their life and work). Because of this harmonization attempt, the CHWs report to either surrender to the algorithm's demands or create workarounds in their routines. The literature also suggests gaming as a third response [53]. In contrast to other use cases of algorithmic management, a CHW's deviation from the algorithmic instruction could have severe consequences for their clients. For example, they could engage in gaming by manipulating the medical algorithm with incorrect data. A female CHW could avoid a single male client by labeling him non-diabetic or not registering him at all if she is afraid of sexual assault. Her self-protecting act might harm her community members if they remain undiagnosed. A workaround found in practice is adapting the schedule to a physical notebook. While this workaround does not have to be critical, it might leave patients without medication if the CHW reschedules without consideration. Yet, strict execution of the algorithm's instruction also has potential downsides. The subordination could lead to overburdening and, in the worst case, attrition of the CHWs.

In summary, our study highlights breakdowns of the socio-technical system as unintended consequences of algorithmic management in community-based NCD care. The resulting response of CHWs to the control vs. autonomy tension not only impacts their empowerment but also directly impacts their community. We propose two measures to avoid these consequences: (1) Researchers and practitioners must recognize CHWs as active members of the health system. This requires critically reflecting on the underlying assumptions discussed in Sects. 2.1 and 4 of this paper. (2) the design of digital tools for CHW-led NCD care must consider the control vs. autonomy tension to harmonize the socio-technical system. Only then can we leverage the empowering potential of digital tools as they can improve organizational support and provide adequate work conditions.

6.3 Discussion of a Potential Solution

In the following section, we describe a scenario proposing preliminary design requirements (summarized in Table 4) based on ongoing research in ComBaCaL. It aims to resolve the control vs. autonomy tension to avoid hazardous behavior in response to the medical algorithm. We describe three solution objectives trying to incorporate identified workarounds and make gaming obsolete.

Table 4. Overview of problems generated by CHT and proposed solution objectives and design requirements to mitigate the identified problems.

Problem	Solution Objectives	Design Requirement
Neglect of personal preferences	(i) Embed work as CHW in the pre-existing network of responsibilities	Capture CHW's preferred working times and suggest a schedule balancing patient and CHW interests
Neglect of external conditions	(ii) Grant CHWs supervised flexibility	Provide CHWs the option to re-schedule tasks within set boundaries by the medical algorithm
Burden of autonomy	(iii) Support CHW in work planning	Provide CHWs with an operationalizable task list including progress overview, urgency indication, suggested task order

Thloko (female) is a 28-year-old Mosotho living in rural Lesotho. She works as a CHW in ComBaCaL because she feels strongly committed to her community. Besides her work as a CHW, she is a subsistence farmer and cares for her two children. Due to her personal responsibilities, Thloko set her preferred working days to Monday through Saturday in the morning. She usually works on her crops in the afternoon and attends church on Sundays (see Fig. 2).

Fig. 2. Proposition to capture CHW's preferred working times.

Initially, there were little to no issues combining her work and personal responsibilities. She starts registering her community during her preferred working hours in the morning. However, the workload steadily increases over time as she continues to register the whole community. As usual, Thloko opens CHT Sunday evening to plan her week. She lands on an overview that displays all planned tasks for the week (see Fig. 3). In the background, the medical algorithm optimized her schedule by harmonizing ComBaCaL's demands and Thloko's preferences and capacity.

This aspect of the proposed solution aims to (i) embed the work as a CHW in the pre-existing network of responsibilities from their private lives. Typically, tasks have a specific urgency. On the one side, medication must be handed out before patients run out of medication, leaving little flexibility for rescheduling. On the other side, yearly checkups could be done within one or two months, offering more flexibility as it is less urgent. Algorithms should incorporate user preferences and task urgency when optimizing work scheduling.

Back to Thloko: She can reschedule tasks in the overview if necessary. For example, she must work a full day on her crops the upcoming Thursday. She reschedules all tasks to Friday, where she works the whole day to compensate for Thursday. For one task, a pop-up notifies her that it cannot be completed later than Thursday. She decides to complete this task Thursday first thing in the morning before working on her crops.

Fig. 3. Proposition for a weekly overview allowing CHWs to plan their work and to re-schedule tasks within set boundaries by the medical algorithm.

On Monday, Thloko is ready to work. Unfortunately, heavy rain rendered the solid ground into streams of mud. She worries about her safety as these conditions can be dangerous, and she does not have health insurance. Thloko opens CHT and looks at her dashboard that shows all tasks for today (see Fig. 4). She immediately recognizes that two tasks must be done today as they are at the top of the list and flagged with a red exclamation mark. The remaining tasks are not as urgent, so she reschedules all but one task. The last task is a quick checkup with her neighbor. Even though it is not urgent, she wants to complete it and not delay it unnecessarily. Unfortunately, despite Thloko's reminder the previous evening, her neighbor is not home. She reschedules the task and remarks on the neighbor's absence as justification. In the background, the algorithm adjusts Thloko's schedule for the remainder of the week based on task urgency to balance her workload. Once the rain eases, she attends to her two clients for today and returns home safely. She checks CHT one last time and knows her community is well cared for as she sees a completed progress bar.

The system (ii) grants Thloko supervised flexibility in two instances. When planning her week, she can adjust the algorithm-generated schedule as her preferences for this week changed (i.e., personal responsibilities on Thursday, CHW work on Friday). To ensure patient safety, the system prompts CHWs if a rescheduling attempt is not in line with medical guidelines (e.g., medication must be handed out before or on Thursday). After the weekly planning, Thloko wants to reschedule the task due to bad weather allowing her to respond to her context. Furthermore, the system (iii) supports CHW in work planning by indicating urgency with an exclamation mark and importance with task order. This proposition aims at reducing the potential burden of autonomy without exerting control by offering the CHWs an anchor for their daily planning.

Fig. 4. Proposition of a dashboard with an operationalizable task list, including progress overview, urgency indication, and suggested task order.

6.4 Conclusion

This paper hints at the downsides of digital tools such as CHT by studying the breakdowns of the socio-technical system. Generally, algorithmic management can empower CHWs to assume broader responsibility by supporting their work and ensuring patient safety. This study demonstrates how CHT is designed to empower CHWs to assume these responsibilities. We show the general suitability of CHT for community-based NCD care using the example of ComBaCaL. However, CHT's design creates a tension between control and autonomy when confronted with reality, forcing CHWs to make undesirable decisions. This tension stems from a discrepancy between the traditional understanding of CHWs as sensors and the emerging, more active role they are being assigned in many programs. If not resolved, this tension could lead to disempowerment and attrition among CHWs [49].

Accentuated by the increasing complexity of tasks, the paradigm shift from sensors to actors uncovers a deep-rooted neglect of the social system in favor of the technical system. CHWs as sensors could be disguised as part of the latter allowing health facilities to reach where they could not reach to execute their tasks. Hence, this paradigm shift requires a holistic consideration of the socio-technical system of community-based healthcare. Acknowledging CHWs as "agents of social change" [21] requires acknowledging personal preferences and the context within which the CHWs act. We offer an initial set of design requirements to attend to this new perspective to introduce algorithmic management as a blessing by mitigating its potential curse. For this, we propose design adaptations for CHT to balance work and personal responsibility and control and autonomy.

Future research could continue to explore this paradigm shift and its consequences by addressing to limitations of this study. First, a larger sample size could provide deeper insights into the longitudinal mechanics of digital empowerment. For example, it is unclear how the work conditions impact the perceived empowerment of CHWs as they gain more experience in their work. Second, an instantiation of our design propositions could evaluate their validity and advance our design knowledge in the digital empowerment of CHWs and algorithmic management.

Acknowledgments. This study is part of the Community-based chronic care project Lesotho (ComBaCaL; www.combacal.org). The ComBaCaL project is funded by the TRANSFORM grant of the Swiss Agency for Development and Cooperation (Project no. 7F-10345.01.01) and a grant by the World Diabetes Foundation to SolidarMed. The authors would like to thank the VHWs interviewed in this study, and all involved ComBaCaL staff members, especially Thabo Lejone, who assisted with the interviews. Further, we would like to thank Damaris Schmid from the University of Zurich for her support in the interviews.

References

1. Aninanya, G.A., Williams, J.E., Williams, A., Otupiri, E., Howard, N.: Effects of computerized decision support on maternal and neonatal health-worker performance in the context of combined implementation with performance-based incentivisation in Upper East Region, Ghana: a qualitative study of professional perspectives. BMC Health Serv. Res. **22**, 1581 (2022)
2. Bai, B., Dai, H., Zhang, D.J., Zhang, F., Hu, H.: The impacts of algorithmic work assignment on fairness perceptions and productivity: evidence from field experiments. Manuf. Serv. Oper. Manag. **24**, 3060–3078 (2022)
3. Bakibinga, P., Kamande, E., Omuya, M., Ziraba, A.K., Kyobutungi, C.: The role of a decision-support smartphone application in enhancing community health volunteers' effectiveness to

improve maternal and newborn outcomes in Nairobi, Kenya: quasi-experimental research protocol. BMJ Open **7**, e014896 (2017)

4. Bandura, A.: Self-efficacy: Toward a Unifying Theory of Behavioral Change 25 (1977)
5. Bangor, A., Kortum, P.T., Miller, J.T.: An empirical evaluation of the system usability scale. Intl J. Human-Computer Interaction **24**, 574–594 (2008)
6. Bannon, L.: Reimagining HCI: toward a more human-centered perspective. Interactions **18**, 50–57 (2011)
7. Bemelmans, M., et al.: Providing universal access to antiretroviral therapy in Thyolo, Malawi through task shifting and decentralization of HIV/AIDS care: task shifting to support universal access to ART. Tropical Med. Int. Health **15**, 1413–1420 (2010)
8. Berman, P.A., Gwatkin, D.R., Burger, S.E.: Community-based health workers: Head start or false start towards health for all? Soc. Sci. Med. **25**, 443–459 (1987). https://doi.org/10.1016/0277-9536(87)90168-7
9. Bhatia, K.: Community health worker programs in India: a rights-based review. Perspect. Public Health **134**, 276–282 (2014)
10. Bhutta, Z.A., Lassi, Z.S., Pariyo, G., Huicho, L.: Global experience of community health workers for delivery of health related millennium development goals: a systematic review, country case studies, and recommendations for integration into national health systems. Global Health Workforce Alliance **1**, 61 (2010)
11. Briggs, R.O., De Vreede, G.-J.: ThinkLets: Building Blocks for Concerted Collaboration. University of Nebraska, Center for Collaboration Science Omaha (2009)
12. Chandra Kruse, L., Seidel, S., vom Brocke, J.: Design archaeology: generating design knowledge from real-world artifact design. In: International Conference on Design Science Research in Information Systems and Technology. Springer, pp. 32–45 (2019). https://doi.org/10.1007/978-3-030-19504-5_3
13. Christopher, J.B., May, A.L., Lewin, S., Ross, D.A.: Thirty years after Alma-Ata: a systematic review of the impact of community health workers delivering curative interventions against malaria, pneumonia and diarrhoea on child mortality and morbidity in sub-Saharan Africa. Hum. Resour. Health **9**, 27 (2011)
14. Cronin, P.R., Kimball, A.B.: Success of automated algorithmic scheduling in an outpatient setting. Methods (2012)
15. Flanagan, J.C.: The critical incident technique. Psychol. Bull. **51**, 327 (1954)
16. Harrison, A., Short, S.E., Tuoane-Nkhasi, M.: Re-focusing the gender lens: caregiving women, family roles and HIV/AIDS vulnerability in Lesotho. AIDS Behav. **18**, 595–604 (2014)
17. Holeman, I., Kane, D.: Human-centered design for global health equity. Inf. Technol. Dev. **26**, 477–505 (2020)
18. Ismail, A., Kumar, N.: Empowerment on the margins: the online experiences of community health workers. In: Proceedings of the 2019 CHI Conference on Human Factors in Computing Systems, pp. 1–15 (2019)
19. Jarrahi, M.H., Sutherland, W.: Algorithmic management and algorithmic competencies: understanding and appropriating algorithms in gig work. In: International conference on information. Springer, pp. 578–589 (2019). https://doi.org/10.1007/978-3-030-15742-5_55
20. Källander, K., et al.: Mobile health (mHealth) approaches and lessons for increased performance and retention of community health workers in low- and middle-income countries: a review. J. Med. Internet Res. **15**, e17 (2013). https://doi.org/10.2196/jmir.2130
21. Kane, S., et al.: Limits and opportunities to community health worker empowerment: a multi-country comparative study. Soc. Sci. Med. **164**, 27–34 (2016)
22. Kanter, R.M.: Men and Women of the Corporation: New edition. Basic books (1977)
23. Kaphle, S., Chaturvedi, S., Chaudhuri, I., Krishnan, R., Lesh, N.: Adoption and usage of mhealth technology on quality and experience of care provided by frontline workers: observations from Rural India. JMIR mHealth uHealth **3**, e61 (2015)

24. Kateera, F., et al.: The effect and feasibility of mhealth-supported surgical site infection diagnosis by community health workers after cesarean section in Rural Rwanda: randomized controlled trial. JMIR Mhealth Uhealth **10**, e35155 (2022)
25. Laschinger, H.: A theoretical approach to studying work empowerment in nursing: a review of studies testing Kanters theory of structural power in organizations. Nurs. Adm. Q. **20**, 25–41 (1996)
26. Laschinger, H.K., Finegan, J., Shamian, J., Wilk, P.: Impact of structural and psychological empowerment on job strain in nursing work settings: expanding kanter's model. JONA: The Journal of Nursing Administration, pp. 260–272 (2001)
27. Lee, M.K., Kusbit, D., Metsky, E., Dabbish, L.: Working with machines: the impact of algorithmic and data-driven management on human workers. In: Proceedings of the 33rd Annual ACM Conference on Human Factors in Computing Systems, pp. 1603–1612 (2015)
28. Leong, C.M.L., Pan, S.L., Ractham, P., Kaewkitipong, L.: ICT-enabled community empowerment in crisis response: social media in Thailand flooding 2011. J. Assoc. Inf. Syst. **16**, 1 (2015)
29. Levy, K., Barocas, S.: Privacy at the Margins| refractive surveillance: monitoring customers to manage workers. Int. J. Commun. **12**, 23 (2018)
30. Maes, K., Closser, S., Kalofonos, I.: Listening to community health workers: how ethnographic research can inform positive relationships among community health workers, health institutions, and communities. Am. J. Public Health **104**, e5–e9 (2014)
31. Mastellos, N., et al.: Training community healthcare workers on the use of information and communication technologies: a randomised controlled trial of traditional versus blended learning in Malawi, Africa. BMC Med. Educ. **18**, 1–13 (2018)
32. Maynard, M.T., Gilson, L.L., Mathieu, J.E.: Empowerment—fad or fab? a multilevel review of the past two decades of research. J. Manag. **38**, 1231–1281 (2012). https://doi.org/10.1177/0149206312438773
33. Medic. The Community Health Toolkit's Core Framework: An Overview (2023). https://static1.squarespace.com/static/5bd25eea65a707ad54c1e8ca/t/5db502b9628b613d418ce7be/1572143837269/Core+Framework+Overview.pdf. Accessed 27 Jan 2023
34. Menon, S.: Employee empowerment: an integrative psychological approach. Appl. Psychol. **50**, 153–180 (2001). https://doi.org/10.1111/1464-0597.00052
35. Ngugi, A.K., et al.: Prevalence, incidence and predictors of volunteer community health worker attrition in Kwale County. Kenya. BMJ Glob Health **3**, e000750 (2018)
36. Nicolini, D.: Articulating practice through the interview to the double. Manag. Learn. **40**, 195–212 (2009)
37. Olang'o, C.O., Nyamongo, I.K., Aagaard-Hansen, J.: Staff attrition among community health workers in home-based care programmes for people living with HIV and AIDS in western Kenya. Health Policy **97**, 232–237 (2010)
38. Olaniran, A., Smith, H., Unkels, R., Bar-Zeev, S., van den Broek, N.: Who is a community health worker? – a systematic review of definitions. Glob. Health Action **10**, 1272223 (2017). https://doi.org/10.1080/16549716.2017.1272223
39. Parent-Rocheleau, X., Parker, S.K.: Algorithms as work designers: how algorithmic management influences the design of jobs. Hum. Resour. Manag. Rev. **32**, 100838 (2022)
40. Payne, J., Razi, S., Emery, K., Quattrone, W., Tardif-Douglin, M.: Integrating community health workers (CHWs) into health care organizations. J. Community Health **42**, 983–990 (2017). https://doi.org/10.1007/s10900-017-0345-4
41. Perry, H.B., Zulliger, R., Rogers, M.M.: Community health workers in low-, middle-, and high-income countries: an overview of their history, recent evolution, and current effectiveness. Annu Rev Public Health **35**, 399–421 (2014)

42. Rassi, C., et al.: Improving health worker performance through text messaging: a mixed-methods evaluation of a pilot intervention designed to increase coverage of intermittent preventive treatment of malaria in pregnancy in West Nile. Uganda. PLOS ONE **13**, e0203554 (2018)

43. Rawal, L., Jubayer, S., Choudhury, S.R., Islam, S.M.S., Abdullah, A.S.: Community health workers for non-communicable diseases prevention and control in Bangladesh: a qualitative study. Global Health Research and Policy **6**, 1 (2021)

44. Rodrigues, S.M., Kanduri, A., Nyamathi, A., Dutt, N., Khargonekar, P., Rahmani, A.M.: Digital health-enabled community-centered care: scalable model to empower future community health workers using human-in-the-loop artificial intelligence. JMIR Form Res **6**, e29535 (2022). https://doi.org/10.2196/29535

45. Rosenberg, N.E., et al.: Development of a blended learning approach to delivering HIV-assisted contact tracing in malawi: applied theory and formative research. JMIR Formative Res. **6**, e32899 (2022)

46. Ryan, R.M., Deci, E.L.: Self-Determination Theory and the Facilitation of Intrinsic Motivation, Social Development, and Well-Being. American Psychologist **67** (2000)

47. Schildt, H.: Big data and organizational design–the brave new world of algorithmic management and computer augmented transparency. Innovation **19**, 23–30 (2017)

48. Scott, K., et al.: What do we know about community-based health worker programs? a systematic review of existing reviews on community health workers. Hum Resour Health **16**, 39 (2018). https://doi.org/10.1186/s12960-018-0304-x

49. Spence Laschinger, H.K., Leiter, M., Day, A., Gilin, D.: Workplace empowerment, incivility, and burnout: Impact on staff nurse recruitment and retention outcomes. J. Nurs. Manag. **17**, 302–311 (2009)

50. Spreitzer, G.M.: Psychological, empowerment in the workplace: dimensions, measurement and validation. Acad. Manag. J. **38**, 1442–1465 (1995). https://doi.org/10.2307/256865

51. Staehelin, D., Greve, M., Schwabe, G.: Empowering Community Health Workers with Mobile Health: Learnings from two Projects on Non-Communicable Disease Care. In: ECIS 2023 Research Papers (2023)

52. Tan, H., Yan, M.: Collaborative Diabetes Management in China: A Digital Empowerment Perspective **10** (2020)

53. Tarafdar, M., Page, X., Marabelli, M.: Algorithms as co-workers: human algorithm role interactions in algorithmic work. Information Systems Journal (2022)

54. Unruh, C.F., Haid, C., Büthe, T., Fottner, J.: Algorithmic Scheduling in Industry: Technical and Ethical Aspects (2022)

55. de Vries, D.H., Pool, R.: The influence of community health resources on effectiveness and sustainability of community and lay health worker programs in lower-income countries: a systematic review. PLoS ONE **12**, e0170217 (2017)

56. Whidden, C., et al.: Improving community health worker performance by using a personalised feedback dashboard for supervision: a randomised controlled trial. Journal of Global Health **8** (2018)

57. WHO. Global Strategy on Human Resources for Health: Workforce 2030 (2016)

58. Yadav, D., et al.: Sangoshthi: Empowering community health workers through peer learning in rural India. In: Proceedings of the 26th International Conference on World Wide Web, pp. 499–508 (2017)

59. Zaman, S.B., et al.: Feasibility of community health workers using a clinical decision support system to screen and monitor non-communicable diseases in resource-poor settings: study protocol. mHealth **7**, 15 (2021). https://doi.org/10.21037/mhealth-19-258

Explorative Study of Perceived Social Loafing in VR Group Discussion: A Comparison Between the Poster Presentation Environment and the Typical Conference Environment

Koutaro Kamada[1]([⊠]) [iD], Ryuya Watarai[2], Tzu-Yang Wang[1], Kentaro Takashima[1], Yasuyuki Sumi[2], and Takaya Yuizono[1]

[1] Japan Advanced Institute of Science and Technology, Nomi, Japan
kamada@jaist.ac.jp
[2] Future University Hakodate, Hakodate, Japan

Abstract. Social loafing is a phenomenon in which members of a group reduce individual motivation and effort. We explored the difference between social loafing perceived by the loafer himself/herself (Self Perceived Social Loafing; SPSL) and social loafing perceived by other group members in VR group discussion (Others Perceived Social Loafing; OPSL). We also investigated how this difference changes in two types of group discussion: the poster presentation environment and the typical conference environment. An experiment with a between-participant design was conducted, and participants conducted a desert survival task through VR group discussion. The results showed that, overall, there was only a weak positive correlation and not much agreement between SPSL and OPSL. The results also suggested that there were significant positive correlations between the indicators relating to conversation behavior and OPSL in the typical conference environment but not in the poster presentation environment. In addition, an analysis by Lasso was conducted to examine the relationship between OPSL and these indicators and found that three indicators relating to participants' conversation behavior were selected in the typical conference environment, but none were selected in the poster presentation environment. Our study suggested that, in the typical conference environment, people judged the other people's social loafing through their conversation behavior; on the other hand, people's conversation behavior may not be used as significant indicators for social loafing in the poster presentation environment.

Keywords: Social Loafing · Perceived Social Loafing · VR Group Discussion · Social VR · Metaverse

1 Introduction

VR group discussion has become more important in the last few years because of the development of VR technology and the COVID-19 pandemic. People use avatars to attend in a virtual environment, and they perform group discussion in that environment.

J. Abdelnour Nocera et al. (Eds.): INTERACT 2023, LNCS 14144, pp. 115–134, 2023.
https://doi.org/10.1007/978-3-031-42286-7_7

However, just like other group works, social loafing that members in a group reduce individual motivation and effort are also expected to occur in VR group discussion [21]. Indeed, it has previously been shown that social loafing occurs in remote collaborative work [23, 33]. Social loafing has a negative impact on group members and has traditionally been desired to be controlled [21]. If the task involves interaction with other members, as in VR group discussion of this study, the bad effects on the members are likely to occur when they perceive social loafing [1, 25]. Therefore, we focused specifically on perceived social loafing. That is, the criterion is not whether social loafing is actually occurring, but whether or not the person is aware that social loafing was occurring. There are two types of perceived entities: self (Self Perceived Social Loafing; SPSL) and others (Others Perceived Social Loafing: OPSL).

Additionally, we focused on the VR space. This is because VR group discussions take place in a variety of VR environments and perceived social loafing can be affected by them. In fact, group cohesion, which has been reported to be associated with social loafing, has also been found to be affected by VR environments [13, 16].

Considering the above, to understand the elementary mechanism of perceived social loafing in VR group discussions, we set the following Research Questions (RQs).

First of all, the question arose as to how the estimation ability of other people's evaluations is. In other words, even if we think we are taking ourselves seriously, others may not think so, and vice versa. Therefore, we examined how well other people's evaluations match their personal evaluations.

– RQ1: How different is Others Perceived Social Loafing from Self Perceived Social Loafing in VR group discussions?

Next, we considered the possibility that the VR environment could affect others' perceptions of social loafing. Therefore, we examined whether changes in the VR environment affect the degree of agreement between self and others' evaluations.

– RQ2: Does the type of the VR environment influence the degree of agreement between Self Perceived Social Loafing and Others Perceived Social Loafing?

Finally, we focused specifically on the evaluation of others. This was because we consider that, unlike self-evaluations, judgments are made based on objective event cues. Differences in VR environments should affect this cue. That is, we decided to investigate how they perceive social loafing of others and what indicators they use to rate it.

– RQ3: How does the type of the VR environment affect the rating of Others Perceived Social Loafing?

Since there has been no research investigating social loafing in the VR space, these three RQs are a first step toward understanding perceived social loafing in VR.

2   Related Work

2.1   Concepts of Social Loafing

In the real world, performing tasks in groups is essential and one in which the individual members combine their strengths. Groups must be more efficient and effective than when performing tasks individually. This is because groups utilize more resources than individuals. However, in the real world, performing tasks in groups often reduce individual productivity. This loss of productivity was referred to by Steiner as process loss [32]. Social loafing, a form of process loss, has been studied in the field of social psychology. According to them, the traditional definition of social loafing is "the reducing effort or motivation by an individual in a group task". Laboratory experiments and field studies were conducted on a variety of tasks. The results revealed the occurrence of social loafing. Karau and Williams categorized tasks in which social loafing occurs as physical tasks (e.g., rope pulling [21]), cognitive tasks (e.g., decision making [15]), evaluative tasks (e.g., evaluating poetry [26]), and perceptual tasks (e.g., maze performance [14]) [17].

Research on social loafing has also been conducted in the field of HCI and CSCW. It has been observed to occur in cognitive tasks in remote collaboration [23, 33]. However, the mechanisms of social loafing in the VR space have not yet been investigated. With the current emphasis on social VR, we consider it important to understand social loafing in virtual space.

2.2   Evaluation Methodology of Social Loafing in Group Discussion

How to measure social loafing is an important issue and at the same time can be very difficult for some tasks. Unfortunately, group discussion is one of the most difficult tasks to measure social loafing.

In the research on group discussion, measures of effort or motivation can be broadly divided into objective and subjective evaluations. Objective evaluation is a method that measures the quantity of output, while subjective evaluation is a questionnaire-based method.

Objective evaluation is an important method for measuring social loafing. However, there are few objective evaluation methods for social loafing in group discussions [15]. This is because objective evaluation is thus used when individual and group output can be treated quantitatively such as the strength of a rope pull. In the experiment, the strength of an individual's rope pull was regarded as effort or motivation, and the pull strength per person is compared when the rope is pulled by one person and when the rope is pulled by a group [21]. On the other hand, the few existing studies on group discussion measure social loafing from the amount of information recalled prior to decision making [15]. In the experiment, the task was to assume decision-making regarding a civil trial and to recall as much as possible of the 80 items of information contained in a complex civil litigation scenario. That is, the number of information recalled by individuals and groups is used as an objective measure.

Subjective evaluation method measures an individual's perception of social loafing, rather than actual social loafing, and is measured using a questionnaire. Subjective evaluation can be based on the concept of perceived loafing advocated by Comer [6]. Perceived loafing is "the perceived low contribution of one or more other members to the group" [6]. However, this definition is not sufficient. This is because it only covers methods that measure the perception of others' social loafing and not the perception of self-social loafing [12]. A method to measure one's own social loafing is also an important concept [27]. For tasks that involve interaction among group members, such as group discussions, it is more important whether the social loafing of others is recognized than whether social loafing actually occurs. This is because individual effort or motivation is supposed to be influenced by the perceived effort or motivation of others [1, 25]. For example, when people perceive that group members other than themselves are putting enough effort or motivation into a task, they are known to reduce their effort and motivation, thinking that they can rely on them to do the task [17]. Also, the results were shown for virtual work [23]. Therefore, we decided that it was appropriate to investigate perceived social loafing in a subjective evaluation. Therefore, in this study, we extend perceived loafing and propose two concepts: Self Perceived Social Loafing (SPSL) and Others Perceived Social Loafing (OPSL). We defined SPSL as social loafing perceived by the loafer himself/herself and OPSL as social loafing perceived by other group members in VR group discussion. In this study, these are collectively referred to as perceived social loafing. This paper investigates perceived social loafing (SPSL and OPSL) in VR group discussions using a subjective rating scale.

2.3 VR Environment and Perceived Social Loafing

We consider that we should focus on the VR space. As previously stated, VR group discussions can take place in a variety of VR environments. It is possible that VR space will have an impact on perceived social loafing. Related studies have reported that VR spaces influence social behavior [13]. For example, group cohesion, which is considered an indicator closely related to social loafing, is influenced by VR space (closed and open space) [13, 16].

In this study, we chose two representative types of group discussion: the poster presentation environment and the typical conference environment. The poster presentation environment is an environment that promotes the movement of avatars; the typical conference environment is an environment does not promote participants' movement. Because VR allows users to move freely in the environment, various group discussions can be applied. Although we could not cover all types, we considered the movement affects users' judgment of social loafing and selected the two ends of the group discussion types in this work: the conference type with no movement required and the poster type with movement required. That is, we hypothesized that people's way of perceiving social loafing differs between the two environments.

3 Preliminary Investigation

In this paper, for answering the three RQs mentioned above, we conducted an experiment to simulate VR group discussion and to investigate perceived social loafing. Before the experiment, we conducted a preliminary investigation to find the following: How long could the discussion last before social loafing occurs and what parameters could be used to judge social loafing based on in remote conferences. The findings were used to set the time of the group discussion and what data would be collected in the experiment. This is because, in order to answer the three RQs, social loafing needs to occur in the experiment, and we would like to find out what potential parameters people used to judge others' social loafing.

Amazon Mechanical Turk was used for the investigation. 19 participants (8 females and 11 males) were recruited randomly. The average age was 40.8 years (SD = 11.6). Each participant received compensation of 1.5 dollars. After explaining the definition of social loafing, the participants recalled one of the most significant group discussion experiences when they intentionally reduced their effort. They then answered an open-ended questionnaire, all self-reported, about the features of that.

As a result, 6 people responded that they had experienced perceived social loafing at one of the remote conferences. Additionally, the average time for participants to start reducing their effort was about 22 min (SD = 17.4). In addition, the result showed that the social loafing happened due to the following reasons: 1) the participants have other works to do, 2) the participants felt being ignored, 3) the participants have low interested in the topic, 4) the participants felt that their ideas were not be accepted and their opinion were different, 5) the participants perceived strong dominance from other members, and 6) the participants considered that they did not have to participate in it. Based on the results, we considered that social presence, cohesion, conflict styles, a quantity of conversation, new idea expression, agreement/disagreement, dominance, reaction and interrupting a turn may be associated with social loafing.

4 Experiment

4.1 Experimental Design

An experiment with a between-participant design was conducted, and 39 participants conducted VR group discussion in 8 groups of 4–5 people. Each group of participants only participated in one of the two conditions. The topic of discussion was the desert survival task, which participants negotiate about important items for surviving in the desert after an airplane accident (see details in 4.2). The discussion lasted 40 min based on the result of the preliminary investigation that the mean time of occurrence of social loafing is about 22 min. To explore the effect of VR environment on perceived social loafing, in this experiment, we considered the movement an important potential factor affecting users' judgment of social loafing and compared the two ends of the group discussion types: the poster presentation environment which promotes participants' movement and the typical conference environment which does not promote participants' movement (see Fig. 1). Both were configured with Mozilla Hubs using Spoke [24].

The two VR environments involved a poster that explains the desert survival task in the front of the room, a table, 3D models of the items, and posters of the expert opinion of items. For the poster presentation environment, the items were placed in a distributed manner. For the typical conference environment, they were placed on desks. The way these were arranged implicitly promote or demote the participants to move their avatars during the discussion. Additionally, in both environments, to induce social loafing, two objects which are irrelevant to the desert survival task (an aquarium and a whiteboard with the novel written on it) were placed to induce social loafing.

All participants used the avatar in Fig. 1. The simple white avatar without facial expressions was designed to minimize the possibility that the impression to the participants was affected by the impression of the avatar's design, such as the Proteus effect [37], the color of the avatar [8].

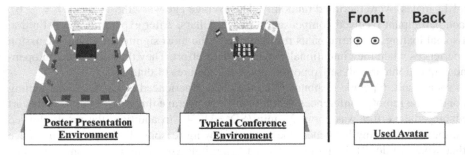

Fig. 1. VR Environment.

4.2 Task

A desert survival task was used as our experiment task to simulate a VR group discussion situation. The desert survival task was developed by Lafferty et al. and widely used in group discussion research [19, 34]. It is a task that requires the selection of goods necessary for survival in the desert. In this study, we modified and used it. In the existing desert survival task, each item is prioritized. However, in this experiment, we determined that it would be difficult to memorize the priorities of all the items, so we asked the participants to choose five items from a list of ten items that were necessary for survival.

The participants were told the task was to select the items for survival because the plane they were on had crashed in the desert. The plane was off the flight plan and it was very far from the crash site to a nearby residence. The desert was too hot, flat plain with nothing but cacti. They were also informed that they wear light clothing (shirt with short sleeves, pants, socks, and sneakers).

The ten items adopted are as follows: 1L water per person, compass, dressing mirror, one coat per person, pistol, 2L vodka, flashlight, table salt, books on desert animals suitable for food, and aerial picture of the surrounding area.

4.3 Participants

40 participants (8 females and 32 males) were recruited from Japan Advanced Institute of Science and Technology (25 people) and Future University Hakodate (15 people). They were native speakers of Japanese. However, one of them withdrew from the experiment before participating, and resulted in 39 people. The average age was 22.6 years old, and the standard deviation was 1.55. At the end of the experiment, each participant received a compensation of 3000 yen.

4.4 Procedure

All participants used their laptop computer with a web camera and participated in the experiment at locations where they could naturally participate in the remote conference (e.g., their own room). The experimenter asked participants to use WebEx and share their screens and activate their webcams. They were recorded.

The experiment was described as follows. After informing them that this was not an experiment to measure their ability to discuss, they were instructed to discuss the task freely and build a consensus as a group. Taking notes during the task was prohibited. They did not reveal any personally identifiable information, such as self-introductions. Therefore, anonymous names were used for the discussion. Each of the 4–5 participants was asked to identify themselves as (A, B, C, D, E). In addition, since we wanted to observe the usual remote discussions, we emphasized that there were no penalties and that the rewards did not fluctuate based on results and asked the participants to keep in mind that they were to discuss as usual. In the VR environment, because Mozilla hubs have various functions, we restricted their use except for those we instructed them to use.

Before the experiment, each participant was individually briefed about the experiment, agreed with the experiment to make an ethical review, set up their computers, and practiced operating their avatars. After that, all experimental conditions proceeded as presented in Fig. 2. In the beginning, the participants were asked to connect to WebEx [36] and Mozilla Hubs [24]. Then, using WebEx, the experiment and the tasks were explained again. Next, the participants were asked to submit their own opinions of selected items for the task using Google Forms. In a submission of individual opinions, they were asked to describe the five selected items and why they chose or did not choose them for all items. After confirming everyone's submissions, they started a 40-min discussion with Mozilla Hubs. After the discussion began with an opening signal, the participants were informed about the time left (20 min, 10 min, 5 min, and 1 min) before the end of the session. Apart from that, we did not interrupt the participants' group discussion. After the discussion, each participant submitted the results of the group consensus and completed a questionnaire. In submission of the group's opinions, they were asked to report on the five items on which the group had reached consensus and to describe, along with reasons, whether they were satisfied with their opinions on all items. Finally, a focus-group interview was conducted. The interviews were semi-structured. The entire session was approximately two hours.

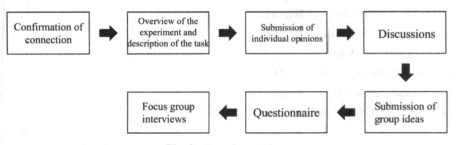

Fig. 2. Experiment Flow.

4.5 Measure

We used a variety of indicators, and it included three broad categories: indicators for measure of perceived social loafing, indicators for measure of discussion quality, and indicators that Amazon Mechanical Turk and previous studies have suggested related to social loafing.

Perceived social loafing was measured using questionnaires. Discussion quality was measured from a variety of indicators: perceived consensus and objective consensus. Indicators suggested to be associated with social loafing include the following: social presence, perceived cohesion, conflict management styles, conversation analysis and morpheme. Those whose units are percentages are divided by the total of all group members and expressed as a percentage.

Perceived Social Loafing. We used the two questionnaires to assess both Self Perceived Social Loafing and Others Perceived Social Loafing. Table 1 is the English version of our questionnaires. This questionnaire was developed based on George [12], and Petty and Williams [27], with modifications to fit the discussion task.

- Self Perceived Social Loafing (SPSL): measures how much effort the participant themselves perceived they put into the discussion. Initially, there were 23 items, but 10 were eliminated due to ceiling and floor effects. Consequently, there were 13 items. The average score of the items were considered as the SPSL of the participants.
- Others Perceived Social Loafing (OPSL): measures other participants perceived a participant whether he/she put effort into the discussion. Each participant judged and selected other participants whether they put effort into the discussion or whether they were involved in the discussion. For each participant, the average of number of being selected was considered as the OPSL of the participant. (0 = Strong social loafing to 4 = Week social loafing). Note that for the group with four participants, we adjusted the score by multiplying it by 4/3.

Table 1. Questionnaire of Perceived Social Loafing.

Self Perceived Social Loafing (SPSL)
I tried as hard as I could
I did not contribute much to the discussion (R)
I did the best I could with the abilities I had
I tried as hard as I could to offer my opinion
I actively tried to speak up
I was not concentrating on the task (R)
I tried to be actively involved in the discussion
I tried to maximize the ability I had

(*continued*)

Table 1. (*continued*)

Self Perceived Social Loafing (SPSL)
I tried to understand the thoughts of the other members
I participated in the discussion, organizing the opinions of the entire group
Relying on other members, I did not express my opinion much (R)
I didn't make an effort harder than the other members (R)
I was more determined to do well than the other members
Others Perceived Social Loafing (OPSL)
Who did you think put the effort into the discussion? Please select 0–4 people, excluding yourself
Who did you think was involved in the discussion? Please select 0–4 people, excluding yourself

Note: item with (R) is the reversed item

Questionnaire. Questionnaires were conducted to investigate regarding the items in Table 2.

To examine the subjective quality of consensus, two types of consensus were measured: Perceived consensus and objective consensus. In perceived consensus, we adopted the scale developed by DeStephen and Hirokawa [7]. There are five component constructs and each of the items was rated on a 7-point Likert scale. A higher value means a higher perceived consensus. The objective consensus was divided into two variables. Participants submitted their individual opinions before the discussion. This was a selection of 5 from 10 items. After the discussion, they individually submitted their group consensus results (selection of 5 from 10 items) and answered whether or not they were satisfied with each selected item. From these data, the percentage of changing opinions and the percentage of agreement were calculated. The percentage of changing opinions is the total number of items whose opinion changed before and after the discussion divided by 10 and expressed as a percentage. Before discussion opinions refer to the five items selected in the individual opinion submission. After discussion opinions are the items selected and agreed upon in the group opinion, and the items not selected and disagreed upon in the group opinion. The percentage of agreement is the percentage of the number of items not agreed upon in the group opinion submission. The total number of group opinions agreed upon is divided by 10 and expressed as a percentage.

Social presence was measured using a questionnaire developed by Biocca and Harms [3]. All items were not used, only items related to co-presence (perception of self and perception of the other) were used. It defines as the "degree of salience of the other person in the interaction and the consequent salience of the interpersonal relationships" [31]. These measure the degree to which the users feel as if they are together in the same space. Each of the items was rated on a 7-point Likert scale. A higher value means a higher social presence.

In this experiment, we measured cohesion, especially task cohesion. To measure perceived task cohesion, we adopted the scale developed by Carless and De Paola [4]. Each of the items was rated on a 7-point Likert scale. A higher value means a higher perceived cohesion. Previous studies have indicated that it is closely related to social loafing [20].

Conflict management styles was a questionnaire developed by Rahim and adapted to suit this task [28]. The items were tailored to examine what conflict management styles were used by the participants in the discussions. Each of the items was rated on a 5-point Likert scale. However, the compromise score was removed because of $\alpha = .125$.

- Avoidance score: is measured with three items. "I tried to avoid stating my opinion in order not to create disagreements.", "I kept my opinions to myself if they disagree with others' opinions." and "I tried to avoid disagreements with others." ($\alpha = .793$).
- Accommodation score: is measured with three items. "When there was a disagreement, I tried to satisfy the needs of the other." "I went along with the desires of others in a conflict situation." and "I went along with the recommendations of others in a conflict." ($\alpha = .656$).
- Confrontation score: is measured with three items. "I used my influence to get my position accepted by others." "I was firm about advocating my side of an issue." and "I stuck to my position during a conflict." ($\alpha = .582$).
- Collaboration score: is measured with three items. "I tried to discuss an issue with others to find a solution acceptable to all of us." "I like to work with others to find solutions to a problem that satisfy everyone." and "To resolve a conflict, I tried to blend the ideas of all of the people involved." ($\alpha = .776$).

Table 2. Questionnaire of Several Indicators.

Questionnaire	Variables
Perceived Consensus	Feelings regarding the group decision
	Feelings regarding the decision process
	Feelings regarding group member relationships
	Feelings regarding individual effectiveness
	Feelings regarding individual opportunity to participate
Objective Consensus	The percentage of changing opinions
	The percentage of agreement
Social Presence	Co-presence (Perception of self)
	Co-presence (Perception of the other)
Perceived Cohesion	Task cohesion
Conflict Management Styles	Avoidance score
	Accommodation score
	Confrontation score
	Collaboration score

Conversation Analysis. All conversations that took place in the discussion were coded by two people. The conversation scripts were created by Whisper [2], which mechanically converted the utterances into text and then manually adjusted them. The speech was reproduced as verbatim as possible, and the speaker was also identified. Even the errors of speech are scripted. We conducted the following conversation analysis in conjunction with the task of this experiment. At first, we coded TCU (turn constructional units) for all conversational scripts. In those coding, we followed the principles advocated by Sacks et al. [30] that a turn is all speech from the time one speaker begins to speak until another person takes over the chance to speak. However, we did not count as turns any utterances that did not have a smooth response or turn changeover during the utterance. The analysis is at the individual level, not at the group level. Then, for these turns, we further coded the following: turn, turns involving new idea expression, interrupting the other's turn, failed turn-taking, times selecting the member, selected times by the member, agreement, disagreement, reactive token, and floor time. Each operation is described below easily.

Turns involving new idea expressions were counted as turns that stated an idea that no one else in the discussion has yet stated. In other words, it represents the number of unique ideas. Interrupting the other's turn was counted as the number of times the participant interrupted and started talking while someone else was speaking. Times selecting the member counted the number of times the speaker was named by a specific person or an unspecified number of persons when making a speaker change. Conversely, Selected times by the member counted the number of times the member was named. The code of agreement/disagreement was counted as agreement or disagreement with the immediately before opinion. The definition of the reactive token is "short utterance by an interlocutor acting as a listener while another interlocutor is speaking" [5]. For example, in Japanese, "Ah", "Um" and so on. The definition of floor is "Time and space in which the speaker perceives that he has the right to speak" [9]. In this study, floor time was defined as the time for someone in particular to lead the conversation. In many cases, this is the person who created a particular topic or raised an issue. We measured the time from the start of floor's speech until the next floor replaced it. We then calculated the total floor time for each member. The floor (%) was then used as a measure of the percentage of the conversation that was dominated. Failed turn-taking counted the number of times the participant was unable to perform turn-taking smoothly. We have performed morphological analysis on all utterances in the conversation script by using MeCab [22]. The number of morphemes was used as an indicator of message quantity. This is because, in Japanese, spacing is not based on words.

5 Result

5.1 Correlation Between SPSL and OPSL

Under two environments, we conducted Pearson's Correlation Analysis between SPSL (Mean = 5.19, SD = 1.02) and OPSL (Mean = 3.06, SD = 0.894) (see Fig. 3). There was a weak positive correlation between the two variables (r = .320, p = < .05, N = 39).

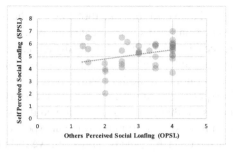

Fig. 3. Scatterplot of the relationship between SPSL and OPSL. Overlapping points are represented darkly.

5.2 Correlation Between Perceived Social Loafing and Several Indicators

For each environment, we conducted Pearson's Correlation analysis (two-sided) between perceived social loafing (SPSL and OPSL) and collected data, and then the correlation coefficient difference test (see Table 3).

There was a positive correlation between SPSL and OPSL in the poster presentation environment ($r = .246$, $P = .309$) and in the typical conference environment ($r = .444$, $P = .05$), and no significant difference in the correlation between the two environments ($P = .516$).

There tended to be more than moderate correlations between SPSL and subjective indicators. In the poster presentation environment, the variables for which strong correlations were obtained were following: individual effectiveness ($r = .725$, $P < .01$), individual opportunity to participate ($r = .675$, $P < .01$), confrontation score ($r = .709$, $P < .01$). The moderately and significantly correlated variables were as following: the group decision ($r = .525$, $P < .05$), avoidance score ($r = -.589$, $P < .01$), accommodation score ($r = -.513$, $P < .05$). In the typical conference environment, the variables for which strong correlations were obtained were following: co-presence (perception of self) ($r = .639$, $P < .01$), group member relationships ($r = .790$, $P < .01$), individual effectiveness($r = .687$, $P < .01$), individual opportunity to participate ($r = .720$, $P < .01$), confrontation score ($r = .619$, $P < .01$), collaboration score ($r = .678$, $P < .01$). The moderately and significantly correlated variables were as following: co-presence (perception of the other) ($r = .575$, $P < .05$), the decision process ($r = .511$, $P < .05$). On the other hand, the just OPSL and subjective indicators that obtained more than moderate correlations were collaboration score (the poster presentation environment $r = .484$, $P < .05$), group member relationships (the poster presentation environment $r = .497$, $P < .05$; the typical conference environment $r = .452$, $P < .05$).

There tended to be more than moderate correlations between OPSL and objective indicators in the typical conference environment. In the typical conference environment, the variables for which strong correlations were obtained were Selected times by the member ($r = -.638$, $P < .01$). The moderately and significantly correlated variables were as following: morpheme ($r = .559$, $P < .05$), morpheme (%) ($r = .580$, $P < .05$), turn (%) ($r = .538$, $P < .05$), turns involving new idea expression (%) ($r = .578$, $P < .05$), times selecting the member(%) ($r = .451$, $P < .01$), reactive token(%) ($r = $

Table 3. Correlation Analysis Result.

Variables	Poster Presentation Environment				Typical Conference Environment				Correlation coefficient difference test between two environments (p-value)	
	SPSL	OPSL	Mean	SD	SPSL	OPSL	Mean	SD	SPSL	OPSL
SPSL	–	.246	5.35	0.900	–	.444*†	5.04	1.13	–	.516
OPSL	.246	–	2.86	0.800	.444*†	–	3.25	0.950	.516	–
Co-presence (Perception of self)	-.110	-.301	5.42	1.16	.639***‡	.346	5.00	1.64	.013	.054
Co-presence (Perception of the other)	.192	-.124	4.87	1.26	.575***†	.145	4.83	1.14	.186	.437
The group decision	.525*†	.236	6.05	0.891	.443†	.101	5.68	1.20	.758	.689
The decision process	.387	.387	5.63	1.08	.511*†	.023	5.48	1.47	.655	.269
Group member relationships	.286	.497*†	5.25	1.41	.790***†	.452*†	4.72	1.64	.026	.868
Individual effectiveness	.725***‡	.251	4.75	1.80	.687***‡	.311	4.48	1.46	.828	.852
Individual opportunity to participate	.675***‡	.207	5.17	1.02	.720***‡	.264	4.86	1.40	.801	.862
Perceived Cohesion	.378	.215	6.21	0.850	.422†	-.186	5.74	1.13	.880	.243
Avoidance score	-.589***†	-.204	2.40	0.821	-.358	.173	2.23	1.22	.387	.273
Accommodation score	-.513*†	-.363	2.89	0.910	-.349	-.084	2.68	0.820	.561	.395
Confrontation score	.709***‡	.241	3.04	0.744	.619***‡	.270	2.77	0.750	.642	.929
Collaboration score	.321	.484*†	4.05	0.536	.678***‡	.181	3.52	1.15	.157	.322
The percentage of changing opinions	-.213	.218	22.11	18.73	.093	-.430†	25.50	16.38	.374	.050
The percentage of agreement	.283	.521*†	91.58	13.85	.349	.304	93.50	11.37	.833	.449

(*continued*)

Table 3. (*continued*)

Morpheme	.000	-.319	363.00	220.57	.110	.559*†	388.80	236.56	.751	.006
Morpheme(%)	.104	-.178	–	0.120	.251	.580**†	–	0.090	.662	.016
Turn	-.146	-.295	58.26	38.79	.426†	.364	52.40	28.76	.084	.049
Turn(%)	.079	-.346	–	0.110	.428†	.538*†	–	0.100	.277	.006
Turns involving new idea expression	-.036	-.192	9.68	6.06	.326	.441†	7.75	4.04	.282	.055
Turns involving new idea expression(%)	.144	-.087	–	0.130	.270	.578**†	–	0.094	.705	.032
Interrupting the other's turn	-.092	-.068	2.21	2.49	.272	.217	1.90	2.29	.286	.407
Interrupting the other's turn(%)	.083	-.297	–	0.190	.276	.268	–	0.200	.566	.095
Failed turn-taking	-.299	-.023	4.84	3.79	-.050	.081	2.75	2.57	.458	.765
Failed turn-taking(%)	-.085	-.189	–	0.120	.138	.260	–	0.120	.520	.189
Times selecting the member	.081	-.546*†	7.16	6.32	.331	.275	7.80	8.64	.451	.010
Times selecting the member(%)	-.098	-.442†	–	0.200	.393	.451*†	–	0.180	.140	.006
Selected times by the member	-.307	-.446†	2.32	1.86	-.214	-.638**†	2.65	3.75	.774	.430
Selected times by the member(%)	-.119	-.248	–	0.170	-.102	-.267	–	0.250	.961	.953
Agreement	-.362	.112	11.58	10.34	.363	.007	8.15	6.34	.029	.762
Agreement(%)	-.133	-.307	–	0.100	.265	.038	–	0.130	.245	.308
Disagreement	-.142	-.053	1.68	1.73	-.035	.151	0.950	1.19	.757	.556
Disagreement(%)	.013	.161	–	0.240	.039	.178	–	0.260	.940	.960
Reactive Token	-.168	-.007	20.47	14.79	.361	.348	19.70	16.65	.116	.288
Reactive Token(%)	.047	-.049	–	0.120	.287	.456*†	–	0.140	.476	.120
Floor Time (%)	-.014	-.119	–	0.160	.303	.438†	–	0.210	.348	.091

Note: *P<.05; **P<.01. Correlation coefficient: .00-.19 = very weak; .20 - .39 = weak; †.40 - .59 = moderate (light red); ‡.60 - .79 = strong (deep red).

.456, P < .05). On the other hand, in the poster presentation environment, none of the variables were strongly correlated. The only one variable that showed moderately significant correlations were times selecting the member (r = -.546, P < .05).

Indicators for which the difference in correlation with SPSL was significant in the two environments were as follows: co-presence (perception of self) (P < .05), group member relationships (P < .05), agreement (P < .05). For OPSL, the indicators were as following: the percentage of changing opinions (P < .05), morpheme (P < .01), morpheme (%) (P < .05), turn (P < .05), turn (%) (P < .01), turns involving new idea expression (%) (P < .05), times selecting the member (P < .01), times selecting the member (%) (P < .01) agreement (P < .05). Marginally significant differences were as following: co-presence (Perception of self) (P < .1), turns involving new idea expression (P < .1), interrupting the other's turn (%) (P < .1), times selecting the member (P < .1), floor time (%) (P < .1).

5.3 Explanatory Variables Selected by Lasso

Lasso (Least Absolute Shrinkage and Selection Operator) was a method for estimation in linear models and was developed by Robert [29]. It minimizes the residual sum of squares while limiting the sum of the absolute values of the coefficients. That is, it can used to automatically select more relevant coefficients. In this study, Lasso was used to find explanatory variables intrinsically related to OPSL.

To conduct the Lasso, we used the R package glmnet [10]. The objective variable was OPSL, and 11 objective indicators were entered as explanatory variables: Morpheme (%), turns involving new idea expression (%), interrupting the other's turn (%), failed turn-taking, failed turn-taking (%), times selecting the member (%), selected times by the member (%), agreement (%), disagreement (%), reactive token (%), and floor time (%). The reason these indicators are percentage unit is that we determined that this social loafing was evaluated relative to the group members.

As a result, no variable had explanatory power in the Poster condition. For the Conference condition, three indicators were selected, namely: morpheme (%), turns involving new idea expression (%), and reactive token (%).

6 Discussion

6.1 Relationship Between SPSL and OPSL

Throughout, there was a significant weak positive correlation between SPSL and OPSL. This means that SPSL and OPSL are rarely in coincidence (RQ1). In addition, when the correlation coefficients between SPSL and OPSL were compared separately between the two environments, the coefficient of the typical conference environment was higher than the coefficient of the poster conference environment. Although the difference was not significant, the result suggested that the difference between SPSL and OPSL was affected by the form of VR environment, and the typical conference environment had a smaller difference (RQ2).

The existence and degree of difference between SPSL and OPSL may be attributed to the extent to which participants know each other. It has been reported that close acquaintances are less likely to have disagreements between self-assessments and others' assessments of them in the related work about personality judgment [11]. In this experiment, the group discussions were conducted anonymously, and group members did not know each other. Thus, the degree of agreement between the SPSL and OPSL might be affected by the VR environments which provide participants with different levels of opportunity to know other participants. In the poster presentation environment, the avatars moved around in the VR space, so the time spent looking at other avatars was likely to be short and difficult to fully observe. Therefore, participants may not get to know other participants better than in the typical conference environment, and it resulted in a larger difference between SPSL and OPSL.

6.2 Relationship between Perceived Social Loafing and Several Indicators

Pearson's Correlation analysis shows that interestingly, in both environments, SPSL tends to correlate significantly with subjective indicators. However, there were more exceptions in the poster presentation environment than in the typical conference environment. For example, co-presence or perceived cohesion and SPSL were only weakly correlated in the poster presentation environment. These indicators were found to be moderately or highly correlated in the preliminary study and related work [23].

On the other hand, our results indicated that OPSL was more likely to be significantly correlated with objective indicators in the typical conference environment while OPSL shows little correlation with indicators in the poster presentation environment. This shows that the participants judged others' social loafing differently in the two environments. The finding is also supported by Lasso's results that three variables are selected in the typical conference environment and no variables are selected in the poster presentation environment. Furthermore, the selected three variables (morpheme, turns involving new idea expression, and reactive token) showed that the participants might have used conversational cues to determine OPSL in the typical conference environment. Conversely, the participants might not have used conversational cues to determine OPSL in the poster presentation environment (RQ3).

We considered that the strategy for default usage of the environment influenced whether or not conversational information was used to determine OPSL. The poster presentation environment is to provide information to others or to explore information, while the typical conference environment is to exchange information or interact with others. In the poster presentation environment, the participants paid little attention to others' conversational behaviors; thus, those behaviors may be less important as cues for OPSL. In contrast, the participants in the typical conference environment expected others and themselves to engage in the discussion; thus, the conversational behaviors were being focused more; therefore, these behaviors may be critical cues for OPSL.

6.3 Design Principles for Designers to Facilitate Communication in VR

From the findings of the result, we discuss some design principles for designers to facilitate communication in VR.

Many facilitating functions focused on how their functions make participants engage more in communication, and they evaluated the objective outcome and the participants' engagement with self-report. For example, focusing on the amount of speech as an outcome, and a subjective self-evaluation using a questionnaire [18]. However, our research findings suggested the importance of considering OPSL while designing facilitation functions. OPSL is an indicator that affects group members and should not be taken lightly [25]. In addition, the results of this study show that OPSL has a complex relationship with SPSL or simple output. Even if SPSL or simple output is improved, it does not necessarily mean that OPSL can be improved.

Furthermore, based on our finding that the type of the VR environment affects the OPSL, we also argue that it is important to consider the interaction between the type of the VR environment and the facilitating functions during design. For example, a facilitating function inducing users to speak more in a typical conference environment may improve his/her OPSL; however, it might not work well in a poster presentation environment. This is because, according to the results of this experiment, in a poster presentation environment, people's interest is not in conversational behavior, and a person who speaks more may still not be perceived to perform less social loafing.

6.4 Limitation and Future Work

In this research, we are aware that there are some limitations and future work.

First, the results of this study were based on a single type of discussion, and the generalizability is one of the limitations. We adopted the desert survival task in the experiment. This kind of negotiation task has a clear procedure and goal, so it may be easier for participants to distinguish others' social loafing. However, real-world group discussion type varies, and they often involve more open-ended topics and involve more physical movement, such as people drawing plans and writing down ideas on whiteboards in a topic involving planning [35]. Moreover, people may also play different roles. People might difficultly judge others' social loafing, and their strategy might change. Thus, it is necessary to conduct experiments with different types of discussion to investigate how SPSL and OPSL differ in different situations and determine robust indicators for estimating perceived social loafing.

Second, we are aware that the individual differences might be biases of our experiment. However, we did not collect much demographic information, such as the expertise level of VR, the knowledge about the tasks, and the participants' personalities. As a future work, it is necessary to investigate whether these individual differences affect the result or not.

Third, in the poster presentation environment, OPSL was not determined based on conversational information. It is possible that OPSL was determined based on other factors. For example, the avatar's gaze and gait information. It is necessary to clarify these factors in future work.

7 Conclusions

The purpose of this paper was to understand the mechanism of perceived social loafing in VR group discussions. In particular, we explored the difference between SPSL and OPSL. We also investigated how this difference changes in the poster presentation environment and the typical conference environment. Therefore, we formulated the three RQs.

For RQ1, the overall SPSL and OPSL had only a significantly weak positive correlation. This means that the SPSL and OPSL are not so consistent in VR conferences.

For RQ2, the correlation coefficients between SPSL and OPSL were higher in the typical conference environment than in the poster presentation environment. However, in this experiment, the results of the correlation coefficient difference test were not significantly different, so at the level of suggestion.

For RQ3, we looked at the relationship between OPSL and various discussion related indicators in the two VR environments. The results showed that in the VR space of a typical conference, there were significant correlations with objective indicators that seemed to be related to Social Loafing. In addition, regression analysis by Lasso calculated three indicators with explanatory power. Thus, those who participated in discussions in the typical conference environment were found to be cued by several objective indicators. On the other hand, in the poster presentation environment, there was little correlation with indicators that might be associated with social loafing. Regression analysis by Lasso also showed no objective indicators with explanatory power. It can be said that in the poster presentation environment, those who participated in the discussion were at least making judgments without using conversational information as a cue. Therefore, we suggest that the criteria for OPSL are different in the poster presentation environment and the typical conference environment.

Acknowledgments. This work was supported by JAIST Research Grant 2022 (Fundamental Research), and JSPS KAKENHI Grant Number 21K11978 and 22H03634.

References

1. Albanese, R., Van Fleet, D.D.: Rational behavior in groups: the free-riding tendency. Acad. Manag. Rev. **10**, 244–255 (1985). https://doi.org/10.2307/257966
2. Alec, R., Jong, W.K., Tao, X., Greg, B., Christine, M., Ilya, S.: Robust Speech Recognition via Large-Scale Weak Supervision (2022). https://doi.org/10.48550/arXiv.2212.04356
3. Biocca, F., Harms, C.: Networked Minds Social Presence Inventory (Scales only version 1.2) (2003). http://cogprints.org/6742/
4. Carless, S., De Paola, C.: The measurement of cohesion in work teams. Small Group Res. **31**(1), 71–88 (2000). https://doi.org/10.1177/104649640003100104
5. Clancy, P.M., Thompson, S.A., Suzuki, R., Tao, H.: The conversational use of reactive tokens in English, Japanese, and Mandarin. J. Pragmat. **26**(3), 355–387 (1996). https://doi.org/10.1016/0378-2166(95)00036-4
6. Comer, D.R.: A model of social loafing in real work groups. Human Relations **48**(6), 647–667 (1995). https://doi.org/10.1177/001872679504800603

7. DeStephen, R., Hirokawa, R.Y.: Small group consensus: stability of group support of the decision, task process, and group relationships. Small Group Behavior **19**(2), 227–239 (1988). https://doi.org/10.1177/104649648801900204

8. Domínguez, I., Roberts, D.: Asymmetric virtual environments: exploring the effects of avatar colors on performance. Proceedings of the AAAI Conference on Artificial Intelligence and Interactive Digital Entertainment **10**(3), 8–14 (2021). https://doi.org/10.1609/aiide.v10i3.12746

9. Edelsky, C.: Who's got the floor? Lang. Soc. **10**(3), 383–421 (1981). https://doi.org/10.1017/S004740450000885X

10. Friedman, J., Hastie, T., Tibshirani, R.: Regularization paths for generalized linear models via coordinate descent. J Stat Softw. **33**(1), 1–22 (2010). https://doi.org/10.18637/jss.v033.i01

11. Funder, D.C., Colvin, C.R.: Friends and strangers: acquaintanceship, agreement, and the accuracy of personality judgment. J. Personality and Social Psychol. **55**(1), 149–158 (1988). https://doi.org/10.1037/0022-3514.55.1.149

12. George, J.M.: Extrinsic and intrinsic origins of perceived social loafing in organizations. Acad. Manag. J. **35**, 191–202 (1992). https://doi.org/10.2307/256478

13. Han, E., et al.: People, places, and time: a large-scale, longitudinal study of transformed avatars and environmental context in group interaction in the metaverse. J. Comput.-Mediat. Commun. (2022). https://doi.org/10.1093/jcmc/zmac031

14. Harkins, S.G.: Social loafing and social facilitation. J. Exp. Soc. Psychol. **23**(1), 1–18 (1987). https://doi.org/10.1016/0022-1031(87)90022-9

15. Henningsen, D.D., Cruz, M.G., Miller, M.L.: Role of social loafing in predeliberation decision making. Group Dyn. Theory Res. Pract. **4**(2), 168–175 (2000). https://doi.org/10.1037/1089-2699.4.2.168

16. Høigaard, R., Säfvenbom, R., Tønnessen, F.E.: The relationship between group cohesion, group norms, and perceived social loafing in soccer teams. Small Group Res. **37**(3), 217–232 (2006). https://doi.org/10.1177/1046496406287311

17. Karau, S.J., Williams, K.D.: Social loafing: a meta-analytic review and theoretical integration. J. Pers. Soc. Psychol. **65**(4), 681–706 (1993). https://doi.org/10.1037/0022-3514.65.4.681

18. Kim, S., Eun, J., Seering, J., Lee, J.: Moderator chatbot for deliberative discussion: effects of discussion structure and discussant facilitation. Proceedings of the ACM on Human-Computer Interaction 5, CSCW1, 87, 1–26 (2021). https://doi.org/10.1145/3449161

19. Lafferty, J.C., Eady, P., Elmers, J.: The Desert Survival Problem. Plymouth. Experimental Learning Methods, Michigan (1974)

20. Lam, C.: The role of communication and cohesion in reducing social loafing in group projects. Business and Professional Communication Quarterly **78**(4), 454–475 (2015). https://doi.org/10.1177/2329490615596417

21. Latané, B., Williams, K.D., Harkins, S.G.: Many hands make light the work: the causes and consequences of social loafing. J. Personality and Social Psychol. **37**(6), 822–832 (1979). https://doi.org/10.1037/0022-3514.37.6.822

22. MeCab: Yet Another Part-of-Speech and Morphological Analyzer. https://taku910.github.io/mecab/. Accessed 18 Jan 2023

23. Monzani, L., Ripoll, P., Peiró, J.M., Dick, R.V.: Loafing in the digital age: the role of computer mediated communication in the relation between perceived loafing and group affective outcomes. Comput. Hum. Behav. **33**, 279–285 (2014). https://doi.org/10.1016/j.chb.2014.01.013

24. Mozilla Hubs. https://hubs.mozilla.com/. Accessed 18 Jan 2023

25. Mulvey, P.M., Klein, H.J.: The impact of perceived loafing and collective efficacy on group goal processes and group performance. Organ. Behav. Hum. Decis. Process. **74**(1), 62–87 (1998). https://doi.org/10.1006/obhd.1998.2753

26. Petty, R.E., Harkins, S.G., Williams, K.D., Latane, B.: The effects of group size on cognitive effort and evaluation. Pers. Soc. Psychol. Bull. **3**(4), 579–582 (1977). https://doi.org/10.1177/014616727700300406

27. Petty, R.E., Harkins, S.G., Williams, K.D.: The effects of group diffusion of cognitive effort on attitudes: an information-processing view. J. Pers. Soc. Psychol. **38**(1), 81–92 (1980). https://doi.org/10.1037/0022-3514.38.1.81

28. Rahim, M.: A measure of styles of handling interpersonal conflict. Acad. Manag. J. **26**(2), 368–376 (1983). https://doi.org/10.2307/255985

29. Robert, T.: Regression shrinkage and selection via the lasso. J. Royal Statistical Society. Series B (Methodological), 267–288 (1996). https://doi.org/10.1111/j.2517-6161.1996.tb02080.x

30. Sacks, H., Schegloff, E.A., Jefferson, G.: A simplest systematics for the organization of turn-taking for conversation. Language **50**(4), 696–735 (1974). https://doi.org/10.2307/412243

31. Short, J., Williams, E., Christie, B.: The Social Psychology of Telecommunications. John Wiley and Sons, London (1976)

32. Steiner, I.D.: Group Process and Productivity. Academia Press (1972)

33. Suleiman, J., Warson, R.T.: Social loafing in technology-supported teams. Computer Supported Cooperative Work (CSCW) **17**(4), 291–309 (2008). https://doi.org/10.1007/s10606-008-9075-6

34. Wang, T., Kawaguchi, I., Kuzuoka, H., Otsuki, M.: Effect of manipulated amplitude and frequency of human voice on dominance and persuasiveness in audio conferences. Proceedings of the ACM on Human-Computer Interaction.2, CSCW, 177, pp. 1–18 (2018). https://doi.org/10.1145/3274446

35. Wang, T., Noaki, Y., Kuzuoka, H.: Exploring how to display referential action to support remote group discussion. In: Asian CHI Symposium 2021. Association for Computing Machinery, pp. 89–96 (2021). https://doi.org/10.1145/3429360.3468188

36. WebEx. https://www.webex.com/ja/index.html. Accessed 18 Jan 2023

37. Yee, N., Bailenson, J.: The effect of transformed self-representation on behavior. Hum. Commun. Res. **33**, 271–290 (2007). https://doi.org/10.1111/j.1468-2958.2007.00299.x

Recommendation Systems and AI Explainability

Blending Conversational Product Advisors and Faceted Filtering in a Graph-Based Approach

Timm Kleemann[✉] and Jürgen Ziegler

University of Duisburg-Essen, Duisburg, Germany
{timm.kleemann,juergen.ziegler}@uni-due.de

Abstract. Today's e-commerce websites often provide many different components, such as filters and conversational product advisors, to help users find relevant items. However, filters and advisors are often presented separately and treated as independent entities so that the previous input is discarded when users switch between them. This leads to memory loads and disruptions during the search process. In addition, the reasoning behind the advisors' results is often not transparent. To overcome these limitations, we propose a novel approach that exploits a graph structure to create an integrated system that allows a seamless coupling between filters and advisors. The integrated system utilizes the graph to suggest appropriate filter values and items based on the user's answers in the advisor. Moreover, it determines follow-up questions based on the filter values set by the user. The interface visualizes and explains the relationship between a given answer and its relevant features to achieve increased transparency in the guidance process. We report the results of an empirical user study with 120 participants that compares the integrated system to a system in which the filtering and advisory mechanisms operate separately. The findings indicate that displaying recommendations and explanations directly in the filter component can increase acceptance and trust in the system. Similarly, combining the advisor with the filters along with the displayed explanations leads to significantly higher levels of knowledge about the relevant product features.

Keywords: Search interfaces · Explanations · Graph-based interaction

1 Introduction

Many e-commerce websites offer an overwhelming selection of products, making it challenging for users to identify the relevant ones. To counteract the resulting information overload and to facilitate finding suitable products in large item spaces, search and filtering techniques have become standard components on most websites [19,57]. These methods, however, require a clearly defined search goal and often also a sufficient level of knowledge about the product domain.

ⓒ The Author(s), under exclusive license to Springer Nature Switzerland AG 2023
J. Abdelnour Nocera et al. (Eds.): INTERACT 2023, LNCS 14144, pp. 137–159, 2023.
https://doi.org/10.1007/978-3-031-42286-7_8

Faceted filtering, for instance, provides users with a high degree of control over the results so that they can effectively and transparently narrow down large item sets until a suitable item is found [31]. This approach can involve considerable interaction effort and requires sufficient knowledge about the meaning of the various filter attributes and how relevant these are with respect to the user's goal [45]. As an alternative to manual filtering, conversational systems have emerged and are commonly used as product advisors on e-commerce websites. In this paper, we will focus on GUI-style dialog-based advisors that guide users through a predefined dialog structure [14] and support them in their decision process in a conversational manner by asking questions about their product-related goals and preferences. With each successive question, the results are refined on the basis of the given answers, suggesting products that fit the requirements increasingly well [17,25]. Since the questions are often framed with an application-oriented focus rather than on the level of (technical) product features, in-depth domain knowledge is mostly not required. However, for experts who know (to some extent) what they are looking for, the structured dialogical approach can be cumbersome–in contrast to filtering systems, there are usually no options for directly specifying desired product features in a targeted manner.

These opposite requirements create a need for approaches that seamlessly integrate interactive filtering and dialogical advisors. This paper presents our contribution to this challenge–a novel method that achieves this integration. When filter mechanisms and conversational advisors are both present, they are mostly presented separately from each other and intended to be used independently, with no data-based connection. To overcome this disintegration, we propose a graph-based method that, in combining the two components, leverages the advantages of both. This allows users to obtain suitable products by answering simple, application-related questions while, at the same time, enabling them to select concrete feature values if they have specific preferences. Furthermore, we introduce a method for explaining which filter values are relevant for the given answers and thus for the items in the result list. Conversely, the advisor, i.e. the application-oriented level, should know which questions and answers are already covered by the selected filters and thus only focus on questions that have not yet been sufficiently answered. In this regard, our research interest is to investigate how a deep integration of filtering and dialogical advisor affects users' perception of the search process as well as their interaction behavior. To answer this question, we conducted a user study in which we compare the integrated approach with a system that keeps the two techniques separated. The results indicate that our approach increases the transparency of the recommendation process and thereby system satisfaction and acceptance. Hence, we conclude that the proposed integration of two interactive components is considered helpful by users in aiding their decision making. Also, we assume, that this integration does not increase cognitive demands or interaction effort, which might be the case if the integration leads to higher complexity.

2   Related Work

To alleviate the search and decision-making challenge, automated recommender systems have become widely used components [16,50] to more actively guide users to relevant content and have been shown in numerous studies to reduce both cognitive load and interaction effort [30,44]. Therefore, most e-commerce websites rely on one-shot recommendations to automatically present items based on historical user preference data [22]. However, interaction is typically rather limited, and users do not have the opportunity to explicitly influence how the recommendations are generated [27,30,35]. In addition, recommender systems are often non-transparent as they make it difficult for users to understand why certain products have been suggested [42]. This is especially relevant if a user's domain knowledge is low or insufficient information about the products is presented [34]. To counteract this, and to increase the trust and perceived transparency of recommender systems and advisors, explanations can be provided to clarify the recommendation process or to justify why certain items were recommended, thereby making the recommendation process more transparent and facilitating decision making [1,3,40,49,52,53]. In addition to static explanations, there are also conversational approaches for explaining recommendations, making it easier for users to scrutinize system decisions and to explore arguments according to their information needs [20]. In addition to textual explanations, methods that use features to show how the characteristics of an item match the user's preferences are widely used [54]. In this work, we provide explanations emanating from the coupling of different decision-support tools to increase the transparency of the recommendation process. Although considerable amount of research has been done on this topic, most approaches have added an explanatory layer to the particular component under consideration without including other existing components.

As an alternative to filter or search systems, conversational systems often help users find suitable results. Conversational systems enable users to respond to recommendations on a more human-like level [21,51]. In this context, a variety of techniques has been explored. These include GUI-style dialog-based product advisors that guide users through a predefined dialog structure [14], which evolved from early, strictly rule-based approaches where users had to answer a given sequence of questions based on a limited set of predefined answers [56]. Through recent advances in deep learning, chatbots are able to mimic natural language conversations [43]. In most systems, however, these conversational advisors are offered separately from the usual filter and search systems, even though it is well known that users typically use several decision aids and switch between them before settling on a product [46,55]. As each component has a different impact on progress towards the goal [8,18], it is reasonable to consider ways in which they can be usefully combined. To date, this problem has only been partially addressed by research into some specific aspects, for example, approaches that combine different interactive recommendation mechanisms [37], a dialog-based advisor with a filtering interface [25], or multiple decision support tools such as filtering mechanisms, recommendations, product advisors, and chatbots

[23]. Some approaches also combine filtering systems with recommender systems to increase the interactivity of the recommendation process and to guide users to their destination more efficiently [13,36].

3   Graph-Based Approach for an Integrated System

Assuming that users will benefit from a closer connection between the components and thus a more seamless experience, we outline an approach for an integrated system that provides a tight coupling of user interactions with filters and an advisor. In addition, the integrated system provides the ability to explain how certain feature values relate to dialog responses or influence recommendation generation. This coupling enables users to see how recommended filter values change when different answers are selected. Coupling with filters also allows for customization; the filter component lets users specify or change the filter values suggested by the advisor.

Our proposed system is meant to provide comprehensive assistance to users interacting with the advisor. Specifically, it should be able (1) to identify relevant items for the chosen answers; (2) to determine which feature values are (not) relevant for the selected answers; and to (3) provide an explanation as to why certain feature values are (not) relevant for a particular answer. As a result, we expect that users will gain a better understanding of the reasoning behind the answers and will be able to make more informed decisions. Results from a previous study [24] indicated that users with a high level of domain knowledge prefer to use the filter component to find suitable items. It has also been observed that these users utilize an advisor for preliminary selection of filter values, although they like to adjust these recommended filters to their needs afterwards. For users who are utilizing the filter component, the integrated system should be able (4) to identify which of the advisor's questions may have already been answered by the interaction with the filter, i.e., by the selection of feature values, and (5) to determine which of the unanswered questions should be presented next.

To achieve these goals, we propose a knowledge graph-based approach that allows us to model relationships between different data entities [33]. Knowledge graphs have become a popular technique for web search, recommender systems, and question-answering systems such as dialog-based advisors or chatbots [9]. Knowledge graph-based recommender systems can build a semantic representation and leverage the underlying knowledge even with little or sparse data and thereby identify potentially interesting or useful items for the target user, either through direct or indirect associations between entities [9,39]. According to [33], knowledge graph-based recommendation approaches can be classified into three categories: ontology-based recommendation, linked open data-based recommendation, and knowledge graph embedding-based recommendation. Zou [58] adds path-based approaches to this list. In addition, graphs are well suited for efficient querying of complex, interconnected data [33] and thus provide a promising basis for combining a dialog-based product advisor with filter mechanisms.

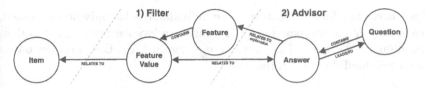

Fig. 1. Graph model that allows filters and advisor to be connected. Relationships between features, feature values, and items are retrieved from datasets. Expert knowledge is required to define relationships between advisor and filters.

3.1 Graph Model

As shown in Fig. 1, the underlying graph of our integrated system is divided into two parts. The first part consists of the features and feature values retrieved from the items of a dataset. This part serves as the basis for the filtering component. The second part of the graph provides the advisor with information and is connected to the vertices of the first part. Based on the selected feature values and/or answers, the items are filtered and ranked according to their relevance. In the following, we first describe the graph and then present the techniques for retrieving appropriate feature values and items based on the interaction with the system. The dataset consists of *items* $I = \{i_1, i_2, i_3, \dots\}$, which differ in at least one feature value. In addition to the item specific feature values, the items may also contain rating information. Further information about user interactions with these items, such as viewing frequency or purchase information, is also conceivable. Each item contains information about all available *features* $F = \{f_1, f_2, f_3, \dots\}$. Each feature (or attribute) has as its domain a subset V_f of all *feature values* $V = \{v_1, v_2, v_3, \dots\}$, which are concrete properties of an item such as its color. Feature values can be categorical, ordinal, or numeric. At the interface level, checkboxes can be used to select categorical and ordinal values, and numeric values can be shown and selected as ranges.

Additionally, we integrate information about the questions and answers used in the dialog-based advisor into the graph. To do this, and to establish the associations between the advisor and the feature values, we require information about the usage of an item and its relevant features. Since this information is not contained in the item dataset, we need expert knowledge. The advisor consists of *questions* $Q = \{q_1, q_2, q_3, \dots\}$. Each question corresponds to a subset of all *answers* $A = \{a_1, a_2, a_3, \dots\}$. Each answer includes information regarding relevant assigned feature values. The relevance $\tau_{a,v} \in [-1, 1]$ between an answer $a \in A$ and a feature value $v \in V$ is defined by domain experts. While positive relevance values indicate recommended feature values, negative relevance values indicate that those feature values do not satisfy this answer. Thus, multiple feature values can be assigned to an answer, but they may have different relevance to the answer. Additionally, the domain expert should provide an explanation $x_{a,f}$ of why certain aspects of a feature f are important for an answer a. Since we assume that it is sufficient to provide this explanation at the feature level and not necessary for each feature value individually, this only needs to be done for each answer feature pair (a, f) for which a relevance value $\tau_{a,v}$ was defined between an answer a and feature value v, where $v \in V_f$. Based on the data, we define a weighted directed graph as

$$G = (I \cup V \cup F \cup A \cup Q, E, w) \tag{1}$$

For the edges between the vertices, we define the edge set E and a weight function $w : E \rightarrow [-1, 1]$. We construct the graph, starting with the edges between the feature and the feature values: For all $f \in F$ and $v \in V$ where $v \in V_f$ there are $(f, v) \in E$. In a graph, the weight function is defined for all edges. However, in our approach we do not consider the edge weights between features and feature values, therefore we set the weight $w((f, v)) = 0$.

For all feature values $v \in V$ and items $i \in I$ where v is included in i, there are $(v, i) \in E$. To prioritize relevant items for selected or recommended feature values in the result list, we define weights for these edges. These weights take into account both the relative frequency of a feature value and the popularity of the related items, since we assume that popular items that contain a selected or recommended feature value are more important to users than items that are not popular, i.e., less well rated. Thus, the weight for the edges $w((v, i))$ expresses the relevance of an item i to a feature value v. To calculate this relevance, we first define the popularity ρ_i for each item i.

$$\rho_i = \frac{k \cdot \bar{r} + c_i \cdot \bar{r}_i}{k + c_i} \tag{2}$$

To calculate the popularity of an item, we include both the average rating $\bar{r}_i$ for an item i and the number of assigned ratings c_i. The average user rating is $\bar{r}_i \in [0, 5]$, where 0 is the lowest and 5 the highest score. Additionally, the mean rating across all items $\bar{r}$ is included, while k is a constant that we set to 100 based on our early experiments with the dataset. These values are then standardized across all items. The relative frequency ϕ_v of a feature value v of a feature f is the number of all items containing v divided by the number of all items containing any feature value of f. The weights for the edges between a feature value v and an item i originate from the relative frequencies ϕ_v and the popularity ρ_i.

$$w((v, i)) = 0.4 \cdot \phi_v + 0.6 \cdot \rho_i \tag{3}$$

A weighting is applied to the input factors to adjust the influence of the popularity ρ_i and the relative frequency ϕ_v. Internal tests indicated that a higher weighted popularity score leads to more appropriate results.

Next, to include the advisor in our graph, we establish the connections between questions and answers, for all $q \in Q$ and $a \in A$, there are $(q, a) \in E$. If a domain expert has defined an optional answer a for question q, we set $w((q, a)) = 0$. Since dialog-based systems can ask users questions that depend on previously given answers which affect the question sequences, we model these dependencies in our graph. Therefore, we define an additional edge when a question q depends on a previously given answer a: For all $a \in A$ and $q \in Q$, there are $(a, q) \in E$ and $w((a, q)) = 0$, if a domain expert has defined that answer a is the prerequisite for asking question q.

To establish connections between the advisor and the filter component, we add edges between the vertices of the answers and the feature values: For all $a \in A$ and $v \in V$ where $\tau_{a,v} \neq 0$, there are edges $(a, v), (v, a) \in E$ with a weight $w((a, v)) = w((v, a)) = \tau_{a,v}$. Additionally, we connect answers with features: For all $a \in A$ and $f \in F$ where a is related to f (i.e. where $x_{a,f}$ is defined by a domain expert), there are edges $(a, f) \in E$ with the weight $w((a, f)) = 0$. The weight is set to 0 because we do not need the weight for our calculations; only the explanation provided by the domain expert is relevant. We can utilize the graph to compute relevant feature values and items from given answers. In addition, we can infer related advisor answers from previously selected feature values.

Feature Value and Item Recommendations. Based on the edges and weights defined in the graph, we calculate which feature values are relevant for selected answers. Selected answers are described as follows:

$$p_A : A \rightarrow \{0, 1\} \tag{4}$$

$$p_A(a) = \begin{cases} 1 & \text{if user has selected answer } a \\ 0 & \text{if user has not selected answer } a \end{cases} \tag{5}$$

In addition to selecting answers, users can deselect recommended feature values so that they are no longer considered. Moreover, users can explicitly select feature values to be included in the considerations even if these were not originally considered in an answer.

$$p_V : V \rightarrow \mathbb{R} \tag{6}$$

$$p_V(v) = \begin{cases} 1 & \text{if user has selected feature value } v \\ -1 & \text{if user has deselected feature value } v \\ \sum_{(a,v) \in E} w((a, v)) \cdot p_A(a) & \text{else} \end{cases} \tag{7}$$

Next, we calculate relevant items based on feature values.

$$p_I : I \rightarrow \mathbb{R} \tag{8}$$

$$p_I(i) = \sum_{(v,i) \in E} w((v, i)) \cdot p_V(v) \tag{9}$$

Then, based on the resulting relevance values $p_I(i)$, the items are sorted in descending order. Through the use of the graph and the calculation of relevance values as described above, the advisor and the filter components can be used together as well as on their own to determine a selection of suitable items.

Answer and Question Recommendations. By means of the graph and the connections between feature values and answers, we are able to retrieve feature value related answers. If a user selects feature values that are associated with an answer, that user is more likely to select that answer when using the advisor. To get relevant answers, we consider a set S of all (de-) selected values $v \in V$.

$$q_A : A \to \mathbb{R} \tag{10}$$

$$q_A(a) = \sum_{(v,a) \in E,\, v \in S} w((v,a)) \cdot p_V(v) \tag{11}$$

If a follow-up question is defined for the answer a with the largest $q_A(a)$, i.e. there are selected feature values associated with an answer a, and there is an edge $(a, q) \in E$, then question q is the most appropriate follow-up question and is displayed next. If no follow-up question is defined for the answer a with the largest $q_A(a)$, the system must decide which question to display next. In this case, the question that contains the answer a with the smallest $q_A(a)$ is displayed next. Also, this question must not be considered already answered by selected filter values (i.e. an answer a' with the largest $q_A(a')$ is not an answer) and must not have been answered directly by the user. We assume, that it might be beneficial for users to let the advisor prioritize questions which are not yet answered. Conversely, if a user has already selected an answer but then selects feature values that are more closely associated with a conflicting answer to the same question, the advisor should notify the user.

4   Prototype

We implemented a prototype of our integrated system with the graph-based approach (Sect. 3.1). We chose laptops as a domain as they are typical search products [48]. Many different factors have to be considered in choosing the right model, and a variety of features are usually available even for single models of a specific brand. The dataset was collected from publicly available laptops in an online store of a notebook retailer. It consists of 2 018 products and information on 19 features as well as of prices and average ratings on a 5-star scale.

Both the questions and the advisor's answers were formulated with a focus on the task users might want to perform with a laptop, reducing the need for specific domain knowledge. The structure of the advisor, as well as the information needed to relate the answers to the laptop's data set, was created with the help of 5 domain experts. They also provided the necessary explanations. Then, the data was transformed into a graph using a *Neo4j*[1] graph database.

The interface of the integrated system (Fig. 2) displays the filter and advisor components simultaneously. Users can narrow down the result set by using filters (1) and range sliders (2) and at the same time receive a list of results that has been tailored to their specific requirements through questions and answers with

---

[1] https://www.neo4j.com/

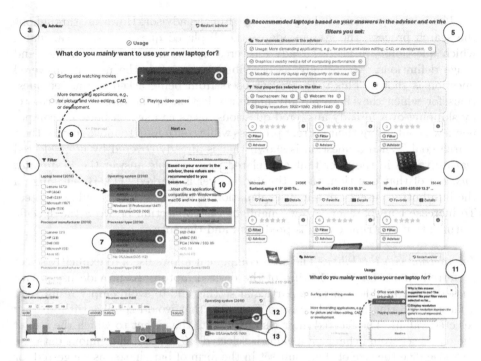

Fig. 2. Screenshots of the prototypical implementation of the integrated system combining advisor and filter mechanisms.

the help of the dialog-based advisor (3). The results list is displayed in the lower part of the right-hand side of the page (4). Initially, this list is sorted based on the popularity of the products, which we define as a weighted product of mean item rating and rating frequency. An explanation of how the result list is generated is displayed in the upper pane (5), along with a summary of the selected answers, filters, and value ranges (6). The result list is updated every time the user changes filters or answers a question in the advisor.

Interacting with the Advisor. Once the user selects an answer, matching filter values are highlighted in green within the filter component. If filter values are defined that do not match this answer, they are highlighted in purple (7). Similarly, numeric feature recommendations appear as ranges below the range sliders (8). In addition, the relationship between the answer and the filter is visualized by an animated arrow (9). This arrow automatically disappears after a short time to avoid cluttering the interface. Explanations (10) about the importance of certain feature values are displayed for the given answer. Note that to avoid information overload, only one explanation is displayed for each related feature. These explanations and the arrow connection to the answer can be toggled on and off by clicking an info button next to the feature value recommendations.

The initial question is always displayed in the advisor. However, throughout the search process, the system adapts the displayed questions as it calculates which questions are likely already answered by the users' selected values and range definitions. Accordingly, as described in Sect. 3.1, the next unanswered question is shown. This is to prevent users from being asked to answer questions for which they have already made a selection in the filter. Furthermore, by skipping over already answered questions, users can switch between components without losing their current progress while continuing to move toward their search goal. When a question is shown that is already covered by user-selected feature values in the filter that are related to a possible answer (i.e., *estimated answer*) of that question, the estimated answer is marked (11). By clicking on the info button, users can see an explanation of why this answer is highlighted. To increase transparency, arrows highlight the connection between the specific features that contribute to this prediction and the answer.

Interacting with the Filter. The filter component allows users to explicitly select preferred values for each feature of the desired laptop. To provide users with cues about available items in a particular setting and to avoid empty result sets, a faceted filtering approach grays out options that would conflict with already selected values. The faceted filter also highlights the extent to which the size of the result set would change if a value is selected [19,57]. For continuous data, we also visualize the size of the result set in the form of bar charts, as suggested for faceted filtering in [26]. When recommendations from the advisor are displayed in the filter component, users can deselect recommended feature values that should not be considered for the result list (12). Non-recommended feature values (i.e., those highlighted in purple) that should still be considered, can be selected by the user (13). Since the recommended ranges are displayed below the range slider, ranges can be constrained with the slider.

5   Empirical Evaluation

A quantitative analysis was performed to determine whether the availability of filter and advisor and their close coupling leads to an improvement of the user experience. Furthermore, we aim to draw conclusions as to whether the chosen form of visualization of the coupling and the associated explanations are comprehensible to the users and provide them with added value. Our hypotheses for this purpose are as follows: Compared to systems where the components are presented separately, the combination of advisor and filter ...

H1 a) ... increases the perceived transparency of the advisory process.
    b) ... increases the perceived control of the advisory process.
    c) ... increases the perceived acceptance of the advisory process.
    d) ... increases the perceived trust in the system.
H2 ... has a positive effect on the perceived explanation quality.
H3 ... results in increased knowledge of relevant features.

5.1 Method

To evaluate the hypotheses, an online user study was conducted. Therefore, in addition to the integrated system described in Sect. 4, two additional system variants were implemented and served as comparable systems:

C *Conventional System*: Participants had access to a number of filters and to the conversational advisor. Each component was located on a separate page, accessible via a navigation menu that was permanently visible at the top. We randomized the navigation menu to cater for potential ordering effects. Both components had their own set of recommended products.

H *Hybrid System*: The filters and conversational advisor were presented on the same page so that participants had access to both components without switching pages. Recommendations were shown in a single combined list of results. The products displayed were generated based on the input from the two available components (as described in Sect. 4). For each product, it was indicated whether it matches the answers and/or the filter set.

HE *Hybrid System with Explanations*: In addition to the system presented in the condition *H* described above, the filter component highlights filter and range value recommendations, as described in Sect. 4, based on answers given in the advisor. Additionally, relationships between given answers and filters are presented and explained.

Furthermore, in all three conditions, participants could inspect the details of a selected product on a separate page. For the purpose of this study, we also implemented a shopping basket. Participants were randomly assigned to the conditions in a between-subjects design.

Questionnaires and Interaction. First, after a brief introduction, we asked for demographic details (age, gender, country, education); measured domain knowledge with self-constructed items; and assessed affinity for technology, using items from [15]. These items and all items described below had 5-point Likert response scales, unless otherwise noted. In addition, we presented a screenshot of a real-world instance of each component featured in the prototype (e.g. a product advisor for bikes), and asked participants about their previous use of and attitude towards this kind of decision-making aid.

At the end of the first questionnaire section, we presented a search task where participants had to interact with the prototype system. The task was presented as follows: *Imagine your current laptop broke down. Please try to find laptops that fit to your personal needs. Using all available interaction possibilities in whatever way you like, including the two components, please try to find at least one suitable laptop for you, and put it into the shopping basket!* We avoided mentioning explicit criteria in the task descriptions so that participants would not be able to simply translate the given requirements into filter criteria.

Participants were next asked to briefly outline their use case for such a replacement laptop. They were then asked to rate a list of 19 features–all available as filters in the prototype–in terms of relevancy to their use case. As an alternative to assessing relevance, an additional feature-specific option allowed users to indicate that they did not have knowledge about it. This is to determine their knowledge of specific features for the use case they described. To assess whether the interaction with the system led to an improvement of the knowledge about the relevant features, we repeated this part of the questionnaire after interacting with the prototype. Participants were then asked to use the prototype system to complete the pre-defined task. They were allowed to complete the task at any time, as long as they put at least one item into the shopping basket.

The second part of the questionnaire evaluated the participants' perception of the interaction with the system and its components. First, we re-evaluated the knowledge about the relevance of the features with respect to the previously described use case. As a reminder, we presented participants with the use case description they had written before the interaction. Next, separately for each component, we used established constructs to measure the related usage effort [28], ease of use, and usefulness [41]. Using constructs from [32], we measured perceived control and understandability as well as acceptance of the components and their transparency [29] the latter with items that had 7-point Likert response scales. Participants were also able to indicate that they had not used a component, which meant that none of the previously mentioned items were displayed for that component. Using self-generated items, we asked participants if they would use the system, the advisor, and the filter component again.

Next, we assessed the general usability by means of the *System Usability Scale* (SUS) [6] and the short version of the *User Experience Questionnaire* (UEQ-S), with items on a 7-point bipolar scale ranging from -3 to 3 [47]. In addition, we measured the participants' satisfaction with the laptop they chose, the perceived difficulty of making that choice, and the perceived quality of results when using the corresponding constructs proposed in [28]. Regarding the system as a whole, we asked questions related to the usage effort, ease of use, and usefulness [28,41]. Furthermore, self-generated questions about the explanatory qualities of the systems were presented, and participants assigned to the *HE* condition were asked additional questions about the visualizations. These self-generated items were designed to test whether participants understood our chosen visualizations. For this purpose, participants were presented with screenshots of the corresponding visualizations and asked to select the correct answer from a list. They were also given the option to indicate that they were not sure. We were interested in whether the participants understood what the visualizations for (non-) recommended feature values and value ranges looked like. In addition, participants were asked questions about manipulating the recommended values (deselecting recommended values; adding non-recommended values). Finally, the constructs related to perceived control, understandability [32], and acceptance of the system and its transparency [29] were assessed again for all participants. This time, however, in relation to the system as a whole.

Participants. We recruited 128 participants on Prolific.[2] Preliminary screening was based on the following criteria to ensure sufficient quality of results: (1) participants had to be fluent in English, (2) their success rate on Prolific had to be greater than 98 %, (3) they had to have completed at least 30 studies, and (4) they were required to use a different device than a smartphone or tablet to ensure that the prototypes were always displayed in an adequate manner.

120 participants, 60 of which were female, finished the study. Given the average duration of 16.50 minutes ($SD = 5.52$), we compensated them with £3.50. Their age ranged from 21 to 71 ($M = 33.48$, $SD = 12.07$). The majority had a university degree (54.2 %), 17.5 % a certificate of secondary education, or a higher education entrance qualification (11.7 %). Most participants were from the United Kingdom (25.0 %), Italy (17.0 %), South Africa (13.3 %), or Germany (12.5 %). Domain knowledge was in an upper medium range ($M = 3.25$, $SD = 1.22$), and participants indicated to have a rather high affinity for technology ($M = 4.05$, $SD = 1.08$). The majority (64.3 %) had searched for a laptop during the last 12 months. Of these, 23.9 % searched during the last 30 d. 22.5 % last looked for a laptop 1–3 years or more than 3 years ago (21.7 %). Conditions, i.e. the three different systems, were equally distributed among participants.

5.2   Results

We used an α-level of .05 for all statistical tests. Tests of the *a priori* hypotheses were conducted using Benjamini-Hochberg adjusted α-levels [4].

Table 1. The use of filter and advisor components prior to and during the study.

(a) Mean values and standard deviations with respect to *prior experience* with components. Higher values indicate better results.

	Filter		Advisor	
	M	SD	M	SD
Usage frequency	4.40	0.80	2.41	1.05
Overall satisfaction	3.73	0.98	2.68	1.05
Trust the advice	3.81	1.06	2.49	1.00
Follow the suggestions	3.91	0.86	2.64	1.02

(b) Percentage usage of components *during the study* across all three conditions. More than one component could be used.

Condition	Filter	Advisor
Conventional	87.0 %	55.0 %
Hybrid	82.0 %	100.0 %
Hybrid Explanations	70.0 %	95.0 %

Prior Experience. As shown in Table 1a, participants had different experiences with and attitudes towards real-world instances of the two components that were available in the prototype. Especially noteworthy is that participants often used filtering mechanisms and were generally satisfied with them. They stated that they usually trust the results obtained with this method and follow them very often. Overall ratings for the advisor were lower.

The component usage during the interaction with the prototype, divided into the three conditions, is shown in Table 1b. Participants in the *C* condition showed similar usage behavior as indicated by the participants in the previous

---

[2] https://www.prolific.co/

Table 2. Perception of the system: Results of 1-way ANOVAs between conditions. Higher values indicate better results. $df=2$, unless otherwise specified. [†]No variance homogeneity consequently interpretation of Welch test, $F(2, 73.315)$

		Conv.		Hyb.		Hyb. Expl.				
		M	SD	M	SD	M	SD	$F(2, 117)$	p	e^2
SUS		72.0	16.68	73.75	16.65	73.81	20.55	0.130	.878	-0.015
UEQ		0.89	0.98	0.82	1.06	1.38	1.21	3.170	.161	0.035
Choice	Difficulty	3.28	1.34	3.55	1.13	3.20	1.36	0.827	.513	-0.003
	Satisfaction	4.45	0.68	4.23	0.83	4.55	0.55	2.284	.247	0.021
	System	3.98	0.92	3.83	1.13	4.18	0.98	1.197	.428	0.003
Use Again	Advisor	2.83	1.55	3.40	1.43	**4.20**	1.32	9.231	<.001*	0.122
	Filter	4.38	1.15	4.05	1.11	3.88	1.02	2.157	.210	0.019
Transparency		5.60	1.26	5.12	1.76	5.92	1.28	3.078	.050	0.034
Control		3.79	0.83	3.78	0.69	3.84	0.89	0.061	.457	-0.016
Acceptance		5.28	0.98	4.93	1.34	**5.62**	1.43	3.006	.041*	0.033
Trust in System		3.60	0.90	3.73	1.01	**4.25**	0.78	5.856	.012*	0.075
Decision Confidence[†]		3.91	0.62	3.46	1.20	4.08	0.85	3.497	.054	0.059
Rec. Quality		4.15	1.00	3.93	0.92	4.30	0.83	1.697	.112	0.012

usage frequency of the components. Most participants used the filter, while just over half used the advisor. In the H condition, conversely, all participants used the advisor, while the filters were used less. In the HE condition, almost all participants used the advisor, but only 70 % relied on the filters (Table 1b).

Perception of the System. Participants rated the general usability of the prototype (SUS) in all conditions as *Good* [2] (Table 2). Multiple one-way ANOVAs were calculated to test for significant differences between conditions. Except for the HE condition, the UEQ values were rather low, although there was no significant difference. The difficulty of choosing suitable items was rated moderate. Choice satisfaction was rated good in all three conditions.

When asked whether they would use the system as a whole and the filters and advisor specifically again, the participants' answers showed a significant difference between the conditions for the advisor (Table 2). Bonferroni post-hoc tests showed a significant difference ($p < .001$) between the conditions HE and C (1.31, 95 %-CI[0.506, 2.11]). Effect size was in an upper medium range.

Perceived recommendation quality was rated equally positive in all three conditions (Table 2). The quality of the results was rated slightly higher in the HE condition. In contrast, the recommendations in the H condition were rated slightly lower than those in the other two conditions, but the differences were not significant.

Transparency and acceptance of the system scored high. Perceived control was also in the upper range. As shown in the lower part Table 2, of the three conditions, the system in the HE condition was rated highest in all factors, followed by the variant of condition C. For the factor *acceptance*, we observed a significant difference with small effect size. Again, a significant difference ($p = .047$) between conditions HE and H was found using post-hoc tests (0.69, 95 %-CI[0.01, 1.38]).

Table 3. Perception of the components: Results of 1-way ANOVAs between conditions. Higher values indicate better results. [†]No variance homogeneity consequently interpretation of Welch test

		Conv.[1]		Hyb.[2]		Hyb. Expl.[3]						
		M	SD	M	SD	M	SD	df_1	df_2	F	p	ϵ^2
Effort	Advisor	3.93	0.91	3.96	0.92	4.21	0.76	2	98	1.080	.344	0.022
	Filter[†]	3.60	0.83	3.55	0.95	3.48	1.14	2	59.25	0.110	.896	-0.018
Ease of Use	Advisor[†]	4.17	1.13	3.91	0.72	**4.41**	0.71	2	50.73	4.680	.014*	0.048
	Filter	4.07	1.03	3.93	0.87	3.73	0.85	2	94	0.716	.491	-0.006
Usefulness	Advisor	4.04	1.14	3.65	1.09	4.11	1.01	2	98	1.994	.142	0.019
	Filter	3.99	1.00	3.53	1.21	3.71	0.95	2	94	1.600	.207	-0.012
Transparency	Advisor[†]	5.33	1.40	4.96	1.94	**5.94**	1.09	2	52.50	4.343	.027*	-0.160
	Filter	6.06	1.25	5.84	1.48	5.94	1.07	2	94	0.247	.469	-0.016
Control	Advisor	3.15	0.42	3.14	0.53	3.33	0.40	2	98	1.991	.142	-0.017
	Filter	3.79	0.82	3.92	0.89	3.82	0.85	2	94	0.213	.404	-0.017
Acceptance	Advisor	5.15	1.48	4.45	1.70	**5.57**	1.53	2	98	4.920	.027*	-0.013
	Filter	5.62	1.25	5.34	1.54	5.57	1.25	2	94	0.394	.507	-0.013

[1] $N_{Advisor} = 23$, $N_{Filter} = 35$; [2] $N_{Advisor} = 40$, $N_{Filter} = 33$; [3] $N_{Advisor} = 38$, $N_{Filter} = 29$

Moreover, we found a significant difference in terms of trust in the system, with a moderate effect size, as shown in Table 2. The HE system was rated significantly ($p = .005$) better than the C system (0.65, 95 %-CI[0.16, 1.14]) and also significantly ($p = .031$) better than the system in condition H (0.53, 95 %-CI[0.04, 1.01]). However, there was no significant difference between the HE and C. In addition, the quality of recommendations was rated equally positive, and participants were confident in their decision in all three conditions.

The detailed evaluation of the individual components with regard to their ease of use and the assessment of effort and usefulness (Table 3) shows that all scores were rather positive in all tested conditions. In terms of ease of use, there was a significant difference between the conditions for the advisor. Post-hoc tests showed a significant difference ($p = .028$) between the conditions HE and H (0.50, 95 %-CI[0.40, 0.95]). Overall, effect sizes were rather small.

Focusing on the individual components with regard to transparency, control, and acceptance, the advisor was rated higher in the HE condition than in the other two conditions (Table 3). In terms of perceived transparency, there was a significant difference between the conditions. However, the effect size was small. Post-hoc tests revealed a significant difference ($p = .019$) between conditions H and HE (0.98, 95 %-CI[0.13, 1.84]). Similarly, there was a difference in acceptance. Again, there was a significant ($p = .007$) difference between the two hybrid conditions (1.12, 95 %-CI[0.24, 1.99]). Perceived control of the filter component was the only factor in which the HE condition performed better (Table 3). Apart from this aspect, the best results were obtained in the C condition. With regard to the filter component, however, there were no significant differences between the conditions for any of the factors tested.

Explanation Quality. In the following, we present how participants perceived the explanations of the advisor. Again, multiple one-way ANOVAs were calculated to test for significant differences between conditions. Perceived explanation quality was rated highest in the *HE* condition. The system in condition *H* consistently received the lowest ratings (Table 4). There were significant differences in all tested factors. While the effect size for explanation relevance was large, the effect sizes for the other factors tested were moderate. Bonferroni post-hoc tests indicated that there was a significant difference ($p = .009$) between *HE* and *H* regarding explanation satisfaction (0.66, 95 %-CI[0.13, 1.19]).

Explanatory relevance was rated significantly ($p < .001$) higher by participants in the *HE* condition than by participants in the *H* condition (1.03, 95 %-CI[0.50, 1.55]). Moreover, the explanatory relevance in the conventional condition was rated significantly ($p = .019$) higher compared to the *H* condition (0.60, 95 %-CI[0.08, 1.12]). Participants rated the sufficiency of the explanation significantly ($p = .002$) higher in the *HE* condition than in the *H* condition (0.80, 95 %-CI[0.23, 1.37]). Similarly, the explanation presentation was rated highest in the *HE* condition. Again, there was only a significant difference ($p = .041$) between the conditions *HE* and *H* (0.60, 95 %-CI[0.02, 1.18]).

Table 4. Explanation quality: Results of 1-way ANOVAs between conditions. Higher values indicate better results. [†]No variance homogeneity consequently interpretation of Welch test; [1]$F(2, 75.324)$; [2]$F(2, 76.656)$

	Conv.		Hyb.		Hyb. Expl.				
	M	*SD*	*M*	*SD*	*M*	*SD*	$F(2, 117)$	p	ϵ^2
Expl. Satisfaction	3.89	0.75	3.45	1.16	**4.11**	0.96	4.790	.007*	0.060
Expl. Relevancy[†,1]	3.93	0.86	3.33	1.23	**4.35**	0.74	10.585	<.001*	0.163
Expl. Sufficiency[†,2]	3.78	0.90	3.21	1.26	**4.01**	0.93	5.230	.007*	0.081
Expl. Presentation	3.88	0.91	3.40	1.22	**4.00**	1.06	3.500	.017*	0.040

Three one-tailed paired *t*-tests were conducted to determine whether participants in the *HE* condition were more likely than participants in the other conditions to appraise which item features were relevant to their intended use.[3] We thus analyzed whether participants were able to indicate the relevance of more features for their use case after the interaction. In order to measure this, we looked at the number of features for which participants were able to indicate relevance–before and after interaction with the respective system variants. Participants in the *HE* condition were able to provide statements regarding relevance for significantly ($t(39) = 3.078$, $p = .006$, $d = -0.49$) more features after interacting ($M = 17.80$, $SD = 2.20$) with the system than before interacting with it ($M = 16.78$, $SD = 3.88$). No significant differences were observed in the other two conditions. However, a positive trend was observed in the *H* condition. Before the interaction, the mean number of relevancies given was 16.83 ($SD = 3.93$); after interacting, the value increased slightly ($M = 17.05$, $SD = 3.95$; $t(39) = -1.778$, $p = .063$, $d = -0.28$). In the *C* condition, the average number of stated relevancies

---

[3] A mixed ANOVA was originally computed, but due to violations of homogeneity of variance and homogeneity of covariance matrices, the results could not be interpreted.

was the same before ($M=16.80$, $SD=3.98$) and after ($M=16.80$, $SD=3.83$) the interaction ($t(39)=0.000$, $p=.500$, $d=0.00$).

Understanding of Visualizations. In the *HE* condition, the majority of participants (77.0 %) were able to make sense of the visualization of the values recommended by the advisor (incorrect: 20.0 %; not sure: 2.5 %). Fewer participants were able to correctly (60.0 %) identify the visualization of values that were not recommended (incorrect: 25.0 %; not sure: 15.0 %). Additionally, less clear was the possibility of manipulating the (non-) recommended values. The ability to deselect recommended values was only noticed by 62.5 % of the participants (incorrect: 22.5 %; not sure: 15.0 %). Similarly, the visualization of selected, but non-recommended values was only recognized by 50 % of the participants (incorrect: 37.5 %; not sure: 12.5 %). However, the majority of participants (85.0 %) were familiar with the advisor's visualization of recommended ranges. (incorrect: 15.0 %). 82.5 % of the participants were aware of the visualization of non-recommended ranges (incorrect: 12.5 %; not sure: 5.0 %). The majority of participants understood the chosen visualization for suggesting appropriate answers in the advisor; 72.5 % were able to correctly identify that the suggestion was based on their previous interaction with the system (incorrect: 17.5 %; not sure: 10.0 %).

5.3   Discussion

In both of our blended systems, with and without explanations, participants almost always used the advisor and less often the filter. This is remarkable insofar as advisors in most online shops are either not available at all or only restrictively available, for example, can only be reached via a separate page. One could, therefore, assume that the orientation towards filters would initially be greater due to greater familiarity with these. As in our study the advisor was directly integrated and presented an easy-to-answer question about the intended use, the inclination to turn to the advisor seems to be rather pronounced. In fact, participants in the *HE* condition were those most likely to say they would use the advisor again. This suggests that the integrated system provides added value to participants, especially in light of their previous experience with advisors, where scores were in the mid-range. Furthermore, no significant differences were found between the conditions in terms of usability, although the interface was more complex due to the simultaneous display of the components and additional information which could lead to a higher cognitive load.

In terms of component perception, ease of use was rated higher in the *HE* condition than in the other conditions. Here, the presence of additional explanations, arrow animations, and filter recommendations may have had a positive effect by clarifying the implications of choosing an answer. We only observed significant differences between the conditions *H* and *HE* when evaluating the advisor component in terms of transparency and acceptance. Similar results between the *C* and *HE* conditions may be explained by the combined result list of the integrated system. Due to the missing explanations, the presentation and thus the recommendation process was not understandable, leading to limited perceived transparency, control, and acceptance. Since the hybrid system with explanations performed as well as the conventional system, we must reject *H1*.

While there were no significant differences between the tested conditions in terms of usability, there were significant differences in terms of transparency of results and acceptance. This may be due to the fact that the usability questionnaires covered broader aspects so that the differences between the conditions were less pronounced. The more specific transparency and acceptance questionnaires capture the differences between the conditions more clearly.

Finally, the explanation quality of the system was rated best in the *HE* condition. However, the perceived recommendation quality was also rated rather positively in the *C* condition–significantly better than in the *H* condition i.e. in the hybrid system without explanations. This could be due to the fact that the combination of both components and the presentation of the results in a combined list requires more explanation than when both components are available separately. This is particularly clear regarding the explanation sufficiency, where the *H* system scored the lowest. Since only one of the two tested conditions of the hybrid system was rated better than the system in the *C* condition in terms of explanation quality, i.e. the system with additional explanations, we can only partially accept *H2*. However, the ability of participants in the *HE* condition to indicate relevance to their use case for significantly more features after the interaction demonstrates the usefulness, at least for the *HE* system, suggesting a partial acceptance of *H3*. Hybrid systems that combine different components should clearly present and communicate this combination. The importance of explanations and clear presentation can be observed in the evaluation of the visualizations chosen in condition *HE*. While most of the visualizations and color schemes were correctly understood by a majority of participants, the manipulation options of the displayed recommendations were not fully intelligible to all participants–despite explanatory tooltips.

Since the proposed system has not been tested in a real-world environment with actual customers, which would allow for realistic user data, the results discussed were based on an artificial study environment and rely on a cover story. We conducted our study through a crowd-sourcing platform, which allowed us to recruit a larger (but still not representative) sample than in a laboratory setting. However, due to the pre-screening process (Sect. 5.1), which only allowed participants who were fluent in English to participate, and the short time available for reaching the desired sample size, the diversity of participants was limited. Although it is difficult to replicate the search and decision behavior of real users in an artificial study environment, we expect that the results are at least indicative of the expected user experience of such a system.

Finally, our current approach requires a potentially large amount of effort to manually build parts of the graph model, especially to establish connections between the advisor and the product features. While we rely on domain experts to create relevant connections between the advisor and the product features and to write explanations, there are approaches that can mitigate this effort, e.g., by reusing existing ontologies [7,10,38] or by automatically extracting structures from textual sources like product descriptions or reviews [5,11,12].

6   Conclusions

With the conducted user study, we have shown that our proposed integration of a dialog-based product advisor into a filtering system through a graph-based approach was well accepted by the participants. We were able to show that by displaying recommendations and explanations directly in the filter component, acceptance and trust in the system can be increased. Similarly, combining the advisor with the filters along with the displayed explanations increased trust in the advisor. However, in future work, we plan to investigate how the graph-based approach can be improved by incorporating additional information, such as user behavior, to update the edge weights and improve the recommendations. Since the chosen product domain of laptops is very specific, future work should investigate whether our approach is also applicable and advantageous in other product domains. Furthermore, we will explore whether other decision support tools in online stores, such as chatbots, can also benefit from an integration into a filtering system.

References

1. Al-Natour, S., Benbasat, I., Centefelli, R.: Trustworthy virtual advisors and enjoyable interactions: designing for expressiveness and transparency. In: Alexander, P.M., Turpin, M., van Deventer, J.P. (eds.) Proceedings of the 18th European Conference on Information Systems, p. 116. ECIS '10 (2010)
2. Bangor, A., Kortum, P., Miller, J.: Determining what individual SUS scores mean: adding an adjective rating scale. J. Usability Stud. 4(3), 114–123 (2009)
3. Benbasat, I., Wang, W.: Trust in and adoption of online recommendation agents. J. Assoc. Inf. Syst. 6(3), 4 (2005)
4. Benjamini, Y., Hochberg, Y.: Controlling the false discovery rate: a practical and powerful approach to multiple testing. J. Royal Stat. Soc. Ser. B (Methodological) 57(1), 289–300 (1995)
5. Bing, L., Wong, T.L., Lam, W.: Unsupervised extraction of popular product attributes from e-commerce web sites by considering customer reviews. ACM Trans. Internet Technol. 16(2) (2016). https://doi.org/10.1145/2857054
6. Brooke, J.: SUS: a "quick and dirty" usability scale. Usability Evaluation in Industry 189 (1996)
7. Buitelaar, P., Cimiano, P., Frank, A., Hartung, M., Racioppa, S.: Ontology-based information extraction and integration from heterogeneous data sources. Int. J. Hum.-Comput. Stud. 66(11), 759–788 (2008). https://doi.org/10.1016/j.ijhcs.2008.07.007
8. Castagnos, S., Jones, N., Pu, P.: Recommenders' influence on buyers' decision process. In: Proceedings of the 3rd ACM Conference on Recommender Systems, pp. 361–364. RecSys '09, ACM, New York, NY, USA (2009)
9. Chicaiza, J., Valdiviezo-Diaz, P.: A comprehensive survey of knowledge graph-based recommender systems: technologies, development, and contributions. Information 12(6), 232 (2021). https://doi.org/10.3390/info12060232

10. Di Noia, T., Mirizzi, R., Ostuni, V.C., Romito, D., Zanker, M.: Linked open data to support content-based recommender systems. In: Proceedings of the 8th International Conference on Semantic Systems, pp. 1–8. I-SEMANTICS '12, Association for Computing Machinery, New York, NY, USA (2012). https://doi.org/10.1145/2362499.2362501

11. Dong, R., Schaal, M., O'Mahony, M.P., McCarthy, K., Smyth, B.: Opinionated product recommendation. In: Delany, S.J., Ontañón, S. (eds.) Case-Based Reasoning Research and Development, pp. 44–58. Springer, Berlin Heidelberg, Berlin, Heidelberg (2013)

12. Donkers, T., Kleemann, T., Ziegler, J.: Explaining recommendations by means of aspect-based transparent memories. In: Proceedings of the 25th International Conference on Intelligent User Interfaces, pp. 166–176. IUI '20, Association for Computing Machinery, New York, NY, USA (2020). https://doi.org/10.1145/3377325.3377520

13. Dooms, S., De Pessemier, T., Martens, L.: Improving IMDb movie recommendations with interactive settings and filters. In: Proceedings of the 8th ACM Conference on Recommender Systems. Poster-RecSys '14, vol. 1247. ACM (2014)

14. Felfernig, A., Friedrich, G., Jannach, D., Zanker, M.: An integrated environment for the development of knowledge-based recommender applications. Int. J. Electron. Commerce **11**(2), 11–34 (2006). https://doi.org/10.2753/JEC1086-4415110201

15. Franke, T., Attig, C., Wessel, D.: A personal resource for technology interaction: development and validation of the affinity for technology interaction (ATI) scale. Int. J. Hum.-Comput. Interact. **35**(6), 456–467 (2019). https://doi.org/10.1080/10447318.2018.1456150

16. Gomez-Uribe, C.A., Hunt, N.: The Netflix recommender system: algorithms, business value, and innovation. ACM Trans. Manage. Inf. Syst. **6**(4), 13:1-13:19 (2015)

17. Häubl, G., Murray, K.B.: Double agents: assessing the role of electronic product recommendation systems. Sloan Manage. Rev. **47**(3), 8–12 (2005). https://doi.org/10.2139/ssrn.964191

18. Häubl, G., Trifts, V.: Consumer decision making in online shopping environments: the effects of interactive decision aids. Market. Sci. **19**(1), 4–21 (2000)

19. Hearst, M.A.: Search User Interfaces. Cambridge University Press, USA (2009)

20. Hernandez-Bocanegra, D.C., Ziegler, J.: Explaining recommendations through conversations - dialog model and the effects of interface type and degree of interactivity. ACM Trans. Interact. Intell. Syst. (2023). https://doi.org/10.1145/3579541

21. Jannach, D., Manzoor, A., Cai, W., Chen, L.: A survey on conversational recommender systems. ACM Comput. Surv. **54**(5) (2021). https://doi.org/10.1145/3453154

22. Jawaheer, G., Weller, P., Kostkova, P.: Modeling user preferences in recommender systems: a classification framework for explicit and implicit user feedback. ACM Trans. Interact. Intell. Syst. **4**(2), 8:1-8:26 (2014)

23. Kleemann, T., Loepp, B., Ziegler, J.: Towards multi-method support for product search and recommending. In: Adjunct Proceedings of the 30th ACM Conference on User Modeling, Adaptation and Personalization, pp. 74–79. UMAP '22 Adjunct, Association for Computing Machinery, New York, NY, USA (2022). https://doi.org/10.1145/3511047.3536408

24. Kleemann, T., Wagner, M., Loepp, B., Ziegler, J.: Modeling user interaction at the convergence of filtering mechanisms, recommender algorithms and advisory components. In: Proceedings of the Conference on Mensch und Computer, pp. 531–543. MuC '21, ACM, New York, NY, USA (2021)

25. Kleemann, T., Ziegler, J.: Integration of dialog-based product advisors into filter systems. In: Proceedings of the Conference on Mensch und Computer, pp. 67–77. MuC '19, Association for Computing Machinery, New York, NY, USA (2019). https://doi.org/10.1145/3340764.3340786

26. Kleemann, T., Ziegler, J.: Distribution sliders: visualizing data distributions in range selection sliders. In: Proceedings of the Conference on Mensch und Computer, pp. 67–78. MuC '20, Association for Computing Machinery, New York, NY, USA (2020). https://doi.org/10.1145/3404983.3405512

27. Knijnenburg, B.P., Willemsen, M.C., Gantner, Z., Soncu, H., Newell, C.: Explaining the user experience of recommender systems. User Model. User-Adapted Interact. **22**(4), 441–504 (2012). https://doi.org/10.1007/s11257-011-9118-4

28. Knijnenburg, B.P., Willemsen, M.C., Kobsa, A.: A pragmatic procedure to support the user-centric evaluation of recommender systems. In: Proceedings of the Fifth ACM Conference on Recommender Systems, pp. 321–324. RecSys '11, Association for Computing Machinery, New York, NY, USA (2011). https://doi.org/10.1145/2043932.2043993

29. Köhler, C.F., Breugelmans, E., Dellaert, B.G.C.: Consumer acceptance of recommendations by interactive decision aids: the joint role of temporal distance and concrete versus abstract communications. J. Manage. Inf. Syst. **27**(4), 231–260 (2011)

30. Konstan, J.A., Riedl, J.: Recommender systems: from algorithms to user experience. User Model. User-Adapted Interact. **22**(1–2), 101–123 (2012)

31. Koren, J., Zhang, Y., Liu, X.: Personalized interactive faceted search. In: Proceedings of the 17th International Conference on World Wide Web. p. 477–486. WWW '08, Association for Computing Machinery, New York, NY, USA (2008). https://doi.org/10.1145/1367497.1367562

32. Liang, Y., Willemsen, M.C.: Interactive music genre exploration with visualization and mood control. In: Proceedings of the 26th International Conference on Intelligent User Interfaces, pp. 175–185. IUI '21, ACM, New York, NY, USA (2021)

33. Liu, C., Li, L., Yao, X., Tang, L.: A survey of recommendation algorithms based on knowledge graph embedding. In: Proceedings of the 2019 IEEE International Conference on Computer Science and Educational Informatization, pp. 168–171. CSEI '19, IEEE (2019). https://doi.org/10.1109/CSEI47661.2019.8938875

34. Loepp, B., Donkers, T., Kleemann, T., Ziegler, J.: Impact of item consumption on assessment of recommendations in user studies. In: Proceedings of the 12th ACM Conference on Recommender Systems, pp. 49–53. RecSys '18, ACM, New York, NY, USA (2018)

35. Loepp, B., Donkers, T., Kleemann, T., Ziegler, J.: Interactive recommending with tag-enhanced matrix factorization (TagMF). Int. J. Hum.-Comput. Stud. **121**, 21–41 (2019)

36. Loepp, B., Herrmanny, K., Ziegler, J.: Blended recommending: integrating interactive information filtering and algorithmic recommender techniques. In: Proceedings of the 33rd Annual ACM Conference on Human Factors in Computing Systems, pp. 975–984. CHI '15, Association for Computing Machinery, New York, NY, USA (2015). https://doi.org/10.1145/2702123.2702496

37. Loepp, B., Ziegler, J.: Towards interactive recommending in model-based collaborative filtering systems. In: Proceedings of the 13th ACM Conference on Recommender Systems, pp. 546–547. RecSys '19, ACM, New York, NY, USA (2019)

38. Musto, C., Basile, P., Lops, P., de Gemmis, M., Semeraro, G.: Introducing linked open data in graph-based recommender systems. Inf. Process. Manage. **53**(2), 405–435 (2017). https://doi.org/10.1016/j.ipm.2016.12.003

39. Musto, C., Basile, P., Semeraro, G.: Hybrid semantics-aware recommendations exploiting knowledge graph embeddings. In: Alviano, M., Greco, G., Scarcello, F. (eds.) AI*IA 2019. LNCS (LNAI), vol. 11946, pp. 87–100. Springer, Cham (2019). https://doi.org/10.1007/978-3-030-35166-3_7

40. Pu, P., Chen, L.: Trust building with explanation interfaces. In: Proceedings of the 11th International Conference on Intelligent User Interfaces, pp. 93–100. IUI '06, Association for Computing Machinery, New York, NY, USA (2006). https://doi.org/10.1145/1111449.1111475

41. Pu, P., Chen, L., Hu, R.: A user-centric evaluation framework for recommender systems. In: Proceedings of the 5th ACM Conference on Recommender Systems, pp. 157–164. RecSys '11, Association for Computing Machinery, New York, NY, USA (2011). https://doi.org/10.1145/2043932.2043962

42. Pu, P., Chen, L., Hu, R.: Evaluating recommender systems from the user's perspective: survey of the state of the art. User Model. User-Adapted Interact. **22**(4), 317–355 (2012). https://doi.org/10.1007/s11257-011-9115-7

43. Ramesh, K., Ravishankaran, S., Joshi, A., Chandrasekaran, K.: A survey of design techniques for conversational agents. In: Kaushik, S., Gupta, D., Kharb, L., Chahal, D. (eds.) Information, Communication and Computing Technology, pp. 336–350. Springer, Singapore (2017). https://doi.org/10.1007/978-981-10-6544-6_31

44. Ricci, F., Rokach, L., Shapira, B.: Recommender systems: techniques, applications, and challenges, pp. 1–35. Springer, US, New York, NY (2022). https://doi.org/10.1007/978-1-0716-2197-4_1

45. Sacco, G.M., Tzitzikas, Y.: Dynamic taxonomies and faceted search: theory, practice, and experience, vol. 25. Springer Science & Business Media (2009)

46. Schaffer, J., Humann, J., O'Donovan, J., Höllerer, T.: Contemporary research: models, methodologies, and measures in distributed team cognition, chap. quantitative modeling of dynamic human-agent cognition, pp. 137–186. CRC Press, Boca Raton, FL, USA (2020)

47. Schrepp, M., Hinderks, A., Thomaschewski, J.: Design and evaluation of a short version of the user experience questionnaire (UEQ-S). Int. J. Interact. Multimedia Artif. Intell. **4**(6), 103–108 (2017)

48. Senecal, S., Nantel, J.: The influence of online product recommendations on consumers' online choices. J. Retail. **80**(2), 159–169 (2004). https://doi.org/10.1016/j.jretai.2004.04.001

49. Sinha, R., Swearingen, K.: The role of transparency in recommender systems. In: Extended Abstracts on Human Factors in Computing Systems, pp. 830–831. CHI EA '02, Association for Computing Machinery, New York, NY, USA (2002). https://doi.org/10.1145/506443.506619

50. Smith, B., Linden, G.: Two decades of recommender systems at Amazon.com. IEEE Internet Comput. **21**(3), 12–18 (2017)

51. Sun, Y., Zhang, Y.: Conversational recommender system. In: The 41st International ACM SIGIR Conference on Research & Development in Information Retrieval, pp. 235–244. SIGIR '18, Association for Computing Machinery, New York, NY, USA (2018). https://doi.org/10.1145/3209978.3210002

52. Tintarev, N.: Explanations of recommendations. In: Proceedings of the 2007 ACM Conference on Recommender Systems, pp. 203–206. RecSys '07, Association for Computing Machinery, New York, NY, USA (2007). https://doi.org/10.1145/1297231.1297275

53. Tintarev, N., Masthoff, J.: Effective explanations of recommendations: user-centered design. In: Proceedings of the 2007 ACM Conference on Recommender

Systems, pp. 153–156. RecSys '07, Association for Computing Machinery, New York, NY, USA (2007). https://doi.org/10.1145/1297231.1297259

54. Vig, J., Sen, S., Riedl, J.: Tagsplanations: explaining recommendations using tags. In: Proceedings of the 14th International Conference on Intelligent User Interfaces, pp. 47–56. IUI '09, Association for Computing Machinery, New York, NY, USA (2009). https://doi.org/10.1145/1502650.1502661

55. Virdi, P., Kalro, A.D., Sharma, D.: Online decision aids: the role of decision-making styles and decision-making stages. Int. J. Retail Distrib. Manage. **48**(6), 555–574 (2020). https://doi.org/10.1108/IJRDM-02-2019-0068

56. Weizenbaum, J.: Eliza-a computer program for the study of natural language communication between man and machine. Commun. ACM **9**(1), 36–45 (1966)

57. Yee, K.P., Swearingen, K., Li, K., Hearst, M.: Faceted metadata for image search and browsing. In: Proceedings of the SIGCHI Conference on Human Factors in Computing Systems, pp. 401–408. CHI '03, Association for Computing Machinery, New York, NY, USA (2003). https://doi.org/10.1145/642611.642681

58. Zou, X.: A survey on application of knowledge graph. In: 4th International Conference on Control Engineering and Artificial Intelligence. CCEAI '20, vol. 1487. IOP Publishing (2020). https://doi.org/10.1088/1742-6596/1487/1/012016

Everyday-Inspired Movies: Towards the Design of Movie Recommender Systems based on Everyday Life through Personal Social Media

Abhishek Kulkarni[1]([envelope]) [iD], Larry Powell[2] [iD], Shaina Murphy[1] [iD], Nanjie Rao[1] [iD], and Sharon Lynn Chu[1] [iD]

[1] University of Florida, Gainesville, FL 32611, USA
{kulkarniabhishek,shainanmurphy,raon,slchu}@ufl.edu
[2] Texas A&M University, College Town, TX 77843, USA
larry.powell@tamu.edu

Abstract. This paper proposes the idea of movie recommenders that draw from the users' everyday life happenings as documented through their personal social media posts to produce relevant recommendations. We conducted an experimental study to understand the important dimensions to consider in the design of such a recommendation system. We began with the design hypothesis that matching keywords and categories from users' social media posts to those from movie plots may increase users' perceived relevance of movie recommendations. Our analysis revealed that beyond keywords and categories, emotional context and genre of movies are important aspects to consider. Based on these findings, we discuss the implications on the design of movie recommendation systems leveraging users' everyday life through social media posts.

Keywords: Movie Recommender Systems · Social Media · Everyday Life · Personalized Recommendations

1 Introduction

Media streaming services such as Netflix typically focus on delivering tailored recommendations based on media genre, ratings, popularity, and user interaction history within their platform. Current recommendation approaches do not capture users' everyday life outside of the activity space of the media platform. Everyday life here includes life experiences of people and how they typically act, think, and feel in their daily life in response to different events and happenings [1]. Our research investigates the use of users' daily life feelings, experiences, and happenings to assist in generating relevant media recommendations. We propose that one way to access people's daily life feelings, experiences, and happenings is through their social media. Research has shown that people tend to turn to

J. Abdelnour Nocera et al. (Eds.): INTERACT 2023, LNCS 14144, pp. 160–169, 2023.
https://doi.org/10.1007/978-3-031-42286-7_9

social sharing as a means to deal with and make sense of events and interactions in their life [2,3]. Text-based social media platforms have been shown to hold valuable personal information about their users' everyday life events [4]. The main goal of this work was to understand what dimensions need to be taken into account in the design of a movie recommender system when using users' social media posts as an index to their everyday life. To enable our investigation, we implemented a basic movie recommendation system and a companion interface. We then conducted a study where participants rated their perceived relevance of movie recommendations generated by the system from their social media posts.

2   Background and Related Work

Collaborative and content-based filtering are the two main methods recommender systems use to personalize content for users [5]. Collaborative filtering leverages the preferences of similar users while content-based methods account for the user's own past interests in similar items [6]. Neither method is without its flaws or is applicable to every situation. Reliance on similar users can hinder collaborative filtering if there are initially no other users from which to base recommendations [5,7]. Similarly, the content-based approach suffers when there is a lack of information on user preferences in the initial and early stages of use [5,7]. To sidestep these pitfalls, researchers have melded the advantageous aspects of both into hybrid filtering methods [7]. Cross-domain recommender systems share knowledge of user interest and preference from domains outside of the activity space of the system to try to mitigate these problems [8]. Social media-based recommender systems can be considered a type of cross-domain recommender system where the users' social media is a domain from which to pull user interests. Prior work have been done in this direction, however many focus on exploiting meta-level aspects of the users' social media such as their likes [9], navigation [10], or social tagging [11–13]. Work that have analyzed directly the content of social media posts for recommender systems typically extract specific items such as user demographics [14], emotions [15], relationships, or scenarios [16]. Our research seeks to analyze social media posts as a source of users' possible current interests. One previous work [17] explored a similar idea, but no recommender system was built in that work. Instead, recommendation was generated manually by researchers following a systematic predefined protocol. Yet, this work still helps provide confidence in the idea that personal social media posts can effectively be used to produce movie recommendations that users deem relevant to their lives. Their study found a marginally significant difference in life satisfaction ratings after participants watched a social-media-based movie recommendation, as opposed to one selected randomly, with the former having higher ratings than the latter [17].

In contrast to that earlier work, this paper investigates the design of a recommender system embodying the idea of using personal social media posts as an input to produce assumedly personally relevant movie recommendations. Of note, our work does not attempt to investigate methods of natural language processing to analyze text in social media posts. Much other work such as Zhao et al.'s [18] address that challenge. Nor do we address new machine learning approaches for recommendation engines. The bulk of literature on recommender systems already tackle that topic. Our focus is on understanding the design factors that are important to consider in the design of a social-media-based recommender system (SMbRS) to produce personally-relevant movie recommendations.

3   System Design

The SMbRS was comprised of a 'social media post handler' and a 'movie handler'. The MovieLens database allowed the system access to over 26,780 movie titles, IMDB IDs, and plots [19]. IBM Watson Natural Language Processing API [20] was used to extract keywords and categories from both movie plots and social media posts. For both movie plots and social media posts' text inputs, we extracted at most 5 hierarchical category groups and 50 keywords.

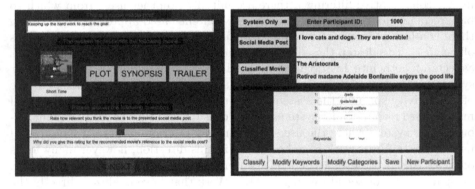

Fig. 1. (Left) Participant's user interface of the recommender system; (Right) Researcher's companion interface

Matching of keywords and categories of social media posts to those of movie plots to produce a movie recommendation was done using a nearest neighbor algorithm. A relevance value was calculated for each Social Media post-movie (thereafter referred to as SM-movie pair) such that each matching keyword contributed a value of 1. The relevance value associated with categories was influenced by a weighted value that reflected the level of specificity and closeness of the subcategories. For instance, if a movie matched to the first and most general category, the relevance value increased by 1. However, as the movie matched more specific categories, the weight was adjusted accordingly, ranging from 1 to 5. This weighting mechanism enabled the algorithm to recognize movies that aligned more closely with the user's social media post. Once both the relevance values were calculated, they were combined to give a composite score.

The algorithm then proceeded to select the movie with the highest relevance value as the primary recommendation.

We also implemented a companion interface that gave researchers the ability to modify the system-identified categories and keywords. The idea was that analyzing the human assistance given to the system would enable us to understand what is missing from the system from a design requirements point-of-view. A researcher was able to change, add, or remove individual keywords or categories, and then regenerate a movie recommendation. Figure 1 shows participants' interface of the movie recommender system and the companion interface.

4 Study Design and Methodology

Our approach to an investigation of the design factors was as follows: we first built the basic SMbRS as elaborated on in Sect. 3 to derive recommendations by extracting and matching keywords and categories between social media posts and movie plots. We then used the system as a platform to investigate what else needs to be added to optimize users' perceived relevance of the movie recommendations generated. We conducted a within-subjects study with two parts. Part A assessed whether keyword- and category-matching used in our recommender system is sufficient to produce relevant recommendations by comparing perceived relevance ratings of movie recommendations made by our system to a baseline condition of recommendations made from human judgment. In Part B, we wanted to understand how movie recommendations from the system could be improved. To that end, we used the companion interface to manipulate initial system recommendations and generated new improved ones, and then analyzed the kinds of manipulations that were done for improvement. The research questions for the study were:

RQ1: *Is there a significant difference in perceived relevance of movie recommendations based on social media posts when the recommendations are generated using the recommender system as opposed to with human judgment?*

RQ2: *What kinds of human manipulations done to the movie recommender system led to higher perceived relevance for the movie recommendations?*

For both Parts A and B of the study, the dependent variable of *perceived relevance of movie recommendations to social media posts*, was measured using a single item: "Rate how relevant you think the movie is to the presented social media post" on a 7-point Likert scale.

4.1 Study Procedures

Twenty-one participants (12 Male, 9 Female; Mean Age: 24 years; Age Range: 19 to 36) took part in the study remotely on Zoom. Based on a pre-study survey, almost half of the participants watched a movie monthly, 2 watched every 2–3 days, and the rest watched weekly. 17 participants spent an hour while 4 spent two hours daily on social media. We also collected five of each participant's existing and most recent text-based social media posts. In total, we collected 105 social media posts from the participants in the study (5 posts per X 21 participants). For each participant, 3 random posts out of the collected 5 were used for the study after applying exclusion criteria such as 'length of post must exceed 2 words'. The chosen posts were then fed into the recommender system to generate personal movie recommendations for each participant ahead of the scheduled study.

At the start of the study, participants were briefed about their task and the SMbRS was demonstrated. Participants were then given access to the system. In the SMbRS interface, participants rated movie recommendations generated by the system based on their social media posts for perceived relevance. For Study Part A, each participant rated 6 SM-movie pairs (3 movies generated by the system only and 3 movies generated from human judgment), presented in random order. For the *human judgment* study condition, to maintain consistency among researchers, a method was set up to select movie recommendations. Researchers identified keywords from participants' social media posts and entered "movies about [keywords]" in the Google search engine. The researchers then used the search results to identify relevant movies. To arrive at a decision about relevance, researchers navigated to IMDB, a well-known online movie database, where they could access the plot and synopsis of the movie. A final movie was then selected and entered into the interface for recommendation to participants.

For Study Part B, a researcher reviewed the parameters (keywords and categories) that were automatically detected by the recommender system for each movie recommendation for a participant in order to generate a more relevant recommendation. Manipulations (change, add, remove) to be done were left up to the reasoned judgment of the researcher. Changing the parameters of the system resulted in a new movie recommendation. For this part of the study, participants rated SM-movie pairs from researcher-manipulated generations. A participant rated up to 3 SM-movie pairs in this part of the study, depending on the number of researcher-manipulated movie recommendations obtained from that participant's social media post. If a participant had no researcher-manipulated movie recommendations because the automatically-generated system parameters were deemed to be already accurate for all of their social media posts, then that participant did not participate in Part B of the study. On average, the study lasted 45 min in total for a participant.

5   Data Analysis and Study Results

RQ1 asked if there was a significant difference in perceived relevance of movie recommendations based on social media posts when the recommendations were produced by the recommender system as opposed to a baseline in the form of human judgment. A paired-samples t-test showed that participants rated *recommendations made using human judgment* ($M = 5.56$, $SD = 1.77$) significantly higher than *recommendations generated only by the recommender system* ($M = 3.27$, $SD = 2.36$), $t(54) = 6.232$, $p < 0.001$. The means are shown in Fig. 2.

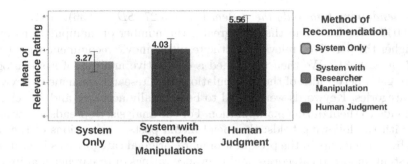

Fig. 2. Means with Error Bars for Perceived Relevance Ratings of Movie Recommendations based on Method of Recommendation

Emergent qualitative coding was performed on the open-ended responses that participants gave to explain their given relevance rating for each SM-movie pair. We only coded responses for relevance ratings that were 2 or below (out of a 7-point likert scale). A response could be tagged with more than one code. Among the codes that emerged, we present those that contained more valuable insights:

Closely related words: Respondents identified that the movie does not relate to keywords in the social media post in the intended meaning. E.g., "The movie depicted does mention 'beauty' but its a different kind."

Mismatched emotions: Participants determined movie and post did not convey similar emotion. E.g., "Although the movie talks about parent it seems to be in a negative tone unlike the post which is of a good occasion."

Brief mention: Participants felt the post only briefly mentioned something. E.g., "Although there is a mention of rain on the movie plot but i don't find the movie to match the overall theme of the post."

Genre: Participants mentioned genre. E.g., "This is clearly a mockumentary horror movie whereas the social media post is about a cartoon (happier)."

Cultural references: Participants indicated that they were unfamiliar with cultural references made in the movie. E.g., "I am unfamiliar with what ganesh chaturthi is."

Current affairs references: Participants found that while the post mentioned issues related to current affairs that most people would be aware of, the movie did not address that issue in the light of current affairs. E.g., "Standing with you #blackouttuesday".

RQ2 asked what kinds of human manipulations were done to the movie recommender system to generate more relevant movie recommendations. First, we validated that researcher-manipulated movie recommendations were perceived as more relevant than recommendations from the system only. A paired-samples t-test showed that participants did rate the *recommendations from the system with human manipulations* ($M = 4.03$, $SD = 2.29$) significantly higher than *recommendations from only the system* ($M = 3.27$, $SD = 2.36$), $t(54) = 1.708$, $p = 0.047$. We also found that the greater the number of manipulations made, the higher the perceived relevance of the resulting movie recommendation ($r(48) = .27$, $p = 0.031$). We then performed a qualitative analysis of system-logged data to get a better idea of the manipulations that researchers made to keywords and categories. Keywords were found to be generally accurate and few changes were made to them during manipulation. For the analysis, a spreadsheet was created with the following fields: the social media posts, descriptions of the posts given by participants in the pre-questionnaire, original categories as identified by the system, modified categories, and relevance ratings of researcher-manipulated movie recommendations. The spreadsheet was sorted by relevance ratings, and only posts with researcher-manipulated movie recommendation ratings 4 and above (on a 7-point scale) were considered for analysis. The fields above were then used to identify what changes were made and why. Codes were generated for the changes made.

Specific references are unknown to system. The system did not take into account specific references made in the posts and instead focused on general subject matter. E.g., in the post 'My hairs almost long enough to pull off Sokka's', 'Sokka' is a popular fictional character but unknown to the system. The system extracted the category '/style and fashion', and researcher manipulations added '/art and entertainment'.

Multiple possible interpretations of a word. The system sometimes came across words that could be interpreted differently in different contexts. E.g., in the post 'Mesmerizing old memories while on journey to make new ones', 'old' could be interpreted as 'past/in the past' or in the context of old age. In the latter case, 'society/senior living' category was added by the researcher.

System may fixate on less important words in a post and miss the main context. In some cases, the system fixated on unimportant words from posts and based categories around them. E.g., in the post 'well we made it to day two before class time became pasta time', the system focused on 'pasta' with categories like '/food and drink'. Researcher manipulations instead added '/education/graduate life'.

System cannot understand sarcasm/hyperbole. In a handful of instances, a post included sarcasm or a hyperbole. E.g., 'If [political candidate] wins I will shoot myself in the foot just like America has decided to shoot itself in the foot'. In such instances, the system took the literal meaning of shooting and identified categories such as 'sports/hunting and shooting'. Researcher manipulations changed these to '/law, govt and politics'.

6   Discussion and Conclusion

RQ1 looked at the comparison of the recommender system to the human judgment baseline. As expected, the results showed that human judgment recommendations scored higher than those generated by the system. This result simply

Table 1. Findings and Design Implications from qualitative analyses

Findings	Descriptions	Design Implications
Closely related words/ Multiple word interpretations	System cannot identify the correct interpretation of a word used in the post	**DI-1**: System needs to consider varied interpretations of key words in a post
Mismatched emotions; Sarcasm/hyperbole	System cannot detect emotional valence of post	**DI-2**: System needs to account for emotional valence of text in a post
Brief mention; Fixation on less important words	System cannot identify the importance of different words in a post	**DI-3**: System needs to identify overall importance of a word in a post
Genre	System is not aware of the different tones posts can have	**DI-4**: System needs to account for connotation of post
Cultural references/ Unknown specific references	System does not understand cultural references used in a post	**DI-5**: System needs to be culturally aware, especially to the culture of the user
Current affairs references	System cannot relate to current affairs that a post may refer to	**DI-6**: System needs to be aware of issues in current affairs

confirmed that the recommender system, built using a keyword- and category-matching approach, needs improvement. Part of the results for RQ2 comparing the relevance ratings for movie recommendations from the recommender system and researcher-manipulated recommendations then showed that with manipulations of categories extracted from social media posts, more relevant recommendations can indeed be generated. The more interesting, and important, part of our findings was to understand why the system failed to produce relevant recommendations. This understanding can be gained from our analysis of participants' explanations of their ratings and the analysis of manipulations done through the companion interface. We synthesized the findings from both of these analyses in Table 1, and list design implications derived from these findings.

The design implications that we present inform what should be taken into account in the design of recommender systems (investigated within the domain of movies in this work) based on user's personal social media posts as an index into their everyday life happenings. Some of the implications can most likely be addressed using existing techniques such as sentiment analysis for detecting emotional valence, adding weights to words to avoid over-reliance on a few words, training the system on a bigger dataset to help it detect specific references, or enabling the system to mine the Web for current affairs issues. Addressing other implications such as resolving multiple word interpretations and making the system culturally sensitive is less apparent and may need further research to be operationalized effectively. We also acknowledge that our work had limitations, including the use of only one database and one publicly available NLP system, along with a small sample size. Utilizing richer databases and advanced NLP systems with a bigger sample size could lead to interesting insights. We hope this work promotes the vision of recommender systems driven by users' everyday lives.

Acknowledgements. This project was partially supported by NSF grant #1942937, CAREER: Bridging Formal and Everyday Learning through Wearable Technologies: Towards a Connected Learning Paradigm.

References

1. Hektner, J.M., Schmidt, J.A., Csikszentmihalyi, M.: Experience sampling method: measuring the quality of everyday life. Sage (2007)
2. Rimé, B., Paez, D., Kanyangara, P., Yzerbyt, V.: The social sharing of emotions in interpersonal and in collective situations: Common psychosocial consequences. In Emotion regulation and well-being, pp. 147–163. Springer, New York (2011). https://doi.org/10.1007/978-1-4419-6953-8_9
3. Veer, E., Ozanne, L.K., Michael Hall, C.: Sharing cathartic stories online: the internet as a means of expression following a crisis event. J. Cons. Behav. **15**(4), 314–324 (2016)
4. Bazarova, N.N., Choi, Y.H., Sosik, V.S., Cosley, D., Whitlock, J.: Social sharing of emotions on Facebook: channel differences, satisfaction, and replies. In: Proceedings of the 18th ACM Conference on Computer Supported Cooperative Work & Social Computing, pp. 154–164 (2015)
5. Adomavicius, G., Tuzhilin, A.: Toward the next generation of recommender systems: a survey of the state-of-the-art and possible extensions. IEEE Trans. Knowl. Data Eng. **17**, 734–749 (2005)
6. Lops, P., de Gemmis, M., Semeraro, G.: Content-based recommender systems: state of the art and trends. In: Ricci, F., Rokach, L., Shapira, B., Kantor, P.B. (eds.) Recommender Systems Handbook, pp. 73–105. Springer, Boston, MA (2011). https://doi.org/10.1007/978-0-387-85820-3_3
7. Bobadilla, J., Ortega, F., Hernando, A., Gutiérrez, A.: Recommender systems survey. Knowl.-Based Syst. **46**, 109–132 (2013)
8. Cantador, I., Fernández-Tobías, I., Berkovsky, S., Cremonesi, P.: Cross-domain recommender systems. In: Ricci, F., Rokach, L., Shapira, B. (eds.) Recommender Systems Handbook, pp. 919–959. Springer, Boston, MA (2015). https://doi.org/10.1007/978-1-4899-7637-6_27
9. Pham, X.H., Jung, J.J., Vu, L.A., Park, S.-B.: Exploiting social contexts for movie recommendation. Malays. J. Comput. Sci. **27**(1), 68–79 (2014)
10. Das, D., Chidananda, H.T., Sahoo, L.: Personalized movie recommendation system using twitter data, pp. 339–347 (2018)
11. Dooms, S., Martens, L.: Harvesting movie ratings from structured data in social media by Simon Dooms and Luc Martens with Ching-man Au Yeung as coordinator. ACM Sigweb Newsl. **2014**, 4 (2014)
12. Schedl, M.: Ameliorating music recommendation: integrating music content, music context, and user context for improved music retrieval and recommendation. MoMM 2013, pp. 3–9, December (2013)

13. Wei, S., Zheng, X., Chen, D., Chen, C.: A hybrid approach for movie recommendation via tags and ratings. Electron. Commer. Res. Appl. **18**, 83–94 (2016)

14. Evgenia Wasserman Pritsker, Tsvi Kuflik, and Einat Minkov. Assessing the Contribution of Twitter's Textual Information to Graph-based Recommendation. pages 511–516, March 2017

15. Leung, J.K., Griva, I., Kennedy, W.G.: Making use of affective features from media content metadata for better movie recommendation making. ArXiv (2020)

16. Chien, C.-Y., Qiu, G.-H., Lu, W.-H.: A movie trailer recommendation system based on pre-trained vector of relationship and scenario content discovered from plot summaries and social media. In: 2019 International Conference on Technologies and Applications of Artificial Intelligence (TAAI), pp. 8959918, November (2019)

17. Chu, S.L., Brown, S., Park, H., Brittnie Spornhauer. Towards personalized movie selection for wellness: investigating event-inspired movies. Int. J. Hum-Comput. Interact. **36**(16), 1514–1526 (2020)

18. Zhao, D., Du, N., Chang, Z., Li, Y.: Keyword extraction for social media short text. In: 2017 14th Web Information Systems and Applications Conference (WISA), pp. 251–256 (2017)

19. GroupLens Research. Movielens. https://movielens.org/

20. IBM Natural Language Processing. https://www.ibm.com/cloud/watson-natural-language-understanding

Towards a Practice-Led Research Agenda for User Interface Design of Recommender Systems

Aletta Smits[(✉)] and Koen van Turnhout

HU University of Applied Sciences, Utrecht, The Netherlands
aletta.smits@hu.nl

Abstract. The design of recommender systems' graphical user interfaces (GUIs) is critical for a user's experience with these systems. However, most research into recommenders focuses on algorithms, overlooking the design of their interfaces. Additionally, the studies on the design of recommender interfaces that do exist do not always manage to cross the research-practice gap. This disconnect may be due to a lack of alignment between academic focus and the most pressing needs of practitioners, as well as the way research findings are communicated. To address these issues, this paper presents the results of a comprehensive study involving 215 designers worldwide, aiming to identify the primary challenges in designing recommender GUIs and the resources practitioners need to tackle those challenges. Building on these findings, this paper proposes a practice-led research agenda for the human-computer interaction community on designing recommender interfaces and suggestions for more accessible and actionable ways of disseminating research results in this domain.

Keywords: Recommender system · Interface design · Research-practice gap · Algorithmic affordances

1 Introduction

Recommender systems are omnipresent [1–4]. Most people in Western society will – consciously or not – have consulted multiple recommenders (social media timelines, news feeds, audio apps, journey planners) before their day has properly started. Professionals – doctors, financial advisors, and teachers, to name a few – have their own recommender systems, in the form of decision support systems, to inform their services. Recommenders play a crucial role in both our personal and professional lives and are indispensable in a world overloaded with information and options [5].

Consequently, design professionals can hardly avoid designing recommender user interfaces (GUIs). However, working on front ends for recommenders introduces artificial intelligence into the design process, an entirely 'new design material [6].' With that comes a multitude of new design challenges [6–9]. These challenges may include issues such as explaining the recommended results and straightforwardly presenting

© The Author(s), under exclusive license to Springer Nature Switzerland AG 2023
J. Abdelnour Nocera et al. (Eds.): INTERACT 2023, LNCS 14144, pp. 170–190, 2023.
https://doi.org/10.1007/978-3-031-42286-7_10

these explanations to the user or allowing the user to modify recommended results. These examples can be considered questions concerning transparent, efficient, and enjoyable communication between the algorithm and the user [9, 10]. They are, therefore, inherently linked to designing interfaces for an artificial intelligence or data-driven system.

To accommodate for such a significant design shift, practitioners require access to all available resources, including current, relevant research presented in a manner that resonates with their professional needs. While studies on the accuracy, efficiency, and effectiveness of recommender algorithms abound for engineers working on the backend of the system [2, 3, 11–14], the same cannot be said for professionals working on the front end of screen-based recommenders, as the number of studies in this area is limited [2–4, 13]. Even lower is the number of studies that find their way into design practice [15, 16]. This deprives design professionals of the latest insights in this emerging field and limits researchers from observing their results in real-world scenarios [17–19]. The reasons for this lack of transfer between research and practice are varied, but two long-standing hypotheses have been put forth in the past 2–3 decades [15–17, 20–23]. Firstly, the HCI research agenda could be more practitioner-led [7, 20, 24], with research topics more closely aligned with the challenges that practitioners encounter. Secondly, research findings should, also, be presented in a manner that resonates with practitioners' problem-solving approach [7, 25–27].

This paper aims to help bridge the research-practice gap for the new design challenges associated with creating recommender GUIs. Based on a comprehensive study among 215 design professionals worldwide, this paper identifies the challenges faced by designers of these data-driven GUIs. Furthermore, it provides an overview of the resources designers would like to have at their disposal to address these challenges. These results lead to a practitioner-led research agenda for this field and suggest an exemplar-driven pattern library, that also includes annotated examples, as a means of disseminating research findings. The contributions of this paper are, therefore, as follows:

1. an overview of the unique design challenges faced by practitioners when designing recommender GUIs, resulting in a research agenda for the Human-Computer Interaction community;
2. a summary of the resources that designers wish to have access to in order to tackle these challenges;
3. a proposal for disseminating the findings of this research agenda in a manner that may help close the gap between academia and practice.

2 Related Work

2.1 A Short History of User Interface Research in Recommenders

Since Resnick and Varian helped popularize the term "recommender systems" in 1997 [1], the majority of research in this field has focused on improving and evaluating the accuracy of recommender algorithms [2–4]. However, after it was recognized that a successful recommender system requires more than simply accuracy [2, 28], research started to also consider design qualities such as diversity, novelty, transparency, and explainability [29–35]. One result of this shift was that recommender system evaluation frameworks also started to incorporate user-centric criteria [11, 12, 36, 37].

Despite the growing emphasis on user experience, however, the research into these user-centric design qualities still very much remained the domain of the data scientist [2, 38, 39]. The research included questions such as 'how to adapt algorithmic calculations to generate a still accurate yet novel and diverse list of recommendations' (for the design qualities novelty and diversity) [40, 41] or 'how to extract explanations from complex algorithms' (for transparency) [35]. However, these design qualities could and should also be implemented in the recommender's user interface and with the user in mind [39]. Then, questions are 'if and how to mark novel items explicitly in a list of recommendations' (for novelty and diversity) or 'how, when, and where to present the extracted explanations for the recommendations' (for transparency) [13, 40]. Section 2.2 explores a selection of studies that address such questions by comparing and contrasting various interfaces and interface elements of recommender GUIs.

2.2 Comparing and Contrasting User Interfaces

One of the pioneering studies that compared multiple user interface designs for recommender systems was conducted by Herlocker, Konstan, and Riedl [42]. Their study focused on incorporating transparency into the interface of a movie recommender system using explanations. Through an experiment with 210 participants, they evaluated 21 different explanatory elements (such as text, icons, and graphs) to determine user preferences. An important finding was that experts preferred a higher information density in the recommendation list and more complex graphs to explain recommendations, demonstrating that results cannot be easily generalized across different user groups.

In a 2021 study, Beel and Dixon also compared various methods for presenting recommended items [2]. They concluded that their respondents showed less interest in item lists that displayed a clear ranking (#1 recommendation, #2 recommendation, etc.). This is surprising, as explicit ranking could be seen as a form of transparency, and previous research has consistently demonstrated a preference for transparent options [31, 32, 42, 43]]. This, too, highlights the limitations of comparative studies, as findings from individual comparisons do not easily translate to other contexts. At the very least, both studies illustrate a need for a host of studies, more than are currently available, comparing similar elements across different user groups in different contexts.

Verbert et al.'s [34] examination of a "talks recommender" for academic conferences is an example from a final set of studies. In this study, the recommendation space - the set of items an algorithm selects for a particular user - is considered an interactive grouping rather than a list. The organizing principles for the various groupings are combinations of tags that the user can activate and explore. Verbert et al. found that academic users are most satisfied when they can combine social tags (e.g., "who else bookmarked this talk?") with content tags (e.g., "what is the talk about?"). However, this process of selection and navigation increases the cognitive load in the decision-making process [44]. It would be interesting to assess this design in different contest: a non-academic environment, a context where the consequences of choices differ, a context where the decision-making process is more time sensitive. The question remains, therefore, to what extent results can be generalized and how practitioners can translate research results to their own projects.

In addition to navigation spaces (see for more examples [44–48]), other aspects of smart interface design that have been examined in various studies include *onboarding and cold starts* [14] and how different interface designs evoke different *mental models* [5, 49, 50]. Studies in the "compare and contrast" category meticulously examine the impact of different design components on the user experience, making them a valuable resource for both researchers and practitioners. However, as noted by Beel and Dixon [2, 51], most studies in this domain, including their own, suffer from two critical limitations. Firstly, many do not explain *why* a particular design is deemed 'superior' [53]. Secondly, as stated above, studies are seldomly replicated in other domains, with other user groups, or in different decision-making contexts. Additionally, it is rare to find reproductions of studies after a set period of time to assess the evolution of users' 'recommender skills,' which could impact GUI-design options. These limitations introduce uncertainties in the UI design decisions a practitioner might make based on academic research. Section 2.3 will, therefore, discuss work that attempts to formulate guidelines on a more general level (design principles, frameworks, pattern libraries), to assess to what extent those suggestions may be more readily transferrable.

2.3 Guidelines, Frameworks, and Pattern Libraries

Over the past two decades, numerous studies have sought to consolidate the findings from comparative studies into coherent frameworks or guidelines [14, 40]. However, the practicality of these frameworks often encounters similar challenges as previously identified by Beel and Dixon [2]. The underlying studies that inform these frameworks are specific to a particular domain, user group, and temporal context, and therefore complicating transfer to other contexts. For example, in 2002, Swearingen and Sinha [14] were pioneers in presenting a comprehensive set of design principles for movie recommender interfaces based on extensive experimentation with interface elements such as onboarding and cold starts, rating, presentation structures, and information density. The authors concluded that displaying reviews and ratings increases users' trust in the recommendations and advised designers to employ specific input modes for collecting user-provided information. However, since the publication of their study, new input modes for GUIs have been introduced, and users' views on the authenticity and the resulting value of reviews have changed [52]. Consequently, while the study still holds methodological significance, its results are no longer fully current [4].

More recently, in 2010, Ozok et al. [40] also attempted to formulate guidelines, this time for commercial web shops and with college-age students as test subjects. One of their key findings was that users were less interested in ratings and reviews, a contrast to the results found by Swearingen and Sinha a decade prior [14]. It is difficult for practitioners to extract clear directions from existing frameworks without a multitude of supporting studies across various domains and with varying respondents, conducted repeatedly to test the current value of results. This proliferation of studies will also aid in the maturation of the research domain and facilitate comprehensive review studies.

Subsequent studies into guidelines for the user interface of recommender systems are scarce, with the notable exception of the suggestion for a recommender interface design pattern library by Cremonesi, Elahi and Garzotto in 2017 [53], and Tintarev and Masthoff's conceptual framework for explaining recommender results in 2015 [33].

Cremonesi, Elahi and Garzotto make an inventory of known design patterns that are encountered in user interfaces of recommender systems (such as 'pagination') and identify a set of new patterns such as 'ratings elicitation' and 'editor's pick'. Tintarev and Masthoff conduct an in-depth analysis of the various goals and tasks that explanations can support, offering valuable insights into the potential benefits for the user. In the end, however, as noted by Nunes and Jannach [54], it does not provide guidelines on how to implement these explanation concepts in a GUI, information that would be highly sought after by design professionals.

Jannach [4] encounters a similar challenge in his own attempt to develop a framework for implementing algorithmic affordances. Algorithmic affordances, as defined by Hekman et al. [10], enable users to interact directly with algorithms, for example, by adjusting parameters or selecting data sources for the recommender calculation. They provide the user with perceptible control over the algorithm. Such mechanisms have been demonstrated to enhance the user experience as test subjects tend to have greater trust in the outcomes a recommender system when they feel they have some level of control [10, 55]. However, algorithmic affordances are also a prime example of how design qualities must be seamlessly integrated in both the algorithm and the interface - the algorithm must permit customization, while the interface must facilitate the communication of the user's modifications and the resulting changes. For their study, too, Jugovac and Jannach [4] conclude that it is difficult to provide implementation guidelines for their affordance categories due to the limited research on recommender interface design and the lack of sufficient valid output. The first part of a potential HCI research agenda writes itself, therefore: significantly increase research into AI-driven GUIs, whether it focuses on developing general principles and frameworks or on conducting comparison and contrast studies. Additionally, it would be beneficial to revisit earlier studies at set intervals. A multitude of such studies may allow for confident and up-to-date guidelines that could be used in the design practice.

2.4 How to Reach Practitioners

Despite their robustness, the studies discussed in Sects. 2.2 and 2.3, have only sparingly found their way into the design practice. Failing to cross the research-practice gap is not uncommon in the field of Human-Computer Interaction. Zielhuis et al. [16] attribute this to a lack of accessibility in the dissemination of research results. They argue that the complexity of models and frameworks that are the research results, as well as the use of academic jargon that differs from the vocabulary used by practitioners, contribute to the challenge in making these results appealing and easily discoverable.

However, Norman [20] identifies a problem at an earlier stage of the research process. He suggests that the topics the academic community selects for its research may not always align with the most pressing needs of the design practice. A 'practice-led research agenda' [20, 24], based on the actual challenges design professionals encounter, could remedy that problem. This paper intends to add to the notion of a practice-led research agenda also the concept of a practice-led dissemination platform. Section 3, therefore, presents the results of a study among design professionals, which examines their primary challenges faced in recommender interface design and their preferred methods for finding resources to overcome these challenges.

3 Practitioners' Views on Designing for Recommender Systems

3.1 Overall Design: Three Studies

This exploratory study aims to gain insight into the design challenges faced by UX/UI practitioners in designing a recommender's graphical user interface (GUI) and to identify the preferred resources for practitioners to address these challenges.

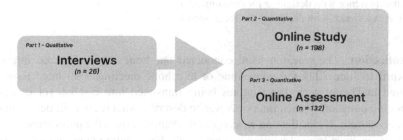

Fig. 1. An explorative sequential mixed methods design

In order to achieve this, an exploratory sequential mixed methods study was conducted [56], consisting of three parts. Part 1 of the study involved semi-structured interviews with 17 junior designers based in The Netherlands. The objective was to gather qualitative data on challenges related to designing for recommenders. The interviews were analysed using a thematic approach [57], and the responses were categorized. These categories served as the basis for Parts 2 and 3 of the study, which were online studies among junior to senior designers based in Europe, the UK, and the US, with experience ranging from 1–22 years.

Part 2 consisted of a survey with 198 participants, while Part 3 questioned a subgroup of 132 participants who chose to continue to Part 3 after having completed Part 2. These two parts were designed to verify the qualitative data obtained in Part 1 of the study. The design of the study is visualized in Fig. 1.

3.2 Part 1: Interview Study

Participants. The participants in the interview study consisted of 17 young practitioners in The Netherlands who graduated between 2018 and 2021 from a design curriculum and are currently employed in design-related positions, either at a product owner such as a bank or a dating app, or at an agency, serving for a range of clients across multiple domains. In Table 1, the asterisk denotes whether a respondent had worked on a recommender's interface design before (7 out of 17 had). A double asterisk indicates subjects who, during the interviews, became aware of the fact that they had worked on a recommender's interface, now that they understood what they were (3 subjects) (for instance, one subject had designed a landing page for a web shop and only realized during the interview that that page qualified as a recommender's GUI).

Table 1. Participants Part 1: Interview Study

Role	Agency	Product owner
UX/UI Designer	**7** (S2, S7*, S9, S10, S11, S12, S13**)	**6** (S1*, S3**, S4*, S5, S6*, S8*)
UX researcher	**4** (S14, S15**, S16*)	**1** (S17*)

* explicit experience with designing for recommenders
** implicit experience with designing for recommenders

Data collection. The research team conducted one-hour semi-structured interviews from April to June 2022 through online or telephone meetings. All interviews were conducted in Dutch, with direct quotes being translated into English for this paper. The opening question of each interview was to describe what recommender systems or recommenders are. If clarification was required, examples from the participants' experiences, such as those from streaming services, web shops, dating apps, and social media platforms, were used to illustrate the concept of recommenders. Subsequently, *recommenders* were loosely defined as "systems that select, and display content tailored to users' preferences," providing participants with a basic understanding. The subsequent interview was structured along the following questions (translated from Dutch):

- Do you have experience with designing graphical user interfaces (GUIs) for recommenders?
- Could you describe one or two of your projects in this domain?

  - If challenges were mentioned: Could you elaborate on those challenges?
  - If challenges were not spontaneously mentioned: do you remember any of the challenges in that project?
  - If challenges were mentioned, spontaneously or after prompting: Do you consider those challenges particular to working on a recommender's GUI?

- What resources did you have available to address these challenges?

If participants did not have prior experience with designing recommender GUIs they were asked about their experience as users of such systems, but their data was not included in the results of Part 1.

Results. As a group, the ten interviewees with experience with recommender systems identified multiple design challenges that they felt were specific to designing interfaces for a recommender system. Their leading candidate for such a challenge was the question of how to *present the recommendations*. Their questions in this challenge concerned the presentation structure of the recommended items and the items' information density. Another prominent concern was the combination of business goals with user goals, and they wondered if and how business-driven items should be marked as such in the presented recommendations.

Concerning solving this challenge, the respondents felt they were mainly limited to their own ideas of presentation structures or to what they could find while researching other platforms ("benchmarking"). They lacked information on 'how layouts affect [a user]' (S3) and felt they did not have the proper terminology to do a valid search for information. S13 stated: "Had I known that I was working on a recommender system's interface, maybe I would have been able to find something. But I have never used that word." Even with the proper terminology available, finding relevant academic papers on the presentation of results was hard. S1 commented that the papers he could find were "so specific that... [we] could not translate them to our app." They added that in the end, "we had to resort to conducting our own experiments. That did yield a result", but "we don't know why this was the best option."

A second design challenge multiple respondents listed was, as S6 called it, the "dreaded filter bubble." Two respondents (S6, S17) first claimed that filter bubbles were probably more of an algorithmic problem but, after consideration, contended that they had UX/UI components in there as well. As S6 noted, the user's experience would probably suffer if novel or diverse recommendations intended to burst the bubble were not adequately marked as such. The concerns about how to present items intended to burst a filter bubble led in three interviews to questions about explanations: should filter-bursting items be just marked or also explained? Should explanations accompany other 'regular' items as well? When should those explanations be presented, and how?

A final design challenge that most respondents mentioned was the *rating process*. This was, in their opinion, definitely a recommendation design challenge since, as S8 commented, people are "now tired of rating everything, but an algorithm still needs that information". Hence, designers must "find ways that make people still want to do this."

Less broadly shared challenges were *onboarding processes* (S4), *mental models of the algorithm* (S6), and *selecting relevant data* (S3). While many platforms other than recommenders offer an *onboarding process* (such as a registration flow), onboarding in recommenders contains a step that is not general in non-intelligent platforms, namely *overcoming the cold start*: the part of the onboarding process where the user provides initial information on preferences with which the algorithm can generate its first set of recommendations. It is vital that a user treats those questions seriously, that the data entry is not too cumbersome, feels relevant, and evokes trust. Those are matters of design, according to (S4).

Selecting relevant data, too, was decidedly a recommender's question, according to S3, but they were unsure if it was an algorithmic problem, a design problem, or both. They felt that design professionals should be involved during the engineering process to make the engineers aware of how data points vary in relevance depending on context. Engineers should know "that users would like to see other movies on Friday night with their partner than on Saturday morning when they are postponing their workout." Also, they considered controls to manipulate data selection to be part of the interface, and therefore a design question. Concerning *mental models*, finally, S6 related how their e-learning environment could frustrate users. When they answer a question correctly, it wins them 2% progress. Answering incorrectly, however, can lose a user 20%. S6 complained that "results should fit how users feel the system [the 'mental model of the algorithm'] works."

When the designers were asked how they approached these challenges, they listed a set of strategies, including Google searches and benchmarking: comparing various recommenders' implementation of particular processes (such as *onboarding*). However, S1 and S13 noted that while benchmarking might solve their immediate problem (they now have inspiration), they would still not know why a particular presentation is better than another (and better for whom?). A similar disadvantage was discussed concerning A/B tests: one of the two options in an A/B test might be better, but why that was best or whether there was a better design to be tested remains unknown. The respondents also stated that when their research could not be facilitated (lack of time, money, respondents, or lack of research to fall back on), they would make design decisions based on 'gut feeling' (S13) or 'intuition' (S8).

Discussion. Table 2 presents the complete list of recommender GUI design challenges, according to practitioner respondents:

Table 2. Seven design challenges for recommender systems' interfaces

Challenge	Description
1	Presentation of recommendations
2	Explanations of why recommendations were selected
3	Mental models of the algorithm
4	Onboarding and cold start
5	Rating of items (in whichever phase)
6	Data selection
7	Filter bubble

Two observations can be made regarding these results:

1. As was stated in Sects. 1 and 2, most of these problems have been discussed in academic literature, although often primarily from an algorithmic perspective. The academic community did find the topics that are pressing for practitioners.
2. All the challenges in Table 2 can be rephrased as an *algorithmic affordance*. That is, they can all be considered as situations in which the user is given control over the algorithm: by rating, by answering cold-start questions, by indicating which data the algorithm should consider, and by understanding the algorithm's reasons for selecting a result. The implementation of 'algorithmic affordances' can, therefore, function as an umbrella category for recommender-specific design challenges.

Resources to tackle these challenges, included go-to solutions, such as small-scale benchmarks, A/B tests, Google, or their intuition. They did, however, indicate that they felt as if they were falling short. They would like easier access to academic research results to understand better how communication between algorithm and user could be shaped. They also felt that the lack of relevant research was partly their own shortcoming: they did not know the words they needed to search for relevant academic papers.

3.3   Part 2 and 3: Online Study

Participants. Following the interviews with the junior designers, in the summer of 2022, the research team conducted an online study with 198 international design professionals with a wide range of experience (see Table 3) to verify the result from the interviews. The respondents were recruited via UX meet-up groups in Amsterdam (53) and via LinkedIn (personal timelines and LinkedIn UX groups) (28). We also recruited design professionals from a commercial database that were paid $15 to participate (117). 60% of these respondents had hands-on experience with recommender GUIs. All 198 participants participated in Part 2 of the study, and a subset of 132 (self-selection) also participated in Part 3.

Table 3. Participants Part 2 and 3: Online Study ($n = 198$ and $n = 132$, respectively)

Based in	Part 2	Part 3	Gender		Part 2	Part 3
N. + W. Europe	32 (16%)	18 (14%)	She/her		154 (27%)	35 (27%)
S. Europe	63 (32%)	48 (36%)	He/him		140 (71%)	95 (72%)
UK	66 (33%)	41 (31%)	They/them		144 (72%)	02 (1%)
USA	37 (19%)	25 (19%)				
Experience in UX	Part 2	Part 3	Main experience with recommender interface design		Part 2	Part 3
0–4 years	68 (34%)	48 (36%)	User research		28 (14%)	11 (08%)
5–9 years	55 (28%)	41 (31%)	Interaction design		36 (18%)	17 (13%
10–14 years	33 (17%)	18 (14%)	User testing		38 (19%)	19 (14%)
15 + years	42 (21%)	25 (19%)	Other		18 (10%)	16 (12%)
			No experience		81 (40%)	69 (52%)

Data Collection. At the beginning of Part 2, respondents were first made aware of the definition of recommender systems through a short explanation and a set of examples. Subsequently, they were asked to indicate whether they had experience designing recommender systems (multiple choice) and if so, to elaborate on their experience. After describing their experiences (open question), they were prompted on any design challenges they may have faced during those experiences (open question). They were then asked to assess to what extent they thought those challenges were specific for designing a recommender's GUI (multiple choice). They were not prompted on the categories that had emerged from the interview study. The challenges that were listed in the open text fields were, however, analysed using the seven-categories model (template coding) that had emerged from Part 1 of the study by two researchers, with disagreements resolved through discussion (Cohen's Kappa = 0,77).

For the 132 participants that continued to the third part of the study, the questioning format was adapted. Respondents were presented with a scenario of designing an interface for a mid-sized library that had recently added audiobooks to its collection and sought to implement a recommender system to suggest titles to members. The participants were asked to select 2–4 design challenges, presented in a random order, from the categories that had emerged from Part 1 of the study, including the overarching category of algorithmic affordances. Each design challenge was accompanied by a brief introduction that defined and scoped the concepts, as seen in Fig. 2, which presents the introduction for the design challenge of "Explanation of Recommended Items."

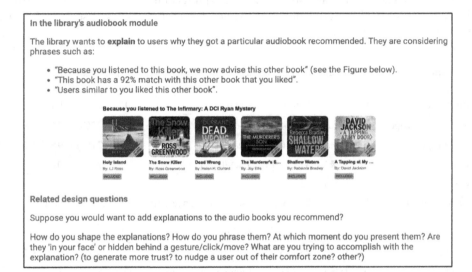

Fig. 2. Introduction to the challenge 'explanations'

After the introduction to a challenge, the participants answered four questions:

1. Do you consider questions related to this challenge specific to designing for recommender interfaces? (multiple choice)
2. Could you elaborate on this answer? Why yes or no? If you said 'no' above, what other contexts do you have in mind? (open question)
3. What tools, research methods or resources do you currently have at your disposal to inform your decisions concerning this design challenge? (open question)
4. What tools, research methods, or resources would you like to have at your disposal (but as far as you know, is not readily available now) to inform your decisions on this design challenge? (open question)

Results. Firstly, as Table 4 shows, all individual challenges reported by the participants in Part 1 were also identified by the participants in Part 2. The one category that was not very pronounced is *the mental model of the algorithm*. Clear-cut examples, such as provided in Part 1, were not encountered in this data set. Secondly, the respondents in Part 2 spontaneously produced problems that can be categorized as 'algorithmic affordances,' the umbrella category that was added in Part I. An example of an answer coded in this category is: "Do people want to manually tweak their recommendation profile (aspects that determine the recommendations)?" Thirdly, respondents listed problems that the research team considered 'general design problems' (example: what font to use), 'technical design problems' (example: how to deal with buffering), 'contextual design problems' (example: how to deal with the difference between financial and entertainment recommenders), and ethical questions ('example: are there ethical problems with the selected items?'). While important, they did not pertain immediately to the core of the study and were not further analysed. Finally, and probably most importantly, no alternative design problems were listed. We can tentatively conclude that the list in Table 4 represents a complete overview of design challenges for recommender GUIs that practitioners report to experience in answer to an open question.

Table 4. Design challenges in recommender projects (Study II)

Category	Example	Freq
Presentation of recommendations	Does the user want the latest watched show to be shown on top? Or under a specific headline like 'watched lately'	27
Explanations of recommendations	How to efficiently broadcast to the user that the recommendation is based on their liked things?	10
Mental models of the algorithm	How do we make it feel/look like the system is thinking with you organically, while it is actually us recommending you items?	6
Onboarding and cold start	Should there be a questionnaire for the user to fill, or should recommendations only be based on activity?	11
Rating of items (in whichever phase)	How can we design an interface that allows users to quickly and easily provide feedback on recommendations?	9
Data selection	Identifying products that are liked by most people	14
Filter bubble	How much personalization is too much? or too little?	12
Umbrella category: Algorithmic Affordances	Do people want to manually tweak their recommendation profile?	10

These results were confirmed in Part 3, where 132 participants each selected 2–4 challenges out of the set of challenges that had emerged from Part 1 (this was the first time these challenges were used as prompts). To the question if a particular challenge could be considered specific to the design of a recommender interface, the participants answered in majority with either 'yes', this is an exclusive challenge for designing a recommender interface, or with 'yes', this is a challenge when designing a recommender interface, but it might be a challenge in other contexts as well (see Fig. 3).

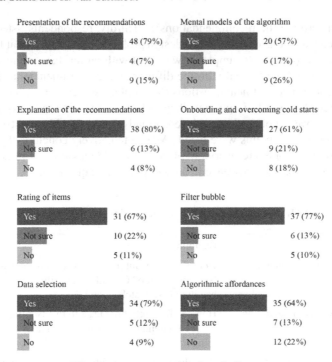

Fig. 3. Assessment of design challenges

Explanations, data selection, the presentation of items, and filter bubbles were the most clearly recognized recommender GUI challenges (between 77–80%). For the other four challenges, most respondents thought they might be related to recommenders but felt they could find other contexts in which this was a design challenge, too. However, when asked for alternative contexts (open question), suggestions were, for instance, "social media timelines" or "web shops," which, of course, are recommenders, too. Mental models of algorithms were most often considered not to be specific to recommenders. While respondents recognized mental models as essential concepts, they felt a mental model is always important, not just the mental model of the algorithm.

In Part 3, respondents also listed the resources they currently employ when addressing these types of challenges (open question). Benchmarking and focus groups were mentioned the most (17% and 22%, respectively), although they should be "treated with circumspection as it is difficult to ensure valid comparisons in complex cases," one respondent stated. Furthermore, their answers included prototyping (tools), various forms of user testing and user research (journeys, personas), and data analysis. However, many respondents lamented the lack time, money, and in quite a few cases, support, either because they needed time from their team members or because they needed a team in the first place. As one respondent put it: he could use "like a team or something. I am just a guy in a room that is low on food".

Concerning benchmarking, quite some respondents volunteered their views on the validity and value of this method (the survey did not ask for it, but the open-question format allowed for this information to be shared). Their concerns align with the draw-backs earlier collected in the interview study and the literature overview. "You cannot know *why* a competing company has chosen this solution," one respondent commented. Others concerns: "benchmarking results in continuing solutions that are dominant in the market already", or "the uncertainty always remains that other solutions might be out there that were not covered in the benchmarking process."

When asked what resources they would like to have available, again focus groups was most frequently mentioned, with qualification such as 'easy access to respondents', 'more time and resources to carry out focus groups,' and 'more run-through time, so there is time to process.' A close second and third were accessible and actionable academic research on designing for recommender interfaces and example libraries or "item databases" with "examples and explanations for implementations".

Regarding academic research, respondents noted, "I would like to have a paper that analysed the effectiveness of out-of-bubble recommendations relating to both time spent on platform and genre of recommendation (political, e-commerce, etc.)" or "I think targeted research papers ... can also help a lot". About exemplar-based resources, respondents comment: "I would like to see a wiki-type guide of solutions to this problem, with a step-by-step guide to solving it," or "An easy guide that all services can look at for inspiration on how to best structure the recommendation systems." or "An item database is what we are heavily missing." Finally, "best design principles" would be appreciated, as well.

Discussion. The findings from Parts 2 and 3 of the study reveal several key obser-vations. Firstly, designers recognize that designing interfaces for intelligent systems presents unique challenges and they identified similar challenges as the participants in Part 1. Secondly, as was also seen in Part 1, the challenges associated with "expla-nations" and "presentation of recommendations" are widely acknowledged as specific to designing GUIs for recommenders. Thirdly, in contrast to Part 1, Part 2 identified some challenges that could be directly classified under the overarching category of algo-rithmic affordances and paraphrased as "how to effectively communicate to users that they have control over the algorithm's recommendations." While engineers are respon-sible for building algorithms that allow such controls, it is the designer's task to make them accessible and foster user confidence in manipulating them. Fourthly, while most respondents considered all challenges specific to designing recommenders, the number of respondents that considered them not specific to recommenders was still 20–40%. Section 4.1 will explore potential explanations for this last finding. Finally, when it comes to their tools to solve the design challenges in recommender GUIs, the most pop-ular resources were accessible academic research [22] and example databases [17, 18, 53]. Participants stated in general, however, that access to academic papers is limited both literally (by paywalls) and metaphorically: the papers were not written in a way that allowed for quick reviews, especially when the practitioner was not familiar with the ter-minology and the most prominent keywords [15, 21]. With regard to example database, the need for them is confirmed by a quick evaluation of the algorithmic affordances pattern library that Van Turnhout et al. [58] and Smits et al. [59] have in preparation. The respondents in Part 3 of the study who selected algorithmic affordances as a theme were presented with one extra question: to evaluate to what extent they would consider a content-rich pattern library such as Hekman et al.'s library could be a helpful resource. 88% responded positively, of which 25% thought it was 'definitely useful,' and 63% could see themselves 'consulting that library regularly.'

4 Discussion and Implications for Future Work

4.1 Practitioners' Perspective on Design Challenges of a Recommender's User Interface

Throughout this paper, three main observations have emerged. Firstly, practitioners consistently identify a similar set of design challenges for designing recommender GUIs regardless of the methodology used to elicit their views on designing for recommenders (interviews in Part 1, open-question survey in Part 2, or assessment study with prompts and multiple-choice format in Part 3). Secondly, however, the exclusivity of these challenges for recommenders is somewhat ambiguous (as seen in Fig. 3). A potential reason for this ambiguity is that designing for recommenders blends with other concerns in two distinct ways. On the one hand, the user experience of a recommender is partly determined by the recommendations themselves, with both the algorithm and the GUI contributing to the overall experience. Although the interface design can be considered a separate problem, the overall user experience cannot, so GUI design may not always be recognized as a separate challenge. On the other hand, a recommender is often integrated into a more extensive user interface with goals that are not necessarily directly related to the recommendation engine's workings. For example, the filtering of a news feed supports users in handling the flow of information, which is their primary task. Algorithmic affordances in the interface, such as liking or sharing a news item, are secondary tasks and that may take focus away from the interface elements relevant to these secondary tasks. However, isolating the design challenges in the recommender's GUI from these two "distractions" allows creators to view the recommender's front end as a separate design layer, creating space for user control between the technical aspect of these systems and their context of use.

As a third observation, all challenges that practitioners consciously encounter, while designing for recommender's GUIs circle around the concept of algorithmic affordances. They all involve processes, such as eliciting rating, presenting results, providing explanations, eliciting onboarding information. And all of these facilitate communication between the algorithm and the user and provide the user with power to exert perceptible influence on the results of those algorithms.

4.2 Resources

The second question in this study concerns the ways in which practitioners tackle the design challenges posed by a recommender's user interface. Currently, they primarily use traditional UX methods such as focus groups, benchmarking, and A/B testing. These methods are comprehensive and can provide a wealth of information, but practitioners often feel that they only scratch the surface of the problem. They would like to have other resources available, such as actionable academic research and example libraries.

There are several reasons for why practitioners felt hat academic research is not actionable. Firstly, the academic discourse does not thoroughly examine the design of recommender interfaces, leaving practitioners unaware of the dilemmas and opportunities at their disposal. An important first step for a research agenda, therefore, is to increase the production of research on interface design of recommenders: in various domains, with various user-groups, and with various tasks, and to reproduce that research regularly to keep up with users' changing preferences.

Secondly, academic discourse is primarily confined to academic circles [15, 22, 60]. It is therefore important to find means to transfer academic research results to the design practice. Thirdly, within academic discussions of recommenders, it is difficult to separate design aspects, technical aspects, and contextual requirements, making it challenging for practitioners to determine the transferability of academic results to their own problems. Practitioners do turn to academic research when accessibility problems or time constraints allow them to, but they do not always find the guidance they seek.

As this study shows, practitioners would like to have access to a collection of examples – a 'wiki-type guide' or a pattern library – at their disposal, and they would like to have access to relevant academic literature that helps them ground their designs. Practitioners believe that a pattern library would be a valuable resource in their often time-constrained search for inspiration. That would solve a first question of the design practice. The second request, accessible research, could be solved if the examples included in the library are enriched by academic research. Then the library also helps transfer research to the design practice and it provides a rationale for design decisions. The provided academically enriched examples then function as generative design knowledge [27], which can be used to inspire innovative solutions for their own challenges.

4.3   A Practice-led Research Agenda

Based on this study, we contend that a practice-led research agenda in the field of recommender GUI-design comprises content and form. Content-wise, the following suggestions are made:

1. *The HCI community should produce more and also more rapid research on recommender GUIs.* An increase in volume of studies in this domain, including revisiting earlier research regularly to monitor developments, will lead to a more mature research domain and more material for review studies, culminating in the creation and maintenance of up-to-date design frameworks for recommender GUIs.

2. *Research on recommender GUI design should focus on algorithmic affordances.* As Sect. 3 showed, practitioners consider questions on the implementation of algorithmic affordances challenges that are uniquely posed by designing for recommender GUIs. It is those challenges, therefore, that should attract the most research. The challenges are: 1. How to implement explanations in an interface; 2. How to present an algorithms' set of recommendations to a user; 3. How to implement the controls that facilitate a user's data selection; 4. How to show the user filter bubble bursts; 5. How to design the various forms of rating (stars, reviews, liking, wish lists, etc.); 6. How to design the onboarding process, including overcoming the cold start; and potentially 7. How interface elements in a recommender GUI help shape a user's mental model

of the algorithm. For all of these how-to-questions, the underlying questions are: how the various implementations affect design qualities such as trust, fun, transparency, serendipity, sense of control.

Form-wise, researchers should publish their findings via traditional academic venues, but also feel a responsibility to present their work in a manner that is easily accessible to practitioners. A pattern library serves as a suggestion for such an accessible venue:

3. *Research results could be disseminated via a pattern library: an online library with examples annotated with up-to-date research, presented in an accessible, transparent format.* This library will sport collections of examples of live implementations of algorithmic affordances in recommenders' GUIs. They are structured according to patterns (eliciting information from the user, presenting items) and the design challenges they address. The accompanying research is specific to structures and diverse enough to include multiple user groups across various domains. Such a library will provide practitioners with a transparent and trustworthy source to turn to for their design challenges when working on a recommender GUI.

Acknowledgments. We are grateful to the Amsterdam UX meetup community, notably Tatiana Siderenkowa, for helping us recruit so many committed respondents. Credits for the graphics in Figure 1 and Figure 3 go to Karine Cardona and Ester Bartels.

References

1. Resnick, P., Varian, H.R: Recommender Systems. Communications of the ACM **40**(3), 56–58 (1997). https://doi.org/10.1145/245108.245121
2. Beel, J., Dixon, H.M: The 'unreasonable' effectiveness of graphical user interfaces for recommender systems. In: 2021 Adjunct Proceedings of the 29th ACM Conference on User Modeling, Adaptation and Personalization, pp. 22–28 (2021). https://doi.org/10.1145/345 0614.3461682
3. Gunawardana, A., Shani, G., Yogev, S.: Evaluating recommender systems. In: Ricci, F., Rokach, L., Shapira, B. (eds) Recommender Systems Handbook, pp. 547–601. Springer, New York, NY (2022). https://doi.org/10.1007/978-1-0716-2197-4_15
4. Jugovac, M., Jannach, D.: Interacting with recommenders—overview and research directions. In: Zhou, M., (ed) ACM Transactions on Interactive Intelligent Systems, **7**(3), pp. 1–46 (2017). Association for Computing Machinery, New York, NY. https://doi.org/10.1145/3001837
5. Ghori, M., Dehpanah, A., Gemmell, J., Qahri-Saremi, H., Mobasher, B.: Does the user have a theory of the recommender? a grounded theory study. In: 2021 Adjunct Proceedings of the 30th ACM Conference on User Modeling, Adaptation and Personalization, pp. 167–174. Association for Computing Machinery, New York (2021). https://doi.org/10.1145/3511047.3537680
6. Holmquist, L.: Intelligence on tap: artificial intelligence as a new design material. Interactions **24**(4), 28–33 (2017). https://doi.org/10.1145/3085571
7. Goodman, E., Stolterman, E., Wakkary, R.: Understanding interaction design practices. In: Proceedings of the 2011 SIGCHI Conference on Human Factors in Computing Systems, pp. 1061–1070. Association for Computing Machinery, New York (2011). https://doi.org/10.1145/1978942.1979100

8. Dove, G., Halskov, K., Forlizzi, J., Zimmerman, J.: UX design innovation: challenges for working with machine learning as a design material. In: Proceedings of the 2017 CHI Conference on Human Factors in Computing Systems, pp. 278–288. Association for Computing Machinery, New York (2017). https://doi.org/10.1145/3025453.3025739
9. Yang, Q., Scuito, A., Zimmerman, J., Forlizzi, J., Steinfeld, A.: Investigating how experienced UX designers effectively work with machine learning. In: Proceedings of the 2018 Designing Interactive Systems Conference, pp. 585–596. Association for Computing Machinery, New York (2018). https://doi.org/10.1145/3196709.3196730
10. Hekman, E., Nguyen, D., Stalenhoef, M., Van Turnhout, K.: Towards a pattern library for algorithmic affordances. In: Joint Proceedings of the IUI 2022 Workshops, **3124**, pp. 24–33. (2022). https://ceur-ws.org/Vol-3124/paper3.pdf
11. Knijnenburg, B.P., Willemsen, M.C., Gantner, Z., Soncu, H., Newell, C.: Explaining the user experience of recommender systems. User Model. User-Adap. Inter. **22**(4), 441–504 (2012). https://doi.org/10.1007/s11257-011-9118-4
12. Pu, P., Chen, L., Hu, R.: A user-centric evaluation framework for recommender systems. In: Proceedings of the Fifth ACM Conference on Recommender Systems 2011, pp. 157–164. Association for Computing Machinery, New York (2011). https://doi.org/10.1145/2043932.2043962
13. Murphy-Hill, E., Murphy, G.: Recommendation delivery: Getting the user interface just right. In Robillard, M., Maalej, W., Walker, R., Zimmerman, T. (eds) Recommendation systems in software engineering, pp. 223–242. Springer, Berlin, Heidelberg (2014). https://doi.org/10.1007/978-3-642-45135-5_9
14 Swearingen, K., Sinha, R.: Interaction design for recommender systems. In Designing Interactive Systems **6**(12), 312–334 (2002)
15. Rogers, Y.: New theoretical approaches for human-computer interaction. In: Cronin, B. (ed) Annual Review of Information Science and Technol. **38**(1), 87–143. Wiley, Hoboken (NJ) (2005). https://doi.org/10.1002/aris.1440380103
16 Zielhuis, M., Visser, F., Andriessen, D., Stappers, P.: What makes design research more useful for design professionals? an exploration of the research-practice gap. J. Design Res. **20**(2), 105–122 (2022)
17. Buie, E., Hooper, C., Houssian, A.: Research-practice interaction: building bridges, closing the gap. In: CHI 2013 Extended Abstracts on Factors in Computing Systems, pp. 13–16. Association for Computing Machinery, New York (2013). https://doi.org/10.1145/2468356.2468813
18. Löwgren, J.: Annotated portfolios and other forms of intermediate-level knowledge. Interactions **20**(1), 30–34 (2013). https://doi.org/10.1145/2405716.2405725
19. Gaver, B., Bowers, J.: Annotated portfolios. Interactions **19**(4), 40–49 (2012). https://doi.org/10.1145/2212877.2212889
20. Norman, D.: The research-practice gap: the need for translational developers. Interactions **17**(4), 9–12 (2010). https://doi.org/10.1145/1806491.1806494
21. Parsons, P., Shukla, P.: Considering the Role of Guidelines in Visualization Design Practice. https://doi.org/10.31219/osf.io/mw376
22. Zielhuis, M.: Discomfort as a starting point: how design research can contribute to design practice. In: Joore, P., Stompff, G., Van den Eijnde, J. (eds.) Applied Design Research, pp. 114–123. CRC Press, Boca Raton (2022)
23. Colusso, L., Bennet, C., Hsieh, G., Munson, S.: Translational resources: reducing the gap between academic research and HCI practice. In: Proceedings of the 2017 Conference on Designing Interactive Systems, pp. 957–968 (2017). https://doi.org/10.1145/3064663.3064667

24. Kou, Y., Gray, C.: A practice-led account of the conceptual evolution of UX knowledge. In: CHI 2019 Conference on Human Factors in Computing Systems, pp. 1–13. Association for Computing Machinery, New York (2019). https://doi.org/10.1145/3290605.3300279

25. Bolin, E., Gray C.: Use of precedent as a narrative practice in design learning. In: Hokanson, B., Clinton, G., Kaminski, K. (eds) Educational Technology and Narrative: Story and Instructional Design, pp. 259–270. Springer Cham, New York (2017). https://doi.org/10.1007/978-3-319-69914-1_21

26. Yang, Q., Banovic, N., Zimmerman, J.: Mapping machine learning advances from HCI research to reveal starting places for design research. In: CHI Conference on Human Factors in Computing Systems, pp. 1–11. Association for Computing Machinery, New York (2018). https://doi.org/10.1145/3173574.3173704

27. Turnhout, K., Smits, A.: Solution repertoire. In: Grierson, H., Bohemia, R., Buck, L. (eds) Proceedings of the 23rd International Conference on Engineering and Product Design Education (2021). https://doi.org/10.35199/EPDE.2021.41

28. Smits, A., Van Turnhout, K., Hekman, E., Nguyen, D.: Data-driven design. In: Buck, L., Bohemia, E., Grierson, H. (eds) Proceedings of the 22nd International Conference on Engineering and Product Design Education (2020). https://doi.org/10.35199/EPDE.2020.10

29. Konstan, J., Riedl, J.: Recommender systems: from algorithms to user experience. User Model. User-Adap. Inter. **22**(1), 101–123 (2012). https://doi.org/10.1007/s11257-011-9112-x

30. Iaquinta, L., Gemmis, M., Lops, P., Semeraro, G.: Introducing serendipity in a content-based recommender system. In: 8th International Conference on Hybrid Intelligent Systems, pp. 168–174. IEEE, New York (2008). https://doi.org/10.1109/HIS.2008.25

31. Kamahara, J., Asakawa, T., Shimojo, S., Miyahara, H.: A community-based recommendation system to reveal unexpected interests. In: Chen, Y. (ed) 11th International Multimedia Modeling Conference 2005, pp. 433–438. IEEE, New York (2005). https://doi.org/10.1109/MMMC.2005.5

32. Schnabel, T., Bennet, T. Joachim, T.: Improving Recommender Systems Beyond the Algorithm (2018). https://doi.org/10.48550/arXiv.1802.07578

33. Tintarev, N., Masthoff, J: Explaining recommendations: design and evaluation. In: Ricci, F., Rocach, L., Shapira, B. (eds) Recommender systems handbook, pp. 353–382. Springer, New York (2015). https://doi.org/10.1007/978-1-4899-7637-6_10

34. Verbert, K., Parra, D., Brusilovsky, P., Duval, E.: Visualizing recommendations to support exploration, transparency, and controllability. In: Proceedings of the 2013 international conference on Intelligent user interfaces, pp. 351–362. Association for Computing Machinery, New York (2013). https://doi.org/10.1145/2449396.2449442

35. Pasquale, F.: The Black Box Society. Harvard University Press, Cambridge, MA (2015)

36. Schoonderwoerd, T., Jorritsma, W., Neerincx, M., Van den Bosch, K.: Human-centered XAI: Developing design patterns for explanations of clinical decision support systems. International Journal of Human-Computer Studies **54**, (2021). https://doi.org/10.1016/j.ijhcs.2021.102684

37. Champiri, Z., Mujtaba, G., Salim, S., Chong, C.: User experience and recommender systems. In: 2nd International Conference on Computing, Mathematics and Engineering Technologies (2019), pp. 1–5. IEEE, New York (2019). https://doi.org/10.1109/ICOMET.2019.8673410

38. Xu, F., Uszkoreit, H., Du, Y., Fan, W., Zhao, D., Zhu, J.: Explainable AI: a brief survey on history, research areas, approaches and challenges. In Natural Language Processing and Chinese Computing: 8th CCF International Conference, NLPCC 2019, Dunhuang, China, October 9–14, 2019, Proceedings, Part II 8, pp. 563–574. Springer International Publishing (2019). https://doi.org/10.1007/978-3-030-32236-6_51

39. Liao, Q.V., Gruen, D., Miller, S.: Questioning the AI: informing design practices for explainable AI user experiences. In: Proceedings of the 2020 CHI Conference on Human Factors in Computing Systems, pp. 1–15 (2020). https://doi.org/10.1145/3313831.3376590

40. Ozok, A., Fan, Q., Norcio, A.: Design guidelines for effective recommender system interfaces based on a usability criteria conceptual model: results from a college student population. Behaviour & Inf. Technol. **29**(1), 57–83 (2010). https://doi.org/10.1080/01449290903004012

41. Zangerle, E., Bauer, C.: Evaluating recommender systems: survey and framework. ACM Comput. Surv. **55**(8), 1–38 (2022). https://doi.org/10.1145/3556536

42. Herlocker, J., Konstan, J., Riedl, J.: Explaining collaborative filtering recommendations. In: Proceedings of the 2000 ACM Conference on Computer Supported Cooperative Work, pp. 241–250. Association for Computing Machinery, New York (2000). https://doi.org/10.1145/358916.358995

43. Tsai, C., Brusilovsky, P.: Designing explanation interfaces for transparency and beyond. In: Joint ACM IUI Workshops (2019), p. 2327 (2017). https://ceur-ws.org/Vol-2327/IUI19WS-IUIATEC-4.pdf

44. Chen, L., Tsoi, H.: Users' decision behavior in recommender interfaces: impact of layout design. In: RecSys 2011 Workshop on Human Decision Making in Recommender Systems (2011). https://ceur-ws.org/Vol-811/paper4.pdf

45. Jannach, D., Jesse, M., Jugovac, M., Trattner, C.: Exploring multi-list user interfaces for similar-item recommendations. In: Proceedings of the 29th ACM Conference on User Modeling, Adaptation and Personalization, pp. 224–228. Association for Computing Machinery, New York, NY (2021). https://doi.org/10.1145/3450613.3456809

46. Chen, L., Pu, P.: Eye-tracking study of user behavior in recommender interfaces. In: Bra, P., Kobsa, A., Chin, D. (eds) User Modeling, Adaptation, and Personalization, pp. 375–380. Springer, Berlin, Heidelberg (2010). https://doi.org/10.1007/978-3-642-13470-8_35

47. Kammerer, Y., Gerjets, P.: The role of search result position and source trustworthiness in the selection of web search results when using a list or a grid interface. International J. Human-Computer Interaction **30**(3), 177–191 (2014). https://doi.org/10.1080/10447318.2013.846790

48. Starke, A., Asotic, E., Trattner, C.: Serving each user: supporting different eating goals through a multi-list recommender interface. In: Fifteenth ACM Conference on Recommender Systems, pp. 124–132. Association for Computing Machinery, New York, NY (2021). https://doi.org/10.1145/3460231.3474232

49. Eslami, M., et al.: First i" like" it, then i hide it: folk theories of social feeds. In: Proceedings of the 2016 CHI Conference on Human Factors in Computing Systems, pp. 2371–2382. Association for Computing Machinery, New York, NY (2016). https://doi.org/10.1145/2858036.2858494

50. Ngo, T., Kunkel, J., Ziegler, J.: Exploring mental models for transparent and controllable recommender systems: a qualitative study. In: Proceedings of the 28th ACM Conference on User Modeling, Adaptation and Personalization, pp. 183–191. Association for Computing Machinery, New York, NY (2020). https://doi.org/10.1145/3340631.3394841

51. Nielsen, J.: Putting A/B testing in its place. Nielsen Norman Group. https://www.nngroup.com/articles/putting-ab-testing-in-its-place/, Accessed 29 Mar 2023

52. Salminen, J., Kandpal, C., Kamel, A., Jung, S., Jansen, B.: Creating and detecting fake reviews of online products. Journal of Retailing and Consumer Services **64**, 102771 (2022). https://doi.org/10.1016/j.jretconser.2021.102771

53. Cremonesi, P., Elahi, M., Garzotto, F.: User interface patterns in recommendation-empowered content intensive multimedia applications. Multimed Tools Appl. **76**, 5275–5309 (2017). https://doi.org/10.1007/s11042-016-3946-5

54. Nunes, I., Jannach, D.: A systematic review and taxonomy of explanations in decision support and recommender systems. User Model. User-Adap. Inter. **27**(3), 393–444 (2017). https://doi.org/10.1007/s11257-017-9195-0

55. Dietvorst, B., Simmons, J., Massey, C.: Overcoming algorithm aversion: people will use imperfect algorithms if they can (even slightly) modify them. Manage. Sci. **64**(3), 1155–1170 (2018). https://doi.org/10.1287/mnsc.2016.2643

56. Creswell, J., Clark, V.: Designing and Conducting Mixed Methods Research. Sage, Thousand Oaks (2009)

57. Gray, C.: It's More of a Mindset Than a Method: UX practitioners' conception of design methods. In: Proceedings of the 2016 CHI Conference on Human Factors in Computing Systems, pp. 4044–4055. Association for Computing Machinery, New York, NY (2016). https://doi.org/10.1145/2858036.2858410

58. Algorithmic Affordances Pattern Library (rudimentary version). https://algorithmicafforda nces.com/. Accessed 29 Mar 2023

59. Smits, A., Bartels, E., Detweiler, C., Van Turnhout, K.: Algorithmic affordances in recommender interfaces. In: Human-Computer Interaction–INTERACT 2023: 19th IFIP TC 13 International Conference, York, UK, August 28–September 1, 2023, Proceedings, Part V 18 (2023)

60. Zielhuis, M., Visser, F., Andriessen, D., Stappers, P.: Making design research relevant for design practice: what is in the way? Des. Stud. **78**(101063), 1–21 (2022). https://doi.org/10. 1016/j.destud.2021.101063

WeHeart: A Personalized Recommendation Device for Physical Activity Encouragement and Preventing "Cold Start" in Cardiac Rehabilitation

Rosa van Tuijn(✉), Tianqin Lu, Emma Driesse, Koen Franken, Pratik Gajane, and Emilia Barakova

Eindhoven University of Technology, Eindhoven, Netherlands
rosavantuijn@gmail.com

Abstract. This paper highlights the importance of physical activity in cardiac rehabilitation as a means of reducing morbidity and mortality rates associated with cardiovascular disease. However, forming physical activity habits is a challenge, and the approach varies depending on individual preferences. We introduce WeHeart, a personalized recommendation device that aims to gradually increase physical activity levels and avoid a "cold start". WeHeart employs a Random Forest classification model that combines both measured and self-reported data to provide personalized recommendations. The system also uses Explainable AI to improve transparency and foster trust. Our study showcases the potential of Machine Learning in providing personalized recommendations for physical activity, and we propose a reinforcement learning approach to improve the system's personalization over time. Overall, this study demonstrates the potential of WeHeart in encouraging physical activity and preventing "cold start" in cardiac rehabilitation.

Keywords: Cardiac Rehabilitation · Physical Activity · Supervised Learning · Habit Formation · Recommendation System · XAI (Explainable AI)

1 Introduction

Cardiovascular disease (CVD) is a global public health concern, and cardiac rehabilitation (CR) is a vital multidisciplinary treatment for reducing secondary cardiovascular risk by improving both optimal physical and psychosocial functioning [1] through exercise training, nutritional interventions, smoking abstinence, etc. [2]. Physical activity (PA) is a key component of CR, with a focus on PA counselling and training [3]. Regular PA can protect the heart and reduce the incidence of cardiovascular events [4]. During CR participation, 70–85% of patients report meeting the recommended PA guidelines [5,6]. However, maintaining PA over the long-term after CR can prove challenging, with only 38–56% of worldwide patients continuing to meet the guidelines a year later [7,8].

© The Author(s), under exclusive license to Springer Nature Switzerland AG 2023
J. Abdelnour Nocera et al. (Eds.): INTERACT 2023, LNCS 14144, pp. 191–201, 2023.
https://doi.org/10.1007/978-3-031-42286-7_11

Thus, it is crucial to encourage PA habit formation among CR and post-CR patients. Habits are believed to promote long-term activity and prevent loss of motivation [9]. To form a habit, a behavior must be performed repeatedly in a consistent environment [10]. The variables that influence the continuation of behavior after initiation must also be taken into account [11]. However, these variables are unique to each individual, making it challenging to develop a one-size-fits-all solution.

As AI is at the heart of healthcare innovation [12], it creates opportunities in applications including personalized treatment and behavior modification [13]. Research has shown promise in the development of personalized recommendation systems through the exploration of deep neural learning models [14] as well as by developing situation-aware recommendation systems utilising wearables to collect several vital inputs [15]. Furthermore, some have proposed that AI recommendation systems utilizing reinforcement learning can help increase user engagement and satisfaction beyond only predicting the users' preferences alone [16].

However, despite the potential benefits, personalized recommendation systems pose several challenges. Firstly, relying solely on reinforcement learning may lead to a so-called "cold start", where the model lacks information about new users which is a common challenge in recommendation systems. Secondly, barriers of trust between the users and the AI can prevent users from using the system due to the user's limited knowledge of AI and the complexity of AI itself [12]. This "black box" problem, which is inherent in some forms of AI [17], can be addressed through explainable AI (XAI). XAI can help the users know how the AI works [18] and thereby increase transparency between the AI system and users, track influencing factors, and improve the predictive models [19]. Lastly, when designing for habit formation habitual tendencies should be considered by incorporating behavior change techniques, such as rehearsal and repetition or self-monitoring of behavior [20]. As this can help users to develop and maintain healthy habits that are beneficial to their health habits such as being physically active [21].

Based on this reasoning motivated by the supporting research, we hypothesize that a smart AI solution that fulfills these habitual tendencies, can prevent a cold start and by including XAI principles would demonstrate the potential of a personalized recommendation system in a CR context. This paper features the design of a personalized recommendation system called "WeHeart" that makes possible testing of this hypothesis and the initial validation of it. The system uses measured and self-reported data from CR patients to provide personalized PA recommendations that vary in time and intensity. WeHeart, placed in the patient's home, uses an algorithm that takes into account personal circumstances when making recommendations. To ensure patient understanding, WeHeart employs Explainable AI (XAI) to show how recommendations are calculated, using Shapley Values to explain the contribution of various factors. This approach helps patients form PA habits, supports long-term activity, and prevents loss of motivation.

2   Methods and Materials

The designed system consists of a recommendation model and a physical prototype called "WeHeart". For the recommendation model, the dataset needs to be selected and preparated for the integration in the overall system. To take the first steps in creating an AI system that creates personalized recommendations for cardiac rehabilitation is by avoiding a cold start. Therefore, this system can provide a recommendation reflecting the current state of the rehabillitee by including self-reported and sensor data and incorporating them in a supervised learning algorithm, specifically a classification model. This is especially important in the context of this paper as inaccurate health recommendations can have undesirable effects. This classification model will make use of PMData [22], a public dataset containing logging data of 16 healthy adults over a period of 5 months. The dataset contains data measured with a Fitbit Versa 2 smartwatch and subjective reporting. This dataset was chosen as it included both sensor and self-reported data and was openly available.

To choose the appropriate recommendation based on the provided data, a supervised classification model is used. Since at this stage, it is unknown which algorithm is best for the system, a total of three algorithms will be compared: decision tree classifier, decision tree regressor, and random forest classifier, to choose the best performing algorithm for the recommender system.

3   Results

3.1   Data Preparation and Classification

The variables used are step count, active minutes, sleep quality, and self-reported data. "PAI" is an existing single indicator of PA [23] which provides an easy-to-understand measure, however, it is processed with an inaccessible algorithm. Therefore a so-called PA score is calculated to be able to grasp the PAI of the potential user. The PA score represents the recommended activity norm of 150 min of moderate intensity by the World Health Organization [24]. And just like the PAI it is based on the heart rate response to PA [23]. The PA score is calculated with the moderately active minutes based on the aforementioned recommendation from World Health Organization, as seen in Eq. 1, which is then added as a separate column called "score" in the final algorithm. With a PA score greater than 100, the user is considered to have performed the standard amount of PA during the week.

$$score = \frac{\text{sum of the moderately active minutes of the past 7 days}}{150} * 100\% \quad (1)$$

The data is classified with the score variable. Whilst the goal is to move towards a score of 100%, a user should not go from 0% to 100% at once. Therefore the mean score of the past 7 days is taken into account. If today's score of the user is above the mean score of the past 7 days with an increment of 5% (as this only adds a small amount of 7,5 min of exercise), the user is not recommended to perform PA. However, if the score is below the described threshold the user is most likely recommended to exercise.

There are many factors that influence a user's state. For example, sleep [25] or stress [26,27] can influence how ready the user is for PA. WeHeart should take into account these factors. Besides sleep and stress, fatigue and mood [25,28] are factors that can impact PA and are available to measure, either through wearable or self-reported data. Therefore, WeHeart will take into account these four features and will skew the recommendation based on this. If they are not already, each input will be translated to a score between 1 and 5.

3.2 Model Selection and Validation

The model is trained to estimate to which category a new observation belongs. The chosen classes for this model are Enough, Light exercise, Medium exercise and Intense exercise. The dataset is split into a training (80%) and a testing (20%) set. To select an appropriate algorithm for the classification model, three variations were considered: decision tree classifier, random forest classifier, and decision tree regressor. The results of the three different algorithms are compared by looking at the accuracy of the model and its confusion matrix, see Fig. 1.

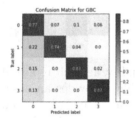 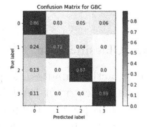 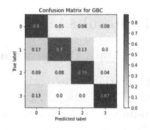

(a) Decision tree classifier; Accuracy: 0.80.   (b) Random forest classifier; Accuracy: 0.86.   (c) Decision tree regressor; Accuracy: 0.81.

Fig. 1. Confusion matrices of the different classification models

First, considering the accuracy, the Random forest classifier has the highest score of 0.86. Second, the confusion matrix shows the probability of classifying wrongly for all the different cases. The worst-case scenario is that someone who should be recommended to perform no exercise is recommended to do a high-intensity exercise. Which is the right top square of the confusion matrix. These cases are the lowest for both the Decision tree classifier and the Decision tree regressor. As the accuracy is the highest for the Random forest classifier, that algorithm will be used to train the model.

In the above cases, the model was trained on all participants together. However, as the goal is to produce personal recommendations a test was performed

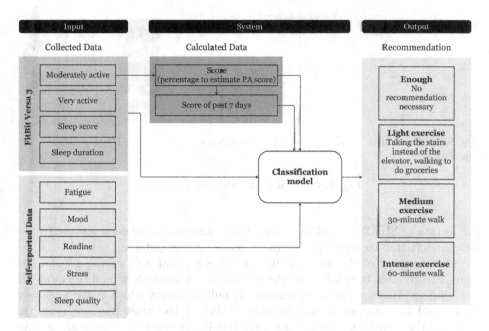

Fig. 2. Input and output data of the classification model.

to see the accuracy of the model and if it would be trained on an individual level. However, this reduced the accuracy of the model to 0.57. Therefore, the model will not be trained on an individual level. Next to that, the classification learning curve showed that at least 400 cases are needed to reach the maximum efficiency of the model.

Graphical visualization of the WeHeart system can be found in Fig. 2, which shows the input and output of the different data types into the classification model.

3.3 The Physical Prototype "WeHeart"

Whilst it is important that the model provides suiting and reliable recommendations, it is just as important to consider how this information is presented to its users. As the target group of this study mostly consists of older adults with limited experience with digital systems, it was decided to design a physical device. This device is placed in the living environment of the user and provides them to interact with the recommendation model by answering questions to provide self-reported data (such as stress and mood), see Fig. 3a, evaluating their current PA score in relation to previous days and requesting a PA recommendation Fig. 3b. Once the user decides to accept the recommendation, they can activate the printing function by pressing the button at the top of WeHeart (Fig. 3c). The recommendation includes the type of exercise, the intensity, and

(a) Self-reported data input   (b) PA score overview.   (c) Physical device.
interface.

Fig. 3. Pictures of the physical prototype.

the duration. SHAP is used to visualize the contribution of each feature to the recommendation to make the algorithm more understandable.

The accuracy of the model is 0.86 which says that 86% of the predictions were correct. This is insufficient information to determine how well the model is performing. Another metric to consider is null accuracy, which is the accuracy that could be obtained by consistently predicting the most frequent class (in this case the target 0). The null accuracy is 0.46. However, the confusion matrix should be examined to learn more about the classification model's performance (see Fig. 4a).

As previously discussed in the preceding section, there exist various categories of errors, each with its own level of severity. These errors are represented by colored lines in Fig. 4b. The green boxes are mistakes that do not cause any direct problems, as in these cases the algorithm proposes a lighter exercise than its original label (False Negatives). However, the red boxes can cause more severe problems, as a more intense exercise is proposed or the worst case scenario in which the user should be recommended to perform no exercise whilst the algorithm proposes a high-intense exercise (False Positives). The false positive rate was computed to be 0.19, which is sub-optimal as it ideally should be 0. The confusion matrix has been analyzed by calculating the sensitivity, specificity, False Positive Rate, and Precision. To calculate this, classes 1–3 are seen as positives, and 0 is seen as negative as it is especially important that the user is correctly recommended to either perform an exercise or not (see Fig. 4c).

Lastly, the model is validated by a 5-fold validation that has been performed and showed that the mean Accuracy is 0.83 with a standard deviation of 0.01. This shows that the results of the model were not biased by the testing and training set used.

3.4   Explainable AI

Considering the personalized recommendations, it is crucial that users can trust the system that they are working with. To achieve trust, we have adopted the Shapley Values as an XAI technique [29] as a visualisation of explaining the models' predictions by calculating feature importance, which provides a framework

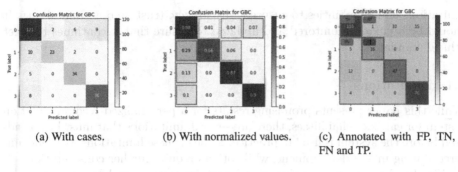

(a) With cases.   (b) With normalized values.   (c) Annotated with FP, TN, FN and TP.

Fig. 4. Confusion matrices

to interpret decision trees and ensemble tree models. WeHeart uses the global interpretability of the Shapely Additive exPlanations (SHAP) model in a Figma concept to demonstrate the extent to which each input variable contributes positively or negatively to the target variable. This greatly increases the transparency of the model used in this paper by explaining to users why they received this recommendation and the extent to which factors influence the results. For example, if a recommendation is different than expected, the user can see it is caused by the high level of stress that the user reported. To sum up, it allows the user to identify and compare the effects of the different factors and make changes accordingly.

4   Discussion

The objective of this research is to develop an AI system that could assist individuals undergoing cardiac rehabilitation in adopting physical activity habits, thereby reducing the likelihood of a future cardiac event [4]. As highlighted in the related works, ensuring that users can trust the recommendations is crucial in a healthcare setting, as offering inappropriate suggestions can have unfavorable consequences. Based on the performed tests and analysis a random forest classifier would be the most suitable model to use with existing data in order to reduce erroneous recommendations and thereby avoid a "cold start". However, at this point, the confusion matrix shows that there are errors where the algorithm proposes a more intense exercise than the user should do. This error is dangerous because it could lead to health risks for the rehabilitees and mistrust of the system. With the random forest classifier, the chance of such an error is the lowest but nonetheless, in future designs, these errors should be avoided. This could be done by applying certain thresholds, for example, by using ROC-Curve as a diagnostic map to find a threshold to minimize the False Positive Rate. Furthermore, in the case where the system is not sure about a recommendation or in the "worst case scenario", it should have a fail-safe mechanism in place to prevent any harm to the patient. For instance, the system could prompt the patient to consult with their healthcare provider before engaging in the activity. Additionally, the system should have a clear and concise explanation of its limitations and capabilities to ensure transparency, trust, and accountability. It should be regularly monitored and updated to ensure that it continues to meet ethical standards.

4.1 Limitations

While this paper presents promising results for a personalized recommendation system for cardiac rehabilitees, there are several limitations that must be considered before the system is used in practice. Some of these limitations were encountered during model development, while others require further consideration.

Firstly, the data set for this model contains data from healthy adults. To further evaluate the model's effectiveness, data should be collected from cardiac rehabilitation patients. It is important to acknowledge that the model's results may vary regarding gradual improvement, as healthy adults already have a baseline level of physical activity. Therefore, it is possible that utilizing data from the target population will lead to necessary changes in the model.

Secondly, the classification of the training and testing data can be further improved. Currently, existing data has been classified by looking at whether someone has reached the minimum amount of PA (score) and at self-reported data (e.g. stress level or mood). Literature showed that these factors have an influence on the performance of PA [25–27]. However, this classification could be improved to research in more detail the weight of different features.

Lastly, the current model also focuses insufficiently on gradual improvement. Specifically, it takes into account if one's current score has increased by 5% from the mean of the past 7 days. Although this prevents someone from going from 0 to 100 at once it is only classified if enough physical exercise was done. Instead of classifying if someone did or did not do enough exercise, other models such as a regression model could be used to actually predict someone's progress and improvements. This could make the recommendations suitable to the needs of the rehabilitee. There are also some limitations to the actual implementation and explainability of the system. While the tangible prototype of the system is designed to provide users with an explanation of the recommendations based on the Shapley Values visualization, its efficacy in promoting user understanding and trustworthiness of the results remains unclear as it has not been evaluated with rehabilitees. It may lead to users disregarding the results, as exemplified by the scenario where, due to bad sleep quality the recommendation is for lower PA than usual, the user might still go for a more intense workout. It might be important to prevent these situations and to also inform someone of the dangers of doing too much physical exercise immediately after a cardiac event [30].

4.2 Future Work

The current paper shows the development of a part of an AI system for supporting PA of cardiac rehabilitees. Following the idea of hybrid (human-artificial) intelligence, there is yet limited knowledge integrated about behaviour change. Although we refer to the Behavior Change taxonomy of Michie et al., [20] it is not (yet) shown how it does relate to the minimal set of recommendations, and we intend to investigate that while personalising via reinforcement learning (RL). RL can also address limitations such as gradual improvement, enhance the long-term effects and capture dynamic sentiments of users, which traditional recommendation systems fail to consider. Previous studies have employed RL in health-related recommendation systems, such as the "Actor-Critic" model proposed by Mulani et al. [31], which continuously updates information-seeking strategies based on user feedback. Another study by Zheng et al. [32], showed that RL methods can lead to recommendations with high concordance with clinicians' prescriptions and improve clinical outcomes.

Among other things, explanations should focus on minimizing the risks for (under and) over-reliance, as discussed in the literature on human needs for explanations, the different types of explanations that can be provided, and the possibility to provide confidence explanations [33,34]. To determine the effectiveness of the recommendations future field research of such a model in the homes of cardiac rehabilitatees could explore the combined effects of the classifier output, explanations and personalisation.

5   Conclusion

This paper reports the first phase of the design of a personalised embodied XAI system that will persuade CA patients to have the adequate amount of physical activity. The findings of this part of the study demonstrate that a classification model, incorporated into a physical system WeHeart, can be used to make personalised suggestions regarding PA, based on wearable sensor data and self-reported data. The use of this recommendation system has the potential to assist cardiac rehabilitees in incorporating PA into their daily lives and reducing the risk of future events and forming habit of doing PA at home. The classification algorithm of WeHeart could be used to start with personal recommendations. Further exploration of reinforcement learning algorithms could contribute to the quality and personalization of the model. Future work could focus on the actual implementation of such a recommendation model with cardiac rehabilitees and on the development of a reinforcement algorithm to make the PA suggestion more aligned with the preferences of the rehabilitees. Overall, the results of this research demonstrate the potential benefits of using data that is easily accessible from wearable sensor data and self-reported data to generate initial recommendations. In addition to the promising results obtained from the use of a classification model to generate personalized PA suggestions, the WeHeart system incorporates explainable artificial intelligence (XAI) in the form of Shapley values. This feature enables the system to provide clear explanations of how and where the recommendations are generated, thus increasing users' trust in the system. By incorporating XAI, WeHeart represents an important step towards developing more personalized, and transparent basis for recommendations as a critical feature for building user trust in AI-powered systems.

References

1. Drwal, K.R., Wakefield, B.J., Forman, D.E., Wu, W.C., Haraldsson, B., El Accaoui, R.N.: Home-based cardiac rehabilitation: experience from the veterans affairs. J. Cardiopulm. Rehabil. Prev. **41**, 93–99 (2021)
2. Kieffer, S.K., Zisko, N., Coombes, J.S., Nauman, J., Wisløff, U.: Personal activity intelligence and mortality in patients with cardiovascular disease: the hunt study. Mayo Clinic Proc. **93**, 1191–1201 (2018)
3. Martinello, N., Saunders, S., Reid, R.: The effectiveness of interventions to maintain exercise and physical activity in post-cardiac rehabilitation populations: a systematic review and meta-analysis of randomized controlled trials. J. Cardiopulm. Rehabil. Prev. **39**, 161–167 (2019)
4. Bassuk, S.S., Manson, J.A.E.: Epidemiological evidence for the role of physical activity in reducing risk of type 2 diabetes and cardiovascular disease. J. Appl. Physiol. **99**, 1193–1204 (2005)
5. Blanchard, C.M., et al.: Demographic and clinical determinants of moderate to vigorous physical activity during home-based cardiac rehabilitation: the home-based determinants of exercise (home) study. J. Cardiopulm. Rehabil. Prev. **30**, 240–245 (2010)
6. Hansen, D., Dendale, P., Raskin, A., Schoonis, A., Berger, J., Vlassak, I., Meeusen, R.: Long-term effect of rehabilitation in coronary artery disease patients: randomized clinical trial of the impact of exercise volume, **24**, 319–327 (2010). https://doi.org/10.1177/0269215509353262
7. Bock, B.C., Carmona-Barros, R.E., Esler, J.L., Tilkemeier, P.L.: Program participation and physical activity maintenance after cardiac rehabilitation, **27**, 37–53 (2016). https://doi.org/10.1177/0145445502238692
8. Izawa, K.P.: Long-term exercise maintenance, physical activity, and health-related quality of life after cardiac rehabilitation. Am. J. Phys. Med. Rehabil. **83**, 884–892 (2004)
9. Gardner, B., Rebar, A.L.: Habit formation and behavior change. Oxford Res. Encycl. Psychol. (2019)
10. Lally, P., Van Jaarsveld, C.H.M., Potts, H.W.W., Wardle, J.: How are habits formed: modelling habit formation in the real world. Eur. J. Soc. Psychol. **40**, 998–1009 (2010)
11. Borland, R.: Habits and temporality: a commentary on Hall and Fong's temporal self-regulation theory. Health Psychol. Rev. **4**, 66–69 (2010)
12. Gille, F., Jobin, A., Ienca, M.: What we talk about when we talk about trust: theory of trust for AI in healthcare. Intell.-Based Med. **100001**(11), 1–2 (2020)
13. Panesar, A.: Machine Learning and AI for Healthcare Big Data for Improved Health Outcomes, 2nd edn. Apress, New York (2021)
14. Zhou, X., Liang, W., Kevin, I., Wang, K., Shimizu, S.: Multi-modality behavioral influence analysis for personalized recommendations in health social media environment. IEEE Trans. Comput. Soc. Syst. **6**, 888–897 (2019)
15. Saad, A., Fouad, H., Mohamed, A.A.: Situation-aware recommendation system for personalized healthcare applications. J. Ambient Intell. Hum. Comput. **1**, 1–15 (2021)
16. Zhang, Q., Lu, J., Jin, Y.: Artificial intelligence in recommender systems. Complex Intell. Syst. **7**, 439–457 (2021)
17. Ferretti, A., Schneider, M., Blasimme, A.: Machine learning in medicine. Eur. Data Protect. Law Rev. **4**, 320–332 (2018)

18. Loh, H.W., Ooi, C.P., Seoni, S., Barua, P.D., Molinari, F., Acharya, U.R.: Application of explainable artificial intelligence for healthcare: a systematic review of the last decade (2011–2022). Comput. Methods Programs Biomed. **226**, 107161 (2022)
19. Pawar, U., O'Shea, D., Rea, S., O'Reilly, R.: Explainable AI in healthcare. In: 2020 International Conference on Cyber Situational Awareness, Data Analytics and Assessment, Cyber SA 2020 (2020)
20. Michie, S., et al.: The behavior change technique taxonomy (v1) of 93 hierarchically clustered techniques: building an international consensus for the reporting of behavior change interventions. Ann. Behav. Med. **46**, 81–95 (2013)
21. Carels, R.A., et al.: A randomized trial comparing two approaches to weight loss: differences in weight loss maintenance. J. Health Psychol., **19**, 296–311 (2014)
22. Thambawita, V., et al.: PMData: a sports logging dataset. In: MMSys 2020 - Proceedings of the 2020 Multimedia Systems Conference, pp. 231–236 (2020)
23. Hannan, A.L.: Effect of personal activity intelligence (PAI) monitoring in the maintenance phase of cardiac rehabilitation: a mixed methods evaluation. BMC Sports Sci. Med. Rehabil. **13**, 1–18 (2021)
24. World Health Organization. Physical activity (2022)
25. Fullagar, H.H.K., Skorski, S., Duffield, R., Hammes, D., Coutts, A.J., Meyer, T.: Sleep and athletic performance: the effects of sleep loss on exercise performance, and physiological and cognitive responses to exercise. Sports Med. **45**, 161–186 (2015)
26. Salmon, P.: Effects of physical exercise on anxiety, depression, and sensitivity to stress: a unifying theory. Clin. Psychol. Rev. **21**, 33–61 (2001)
27. Stults-Kolehmainen, M.A., Sinha, R.: The effects of stress on physical activity and exercise. Sports Med. **44**, 81–121 (2014)
28. Hamer, M., Endrighi, R., Poole, L.: Physical activity, stress reduction, and mood: insight into immunological mechanisms. Methods Mol. Biol. **934**, 89–102 (2012)
29. Lundberg, S.M., Allen, P.G., Lee, S.-I.: A unified approach to interpreting model predictions. In: Advances in Neural Information Processing Systems, vol. 30 (2017)
30. Squires, R.W., Kaminsky, L.A., Porcari, J.P., Ruff, J.E., Savage, P.D., Williams, M.A.: Progression of exercise training in early outpatient cardiac rehabilitation: An official statement from the American association of cardiovascular and pulmonary rehabilitation. J. Cardiopulm. Rehabil. Prev. **38**, 139–146 (2018)
31. Mulani, J., Heda, S., Tumdi, K., Patel, J., Chhinkaniwala, H., Patel, J.: Deep reinforcement learning based personalized health recommendations. Stud. Big Data **68**, 231–255 (2020)
32. Zheng, H., Ryzhov, I.O., Xie, W., Zhong, J.: Personalized multimorbidity management for patients with type 2 diabetes using reinforcement learning of electronic health records. Drugs **81**, 471–482 (2021)
33. Miller, T.: Explanation in artificial intelligence: insights from the social sciences. Artif. Intell. **267**, 1–38 (2019)
34. Schoonderwoerd, T.A.J., Jorritsma, W., Neerincx, M.A., Van Den Bosch, K.: Human-centered XAI: developing design patterns for explanations of clinical decision support systems. Int. J. Hum.-Comput. Stud. **154**, 102684 (2021)

Social AI

"A Solution to a Problem that Didn't Exist?": Exploring Attitudes Towards Smart Streetlight Systems

Anna-Lena Theus[1]([☒]) [iD] and Sonia Chiasson[2] [iD]

[1] School of Journalism and Communication, Carleton University, Ottawa, ON, Canada
annatheus@cmail.carleton.ca
[2] School of Computer Science, Carleton University, Ottawa, ON, Canada
chiasson@scs.carleton.ca

Abstract. We present the first exploration of individuals' expectations for smart streetlights and associated urban data collection practices, with a focus on privacy implications. We conducted an anonymous online survey with 598 participants from across Canada. We found that participants were more accepting of data collection and usage when these were benefiting the community, and when data collection occurred through non-intrusive, privacy-preserving sensors. We also uncovered that participants lacked a coherent understanding of what constitutes a 'smart' streetlight. While unsurprising, these inaccurate mental models can unknowingly expose individuals to privacy risks. Our findings suggest that surveys about smart cities in general are not necessarily applicable to individual technologies such as smart streetlights because these surveys fail to account for the context in which residents encounter streetlights and the disparate impact smart streetlights can have on diverse populations. We highlight the need for cities in collaboration with smart streetlight creators to establish an iterative, resident-centered design approach and emphasize the importance for HCI designers to consider the social, cultural, and political contexts in which smart streetlights are introduced.

Keywords: Smart Streetlights · Sensing Technologies · Resident Perception · Survey

1 Introduction

Smart technology, such as smart streetlights, have been introduced into cities around the world to collect, analyse, and use data to manage, control, and improve city life in real-time, which contributes to a shift from traditional city planning towards smart city development and data driven urbanism [34, 39]. A recent projection estimates that by 2029, 23% of the over 325 million streetlights worldwide will be transformed into their smart counterparts [54]; these can have a variety of embedded features, such as cameras, Wi-Fi antennas, and sensors [19]. Compared to the ordinary lamppost, smart street lighting systems can substantially reduce energy costs and consumption [7, 24, 46, 67] and provide an infrastructure for novel public safety measures [33, 56]. However,

© The Author(s), under exclusive license to Springer Nature Switzerland AG 2023
J. Abdelnour Nocera et al. (Eds.): INTERACT 2023, LNCS 14144, pp. 205–238, 2023.
https://doi.org/10.1007/978-3-031-42286-7_12

smart streetlights can also be used for purposes that may not align with community values or individual rights, such as suppression and surveillance [18]. This emphasizes the asymmetrical power relations between individuals who produce data by interacting with or by merely tolerating these technologies in their vicinity and those who receive, process, act on and benefit from the resulting data, such as governments or private corporations [9, 23].

The presence of smart streetlights also has the potential to significantly shift residents' relationship with their environment. The assumption of being observed or tracked can lead people to perceive themselves and their actions as if under a magnifying glass [62], which in turn can foster self-censorship behaviour [55]. In this context, the deployment of smart streetlights provokes critical questions about residents' privacy and control of data collection practices associated with this technology. Applying a human-computer interaction (HCI) lens to smart streetlights allows an investigation of these questions by exploring individuals' needs and reservations towards this technology on a city level. As smart-city technologies move quickly from design and development to adoption, residents' diverse perceptions of smart city technologies are often under-represented in these development processes [31, 45, 64]. To the best of our knowledge, no prior study has examined citizens' perceptions and concerns about data and privacy practices associated with smart streetlights.

To address this gap, we conducted an anonymous online survey with 598 participants from across Canada to explore individuals' attitudes towards data collection, data self-determination, and privacy with respect to smart streetlights. Our results suggest that the purpose of data collection and usage as well as the type of sensors used for gathering data are strong drivers of participants' acceptance, but that individuals lack a coherent understanding of what a smart streetlight is and for what this technology can be used. Despite the ubiquity of streetlights in everyday live, most individuals are unlikely to consider that every streetlight has the potential for continuous, possibly invasive, networked data collection, similar to those of more explicit surveillance devices (e.g., CCTV). Further, our findings indicate that previously obtained insights into individual's privacy attitudes in a broader smart city context [5] are not directly applicable to specific smart city technologies, such as smart streetlights. Therefore, our results provide guidance for resident-centered smart streetlight design, urban planning, and policy making, and contribute to the existing body of HCI research by providing first insights into the relationship between individuals and smart streetlight technology.

2   Background

2.1   The Technology-Driven Smart City

In spite of its pervasive nature, a universal definition of the smart city is nowhere to be found. Instead, various competing concepts are present in both academic and public domains. But one concept dominates the contemporary discourse: the technology-driven smart city. Guided by the possibilities of Internet of Things (IoT) devices, cloud computing, and Big Data analytics [35], technology-driven smart city projects often rest on the assumption that technology is the main driver needed to solve complex societal challenges [3] and are fueled by the promise that gathering extensive amounts of data will generate insights into how to improve citizens' lives [11, 19, 35].

However, this line of thought has faced some major criticism. For instance, in his book *The smart city in a digital world*, Vincent Mosco [47] challenges the concept of the technology-driven smart city, which he portrays as a driving force that shifts urban governance to private companies, deepens surveillance, and leads to a decline in democracy. He states that for a city to really become smart, the city must commit to a citizen-centred approach rooted in the fundamental right to personal privacy, a commitment to public space, as well as citizens' control over technology. Therefore, it is essential to enforce people's rights to privacy and to establish that data gathered from smart city technologies belongs to the individuals from whom it is collected. Mosco [47] expands an earlier argument made by Hollands [31], who also argued that cities cannot simply be labelled as 'smart' by adopting sophisticated information technology infrastructure. Instead, real smart cities will have to take much greater risks with technology, devolve power, tackle inequalities, and foster input and contribution from its residents, who are under-represented in smart city development processes.

The discourse around the technology-driven smart city has led scholars to conceptualize alternative, socio-technological approaches to smart cities. One of the most prominent examples is the open smart city, a concept introduced by Lauriault et al. [39]. The authors describe the open smart city as a site "where residents, civil society, academics, and the private sector collaborate with public officials to mobilize data and technologies when warranted in an ethical, accountable and transparent way to govern the city as a fair, viable and liveable commons and balance economic development, social progress and environmental responsibility". Thus, in the context of an open smart city, notions of efficiency and technological advancement are closely intertwined with diverse human experiences and values.

2.2 Smart Streetlights

Intelligent street lighting solutions are being introduced into cities around the world [47, 54, 71]. A recent industry report examining the worldwide deployment of connected streetlights found that the top 10 of 111 ranked cities had already installed between 100,000 and 500,000 smart streetlights each [41]. But similar to the concept of the smart city, an agreement of what constitutes a smart streetlight has not yet been reached. Instead, the academic and industrial literature lists different interpretations that range from smart streetlights as an environmentally friendly alternative [7, 46, 67] to smart streetlights as infrastructure that represents the backbone of a city's mesh network and is the host for manifold sensors, meters, or cameras [19, 32, 44].

The decision to implement smart streetlights into a city is usually made by municipal governing bodies eager to use data to tackle urban issues [2]. For example, intelligent street lighting systems with the capacity to adjust brightness levels according to outside lighting conditions or presence of vehicles and pedestrians can substantially reduce energy costs and consumption [7, 24, 46, 67]. Smart streetlights are usually connected to a wireless network and are controlled from a centralized facility [47]. However, this evokes an asymmetry of power and knowledge between governing entities and residents, fostered by the data collection functionalities of smart streetlights and the analytical and computational abilities of public and private institutions [9, 23]. In Canada, several cities, including Montréal [14], Ottawa [58], Halifax [12], and Kitchener [13], have begun to replace ordinary streetlamps with smart streetlights, often as part of larger smart city initiatives. To illustrate, the City of Kitchener completed the conversion of the city's approximately 16,000 ordinary lampposts into smart LED streetlights, each connected to a wireless network and equipped with various smart sensors [65]. The city aims to explore applications beyond dimming lights, such as remotely transmitting gas and water usage information from homes to a central location, tracking of parking spaces, and real-time noise level monitoring.

2.3 Data Practices and Privacy

The widespread distribution of networked sensing technologies that are able to capture personal and non-personal information and the prevalence of automated data processing have led to new forms of electronically mediated everyday surveillance, which makes individuals and groups increasingly vulnerable to informational, decisional, and physical privacy harms [9, 37, 42, 60, 69]. In contrast to more traditional forms of electronic surveillance that monitor peoples' behaviours from a distance (e.g., CCTV cameras, wiretapping), these new algorithmically driven surveillance practices also capture information from individuals' self-monitoring practices [11] and are able to connect previously separate data sets [42]. Put differently, peoples' lives are rendered more and more transparent by applying analytical tools to systematically extract and make sense of individuals' information. As data, initially collected in one context or for a specific purpose, is used for different purposes and given new meanings in novel contexts, formerly excluded parties can gain access to peoples' information, often without the individual's knowledge [8, 37, 42]. However, as people expect data to flow in certain directions depending on the context, their behaviour can unknowingly expose them to serious privacy risks when their expectations of data collection and usage do not mirror reality [51].

Various studies have explored privacy perceptions regarding data practices of IoT devices and in the smart home context [22, 38, 48, 73], many of which mirror previous findings of government surveillance studies, such as individuals' concern that the government is jeopardizing their privacy by collecting, accessing, or using their data for objectionable purposes [36]. To the best of our knowledge, prior work has not yet focused on individuals' perceptions and concerns about data gathering, dissemination, and privacy in the context of smart streetlights. The only closely related work is a recent study by Bannerman and Orasch [5], which examines Canadians' attitudes towards privacy and data collection practices in a general smart city context. Their findings suggest that people are concerned about their privacy in the development of smart cities, desire broader protection and control over their personal data, and that the intended purpose of data gathering impacts peoples' attitudes towards its collection.

2.4 Research Gap

Previous research has engaged with the concept of a smart city [3, 31, 35, 39, 47], has considered potential applications for smart streetlights [7, 44, 46, 67], has produced insights into peoples' attitudes towards data and privacy practices regarding various smart devices [22, 38, 48, 73], and has explored residents' perceptions about smart city technology [5]. However, smart streetlights require additional attention as individuals engage with streetlights in a different context compared to other IoT or smart devices. They encounter them in public spaces where individuals expect (at least in democratic societies) to roam and communicate freely [47]. Individuals are also used to navigating through their communities without paying attention to every single streetlight that they encounter. But in contrast to other technologies present in public spaces, such as CCTV cameras (which are usually labelled as such, installed in places where people tend to gather, and have a primary purpose of monitoring and surveillance), streetlights tend to be perceived as community-serving and non-privacy-threatening objects, since their main purpose is illumination. Given the ongoing trend of privatisation of public spaces which regularly results in increased control and surveillance measures [30, 40, 49], the ubiquitous nature of streetlights which are increasingly being replaced by their smart counterparts [14, 58, 65], and the potential for pervasive and invasive networked data collection practices enabled by smart streetlights, investigating peoples' understanding of and relationship with this technology is of critical importance. Our study contributes to this endeavour by exploring individuals' expectations for smart streetlights and associated urban data collection practices, with a focus on privacy implications.

3   Methodology

In June 2020, we conducted an anonymous online survey with participants from Canada to answer the following research question: What are individuals' attitudes towards data collection, data self-determination, and privacy with respect to smart streetlights? Our study was reviewed and cleared by our University Research Ethics Board. A preliminary study in November 2019 with 60 participants resulted in no major changes to the study design. The data obtained from the preliminary survey is not included in the data set that we analyse in the present study.

3.1   Survey Design

The survey was created using the online survey software Qualtrics[1] and consisted of eight sections with closed and open-ended questions, in the form of multiple choice, Likert-scale, and short answer questions (see Appendix 2). All questions were mandatory and participants needed approximately 15 min to complete the entire survey. The survey covered the following topics:

Section 1 covered participants' demographic information.
Section 2 asked participants whether they believed that the city they live in had installed smart streetlights and how this fact made them feel. It also evaluated their level of comfort regarding the presence of smart streetlights in various city areas and regarding the use of different types of sensors that can be attached to them.

---

[1] https://www.qualtrics.com/core-xm/survey-software/.

Section 3 consisted of questions regarding data usage and control (adapted from Bannerman and Orasch [5]).

Section 4 focused on rights and privileges associated with data collection practices (adapted from [5]).

Section 5 covered questions regarding the need of consulting and informing residents.

Section 6 contained questions about data ownership and data access.

Section 7 evaluated participants' privacy concerns (adapted from [5]).

Section 8 allowed participants to provide additional feedback and comments about smart cities in general and smart streetlights in particular.

We adapted the questionnaire previously used by Bannerman and Orasch [5] for our survey Sects. 3, 4 and 7, by applying the questions to smart streetlights specifically. To illustrate, the question "if I do not want to share my personal information in the way that a service provider sets out in their privacy policy, I should simply not use the service" posed by Bannerman and Orasch [5] was revised into "if I do not want to share my personal information, I should simply avoid areas with smart streetlights". We transformed the remaining questions in a similar manner. For the other sections of the questionnaire, we created original questions. In survey Sect. 2, participants are asked to indicate their comfort level with having smart streetlights present in various areas of a city. The areas included are not mutually exclusive, but rather chosen to provide areas of a city that citizens might identify, e.g., it is often implied that smart streetlights would be beneficial in areas with high crime due to the potential crime reduction effects of this technology [19, 32].

3.2 Data Quality and Analysis

The results presented in this paper represent participants' self-reported, subjective perspectives and attitudes. To ensure participants had a basic understanding of the subject matter, we provided them with a brief explanation of smart streetlights (see Appendix 2, Sect. 2, before question 8) and a clarification about what qualifies as personal information (see Appendix 2, Sect. 2, before question 12). Participants were prevented from progressing with the survey until they showed understanding of the described concepts. We did not provide more detailed explanations because we wanted participants' intuitive reactions to the different scenarios, mirroring real life where they may not have full disclosure about the different technologies and data collection practices. To ensure data quality, we added attention check questions to the survey and disregarded data from respondents who failed to correctly answer them.

To analyse the collected data, we used descriptive statistical methods (i.e., mean values, percentages) as well as the Mann-Whitney U test (a non-parametric statistical method) using a p-value < 0.05 for determining statistical significance. In addition, we performed inductive coding [63] for open-ended questions to complement the quantitative results and to identify emerging themes and patterns in the responses. The primary researcher made a subjective assessment of the positive, negative, or ambivalent nature of each comment. Most were easily categorized due to explicit word choices. Ambiguous responses were discussed with the second author. However, the qualitative data was not as rich as we had initially hoped since not every participant entered detailed open-ended responses. We therefore include representative quotes throughout the paper rather than reporting detailed thematic analysis.

3.3 Participants

We recruited participants and managed the study through Prolific[2], an online crowd-sourcing platform specifically set up to recruit participants for scientific studies. To be eligible, participants had to be either Canadian adults or adults currently residing in Canada with an age of 18 years or older. To access the survey, participants logged into their Prolific account, selected our study from a list of studies, and filled out the survey. After completion, we paid each participant £1.50 GBP[3] (as a British platform, Prolific operates in this currency).

Prolific does not have the option of screening participants by Canadian province or territory, so we released our survey in batches to increase the likelihood of recruiting participants from different time zones. In total, 641 participants were recruited. However, we discarded the data of 43 participants because of quality issues (i.e., one or more wrong answers to attention check questions). Thus, we report the results from 598 valid responses (299 women, 292 men, 2 identified as non-binary, 3 preferred to self-describe, and 2 chose not to answer). Our sample reasonably follows the national population distribution as estimated by Statistics Canada [61], with some imbalance between the two most populous provinces, Ontario and Quebec, possibly because the survey was conducted in English, and the two provinces share a time zone (see Table 1 in Appendix 1 for participant distribution by province and territory).

Participants were relatively young, with a mean age of 31 (age range 18–74), well educated (75% of participants reported having received a Bachelor's degree or higher), and their occupations ranged from students to public and private sector workers. The majority of participants identified as Caucasian or white (58%), followed by 23% of participants who identified as Asian, and 9% who identified as African American or Black. A small fraction of participants identified as Middle Eastern (2%), Latino or Hispanic (1%), and Indigenous (1%). Finally, most participants (72%) reported living in large urban centres with a population of 100,000 residents and more, while 28% indicated that they inhabit more rural areas or small and medium population centres.

4 Results

As prior work has extensively shown that technologies can have discriminatory effects on certain demographic groups [1, 4, 6, 23, 52, 70], we anticipated demographic differences by gender and ethnicity for individuals' level of comfort and privacy concern regarding smart streetlights. We compared populations by gender and ethnicity as follows (number of participants in parenthesis): women (299) vs. men (292); Black, Indigenous, and People of Color (246) vs. Caucasian/white (345). We focus on reporting statistically significant results. We did not compare by other demographics (e.g., other age groups, level of education, area of living) because group sizes were very unevenly distributed. We present the results of our study by themes that align with the survey Sects. 2 to 7.

---

[2] www.prolific.co.

[3] Prolific's recommended "good" payment rate at the time.

4.1 Level of Comfort

Participants were asked whether they believe that the city where they live had installed smart streetlights. Only 23% of participants gave an affirmative answer, while the majority of participants (77%) did not believe that smart streetlights exist in their municipality. To get some insight into the accuracy of participants' assessment, we evaluated the answers of those participants who lived in one of eight large or medium size Canadian cities that had reported implementation of smart streetlights at the time this study was conducted [12–15, 20, 27, 58, 59]. In total, n = 237 participants were identified. Of those participants 33% correctly indicated the presence of smart streetlights. However, the majority of respondents (67%) were under the mistaken impression that this technology had not (yet) found its way into their city.

To get a deeper understanding of participants' attitudes towards this technology, participants who indicated to belief that their city had installed smart streetlights were asked to comment on how this fact made them feel. Their responses suggest that individuals tended to fall into one of three categories: (1) 67% had a positive reaction because they perceived smart streetlights as a valuable technological advancement that can also improve the environment and the thought of having this technology within their city made them feel more safe and secure; (2) 21% were ambivalent but cautious about this technology and perceived smart streetlights as useful but also saw potential for misuse; (3) and 10% clearly perceived smart streetlights as a tool that violates their privacy and made them feel uncomfortable.

Participants who thought that the city they live in had not deployed smart streetlights were also asked to reflect on how this fact made them feel. Participants tended to belong to one of four clusters: (1) 47% were ambivalent: they did not really care, they required more information to form an opinion about smart streetlights, or they perceived them as useful but also saw potential for misuse; (2) 26% of individuals were relieved because they perceived smart streetlights as an unnecessary (financial) investment and not having this technology made them feel safe from privacy invasions or data misuse; (3) 23% of individuals had a negative reaction because the absence of smart streetlights made them feel like their city was lagging by not being innovative enough and introducing this technology would enhance their perceived level of safety; (4) 4% indicated that they were unaware that smart streetlights existed before participating in our study.

To examine how comfortable individuals were with having smart streetlights in different areas of the city and with the various sensors these streetlights can have, participants were asked to indicate their comfort level on a 6-point Likert scale (from "very comfortable" to "very uncomfortable"). As shown in Fig. 1, participants seem to be especially open to having smart streetlights in transportation hubs, such as transit stops (88%) and main streets (84%), as well as in high-density areas, such as districts with vivid night life (87%), high levels of crime (87%), and the city centre (87%). Furthermore, 65% of participants were at least somewhat comfortable having smart streetlights in residential areas and even on their own street (67%). In terms of different types of sensors, participants were comfortable with features viewed as non-intrusive, such as weather (97%), air pollution (96%), and Wi-Fi sensors (90%), but felt less comfortable if smart streetlights were equipped with speakers (66%), cameras (61%), or microphones (41%) (see Fig. 5 in Appendix 1). We found no statistically significant effect by gender or ethnicity for level of comfort regarding the presence of smart streetlights in different city areas or smart streetlight sensors.

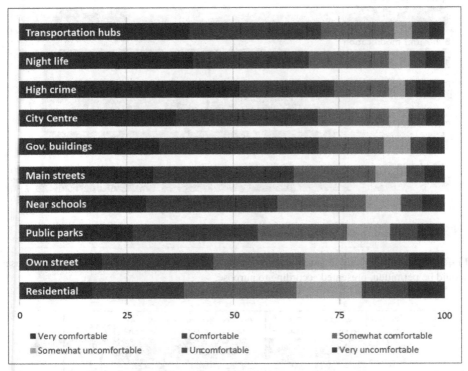

Fig. 1. Percentage of participants selecting each Likert scale response relating to comfort level with smart streetlights in each city area.

4.2 Data Usage and Control

When asked for which purposes the use of personal information collected by smart streetlights should be permitted, the responses showed that participants were hesitant to allow data usage by default and preferred to permit data use under certain conditions only (see Fig. 2). In fact, only a quarter of participants consented to data usage by default for purposes that seemed to benefit the greater good, such as crime prevention (26%) and traffic, transit, or city planning (21%). Participants clearly indicated that data usage should never be permitted for personalized advertising (64%) or behaviour modification purposes (54%). Further, respondents stated that data use by private businesses to improve their profitability (68%) or the sale of personal information collected by smart streetlights (84%) should never be permitted. As one participant summarized, "*I hope that should smart streetlights be rolled out en masse, that it be utilized for the greater good and not for the self-interest of a select few*" (P52).

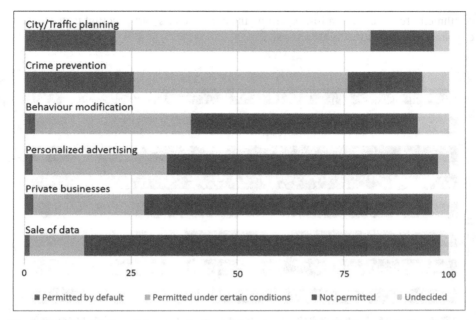

Fig. 2. Percentage of participants selecting each response to the question of whether data use should be permitted, presented according to purpose.

Condition \ Purpose	City/Traffic planning	Crime prevention	Behaviour modification	Personalized advertising	Improve businesses	Sale of data	Mean
Data is aggregated	84%	80%	76%	76%	83%	75%	79%
Ability to opt-out	77%	72%	73%	77%	76%	73%	75%
Ability to view data	74%	71%	68%	73%	65%	65%	69%
Ability to delete data	66%	62%	64%	64%	64%	51%	62%
Ability to opt-in	62%	58%	61%	58%	57%	57%	59%
Notification in fine print	51%	52%	56%	62%	61%	62%	57%
Ability to download data	52%	49%	48%	51%	51%	53%	51%
Ability to correct data	49%	52%	50%	48%	48%	49%	49%

Fig. 3. Percentage of participants selecting each response to the question under which conditions data use should be permitted for different purposes. Darker cells indicate higher levels of agreement; colour changes occur at the 25%, 50%, and 75% marks. The rightmost column shows mean percentages per condition.

Following the initial questions, participants who agreed that data usage could be permitted under certain conditions were presented with a subset of questions to evaluate under which circumstances this should apply. They were instructed to select all of the conditions that they deemed appropriate. As shown in Fig. 3, aggregation (mean of 79%) was the most desired type of data control, followed by the ability to opt out (75%), to view (69%), and to delete (62%) personal data. In contrast, the ability to download (51%) or correct (49%) one's own data were the least preferred methods of control. Participants also strongly preferred having the ability to use areas where smart streetlights are employed without providing personal information (87% agree or strongly agree), instead of needing to avoid these areas when they do not want to share their personal data (15% agree or strongly agree) (see Fig. 4).

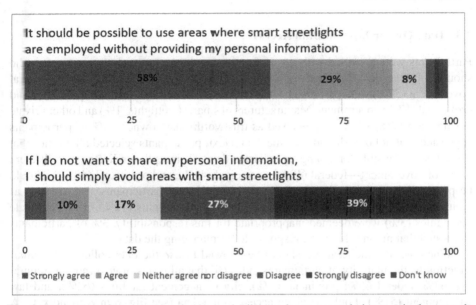

Fig. 4. Percentage of participants selecting each Likert scale response relating to attitudes towards avoiding personal data collection by smart streetlights.

4.3 Consulting and Informing Citizens

The majority of participants (84%) agreed that citizens should be consulted before smart streetlights are introduced. Moreover, their free-text responses revealed five main arguments in favour of consultation: (1) smart streetlights can represent an invasion of privacy; (2) citizens have the right to know about the technology and associated data practices because their personal information will be collected; (3) citizens have the right to be in control of their data and to provide or withhold consent; (4) citizens should become active participants in the planning process to provide feedback, ask questions, and voice concerns; (5) the city is a public space. However, 14% of participants stated that the need for prior consultation depends on the planned location of smart streetlights, the purpose of the data collection, and the type of data that is being collected. Interestingly, a few participants (2%) indicated that citizens do not need to be consulted at all because the implementation of smart streetlights would be in citizens' best interest, a consultation or informing residents would cost too much time, and it would prevent law enforcement from using this technology to fight crime.

When asked how they would like to be informed about the presence of smart streetlights when visiting another city, participants preferred signs in areas with smart streetlights (91%), information on the city's website (67%) and on social media (46%) over other methods, such as ads (22%), printed flyers (19%) or press conferences (15%). In addition, some participants suggested large, obvious signs at airports, train stations, and on roads leading into the city. Notably, only 2% of participants indicated that informing would be unnecessary.

4.4 Data Ownership and Data Access

Participants were provided with a list of entities and asked to pick the one entity who should *own* the data collected by smart streetlights. Citizens (27%) and the federal government (27%) were participants' top choices, followed by the municipal (22%) and provincial (17%) government. Manufacturers of smart streetlights (1%) and other private businesses (0.2%) were not perceived as trustworthy data owners. 3% of participants suggested that nobody should own the data. Next, participants selected all entities that should be responsible for *managing* collected data. Their replies indicated that different levels of government—federal (49%), municipal (49%), and provincial (48%)—should be primarily responsible for managing the data. 23% of participants also saw this as a citizen duty. In contrast, manufacturers of smart streetlights (12%) or other private companies (3%) were deemed inappropriate for this responsibility. 3% of participants suggested that no one should be responsible for managing the data.

When asked which entities should be allowed to *use* the data collected by smart streetlights, the majority of participants indicated that all levels of government (municipal 67%; federal 65%; provincial 64%), city management facilities (62%), and law enforcement (51%) should be given access to the data (see Fig. 6 in Appendix 1). A large number of respondents also agreed to data usage by citizens (44%) and academic institutions (42%), while only a few participants granted this privilege to smart streetlight manufacturers (12%) and other private companies (4%). 3% of participants suggested that no one should be allowed to use this data.

4.5 Privacy Concern

At the end of the survey, participants reported their level of privacy concern regarding smart streetlights. As Fig. 7 (see Appendix 1) shows, 84% of participants reported being at least somewhat concerned about their privacy.

To examine differences in privacy concern by populations (i.e., gender, ethnicity), we conducted Mann-Whitney U tests. The first Mann-Whitney U test indicated that the level of privacy concern was slightly higher for women (Mean rank = 310.96) than for men (Mean rank = 277.59), U = 38305 (Z = −2.473), N = 588, p = 0.013. But the calculated effect size was quite small (r = 0.10). An additional Mann-Whitney U test suggested no significant difference between the level of privacy concern of participants who identified as Caucasian/white and participants who identified as Black, Indigenous, and People of Color (BIPOC), U = 41958 (Z = −.03), N = 588, p = 0.976.

We anticipated that not all participants had heard of smart streetlights before taking part in our study. To ensure that all participants had a comparable understanding of the technology before reporting their perceived level of privacy concern, we placed the question at the end of the survey. We acknowledge that positioning this question at the end of our questionnaire poses the risk of survey ordering bias and that prompting participants to focus on their privacy tends to heighten their level of concern [28]. Therefore, interpretation of these findings should be done with caution.

4.6 Limitations

Our first limitations relate to our participant sample. Our study focused on the Canadian context, therefore generalising our findings to other populations should be done with caution. In addition, our study could have suffered from self-selection bias since we may have been approached by participants who were especially interested in smart streetlights. Our second set of limitations relates to methods. There may have been ordering bias since we asked participants to indicate their level of privacy concern at the very end of our survey after considering several aspects of smart streetlights, and simply prompting participants to reflect on their level of privacy concern might have primed them to rank it higher [28]. Conducting the survey online may have also impacted participants' responses and restricted the capturing of more qualitative data since some participants may not want to type long explanatory responses. Finally, our results may have been influenced by contemporary events, e.g., the #blacklivesmatter and #defundthepolice protests, which may have heightened participants' surveillance awareness.

4.7 Summary of Results

Our results show under which circumstances individuals are more willing to accept urban data collection practices associated with smart streetlights:

- When data collection and usage are for a perceived greater good or for the benefit of the community;
- when data collection occurs through non-intrusive sensors that preserve residents' privacy (about which participants expressed a high level of concern);
- when residents are consulted before smart streetlights are introduced into a city or community;
- and when residents are in control of collection and usage of their personal data (e.g., participants were more open to the usage of their data by the government, while strongly rejecting private business uses).

5 Discussion

5.1 The Notion of Safety and Security

Participants' attitude towards installing smart streetlights was often accompanied by a contradictory narrative of safety and security. About one third of participants expressed that having this technology present made them feel more safe and secure, a notion that became apparent in participants' feedback at the end of our survey. While some participants only provided a general rational, such as "*smart cities and streetlights are a positive change towards a more secure community*" (P577), other respondents suggested more concrete ideas for how smart streetlights could improve public safety, e.g., "*smart streetlights could be very beneficial to law enforcement*" (P547) or "*smart streetlights would work well in tandem with or as a separate public safety measure for emergency alerts*" (P131). Similar suggestions for utilizing smart streetlights can be found in prior work that (among other ideas) proposes emergency call buttons [56] or lighting patterns that allow first responders to quickly locate emergency incidents [33].

In contrast, some participants expressed that a lack of smart streetlights made them feel safe from privacy invasions and data misuse. "*My only concern about this approach is [that] personal data gets hacked by individuals [who] are planning harm against citizens. I would only be ok [with smart streetlights] if it's almost impossible to hack the system*" (P481). This sentiment is shared by other respondents, who indicated that they are especially concerned about the safety of disadvantaged communities should smart streetlights be deployed. As one participant explains, "*I am very worried that smart streetlights will have a disproportionately negative effect on marginalized communities, and I am also concerned about law enforcement and government and their ability to track individuals*" (P16). Another respondent cautions that "*it seems like [smart streetlights]will just be used to continue to police and harass black and indigenous communities. Collecting information from people in their daily lives is dangerous in a police state with a history of harming BIPOC*" (P18). Prior work has extensively shown how technology can be designed and used to discriminate against minority groups [1, 4, 6, 23, 52, 70] and that visible minorities and indigenous people are exposed to higher levels of surveillance by public and private entities, which reproduces existing inequalities and forms of racial domination [6, 10, 25, 57]. For instance, predictive policing software such as PredPol (a crime prediction algorithm for automated risk assessment that produces jurisdiction maps covered with red square boxes that indicate where crime is supposed to occur) is going to be more likely to direct police to disadvantaged neighborhoods because the data that this software is drawing from reflects ongoing surveillance priorities that already target predominantly Black neighborhoods [6]. Our findings demonstrate how smart streetlights with certain sensors could foster the creation of "vertical realities" [6], i.e., distinct realities that result in a higher level of (perceived) safety and freedom for some and heightened surveillance and control for others (e.g., in the form of intensified racialized policing activities), and emphasize the importance of considering the broader social, cultural, and political contexts in which smart streetlights are introduced.

5.2 What About Privacy?

Our results reveal two interesting contradictions relating to smart streetlights and privacy. First, participants reported being generally comfortable with having smart streetlights in different areas of the city (see Fig. 1), including having smart streetlights along their own street. Yet, participants also labelled smart streetlights as a potential threat to their privacy, as one participant made very clear in their feedback at the end of the survey: "*I think that smart streetlights sound like a horrible invasion of privacy*" (P331). Along those lines, another participant commented that "*smart streetlights are fine if they are only lights, but I don't agree with them being equipped with microphones and cameras because it is an invasion of privacy*" (P477). However, we acknowledge that prompting participants to reflect on their level of privacy concern as part of a question prior to providing their feedback might have heightened their focus on privacy invasions [28].

Nevertheless, our results mirror previous findings on peoples' privacy perceptions with respect to novel sensing technologies that are increasingly deployed in smart city contexts [16, 50, 72]. For instance, an investigation into privacy mechanisms for drones conducted by Yao et al. [72] showed that those subjected to the drone's gaze are concerned about their privacy and are in favour of privacy protecting mechanisms such as automatic face blurring.

In the second apparent contradiction, half of participants thought that law enforcement should be allowed to use the data collected by smart streetlights for crime prevention (see Fig. 6 in Appendix 1), but participants also expressed a need for aggregating data to hide one's identity (see Fig. 3), which would likely render the data useless for law enforcement. Prior work suggests that acceptance for different privacy intrusive measures by law enforcement is likely to differ, because individuals' attitudes towards privacy depend on the specific security issue as well as their level of trust in public institutions [68]. However, we strongly advise against labeling these differences as mere personal preferences and instead encourage academics and practitioners to understand them in a broader cultural, historical, and social context to prevent further penalisations of already vulnerable populations. For example, critical race scholars such as Ruha Benjamin [6] and Simone Brown [10] have detailed how scopic vulnerability (i.e., the fact that the mere act of viewing can put the subject of vision at risk) is a pressing reality for many racialized communities and central to their historical and present-day experiences. In other words, not everyone experiences the danger of exposure equally. Ruha Benjamin [6] also illustrates how some technologies fail to see Blackness (e.g., facial recognition software), while others (e.g., predictive policing software) render People of Colour hypervisible and expose them to systems of racial surveillance. Others have demonstrated how social and economic class directs the level of privacy individuals experience, e.g., when the poor are required to trade their rights to privacy to receive welfare and support [25], and how Indigenous people [57], people experiencing homelessness [25], as well as newcomers and immigrants [43] are regularly exposed to higher levels of surveillance and privacy intrusions.

5.3 What Makes a Streetlight Smart?

Overall, participants' responses evoke the question: what does it mean for a streetlight to be considered smart? In academic and industry literature, the smartness of streetlights is often tied to their environmental advantage above ordinary lampposts [7, 46] or their features that allow them to become the sensor equipped backbone of a technology-driven city of the future [19, 32]. However, given that even experts have not reached a consensus on what constitutes a smart streetlight, it is unsurprising that participants are unaware of the range of features that are considered 'smart': "*I had not realized what smart streetlights could possibly do besides harnessing the sun for power and collect weather and traffic data*" (P416).

Our findings also suggest that participants have some difficulties imagining the possible uses of smart streetlights. "*I don't completely understand how my specific information will be used in smart streetlights, or where said information will come from. How can these smart streetlights track me specifically? Or will my data be provided by another company such as Google*" (P460)? Another participant questioned "*if smart streetlights can lower crime rates, for example, then I don't see how the data would be useful for weather monitoring*" (P494). Individuals having vague mental models about the possible functions of smart streetlights is not unexpected, as prior work suggests that individuals hold only rudimentary mental models of objects, technologies or ideas with which they are unfamiliar [26]. A mental model is an image that humans create in their minds through experience, interaction, training, and instruction to help them understand the world around them [53]. Inaccurate mental models of smart streetlights or the associated data collection practices can lead to misconceptions (e.g., about data flows) that can affect behaviours and decisions and can unknowingly expose individuals to privacy risks.

Considering that the functionality of smart streetlights will likely differ by city or even by neighborhood, understanding what functionalities are implied when a streetlight is termed 'smart' is particularly important for individuals to form accurate mental models and to engage in predictable interactions regardless of the space in which they are navigating. In addition, the limited awareness of smart streetlights' potentially extensive data capturing methods and unresolved questions around data ownership and control pose serious risks to individuals' privacy. Interestingly, some participants questioned the desirability of streetlights becoming smart in the first place. As one participant concluded: "*Smart streetlights though, is it a solution to a problem that didn't exist?*" (P505).

5.4 Are Privacy Attitudes Towards Smart Cities Applicable to Smart Streetlights?

Our findings mirror three main results obtained by Bannerman and Orasch [5], whose 2018 study explores peoples' attitudes to privacy in a broader smart city context: (1) participants demonstrated a high level of privacy concern; (2) participants were more open to data use for governmental purposes and objected to data use for improving private businesses; (3) participants desired protection and control over their data.

Besides these similarities, our results also revealed interesting differences. In Bannerman and Orasch's [5] evaluation, 28% of participants were only slightly or not at all concerned about their privacy, but only 15% of our participants reported a similar opinion. Furthermore, 46% of Bannerman and Orasch's [5] participants agreed with the statement "if I do not want to share my personal information in the way that a service provider sets out in their privacy policy, I should simply not use the service." In our study, the statement was slightly reworded for smart streetlights. It read "if I do not want to share my personal information, I should simply avoid areas with smart streetlights." Interestingly, only 15% of our participants agreed with this statement.

Refraining from using a service is often the only option available to individuals, who disagree with a company or service provider's privacy policy. However, in terms of smart city technologies such as smart streetlights installed in public spaces, restricted use is not a plausible option. As one participant pointed out, "*how would it be possible to opt out of something like smart streetlights other than avoiding areas with them?*" (P533). If individuals are uncomfortable with smart streetlights, their only option at this time is to avoid the area. This may be infeasible (e.g., if the area is near the individual's home or work), and it also produces injustices as both available options (i.e., avoiding or not avoiding an area) can result in penalization by either preventing individuals from accessing public spaces or pressuring them into self-exposure. As Jonathan Cohn [17] rightfully points out: "[C]hoices do not lead to agency and freedom; rather, individuals must first be imagined to have agency and freedom in order to have their decisions count as choices" (pp.28). This scenario emphasizes two important factors: First, the immense impact this technology can have on peoples' daily lives due to streetlights' ubiquitous nature. And second, the complexity of ensuring privacy and consent in a smart city context, where privacy is often understood on an individual level (at least in the Western context) while individuals are navigating in collective and public spaces.

One reason for the differing results between the two studies could be that applying Bannerman and Orasch's [5] survey questions to a specific technology (i.e., smart street-lights) might have helped participants to assess the impact of smart city technologies on their own lives in a more concrete manner. Nissenbaum [51] emphasizes that expectations about sharing and withholding (personal) information are dynamic and context dependent. Consequently, using broad questions to assess citizens' attitudes towards smart cities might be too abstract and therefore less helpful for unveiling citizens' concerns and needs regarding specific smart technologies and data flows. Yet another reason could be the dates of data collection. Bannerman and Orasch's [5] data collection occurred during October and November 2018 and our study was conducted in June 2020. During the intervening time, there have been prominent public debates in Canada about the nature of smart city projects, largely initiated by the (now abandoned) collaboration between Sidewalk Labs and Waterfront Toronto in pursuit of a smart neighbourhood built from the ground up [21, 29, 66]. This might have prompted participants to engage with this topic more meaningfully.

Overall, our findings suggest that results obtained in a broader smart city context may not be directly applicable to specific smart city technologies (such as smart streetlights). The nuances, uses, and implications of specific technologies require exploration in their own context.

5.5 Practical Implications of Our Findings

The obtained results provide some practical guidance for resident-centered smart street-light design, urban planning, and policy making. Among other things, we encourage cities in collaboration with smart streetlight creators to apply an iterative, participatory design approach to generate input and feedback from different populations from all over the city and at all stages of the design process (e.g., through focus groups or user stud-ies with members of identified resident groups). Our results indicate that the design of the physical objects (i.e., the smart streetlights), the design of the platform or network system that connects them, and the design of the interactions between streetlights and people are all equally important. An iterative and resident-inclusive approach for gener-ating design ideas and for producing and evaluating prototypes ensures a more thorough understanding of peoples' needs and expectations, mental models, and interactions with this technology in different contexts. In addition, we encourage designers and urban planners to engage in discussions with residents about the consequences of introducing smart streetlights into different city areas, especially with respect to residents' privacy and the potential negative effects on already disadvantaged communities, and to be advocates for equitable smart streetlight design. Other design recommendations are to avoid including unnecessary intrusive sensors (e.g., cameras, microphones), and to include easily accessible identifiers that make smart streetlights distinguishable from ordinary lampposts and that can provide information to residents about how and what kind of data is being collected (and potentially shared). Furthermore, our results lend support to privacy-preserving data collection measures, such as collecting only non-identifying information, blurring identifying features, and aggregating or obfuscating data.

We also recommend that HCI designers and planners incorporate a list of reflective questions about the purpose of a proposed smart streetlighting system into their practices (e.g., what is the goal of the smart streetlight network; who profits from the implementation; who controls the network; how and what kind of data is captured; what is the data used for; who has access to the data; what are potential risks for different populations) to prevent misuse and penalisations of already vulnerable communities, and to consider if specific smart streetlight features and sensors are necessary. The introduction of policies that differentiate between intrusive and non-intrusive sensors along with conditions for installment and usage could also mitigate potential misuse. To further inhibit residents' exposure to privacy harms, data licensing legislation could be introduced requiring those seeking access to data collected via smart streetlights to rationalize and submit documentation (e.g., to an appointed city official) outlining the proposed data use along with privacy protection measures. The provided list of practical applications of our findings is not exhaustive but serves as an invitation to envision additional measures and points towards domains of future research.

6 Conclusion

This study is the first to examine the diversity of opinions and concerns relating to urban data collection practices facilitated by smart streetlights. Participants were more accepting of data collection and use when these are for a perceived greater good (e.g., benefit the community), and when data collection occurs through non-intrusive sensors that preserve their privacy. Participants emphasized the need for resident consultation before installing smart streetlights and reported a high level of privacy concern regarding this technology. In addition, respondents voiced the desire to be in control of collection and usage of their personal data and were more open to the use of their data by the government while strongly rejecting private business applications. We uncovered that participants lacked a coherent understanding of what constitutes a smart streetlight and sometimes held contradictory beliefs. This is cause for concern given the data collection capacities of networked sensing technologies and the disparate impact this technology can have on diverse populations. Other than a small gender difference regarding level of privacy concern, we found no significant differences in attitudes when we compared responses across different participant demographics.

Considering the ubiquitous nature of streetlights in everyday life, our results highlight the need to shift from a technology-focused approach towards a human-centered, socio-technological approach to smart streetlights that addresses residents' concerns and perceptions and actively includes them into planning processes. Our study is relevant to the wider HCI community, as it explores peoples' interactions with an entire technological infrastructure, one that is being continuously updated to allow for more pervasive data collection, at a point in time where we as a HCI community still have the opportunity to shape these interactions. Considering that nearly a quarter of streetlights worldwide will soon be 'smart' [54] and that many cities are installing smart streetlights [12–14, 58, 65], often without citizens' awareness (67% of our study participants living in cities with smart streetlights were under the mistaken impression that this technology was not yet in their city), it is critical to engage with smart streetlights while there remains the opportunity to influence this technology's direction. To this end, our results provide guidance for smart streetlight design, urban planning, and policy making and establish the groundwork needed to spark a broader and diverse conversation about equitable smart streetlight design within the HCI community.

Acknowledgements. This research is supported in part by funding from the Social Sciences and Humanities Research Council Canada - Doctoral Fellowship. Sonia Chiasson acknowledges funding from the Canada Research Chairs and NSERC Discovery Grant programs.

Appendix 1 – Table and Figures

Table 1. Distribution comparison of Canadian population at the time of data collection and participant sample by percentage.

Province/Territory	Statistics Canada Population Estimates Q2 2020	Recruited Participants (N = 598)
Alberta	11.66%	10.03%
British Columbia	13.48%	13.88%
Manitoba	3.63%	3.18%
New Brunswick	2.06%	1.17%
Newfoundland/Labrador	1.37%	2.17%
Northwest Territories	0.12%	0.33%
Nova Scotia	2.58%	4.52%
Nunavut	0.10%	0.00%
Ontario	38.83%	53.34%
Prince Edward Island	0.42%	0.17%
Quebec	22.52%	9.87%
Saskatchewan	3.11%	1.17%
Yukon	0.11%	0.17%

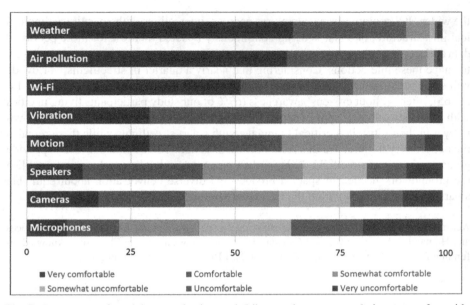

Fig. 5. Percentage of participants selecting each Likert scale response relating to comfort with specific sensors.

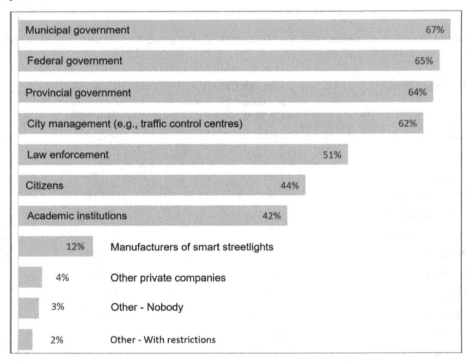

Fig. 6. Percentage of participants selecting each response for which entities should be allowed to use data collected by smart streetlights.

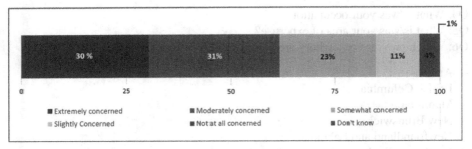

Fig. 7. Percentage of participants reporting each level of privacy concern.

Appendix 2 – Questionnaire

Section 1: Demographics
Q1: Which option below describes you?

– Female
– Male
– Non-binary
– Prefer not to answer
– Prefer to self-describe:

Q2: What is your age?
Q2a: How do you describe your ethnicity?

– African American/Black
– Asian
– Caucasian/White
– Indigenous
– Latino/Hispanic
– Middle Eastern
– Prefer to self-describe:
– Prefer not to answer

Q3: What is your level of education? If you are currently in school, please choose the degree you are enrolled in.

– Less than high school degree
– High school degree or equivalent
– Bachelor's degree
– Master's degree
– Doctoral degree
– Professional degree
– Prefer not to answer

Q4: What is/was your occupation?
Q5: What is/was your area of expertise?
Q6: Which province or territory are you currently living in?

- Alberta
- British Columbia
- Manitoba
- New Brunswick
- Newfoundland and Labrador
- Northwest Territories
- Nova Scotia
- Nunavut
- Ontario
- Prince Edward Island
- Quebec
- Saskatchewan
- Yukon

Q7: Which town or city are you currently living in?
Q7a: How would you describe the area you live in?

- Large urban population center (population of 100,000 or more)
- Medium population center (population between 30,000 and 99,999)
- Small population center (population between 1,000 and 29,999)
- Rural area (population of 999 or less)

Section 2: Smart Streetlights and Personal Information

Transition Page 1: Smart streetlights are being introduced into cities around the country. These smart streetlights are usually connected to a wireless network. They can be equipped with cameras, speakers, microphones, sensors measuring air pollution, Wi-Fi hotspots, digital signs (e.g., for public information or advertising) and more.

Q8: Which smart streetlight equipment was not mentioned on the previous page? (*attention check question*)

- Cameras
- Sensors measuring air pollution
- Digital signs
- Sensors measuring altitude

→ If participants choose "sensors measuring altitude" they get to the next question.
→ If participants choose one of the other three answers, they get back to the previous page with the information about smart streetlights.

Q9: Do you believe the city you are living in has installed smart streetlights?

- Yes

– No

→ If participants choose "*Yes*": **Q9.1**: How does the fact that your city has smart streetlights make you feel?

→ If participants choose "*No*": **Q9.2**: How does the fact that your city does not have smart streetlights make you feel?

Q10: How comfortable are you having smart streetlights in the following areas?

	Very comfortable	Comfortable	Somewhat comfortable	Somewhat uncomfortable	Uncomfortable	Very uncomfortable
The street you are living on						
Near schools						
City centre						
Areas with a lot of night life						
Public transit stops/stations						
Residential areas						
Along main streets						
Public parks						
Near government buildings						
Areas with high crime rates						

Q11: How comfortable do you feel about the different types of sensors smart streetlights can be equipped with?

	Very comfortable	Comfortable	Somewhat comfortable	Somewhat uncomfortable	Un-comfortable	Very uncomfortable
Cameras						
Speakers						
Microphones						
Sensors measuring air pollution						
Weather sensors						

(*continued*)

(*continued*)

	Very comfortable	Comfortable	Somewhat comfortable	Somewhat uncomfortable	Un-comfortable	Very uncomfortable
Wi-Fi hotspots						
Motion sensors						
Vibration sensors						

Transition Page 2: On the following pages the term 'personal information' will appear. Personal information is defined as any information that can identify an individual either on its own, or when combined with other information.

Q12: What is not considered 'personal information'? (*attention check question*)

- Walking route to get home
- Approximate age
- Current temperature
- License plate number

→ If participants choose "*current temperature*" they get to the next question.
→ If participants choose one of the other three answers, they get back to the previous page with the information about smart streetlights.

Section 3: Use of Data Collected by Smart Streetlights
Q13: Please complete the following sentence: Use of my personal information collected by smart streetlights to target me with personalized advertisements …

- should be permitted by default.
- should be permitted, but only if I am granted certain rights and protections for my data.
- should not be permitted.
- not sure / undecided

→ If participants choose "*should be permitted, but only if I am granted certain rights and protections for my data*": **Q13.1**: Under what conditions should the use of your personal data be permitted?

- I'm notified somewhere in the fine print when I agree to use a service.
- I can opt in.
- I can opt out.
- I can view my data.
- I can correct my data.
- I can delete my data.
- I can download my data for my own use.

- My data is aggregated with other data or masked such that my identity is not revealed.
- Don't know/ No response

Q14: Please complete the following sentence: Use of my personal information collected by smart streetlights to prompt me to modify my behaviour ...

- should be permitted by default.
- should be permitted, but only if I am granted certain rights and protections for my data.
- should not be permitted.
- not sure / undecided

→ If participants choose "*should be permitted, but only if I am granted certain rights and protections for my data*": **Q14.1**: Under what conditions should the use of your personal data be permitted?

- I'm notified somewhere in the fine print when I agree to use a service.
- I can opt in.
- I can opt out.
- I can view my data.
- I can correct my data.
- I can delete my data.
- I can download my data for my own use.
- My data is aggregated with other data or masked such that my identity is not revealed.
- Don't know/ No response

Q15: Please complete the following sentence: Use of my personal information collected by smart streetlights for use in traffic, transit, or city planning ...

- should be permitted by default.
- should be permitted, but only if I am granted certain rights and protections for my data.
- should not be permitted.
- not sure / undecided

→ If participants choose "*should be permitted, but only if I am granted certain rights and protections for my data*": **Q15.1**: Under what conditions should the use of your personal data be permitted?

- I'm notified somewhere in the fine print when I agree to use a service.
- I can opt in.
- I can opt out.
- I can view my data.
- I can correct my data.
- I can delete my data.

- I can download my data for my own use.
- My data is aggregated with other data or masked such that my identity is not revealed.
- Don't know/ No response

Q16: Please complete the following sentence: Use of my personal information collected by smart streetlights by police in crime prevention …

- should be permitted by default.
- should be permitted, but only if I am granted certain rights and protections for my data.
- should not be permitted.
- not sure / undecided

→ If participants choose "*should be permitted, but only if I am granted certain rights and protections for my data*": **Q16.1**: Under what conditions should the use of your personal data be permitted?

- I'm notified somewhere in the fine print when I agree to use a service.
- I can opt in.
- I can opt out.
- I can view my data.
- I can correct my data.
- I can delete my data.
- I can download my data for my own use.
- My data is aggregated with other data or masked such that my identity is not revealed.
- Don't know/ No response

Q17: Please choose the colour of the sky during a clear, bright, sunny day (*attention check question*)

- Red
- Blue
- Green
- Yellow

Q18: Please complete the following sentence: The sale of my personal information collected by smart streetlights …

- should be permitted by default.
- should be permitted, but only if I am granted certain rights and protections for my data.
- should not be permitted.
- not sure / undecided

→ If participants choose "*should be permitted, but only if I am granted certain rights and protections for my data*": **Q18.1**: Under what conditions should the use of your personal data be permitted?

- I'm notified somewhere in the fine print when I agree to use a service.
- I can opt in.
- I can opt out.
- I can view my data.
- I can correct my data.
- I can delete my data.
- I can download my data for my own use.
- My data is aggregated with other data or masked such that my identity is not revealed.
- Don't know/ No response.

Q19: Please complete the following sentence: Use of my personal information collected by smart streetlights to plan and refine private businesses to make them more profitable …

- should be permitted by default.
- should be permitted, but only if I am granted certain rights and protections for my data.
- should not be permitted.
- not sure / undecided

→ If participants choose "*should be permitted, but only if I am granted certain rights and protections for my data*": **Q19.1**: Under what conditions should the use of your personal data be permitted?

- I'm notified somewhere in the fine print when I agree to use a service.
- I can opt in.
- I can opt out.
- I can view my data.
- I can correct my data.
- I can delete my data.
- I can download my data for my own use.
- My data is aggregated with other data or masked such that my identity is not revealed.
- Don't know/ No response.

Section 4: Rights and Privileges
Q20: I should have the right to view the personal information collected about me by smart streetlights.

- Strongly Agree
- Agree
- Neither Agree nor Disagree
- Disagree
- Strongly Disagree
- Don't Know

Q21: I should have the right to delete the personal information collected about me by smart streetlights.

- Strongly Agree
- Agree
- Neither Agree nor Disagree
- Disagree
- Strongly Disagree
- Don't Know

Q22: Please select the most negative response (*attention check question*)

- Strongly Agree
- Agree
- Neither Agree nor Disagree
- Disagree
- Strongly Disagree
- Don't Know

Q23: I should have the right to download personal information collected about me by smart streetlights for my own use

- Strongly Agree
- Agree
- Neither Agree nor Disagree
- Disagree
- Strongly Disagree
- Don't Know

Q24: It should be possible to use areas where smart streetlights are employed without providing my personal information.

- Strongly Agree
- Agree
- Neither Agree nor Disagree
- Disagree
- Strongly Disagree
- Don't Know

Q25: If I do not want to share my personal information, I should simply avoid areas with smart streetlights.

- Strongly Agree
- Agree
- Neither Agree nor Disagree
- Disagree
- Strongly Disagree
- Don't Know

Section 5: Consulting and Informing Citizen

Q26: Do you think citizens need to be consulted before smart streetlights are introduced into a city?

- Yes
- No
- It Depends

→ If participants choose *"Yes"*: **Q26.1:** Why do you believe citizens need to be consulted?
→ If participants choose *"No"*: **Q26.2:** Why do you believe citizens do not need to be consulted?
→ If participants choose *"It depends"*: **Q26.3:** Under which circumstances should citizens be consulted?

Q27: If you visited another city, how would you want to be informed about the presence of smart streetlights? Please select all that apply.

- Press conference
- Social media
- City website
- Printed flyers
- Signs in areas with smart streetlights
- Ads
- Other (please elaborate):
- Informing is not necessary

Section 6: Data-Ownership and Data Access

Q28: Who should own the data collected by smart streetlights?

- Federal government
- Provincial government
- Municipal government
- Citizens
- Manufacturer of smart streetlights
- Other private companies
- Other (please elaborate):

Q29: Who should be responsible for managing the data collected by smart streetlights? Please select all that apply.

- Federal government
- Provincial government
- Municipal government
- Citizens
- Manufacturer of smart streetlights
- Other private companies
- Other (please elaborate):

Q30: Who should be allowed to use the data collected by smart streetlights? Please select all that apply.

– Federal government
– Provincial government
– Municipal government
– Citizens
– Manufacturer of smart streetlights
– Other private companies
– Other (please elaborate):

Section 7: Overall Privacy Concern

Q31: How concerned are you about your privacy in the context of smart streetlights?

– Extremely concerned.
– Moderately concerned.
– Somewhat concerned.
– Slightly concerned.
– Not at all concerned.
– Don't know.

Section 8: Further Feedback

Q32: Do you have any further feedback, questions, comments, concerns, or anything else about Smart Cities in general or smart streetlights in particular that you want to share? Please leave a comment below.

Q33: Would you like to get contacted for a potential follow-up interview? If you agree to be contacted about the interview, you will be asked to provide your Prolific ID for sending you study information. Your decision will not impact your payment for the current survey.

– Yes, please contact me for a potential follow-up interview. My Prolific ID is:
– No, I do not wish to be contacted.

References

1. Alkhatib, A.: To live in their utopia: why algorithmic systems create absurd outcomes. Paper presented at the 2021 CHI Conference on Human Factors in Computing Systems, Yokohama, Japan (2021)
2. Attoh, K., Wells, K., Cullen, D.: "We're building their data": labor, alienation, and idiocy in the smart city. Environ. Planning D: Soc. Space **37**(6), 1007 (2019)
3. Baccarne, B., Mechant, P., Schuurman, D.: Empowered cities? An analysis of the structure and generated value of the smart city Ghent. In: Dameri, R.P., Rosenthal-Sabroux, C. (eds.) smart city. PI, pp. 157–182. Springer, Cham (2014). https://doi.org/10.1007/978-3-319-061 60-3_8

4. Baker, P., Potts, A.: 'Why do white people have thin lips?' Google and the perpetuation of stereotypes via auto-complete search forms. Crit. Discourse Stud. **10**(2), 187–204 (2013). https://doi.org/10.1080/17405904.2012.744320

5. Bannerman, S., Orasch, A.: Privacy and smart cities. Can. J. Urban Res. **29**(1), 17–38 (2020)

6. Benjamin, R.: Race after Technology: Abolitionist Tools for the New Jim Code. John Wiley & Sons, Cambridge, UK (2019)

7. Arun Bhukya, K., Ramasubbareddy, S., Govinda, K., Aditya Sai Srinivas, T.: Adaptive mechanism for smart street lighting system. In: Satapathy, S.C., Bhateja, V., Mohanty, J.R., Udgata, S.K. (eds.) Smart Intelligent Computing and Applications. SIST, vol. 160, pp. 69–76. Springer, Singapore (2020). https://doi.org/10.1007/978-981-32-9690-9_8

8. Boyd, D., Crawford, K.: Critical questions for big data: provocations for a cultural, technological, and scholarly phenomenon. Inf. Commun. Soc. **15**(5), 662–679 (2012). https://doi.org/10.1080/1369118X.2012.678878

9. Briggs, P., et al.: Everyday surveillance. Paper presented at the 2016 CHI Conference on Human Factors in Computing Systems, San Jose, CA, US 2016

10. Browne, S.: Dark Matters. Duke University Press, Durham (2015)

11. Budds, D.: How Google Is Turning Cities Into R&D Labs. Fast Company, February 22, 2016. https://www.fastcompany.com/3056964/how-google-is-turning-cities-into-rd-labs. Accessed 18 Mar 2022

12. City of Halifax.: Energy-efficient lighting projects (2017). https://www.halifax.ca/about-halifax/energy-environment/energy-efficent-lighting-projects. Accessed 1 Feb 2022

13. City of Kitchener.: Led streetlight conversion (2017). https://app2.kitchener.ca/digital/text/projects-2017-led-street-light.html. Accessed 1 Feb 2022

14. City of Montréal.: Street lighting: replacement of all light fixtures in Montréal (2021). https://montreal.ca/en/articles/street-lighting-replacement-all-light-fixtures-montreal-20159. Accessed 1 Feb 2022

15. City of Surry.: Street Lights (2020). https://www.surrey.ca/services-payments/parking-streets-transportation/roads-in-surrey/street-lights. Accessed 1 Feb 2022

16. Clothier, R.A., Greer, D.A., Greer, D.G., Mehta, A.M.: Risk perception and the public acceptance of drones. Risk Anal. **35**(6), 1167–1183 (2015). https://doi.org/10.1111/risa.12330

17. Cohn, J.: The Burden of Choice: Recommendations, Subversion, and Algorithmic Culture. Rutgers University Press (2019)

18. Conley, C.: Making smart decisions about smart cities. American Civil Liberties Union of Northern California (2017). https://www.aclunc.org/sites/default/files/20171115-Making_Smart_Decisions_About_Smart_Cities.pdf. Accessed 18 Mar 2022

19. Dale, M.: The backbone of smart cities: Matthew Dale discovers that smart lighting has a lot more to offer than the energy savings associated with LEDs. Electro Optics **280**, 16–20 (2018)

20. Davis, S.: Clear blue technologies illuminates Toronto's Bloor Street with smart city lighting systems. Clear Blue Technologies (2019). https://www.illumient.com/timeline/clear-blue-technologies-illuminates-torontos-bloor-street-with-smart-city-lighting-systems. Accessed 18 Mar 2022

21. Deschamps, T.: Deal allows Waterfront Toronto to block controversial Sidewalk labs project by fall if key issues not resolved. The Globe and Mail, August 2, 2019. https://www.theglobeandmail.com/business/article-deal-allows-waterfront-toronto-to-block-controversial-sidewalk-labs/. Accessed 18 Mar 2022

22. Diamond, L., Fröhlich, P.: Communicating privacy: user priorities for privacy requirements in home energy applications. In: Ardito, C., Lanzilotti, R., Malizia, A., Petrie, H., Piccinno, A., Desolda, G., Inkpen, K. (eds.) INTERACT 2021. LNCS, vol. 12935, pp. 665–675. Springer, Cham (2021). https://doi.org/10.1007/978-3-030-85610-6_38

23. D'Ignazio, C., Klein, L.F.: Data Feminism. MIT Press, Cambridge, MA, USA (2020)
24. Dizon, E., Pranggono, B.: Smart streetlights in smart city: a case study of Sheffield. J. Ambient. Intell. Humaniz. Comput. **12**, 1–16 (2021)
25. Eubanks, V.: Automating Inequality: How High-Tech Tools Profile, Police, and Punish the Poor. St. Martin's Press, New York, NY, USA (2018)
26. Gill, M.J., Swann, W.B., Jr., Silvera, D.H.: On the genesis of confidence. J. Pers. Soc. Psychol. **75**(5), 1101–1114 (1998)
27. Halper, M.: Toronto town settles on smart lights for now. LEDs Magazine, April 11, 2018. https://www.ledsmagazine.com/smart-lighting-iot/article/16701706/toronto-town-settles-on-smart-lights-for-now-updated. Accessed 28 Jan 2022
28. Harper, J., Singleton, S.: With a grain of salt: what consumer privacy surveys don't tell us. Competitive Enterprise Institute (2001). https://cei.org/wp-content/uploads/2010/10/Jim-Harper-With-a-Grain-of-Salt-What-Consumer-Privacy-Surveys-Dont-Tell-Us.pdf. Accessed 18 Mar 2022
29. Hawkins, A.J.: Alphabet's Sidewalk Labs shuts down Toronto smart city project. The Verge, May 7, 2020. https://www.theverge.com/2020/5/7/21250594/alphabet-sidewalk-labs-toronto-quayside-shutting-down. Accessed 18 Mar 2022
30. Henry, K., Lloyd, G., Ritchie, H.: People, power and planning in public places: the making of covenant day. Urban, Planning and Transp. Res. **3**(1), 109–131 (2015)
31. Hollands, R.G.: Will the real smart city please stand up? Intelligent, progressive or entrepreneurial? City **12**(3), 303–320 (2008). https://doi.org/10.1080/13604810802479126
32. Intel: Smart Street Lights for Brighter Savings and Opportunities (2017). https://www.intel.com/content/dam/www/public/us/en/documents/solution-briefs/smart-street-lights-for-brighter-savings-solutionbrief.pdf. Accessed 28 Jan 2022
33. Jin, D., et al.: Smart street lighting system: a platform for innovative smart city applications and a new frontier for cyber-security. Electr. J. **29**(10), 28–35 (2016)
34. Kitchin, R.: The Data Revolution: Big Data, Open Data, Data Infrastructures and their Consequences. Sage, London, UK (2014)
35. Kitchin, R.: The realtimeness of smart cities. TECNOSCIENZA: Ital. J. Sci. Technol. Stud. **8**(2), 19–42 (2018)
36. Königs, P.: Government surveillance, privacy, and legitimacy. Philos. Technol. **35**(1), 1–22 (2022). https://doi.org/10.1007/s13347-022-00503-9
37. Lanzing, M.: "Strongly recommended" revisiting decisional privacy to judge hypernudging in self-tracking technologies. Philos. Technol. **32**(3), 549–568 (2019). https://doi.org/10.1007/s13347-018-0316-4
38. Lau, J., Zimmerman, B., Schaub, F.: Alexa, are you listening? Privacy perceptions, concerns and privacy-seeking behaviors with smart speakers. In: Proceedings of the ACM on Human-Computer Interaction 2(CSCW), pp. 1–31 (2018). https://doi.org/10.1145/3274371
39. Lauriault, T.P., Bloom, R., Landry, J.-N.: Open Smart Cities Guide V1.0. Open North (2018). https://www.opennorth.ca/open-smart-cities-guide. Accessed 19 Mar 2022
40. Low, S.M.: The erosion of public space and the public realm: paranoia, surveillance and privatization in New York City. City & Society **18**(1), 43–49 (2006)
41. Lueth, K.L.: The top 10 cities implementing connected streetlights: Miami, Paris and Madrid on top. IoT Analytics (2018). https://iot-analytics.com/top-10-cities-implementing-connected-streetlights/. Accessed 19 Mar 2022
42. Lyon, D.: Surveillance, snowden, and big data: capacities, consequences, critique. Big Data Soc. **1**(2), 1–13 (2014). https://doi.org/10.1177/2053951714541861
43. Magnet, S.A.: When Biometrics Fail. Duke University Press (2011)
44. Mahoor, M., Hosseini, Z.S., Khodaei, A., Paaso, A., Kushner, D.: State-of-the-art in smart streetlight systems: a review. IET Smart Cities **2**(1), 24–33 (2020)

45. Marrone, M., Hammerle, M.: Smart cities: a review and analysis of stakeholders' literature. Bus. Inf. Syst. Eng. **60**(3), 197–213 (2018)
46. Mohandas, P., Dhanaraj, J.S.A., Gao, X.-Z.: Artificial neural network based smart and energy efficient street lighting system: A case study for residential area in Hosur. Sustain. Cities and Society **48**, 101499 (2019). https://doi.org/10.1016/j.scs.2019.101499
47. Mosco, V.: The Smart City in a Digital World. Emerald Publishing Ltd, Bingley, UK (2019)
48. Naeini, P.E., et al.: Privacy expectations and preferences in an IoT world. Paper presented at the 13th Symposium on Usable Privacy and Security (SOUPS), Santa Clara, CA, USA (2017)
49. Németh, J., Schmidt, S.: The privatization of public space: modeling and measuring publicness. Environ. Plann. B. Plann. Des. **38**(1), 5–23 (2011)
50. Nguyen, D.H., Bedford, A., Bretana, A.G., Hayes, G.R.: Situating the concern for information privacy through an empirical study of responses to video recording. Paper presented at the 2011 SIGCHI Conference on Human Factors in Computing Systems, New York, NY, USA (2011)
51. Nissenbaum, H.: Privacy in Context: Technology, Policy, and the Integrity of Social Life. Stanford University Press, Stanford, CA, USA (2010)
52. Noble, S.U.: Algorithms of Oppression. New York University Press, New York, NY, USA (2018)
53. Norman, D.A.: The Design of Everyday Things: Revised and Expanded Edition. Basic Books, New York, NY, USA (2013)
54. Northeast Group.: Global smart street lighting & smart cities: Market forecast (2020–2029). https://wellnesstg.com/wp-content/uploads/2020/12/Wellness-TechGroup-excerpt_Global-Smart-Street-Lighting-Smart-Cities-2020-2029_Northeast-Group-2.pdf. Accessed 19 Mar 2022
55. Penney, J.W.: Chilling effects: online surveillance and Wikipedia use. Berkeley Technol. Law J. **31**(1), 117–182 (2016). https://doi.org/10.15779/Z38SS13
56. Priyanka, S., Lakshmi, T.U., Sakthy, S.S.: Web–based street light system. Paper presented at the 2019 3rd International Conference on Computing and Communications Technologies (ICCCT), New York, NY (2019)
57. Proulx, C.: Colonizing surveillance: Canada constructs an indigenous terror threat. Anthropologica **56**, 83–100 (2014). http://www.jstor.org/stable/24469643
58. Sagolj, D.: Those bright white streetlights are part of Ottawa's conversion to LED. Capital Current (2018). https://capitalcurrent.ca/those-bright-white-streetlights-are-part-of-ottawas-conversion-to-led/. Accessed 19 Mar 2022
59. Smart Energy International.: Ville de Québec smartens its street lights (2007). https://www.smart-energy.com/regional-news/north-america/ville-de-qu-bec-smartens-its-street-lights/. Accessed 19 Mar 2022
60. Snow, S., et al.: Speculative designs for emergent personal data trails: Signs, signals and signifiers. Paper presented at the 2020 CHI Conference on Human Factors in Computing Systems, Honolulu, HI, USA (2020)
61. Statistics Canada: Table 17-10-0009-01 Population estimates, quarterly (2022). https://doi.org/10.25318/1710000901-eng. Accessed 19 Mar 2022
62. Steinmetz, J., Xu, Q., Fishbach, A., Zhang, Y.: Being observed magnifies action. J. Pers. Soc. Psychol. **111**(6), 852 (2016). https://doi.org/10.1037/pspi0000065
63. Thomas, D.R.: A general inductive approach for analyzing qualitative evaluation data. Am. J. Eval. **27**(2), 237–246 (2006). https://doi.org/10.1177/1098214005283748
64. Thomas, V., Wang, D., Mullagh, L., Dunn, N.: Where's wally? In search of citizen perspectives on the smart city. Sustainability **8**(3), 207 (2016). https://doi.org/10.3390/su8030207

65. Thompson, C.: Kitchener to test smart network to monitor parking, noise levels and water use. The Record, February 7, 2018. https://www.therecord.com/news/waterloo-region/2018/02/07/kitchener-to-test-smart-network-to-monitor-parking-noise-levels-and-water-use.html. Accessed 19 Mar 2022
66. Tusikov, N.: Sidewalk Toronto's master plan raises urgent concerns about data and privacy. The Conversation, July 30, 2019. https://theconversation.com/sidewalk-torontos-master-plan-raises-urgent-concerns-about-data-and-privacy-121025. Accessed 19 Mar 2022
67. Umamaheswari, S.: Smart street lighting in smart cities: a transition from traditional street lighting. In: Tamane, S.C., Dey, N., Hassanien, A.-E. (eds.) Security and Privacy Applications for Smart City Development. SSDC, vol. 308, pp. 117–133. Springer, Cham (2021). https://doi.org/10.1007/978-3-030-53149-2_6
68. van den Broek, T., Ooms, M., Friedewald, M., van Lieshout, M., Rung, S.: Privacy and security: citizen's desires for an equal footing. In: Michael Friedewald, J., Burgess, P., Čas, J., Bellanova, R., Peissl, W. (eds.) Surveillance, Privacy and Security: Citizens' Perspectives, pp. 15–35. Routledge, London (2017). https://doi.org/10.4324/9781315619309-2
69. Wade, K., Brubaker, J.R., Fiesler, C.: Protest privacy recommendations: an analysis of digital surveillance circumvention advice during black lives matter protests. Paper presented at the 2021 CHI Conference on Human Factors in Computing Systems, Yokohama, Japan (2021)
70. West, S.M., Whittaker, M., Crawford, K.: Discriminating systems. AI Now Institute (2019)
71. Woods, E.: From Connected Street Lights to Smart Cities. Forbes, June 4, 2018. https://www.forbes.com/sites%20/pikeresearch/2018/04/06/smart-cities/#59623c7613c8. Accessed 19 Mar 2022
72. Yao, Y., Xia, H., Huang, Y., Wang, Y.: Privacy mechanisms for drones: perceptions of drone controllers and bystanders. Paper presented at the 2017 CHI Conference on Human Factors in Computing Systems, Denver, CO, USA (2017)
73. Zheng, S., Apthorpe, N., Chetty, M., Feamster, N.: User perceptions of smart home IoT privacy. Proc. ACM Hum.-Comput. Interact. 2(CSCW), 1–20 (2018). https://doi.org/10.1145/3274469

AI in the Human Loop: The Impact of Differences in Digital Assistant Roles on the Personal Values of Users

Shakila Shayan[1]([✉]), Marlies van Steenbergen[1], Koen van Turnhout[1], Zelda Zeegers[1], Somaya Ben Allouch[2,3], Maaike Harbers[4], Guido Evertzen[1], Janna Bruijning[1], Wieke van Boxtel[1], and Katarina Jerkovich[1]

[1] Utrecht University of Applied Sciences, 3584 CH Utrecht, The Netherlands
shakila.shayan@hu.nl
[2] Amsterdam University of Applied Sciences, 1097 DZ Amsterdam, The Netherlands
[3] Informatics Institute, University of Amsterdam, 1098 XH Amsterdam, The Netherlands
[4] Rotterdam University of Applied Sciences, 3015 GG Rotterdam, The Netherlands

Abstract. As AI systems become increasingly prevalent in our daily lives and work, it is essential to contemplate their social role and how they interact with us. While functionality and increasingly explainability and trustworthiness are often the primary focus in designing AI systems, little consideration is given to their social role and the effects on human-AI interactions. In this paper, we advocate for paying attention to social roles in AI design. We focus on an AI healthcare application and present three possible social roles of the AI system within it to explore the relationship between the AI system and the user and its implications for designers and practitioners. Our findings emphasise the need to think beyond functionality and highlight the importance of considering the social role of AI systems in shaping meaningful human-AI interactions.

Keywords: Human-AI collaboration · Human-AI relationship · Social AI · Value Sensitive Design

1 Introduction

Artificial Intelligence (AI) has become ubiquitous in various industries and applications and is transforming how we live and work. As AI is becoming more widespread, contemplating the role of AI systems in our life is essential to ensure that it is used ethically, responsibly, and effectively [1]. Within the field of Human-AI collaboration, it is also vital to know how humans and AI systems can work together effectively and how to ensure that AI systems are aligned with human values and goals [2].

Historically, the AI field focused on creating fully autonomous systems that can perform tasks with the accuracy and efficiency of a machine and replace humans in tasks they cannot or do not want to perform. With the growth of adaptive systems which can collaborate and communicate with humans, the quality of the interaction with AI systems and the social components of that interaction is getting more attention [3]. At

J. Abdelnour Nocera et al. (Eds.): INTERACT 2023, LNCS 14144, pp. 239–249, 2023.
https://doi.org/10.1007/978-3-031-42286-7_13

times this attention has resulted in shifting focus from the functionality of the AI to its social relation in what is referred to as functional AI vs social AI [4]. In Functional AI completing the task at hand is the priority, while with social AI maintaining the social relationship with the user takes precedence [4].

In human-human collaboration, the quality of social relationships among humans can affect the partnership dynamics and the task outcomes [5–7]. Emotional support, which involves providing reassurance of worth and esteem, creates an encouraging and trustworthy environment, serves as a foundation for effective persuasion and motivates individuals to actively participate and contribute their best efforts [8, 9]. Appraisal support, which encompasses offering guidance, and constructive feedback, helps individuals refine their skills, make informed decisions, and continuously improve their performance within the activity [8]. When individuals feel that their autonomy and personal choices are respected and supported, they feel more in control, are more likely to be actively engaged and committed to the cooperative endeavour and their motivation to engage in the task and perform at their best increases [6, 10–12]. These findings are incorporated into the design of social AIs, where the goal is to create systems that can interact with humans in an engaging and effective manner [5]. Furthermore, research on computers as social actors shows that people tend to form relationships with machines when given appropriate social cues. [13, 14]. These results suggest that, like in human-human interactions, the quality of social interaction in human-AI systems can shape and influence individuals' personal values and affect task performance and outcome.

Interest in the impact of technology on human values has been increasing over the last few years. One of the most extensive accounts is the Value Sensitive Design approach introduced by Friedman in the 1990s [15]. In this approach, values are defined as "what a person or group of people consider important in life" [16]. Examples of values that may be affected by the design of technology include *human welfare, ownership and property, privacy, freedom from bias, universal usability, trust, autonomy, informed consent, accountability, courtesy, identity, calmness, and environmental sustainability* [17].

Attention to human values is important both from a responsible AI perspective and an adoption perspective. Differences in power dynamics between an AI system and its user can interfere with the user's values and behaviour [18]. Suppose an AI system with a higher level of control over the user's decisions; in that case, it may influence the user's priorities in ways that align with the AI system's goals rather than the user's. In this case, power imbalance affects the user's autonomy and agency. For instance, in the context of a highly automated self-driving car, the AI system makes decisions without human intervention, leading to low human autonomy. If the driver is on a road trip and wants to take the scenic route, the self-driving car's programming may override the driver's input and takes a more direct route instead of allowing the driver to overrule the car's programming. Such interference may make the driver feel frustrated or powerless. In contrast, when an AI-based voice assistant is designed such that the user has an active role and a lot of control over the tasks and decisions of the AI system, the user has more autonomy and will probably feel more in power.

Recent empirical studies are investigating how the social roles of AI systems affect users' relationships with them and how in turn, it may change power dynamics between people and technology [19, 20]. Dietvorst and colleagues [19], for instance, found significant differences in acceptance of AI-generated advice, depending on the interaction and whether users were given enough autonomy and control to adjust the advice. In other studies, the choice of female voice for Siri, Alexa and most other voice assistants and its potential impact on users' values has raised concerns among scholars. [20, 21]. Guzman [20], for instance, argues that Siri as a "female assistant" has a noticeable link to what is stereotypically associated with women's work. She writes, "With Siri, the power dynamics can extend beyond our understanding of machines onto our understanding of humans. Siri not only reflects gender stereotypes but has the potential to reinforce them".

In this paper, we examine how the social relationship between an AI system and its user affects the human values of the user. By analysing such an impact, we aim to gain insights into how users' values, attitudes, and behaviours may be influenced by their interactions with AI systems. We investigate three potential social roles that an AI healthcare application could take and explore how these roles impact the user's values. Understanding these variations and nuances in interaction would enable us to identify the potential implications for designers and practitioners.

2 Case

We investigated the social role of an "AI system" as part of a Human-Human advisory context, in which AI supported one human in advising another human. We chose the context of preventive health care and promoting 'positive health', which views health as a broader concept that focuses on *enhancing the quality of life, building resilience,* and *encouraging active participation* rather than just treating illness. In this context, the end goal of a conversation with a client is not always clearly defined. The Clients' problems could be "I don't know where to check for a healthy lifestyle" or "I don't know where to go in my neighbourhood to find a friend", but often, no decision is needed, and the client is recommended to follow the path towards positive change.

Allied Health students may struggle with conducting open conversations, as they are accustomed to focusing on specific health issues that require their expertise; therefore, they are more inclined to shift the conversation to their health practice in which they feel confident and knowledgeable. Instead, they should level their language to the client's level and start the conversation broadly, such as, "Why are you here today?", "Are you happy in general?", "How is your quality of life?". Then, dig deeper into the problems or areas of improvement that might arise to make more specific suggestions.

We chose the health check program because of its flexibility to allow for experimentation with different roles of an AI assisting system. We designed an AI prototype that would assist students in conversing with clients and would take on various roles. Given the complexity of the design space and to better address the context-specific questions concerning AI-Human Interaction, we limited the roles that AI could take to three roles based on existing models in the context of AI-Human collaboration. We named the roles: AI as Decision-Maker, AI as Coach and AI as Information-Provider. We explored how these three roles of AI impact users' values. The underlying assumption was that a proactive authoritative AI in the role of Decision-Maker activates values such as autonomy and agency differently than a reactive AI in the role of Information-Provider that waits for the user to take the initiative.

3 Design

3.1 Distinguishing Roles

The prototype design emerged from co-creation workshops with experts in AI, UX design, and preventive health practices. We aimed for an AI system knowledgeable in the broad mental and physical health domain instead of highly specialised medical expertise. Students could use AI to broaden their scope and ask open questions instead of focusing on their specific medical field. They could also use it to identify emerging issues in the talk, give general advice and wrap up the conversation.

We defined features that would distinguish the three roles through the interaction with the student. We wanted the elements to resemble the human roles of a decision-maker, a coach and an informer. Table 1 shows how the roles were distinguished at an abstract level. On the one end is the Decision-Maker role with the highest level of autonomy and control, which makes top-down decisions and interrupts and guides proactively. On the other end, an Information-Provider gives information only reactively and does not interrupt or intervene without explicit request. In between is the Coach, who offers suggestions, but in a more restrained manner than the Decision-Maker.

Table 1. Differences between the three roles assigned to AI

Decision-Maker	Coach	Information-Provider
Make decisions PROACTIVELY	Co-create and facilitate in MIXED INITIATIVE	Provide information REACTIVELY:
Provide the next step without asking Prioritise the problem for the student Provide exact advice or questions to ask Intervene when necessary	Provide guidance and information upon request Provide positive or negative feedback proactively when necessary	Get the question as input and provide the information No intervention or interruption without request

3.2 Design of the Prototype

The Positive Health Spider Web framework, developed at the Institute for Positive Health[1], was used as the structuring basis of the prototype. The starting page of the prototype is the same for all three roles; Irrespective of the pre-set role of the AI, the interface consists of a web schematic image of the framework (see Fig. 1). This screen is intractable, and the student can click on each section of the image to get additional information (e.g. suggestions of questions the student could ask). Upon clicking, the AI

---

[1] Interface was designed based on the research of the Positive Health Institute (https://www.iph.nl).

would interact differently with the student depending on the assigned role. The differences, however, are subtle; while the interface remains the same, the content or tone of language or level of reactiveness would differ. During the conversation with the client, the student could go back and forth to the main page to discuss other aspects of a healthy lifestyle that might need attention. Figure 1 depicts the differences between the three roles in more detail.

Role-1 Information-Provider

- Students can navigate through the spider web and choose what topic to discuss, and ask the client questions about that topic.
- Students can request information from the AI using a search bar.
- App responds to a question from the student with general information and in an informative tone.

Role-2 Coach

- Instead of the search bar, the App responds to the *"I don't know what to do"* button
- Student can navigate through the spider web and search for **what to ask**, the text hints on specific questions relevant to each topic.
- App sends suggestions and compliments to the student in a pop up **proactively** in green color, with a **neutral** to **positive** tone.

Role-2 Decision-Maker

- Students can navigate through the spider web; provided information has a dictating tone with exact questions the student should ask.
- The App takes a further proactive step and lights up a Positive Health dimension relevant to the problem of the client based on the conversation.
- App proactively sends a neutral/positive decision to the student with a green colour.
- App proactively sends negative/correcting decisions to the student with a red colour.
- App proactively sends keywords as a hint to the student to talk.

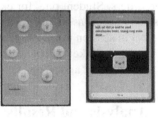

Fig. 1. Differences between the three roles as implemented in the prototype

The prototype was operated in the Wizard of OZ manner [22–24]. Wizard of Oz (WOZ) prototyping is a design methodology used to evaluate and improve the user experience of a design concept before it is turned into a product. This means we did not build a functioning AI system for this research. Instead, we used The WOZ methodology and the knowledge of the experts to operate the prototype and simulate the AI's behaviour. WOZ prototyping requires three things: a human "wizard" who runs the prototype, a script that provides instructions for this operation, and a person who plays the end user role. In our case, teachers and researchers from the Innovations in Preventive Healthcare group played the wizard and operated the prototype using a prewritten script for each role. In our Human-Human interaction setup, only the person interacting with the "AI system" (student) was considered the end user. Students of the Institute of Allied Health program were recruited for this purpose. Actors were recruited to play the role of the other human. These actors were given a predefined role and an accompanying script to play.

4   Evaluation

The AI prototype was tested in pilot sessions with two students and six clients online via MS Teams. After fixing minor issues, more students were recruited from various health study programs for in-person testing on location. Each student participated in three sessions, testing the prototype in different roles with different clients. Before the test, students were given a general overview of the research without mentioning the AI roles or differences between sessions. During the sessions, students' interactions with the prototype were recorded, and they participated in semi-structured interviews after each session to give feedback on the overall experience, app features, and evaluation. One professional actor and three drama school students played the client role with pre-assigned roles and scripts. We created three personas for clients based on standard and challenging cases. The order of the actors in each session was consistent, the AI prototype's role was counterbalanced across sessions, and students were randomly assigned to specific role orders. Student one, for example, had AI as Information-Provider with actor-1 in session one, AI as a Coach with actor-2 in session two, and AI as Decision-Maker with actor-3 in session three. Student two had AI as a Coach with actor-1 in session one, AI as Decision-Maker with actor-2 in session two, AI as Information-Provider with actor-3 in session three, and so on.

5   Analysis and Results

5.1   Coding Process

The prototype has been tested with seven students, each completing three sessions of interacting with the "AI system". We transcribed the 10-min interviews after each session (three interviews per student) and coded them using Atlas.ti[2]. We started with bottom-up

---

[2] ATLAS.ti Scientific Software Development GmbH [ATLAS.ti 22 Windows]. (2022). Retrieved from https://atlasti.com.

open coding. Five authors performed the first round of coding. One author coded all 21 sessions, while the other four coded six sessions each for verification purposes. This first coding round was done without predefined codes to let the concepts and values emerge from the context. Coders each added notes to the relevant conversation pieces when they found information that conveyed either a positive or negative general comment. Next, the authors went through the collection of these annotations together and agreed upon a coding approach. By employing this approach, one author coded all the interview conversations. In the second round, the codes that emerged from the open coding were discussed and grouped into bigger value-based code categories.

5.2 Distinguished Values

The following four values emerged from the interviews:

Autonomy in the context of this study can be described as the ability to make your own decisions without being controlled by anyone else. In the interviews, the students made remarks on the degree to which they felt compelled by the AI to ask specific questions. The AI was occasionally perceived as intrusive, but on the whole, students felt free to ignore the suggestions, even though sometimes it felt a little uncomfortable to do so. This feeling of intrusiveness was associated with the proactive pop-up of messages sent by the Decision-Maker and the Coach. Interruptions of the AI in these roles seemed to harm autonomy. Additionally, one student stated that formulating the topics as questions was distracting. This student would have preferred keywords, leaving more space to prepare questions in her own words.

Agency refers to the ability of a person to take purposeful action towards a specific objective. The students primarily talked about agency as being able to ask questions or look for information from the app: "..it just feels like one direction. I'm just receiving, and I don't feel like I can enter anything or search anything" (#4 on the Information-Provider). The same student on the Decision-Maker: "So what [I noticed] was different now, is that I get a response. Unsolicited. I like that. So you kind of have an idea that an assistant is helping out." (#4). Student 7 about the Coach: "That you indicate yourself when you need it, and when you don't."

Self-confidence emerged from the interviews in the sense of trust in one's abilities, qualities, and judgment. The prototype is experienced as supportive when the student is not entirely confident about what questions to ask. "So why would one need the app? Maybe a little bit of security for yourself." (#6 on the Coach role). Some students also had to learn that they did not need to ask all the suggested questions and that they could decide whether or not all of those questions were relevant or necessary: "Whether all those questions have to be asked. I don't know. I don't know if I had done it right." (#2).

Pop-up messages were not always evaluated negatively. Students respond positively to the proactive feedback messages, both to those that confirmed and supported their actions and the messages that corrected them and suggested different ways of proceeding. As student 5 formulated it: "Yes, sometimes I also got, for example, a: "Good job!". Because it is my first time using this, and that I have such a conversation, it's nice when someone says, "You're doing well" (#5 about the coach). And student 1 said, "It kind of makes you feel like, okay, I'm on the right track. That gives you a little confidence. So that feedback is nice" (#1 about the decision-maker).

Professional dignity in our context refers to the significance and value an individual holds in their professional capacity. It can be a factor in earning respect from others or in fostering self-respect. Professional dignity did not seem to be an issue for most students, except for student 7: "..you have to put your pride aside. Okay: "I don't know everything"….And in a sense, some kind of expert authority diminishes that a bit." (#7).

Besides these values, students also remarked on some themes related to the app's usability, such as the feedback and guidance provided by the app and the embedding of usage of the app in the conversation.

6 Discussion

Although our sample size is too small to draw firm conclusions at the moment, we see an indication that students did experience interacting with the three different roles of AI differently. Not only did they observe dissimilarities among the three roles, but they also evaluated these roles in different ways.

Our preliminary findings show that all three roles supported the student and boosted their confidence. The structure provided by the positive health model of the information provider helped the students with an overview and alleviated their concerns on how to continue the conversation and which question to ask next. It also enabled them to ask questions outside their field of expertise. The supportive messages from the coach gave the students a much-appreciated confirmation that they were doing all right. The corrective and directive messages from the decision maker provided clear and to-the-point guidance and gave the feeling of a real assistant.

Furthermore, it appears that different roles might have evoked different values simultaneously. For example, the supportive, positive messages from the coach and the more directive, sometimes corrective messages from the decision maker helped students develop self-confidence, as long as these messages were not too intrusive to interfere with their autonomy or call out for immediate attention. The students also seemed to feel more agency with the coach and decision-maker than with the Information-Provider. This appears to be related to the fact that the first two roles give a greater sense of inter-action. Having a kind of dialogue felt like having a helpful assistant. However, too much interference by the Decision-Maker felt authoritative and reduced that effect.

Experts have emphasised that human agency and the potential loss of autonomy and control over one's decisions are significant concerns regarding AI in the future [25, 26]. Research on how humans experience autonomy, agency, trust and motivation while inter-acting with AI in various everyday contexts has emphasised concerns regarding humans experiencing a loss of control over their goals, decisions, and actions when engaging with AI [27–31]. Recognising this, organisations like the European Commission have also released ethical guidelines, prioritising the development of trustworthy AI that would align with users' values [32, 33].

Values such as autonomy, agency, and professional dignity are intrinsic to human social relationships. They play a fundamental role in establishing healthy, balanced, and fulfilling individual relationships. Incorporating these values through relationship elements, such as emotional support, appraisal support, autonomy support, and a sense of belonging and identity, is vital in promoting empowerment, respect, and mutual trust and fostering collaborative efforts, engagement and meaningful interaction [5–12].

Hence, it is crucial to draw insights and lessons from human-human relationships and collaborations when designing AI systems that align with user values and expectations. By understanding the dynamics, principles, and values inherent in human relationships, we can create AI systems that foster similar qualities and promote positive interactions. This approach ensures that AI systems are designed with a user-centric perspective, taking into account the fundamental aspects of human relationships that contribute to trust, respect, autonomy, and collaboration.

7 Conclusion

The results presented in this paper are preliminary and must be validated in future research. Nevertheless, we have observed indications that variances in attitude exhibited by the AI could interfere with the user's perception and experience of AI support. Additionally, we identified the interplay between the design features of AI roles and values such as self-confidence, agency, and autonomy—differences in the role of the AI system during an interaction activated specific values more than others. Further investigation is necessary to delve into the design features of specific social roles of AI and how these features can potentially hinder or impede users' values.

The idea of mapping different AI roles to social relationships has not been systematically investigated in human-computer interaction research. However, some social components of interacting with AI have been explored in designing social AI systems [3], and findings suggest that people, in general, are not entirely on board with the current social AI systems [34, 35]. We advocate for greater attention to the design of the intended social role of an AI system to ensure that users' needs and values are met when interacting with the AI.

We believe that utilising social relationship models as generative metaphors in design is a valuable starting point for designing social roles in AI systems. These models offer designers a framework that facilitates the comprehension of how AI systems interact with humans. By employing such models, designers can consider the intricacies of human interaction more accurately, resulting in the creation of AI systems that align closely with users' needs, values, and expectations. Ultimately, this approach enhances users' acceptance and satisfaction with AI systems.

References

1. Agarwal, S., Mishra, S.: Responsible AI Implementing Ethical and Unbiased Algorithms. Springer International Publishing (2021). https://doi.org/10.1007/978-3-030-76860-7
2. Christian, B.: The Alignment Problem: Machine Learning and Human Values. WW Norton & Company, New York (2020)
3. Guzman, A.L., Lewis, S.C.: Artificial intelligence and communication: a human-machine communication research agenda. New Media Soc. 22(1), 70–86 (2020)
4. Kim, J., Merrill, K., Jr., Collins, C.: AI as a friend or assistant: the mediating role of perceived usefulness in social AI vs. functional AI. Telematics Inform. 64, 101694 (2021)
5. Bickmore, T.W., Picard, R.W.: Establishing and maintaining long-term human-computer relationships. ACM Trans. Comput.-Hum. Interact. (TOCHI) 12(2), 293–327 (2005)

6. Gabarro, J.: The development of working relationships. In: Galegher, J., Kraut, R., Eido, C. (eds.) Intellectual Teamwork: Social and Technological Foundations of Cooperative Work, pp. 79–110. Lawrence Erlbaum Associates, Hillsdale, New Jersey (1990)

7. Holtzblatt, K., Beyer, H.: Contextual Design: Defining Customer-Centered Systems. Elsevier (1997)

8. Berscheid, E., Reis, H.T.: Attraction and close relationships. In: Gilbert, D.T., Fiske, S.T., Lindzey, G. (eds.) The Handbook of Social Psychology, pp. 193–281. McGraw-Hill (1998)

9. Petty, R.E., Wegener, D.T.: Attitude change: multiple roles for persuasion variables. In: Gilbert, D.T., Fiske, S.T., Lindzey, G. (eds.) The Handbook of Social Psychology, pp. 323–390. McGraw-Hill (1998)

10. Borhani, K., Beck, B., Haggard, P.: Choosing, doing, and controlling: implicit sense of agency over somatosensory events. Psychol. Sci. **28**, 882–893 (2017). https://doi.org/10.1177/095679 7617697693

11. Caspar, E.A., Christensen, J.F., Cleeremans, A., Haggard, P.: Coercion changes the sense of agency in the human brain. Curr. Biol. **26**, 585–592 (2016). https://doi.org/10.1016/j.cub. 2015.12.067

12. Deci, E.L., Ryan, R.M.: The "what" and "why" of goal pursuits: human needs and the self-determination of behavior. Psychol. Inq. **11**, 227–268 (2000). https://doi.org/10.1207/S15327 965PLI110401

13. Nass, C., Steuer, J., Tauber, E.R.: Computers are social actors. In: Proceedings of the SIGCHI Conference on Human Factors in Computing Systems, Boston, MA, 24–28 April, pp. 72–78. ACM, New York (1994)

14. Nass, C., Moon, Y.: Machines and mindlessness: social responses to computers. J. Soc. Issues **56**(1), 81–103 (2000). https://doi.org/10.1111/0022-4537.00153

15. Friedman, B.: Value-sensitive design. Interactions **3**(6), 16–23 (1996)

16. Friedman, B., Kahn, P.H., Borning, A., Huldtgren, A.: Value sensitive design and information systems. In: Doorn, N., Schuurbiers, D., Poel, I., Gorman, M.E. (eds.) Early Engagement and New Technologies: Opening Up the Laboratory. PET, vol. 16, pp. 55–95. Springer, Dordrecht (2013). https://doi.org/10.1007/978-94-007-7844-3_4

17. Friedman, B., Harbers, M., Hendry, D.G., van den Hoven, J., Jonker, C., Logler, N.: Eight grand challenges for value sensitive design from the 2016 Lorentz workshop. Ethics Inf. Technol. **23**(1), 5–16 (2021). https://doi.org/10.1007/s10676-021-09586-y

18. Vereschak, O., Bailly, G., Caramiaux, B.: How to evaluate trust in AI-assisted decision making? A survey of empirical methodologies. Proc. ACM Hum.-Comput. Interact. **5**(CSCW2), 1–39 (2021)

19. Dietvorst, B.J., Simmons, J.P., Massey, C.: Overcoming algorithm aversion: people will use imperfect algorithms if they can (even slightly) modify them. Manage. Sci. **64**(3), 1155–1170 (2018)

20. Guzman, A.L.: Making AI safe for humans: a conversation with Siri. In: Socialbots and Their Friends, pp. 85–101. Routledge(2016)

21. Kudina, O.: Alexa does not care. Should you? Media literacy in the age of digital voice assistants. Glimpse **20**, 107–115 (2019). https://doi.org/10.5840/glimpse2019207

22. Dahlbäck, N., Jönsson, A., Ahrenberg, L.: Wizard of Oz studies: why and how. In: Proceedings of the 1st International Conference on Intelligent User Interfaces, pp. 193–200 (1993)

23. Riek, L.D.: Wizard of oz studies in hri: a systematic review and new reporting guidelines. J. Hum.-Robot Interact. **1**(1), 119–136 (2012)

24. Porcheron, M., Fischer, J.E., Reeves, S.: Pulling back the curtain on the wizards of Oz. Proc. ACM Hum.-Comput. Interact. **4**(CSCW3), 1–22 (2021)

25. Van de Poel, I.: Embedding values in artificial intelligence (AI) systems. Mind. Mach. **30**(3), 385–409 (2020)

26. Anderson, L.R.J., Luchsinger, A.: Artificial Intelligence and the Future of Humans (2018). https://www.pewresearch.org/internet/2018/12/10/artificial-intelligence-and-the-future-of-humans/

27. Abbass, H.A.: Social integration of artificial intelligence: functions, automation allocation logic and human-autonomy trust. Cogn. Comput. **11**(2), 159–171 (2019)

28. Kraus, M., Wagner, N., Minker, W.: Effects of proactive dialogue strategies on human-computer trust. In: Proceedings of the 28th ACM Conference on User Modeling, Adaptation and Personalization, pp. 107–116 (2020)

29. Sankaran, S., Zhang, C., Funk, M., Aarts, H., Markopoulos, P.: Do I have a say? Using conversational agents to re-imagine human-machine autonomy. In: Proceedings of the 2nd Conference on Conversational User Interfaces, pp. 1–3 (2020)

30. Sankaran, S., Zhang, C., Aarts, H., Markopoulos, P.: Exploring peoples' perception of autonomy and reactance in everyday AI interactions. Front. Psychol. **12**, 713074 (2021)

31. Zhang, C., Sankaran, S., Aarts, H.: A functional analysis of personal autonomy: how restricting 'what', 'when' and 'how' affects experienced agency and goal motivation. Eur. J. Soc. Psychol. **53**(3), 567–584 (2023)

32. High-Level Expert Group on Artificial Intelligence. Ethics guidelines for trustworthy AI. European Commission (2019)

33. European Commission: White Paper on Artificial Intelligence: a European approach to excellence and trust 2020. https://commission.europa.eu/publications/white-paper-artificial-intelligence-european-approach-excellence-and-trust_en

34. Ray, C., Mondada, F., Siegwart, R.: What do people expect from robots? In: IEEE/RSJ International Conference on Intelligent Robots and Systems, Nice, France, pp. 3816–3821(2008). https://doi.org/10.1109/IROS.2008.4650714

35. Dautenhahn, K., et al.: What is a robot companion - friend, assistant or butler? In: 2005 IEEE/RSJ International Conference on Intelligent Robots and Systems, Edmonton, AB, Canada,, pp. 1192–1197 (2005). https://doi.org/10.1109/IROS.2005.1545189

Evaluation of the Roles of Intelligent Technologies in Shared Activity Spaces of Neighborhood Communities

Jouko Makkonen[✉] ⓘ, Rita Latikka ⓘ, Rosana Rubio-Hernández ⓘ,
and Kaisa Väänänen ⓘ

Tampere University, Kalevantie 4, 33014 Tampere, Finland
jouko.makkonen@tuni.fi

Abstract. The use of shared spaces in urban neighborhoods can advance sustainability and residents' sense of community. Intelligent technologies may take different roles in supporting activities in shared spaces. We conducted an evaluation study of technology roles for space sharing in the context of a new residential area in Tampere, Finland. This area, called Hiedanranta, is planned to accommodate shared spaces in novel ways. Four previously defined roles were addressed: community sheriff, matchmaker, facilitator, and tutor. Overall, the roles were considered positive; however, the participants experienced the sheriff as being inefficient and the matchmaker as being intrusive. The facilitator was considered a potential source for pragmatic support, and the tutor was thought of as an add-on to the other roles. In addition to pragmatic benefits, intelligent technologies with these roles have the potential to lower the social threshold of using activity spaces. However, the participants were concerned about their privacy and the intrusiveness of technology. The findings contribute to the research of sustainable technologies for supporting shared spaces and activities in urban residents' local communities.

Keywords: intelligent technologies · technology roles · shared activity spaces · neighborhood communities · evaluation study

1 Introduction

Globally, more than half of the people live in urban areas, and the urban population is estimated to rise rapidly [31]. Even though in Finland the COVID-19 pandemic slowed the growth of the population in the metropolitan area of the capital, Helsinki, many other Finnish cities, for instance, Tampere, increased their population [30]. This urban development creates ecological, social, economic, and spatial needs for balancing independent homes with shared spaces in urban areas [10, 16, 17, 19]. Residents' motivations to use shared spaces in their city block or neighborhood are diverse [2, 5, 6, 8, 28]. Some of the reasons are linked to activities [20]: first, shared spaces would enable residents to engage in activities that cannot be undertaken in their private homes (such as unclean handcraft

Supplementary Information The online version contains supplementary material available at https://doi.org/10.1007/978-3-031-42286-7_14.

and repair or activities that require space), and second, the activities could be performed together with other residents. Thus, shared spaces, on the one hand, expand the spatial possibilities of private homes, in terms of dimensions and facilities, in an affordable manner [20]. On the other hand, they support the balance of privacy and communality in living contexts [20]. These needs are recognized in the planning of a new innovation-and sustainability-oriented residential area of Hiedanranta in Tampere, Finland, where residential blocks are being planned to increase the sharing of yards, common spaces, services, and utilities [27].

Intelligent technologies have been proposed for advancing the use of shared spaces, aiming at providing benefits for costs, energy or resource sufficiency, or well-being [20, 26]. By *intelligent technology*, we refer to data-driven and proactive technology applications that involve some form of Artificial Intelligence (AI) in their functionality. This relatively novel context of applying intelligent technologies into shared activity spaces of neighborhood communities is lacking well-grounded theories. In this study, we used roles from study by Makkonen et al. (2022) for informing and structuring the investigation. Makkonen et al. [20] found that intelligent technology solutions could advance space sharing by facilitating a fluent use of spaces, activities in the spaces, social interaction, and communality in the neighborhood; based on the findings, they proposed four roles for intelligent technology: community sheriff, matchmaker, facilitator, and tutor.

In this study, we evaluated these roles from the user experience standpoint in the context of shared activity spaces in urban neighborhood communities. We used the Hiedanranta area as the study context because it is planned to accommodate sharing of spaces in novel ways and therefore exemplifies an urban neighborhood where the roles of intelligent technologies for advancing space sharing could be applied to. We used a mixed-method approach by combining survey and focus group (FG) data. In this context, we define the concept of *role* to include the use purposes, goals, possible actions, and social behaviors of technology in its interaction with users [14, 18, 20]. The consideration of roles provides a way to broadly evaluate the user experience and expectations of intelligent technologies in a novel use context where technical solutions are not set, because the roles are not limited to certain devices or software.

Our general research question (RQ) was:

How do residents perceive the predefined roles of intelligent technologies for advancing space sharing?

To gain more nuanced information about the perception, we also asked:

RQa: What are the expected benefits of the roles of intelligent technologies for advancing space sharing?

RQb: What are the expected challenges of the roles of intelligent technologies for advancing space sharing?

These questions were established to investigate the residents' perceptions, expectations, and experiences of the roles of intelligent technologies in supporting space sharing in urban residential areas. The findings contribute to the field of human-computer interaction (HCI) and user experience (UX) by increasing the knowledge of how interactive technologies can advance sustainable living in future societies.

2 Background and Related Work

The study of roles has been applied to different types of technologies and in several contexts. In the context of residential living and related to the social roles of technology, for instance De Graaf and Allouch [11] studied the acceptance of three potential roles for domestic social robots in an online questionnaire: (1) *a butler robot* described as a servant that does chores, (2) *an information source* as a database that answers all of the user's questions, and (3) *a companion* as "a sociable intellect that builds on online shared stories and with whom users can talk when feeling down or lonely" [11]. De Graaf's and Allouch's results suggested that participants favor the more pragmatic roles of the robot (butler and information source) instead of the companion. Based on their results, the companion robot was evaluated negatively compared with others on different acceptance factors, i.e., usefulness, enjoyment, social presence, and experienced social influence [11]. Herczeg [12] discussed the roles and values of *smart, intelligent, and wise* interactive systems, presenting smart systems as "hidden and silent performers" that meet general consumers' needs by just doing "what they are expected to do", i.e., sense and act. Herczeg's intelligent systems are "mind tools" or "assistants" capable of solving problems rationally, whereas wise social systems classify, combine, and reflect human knowledge and wisdom [12].

HCI and UX have been studied scarcely in the context of shared residential spaces. Sánchez et al. [26] presented an IoT and iTV system for monitoring, automation, and helping with decision-making about residents' common areas, showing potential benefits for the measurement of air quality, optimization of utilities, and maintenance of leisure spaces like pools and gardens. Intelligent technologies in shared spaces relate to smart-city and urban informatics research [7], where privacy and data gathering have been found to concern residents [21]. As a response to anxieties about control, Mann et al. [21] proposed citizens' sovereignty over technology and data in the context of smart cities. By this they referred to ownership and control over personal data, to provide a more transparent and democratic design of smart-city technologies and to provide citizens with more autonomy instead of being source of technology providers' data [21]. Smart-city development has encountered both expectations for sustainable urban development and critiques of it: e.g., excessive optimism toward technology, risks for social equity, or instrumentalizing citizens as data sources [9, 13, 23]. In the domestic sphere, trust and security risks play a significant role in the acceptance of smart homes [1], and constant data gathering causes potential privacy and security risks [29]. Wang et al. [29] found, however, that individuals tend to ignore the risks and focus on potential benefits instead. Marky et al. [22] suggested that visitors of smart homes have a limited understanding of how smart home technologies collect their personal data, and therefore, they are missing the needed awareness to protect their privacy.

The application of technologies with roles in the context of shared spaces in residential areas is limited. Research on social functions of the technology roles or the roles as advancers of the use of shared spaces is also scarce. Makkonen et al. [20] presented four roles for intelligent technologies in the context of sharing spaces in residential areas. These roles for space sharing considered the identified needs, expectations, and challenges of residents living in a similar area than Hiedanranta. The roles aim at being parallel with factors that support space sharing from the resident perspective, i.e., the proximity of the space, presence of activities, and experience of ownership of the space [20, 25], or factors that mitigate the experienced challenges of space sharing [20]. The role of *the community sheriff* is an objective observer that gently pushes people toward positive behavior and promotes the common rules of the space. *The matchmaker* matches, recommends, and connects people, places, and activities. The function of *the facilitator* is to organize and remove obstacles and extra work in using the space. *The tutor* teaches, motivates, and helps to share skills needed in hobbies [20]. The roles are expected to utilize AI recommendations in their functions. They serve several use-purposes for intelligent technologies, which can be categorized as "organizing and facilitating"; "matching, recommendation, and connecting"; and "supportive intelligent technologies for space and activities" [20]. In comparison, the roles of the butler and information source presented by de Graaf and Allouch [11] are partially overlapping with the facilitator and tutor [20]. Some of the roles for space sharing aim at inviting residents to use spaces, do activities, volunteer, and be socially and physically involved in the community of residents. Regarding volunteering, Lund and Juujärvi [19] indicated that residents' participation in the neighborhood begins with everyday actions, and the development of residents' agency needs a sense of community and interaction between residents and common spaces.

3 Methods

This mixed-method study is based on survey data with quantitative and open-ended text questions and qualitative data from three FG discussions of Finnish respondents. This setting enabled the evaluation of residents' perceptions regarding benefits and challenges of roles, both qualitatively and quantitatively. The survey focused on measuring the attitudes toward the roles and transferring the answers to comparable numerical values. FGs enabled the evaluation of the roles qualitatively in a dynamic social setting formed by the FGs. The data gathered in the survey and the FGs support each other: the survey informed preparing the FGs and in the analysis phase, the FGs provided in-depth qualitative view to support the survey findings. Together, these methods provided insight into the expected benefits and challenges of using intelligent technologies with the roles for space sharing in residential settings.

3.1 Survey

We collected online survey data from Finnish respondents from June to August 2021 ($N = 85$). The survey data was collected as part of a larger survey on shared spaces and technologies in residential areas of the near future. The survey addressed space sharing concepts in urban residential areas, attitudes and perceptions on different features of the predefined technology roles or space sharing, and features of potential intelligent technology solutions with the roles.

Participants. The survey targeted people living in apartment buildings in Tampere, Finland. It was distributed on local social media groups, on mailing lists of local and Hiedanranta-related stakeholders in the Tampere area, and through internal communication channels for residents of six apartment buildings with contemporary shared spaces located next to the planned Hiedanranta area. The respondents were 64.7% female, and the average sample age was 44.3 years (SD = 15.1). Most respondents had a university degree (65.9%) and were working full-time (50.6%). Most of the respondents lived in an apartment building (80.0%). The respondents were informed about the aims of the research, and answering the survey was fully voluntary. The respondents were allowed to quit the survey at any point if they wanted to. The respondents were not monetarily compensated for participating in the study.

The Survey Structure. The survey begun with questions on background information. To evaluate the general aims of the technology roles for space sharing, the participants were asked about their interests in receiving recommendations in general on activities, shared spaces, and company for hobbies in their residential area. More questions were asked regarding a shared space and technology concept that was presented to participants through a written scenario and an illustration where it was located in the planned urban residential area of Hiedanranta (Fig. 1). The concept utilizes intelligent technologies with the roles for space sharing in a network of shared activity spaces. AI gives recommendations on activities, spaces, and company for hobbies. Spaces enable activities, e.g., unclean handcraft and repair, cooking, exercise, and gardening. Referring to this scenario, participants were queried on their perceptions of the attributes of the concept and the investigated roles for space sharing (i.e., participants' positivity towards the key functions of the roles, participants' readiness for the user's involvement that some of the intelligent technologies with roles would invite users to, and expected problems of the concept), recommendations, and data gathering (i.e., affective perceptions towards data gathering of topics that are required for intelligent technology to give recommendations on activities, wanted subjects of recommendations, and opinions on who owns and administrates the data), and privacy related issues. A full list of survey measures can be found in the supplementary material.

Analysis Method. We analyzed the quantitative data using descriptive methods. We report percentages (%) for categorical variables and means (M) and their standard deviations (SD) for continuous variables. For analyzing the open-text answers, we used content analysis, which was considered the most suitable for identifying attitudinal and behavioral responses and categorizing the data [3, 24]. The analyses were mainly conducted by the first author, but other authors were also involved in the process by providing critical comments.

3.2 Focus Groups

We conducted three FG discussions online from November 2021 to April 2022 (N = 13).

Participants. The total number of participants was 13. The participants' age varied from 20 to 60 years. The FGs included residents living in apartment buildings in Tampere, active members or personnel of third-party civic organizations or activist groups, and the City of Tampere urban developers. The distribution of participants in the focus groups is presented in Table 1.

Participants were recruited through local social media groups and direct contact. Participants received a movie ticket for participation.

Fig. 1. The planned Hiedanranta area and potential types of shared spaces: handcraft and repair workshop, shared kitchen and dining room, exercise space, and garden. The image was used in the survey and the focus groups.

Table 1. The distribution of participants in the FGs by the group they represent. (* In FG2, one participant was affiliated with both residency and civic organizations. ** One representative of city of Tampere urban developers participated both FG1 and FG2.)

	FG1	FG2	FG3	Total
Number of participants	5	6*	3	13*
Residents	3	3*	3	9
Civic organization representatives		3*		3
City of Tampere urban developers	2	1		2**

The Process of the FGs. The FGs were held online on the Teams platform. A canvas in the Mural online whiteboard application was used for online collaboration and real-time documentation, grouping and visualization of the discussion content. The same shared space and technology concept that was used in the survey was illustrated and explained on the canvas and by verbal explanation. Audio and activities on the Mural canvas were recorded. The FG discussions were transcribed. All focus group discussions lasted approximately 1 h and 20 min.

In the FG discussions, we aimed at investigating the perceptions of residents and other stakeholders relevant to residential area activities, particularly about intelligent technologies with the predefined roles for space sharing. We presented each role through a description and a use scenario on the Mural canvas and read them aloud. The role descriptions were summarized from the roles of Makkonen et al. (2022). The scenarios were built around example use cases described in the original role descriptions, written in a form where imaginary users are utilizing the system. As an example of a role description, we described the community sheriff as an independent observer of shared spaces, which, when needed, guides people towards good behavior and to comply with the common rules of the space. The descriptions were followed by a discussion that was supported by questions related to the first impressions, positive and negative factors, use purposes, and thoughts on how the roles could advance the use of activity spaces. The order of the questions was not set; however, the discussion was guided to ensure each topic was discussed.

In FG1 and FG2 one researcher lead the interview and facilitated the discussion, presented the scenarios, and guided through tasks in the Mural canvas, while another researcher was responsible for notetaking, and additional questions. FG3 was ran by only one researcher for practical reasons.

Analysis Method. The focus group data was analyzed using thematic analysis to present the findings in the form of themes [4]. This included familiarizing oneself with the data and coding and creating initial themes. The first author sketched the initial themes, which were then reviewed by other authors. Qualitative analysis software Atlas.ti was used in the analysis.

4 Results

The first section presents the survey results about residents' general attitudes toward and perceived challenges of the space and technology concept that utilizes intelligent technologies with the roles for space sharing. After that, the presentation order follows the themes found in the analysis of the FG data. The general RQ is answered trough the survey results and found themes. Survey results relevant to the topic of the theme are presented in the same section as the FG results. Starting from Sect. 4.2, each section presents a theme, and each subsection a subtheme. As an exception, in the last subsection of Sect. 4.2 we present survey results on the functions of the roles. The first two sections of this results chapter answer to both sub-questions RQa and RQb, Sects. 4.3 and 4.4 to RQa and Sects. 4.5 and 4.6 to RQb.

In the analysis of the FG data, five themes were found: *Role-specific findings* (Sect. 4.2), *Pragmatic benefits are appreciated as advancers of space use* (Sect. 4.3), *Technologies with predefined roles have the potential to lower residents' social threshold for using shared spaces* (Sect. 4.4), *Residents are concerned about intrusiveness, privacy issues, and data gathering* (Sect. 4.5), and *Potential negative consequences of limitations or excessive use of intelligent technology in the residential context* (Sect. 4.6).

4.1 Residents' Attitudes and Perceived Challenges of Shared Activity Space Use and Recommendations by Intelligent Technology

Majority of the survey respondents (71.8%) wanted recommendations for shared spaces, activities, and company (e.g., a partner) for hobbies in their neighborhood. Each of the 24 open comments for the question regarding interest in receiving recommendations communicated the need for more information on activities and spaces. Spaces and activities were assumed to be unknown and hard to find, and the use potential of spaces was lowly utilized. Open answers also revealed that some respondents considered in this question rather general communications or advertisement for groups on a scale of a housing company or a neighborhood instead of personally targeted recommendations. One participant directly mentioned that the recommendations should be general and not overly targeted. Regarding more detailed topics pertaining to activity recommendations, two mentioned exercise, and one mentioned guidance with digital tools.

Regarding subjects of AI recommendations 72.9% of the respondents wanted recommendations from AI on suitable shared spaces, 65.9% on activities, and 64.7% on schedules for the use of spaces and hobbies. The popularity of recommendations that involve other residents was lower, with percentages of 36.5% for other residents in the area who are interested in doing activities together, 35.3% for other residents in the area who can teach you skills needed for hobbies, and 18.8% for other residents in the area whom you could teach skills needed for their hobbies. 14.1% chose none of the above.

Considering readiness for user involvement, 42.4% reported they would be ready to volunteer as a company for hobbies to others, and 31.8% would teach other people skills needed for their hobbies. There was a drop in letting AI recommend similar things: 27.1% were ready to let AI recommend them as a hobby company, and 20.0% would let AI recommend them to teach other people skills needed for their hobbies. 40.0% chose the option none of the above.

The open question "What problems can be associated with the described shared space for hobbies?" was answered by 41 respondents. The analysis resulted in 17 different problem codes. Most of the reported problems were related to the space or the concept as a whole, rather than the intelligent technology in it; however, eight of the codes considered problems of assumed AI solutions, answering RQb directly. These expected challenges of intelligent technology were high costs, data gathering, privacy issues, problems in security, lack of control, meeting the versatility in users' expectations, difficulties in motivating the community members to participate and take responsibility, potential usability issues, and disturbing recommendations. Considering the problems linked to the space concept, 11 of them were such that the investigated roles for space sharing aim at solving. In most cases (10), this considered the role of the sheriff and regarded problems in tidiness and hygiene, rules and responsibilities, misbehavior and vandalism, unauthorized use or disappearance of objects, meeting the versatility of users' expectations, breakages, noise, security, surveillance and control, as well as motivating the community members to participate and take responsibility. One recognized problem regarding the viability of the space concept matched the aims of the facilitator role.

4.2 Role-Specific Findings

This section presents findings that are related to specific roles.

The Authority of the Sheriff is Questioned. The role of the sheriff had a twofold reception in the focus groups with its positively experienced goals and questionable efficiency. In the discussions of each group, the role of the sheriff was seen as interconnected to the residential community and social pressure. It was considered to reduce stigma and social pressure caused by the rules of shared space and the potential or actual breakage of those rules because the feedback would come from technology instead of a person. However, the same reasoning questioned the efficiency of the feedback because of the lack of authority and lessened or absence of social pressure as a motivator. The sheriff was considered to have the potential to unify standards, which can vary among the users of the shared spaces.

Several potential use areas were found for the sheriff. It could supervise, for instance, correct use of parking areas, storage spaces, recycling areas, or location of tools in a workshop. Also, safety and security were seen as suitable application areas. The sheriff's role is dependent on the technical capabilities. The mistakes or misinterpretations of technology appeared as a concern in the FG discussions. From the community perspective, FG3 discussed a problem of common ground in shared spaces, where no one takes responsibility. They saw that the sheriff has the potential to tackle this problem by advancing the experience of ownership of the shared spaces.

The Matchmaker Balances Positive Outcomes and Intrusiveness. In the FGs, first impressions of the matchmaker role varied from *great* to *horrible*. It can be summarized to have positive goals but concerning means. The negative comments related to intrusiveness. The matching related to the role, proposing meetings and meeting times, and letting the matchmaker technology access one's calendar, was considered intrusive and *too much* by some participants. However, these participants also appreciated most of the expected benefits of the matchmaker, i.e., mediating help in the neighborhood, organizing, and sharing information about the shared spaces. The matchmaker was expected to have the potential to increase the interest in shared space and lower the threshold in using the spaces. According to the workers of civic organizations who participated in FG2, the matchmaker would answer to the real needs of, for instance, older adults who need help. Mutually, the participants noted that people are happy to help others.

The participants suggested that the matchmaker can be utilized for sharing or borrowing tools or other things, sharing skills and know-how, or looking for company for sports or other hobbies. The discussed risks were related to misuse or misbehavior (e.g., harassment) and potential burdening of often matched people. The participants called for a high level of control for users over the system.

The Facilitator is Valued for Its Pragmatic Benefits. In FG2 and FG3, the participants showed enthusiasm about the pragmatic benefits of the role of facilitator, i.e., saving time, removing tasks from the user, automating the space, and organizing activities. Most of these benefits, however, were based on an assumption that the space is highly automated. In FG1, the discussion took another path, and attitudes were more reserved toward the facilitator than in FG2 and FG3: these participants called the role *strange* and *distant* and spent time discussing the challenges, e.g., the risk of segregation between living areas because of advanced technology being used in some but not all areas.

The facilitator was considered to advance sustainability and create value for individuals by optimizing the use rate of the space and by creating the most suitable circumstances, e.g., time- and money-wise for the user. Regarding the potential application areas of the facilitator, the participants proposed spaces, services, or facilities that can be booked for private use, for instance, saunas and laundry facilities.

Spontaneous recommendations for hobbies divided opinions. For some, it was a distant idea to get propositions on hobbies, whereas others were enthusiastic about it. In FG3, the discussions were positive about hobby recommendations, which were thought to provide benefits for individuals and the community of residents, for instance, by reducing perceived loneliness and increasing the social activity in the community.

Tutor's Potential is in Its Cooperation with Other Roles. The tutor was experienced positively in the FGs. The participants saw potential in the tutor's capabilities to lower the barriers of using shared spaces or doing activities, as well as in marketing spaces, resulting in increasing the use rate of shared activity spaces. However, the usefulness of one of the key tasks of the tutor role, providing information, was questioned. The participants in FG3 suspected they would not use it because they would seek the same information that the tutor provides from a search engine that they usually use. However, the participants in FG3 proposed adding value by optimizing the tutor for the housing company it operates in, i.e., instructing the residents about what can be done in the spaces and the facilities that are available.

FG1 and FG2 associated the tutor with other roles, so the previously mentioned potential benefits were not necessarily benefits of the tutor independently, but rather the combination of the tutor and the matchmaker and, in some cases, the tutor and the sheriff. In addition to gardening, which was given in the example scenario, the participants proposed potential subjects of instruction: sports activities, cooking, digital skills, and the use of tools in the handcraft workshop. Together with the roles of sheriff and matchmaker, it could mediate help and assistance in the neighborhood or work as a companion technology. The tutor was considered to benefit mostly the new residents in the area or a housing company; however, some participants considered it likely that it would lose its usefulness after residents familiarized themselves with the neighborhood. Another expected challenge was keeping the information up to date.

Residents Are Mildly Positive Toward the Functions of the Roles for Space Sharing. The respondents reported being mildly positive toward the functions of the roles for space sharing. Nevertheless, the most positively experienced option was the non-AI option given as a reference point *(d) ...something other than AI motivates one to use spaces, guides and teaches in spaces, and invites people of the neighborhood together* ($M = 4.9, SD = 1.6$). Continuing, the open field question *If you wanted something other than AI to handle your data and guide and organize the use of spaces, what or who would this be, and why?* was answered by 39 participants. In 12 of these respondents expected it to be challenging for AI to interact with people in the social context of a neighborhood; a human was seen as more approachable and better at motivating people. Four participants considered that using AI for these matters might reduce human contacts; however, three comments supported using AI for routine matters. Three participants stated a need for the data gathering to be done in an ethically acceptable manner.

The answer option connected to the role of sheriff *(b) ...AI would guide and motivate you to follow the agreed rules of a shared space*, was reported the most positive of the role connected options ($M = 4.8, SD = 1.8$). Second positively rated was the option connected to the role of tutor, *(a) ...AI would teach you the skills needed for hobbies* ($M = 4.4, SD = 1.7$), and as the least positively experienced was the option connected to the roles of facilitator and matchmaker *(c) ...AI would invite people from the neighborhood together, for instance, for a communal cooperative work meeting (i.e., a communal work gathering) (M* = 4.2, *SD* = 1.9). The distribution of the answers is presented in Fig. 2.

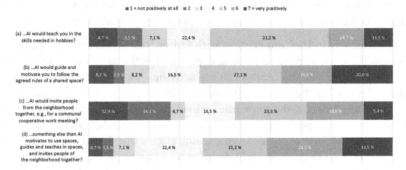

Fig. 2. Distribution of the answers to the question "Regarding shared spaces, how positive are you toward…"

4.3 Pragmatic Benefits Are Appreciated as Advancers of Space Use

The participants in each FG listed several concrete and pragmatic benefits of the intelligent technologies with roles that are linked to advancing the use of activity spaces. The described pragmatic benefits were gained by either the spaces or the users of spaces, for instance, resulting in a well-kept space or a space user with added value. They were also considered to save resources on maintenance and make it more efficient.

> *The first thing that came to my mind was that it [the sheriff] would be handy. – – No need to send messages afterwards – – Instead, one could fix one's error already during the same day or during the reservation. (P4)*

These pragmatic benefits, as advancers of space use, were connected to each of the roles and several use contexts of the roles. For instance, the role of the sheriff was considered to increase residents' trust in the good condition of shared activity spaces, as well as the space users' certainty about the condition of a space after its use. The sheriff was expected to unify the standards among space users, which was expected to result in spaces being more attractive to use. Using the roles in the context of facilities like storages or waste management, or to advance communication or assistance between neighbors were also considered to be linked with pragmatic benefits.

4.4 Technologies with the Predefined Roles Have the Potential to Lower Residents' Social Threshold for Using Shared Spaces

The potential of intelligent technology to lower the threshold to use activity spaces was discussed in each group, and it was connected to each of the roles. Different kinds of thresholds were discussed, as well as different mechanisms for lowering them. Mostly, the thresholds described by the participants were social by their nature. These social thresholds to use activity spaces, as categorized in the analysis of the FG data, included versatility in their root causes. For instance, personal social barriers, i.e., shyness or fear of getting negative feedback from other residents or space users, were mentioned several times as reasons that might cause perceived social thresholds.

Technology functioning in the role of sheriff was considered to have the potential to lower the threshold by giving critical feedback as a *faceless technology* and by removing the kind of social interactions that are unpleasant for some. Participants felt that feedback from technology would have a more constructive impact than feedback from people who are active in communicating with passive-aggressive notes on the bulletin board. On the other hand, technologies with matchmaker and facilitator roles were expected to have the potential to advance the communality in the neighborhood, thus making the social interaction that happens in activity spaces easier for those who experience a greater social barrier with strangers:

If you move in, it would be easier to get into the community of the condominium with that kind of application [referring to the matchmaker]. Some, perhaps smaller condominiums might have so tight community, that it is difficult to get into. (P9)

Sharing or increasing information was considered a factor in reducing barriers. Space users' uncertainty of their capabilities in using the space or doing activities in the space was mentioned as a cause of social thresholds. The participants believed that the role of the tutor could help in that regard by teaching and strengthening space users' skills, know-how, and confidence. The matchmaker was expected to help in the same issue by matching people based on needed and shared skills and know-how, as described in the matchmaker scenario in the FGs.

Advancing communality and increasing information, done by the intelligent technologies with the roles, were both seen as key aspects in indirectly lowering social thresholds for using activity spaces. In the FG discussions, lowering social barriers in space use, social interaction and activities, and social and communal benefits of technologies with the roles were interconnected. In addition, the analysis showed a connection between lowering social barriers and other positive outcomes of intelligent technologies with roles, i.e., *organizing, mediating help, benefits of communication,* and *increasing use rate.*

4.5 Residents Are Concerned About Intrusiveness, Privacy Issues, and Data Gathering

In the focus groups, the most significant cluster of concerns was formed around data gathering, privacy, and intrusiveness or similar to avoid repetition. Data gathering raised privacy concerns in participants and caused questions, for instance, what data would be gathered, who would gather it and for what purpose, and where and for how long it would be stored.

In the survey, 34 participants answered the open field question *What kind of privacy-related thoughts does the shared space for hobbies provoke in you?* Their answers underlined the importance of privacy and data security for the participants by directly stating the importance and stating the unpleasantness of gathering personal data. However, several participants considered the concept free of privacy challenges. Some mentioned this as a current reality anyway. The shared spaces were considered public space; however, some mentioned a risk of other people's misbehaviors that can compromise other's privacy (e.g., other space users' social media posts with pictures of bystanders, or misuse of the gathered data). Intelligent solutions were considered a trade-off of where data gathering is accepted to gain the benefit of using the solution.

Regarding the question *How would you feel if data about you were gathered to provide recommendations on...*, the most pleasantly experienced option was, on a scale from 1 to 7, the option *(a) ...how often and what times do you visit shared spaces? (M = 4.2, SD = 1.7)*, second pleasantly experienced option was *(b) ...what do you do in a shared space? (M = 3.7, SD = 1.8.)*, and third, the option *(d) ...your hobbies? (M = 3.7, SD = 1.7)*. The option that was experienced the most unpleasant subject of data gathering was *(c) ...your movements in the neighborhood? (M = 2.9, SD = 1.8)*. The distribution of the answers is presented in Fig. 3.

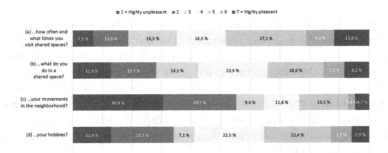

Fig. 3. Distribution of the answers to the set of questions about "How would you feel if data about you were gathered to provide recommendations on..."

The matchmaker was believed to be intrusive by several participants. Some participants described that it would be highly intrusive that intelligent technology in the role of matchmaker could access their personal calendar to search for free time slots and recommend suitable activities for those times. They described it as interference in their private life and independence:

It makes me think, how far it is wise to go – – this application intrudes my private life and tries to control me. There are some limits. (P3)

This was an experience of only few participants; however, its intensity was high. One participant described similar type of intrusiveness regarding the role of the sheriff, which was caused by surveillance. The experience of intrusiveness was linked to fear or uncertainty of personal information being visible to others. The participants, however, expected positive outcomes from the use of the same technologies and considered using the technologies a trade-off between intrusiveness and benefits.

The FG data underlined the importance of user control, visibility, and understandability of data gathering, recommendations, and other functionalities of technology. FG discussions revealed uncertainty about what data would be gathered, what would it be used for, and what the technologies would do. Regarding a real-life setting, participants of the FGs and the survey expected more clarity and transparency about data protection, and full control to decline all data gathering and use of technology. Moderation of the technologies was considered a potential concern regarding who has access to the data, but also a necessity to mitigate intrusiveness, privacy issues, and misuse.

When asked in the survey, *What kind of operators can function as administrator and owner of the data gathered by AI?*, 64.7% of the participants chose *Finnish public operator*, 55.3% chose *your hometown municipality*, 40.0% chose *people of the neighborhood community themselves*, 14.1% chose *domestic commercial company*, 9.4% chose *none of the above*, and 3.5% chose *multinational corporation*.

4.6 Potential Negative Consequences of Limitations or Excessive Use of Intelligent Technology in Residential Contexts

In addition to intrusiveness, privacy issues, and data gathering related concerns, the participants also expected intelligent technology with the roles to have other negative consequences for the community and individuals. In the FG discussions, these negative consequences were assumed to be caused by the limitation and errors of intelligent technology, but also its supremacy and overuse of it. These negative consequences are described in the following subthemes.

Limitations and Wrong Decisions of Intelligent Technology Can Harm the Community. Several participants were suspicious of how technologies with the roles would be practically implemented to consider the complex and social neighborhood context. The limitations and potential wrong decisions of intelligent technology were considered a risk for the sense of communality in the neighborhood. For instance, wrong decisions made by technology in the role of the sheriff in observing the common rules of activity spaces were considered a risk to the development of communality by mitigating trust or creating shame that can become an obstacle to the interaction between people. The role of the sheriff had the strongest associations with this subtheme with the deepest assumed impacts on the community.

Expected Negative Consequences for Individuals Caused by the Use of Technologies with the Roles. The participants expected that the use of technologies with the roles would also cause negative consequences for individuals; however, this had less emphasis than the community impacts. In contrast to seeing social pressure as a positive factor, as reported earlier, one type of potential negative outcome for individuals was summarized as social pressure, shame, and stigmatization. Dependent on a person and the situation, these similar factors can either support the positive goals of the roles, create unwanted negative emotions, or even do both at the same time. In the negative meaning, these factors were linked to the role of the sheriff if the feedback given by the sheriff would cause negative pressure or shame, and to the facilitator, if someone might experience being pushed reluctantly toward an activity by social pressure or be stigmatized and feel ashamed for not attending.

Another expected risk in the context of the facilitator role was burden on the users. Some participants mentioned a risk that the most active members might get an excessive number of recommendations, which can cause an experience of an internal or external duty to participate in the activities and an excessive amount of activity as a result.

Risk of Technology Reducing Human Contact. The participants in the FG saw a risk of reduced human contact in a neighborhood, because of technology overuse or superiority, if it is not taken into consideration in the design and implementation of the technology. This was also recognized by some participants in the survey. This was directly mentioned only in the context of the sheriff in FG2 with an example that the technology might not replace only the unwanted negative associated communication, but also other interactions between residents. The mechanism of technology and automation as replacers of the pragmatic interactions between residents touched also upon the other roles in other FGs. Therefore, this subtheme is connected to all roles, however, lightly.

Advanced Technology Can Lead to Segregation Between Living Areas. As an indirect result of implementing novel technology in a residential area, the participants expected segregation between areas. This was discussed in FG1 in the context of the facilitator role, assuming it would be something that would divide people by their social or economic status and be economically available only in areas where residents have the economic power to pay for it. Connected to segregation, on an individual level, the participants were concerned about the accessibility of these technologies.

5   Discussion and Conclusion

The results of this study indicate that intelligent technologies with predefined roles for space sharing have a versatile potential to advance residents' use of shared activity spaces. The major challenges are connected to privacy, intrusiveness, and the social context of the neighborhood. Our results draw an image of a positive sphere of technologies with roles and community development supporting each other, however, this requires more research to be validated. Residents' responses were positive toward the social functions of the roles; however, they were unsure of the technologies' capabilities to successfully implement those roles.

As an answer to our first sub question (RQa), first, both the survey and focus group results underline that residents value pragmatic benefits that intelligent technologies with the roles could provide. Earlier research on the roles and user experience of domestic or neighborhood technologies has brought up similar findings, with pragmatic reasons being the most concrete factor in using technology [11, 20, 26]. Our results link the context of shared spaces to this area of research. In shared activity spaces, the most reported challenges, however, are related to actions or behavior of humans and social issues in the neighborhood community, instead of pragmatic issues [20]. For the resolution of such social and behavioral issues, our results are promising. Unlike De Graaf and Allouch's [11] negative findings on the companion role of technology, in our results, social aspects were the second largest factor regarding the potential in advancing space sharing. In residents expectations the roles for space sharing shape the intelligent technologies towards rational and social problem solvers, thus resembling Herczeg's [12] intelligent and social systems. Technologies with the roles have a vast potential in supporting community development and interaction between residents and common spaces, both of which have been presented as the advancers of resident participation, agency, and volunteering in neighborhoods [19]. To work with their full potential, some of the roles assume active participation and volunteering from residents [20].

The sheriff has a large potential in both pragmatic and social matters. Both the survey and focus groups support the idea that the goals set for the role of the sheriff are justified in the context of activity spaces. However, the participants questioned the sheriff's capability to have an impact on the people of the community, and this would require more development and testing. On the other hand, stigmatization and social pressure caused by the rules of shared spaces were detected in a previous study as challenges for the residential community in sharing activity spaces [20]. The present study gives more support for the role of the sheriff as a mitigator of those challenges.

Intelligent recommendations and matchmaking in the context of neighborhood activities have the potential to advance the use of activity spaces, as well as support the community. The high positivity in the survey toward recommendations for shared spaces and social activities in the respondents' neighborhoods indicate acceptance towards the use purposes of the matchmaker and certain functions of other roles. However, based on the open answers, it remained unclear how participants understood recommendations when answering the question, especially considering how targeted the recommendations would be. Activities, spaces, and schedules were popular topics for recommendations, while the popularity of recommending other residents as hobby company to others was lower. This suggests better viability for the matchmaker to recommend things instead of people. Direct matching of residents to do activities together in the neighborhood may hold a risk of being considered intrusive. Therefore, the results indicate a low potential for matching people to teach skills to each other, a function that was associated with both the matchmaker and tutor. The participants' readiness to let intelligent technology suggest activities that require volunteering or high user involvement was low, according to the survey. The matchmaker met divided opinions in both the survey and focus groups. The differences in the favored topics of recommendations found in the survey could explain some of the variance, accompanied by the experienced intrusiveness found in the focus groups.

Besides supporting the findings of earlier research by Makkonen et al., that was the origin of the roles, [20] the survey and focus group results also challenged them. The roles of the facilitator and the tutor were seen as vague by the participants. It is worth considering whether they should be treated as independent roles or whether their functions should be integrated into other roles. In the case of the tutor, the questioned usefulness in the key tasks of the role and the expected need for the tutor to be heavily optimized for the use context raises a question about its viability.

Regarding the expected challenges for residents in adapting intelligent technologies with predefined roles for space sharing (RQb), privacy and intrusiveness were evident in the results of both the survey and focus groups. These results expand the findings of earlier studies regarding smart cities and domestic technology in the context of shared spaces in neighborhoods [1, 7, 21, 22, 29]. Also, the tendency to ignore the risks in the trade-off for benefits has been found in the smart home context [29]. Regarding data ownership and autonomy, the participants in the present study were reluctant to allow corporations to gather their data; however, our Finnish sample had a strong trust in Finnish public operators. Also, 40% of the respondents were willing to let the people of the neighborhood community themselves administrate and own their data, which was most closely linked to the proposition of Mann et al. on technological sovereignty [21]. Intrusiveness and privacy concerns were dependent on what data is gathered. According to the survey, tracking movements in the neighborhood was experienced as the most unpleasant subject of data gathering. In the FGs, sharing schedules or personal calendar information with technology raised the most negative comments. It remains open if the real problem for participants was that technology could access their calendar information or if the experience was more about fear of other people getting access to the data. The social context of neighborhood is also connected to the several potential challenges described in the theme *Potential negative consequences of limitations or excessive use of intelligent technology in residential contexts*. The risk of the technology-oriented design is plausible if the social context is not given enough attention in the design of technologies using the roles.

This study extends the research of roles of technologies, as well as user experience research of intelligent technologies, to the context of shared spaces in urban residential areas. The results reveal the initial potential for the technology roles for space sharing. Applying intelligent technologies with the roles to the context of shared activity spaces calls for further research of the topics, such as designing and implementing actual technology solutions and evaluating them in diverse types of neighborhoods.

5.1 Limitations

We acknowledge certain limitations in this study. The participants of this study were limited to Finnish, mostly from the city of Tampere and its surroundings. The scenarios of the activity space concept were described in the context of a planned residential area in Tampere. These factors introduce limitations to the generalizability of the results. Studying intelligent solutions of near future by using scenarios is also prone to be influenced by the placebo effect of AI [15]. This needs to be recognized when interpreting the results by acknowledging that the assumed involvement of AI might lead to more nonneutral expectations.

Considering methods, focus groups provided less understanding of individuals' perceptions and more on the groups'; however, in the context of this study it is more of a remark than a limitation, the group perceptions are at least as important, and together with the survey, they provided a balanced set of data. In the research setting we focused on the roles of intelligent technology; however, we left the detailed specification of the forms of technologies undefined. Although in focus groups the scenarios used examples of technologies, and in some cases, the discussions remained around some specific image of an application of a role, partially the results remain in an abstract level. Some of the roles were seen vague by participants, which can partly be a result of the role's definition or the given scenario in the focus groups. In the survey, there is a chance of variance how respondents understood the questions and the scenarios, which might affect the answers.

Our methodological choices were made according to what best serves our research goals, i.e., to assess on a general level how people perceive the technology roles and what are the benefits and challenges of the roles. We studied how participants reacted to the presented scenarios and technology-related questions. Future studies could delve deeper into the factors predicting acceptance. The survey and the focus groups, however, provided also qualitative data regarding the explanations behind residents' perceptions. Some themes might have remained unidentified due to the small number of participants in the focus groups. However, we gained rich data from the focus groups, which was supported by the survey. We argue that most likely the main themes were found with this number of participants.

5.2 Conclusion

This study contributes to the research on the design of intelligent solutions that consider the social aspects in the sphere of neighborhood communities and shared spaces. The technology roles for space sharing have the potential to provide pragmatic and social benefits for neighborhood communities; however, their implementation requires a careful human-centered design to avoid the pitfalls – especially related to privacy – presented in this study. There are several use cases and purposes for intelligent technologies with the predefined roles for space sharing; however, their feasibility and viability require deeper evaluation.

The results reveal potential residents of the area of Hiedanranta to be open to the applications of intelligent technology with the presented roles, with the aim of advancing neighborhood space sharing. This can support the socially sustainable development of Hiedanranta and other similar areas. However, residents value their privacy, and technologies with the roles hold a risk of intrusiveness, which needs to be taken seriously in the actual implementation of the technology solutions.

References

1. Aldossari, M.Q., Sidorova, A.: Consumer acceptance of internet of things (IoT): smart home context. J. Comput. Inf. Syst. **60**(6), 507–517 (2020). https://doi.org/10.1080/08874417.2018.1543000
2. Beck, A.F.: What is co-housing? Developing a conceptual framework from the studies of Danish intergenerational co-housing. Hous. Theor. Soc. **37**(1), 40–64 (2020). https://doi.org/10.1080/14036096.2019.1633398
3. Bengtsson, M.: How to plan and perform a qualitative study using content analysis. NursingPlus open **2**, 8–14 (2016). https://doi.org/10.1016/j.npls.2016.01.001
4. Braun, V., Clarke, V.: Using thematic analysis in psychology. Qual. Res. Psychol. **3**(2), 77–101 (2006). https://doi.org/10.1191/1478088706qp063oa
5. Bresson, S., Denèfle, S.: Diversity of self-managed co-housing initiatives in France. Urban Res. Pract. **8**(1), 5–16 (2015). https://doi.org/10.1080/17535069.2015.1011423
6. Droste, C.: German co-housing: an opportunity for municipalities to foster socially inclusive urban development? Urban Res. Pract. **8**(1), 79–92 (2015). https://doi.org/10.1080/17535069.2015.1011428
7. Foth, M., et al.: Urban informatics. In: Proceedings of the ACM 2011 Conference on Computer Supported Cooperative Work, pp. 1–8. Association for Computing Machinery, New York, NY, USA (2011). https://doi.org/10.1145/1958824.1958826
8. Fromm, D.: Collaborative Communities: Cohousing, Central Living, and Other New Forms of Housing with Shared Facilities. Van Nostrand Reinhold, New York (1991)
9. Gabrys, J.: Programming environments: environmentality and citizen sensing in the smart city. Environ. Plan. D. **32**(1), 30–48 (2014). https://doi.org/10.1068/d16812
10. Glaeser, E.L., et al.: Inequality in cities. J. Reg. Sci. **49**(4), 617–646 (2009). https://doi.org/10.1111/j.1467-9787.2009.00627.x

11. de Graaf, M.M.A., Allouch, S.B.: The evaluation of different roles for domestic social robots. In: 2015 24th IEEE International Symposium on Robot and Human Interactive Communication (RO-MAN), pp. 676–681 (2015). https://doi.org/10.1109/ROMAN.2015. 7333594

12. Herczeg, M.: The smart, the intelligent and the wise: roles and values of interactive technologies. In: Proceedings of the First International Conference on Intelligent Interactive Technologies and Multimedia, pp. 17–26. Association for Computing Machinery, New York (2011). https://doi.org/10.1145/1963564.1963567

13. Hollands, R.G.: Critical interventions into the corporate smart city. Cambridge J. Reg. Econ. Soc. **8**(1), 61–77 (2015). https://doi.org/10.1093/cjres/rsu011

14. Jarusriboonchai, P.: Understanding Roles and User Experience of Mobile Technology in Co-located Interaction. Tampere University of Technology, Tampere (2016)

15. Kosch, T., et al.: The placebo effect of artificial intelligence in human-computer interaction. ACM Trans. Comput. Interact. **29**(6), 1–32 (2022). https://doi.org/10.1145/3529225

16. Kuo, F.E.: Fertile ground for community: inner-city neighborhood common spaces. Am. J. Community Psychol. **26**(6), 823–851 (1998). https://doi.org/10.1023/A:1022294028903

17. Kuoppa, J., et al.: Houkuttelevan asumisen ainekset. Yhdyskuntasuunnittelu-lehti **58**(2), 10–32 (2020). https://doi.org/10.33357/ys.95604

18. Larivière, B., et al.: "Service Encounter 2.0": an investigation into the roles of technology, employees and customers. J. Bus. Res. **79**, 238–246 (2017). https://doi.org/10.1016/j.jbusres. 2017.03.008

19. Lund, V., Juujärvi, S.: Residents' agency makes a difference in volunteering in an urban neighbourhood. Voluntas **29**(4), 756–769 (2018). https://doi.org/10.1007/s11266-018-9955-4

20. Makkonen, J., Latikka, R., Kaukonen, L., et al.: Advancing residents' use of shared spaces in Nordic superblocks with intelligent technologies. AI & Soc. **38**, 1167–1184 (2023). https:// doi.org/10.1007/s00146-022-01604-x

21. Mann, M., et al.: #BlockSidewalk to Barcelona: technological sovereignty and the social license to operate smart cities. J. Assoc. Inf. Sci. Technol. **71**(9), 1103–1115 (2020). https:// doi.org/10.1002/asi.24387

22. Marky, K., et al.: Roles matter! Understanding differences in the privacy mental models of smart home visitors and residents. In: 20th International Conference on Mobile and Ubiquitous Multimedia, pp. 108–122. Association for Computing Machinery, New York (2021). https:// doi.org/10.1145/3490632.3490664

23. Martin, C.J., et al.: Smart and sustainable? Five tensions in the visions and practices of the smart-sustainable city in Europe and North America. Technol. Forecast. Soc. Chang. **133**, 269–278 (2018). https://doi.org/10.1016/j.techfore.2018.01.005

24. Neuendorf, K.A.: The Content Analysis Guidebook. SAGE Publications, Inc (2017). https:// doi.org/10.4135/9781071802878.

25. Nugent, J.: Residential common spaces that really work: a post-occupancy study. Plan. High. Educ. **41**(1), 234–243 (2012)

26. Sánchez, H., et al.: IoT and iTV for interconnection, monitoring, and automation of common areas of residents. Appl. Sci. **7**(7), 696 (2017). https://doi.org/10.3390/app7070696

27. Sjöblom, J., et al.: Crafting a planning issue with citizens in the context of planning competition: a case of 'Nordic Superblock.' J. Urban Des. **26**(1), 117–131 (2021). https://doi.org/ 10.1080/13574809.2020.1832886

28. Tummers, L.: Understanding co-housing from a planning perspective: why and how? Urban Res. Pract. **8**(1), 64–78 (2015). https://doi.org/10.1080/17535069.2015.1011427

29. Wang, X., et al.: I want it anyway: consumer perceptions of smart home devices. J. Comput. Inf. Syst. **60**(5), 437–447 (2020). https://doi.org/10.1080/08874417.2018.1528486

30. Tilastokeskus: Pääkaupunkiseutu menetti väestöä muualle Suomeen vuonna 2020 (2021). https://www.tilastokeskus.fi/til/muutl/2020/muutl_2020_2021-05-12_tie_001_fi.html
31. United Nations: World Urbanization Prospects: The 2018 Revision, New York (2019). https://www.un.org/development/desa/pd/news/world-urbanization-prospects-2018

Problematizing "Empowerment" in HCAI

John S. Seberger[1]([envelope])[iD], Hyesun Choung[2][iD], and Prabu David[2][iD]

[1] Drexel University, Philadelphia, PA 19104, USA
jss436@drexel.edu
[2] Michigan State University, East Lansing, MI 48824, USA

Abstract. Human-centered artificial intelligence (HCAI) seeks to assuage fears about ubiquitous machine agency by framing AI in relation to observable human benefits. Such benefits limn a nebulous future condition of AI-driven "empowerment." Yet the rhetorics of HCAI generally preempt consideration of the power structures that subtend imaginaries of AI ubiquity: imaginaries wherein empowerment is bestowed, top-down, through an assumed prior forfeiture of users' bottom-up agency to choose or refuse enrolment in AI futures. Answering calls to examine the language of AI research, we focus on "empowerment" and its use in, and relationship to, three visions of HCAI published between 2019 and 2022. We use close reading to begin answering one research question: "What is the conceptual structure of 'empowerment' across complementary visions of HCAI?" We contend that empowerment in HCAI represents little more than paternalistic *conditional* empowerment. Our work demonstrates the value of language-centric analysis in AI and presents a plea to explicitly account for the discourses – their histories, grammars, power distributions – that are used to rationalize the looming ubiquity of AI.

Keywords: Empowerment · HCAI · HCI · AI · language · discourse

1 Introduction

Human-Centered AI (HCAI) is an emergent domain located, in-part, at the intersection of human-computer interaction (HCI) and artificial intelligence (AI). HCAI is dedicated to "empowering and enabling" [8] people via AI systems that "amplify, rather than erode, human agency" [28]. Such dedication exists in direct contrast to ongoing problems of AI-hype [4,14,30], in which AI is popularly understood to prime futures of reduced human agency, deep-seated systematic injustice, and, more generally, the continued "darkening of the digital dream" [32].

Answering calls from HCI for language-centered analysis of work in AI [27, 29], this humanistic HCI [3] essay provides *initial* critical foundations for understanding the conceptual structure of "empowerment" in HCAI. Through close readings of three visions of HCAI published between 2019 and 2022 (e.g., [19,20,27–29]), we provide foundations for answering one key question:

J. Abdelnour Nocera et al. (Eds.): INTERACT 2023, LNCS 14144, pp. 270–279, 2023.
https://doi.org/10.1007/978-3-031-42286-7_15

- **RQ1**: What is the conceptual structure of "empowerment" across complementary visions of HCAI?

After briefly situating the discourse of "empowerment" in HCI, we argue that its deployment in HCAI is likely misleading – rhetorically appealing, but misleading. In the present discourse, empowerment in HCAI is paternalistic. To be empowered through HCAI requires submitting to sociotechnical advancements over which everyday users have little to no power; it requires a paradoxical objectification of individuals and communities such that they might be "empowered" post hoc through the preliminary and fundamental forfeiture of the agency to opt in or opt out of AI-driven "interpellation" [11]. Essentially, "empowerment" in and through HCAI is received rather than *achieved*; it is predicated on the (naively assumed) voluntary enrolment of users into futures of AI ubiquity. Subsequent to our analysis, we suggest the triad of consent, collaboration, and the co-creation of values [10] as an analytical lens that may allow us to move beyond the reductive and misleading language of "empowerment."

2 Background

Various institutions (e.g., banks, healthcare and insurance systems, platforms, etc.) deploy different forms of AI. Users rarely have the ability to opt out of AI-driven analysis when engaging with such institutions (e.g., applying for a loan). What does it mean to be empowered *by* AI in the absence of the agency to decide whether one will be interpellated [11] *through* AI? A succinct summary of empowerment provided by Agre [2, p. 170] illuminates this question:

> We can articulate precisely the ethical appeal of the word "empowerment". Inasmuch as "empower" is a transitive verb, to "empower" someone is to perform some action upon them. The liberal ideal of individual self-determination would normally object to this kind of operation. People are supposed to be able to define themselves and to choose their own identities and desires and intentions. And this ideal is normally violated when people show up as the objects of transformative verbs. But it is the special claim of empowerment to escape this objection. The person upon whom this action is performed, having been "empowered", is, by definition, in a position to take actions of his or her own. [...] Empowerment thus presents itself not as some kind of programming, but precisely as the removal of any susceptibility to programming.

Thus one passes through a state of objectification so as to be imbued with agency – to be *empowered*. For example, one passes through the objectified state of being a "user" in order to be "empowered" through coupling with a smartphone, an app, a platform, etc.; the same can be said of the banking, insurance, and healthcare systems mentioned above. Yet Agre [2] traces the roots of empowerment as a political discourse to the mid twentieth century, in which individuals and communities organized through grass-roots efforts to amplify their collective political voice. Such empowerment – the ethically appealing empowerment grounded in increased political participation – is *achieved* rather than bestowed. Genuine, bottom-up empowerment signifies a reclamation of agency *in spite of* the power distributions instantiated by sociotechnical systems.

Despite Agre's work [2], there remains a prominent view in computing that "empowerment" can be bestowed to people from the top-down.[1] Contrary to such a top-down view, and aligning with Agre [2], Seberger et al [23] used the work of Schneider et al [21] to introduce the concept of "conditional empowerment." Individuals or communities who are conditionally empowered [23] receive *apparently* heightened levels of agency in relation to technology; however, such heightened agency – the *power to* [21,23] – is always already bounded by networks of actants (e.g., software, devices, institutions, etc.) that exert *power over* [21,23] individuals or communities. Conditionally empowered individuals and communities are empowered to do only that which they are *allowed* to do by those networks of actants possessing *power over* them. Such a form of empowerment is received rather than achieved [2]. For example, one might be able to choose which bank from which to seek a loan, but one cannot generally choose between banking systems that have or have not embraced AI-driven decision-making. The banking system's *power over* subsumes one's *power to*. Thus technologically-allowed empowerment often reduces to mere enrolment in [7], and normalization of [25], imbalanced power structures. Such reduction motivates the research question presented in Sect. 1.

3   Method

Close reading (CR) is an interpretive mode of textual analysis. It generates an interpretation of a text (i.e., a corpus) through examination of the relationship among: (i) a text; (ii) a reader; (iii) an external world that encompasses both. CR has been used in HCI with some frequency over the past twenty years. Cockton [9] employed the method to analyze how the central tenets of designing for usability have evolved over time. Knouf [17] used CR to identify political and social discourses that are absent from corporate visions of computational futures. Most recently, Burtscher and Spiel [6] engaged in CR of gender sensitivity in HCI literature. Close reading is not intended to produce generalizable results in the way that a systematic survey of literature would [6]. The openness [13] of HCAI agendas (i.e., the extent to which HCAI scholars envision fundamentally creative/designerly futures that are, in the present tense, little more than fictions) warrants such non-generalizable and interpretive work.

4   Analysis

Here we tie a thread between three recent and complementary examples of work in HCAI focusing on different aspects: explianability [19]; interaction [20]; and

---

[1] This has much to do with the historical dichotomy and related imbalance of power between "programmers" and "users" (see: [16]).

the production of a unified HCAI agenda [27–29]. We chose these works because they are remarkable in and of themselves, but illustrate problems of scope and scale facing the unification of disparate research into an agenda.

4.1   Capacities and a Two-Way Street

Here we focus on the subtext of empowerment as presented by Riedl [19]. Such subtext, rooted in problems familiar to those working in the area of explainability, manifests in effective communication between AI agents and human users. He provides the following definition: "[HCAI] is a perspective [. . .] that intelligent systems must be designed with awareness that they are of a larger system consisting of human stakeholders, such as users, operators, clients, and other people in close proximity."

Here one reads tacit acknowledgement that HCAI seeks to remedy the exclusion of users (i.e., everyday people) from the historical design and deployment of AI technologies. Thus, HCAI appears as a form of AI-apologism: a post hoc attempt to compensate for the exclusion of users during AI's golden decade. Riedl roughly envisions a two-way street that might remedy such exclusion of the human user from historical AI developments. The realization of HCAI requires scrutable flows of information in two directions: (i) from AI to human; and (ii) from human to AI [19]. Humans, including non-experts, need to be able to understand what an AI agent is doing and why; reciprocally, AI agents need to be able to parse human behavior in meaningful ways. Each set of agents needs to possess the capacity to communicate meaningfully via a theory of mind regarding the other. Riedl [19] frames this bi-directional loop in terms of "critical capacities": each direction of information flow constitutes one capacity.

In this reading, "empowerment" is bi-directional and proportional to the level of communicative efficacy exerted in either direction. In this vision of HCAI, AI agents and human users mutually empower each other through a kind of communicative bootstrapping. Such a reading may hint at the empowerment of AI systems through and by means of their adoption as a primary goal of HCAI, despite its rhetorical framing in the language of human-centeredness. But human empowerment in this context is predicated on an overlooked forfeiture of agency: an assumption that all users will have exerted agency to explicitly enroll in the use of AI systems.

4.2   Control in the Two-Way Street

Schmidt [20] frames HCAI as follows: "the central question is how to create [AI tools] for amplifying the human mind without compromising human values." Agency, it is worth noting, is a fundamental liberal human value [2] and necessarily includes the agency to choose whether to be interpellated through AI. Still, Schmidt [20] focuses on the interactivity of HCAI systems.

Implicitly assuming the vantage of users who have voluntarily enrolled in the use of AI systems, Schmidt [20] provides a list of eight properties that should be possessed by successful HCAI systems. Where Riedl's work [19] adopted a position familiar to those working in explainable AI, Schmidt's approach is more clearly grounded in HCI. We focus on two of Schmidt's properties here: (i) that "individuals can interact in real-time with the algorithms, models, and data and manipulate and control all relevant parameters;" and (ii) that "it is visible who has control of the artificial intelligence, in particular who has the power over data, models, and algorithms." Absent voluntary enrolment (i.e., the exertion of a form of agency that constitutes a pillar of liberal human values [2]), focus on such properties begs the question: it assumes that AI is empowering, *per se*, despite its inherently top-down deployment.

Schmidt deploys what is essentially a functionalist framework to posit that the *feeling of control* is important at higher levels of abstraction: for an air-traveler, it matters more where the plane is going to land than the exact path it takes to reach that point [20]. In continuation of this metaphor, control over the outcomes of AI use matters more than the precise means by which such outcomes are reached [20]. Such a functionalist approach allows for the possibility that end-users interacting with AI agents may avoid the overburdening effects of end-user controls by focusing solely on the bigger picture; HCAI users may be functionally empowered by and through ignorance of how an AI agent does what it does. That is, they may be "empowered" through indifference or adherence to the top-down proclamation that AI is empowering simply by virtue of being AI. As with Riedl's vision [19], the agency to decide whether or not to enroll in AI futures is overlooked entirely. Implicitly, users of HCAI systems are "empowered" because they benefit from a top-down, paternalistic sense of "what is best" produced by powerful expert programmers and designers in the field of AI. Such top-down empowerment resurrects outdated assumptions about the nature of empowerment (cf. [2]) and resembles conditional empowerment [23] more than a genuine increase of capacity *in spite of* sociotechnical power structures.

4.3   From Capacity and Control to Empowerment

Shneiderman also provides a two-part organizational framework for under-standing HCAI: processes and products. In discussing *processes*, Shneiderman describes the application of traditional HCI methods in the development of HCAI technologies. Such methods include user testing, observation, and engagement with stakeholders, to name a few [29]. Given their foundations in empiricism, such methods comprise the passage of the individual user into an objectival onto-grammatical realm so as to receive some form of "empowerment;" through empirical methods, users are represented by data, and data are always already little more than objectival representations of phenomena (see: [1,15]). On the other hand, Shneiderman [29] describes the *products* of HCAI as grounded in the production and maintenance of human control over AI technologies – the perpetuation and improvement of the user's agency in and through the tech-nologies they use. Shneiderman writes that HCAI products should "empower and enhance human performance" [29, p. 9].

Shneiderman engages with HCAI through a more broadly philosophical lens. He gives open consideration to the problems of language that surround and, indeed, define the field of HCAI [27]. He notes not only definitional problems core to AI itself [27], but regularly relies on comparative epistemology (e.g., rationalism vs. empiricism) and discusses a "second Copernican revolution," in which the nebulous language of "the human" replaces a similarly nebulous bit of language, "Algorithms & AI," as the point around which the practices of HCAI revolve [27–29]. He does so by considering which set of agents should be seen as "central" to the process of AI design, development, and deployment.

Echoing the comparatively long history of humans-in-the-loop (HITL) arguments, Shneiderman effects an inversion in this conceptualization – another implicit form of apologism regarding the heretofore absence of users (i.e., humans) from the design of AI systems. He provides the slogan, "Humans in the group, computers in the loop" as a pithy representation of such inversion. Shneiderman's rhetorical move to "empowerment" through and by means of a specific focus on humans that may use AI systems as a motivation for HCAI does not exist in a discursive vacuum. Absent a vacuum, capacity, control, and empowerment do not align cleanly or clearly within HCAI – unless one takes as a given that users have no choice but to enroll in AI futures.

4.4   Summary of Analysis

The aspiration of AI-driven empowerment in and through HCAI emerges as a gestalt effect of the motivations described above: capacity achieved through understandable information flows (i.e., explainability); end-user *feelings* of control over high-level functionality; and an infrastructural inversion [5] of the central agents in AI work (i.e., human and AI agents). Yet nowhere in these visions is the user's agential consent to be interpellated through AI present. Thus empowerment in and through HCAI is bestowed top-down. Such empowerment is not the bottom-up empowerment we historically associate with the term's ethical appeal [2], but rather a paternalistic form of conditional empowerment [23] in which those who are "empowered" are merely enmeshed in a network of actants that always already possesses greater *power over* than users' *power to*.

In a sense, the empowerment-based rhetorical motivations of HCAI appear as tautological: HCAI empowers people because AI is empowering; future humans will be empowered by AI because AI is the future. Future research should seek to understand the role that affect plays in perceived control over AI; it should focus on understanding users as affective agents rather than primarily rational ones [18,25]. If, as Schmidt [20] posits, control is a question of affective comfort and abstraction, and HCAI is to empower people through heightened control over AI [29], then HCAI agents require affect-centered design. Yet the ethical development of such a design position, in which HCAI may mitigate against speculative vulnerabilities [24] brought about by misleading promises of "empowerment," requires evidence that AI is *capable* of solving present-tense societal problems, rather than merely serving as a unproven future-oriented panacea [4,14]. It may further require a substitution for the language of "empowerment," which we discuss in the following section.

5   Discussion and Implications

We argue that in the present discourse of HCAI, to be "empowered" requires an initial submission to the inevitability and hypothesized beneficiality of AI itself. The use of "empowerment" as a rhetoric within HCAI implicitly necessitates a prior forfeiture of agency so that other agency might be acquired. Without consent from users to enroll in AI futures – consent that we know to be absent through interaction with banks, medical institutions, insurance institutions, etc. – any such empowerment that may derive *from* the use of HCAI technologies is always already predicated on a fundamental breach of values (i.e., agency). Given the misuse of extant technologies and their propensity to unnerve users [22,23,25,31], it is naive to assume that users would universally enroll into AI futures through consent-driven agency. Thus, empowerment that is bestowed upon users through the design and deployment of AI agents always already risks reducing to a form of conditional empowerment [23].

In Shneiderman's words, "we are at a decisive moment" in history [28]. HCI scholars and practitioners are playing important roles in this decisive moment. We are tasked with designing (and normalizing) interactions between humans and AI-driven systems. Such responsibility requires great care; such care must manifest, in-part, in heightened sensitivity to the ways in which our language resonates through historical discourse. Language connects novelty with history; it connects contemporary contexts to those which are historically analogous. We do justice to neither history nor AI and the futures AI contains by haphazardly deploying such powerful terms as "empowerment" as a motivation for research, development, and deployment. Such haphazard use of "empowerment" – use that may prime individuals to understand AI as liberatory in a fashion similar to engagement in the bottom-up political empowerment of the mid 20th century [2] – may potentiate future moral injury to users, researchers, and practitioners alike: a moral injury in which the optimism of deploying of AI, motivated by such language as "empowerment," may prove to be ill-placed.

But what might replace the misleading language of "empowerment" while remaining true to the motivations such rhetoric represents? Each of the complementary visions of HCAI that we analyzed describes flows between user and device (e.g., the critical capacity of explainability [19]; the fostering of feelings of control [20], etc.). Focus on such flows presents a possible alternative to the use of "empowerment" as a rhetoric to assuage fears about AI ubiquity. Rather than providing proclamations of HCAI's "empowering" qualities, we identify an obligation to enfold sociotechnical studies of empowerment's mechanics into HCAI work. Through a truncated close reading, we have surfaced the idea that "empowerment" is not a simple process; nor does "empowerment" have a sole referent. The bottom-up achievement of empowerment is simply not the same as the top-down receipt of conditional empowerment. How do we move beyond the apparently conditional empowerment [23] manifest in visions of HCAI, while retaining the human-centered care for users that "empowerment" (misleadingly) represents?

We contend that a framework of consent, collaboration, and the co-creation of value [10] should be central to HCAI – indeed, to all AI research, design, development, and deployment. Such a framework may provide the means by which we in HCI can understand the temporality, transience, and multi-institution interactions that characterize the *achievement*, rather than *receipt*, of empowerment through AI. Such a framework may allow us to move beyond the rhetorical appeal of "empowerment" toward a systematic understanding of the complex sociotechnical events and processes that may yield true empowerment: heightened agency achieved *in spite of* existing power structures.

6 Conclusion

Empowerment derived from enrolment into the imagined futures of AI is both rhetorically appealing and potentially misleading. The achievement of empowerment via HCAI assumes the forfeiture of users' agency (i.e., the individual's right to decide whether they want to be interpellated [11] by AI at all) in the name of acquiring other, nebulous and future-oriented abilities. We contend that "empowerment" in HCAI is not the ethically appealing empowerment characterized by grass-roots construction of heightened agency *in spite of* imbalanced power distributions [2], but rather a form of conditional empowerment [23] in which *being empowered* constitutes only what end users are allowed to do by more powerful assemblages of actants.

Based on our exploratory and preliminary deployment of CR, we conclude that the conceptual structure of "empowerment" in HCAI, then, is load-bearing [12] if and only if all users of HCAI or AI systems have first consented to be interpellated through the "alien" [19, p. 33] computational phenomenology of AI [26]. Such a condition is not realistic in light of widespread discomfort and fear about the looming ubiquity of AI. Thus, it becomes necessary to delve more deeply into the meaning and historical discourse of "empowerment" before we may ethically leverage such a term to enroll users into AI futures. We suggest the triadic framework of consent, collaboration, and co-creation of values [10] as a means by which we might develop a sufficiently rich understanding of "empowerment" so as to use it as a motivation for HCAI. HCAI may yet empower individuals, but such a possibility is dependent on what we mean by "empowerment." Given what is at stake in the looming ubiquity of AI, it is simply not sufficient to risk mere conditional empowerment. Although our current historical mode of being – shaped by networking, the information revolution, and mobile technology – was sold to us for the price of "empowerment," we must be vigilant as AI approaches ubiquity. We must help users achieve a voice in who they – *we* – are becoming. Such a voice is not *given*, but can be encouraged through careful engagement and values-driven redistribution of power among institutions and individuals.

References

1. Ackoff, R.L.: From data to wisdom. J. Appl. Syst. Anal. **16**(1), 3–9 (1989)
2. Agre, P.E.: From high tech to human tech: empowerment, measurement, and social studies of computing. Comput. Support. Cooper. Work (CSCW) **3**(2), 167–195 (1994)
3. Bardzell, J., Bardzell, S.: Humanistic HCI. Interactions **23**(2), 20–29 (2016). https://doi.org/10.1145/2888576
4. Bender, E.M.: Policy makers: please don't fall for the distractions of #aihype (2023). https://medium.com/@emilymenonbender/policy-makers-please-dont-fall-for-the-distractions-of-aihype-e03fa80ddbf1
5. Bowker, G.C.: Science on the run: information management and industrial geophysics at Schlumberger, 1920–1940. MIT Press (1994)
6. Burtscher, S., Spiel, K.: "but where would i even start?": Developing (gender) sensitivity in HCI research and practice. In: Proceedings of the Conference on Mensch Und Computer. MuC '20, pp. 431–441. Association for Computing Machinery, New York, NY, USA (2020). https://doi.org/10.1145/3404983.3405510
7. Callon, M.: Some elements of a sociology of translation: domestication of the scallops and the fishermen of St Brieuc Bay. Sociol. Rev. **32**(1_suppl), 196–233 (1984)
8. Capel, T., Brereton, M.: What is human-centered about human-centered AI? A map of the research landscape. In: Proceedings of the 2023 CHI Conference on Human Factors in Computing Systems. CHI '23, pp. 431–441. Association for Computing Machinery, New York, NY, USA (2023). https://doi.org/10.1145/3544548.3580959
9. Cockton, G.: Revisiting usability's three key principles. In: CHI '08 Extended Abstracts on Human Factors in Computing Systems. CHI EA '08, pp. 2473–2484. Association for Computing Machinery, New York, NY, USA (2008). https://doi.org/10.1145/1358628.1358704
10. David, P., Shroff, P., Gupta, S.: Leadership and Governance for the Digital Future: Value Ethics as Guardrails. Routledge, New York (in press)
11. Day, R.E.: Indexing it All: The Subject in the Age of Documentation, Information, and Data. MIT Press, Cambridge (2014)
12. De Bolla, P.: The Architecture of Concepts: The Historical Formation Of Human Rights. Fordham Univ. Press (2013)
13. Eco, U., et al.: The Open Work. Harvard University Press, Cambridge (1989)
14. Gebru, T., Bender, E.M., McMillan-Major, A., Michell, M.: Statement from the listed authors of stochastic parrots on the "AI pause" letter (2023). https://www.dair-institute.org/blog/letter-statement-March2023
15. Gitelman, L.: Raw Data is an Oxymoron. MIT Press, Cambridge (2013)
16. Gould, J.D., Lewis, C.: Designing for usability-key principles and what designers think. In: Proceedings of the SIGCHI Conference on Human Factors in Computing Systems. CHI '83, pp. 50–53. Association for Computing Machinery, New York, NY, USA (1983). https://doi.org/10.1145/800045.801579
17. Knouf, N.A.: HCI for the real world. In: CHI '09 Extended Abstracts on Human Factors in Computing Systems. CHI EA '09, pp. 2555–2564. Association for Computing Machinery, New York, NY, USA (2009). https://doi.org/10.1145/1520340.1520361
18. Nussbaum, M.C.: Upheavals of Thought: The Intelligence of Emotions. Cambridge University Press, Cambridge (2003)

19. Riedl, M.O.: Human-centered artificial intelligence and machine learning. Hum. Behav. Emerg. Technol. **1**(1), 33–36 (2019). https://doi.org/10.1002/hbe2.117, https://onlinelibrary.wiley.com/doi/abs/10.1002/hbe2.117

20. Schmidt, A.: Interactive Human Centered Artificial Intelligence: A Definition and Research Challenges. Association for Computing Machinery, New York, NY, USA (2020). https://doi.org/10.1145/3399715.3400873

21. Schneider, H., Eiband, M., Ullrich, D., Butz, A.: Empowerment in HCI - a survey and framework. In: Proceedings of the 2018 CHI Conference on Human Factors in Computing Systems. CHI '18, pp. 1–14. Association for Computing Machinery, New York, NY, USA (2018). https://doi.org/10.1145/3173574.3173818

22. Seberger, J.S., Bowker, G.C.: Humanistic infrastructure studies: hyper-functionality and the experience of the absurd. Inf. Commun. Soc. **24**(12), 1712–1727 (2021)

23. Seberger, J.S., Llavore, M., Wyant, N.N., Shklovski, I., Patil, S.: Empowering resignation: there's an app for that. In: Proceedings of the 2021 CHI Conference on Human Factors in Computing Systems, pp. 1–18 (2021)

24. Seberger, J.S., Obi, I., Loukil, M., Liao, W., Wild, D., Sameer, P.: Speculative vulnerability: uncovering the temporalities of vulnerability in people's experiences of the pandemic. Proc. ACM Hum.-Comput. Interact. **6**(CSCW) (2022, in press)

25. Seberger, J.S., Shklovski, I., Swiatek, E., Patil, S.: Still creepy after all these years: the normalization of affective discomfort in app use. In: Proceedings of the 2022 CHI Conference on Human Factors in Computing Systems. CHI '22. Association for Computing Machinery, New York, NY, USA (2022). https://doi.org/10.1145/3491102.3502112

26. Seberger, J.S., Slaughter, R.A.: The mystics and magic of latent space: becoming the unseen. Membrana-J. Photogr. Theory Vis. Cult. **5**(1), 88–93 (2020)

27. Shneiderman, B.: Human-centered artificial intelligence: three fresh ideas. AIS Trans. Hum.-Comput. Interact. **12**(3), 109–124 (2020). https://doi.org/10.17705/1thci.00131

28. Shneiderman, B.: Human-centered AI. Issues Sci. Technol. **37**(2), 56–61 (2021). https://issues.org/human-centered-ai/

29. Shneiderman, B.: Human-Centered AI. Oxford University Press, Oxford (2022)

30. Slota, S.C., et al.: Good systems, bad data?: interpretations of AI hype and failures. Proc. Assoc. Inf. Sci. Technol. **57**(1), e275 (2020)

31. Tene, O., Polonetsky, J.: A theory of creepy: technology, privacy and shifting social norms. Yale JL Tech. **16**, 59 (2013)

32. Zuboff, S.: The Age of Surveillance Capitalism: The Fight for a Human Future at the New Frontier of Power. PublicAffairs, New York (2019)

Social and Ubiquitous Computing I and II

"Draw Fast, Guess Slow": Characterizing Interactions in Cooperative Partially Observable Settings with Online Pictionary as a Case Study

Kiruthika Kannan(✉), Anandhini Rajendran, Vinoo Alluri,
and Ravi Kiran Sarvadevabhatla

International Institute of Information Technology, Hyderabad, India
kiruthika.k@research.iiit.ac.in, anandhini.rajendran@students.iiit.ac.in,
{vinoo.alluri,ravi.kiran}@iiit.ac.in

Abstract. Cooperative human-human communication becomes challenging when restrictions such as difference in communication modality and limited time are imposed. We use the popular cooperative social game Pictionary as an online multimodal test bed to explore the dynamics of human-human interactions in such settings. As a part of our study, we identify attributes of player interactions that characterize cooperative gameplay. We found stable and role-specific playing style components that are independent of game difficulty. In terms of gameplay and the larger context of cooperative partially observable communication, our results suggest that too much interaction or unbalanced interaction negatively impacts game success. Additionally, the playing style components discovered via our analysis align with select player personality types proposed in existing frameworks for multiplayer games.

Keywords: Cooperative partially observable games · Communication modalites · Gameplay · Game interactions · Game difficulty · Game Outcome · Playing styles

1 Introduction

Cooperative human communication in a shared goal setting is ubiquitous. However, constraints often exist despite the cooperative setting. For instance, travellers throughout history have needed to communicate and convey intent despite constraints such as unknown language and cultural barriers. Gestures and pictorial representations are often utilized to overcome these barriers. Shared understanding is achieved in such cases through iterative feedback. Studying these processes in a casual game setting can provide insights into these fundamental human interactions occurring in constrained communication settings. With this motivation, we study Pictionary, a popular social casual game involving drawing and guessing.

Supplementary Information The online version contains supplementary material available at https://doi.org/10.1007/978-3-031-42286-7_16.

Pictionary is an interesting example of cooperative gameplay to achieve a shared goal in communication-restricted settings [16, 37]. The game of Pictionary consists of a time-limited episode involving two players - a *Drawer* and a *Guesser*. The *Drawer* is tasked with conveying a given target phrase to a counterpart *Guesser* by sketching on a whiteboard within a time limit [16]. Crucially, the rules of Pictionary forbid the *Drawer* from writing text on the whiteboard. Since the target phrase is not observable, this restriction leads to partial observability in an otherwise cooperative game. Coupled with time limit per game episode, the restriction also tends to unleash fascinating diversity and creativity in player responses and generated content.

The study of cooperative guessing games is not new [1, 2, 19]. However, existing works assume a *single* and *common* modality for communication (e.g. text). By contrast, players in Pictionary employ different modalities – the *Drawer* draws visual patterns on a 2-D canvas while the *Guesser* enters text guesses. In addition, the players employ out-of-modality 'iconic gestures' (e.g. the *Drawer* signaling 👎, 👍 to *Guesser* to convey the proximity of the guess phrase to the target phrase). Throughout the game, the players are forced to adopt strategies distinct from a single modality setting. This sets the stage for a multimodal theory of mind in which a player is required to 'imagine' other player's state of mind and that too, from responses expressed in a modality different from theirs. As we shall show, players exhibit different styles of interactions to achieve this multimodal communication. Examining these strategies and interaction styles could potentially be of relevance to game developers, researchers developing AI-based cooperative game agents, social scientists studying dynamics in social games, amongst other stakeholders.

In our study, we explore aspects of playing styles in an online version of Pictionary and associations between player actions and the game outcome using a data-driven approach. We use a large corpus of game telemetry data recorded from an online version of Pictionary game for our analysis. We identify attributes of player actions for each role and the interplay between them. We use Principal Component Analysis (PCA) to determine role-specific playing style components. We then investigate the impact of game difficulty on game attributes and playing style components. Finally, we discuss the relationship between player behaviour and game outcome. Although prior works have investigated player behavior and performance in cooperative gameplay [3, 8, 36, 38], these studies do not explore player interactions in a setting with restricted communication. We aim to address this research gap.

In this paper, we investigate the following research questions:

RQ1: What are the different types of playing style components observed in a Cooperative Partially Observable (CPO) game such as Pictionary?

RQ2: Does the game's difficulty impact the playing style components and interplay attributes?

RQ3: Which playing style components and interplay attributes are associated with successful game outcomes?

Please refer to supplementary for a video overview of our work.

2   Related Work

Cooperative Partially observable (CPO) Games: Cooperative partially observable games are those in which certain information remains hidden from team players despite having a shared goal. Bard et al. [5] introduced the card game Hanabi as a new challenge exhibiting a combination of cooperative gameplay and imperfect information. Eger et al. [14] demonstrated the use of intentionality and communication theory for designing Hanabi agents. Iconary [10] is a CPO game similar to Pictionary where the *Guesser* tries to guess a phrase instead of a word and the *Drawer* repeatedly revises the icons on canvas to help the *Guesser* identify the phrase. Charades is a CPO game similar in spirit to Pictionary wherein the player has to act instead of drawing [4,18,33] and the role of *Guesser* remains similar to that in Pictionary. Ashktorab et al. [1,2] used a word guessing game, *Wordgame* where a player, *'Giver'* is given a target word and asked to convey the word to the teammate, *'Guesser'* as in the case of Pictionary. Unlike Pictionary, this game uses a single modality of communication, viz. text.

Characterizing Communication in Games: Analysis of multiplayer games is a widely researched area involving study of communication between players with both cooperative [1,7,42] and competitive [13,23,25] goals. Emmerich et al. [15] studied the influence of various game design patterns on player interactions. They found that high player interdependence implies more communication. Toups et al. [40] analysed 40 digital games using a theoretical approach to develop a framework for cooperative communication game mechanics. They observed that players had lesser ability to request information from their partners and might develop emergent cooperative communication mechanics to compensate insufficiency in existing game design. Thus, cooperative communication mechanics is not generalizable to all game designs since it is dependent on the modality of communication, player motivation and player skills. Different modalities such as text messages, audio and video communication, and game specific activity such as sharing customized icons, cards and location are commonly used in games. Spyridonis et al. [39] compared three communication modalities namely, voice, textual chat and pre-determined commands to propose an efficient communication model for games. They concluded that pre-existing commands lead to faster completion times compared to other modalities such as textual chat. Communication in Pictionary happens through three modalities namely, sketches on canvas, text for guesses and pre-existing commands such as icons 👎 and 👍. The modalities are role-specific and hence, differ with direction of communication (i.e. *Drawer* interacts by sketching and icons and *Guesser* by text and icons). Ashktorab et al. [1] found that in *Wordgame*, the directionality of communication (as from *'Guesser'* or from *'Giver'*) caused significant differences in gameplay outcome and social perceptions of players. Our analysis also explores playing style components of each role (*Drawer* and *Guesser*) separately.

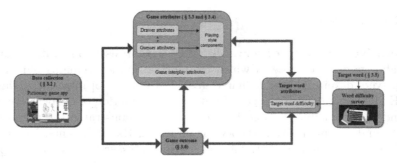

Fig. 1. An illustration of Pictionary game analysis components. ↔ indicates that we perform statistical analysis between the linked components. (Color figure online)

Playing Styles and Gameplay Analysis: Existing works have extensively researched on playing styles along numerous bases such as psychographic, behavioral and in-game demographics for various games [20,41]. One of the earliest works on playing styles proposed by Bartle et al. [6] classified players as *Killers* and *Achievers* or *Socializers* and *Explorers*. Though the study done by Bartle et al. [6] was based on Multi-User Dungeons games, this categorization was commonly adapted for many massively multiplayer online games [9,28]. Loria et al. [29] classified player behavior into more elaborate types such as *competitive, striving, active, committed, purpose-driven*, amongst others. However, these player classifications do not examine the cooperative aspects of gameplay. Ferro et al. [17] classified pre-existing player models into five types namely *Dominant, Objectivists, Humanists, Inquisitive,* and *Creative* based on personality traits and game mechanics. Although we focus only on cooperative game mechanics, our distinctive playing style components are comparable to only few of these player types. Kirman et al [24] classified players based on social interactions in a game. Unlike Kirman et al [24], our analysis takes into account the different styles of interaction between players.

Player types are identified either by user surveys in which the players report [2] or observational classification of the recorded gameplay [22]. Such analyses are not scalable and require manual intervention [20]. To overcome this, we use a data-driven approach on the game telemetry data to identify inherent laying style components in a cooperative game. The commonly used data-driven approaches for gameplay analysis include clustering algorithms [13,23,34], Hidden Markov Models [32], Archetypal Analysis [30] and Principal Component Analysis (PCA) [11,26,31,35]. In our analysis, we use PCA to identify role-specific playing style components in Pictionary.

3 Methodology

We begin by describing the data collection for our game (Sect. 3.2). In Sect. 3.3, we introduce attributes of the game. We introduce the statistical analysis for identifying playing style components in Sect. 3.4 from game attribute data. In

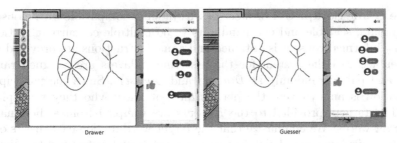

Fig. 2. Screenshot of our online Pictionary app used for data collection.

Sect. 3.5, we introduce attributes of game target phrase and methods to study target phrase's influence on game outcome. In Sect. 3.6, we describe our approach for analyzing the relationship of game outcome with the other attributes of our game. Fig. 1 shows the outline of our methodology.

3.1 Pictionary: A Multimodal Cooperative Partially Observable Game

Pictionary is a popular casual social game played by people of all age groups. In Pictionary, a team of two or more players play together towards a shared goal. One player of the team is chosen as the *Drawer* while the other player or players is the *Guesser*. The *Drawer* is given a randomly chosen *target word* which can be of any category like a name of an object, movie, action or phrase. The other players do not know what this word is. The goal of the game is for the *Drawer* to convey the *target word* by sketching to the teammate *Guesser* within a time limit. The *Drawer* is provided with a canvas on which the *Drawer* can sketch the *target word* or hints related to the *target word*. However, the *Drawer* is not allowed to write any text on the canvas. Also, the *Drawer* is not allowed to communicate by speaking or acting. The *Guesser* looks at the canvas and provides guesses of the *target word*. The game ends successfully when the *Guesser* correctly guesses the *target word* and the players earn points. The game ends in a failure if the time runs out without the *Guesser* guessing the *target word*. We consider a version of the game with a single *Drawer* and *Guesser*.

3.2 Data Collection

To study the game of Pictionary, we first require a large, diverse dataset of Pictionary game sessions with actual human players. However, large-scale data collection for a physically embodied game entails several technological and logistical barriers. Therefore, we designed an online browser-based Pictionary game playing app. We designed the app to make the game-playing experience closely mimic the real-world counterpart. Our main focus was to facilitate and capture all the possible interactions between the *Drawer* and the *Guesser*. A screenshot of our web app is shown in Fig. 2.

Online Game Setup: Our browser-based system is compatible with mouse and touch inputs, scalable and can handle up to 50 multiple concurrent Pictionary sessions. Informed consent is obtained and game instructions are provided when a player accesses the system for the first time. Players are assigned random names and paired randomly as *Drawers* and *Guessers*. Since the participants' information is anonymized, the players did not know who they were playing with. The targets provided to the *Drawers* are sampled from a dictionary of 200 target words. We emphasize that the target word dictionary consists of 138 nouns (e.g. airplane, bee, chair), 51 verbs (e.g. catch, call, hang) and 11 adjectives (e.g. happy, lazy, scary). To ensure uniform coverage across the dictionary, the probability of a target word being selected for a session is inversely proportional to the number of times it has been selected for elapsed sessions. The game has a time limit of 120 s. The game ends when the *Guesser* enters a word deemed correct by the *Drawer* or when the time limit is reached.

For the *Guesser*, a text box is provided for entering guess phrases. For the *Drawer*, the interface provides a canvas with tools to draw, erase and highlight locations (via a time-decaying spatial animation 'ping') for emphasis. In addition, thumbs up (👍) and thumbs down (👎), buttons enable *Drawer* to provide 'hot/cold' feedback on guesses. A question (❓) button is provided to the *Guesser* for conveying that the canvas contents are not informative and confusing. The canvas strokes are timestamped and stored in Scalable Vector Graphic (SVG) format for efficiency. In addition to canvas strokes (drawing and erasure related), guesses and secondary feedback activities mentioned previously (👎, 👍, ❓, highlight) are also recorded with timestamps as part of the game session.

Participants: Using our online Pictionary game, we collected data of 3220 game sessions from 479 participants of diverse age groups (19 to 60 years, mean: 32.02, SD: 13.07), gender (328 male and 98 female), handedness (388 right handed and 38 left handed) and educational demographics (middle and high school students, graduate and undergraduate university students and working professionals). We chose participants with English as primary language. Participants were not selected with any specific drawing skill.

3.3   Game Attributes

To characterize player behavior and interactive gameplay, we selected attributes that describe the player's actions and game interactions (see Table 1). The attributes quantify the degree of interaction and feedback provided. We broadly defined attributes based on player-role (i.e. *Drawer*, *Guesser*), and interactive aspects of the game (i.e. *Drawer-Guesser Interplay*).

We selected five *Drawer* attributes to describe the primary action (i.e. sketching) - see Table 1. Among the primary action attributes, `canvas area` is used as a measure of the canvas space utilized by the *Drawer*. The temporal aspects of the sketching activity are measured in terms of the time related attributes (e.g. instants of first and last sketch stroke, stroke frequency). We also selected

Table 1. List of game attributes describing the player actions in Pictionary.

	Action	Attribute	Abbreviation
Drawer	Sketch	Area of canvas used	canvas area
		Time of first stroke	first stroketime
		Time of last stroke	last stroketime
		Time between first and last stroke	stroke duration
		Frequency of strokes	stroke freq
	Erase and highlight	Percentage of games with erase and highlight	erase highlight usage
	Thumbs up	Percentage of games with thumbs up	thumbs up usage
	Thumbs down	Percentage of games with thumbs down	thumbs down usage
Guesser	Guess	No of guesses	guess count
		Entropy of guesses	guess entropy
		Time of first guess	first guesstime
		Time of last guess	last guesstime
		Time between first and last guess	guess duration
	Confusion	Percentage of games with confusion	confusion usage
Drawer-Guesser Interplay	Interactions	No of UI interactions	feedback-laden
		Largest time of contiguous events of *Drawer/Guesser*	one-sided play

attributes of secondary actions such as erase, highlight, thumbs up (👍) and thumbs down (👎). These actions are relatively rare. Hence, we record the percentage of games containing these actions for each *Drawer*.

For the *Guesser*, we selected six *Guesser* attributes to describe the primary action (i.e. guessing) and secondary action (i.e. confusion ❓) - see Table 1. We record the number of guesses in a session. Similar to the *Drawer* temporal attributes, we record the time of first guess, time of last guess, and duration of guessing. In addition to this, we calculate the entropy of the guess distribution by considering each guess as an impulse on the timeline of the game session. Since the secondary action (i.e. confusion ❓) is present sparingly, the percentage of games where confusion is indicated by the *Guesser* is recorded.

For a player in *Drawer*'s role, we consider all sessions of the player in this role. For each *Drawer* attribute, the median attribute value across the sessions is considered the aggregated attribute score. A similar procedure is used to obtain the player's *Guesser* aggregated attribute scores by considering all the sessions with the player in *Guesser*'s role. The attribute scores for all the players are analyzed together to identify intra/inter-role associations and interplay dynamics between the *Drawer* and *Guesser*.

3.4   Characterization of Playing Style Components

To identify role-specific playing style components in a data-driven fashion, we perform Principal Component Analysis (PCA) on the corresponding *Drawer* and *Guesser* attributes separately. To estimate the number of relevant components, we use parallel analysis. Subsequently, we examine the component loadings to label the playing style components. To examine the associations between the role-specific playing style components, we perform correlation between the *Drawer* and *Guesser* playing style scores obtained via the aforementioned PCA procedure.

3.5   Target Word

Games that are either too difficult or too simple have a greater churn risk [27]. Hence, game difficulty is an important parameter in game studies [43]. The difficulty of a Pictionary game is primarily determined by attributes of target word such as part of speech. For instance, a simple noun such as 'tree' or 'boat' can be easily sketched. Verbs or adjective target words such as 'listen' or 'lazy' may require a more complex illustration. To quantify target word difficulty, we conduct a survey. Subsequently, we analyze the influence of target word difficulty on game attributes, playing style components and game outcome.

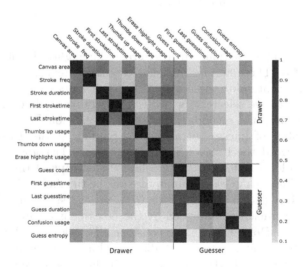

Fig. 3. Spearman's correlation between player attributes.

Target Word Difficulty: 40 participants (age: mean $= 21.83$, SD $= 2.34$, 17 females) rated the perceived sketching difficulty of the 200 target words. Each participant rated a subset (100 words) on a 5-point Likert scale ranging from 'very easy' to 'very difficult'. First, we assess the internal consistency of the acquired ratings by using Cronbach's alpha as a reliability measure. This measure was calculated on both subsets separately. Then, we use the median value of the resulting 20 ratings for each word as a measure of target word difficulty. All target words with a median rating of three and above were classified as 'difficult' while the rest were classified as 'easy'.

Influence of Target Word: We examine the influence of target word difficulty on game attributes and playing style components. To do this, we first divide the game sessions per player into two categories (i.e. 'easy' and 'difficult') based on target word difficulty. We then recalculate game attributes (Sect. 3.3) for each category separately. For difficult words, we expect an increase in amount of interaction and feedback, as well as a delayed response by both *Drawer* and *Guesser*, reflected by an increase in all the game attributes. We use Wilcoxon signed-rank test to examine the differences in game attributes based on target word difficulty level ('easy' and 'difficult'). Owing to multiple statistical testing, we perform Benjamini-Hochberg procedure to control for the false discovery rate.

Next, we obtain the playing style components for each category ('easy' and 'difficult') by performing category-wise PCA (as described in Sect. 3.4). We then examine the category-wise component loadings to determine if the playing style components are influenced by word difficulty. Finally, we perform paired t-test between the difficulty levels ('easy' and 'difficult') for all the scores of playing style components found with PCA.

3.6 Game Outcome

The outcome of Pictionary is binary: a success or a failure. We investigate the relationship between game outcome and other aspects discussed above (i.e. playing style components, *Interplay* attributes and target word difficulty) by performing point bi-serial correlation. Next, we group game sessions into two categories based on game outcome (success and failure). We recalculate *Interplay* attributes for each category separately. We then perform a Mann-Whitney U test to check for differences in *Interplay* attributes grouped by game outcome. Finally, to assess the relationship between the target word and game outcome, we compute the point bi-serial correlation between game outcome and word difficulty. We expect the evidence to support a negative association between the target word difficulty and game outcome.

4   Results

As a part of our overall analysis, we study the role of game difficulty, how it affects the game interplay and the role-specific playing style components. In Sect. 4.1, we report the playing style components exhibited by the *Drawer* and *Guesser*. In Sect. 4.2, we demonstrate the effect of word difficulty on *Drawer*, *Guesser*, and *Interplay* attributes and playing style components. Finally, we demonstrate the association between the game outcome and aforementioned attributes in Sect. 4.3.

4.1 Playing Style Components

As can be seen in Fig. 3, greater number of significant intra-role correlations are observed than inter-role correlations.

Table 2. PCA Component Loadings of *Drawer* attributes.

	PC1	PC2	PC3
Time between first and last stroke	**0.58**	0.01	−0.06
Time of first stroke	**0.36**	−0.13	0.15
Time of last stroke	**0.60**	−0.01	−0.04
% games with Thumbs up	−0.11	**0.70**	0.06
% games with Thumbs down	0.25	**0.37**	−0.22
% games with erase and highlight	0.14	**0.57**	0.08
Area of canvas used	0.26	−0.13	**0.57**
Frequency of strokes	−0.12	0.11	**0.77**
Explained Variance	46.30%	15.84%	11.95%
	Paced	Feedback	Intense

Table 3. PCA Component Loadings of *Guesser* attributes.

	PC1	PC2	PC3
No of guesses	**0.54**	−0.07	−0.02
Entropy of guesses	**0.56**	−0.12	−0.03
Time between first and last guess	**0.52**	−0.01	0.03
Time of last guess	**0.35**	**0.48**	0.02
Time of first guess	−0.08	**0.87**	−0.01
% games with confusion	0	0	1
Explained Variance	56.37%	20.90%	14.84%
	Intense	Delayed	Feedback

Drawer Playing Style Components: Parallel Analysis on *Drawer* attributes revealed an intrinsic dimensionality of three components. Subsequently, the three components obtained via PCA on the *Drawer* attributes explained a cumulative variance of 74.11%. As can be seen in Table 2, the first component ($PC1$), which we refer to as **Paced**, showed a high positive loading for attributes stroke duration, first stroketime and last stroketime. *Drawers* with higher values of **Paced** take longer to start sketching and spend a considerable amount of time drawing (see Fig. 7(a) and Fig. 7(b)). The second component ($PC2$), which we refer to as **Feedback**, showed high positive loadings for *Drawer* feedback attributes (`thumbs up usage`, `thumbs down usage`, and `erase highlight usage`). *Drawers* with higher values of **Feedback** use a significant amount of feedback elements on the GUI (see Fig. 7(c) and Fig. 7(d)). The third component (*PC3*) labelled as **Intense**, shows a high positive loading for `stroke freq` and a moderate positive loading for `canvas area`. *Drawers* with higher values of **Intense** draw fast and also use a large area to sketch (see Fig. 7(e) and Fig. 7(f)).

Table 4. Correlation between playing style components.

Playing style components		Guesser		
		Intense	Delayed	Feedback
Drawer	Paced	0.325***	0.252***	−0.033
	Feedback	0.230***	0.164***	−0.034
	Intense	0.286***	0.170***	−0.059

Note: *p < .05, **p < .01, ***p < .001

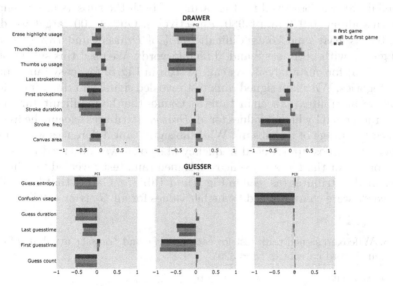

Fig. 4. PCA component loadings of *Drawer* and *Guesser* for first games of players and all but first game of players.

Guesser Playing Style Components: Parallel Analysis on *Guesser* attributes revealed three components. Subsequently, the three components obtained via PCA on the *Guesser* attributes explained a cumulative variance of 92.13% (Table 3). The first component (*PC1*), labeled as **Intense**, has high positive loadings for `guess count`, `guess entropy`, `guess duration`. *Guessers* with higher values of **Intense** make a lot of guesses over a significant time duration (see Fig. 8(a) and Fig. 8(b)). The second component ($PC2$), referred as **Delayed**, shows *Guesser* activity marked by high loading for the `first guesstime` and `last guesstime`. *Guessers* with higher values of **Delayed** wait for some time before guessing or guess only when they are confident (see Fig. 8(c) and Fig. 8(d)). The third component ($PC3$), labelled as **Feedback** has a high positive loading for `confusion usage`. *Guessers* with higher values of **Feedback** frequently use the confusion GUI button (see Fig. 8(e) and Fig. 8(f)).

Spearman's correlation between *Drawer* and *Guesser* playing style components can be seen in Table 4. Significant positive correlations were observed between **Paced**, **Feedback** and **Intense** drawing style components and **Delayed** and **Intense** guessing style components. To ensure the playing style components are not affected by players playing for the first time, we repeated PCA analysis after removing the first game of each player (see Fig. 4). We found that PCA loadings were near identical. This suggests that these playing style components are unaffected by the player's familiarity with the game app.

4.2   Target Word Difficulty

High reliability was observed for the ratings of both the subsets as evidenced by Cronbach's alpha (0.976 and 0.980 respectively). Out of 200 target words, 124 were rated as 'easy' and 76 as 'difficult'. 77% of *Drawers* and 73% of *Guessers* played games with both 'easy' and 'difficult' words. We used this subset of players ($n = 326$) for our analysis. As can be seen in Fig. 5, for 'easy' and 'difficult' word categories, Wilcoxon signed rank test revealed significant differences for several *Drawer* attributes (as seen in Table 5). Games that had 'difficult' target words were characterized by higher values for all *Drawer* attributes except the frequency of strokes and usage of thumbs up. While no significant differences were observed for usage of thumbs up, reduced frequency of strokes was observed for 'difficult' target words. For the *Guesser*, Wilcoxon signed rank test revealed significant differences in all attributes (as seen in Fig. 5 and Table 5). Games that had 'difficult' target words were characterized by higher values for all *Guesser* attributes.

Table 5. Wilcoxon signed rank test for each *Drawer* and *Guesser* attributes for 'easy' and 'difficult' word categories ($n = 326$).

Drawer Attributes	W	p	*Guesser* Attributes	W	p
Canvas area	12954	8.82e-16			
First stroketime	11948	5.90e-18	Guess count	8328	2.58e-20
Last stroketime	8066	1.00e-27	First guesstime	12554	1.26e-16
Stroke duration	9100	6.67e-25	Last guesstime	7902	3.47e-28
Stroke frequency	21322	1.75e-03	Guess duration	7801	5.65e-25
Thumbs up usage	16265	4.99e-02	Guess entropy	7868	3.38e-20
Thumbs down usage	9210	2.41e-06	Confusion usage	1200	5.93e-2
Erase highlight usage	8487	4.37e-04			

PCA on *Drawer* and *Guesser* attributes separately for games with 'easy' and 'difficult' words revealed highly similar component loadings (Fig. 6). This suggests no influence of target word difficulty on playing style components. Paired t-tests revealed no significant differences (refer Table 6) between the obtained playing style component scores at varying levels of word difficulty (i.e. 'easy' and 'difficult').

Spearman's correlation between target word difficulty and *Interplay* attributes revealed a positive correlation for both attributes, `feedback-laden` ($r = 0.41$, $p < 0.001$) and `one-sided` ($r = 0.47$, $p < 0.001$) interplay. Thus, we observed an increased usage of feedback and reduced activity from one of the players when faced with a 'difficult' target word.

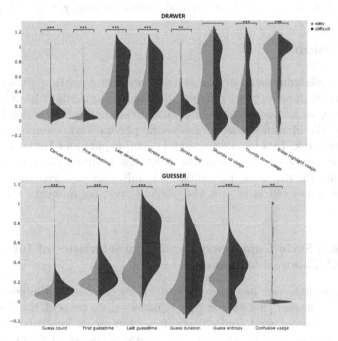

Fig. 5. Distribution of *Drawer* and *Guesser* Attributes for different levels of word difficulty. In the figure, ***$p < 0.001$, **$p < 0.01$ and *$p < 0.05$ where p is the p-value of Wilcoxon signed rank test (Sect. 4.2).

4.3 Game Outcome

Point biserial correlation between drawing style components and game outcomes revealed a significant negative correlation for **Paced** drawing style component ($r = -0.37$, $p < 0.001$), suggesting that slow and prolonged sketching is associated with greater incidence of unsuccessful games. On the other hand, **Intense** drawing style component was positively correlated ($r = 0.09$, $p < 0.001$), albeit a small effect, with game outcome, suggesting that the games with higher frequency of sketching are mildly associated with success. Within guessing style components, **Intense** ($r = -0.19$, p < 0.001) and **Delayed** ($r = -0.19$, p < 0.001) were negatively correlated with game success. A negligible correlation was also found for **Feedback** guessing style component ($r = -0.07$, p < 0.001). This suggests that excessive or belated guessing is associated with unsuccessful game outcome.

Mann-Whitney U test revealed significant differences for *Interplay* attributes grouped by game outcome (`feedback-laden`: $statistic = 990378.5$, $p = 1.14e - 97$ and `one-sided`: $statistic = 1073613.0$, $p = 3.62e - 142$). Significant negative correlation was observed between *Interplay* attributes and game outcome (`feedback-laden`: $r = -0.31$, p < 0.001 and `one-sided`: $r = -0.46$, p < 0.001), suggesting that too little or too much of interaction is associated with unsuccessful game outcomes. Finally, as hypothesized, significant negative correlation was observed between word difficulty and game outcome ($r = -0.59$, p < 0.001).

5   Discussion

Characterizing communication in a partially observable setting gives us interesting insights into how humans interact to convey information. In our paper, we use Pictionary as a case study to understand communication styles in a shared goal setting. We identified three role-specific playing style components namely, **Paced, Feedback, Intense** drawing style components and **Intense, Delayed, Feedback** guessing style components. Next, we analysed the impact of target word difficulty on the game interactions. Finally, we explored the relationship between the game outcome and the playing style components and *Interplay* attributes.

5.1   Playing Style Components and Characteristics of Interactions in a Collaborative Game

Though player behavior has been extensively researched in the context of different kinds of games [20], to our best knowledge, we present the first attempt on analysing playing style components in a communication-restricted environment. Our analysis explores the dynamic nature of cooperative interaction. The attributes investigated in our study not only characterize the aggregated properties of the game but also includes the temporal aspects of gameplay. In line with Loria et al. [30], we find that both aggregated and temporal aspects are needed to understand the dynamics of the gameplay system.

Based on player actions obtained from Pictionary, we observe three types of playing style components for each role (*Drawer* and *Guesser*). The player attributes are classified by quantity and speed of interactions (**Intense** drawing and guessing style components), nature of temporal interactions (**Paced** drawing style component and **Late** guessing style component) and the quantity of feedback (**Feedback** drawing and guessing style components). We observe that the playing style components in Pictionary are comparable to the classification of player typology by Ferro et al. [17]. Ferro et al. [17] group the player types and personality traits from literature into five categories namely, *Dominant, Objectivist, Humanist, Inquisitive, Creative*. The strong correlation we found between **Intense** drawing style component and **Intense** guessing style component appears to be suggestive of *Dominant* player type characterized by aggressiveness [17], exhibited in our study as intensive gameplay in terms of both speed and quantity. Furthermore, the playing style components, **Paced** drawing and **Delayed** guessing demonstrate traits of players who do not appear to be rushed despite the temporal constraint. Ferro et al. [17] describe *Objectivist* players as those who build upon their knowledge by focusing on self-directed tasks, which in our case is either to draw or to guess. The **Feedback** drawing and guessing style components involve responding with greater amount of icon-based feedback to the activity of the teammate. This style of playing is similar to *Humanist* player type, who involve themselves in tasks that rely on social engagement to solve problems.

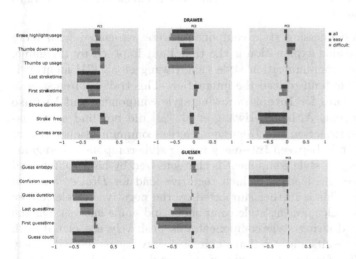

Fig. 6. PCA component loadings of *Drawer* and *Guesser* roles for different levels of word difficulty.

Table 6. Paired t-test for playing style component scores between the categories 'easy' and 'difficult'.

Drawer ($n = 326$):

	T	p
Paced	−0.32	0.74
Feedback	−0.03	0.97
Intense	−0.53	0.59

Guesser ($n = 326$):

	T	p
Intense	−0.71	0.48
Delayed	−1.63	0.10
Feedback	−0.28	0.77

The identified playing style components from our analysis allow us to draw parallels to communication styles in general. Hwang et al. [21] classify communication styles of casino dealers and their influence on player satisfaction. They propose nine communication styles that affect player satisfaction. We find that two of these playing style components *Relaxed* and *Dominant* are relevant to playing style components in Pictionary. *Relaxed* communicators tend to express themselves in an unperturbed and calm manner. Such a trait is seen in players with higher scores for **Paced** drawing and **Delayed** guessing style components. Hwang et al. [21] show that *Relaxed* communication style had a positive influence on player satisfaction. Although we do not have player satisfaction data, a potential proxy could be game outcome. We found that both higher **Paced**

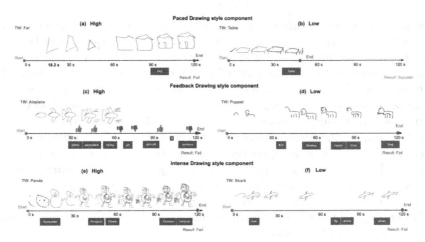

Fig. 7. Example of game with each *Drawer* playing style components. Also, see video example in supplementary.

drawing and **Delayed** guessing style components were associated with more failed games. One possible explanation is the time limit imposed by the game. The *Dominant/Active* communication style that Hwang et al. [21] identify is reflective of players who tend to lead the interaction. This trait is often seen in players with higher scores for **Intense** drawing style component and **Intense** guessing style component. Although Hwang et al. [21] did not find a correlation between player satisfaction and *Dominant/Active* communication style, we find a negative correlation between **Intense** guessing style component and game success. **Intense** guessing style component is characterized by high volume and frequency of text messages leading to high cognitive load for *Drawer* and can be highly distracting. This is further supported by the negative correlation we found between **Feedback** guessing style component and game success. On the other hand, **Intense** drawing style component was positively associated with game success. These results suggest that aggressive drawing paired with early guessing in a controlled fashion may result in successful communication in Pictionary.

While analysis of individual playing style components outlines role-specific behavior, the *Interplay* attributes `feedback-laden` and `one-sided` revealed the overarching gameplay dynamics. The negative correlation of `feedback-laden` interplay with game outcome reinforces our earlier discussion that too much feedback can be distracting to players. Furthermore, we observe that `one-sided` interplay is significantly associated with failure in games. This suggests that balanced interactions between roles are vital for successful communication.

5.2   Impact of Target Word Difficulty on Gameplay

From our analysis, we found that the target word difficulty is associated with significant differences in most player actions. As expected, a difficult target word is associated with an increase in most of the *Drawer* and *Guesser* attributes.

This indicates an increase in quantity of interactions and feedback and a delayed response from the players of both roles. Interestingly, we see a small decrease in the frequency of sketching for difficult words. This is in contrast to the expectation that a more difficult word requires more intense drawing.

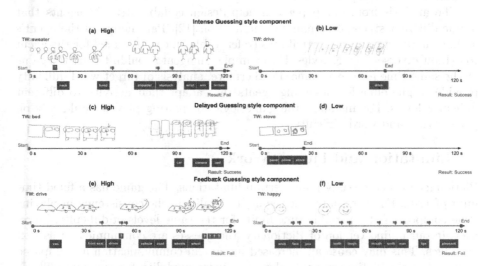

Fig. 8. Example of game with each *Guesser* playing style components. Also, see video example in supplementary.

While Fig. 5 demonstrates differences in player attributes across word difficulty, the covariance between these attributes as demonstrated in the loadings (Fig. 6) remains intact. Furthermore, paired t-tests on playing style components scores between 'easy' and 'difficult' words (Table 6) revealed no significant differences (p>0.05). This implies that while there exist changes in player attributes, the overall playing approach seems to be constant. For instance, when a player is performing a task involving higher cognitive load (i.e. 'difficult' words) vs lower cognitive load (i.e. 'easy' words), the activity of the players may differ based on the demands of the task, while the players approach to performing the task might remain stable. For example, a player playing a game with a 'difficult' word might draw for a longer period of time. However, the overall pace of the player (Paced playing style component) does not change. Thus, the playing style components identified in our analysis are inherent to the player and are not influenced by game difficulty.

5.3 Implications on Game and AI Agent Design

Determining playing style components can help in designing games that appeal to a diverse range of players. Delayed start in communication as observed in playing style components **Paced** drawing, **Delayed** guessing and intervals of inactivity as observed in one-sided interplay have higher churn risk. To address this, we can design a feature in the game which prompts a message to other players indicating that they are thinking or asking them to wait when they are inactive for a brief period. On the other hand, intensive interaction as seen in playing style components **Intense** drawing and **Intense** guessing might overwhelm the other player. To prevent this, the systems can incorporate suggestive mechanisms for players to match player speeds.

The analysis from our paper can help design collaborative AI agents that mimic different styles of human communication [12]. Parameters of the agent's action, similar to our game attributes (refer Table 1), can be tuned for the agent to exhibit diverse playing styles. For example, an agent shouldn't start the game at the same time for every game. Furthermore, analysis of target word difficulty provides a guideline for designing agents that adapt their activity to different difficulty levels. For instance, the game logic for pairing players could rely on player types and word difficulty.

6   Limitation and Future Work

Pictionary as a case study poses certain limitations. The game has a fixed time limit of 120 s. Further analysis is required to validate the consistency in playing style components for variable time limits for the same levels of difficulty. More-over, in our online version of Pictionary, the guesses are communicated as text messages. This may cause an increased latency in communication as compared to a real-world Pictionary game that uses voice modality for guessing [39]. To achieve a thorough analysis of multi-modal communication, further studies can be designed to use both text and voice modes of communication. Apart from Pictionary, similar games such as Wordgame [2] and Charades [33] are also interesting case studies that can be explored to better understand the differences caused by modality of communication in partially observable environment. A limitation of our analysis is that we do not take into account the drawing proficiency or prior experience of players. However, we use data from players of diverse age groups and demographics. Future work can also incorporate a post-game survey to rate social perceptions and player satisfaction to enhance communication in cooperative games.

7   Conclusion

In this novel work, we characterized interactions in a cooperative partially observable setting using the popular multimodal social game Pictionary as a case study. We found stable role-based *Drawer* and *Guesser* playing style components unaltered by word difficulty. The playing style components reinforce the existence of certain personality types in games put forth by existing theoretical frameworks. In terms of gameplay and in the larger context of cooperative partially observation interaction, our results demonstrate that too much interaction or unbalanced interaction leads to unsuccessful communication. In future, our study can help in designing AI agents which mimic human behavior. In addition, our work also establishes a precedence for future studies on Cooperative Partially Observable games.

References

1. Ashktorab, Z., et al.: Effects of communication directionality and AI agent differences in human-AI interaction. In: Proceedings of the 2021 CHI Conference on Human Factors in Computing Systems, pp. 1–15 (2021)
2. Ashktorab, Z., et al.: Human-AI collaboration in a cooperative game setting: measuring social perception and outcomes. Proc. ACM Hum.-Comput. Interact. 4(CSCW2), 1–20 (2020)
3. Ashton, M., Verbrugge, C.: Measuring cooperative gameplay pacing in world of warcraft. In: Proceedings of the 6th International Conference on Foundations of Digital Games, pp. 77–83 (2011)
4. Bafadal, M.F., Humaira, H.: The use of charades games in teaching vocabulary to the junior high school students. Linguist. ELT J. 6(2), 14–21 (2019)
5. Bard, N., et al.: The Hanabi challenge: a new frontier for AI research. Artif. Intell. 280, 103216 (2020)
6. Bartle, R.: Players who suit muds. J. MUD Res. 1(1) (1996)
7. Bauer, A., Popović, Z.: Collaborative problem solving in an open-ended scientific discovery game. Proc. ACM Hum.-Comput. Interact. 1(CSCW), 1–21 (2017)
8. Beznosyk, A., Quax, P., Coninx, K., Lamotte, W.: The influence of cooperative game design patterns for remote play on player experience. In: Proceedings of the 10th Asia Pacific Conference on Computer Human Interaction, pp. 11–20 (2012)
9. Borges, S.S., Mizoguchi, R., Durelli, V.H.S., Bittencourt, I.I., Isotani, S.: A link between worlds: towards a conceptual framework for bridging player and learner roles in gamified collaborative learning contexts. In: Koch, F., Koster, A., Primo, T., Guttmann, C. (eds.) CARE/SOCIALEDU -2016. CCIS, vol. 677, pp. 19–34. Springer, Cham (2016). https://doi.org/10.1007/978-3-319-52039-1_2
10. Clark, C., et al.: Iconary: a pictionary-based game for testing multimodal communication with drawings and text. In: Proceedings of the 2021 Conference on Empirical Methods in Natural Language Processing, pp. 1864–1886 (2021)
11. Colwell, J., Kato, M.: Investigation of the relationship between social isolation, self-esteem, aggression and computer game play in Japanese adolescents. Asian J. Soc. Psychol. 6(2), 149–158 (2003)
12. Conroy, D., Wyeth, P., Johnson, D.: Modeling player-like behavior for game AI design. In: Proceedings of the 8th International Conference on Advances in Computer Entertainment Technology, pp. 1–8 (2011)
13. Drachen, A., Sifa, R., Bauckhage, C., Thurau, C.: Guns, swords and data: clustering of player behavior in computer games in the wild. In: 2012 IEEE conference on Computational Intelligence and Games (CIG), pp. 163–170. IEEE (2012)
14. Eger, M., Martens, C., Córdoba, M.A.: An intentional AI for Hanabi. In: 2017 IEEE Conference on Computational Intelligence and Games (CIG), pp. 68–75. IEEE (2017)
15. Emmerich, K., Masuch, M.: The impact of game patterns on player experience and social interaction in co-located multiplayer games. In: Proceedings of the Annual Symposium on Computer-Human Interaction in Play, pp. 411–422 (2017)
16. Fay, N., Walker, B., Swoboda, N.: Deconstructing social interaction: the complimentary roles of behaviour alignment and partner feedback to the creation of shared symbols. In: CogSci (2017)
17. Ferro, L.S., Walz, S.P., Greuter, S.: Towards personalised, gamified systems: an investigation into game design, personality and player typologies. In: Proceedings of The 9th Australasian Conference on Interactive Entertainment: Matters of Life and Death, pp. 1–6 (2013)

18. Frans, K.: Ai charades: Language models as interactive game environments. In: 2021 IEEE Conference on Games (CoG), pp. 1–2. IEEE (2021)
19. Gero, K.I., et al.: Mental models of AI agents in a cooperative game setting. In: Proceedings of the 2020 CHI Conference on Human Factors in Computing Systems, pp. 1–12 (2020)
20. Hooshyar, D., Yousefi, M., Lim, H.: Data-driven approaches to game player modeling: a systematic literature review. ACM Comput. Surv. (CSUR) 50(6), 1–19 (2018)
21. Hwang, J., Park, S.: An exploratory study of how casino dealer communication styles lead to player satisfaction. J. Travel Tour. Mark. 35(9), 1246–1260 (2018)
22. Iacovides, I., Cox, A.L., Avakian, A., Knoll, T.: Player strategies: achieving breakthroughs and progressing in single-player and cooperative games. In: Proceedings of the First ACM SIGCHI Annual Symposium on Computer-Human Interaction in Play, pp. 131–140 (2014)
23. Jiang, J., Maldeniya, D., Lerman, K., Ferrara, E.: The wide, the deep, and the maverick: types of players in team-based online games. Proc. ACM Hum.-Comput. Interact. 5(CSCW1), 1–26 (2021)
24. Kirman, B., Lawson, S.: Hardcore classification: identifying play styles in social games using network analysis. In: Natkin, S., Dupire, J. (eds.) ICEC 2009. LNCS, vol. 5709, pp. 246–251. Springer, Heidelberg (2009). https://doi.org/10.1007/978-3-642-04052-8_28
25. Kou, Y.: Toxic behaviors in team-based competitive gaming: the case of league of legends. In: Proceedings of the Annual Symposium on Computer-Human Interaction in Play, pp. 81–92 (2020)
26. Lange, A., Somov, A., Stepanov, A., Burnaev, E.: Building a behavioral profile and assessing the skill of video game players. IEEE Sens. J. 22(1), 481–488 (2021)
27. Li, J., et al.: A difficulty-aware framework for churn prediction and intervention in games. In: Proceedings of the 27th ACM SIGKDD Conference on Knowledge Discovery and Data Mining, pp. 943–952 (2021)
28. Lopez, C.E., Tucker, C.S.: The effects of player type on performance: a gamification case study. Comput. Hum. Behav. 91, 333–345 (2019)
29. Loria, E., Marconi, A.: Player types and player behaviors: analyzing correlations in an on-the-field gamified system. In: Proceedings of the 2018 Annual Symposium on Computer-Human Interaction in Play Companion Extended Abstracts, pp. 531–538 (2018)
30. Loria, E., Rivera, J., Marconi, A.: Do they play as intended?-Comparing aggregated and temporal behavioral analysis in a persuasive gamified system. In: HICSS, pp. 1–10 (2021)
31. Mader, S., Tassin, E.: Playstyles in tetris: beyond player skill, score, and competition. In: Göbl, B., van der Spek, E., Baalsrud Hauge, J., McCall, R. (eds.) ICEC 2022. LNCS, vol. 13477, pp. 162–170. Springer, Cham (2022). https://doi.org/10.1007/978-3-031-20212-4_13
32. Matsumoto, Y., Thawonmas, R.: MMOG player classification using hidden Markov models. In: Rauterberg, M. (ed.) ICEC 2004. LNCS, vol. 3166, pp. 429–434. Springer, Heidelberg (2004). https://doi.org/10.1007/978-3-540-28643-1_55
33. Rahmah, A., Astutik, Y.: Charades game: does it affect students' learning on English vocabulary. EnJourMe (Engl. J. Merdeka) 5(1), 75–89 (2020)
34. Ramirez-Cano, D., Colton, S., Baumgarten, R.: Player classification using a meta-clustering approach. In: Proceedings of the 3rd Annual International Conference Computer Games, Multimedia and Allied Technology, pp. 297–304 (2010)

35. Rodrigues, L.A., Brancher, J.D.: Improving players' profiles clustering from game data through feature extraction. In: 2018 17th Brazilian Symposium on Computer Games and Digital Entertainment (SBGames), pp. 177–17709. IEEE (2018)
36. Rogerson, M.J., Gibbs, M.R., Smith, W.: Cooperating to compete: the mutuality of cooperation and competition in boardgame play. In: Proceedings of the 2018 CHI Conference on Human Factors in Computing Systems, pp. 1–13 (2018)
37. Sarvadevabhatla, R.K., Surya, S., Mittal, T., Babu, R.V.: Pictionary-style word guessing on hand-drawn object sketches: dataset, analysis and deep network models. IEEE Trans. Pattern Anal. Mach. Intell. **42**(1), 221–231 (2018)
38. Seif El-Nasr, M., et al.: Understanding and evaluating cooperative games. In: Proceedings of the SIGCHI Conference on Human Factors in Computing Systems, pp. 253–262 (2010)
39. Spyridonis, F., Daylamani-Zad, D., O'Brien, M.P.: Efficient in-game communication in collaborative online multiplayer games. In: 2018 10th International Conference on Virtual Worlds and Games for Serious Applications (VS-Games), pp. 1–4. IEEE (2018)
40. Toups, Z.O., Hammer, J., Hamilton, W.A., Jarrah, A., Graves, W., Garretson, O.: A framework for cooperative communication game mechanics from grounded theory. In: Proceedings of the First ACM SIGCHI Annual Symposium on Computer-Human Interaction in Play, pp. 257–266 (2014)
41. Tuunanen, J., Hamari, J.: Meta-synthesis of player typologies. In: Proceedings of Nordic Digra 2012 Conference: Games in Culture and Society, Tampere, Finland (2012)
42. Tylkin, P., Radanovic, G., Parkes, D.C.: Learning robust helpful behaviors in two-player cooperative atari environments. In: Proceedings of the 20th International Conference on Autonomous Agents and MultiAgent Systems, pp. 1686–1688 (2021)
43. Wheat, D., Masek, M., Lam, C.P., Hingston, P.: Modeling perceived difficulty in game levels. In: Proceedings of the Australasian Computer Science Week Multiconference, pp. 1–8 (2016)

Experience by Cohabitation: Living in a Smart Home Initiated by Your Partner

Annika Sabrina Schulz[1,2](✉) [iD], Johanna Müller[2] [iD], and Frank Beruscha[2] [iD]

[1] Bauhaus-Universität Weimar, Geschwister-Scholl-Straße 8,
99423 Weimar, Germany
annikasabrina@web.de
[2] Robert Bosch GmbH, Robert-Bosch-Campus 1, 71272 Renningen, Germany

Abstract. Setting up a smart home network in a shared household is typically initiated by individuals with a strong interest in technology, who consider the corresponding research, purchases, installation, and maintenance required, a hobby. Other people living in the same household, such as partners, are thus exposed to the technology. We interviewed 12 female users whose partners set up smart home networks in the shared home. From the perspective of the individuals confronted with technology usage, we explored adoption and acceptance processes and how they collaborate as a couple in designing their shared, connected home. To form the interview guideline, we conducted a pre-study in which we analyzed a sample of online forum threads, in which smart home hobbyists discuss challenges and tensions that arise with their partners. Proceeding from the insight that creating a shared smart home is a process highly influenced by the roles users assume in the household, we contribute to understanding the perception of smart home benefits, appreciation, and participation from the angle of users who did not initiate the setup of the network.

Keywords: shared smart home · collaborative use · secondary users

1 Introduction

The revenue of the European smart home (SH) market was projected to reach 28.58 billion USD by 2022, penetrating 17.8% households [36]. By 2027, 40.9% of European households are expected to be equipped with connected devices [36]. Users who adopt smart home products at a large scale are often persons with a strong intrinsic motivation, seeing the implementation of use cases and scenarios rather as a leisure activity [6, 21, 35]. However, remodeling the family home does not only concern the person who pursues this hobby but has an impact on other people who share their lives with them. For instance, the partners of smart home initiators represent one group of users who get confronted with technology usage and consequently must come to terms with handling devices.

© The Author(s), under exclusive license to Springer Nature Switzerland AG 2023
J. Abdelnour Nocera et al. (Eds.): INTERACT 2023, LNCS 14144, pp. 304–323, 2023.
https://doi.org/10.1007/978-3-031-42286-7_17

This work focuses on the experience of the individuals in a household who did not initiate living in a self-built smart home. There is little research on this perspective. Publications with insights about cohabitation in smart homes mostly result from user studies, in which either only the initiating person or both initiator and less-involved cohabitants participated [6,10].

A further avenue for insight into cohabitation experiences is through online discussions from SH enthusiasts, which provide information on how those people who buy and install smart home technology (SHT) think and talk about their household partners. A frequently used term within these discussions is the abbreviation WAF (Woman/Wife Acceptance Factor), which, whilst somewhat controversial, we used as a lens for our search within a pre-study, which we then contrast with our findings from interviews with non-initiating smart home users.

In the pre-study we analyzed a sample of online forum threads, in which smart home community members discuss thoughts and experiences with their SHT projects in interplay with their household members. We then conducted semi-structured interviews with smart home users whose partners initiated the purchase and implementation as a hobby.

The goal of this research was to understand how individuals who did not initiate the purchase and set-up of devices experience the beginning of living with smart home technologies and how cohabiting with a SH enthusiastic partner impacts this journey.

2   Related Work

2.1   User Types and Gender

Several researchers identified different types of smart home users in shared households, typically differentiating depending on their level of engagement [14,24,26]. If the gender of the participants is mentioned, female users are often assigned to a user type characterized by less engagement with SHT.

Poole et al. [26] identified for example the three user types *gurus*, *assisters*, and *passive users/consumers*. Information about the gender of classified smart home users was not reported in this work. *Gurus* are the smart home initiators in the household and responsible for setting up, maintaining, and repairing the SH network and generally show greater knowledge about the network than other household members, likely learned through training [26]. The *assisters* support *gurus* in maintaining the SH network [26]. This group typically can provide general information on how the network functions. Lastly, *passive users* or *consumers* solely utilize the SH infrastructure but do not engage in any network maintenance. *Passive users* are overall less involved in decision-making and leave planning to the *guru* in the household.

Koshy et al. suggest that *pilot-passenger* relationships are common in shared smart home households, in which individuals are located on a spectrum since responsibilities in device management might be shared [21]. In this study, the justification for taking the role of the *passengers* in the household was a lack of tech-savviness, and that it is more of a hobby to the *pilots* [21]. In such households, the *passengers* perceived the benefits of their smart home as limited. In other households, *passengers* got engaged with the devices [21]. One couple described, for example, that she created most routines for which her partner then set up all the devices. Regarding acquiring knowledge about the smart home, *pilots* typically taught *passengers* in their homes. Some *passengers* perceived that the *pilots* had more knowledge about the devices in the home, which makes their interaction with the installed devices occur more fluently in everyday usage [21]. *Passengers* need to invest more effort to adapt to the habits and do typically not share enthusiasm about the technology with their cohabitants; they engage only because of external triggers. In the eyes of a *pilot*, task distribution consolidates unequally over time, with them putting all the effort into managing the devices, benefiting the other household members [21]. Of the participants in [21], most of the *passenger users* were female. More specifically, all wives were classified as *passengers*.

Another way of framing SH user comes from Geeng and Roesner (2019) who classified users of shared smart homes as *smart home drivers* and as *passive users* [14]. The authors present chronological points when multi-user interaction or tensions occur: from device selection and installation, regular device usage when things go wrong, and in the long run. *Smart home drivers* typically perform selection and installation, and the majority of them stated to be the only person in the home installing smart home devices. Only a few individuals consulted with their partners about the purchases, mainly for financial reasons. This insight is in line with the results of Koshy et al., according to whom money and space are the primary concerns of *passenger users* [21]. Further, some *smart homs drivers* reported in this study that they anticipated the concerns of their partners based on experience from earlier situations [14]. Geeng and Roesner found, that in everyday life, the *driver* has control over data and functionality in the network by default [14]. Accordingly, other users must request changes, such as privacy settings, in consultation with this person. When things go wrong, the differences in power and control are often the source of conflict between people [14].

Wilson and Hargreaves describe a socio-technical view on smart home publications in which the relationship between technology and society co-evolve [35, p. 466]. In turn, this may reinforce identities, especially gender roles following major household practices [35]. According to the Socio-Technical Gender Model introduced by Rode and Poole, gender identity and technical identity are co-constructed [27]. Technical identity constitutes the authors' understanding of the technical abilities people have acquired and how they present self-efficacy and agency in handling technology [27].

Rode and Poole observed in their studies that the division of labor involving digital housekeeping did not occur in terms of skills but according to the gendered expression of specific behavior. The authors identified different strategies that male or female-identifying individuals apply concerning using home technology and present them as archetypes for identity work [27]. Regarding masculine behavior, they identified the three categories of *the chivalrous gentleman, the helpful (posturing) man,* and *the technical in other ways man.* One strategy to demonstrate masculinity, they identified, is to provide technical support in form of *digital chivalry*, which does not necessarily equal technical expertise. This archetype may lack contextual or technical knowledge and make changes inappropriate for the given context [27]. Rode and Poole draw the comparison that "being a technology czar is the digital equivalent of walking a woman home at night" [27]. Men showing this behavior try to achieve protection by controlling the computer, including its activities and users [27].

Also Ehrenberg and Keinonen found by investigating how SH usage shapes the flow of information and power in shared households; with the intent of gaining control over the SH networks, often, users exercise control over the inhabitants [13]. Power imbalance becomes evident as the SH administrator often performs direct and indirect observations, constrains the interactions of users, regulates commodities (e.g., water access to save energy), and pre-defines practices in the network. This person is typically male [13]. However, the insights of Ehrenberg and Keinonen represent mostly the male gaze since the speech portion of the male smart home initiators was higher [13].

Regarding showcasing femininity, Rode and Poole identified the four archetypes *the geek, the good woman, the damsel in mistress*, and *the technophobe. The geek* characterizes a female individual who presents herself as comfortable with technology. Often, she holds a higher academic degree in a technology-related discipline, and is thus, already used to masculine technical culture [27]. The other three archetypes apply strategies to construct their technical identity, conforming to gender roles of hetero-normative society norms. So does *the good woman* have strong technical abilities that she often downplays in social interactions, but applies in everyday life to fulfill societal normative roles (e.g., a "'good' homemaker, mother, widow, or daughter" [27]). Rode and Poole forecast, that this behavior contributes that technical work performed by women might become gendered as feminine and, consequently, invisible as with earlier technologies such as ovens and telephones. The *damsel in distress* describes an archetype of a woman who seeks technical support from the men in her life encouraging *digital chivalry.* She typically performs everyday tasks concerning digital housekeeping by herself. For major issues, she would ask for support. The *technophobe* describes the strategy of presenting herself as separate or fearful from technology.

In this work, we describe the experience with smart home technology from the perspective of the individuals to whom other authors often refer as *passive users*[14], *passengers* [21] or *consumers* [26], which implies a hierarchical classification of the different roles. Furthermore, the names *passenger* or *consumer* describe roles that appear in other contexts, in which the relationship between several parties is characterized by a sense of entitlement. By using these terms to describe the relationship of individuals using technology jointly, such as for couples cohabiting in smart homes, this hierarchy is transferred implicitly. *Secondary user* [20] seems to be the most neutral designation in this context, considering the individual's chronological order or dedicated time to smart devices. However, although not fulfilling the administrator role, in everyday usage of smart devices, persons belonging to this group are, from our understanding, still active users.

2.2   The WAF (Woman Acceptance/Wife Approval Factor)

According to Volmar, the abbreviation WAF was first used in the context of hi-fi technology in the magazine *Stereophil*, in which female users are said not to value listening experiences but assessed the technology mostly on appearance [34]. The discourse in the lifestyle magazine presents hi-fi culture as a purely male hobby, which might hinder individuals identifying as another gender from participating [34].

Considering the abbreviation's usage in smart home culture, we believe the same is taking place in this context. The WAF can be considered as a misogynist expression and method of *online othering*, a behavior of virtual groups seeking to shape regulations regarding which people are tolerated to participate and individuals who are not [18]. Criteria that individuals apply to exclude others are typically based on discrimination (e.g., racism, sexism, or ableism).

In academic publications, we came across the term in a satirical glossary of acronyms used in the electronics industry [29]. Among mostly technical acronyms describing methods or technologies, Santo defines the WAF as "A product feature or modification sufficiently appealing to women that they will permit their husbands to buy the product" [29]. As example for a product with high WAF, they mention "the ability of Sony's PlayStation Portable to play children's movies" [29]. Further, we found the WAF in the author's descriptions of the anthology "Smart Home Hacks", in which the author Richard (Rick) Tinker presents his personal "automation items that have the highest WAF [...] the laundry washer and dryer reminders" [25]. Both these examples use the WAF in the context of care work, stereotypically assigned to women.

In 2022, Aagaard published a more detailed examination of the WAF in context of smart homes [6]. In an interview study with Danish couples, one participant explained from his experience of running a blog with reviews of smart home technologies that it was "the key factor in determining whether his (male) readers would approve" a device [6]. This observation supports our assumption that the acronym is widespread in online communities. Aagaard found in their investigation that, although used only by a few participants, content-wise, the WAF was important to all participants [6]. Further, they report that the WAF does not give information about technology acceptance on a scale, but rather the feeling of smart home hobbyists whether the aesthetics of a device corresponds to the preferences of their (female) partners [6].

To investigate technology acceptance of smart homes, researchers mostly adapted prevalent acceptance models [7,8,16], especially the "Technology Acceptance Model" (TAM) [11] or the "Unified Theory of Acceptance and Use of Technology" (UTAUT) [32] to the context. While the acceptance models and their respective extensions largely originated in the organizational context, UTAUT2 provides a framework for the consumer context [33]. Notably, the factor *voluntariness of use* was excluded in UTAUT2, based on the assumption that the consumers' usage of a specific technology is generally voluntary. However, in shared technology usage, this might not always the case and simplifies the dynamics between cohabitants and the impact of the roles individuals assume.

Some authors suggested gender-neutral versions of the WAF, such as the Spouse Acceptance Factor (SAF) [25] or the Household Acceptance Factor (HAF) [10]. In both publications, the authors mention the factor only incidentally.

Throughout this work, we decided to stay with the gendered terminology to consider the socio-technical effects on gender roles impacting information and power dynamics in smart homes [13,17,22,27] aiming to avoid neutralizing the factor as cultural phenomenon.

In using the term as a search keyword, we would like to make clear that we distance ourselves from the construct and associated beliefs and are fully aware of its problematic nature and not seeking to promote its usage. We came across the WAF in a previous conversation with a SH enthusiast and recognized the opportunity to investigate the perspective and role on a specific group of non-initiating SH users through an exploratory approach to discussions around the WAF and its influencing factors. Conducting consecutive interviews with the household members who got to experience smart home technology by having it installed in their shared households by their partner, we provide more information on the requirements of this user group compared to the assumptions stated in online communities.

3   User Study

The following section describes the procedure we followed to investigate couple dynamics with self-built smart homes from the perspective of the secondary users. Figure 1 visualizes the approach, starting with an exploratory study to learn about the WAF in online SH communities. Based on a qualitative analysis of a sample of threads, we then led 12 semi-structured interviews with SH users whose partners set up the networks in their shared households.

Throughout our research, we cautioned to make ourselves aware of personal biases or stereotypical assumptions. All interviewees in this study identified as female and led a relationship with a man. Both partners pursued higher academic education and belonged to the middle or upper class of society living in Central Europe.

3.1   Exchange About Cohabitation: Analyis of SHT Online Forum

We aimed to collect a data sample and analyze it qualitatively to gain a broader understanding of how SH enthusiasts talk about their cohabitants and their challenges with living in their self-built smart home. To define a suitable sample of online forum threads, we used the Social Media Listening tool Brandwatch [2]. To limit the amount of data, we set the time frame to roughly 2 years (from March 1st, 2020, to March 31st, 2022).

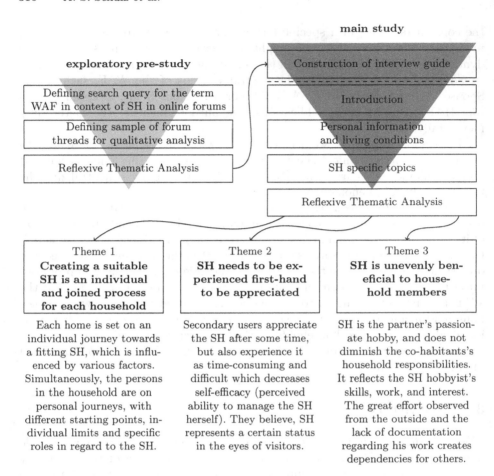

Fig. 1. Study Outline

We used the WAF in the context of SH as a keyword to filter for relevant discussions in an iterative procedure since it comprises how primary SHT users think and exchange about their cohabitants, a group of individuals academically often referred to as secondary [20], passenger [21] or passive [14] users. Using these terms as keywords in an analysis of online forums would not provide the same results.

We reviewed the resulting threads and narrowed the search down by excluding additional keywords. This procedure was challenging, on the one hand, since the abbreviation WAF contains various terminology from different contexts; on the other hand, we learned that the WAF is discussed in various domains, especially concerning purchase decisions. Consequently, we decided to restrict the search to specific online forums.[1] Brandwatch provided us a list of top sites for

---

[1] The query that we used for the Brandwatch search can be found here: https://drive.google.com/file/d/1jHxW8msLg4I7S6ySUoetqjcN1e92pl-V/view?usp=drive_link.

discussing the searched topic. We included the online forums that specifically concerned SH topics and were listed in the Brandwatch search result with a minimum of 10 mentions. Table 1 contains the eight online forums we considered in the analysis.

Table 1. Analyzed online forums

Forum	# of mentions	Threads qualitatively analyzed
knx-user-forum.de	169	70 (in German)
mikrocontroller.net	162	–
homematic-forum.de	151	–
fhem.de	116	–
loxforum.com	30	1 (in English)
athom.com	21	9 (in English)
homey.app	14	6 (in English)
domoticaforum.eu	14	5 (in English)

The query resulted in 676 mentions of the WAF written by 272 unique authors, however multiple counts of mentions may relate to the same post including the WAF due to the set-up of threads in online forums.

Furthermore, we faced some challenges with Brandwatch's traceability [19]. Typically, the software is used for consumer research to keep track of real-time data (e.g., on social media), while we investigated historical data. Consequently, it was not comprehensible how the tool decided which sources to consider.

According to the descriptive results provided by Brandwatch, 87% of these mentions were written by male users mainly located in Germany, followed by the Netherlands, Switzerland, and Austria. Most entries were posted Monday to Friday. The sentiment of the discussions is, according to Brandwatch, overall neutral (92% of the data), distributing with only 4% each among negative and positive valence. Regarding the share of emotions, Brandwatch recognized 82% of anger in the online discussions and 18% joy. However, the reliability of sentiment and emotion data needs to be considered carefully, according to Hayes et al.[19].

To define a feasible data sample for the subsequent qualitative analysis, we proceeded as follows: due to the limited number of English threads, we analyzed threads in German and English jointly, but needed to define a more workable sample of posts for the German threads. We started with a sample of 50 threads from the online forum with the most mentions - the knx-user-forum. We included data by following the link to the original posts listed in Brandwatch according to their timely relevance. Subsequently, we added another 20 threads, after which we stopped according to the concept of saturation [15]. In the German threads, incidentally, the WAF was not translated, but the English abbreviation was used.

In all analyzed online forums, users publish content under pseudonyms, and we removed the link between nicknames or user IDs and the original quotes to ensure anonymity. We analyzed the collected online forum and interview data in a Reflexive Thematic Analysis (RTA), a qualitative data analysis method that acknowledges personal biases and encourages critical reflection of the analysis process [9]. Overall, analysis of the online forum data sample occurred within an experimental framework [9].

In a rather semantic analysis, we focused on interpersonal and social aspects of living with SHT to capture meaning when users described their experiences and opinions about other household members in forum posts. One researcher assigned more than 100 labels to text sections in MAXQDA2022 [3] in an inductive approach. Codes were clustered into 9 topics with varying levels of subtopics.

Subsequently, several researchers were involved in defining, reviewing, and redefining themes on an instance of the collaborative whiteboard tool Miro [5] in iterations before finalizing and naming four themes titled *"Smart home remains male-dominated"*, *"Smart home hobbyists share the goal of achieving a high WAF"*, *"Smart home hobbyists assume three different roles during decision-making"*, and *"A winning formula for a high WAF seems to exist"*.

The exploration of the WAF in online communities convinced us of the importance of a scientific understanding of the smart home hobby culture. However, considering the analysis of only a few threads in German and the limited transparency in Brandwatch, we believe an intensive examination of the discourse merits its own study.

Still, we used the following gained insights as input for the interview guide: Like the abbreviation WAF already implies, the online space feels misogynist. As female researchers, the overall prevailing tone of voice did not feel welcoming. Forum users refer to their partners with nicknames, such as *"mousey"*. Besides, they considered technical tasks assigned to themselves as the male person in the household. One user stated that women *"may romp around in the bath-room+kitchen, the man with electronics"*. Some forum users take it for granted that setting up the devices allows to *"manipulate [her], or rather train your wife"*.

The abbreviation WAF was understood without explanation by most forum participants. Active community members seem to immediately dispel emerging discussions on the political correctness of the term. Still, as reported in [6], the approval of their partners seems to be necessary and important for them. Concerning some areas of the home, a solution with an expected high WAF even outweighs personal preferences. Discussing the needs and requirements of women or wives along the WAF might be another expression of digital chivalry in online communities [27], we believe.

The discussions of the forum members give the impression that they are convinced to know their partners' wishes: correct functionality, cost-effective, intuitive, and visually supported control of the system, fast troubleshooting, white or invisible components, and personalized solutions seem to be the *"recipe to success"*.

The wording suggests that the SH hobbyists make the decisions alone, since many forum users wrote mainly about themselves throughout their posts, although they do not live alone. One user stated, for example: *"I have the problem, that I have many windows on the South side"*. Some distinguished between *"our home"* and *"my SH components"*. Only a few described their requirements in the we-form.

In summary, the assumptions about the preferences and requirements of their female partners that the online forum users imply, depict a traditional stereotype of femininity describing a lack of interest and capability in handling technology, and a primary interest in the aesthetics of the home. Females are presented as if they constantly complain and demand their partner's effort in maintaining and configuring their SHT. Some forum members see themselves in the position to manipulate their partners consequently so they can follow their own interests.

One must take into account, however, that the forums we selected are special interest communities for SHT, partly of specific providers. Individuals who actively engage in these discussions do not represent the male gender or people who initiated living in a smart home in general.

3.2   Experience by Cohabitation: Interviews with Smart Home Users

In our main study, we conducted semi-structured interviews to gather the perspective of individuals confronted with SHT that their partner set up in their shared home as a hobby.

The interview guide followed a funnel-shaped pattern, from general questions to more specific topics. Initially, they shared demographic information describing their relationship, living conditions, and interest in SH. Based on insights we received about the journey with SHT from the online forum analysis, we asked the participants how they first got in touch with it, followed by how communication, decision-making, and troubleshooting concerning SH components occur in their household. To conclude, they shared experiences about how other people handled their personal SH, such as visitors or children. We introduced the WAF to the participants and asked how they felt about the term only at the end of the conversation to avoid biasing towards gender stereotyping.

We conducted 12 interviews, whereas the first served as a pilot. The conversations were audio-recorded with the participants' informed consent and transcribed with Adobe Premiere Pro [1]. We listened again to the audio recording to correct errors created in the automated transcription.

The participation criteria were that the current SH setup in their living space consisted of several connected devices that their partners set up as leisure activity. To recruit participants, we used snowball sampling, starting in the professional and personal surrounding of the researchers.

All interviewees were female and were located in Germany (9) and the Netherlands (3). Table 2 includes a more detailed description of the participants. Interviews lasted between 32 to 48 min and were carried out online via Microsoft Teams [4] between April and May 2022.

Table 2. Participants' demographics including information about their profession, living situation, relationship status, and children

#	Home	Location	Occupation	Married	Children
P1	Apartment	Germany	Student	No	No
P2	Apartment	Netherlands	Student	No	No
P3	Apartment	Germany	Digital analyst	No	No
P4	Apartment	Germany	Digital engineer	No	No
P5	Apartment	Netherlands	Student	No	No
P6	Apartment	Germany	Teacher	Yes	Yes, 1
P7	House	Germany	IT project manager	Yes	Yes, 1
P8	Apartment	Germany	IT consultant	Yes	No
P9	Apartment	Netherlands	Project manager	No	No
P10	House	Germany	Product owner IoT	Yes	Yes, 2
P11	House	Germany	Lawyer	No	No
P12	House	Germany	Processing SAP	Yes	Yes, 2

Throughout the interview data analysis, we followed the same process to conduct RTA [9] as we did in the analysis of online forum data. We again followed an inductive approach with an experimental framework while considering semantic meanings throughout the data with no pre-determined theoretical foundation.

4   Results

In the following section, we provide insights into the experiences of SH users confronted with technology by cohabiting with smart home hobbyists.

4.1   Theme 1: Creating a Suitable SH Is an Individual and Joined Process for Each Household

This theme refers to each household's highly individual path in creating their SH, as each person has another approach, attitude, and level of experience with the technology. One challenge arises from the fact that the users embark on the journey at different times.

In the household constellation we investigated, one person has already been intensively engaged with the idea of the SH, while the others are gradually learning about it. From the perspective of most participants, committing to a relationship with their partner led implicitly to the confrontation with SH technology since their partners have already pursued the hobby before they met. At the time of the initial set-up of their shared SH, most interviewees hardly showed interest in collaborating. Encountering first working prototypes, however, required them to deal with it since established habits got interrupted.

Entry-level projects typically concerned smart lighting, often combined with automation or new interfaces instead of the switches they were used to. According to the participants, the beginnings involved a high cognitive load in changing their behavior and learning the new controls. One participant stated, for example, *"well, [getting used to the SH] comes step by step. It was just too much for me in the beginning"* (P4). P2 reported that her partner typically changed the set-up without informing her: *"This is why I am confused sometimes. Where is what now? Because he just renews things"*.

While getting used to handling the devices, some participants reached out to their partners for explanations, whereas others preferred to deal with it themselves. Most of them started in this phase to reflect on their personal boundaries and needs, especially regarding data protection, privacy, and the necessity for the household. P1, for example, explained: *"I vetoed the idea of having such a thing [smart speaker] in the bathroom, and I think it is a good thing that we do not have one in the home office room, especially because of data protection, work, and so on"*.

Gradually, for some couples, planning, strategizing, and sharing information around expanding the SH became a collaborative interest. For instance, P3 described conversations with her partner revolving around *"what we can imagine having, what we need, what we want"*.

Other interviewees said they left all decisions up to their partners. P6 explained, for instance, *"I was not asked, but that is obvious, I never get asked, because I don't care. He has fun [with SH], and in the end, I also benefit from it. However, it's not like we need to talk about it"*.

Some individuals reported that they held back their interest consciously. They justified this behavior with the arguments that their partners had, on the one side, more expertise than themselves, and on the other, they did not wish to limit their partners in their passion. P4 explains *"I don't want to decide over him or his wishes. He also lets me be free in what I want to do"*.

4.2 Theme 2: SH Needs to Be Experienced First-Hand to Be Appreciated

After getting used to dealing with connected devices in everyday life, some participants to started to get interested in expanding their SH. They began to dig into additional components and inter-compatibility, communicated their needs and requirements, and motivated their partners to proceed with projects.

Simultaneously, most participants reported that they knew their partners had already planned further implementations. Thus, they tried to get involved in prioritizing the new projects. For instance, P8 assumed the role of the person who asks *"does it make sense or does it not make sense and constantly wants to know, what do we need this for?"*, as she started to see the value in their connected home.

The interviewees described to be patient and understanding regarding the speed of new implementations since they see their partners' efforts considering that it is still a hobby for their partner. Especially in case of malfunctioning, the participants appreciate their partner's work. Most of the participants reported they do not consider troubleshooting their *"area of responsibility"* (P6). On the one hand, they are annoyed with it, and on the other hand, they are afraid to break something. Even individuals who theoretically have the necessary skills said that the lack of documentation makes it impossible to resolve issues independently with reasonable effort. P5 described her perceived ability to handle malfunctioning smart home components low: *"I really don't know how to put up all those things. [...] And then if it breaks, I don't know what to do."*.

According to our interviewees, welcoming visitors is a positive experience for both individuals of the couple. They described that they are proud to present their SH together. They are excited to give explanations and instructions to the visitors. In addition, the SH creates a joined status and image. According to P12, the SH represents *"you are modern and up-to-date"*.

4.3   Theme 3: SH is Unevenly Beneficial to Household Members

The participants' descriptions suggested that the functionalities of their SH, first and foremost, deal with household chores that are already uncomplicated, such as turning on lights automatically. The inhabitants still carry out more time-consuming or complex tasks.

Further, setting up and maintaining the network adds up to digital housekeeping, enabling their partner to contribute to the household while pursuing the hobby. In comparison, the interview participants described how most remaining, rather annoying, chores are their responsibility.

Additionally, some interviewees reported to contribute to building the shared SH by taking on the rational voice regarding the usefulness and prizing of new components - a role they do not enjoy to fulfill but assume because they believe no one else would do it otherwise.

Conclusively, multiple participants mentioned that, in the first place, the SH allows their partner to show off their interests and skills while making them tangible for family and friends. Thus, the implemented features serve demonstration purposes and pleasure and are not necessarily useful.

The lack of documentation makes it difficult to get involved independently or ask for external support, thus reinforcing dependencies and determining power distributions. P5 mentioned, for example, that she would want to change the nickname she was given in the system by her boyfriend and stated: *"I cannot do anything. I cannot put another name in there. I just have to deal with it"*.

Furthermore, various interviewees described it as difficult to keep track of their partner's ever-changing and evolving implementations. Paying continuously conscious attention to the interaction is draining for them.

4.4   Opinion of Female Smart Home Users on the WAF

At the end of the interviews, the participants reflected on the WAF. Several participants emphasized the relevance of considering other people possibly affected by decisions concerning the SH since *"they also have to be able to handle it"* (P2) but various participants questioned the term, especially its reference to the female gender.

They criticized the term for only considering the female partner, excluding other family members and relationship models (e.g., P2). To some participants, this felt *"sexist"* (P4) or *"cliché"* (P11). One participant remarked that it *"reinforces the understanding of one's role"* related to gender (P10). Others associated it with men being dominated by their wives (P1, P12).

5 Discussion

The interviews with people living with SHT who did not initiate their installation in their homes highlighted the fact that designing and appropriating the technology is a highly personal journey for each household, but also for each individual. In cohabitation with a SH enthusiast it seems to be initially that person who sets the requirements, as all interviewees reported that their partner had already pursued SHT as a hobby before they met, so whether to own a smart home in cohabitation was not questioned. Hence, it seems not all household members use the smart home fully voluntarily, as usually assumed in acceptance of consumer technology [33].

Still, after getting started to use SHT in everyday life, they reflect on this and build own opinions over time, specifically understanding their boundaries. The interviewees describe getting used to handling the SHT as cognitively draining. They especially struggled to keep up with changes since the set-up evolved dynamically.

With incorporating SHT in their daily routines, they reported to start appreciating some elements and getting engaged with the conceptual design of their SH, especially concerning use cases and the prioritization of projects. At the same time, seeing how much effort their partner puts into administration negatively affects the users' self-efficacy and agency.

Even for individuals with the necessary technological expertise, the missing documentation of the network makes it impossible to change anything with reasonable effort. Consequently, they might tend, despite the wish to engage more with SH, to take rather stereotypical roles that are more in line with their technical and co-constructed gender identity [27].

To support users of a shared smart home in the process of appropriating it, and meeting the requirements of all inhabitants, it is necessary to focus on the individual user journeys and their interplay. The differences of the individual's starting points of getting acquainted with SHT, technological knowledge and personal interest require special attention. In research and development of SHT, methods and tools are required to enable SH end-users to communicate and collaborate effectively.

We found in our interviews that users started to appreciate the installed SHT after they used it over some time. However, in their case, they only got acquainted with the technology with being installed in their personal surroundings at home. Thus, the question arises whether they got indeed comfortable with the technology or normalized feeling uncomfortable in order to reduce cognitive dissonance. Still, this finding can be meaningful to achieving SHT acceptance. This is for example relevant for such households investigated in this research, in which one member is keen on the idea of living in a smart home while the others are still skeptical. For others, SHT might serve as assistive technology or to achieve higher accessibility [23], which individuals might reject initially for various reasons.

Providing interactive experiences in public or semi-public spaces would result in additional touch points and create opportunities for prospective users in which they get the chance to explore and experience the technologies before purchasing devices. An example could be to create exhibitions or equipping public buildings or rental accommodations with SHT. Targeting especially others than the primary user, ideally collaboratively could foster communication and joint decision making.

Our finding that both the secondary and the primary user seem to enjoy presenting their smart homes to visitors and friends could be integrated in the endeavor of providing SHT experiences before purchasing, for example by creating user communities that are not virtual and organizing events for them (e.g., SHT parties or meet-ups hosted at a user's home). Beyond existing online communities such as the analyzed forums, bringing people with interest in SHT together in real life might enable people to connect with each other and be more inclusive to others than the primary user or SHT enthusiasts.

Our research indicates that individuals who did not initiate the purchase of SHT, indeed would like to contribute in shaping their smart home but seem to lack opportunities to engage in the process. Starting initiatives that involve other smart home users than enthusiasts in the process might help in developing smart home features that indeed support with household tasks unlike current implementations as described in our results and described in [21].

The interviewees who got involved in shaping their SH described that they conducted their own research about components, their incompatibility and financial aspects, and questioned the usefulness of features. In the communication with the SHT enthusiast in their household, they typically took the rational voice, which can be considered as a form of care work [12].

The circumstance that the smart home is a hobby for the initiator seems to add another layer of complexity to the couple's handling of their smart home. Several interviewees described that they restrained themselves from interfering with the smart home to avoid spoiling the fun for their partner. They justified this behavior with the wish not to be limited by their partners in pursuing their hobby in return, ignoring that their leisure activities are unlikely to affect others comparably.

Several authors refer to the maintenance of a smart home network as digital housekeeping, that typically men perform [6, 13, 27]. However, with the circumstance that the smart home is an individual's hobby, the participants in our study described that housework is distributed unequally among the two: one person gets to do the work that is fun for them while the other person remains with the annoying parts.

Consequently, concerning the execution of chores regarding the smart home, our interviewees stated to hold back with demands and wait patiently since they do not want to pressure their partners in pursuing their hobby. If they would, they believe the SHT enthusiast's motivation to take care of the smart home network might change. Koshy et al. found this to be true: SHT maintainers feel like they put all the effort into managing the smart home, while others only benefit [21]. This interplay demonstrates that for both individuals the SHT becomes a burden and reinforces gendered distribution of labor [6,28].

For SHT researchers and providers this finding should serve as motivation to invest effort in the development of functionalities that actually facilitate household chores. A large component of mastering everyday life, especially in cohabitation, is cognitive and mental load [12,30]. Technology can support humans in managing these tasks effectively. Besides, it should be noted that living in an SHT creates new chores as part of digital housekeeping [31]. People in cohabitation should be supported in the endeavor of distributing tasks among each others by design of IoT and SHT applications.

5.1 Limitations and Future Work

In this work, we investigated the experience of smart homes from the perspective of users whose partners set up a smart home network in their shared households in their free time. We interviewed individuals who lived as secondary users in a self-built connected home. They all identified as female and led relationship with men, sharing no details whether they lived monogamously. The dynamics might differ in other forms of relationship or cohabitation and should be the topic of future work. Further, one must take into account that gender identities are a continuum, considering that individuals can express their genders fluidly. The same might apply to co-constructed technical identities and the role a person assumes in cohabitation.

Most interviewees had high educational qualifications and lived in Central Europe, thus represented only a subset of couples sharing a smart home. Some participants lived also with children; however, this was not sufficiently discussed in the interviews.

Regarding the WAF, we provided insights from a forum analysis describing how community members use the abbreviation. This investigation was highly exploratory to gain insights of how SH enthusiasts depict their partners concerning dealing with SHT. The abbreviation characterizes threads of an online community expressing misogynist thoughts in these spaces. With this research, we do not want to support reproducing it but encourage a reflective handling of such phenomenon and promote a constructive and critical dialogue about intersectionality in the context of different user groups. Exploring the abbreviation WAF in a small sample of online forum threads suggested that this approach provides information about the smart home hobby culture revealing users' conflicts, tensions, and thoughts. A thoroughly conducted analysis of the term and other discussions about interpersonal topics in the smart home seems promising to understand user behavior in the wild. However, insights derived from such online communities should be handled with care since they include discussions of special interest forums in which users exchange opinions that might be extreme. They might paint an exaggerated picture. The thread sample we analyzed originated from European online forums that are related to specific systems and included mostly posts in German.

The insights of the pre-study in combination with the results of our interviews demonstrate the need to keep the dynamic of relationships in mind when designing technology for shared use. In the context of couples cohabiting smart homes, systems should support users in collaborating and communicating about their home, sharing associated knowledge and, thus, the resulting design opportunities of the living spaces. A crucial element is to focus not only on the initiators and enthusiasts of SHT but focus on all individuals living in connected spaces. Involving secondary users in future research with appropriate speaking parts could help to provide new perspectives and lead to product designs more beneficial to all individuals.

A further approach could include participation-fostering elements for secondary users in user experience designs. One way to do this could be to create new touch points with SHT before purchase decisions that users can explore collaboratively, such as in targeted events and exhibitions.

To support individuals to engage with SHT, products that comprise end-user implementations should include user interfaces appropriate to different identities and interests. Communication and social interaction fostering elements in the user experience design could make the joint journey in cohabitation more enjoyable.

This work focuses on the experiences with the smart home in the initial stage. Future research should investigate more specifically how users move from the playful handling of the smart home as a hobby to professionalizing the usage of the technology when its maintenance adds to the list of chores since inhabitants start to rely on features in their everyday life. For instance, designing meaningful representations of the system to stimulate awareness and reflection on the role users take in collective use could foster self-determination in interaction with ubiquitous technology at home.

6 Conclusion

The main contribution of this work lies in the perspective of smart home users whose partners implemented the network as a hobby and who are often portrayed as passive [14,26]. However, in everyday life, they experience the technology as active users.

Ideally, equipping the house with IoT technologies would be a collaborative process that leads to a shared smart home in which all cohabitants profit from an increased quality of life. The interviews with individuals whose partner initiated living together in a smart home showed that, currently, their smart home mostly represents the preferences of one person and thus, seems to benefit users in shared households unequally. First purchases are often made out of one person's curiosity and personal interests, which, in the further course, make the joint user journey remain one-sided, reinforced by dynamics of the relationship, the initial start as a hobby and the roles individuals take in cohabitation.

For a user getting acquainted with SHT by experiencing it in their own living spaces, the cognitive load increases at the beginning significantly while they learn about the devices, form an opinion about personal interests, wishes, and limits, understand user interfaces, and often simultaneously keep up with continuous changes in their set-up.

Our results showed that many individuals would like to engage and contribute conceptually in shaping their smart home, but experience a decreased sense of agency since they perceive the effort their partners invest as intimidating.

Further, they consciously hold back with intervening not to restrict the other person in pursuing their hobby. Still, as the smart home evolves, the leisure activity transforms to a chore as part of digital housekeeping [21].

The dynamics of the relationship in combination of the different user experiences of the individuals contribute to reinforcing stereotypical understanding of gender roles and distribution of labor, as already pointed out by [6,13,27,35].

In order to create smart homes in which several individuals can feel comfortable [30], research and development of smart home technologies should put more focus in providing opportunities for individuals with diverse personal interests and technical identities to engage and contribute to shaping their shared living spaces.

References

1. Adobe Premiere Pro CC (2022)
2. Brandwatch (2022). https://www.brandwatch.com/
3. MAXQDA Standard, November 2022. https://www.maxqda.de/
4. Microsoft Teams (2022). https://www.microsoft.com/de-de/microsoft-teams/group-chat-software
5. Miro (2022). https://miro.com/app/dashboard/
6. Aagaard, L.K.: When smart technologies enter household practices: the gendered implications of digital housekeeping. Housing Theory Soc. 1–18 (2022). https://doi.org/10.1080/14036096.2022.2094460, publisher: Routledge _eprint
7. Aldossari, M.Q., Sidorova, A.: Consumer acceptance of internet of things (IoT): smart home context. J. Comput. Inf. Syst. 60(6), 507–517 (2020). https://doi.org/10.1080/08874417.2018.1543000, publisher: Taylor & Francis _eprint
8. Baudier, P., Ammi, C., Deboeuf-Rouchon, M.: Smart home: highly-educated students' acceptance. Technol. Forecast. Soc. Change 153, 119355 (2020). https://doi.org/10.1016/j.techfore.2018.06.043, https://www.sciencedirect.com/science/article/pii/S0040162518300192
9. Braun, V., Clarke, V.: Thematic Analysis: A Practical Guide. SAGE Publications Ltd, Los Angeles, London, New Delhi Singapore Washington DC Melbourne (Nov 2021)
10. Brütting, A., Golle, D., Niklas, C., Thiel, C.: Das verbraucherfreundliche Smart Home (2022)

11. Davis, F.D.: Perceived usefulness, perceived ease of use, and user acceptance of information technology. MIS Q. **13**, 319–340 (1989), place: US Publisher: Management Information Systems Research Center. https://doi.org/10.2307/249008

12. Dean, L., Churchill, B., Ruppanner, L.: The mental load: building a deeper theoretical understanding of how cognitive and emotional labor overload women and mothers. Community Work Family (2021). https://doi.org/10.1080/13668803.2021.2002813. Nov

13. Ehrenberg, N., Keinonen, T.: The technology is enemy for me at the moment: how smart home technologies assert control beyond intent. In: Proceedings of the 2021 CHI Conference on Human Factors in Computing Systems, pp. 1–11. ACM, Yokohama Japan, May 2021. https://doi.org/10.1145/3411764.3445058, https://dl.acm.org/doi/10.1145/3411764.3445058

14. Geeng, C., Roesner, F.: Who's in control?: Interactions in multi-user smart homes. In: Proceedings of the 2019 CHI Conference on Human Factors in Computing Systems, pp. 1–13. ACM, Glasgow Scotland UK, May 2019. https://doi.org/10.1145/3290605.3300498, https://dl.acm.org/doi/10.1145/3290605.3300498

15. Glaser, B.G., Strauss, A.L.: The Discovery of Grounded Theory: Strategies for Qualitative Research. Routledge, New York (2017). https://doi.org/10.4324/9780203793206

16. Gross, C., Siepermann, M., Lackes, R.: The acceptance of smart home technology. In: Buchmann, R.A., Polini, A., Johansson, B., Karagiannis, D. (eds.) BIR 2020. LNBIP, vol. 398, pp. 3–18. Springer, Cham (2020). https://doi.org/10.1007/978-3-030-61140-8_1

17. Hargreaves, T., Wilson, C.: Smart Homes and Their Users. Human-Computer Interaction Series, Springer, Cham (2017). https://doi.org/10.1007/978-3-319-68018-7, http://link.springer.com/10.1007/978-3-319-68018-7

18. Harmer, E., Lumsden, K.: Online Othering: An Introduction, pp. 1–33, April 2019. https://doi.org/10.1007/978-3-030-12633-9

19. Hayes, J.L., Britt, B.C., Evans, W., Rush, S.W., Towery, N.A., Adamson, A.C.: Can social media listening platforms' artificial intelligence be trusted? Examining the accuracy of Crimson Hexagon's (Now Brandwatch Consumer Research's) AI-driven analyses. J. Advertising **50**(1), 81–91 (2021). https://doi.org/10.1080/00913367.2020.1809576, publisher: Routledge _eprint

20. Jang, W., Chhabra, A., Prasad, A.: Enabling multi-user controls in smart home devices. In: Proceedings of the 2017 Workshop on Internet of Things Security and Privacy. IoTS&P '17, pp. 49–54. Association for Computing Machinery, New York, NY, USA, November 2017. https://doi.org/10.1145/3139937.3139941

21. Koshy, V., Park, J.S.S., Cheng, T.C., Karahalios, K.: "We just use what they give us": understanding passenger user perspectives in smart homes. In: Proceedings of the 2021 CHI Conference on Human Factors in Computing Systems. CHI '21, pp. 1–14. Association for Computing Machinery, New York, NY, USA (2021). https://doi.org/10.1145/3411764.3445598

22. Laschke, M., et al.: Otherware needs Otherness: understanding and designing artificial counterparts. In: Proceedings of the 11th Nordic Conference on Human-Computer Interaction: Shaping Experiences, Shaping Society, pp. 1–4, No. 131. Association for Computing Machinery, New York, NY, USA (2020). https://doi.org/10.1145/3419249.3420079

23. Layton, N., Steel, E.: The convergence and mainstreaming of integrated home technologies for people with disability. Societies **9**(4), 69 (2019). https://doi.org/10.3390/soc9040069, https://www.mdpi.com/2075-4698/9/4/69, number: 4 Publisher: Multidisciplinary Digital Publishing Institute

24. Mennicken, S., Huang, E.M.: Hacking the natural habitat: an in-the-wild study of smart homes, their development, and the people who live in them. In: Kay, J., Lukowicz, P., Tokuda, H., Olivier, P., Krüger, A. (eds.) Pervasive 2012. LNCS, vol. 7319, pp. 143–160. Springer, Heidelberg (2012). https://doi.org/10.1007/978-3-642-31205-2_10

25. Meyer, G.: Smart Home Hacks: Tips & Tools for Automating Your House. O'Reilly Media, Inc. (2004)

26. Poole, E.S., Chetty, M., Grinter, R.E., Edwards, W.K.: More than meets the eye: transforming the user experience of home network management. In: Proceedings of the 7th ACM Conference on Designing Interactive Systems - DIS '08, pp. 455–464. ACM Press, Cape Town, South Africa (2008). https://doi.org/10.1145/1394445.1394494, http://portal.acm.org/citation.cfm?doid=1394445.1394494

27. Rode, J.A., Poole, E.S.: Putting the gender back in digital housekeeping. In: Proceedings of the 4th Conference on Gender and IT. GenderIT '18, pp. 79–90. Association for Computing Machinery, New York, NY, USA (2018). https://doi.org/10.1145/3196839.3196845

28. Sadowski, J., Strengers, Y., Kennedy, J.: More work for big mother: revaluing care and control in smart homes. Environment and Planning A: Economy and Space, p. 0308518X211022366 (2021). https://doi.org/10.1177/0308518X211022366, publisher: SAGE Publications Ltd

29. Santo, B.R.: Acronym Addiction. IEEE Spectrum 43(10), 28–33 (2006). http://www0.cs.ucl.ac.uk/staff/ucacdxq/others/acronym.pdf

30. Schulz, A.S., Hornecker, E.: Can you please cover both the "smart" and the "home"? Exploring expectations on smart homes considering changing needs. In: Proceedings of the 21st International Conference on Mobile and Ubiquitous Multimedia. MUM '22, pp. 128–137. Association for Computing Machinery, New York, NY, USA (2022). https://doi.org/10.1145/3568444.3568447

31. Strengers, Y., Gram-hanssen, K., Dahlgren, K., Aagaard, L.K.: Energy, emerging technologies and gender in homes. Buildings Cities 3(1), 842–853 (2022). https://doi.org/10.5334/bc.273, http://journal-buildingscities.org/articles/10.5334/bc.273/

32. Venkatesh, V., Morris, M.G., Davis, G.B., Davis, F.D.: User acceptance of information technology: toward a unified view. MIS Q. 27(3), 425–478 (2003). https://doi.org/10.2307/30036540, https://www.jstor.org/stable/30036540, publisher: Management Information Systems Research Center, University of Minnesota

33. Venkatesh, V., Thong, J.Y.L., Xu, X.: Consumer acceptance and use of information technology: extending the unified theory of acceptance and use of technology. MIS Q. 36(1), 157–178 (2012). https://doi.org/10.2307/41410412, https://www.jstor.org/stable/41410412, publisher: Management Information Systems Research Center, University of Minnesota

34. Volmar, A.: Experiencing High Fidelity, vol. 1. Oxford University Press, Oxford (2018). https://doi.org/10.1093/oxfordhb/9780190466961.013.19, https://academic.oup.com/edited-volume/34658/chapter/295315910

35. Wilson, C., Hargreaves, T., Hauxwell-Baldwin, R.: Smart homes and their users: a systematic analysis and key challenges. Person. Ubiquitous Comput, 19(2), 463–476 (2015). https://doi.org/10.1007/s00779-014-0813-0, https://link.springer.com/10.1007/s00779-014-0813-0

36. Zavialova, S.: Smart Home - Market Data & Forecast. Technical report, statista, December 2022. https://www.statista.com/outlook/dmo/smart-home/europe

Towards a Socio-Technical Understanding of Police-Citizen Interactions

Min Zhang[1]([✉]), Arosha K. Bandara[1], Richard Philpot[2], Avelie Stuart[3],
Zoe Walkington[1], Camilla Elphick[1], Lara Frumkin[1], Graham Pike[1], Blaine Price[1],
Mark Levine[2], and Bashar Nuseibeh[1,4]

[1] The Open University, Walton Hall, Milton Keynes MK7 6AA, UK
{min.zhang,arosha.bandara,zoe.walkington,camilla.elphick,
lara.frumkin,graham.pike,blaine.price,
bashar.nuseibeh}@open.ac.uk
[2] Lancaster University, Bailrigg, Lancaster LA1 4YW, UK
{richard.philpot,mark.levine}@lancaster.ac.uk
[3] University of Exeter, Exeter EX4 4SB, Devon, UK
a.stuart@exeter.ac.uk
[4] Lero, University of Limerick, Limerick, Ireland
bashar.nuseibeh@lero.ie

Abstract. The growing uptake of technology in policing provides the opportunity to revisit police-citizen interactions. This paper explores police-citizen interactions from a socio-technical systems perspective, drawing on community policing in the HCI literature, as well as the experience of both citizens and the police. For the latter, we report on a qualitative study with 29 participants including citizens, parish councilors, and police officers in England. Our findings use a socio-technical systems lens to highlight both social and technological challenges in police-citizen interactions, leading to several implications for practice and HCI design. These challenges include those arising from divergent viewpoints, power, and information imbalances between stakeholders, and technical systems that duplicate functionality or limit police-citizen interactions. Thus, our work contributes to extending HCI insights into the socio-technical infrastructure of policing contexts, and a better foundation for future research in the design and use of technologies to enhance community policing.

Keywords: Socio-technical system · Community policing · Policing · Police-citizen interaction

1 Introduction

Good police-citizen relations are imperative to effective law enforcement [1, 2]. In the policing literature, there is an increasing interest in exploring how to improve police-citizen relations [3]. One way to encourage positive police-citizen interactions is through community policing [4], which engages community resources to achieve more effective crime control and prevention [5, 6]. The widespread uptake of community policing has

J. Abdelnour Nocera et al. (Eds.): INTERACT 2023, LNCS 14144, pp. 324–345, 2023.
https://doi.org/10.1007/978-3-031-42286-7_18

provided a great opportunity to explore routine day-to-day police-citizen interactions [1, 7]. However, scholarly attention has often focused on negative, police-initiated enforcement interactions with citizens [8], e.g., traffic stops because the *'negative bias theory'* [9] was found in policing that negative police-citizen contacts have stronger influences on citizen satisfaction with police than positive interactions [10]. Moreover, comparatively less research examines routine police-citizen interactions from a socio-technical systems perspective. This is a significant gap, given that law enforcement agencies increasingly adopt digital technologies to engage with the public and the critical importance of effective citizen-police relations in modern societies.

The socio-technical systems (STS) approach is a framework for analyzing complex systems of actors, social and technological elements, and the interactions between them [11, 12]. This approach emphasizes the intersecting effects of social actors and technological systems rather than the sole reliance on technological solutions [13]. It is widely recognized that STS could lead to a system that is more acceptable to stakeholders [14]. Policing is a complex socio-technical system due to dynamic interactions between people, procedures, policy, technology, and the environment. In this paper, we examine the police-citizen interactions based on Davis et al.'s STS framework [12], which comprises six pillars: *people, goals, culture, infrastructure, process,* and *technology.*

The aim of this research is to understand and highlight some of the perceived constraints in current routine police-citizen interactions from a socio-technical systems perspective. We conducted semi-structured interviews with 29 participants, including citizens and law enforcement stakeholders from England, to explore how they interact with police or citizens. To the best of our knowledge, this is the first work that empirically explores routine police-citizen interactions in a socio-technical way. The contributions of this paper are twofold: firstly, our work extends HCI insights on socio-technical infrastructure by applying an STS approach to the policing context; secondly, we propose implications for both practice and HCI design in the field of community policing. We conclude by discussing the added value of applying a socio-technical approach in understanding and identifying both challenges and opportunities for HCI researchers to explore the police-citizen interaction sphere.

2 Related Work

For this work, we draw from prior research on police-citizen interaction, community policing, and socio-technical systems.

2.1 Police-Citizen Interaction

Police-citizen interaction is used interchangeably with police-citizen contact [15] or encounter [16]. Law enforcement has been reformed since the 1970s [17] to ensure more effective, accountable, responsive, and 'soft' policing [18]. As policing shifts gradually towards community policing worldwide [5, 19], citizens have been provided with greater opportunities to actively take part in crime prevention and investigation [5]. Voluntary community participation [20, 21] assisted the police by reporting incidents or suspicious individuals face-to-face or via phone lines, such as through schemes like Neighborhood

Watch and StreetWatch [22], and citizens are increasingly taking shared responsibility for security in their local communities [5]. One typical example is the citizen-initiated 'cyber-vigilantes' who assisted the police in the criminal investigation of the Boston Marathon bombing in 2013 [23].

Existing work in police-citizen interaction has mainly explored factors affecting negative police-citizen interactions or encounters [24] and how to alleviate the negative impacts [25] on police legitimacy and accountability [26]. For example, Bottoms and Tankebe [27] argued that the normality of police as the 'powerholder' and the community being 'policed' was still implicitly rooted among the police and citizens. As Radburn et al.'s study [28] suggested, police interactions with citizens are not purely interpersonal but inter-group in nature, because police distinguish themselves as a 'powerful social group' and the boundary between 'us' and 'them' were rhetorically constructed [16]. On the other hand, Famosaya's work [8] highlighted the importance of the overlooked 'ordinary' police-citizen encounters, such as language and actions on a daily basis, which may transform into extraordinary negative interactions. The increased dynamics in police-citizen interactions resulting from the 'soft' policing shift provide opportunities to re-examine the routine, day-to-day actions and experiences of police-citizen interactions.

2.2 Community Policing Technology

The definition of Community Policing (CP) is still vague [29] due to the undefined concept of 'community' in various contexts. One popular definition is coined by Myhill [30]: *"Community policing is the process of enabling the participation of citizens and communities in policing at their chosen level"*. There are three agreed features of CP: police-community collaboration, problem-solving approach, and organizational decentralization [30]. The collaboration between police and external stakeholders is at the core of community policing [31]. Traditional community policing often emphasizes the visibility of police officers and the availability of citizen initiatives within local settings. Information and communication technology (ICT) has altered police practice [32] and the way citizens interact with the police [33].

HCI scholars have investigated how technology can facilitate community policing activities. New styles of community policing are often characterized by their adoption of mobile technologies [34, 35] and social media platforms [36–38]. For example, Kadar et al. [35] designed a crime prevention system allowing people in Switzerland to report crimes in real time, and residents could be notified about the safety of their neighborhood through other community members' reporting [34]. Brush et al. [39] integrated home surveillance cameras to build a digital neighborhood watch network. In the Netherlands, citizens-initiated WhatsApp neighborhood crime prevention groups [36] to patrol neighborhoods digitally. Similarly, South African citizens initiated a Community Policing Forum on Facebook, which increased community cohesion [37]; and Erete [38] found that online community participation in America improved community engagement in the real world.

The practical implementation of community policing varies based on the sociodemographic characteristics of the community and of police organizations [40]. The most recent work by Erete et al. [41] has revealed the complexity of community policing in violence prevention. Brewster et al. also claimed that there is no one-size-fits-all approach that could be implemented in diverse socio-cultural and socio-economic contexts [42]. The effectiveness of community policing has been a matter of considerable debate in practice. For example, researchers highlighted its success in crime reduction [43], violence prevention [44], and increasing social control [36], while other work pointed out issues and limitations, e.g., Terpstra [19] suggested that the police are only enthusiastic about initiatives that are likely to provide a source of useful information. Thus, it is imperative to consider social factors, as well as organizational and policy factors when deploying technological interventions.

2.3 Socio-Technical Systems

Socio-technical systems (STS) theory was first proposed by Trist [11] in 1960 to describe a coal mining system, which consists of complex interactions between people, machines, and the environment. Socio-technical systems thinking is now widely used as a philosophy to understand complex systems [14] where non-technological factors are intertwined with technological issues.

Researchers have proposed several potential frameworks of socio-technical systems. Ottens et al. [45] proposed an STS model with three elements (*actor*, *social elements*, and *technological elements*). Leavitt proposed a diamond organizational model [46] which consists of four interactive components (*people*, *task*, *structure*, and *technology*), Challenger and Clegg [47] further extend the diamond model into a hexagon model by adding more social elements: *people*, *goals*, *processes*, *culture*, *technology*, and *infrastructure*. In the hexagon model, *people* work within a physical *infrastructure* with *culture*, using a range of *technologies* and tools via *processes*, to achieve a set of *goals*. People have knowledge, skills, values, awareness, attitudes, and needs; where *culture* refers broadly to the shared values, norms, and beliefs of a group of people. The application of the hexagon model has been demonstrated in novel domains, e.g., crowd event management [48], environmental sustainability [12], and digital sterilization [49].

Inspired by Davis et al.'s work [12, 47], we deploy a socio-technical systems framework as the theoretical underpinning to analyze and understand existing police-citizen interactions, which is an open system involving interactional dynamics between the police and citizens [13]. We present findings based on the first-hand knowledge and experience of front-line police officers, victims, witnesses, parish councilors, and Street Watch volunteers. To ensure equal consideration of social, technological, and organizational aspects, we first outline each element of the socio-technical systems hexagon model, followed by highlighting social and technological challenges.

3 Methodology

The study was conducted between September and December 2019 at multiple sites. We completed semi-structured interviews with 29 participants (11 males and 18 females; age range 24–60; median age 38) in 11 sessions, which include both individual interviews and pair- or group-based discussions (see Table 1). The rationale behind the different number of participants in each session is to keep people of similar role in a group to reduce both hierarchy and power issues [50]. In England, police officers are ranked from low to high with different legal power and responsibility as follows: Police Community Support Officers (PCSO), constable, sergeant, inspector, chief inspector, superintendent, chief superintendent, assistant chief constable, deputy chief constable/commander, and chief constable[1]. There are also civilian roles working for the police force, such as forensic investigator/coordinator and control room call handler. The participants included 12 citizens from semi-urban areas in England (7 witnesses or victims, 5 parish councilors, with two citizens also having StreetWatch [22] experience), 1 prosecutor, and 16 police officers from two police forces in England. The study was approved by our Institutional Review Board in accordance with standard practice. Participants were given the option to withdraw their participation at any time. The citizen participants were recruited through campus-wide emails and noticeboards, with the criteria of having experience interacting with the police. The police participants comprised (PCSOs), police officers, and one leader from three police forces in England, recruited through the Centre for Policing Research and Learning at the Open University. All citizen participants were interviewed at the same place on campus, while we visited police stations and a control room to conduct group or individual interviews and observations with the police participants.

Table 1. Participant code and stakeholders' roles.

Participant code	Stakeholder's role	Participant code	Stakeholder's role
P1	Prosecutor	P15	PCSO
P2	Police officer & Witness	P16	PCSO
		P17	PCSO
P3	Citizen – Victim, Witness	P18	Police officer
P4	Citizen – Victim	P19	Police officer supervisor
P5	Parish councilor	P20	Police officer
P6	Parish councilor		
P7	Parish councilor	P21	Deputy Commander
P8	Parish councilor	P22	Citizen – Victim
		P23	Citizen – Witness
P9	PCSO	P24	Citizen – Victim, volunteer
P10	PCSO		
P11	Police constable	P25	Citizen – StreetWatch volunteer
P12	Police officer	P26	Citizen – Witness
P13	Civilian police officer		
P14	Parish councilor, StreetWatch volunteer	P27	Social media police officer
		P28	Contact resolution officer
		P29	Contact resolution officer

---

[1] https://lineofduty.fandom.com/wiki/UK_Police_Ranks.

Each participant was first asked to introduce their experience with the police or citizens. They then played with the storytelling toolkit (Fig. 1), pen, paper and post-it notes. In each toolbox, each type of item (e.g., building, character) has 10 copies of laminated pictures and were put into a small grid of toolbox, so participants could share the toolbox during the group session. We provided three same toolkit boxes in each session so participants could work individually or in a pair if they have similar experiences and willing to work together. Our participants all chose to work on their individual storytelling to represent their own experience of police-citizen interaction and then shared their story in the session. Then a semi-structured interview was conducted, which asked questions about the challenges of interactions with the police/citizen, what technologies they used in these interactions, and the expected features of the technology that could help (see supplemental material for interview guide). These tangible toolkit materials were used because of their effectiveness in facilitating storytelling in a visual way, as well as catalyzing new ideas [51]. Each session lasted 1.5–2 h, and each citizen participant was compensated with £10 in high-street shopping vouchers and travel costs. The interviews were audio-recorded and transcribed, and data analysis involved the standard inductive-deductive technique of coding [52], including literature-based codes, such as the six elements of the STS framework [12, 47], and codes emerging from data which were iteratively revised through weekly meetings between the first two authors and monthly meetings among all authors.

Fig. 1. The study setting (left) and storytelling toolkit (right).

4 Findings

Here we report the socio-technical systems perspective of routine police-citizen interactions by using the STS framework to provide a deductive structure for our analysis. This is supplemented by sub-themes that were developed inductively from the collected data, together with a set of socio-technical challenges.

4.1 Socio-Technical Systems Perspective

This section describes six pillars of the socio-technical systems hexagon model [12] in police-citizen interactions: *people, goals, culture, infrastructure, processes,* and *technology* (deductive analysis) and emerging sub-themes (inductive analysis) (Fig. 2).

People. Our findings indicate that police-citizen interactions involved groups of different stakeholders, e.g., citizens, law enforcement agencies (police force, Crown Prosecution Service (CPS), the court, etc.), third-party organizations, government, and volunteers who were actively involved in safety preservation in the community. From our interviews, the police force in England was still hierarchically organized and centralized [P21]. There were both sworn police officers and civilians within the police organizational structure, and citizens could normally interact directly with the control room officers, civilian liaison officers, and frontline police officers including both police officers and Police Community Support Officers (PCSOs).

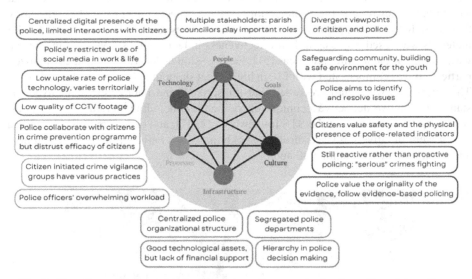

Fig. 2. Six pillars of the social-technical systems framework of police-citizen interactions.

Findings indicate that parish councilors played important roles in building bridges between residents and the police. Parish councilors are elected by residents as representatives of a local area, and they were trained to advise citizens towards appropriate support or assistance services. Additionally, they acted as a consultant to the local government agency (e.g., borough/city/county council) and the police [P8] and "registered" or "liaise" with the police [P23], and they served their local community voluntarily in all aspects (crime, health, education, housing, etc.) and mitigated the criminal activities. As P5 stated: "...*say drinking outside, if I go and speak to them and ask them to move or bring a black sack and ask them to put the rubbish in there, they will do it for me. You get to their level to talk to them... Whereas, the police would turn up, they would not bring the black bag, they would not talk with them, they would be quite intimidating. Not always they get the results, or they will move then come back.*"

Goals. The primary goal of police working collectively with citizens was to identify and resolve issues in the community. A key finding is that police and citizens had different expectations of police-citizen interactions. For example, regarding crime reporting, citizens expected a quick and easy process [P14, P22–23], options to be anonymous [P23], and reporting digitally without creating accounts [P24] or needing to disclose personal details [P22]. While police officers preferred to set up strict parameters for what type of issues citizens could report to police officers [P18], with a great number of details used for verification, risk assessment, and making decisions [P12]. Citizens also expected to be able to follow up the updates on the reported case [P24]: *"it is a peace of mind... if you think what you're saying to them is going to get taken seriously and potentially lead somewhere and then get wrapped-up, that would be really useful to know. I think it would be promoting trust."* However, the police officers were concerned about the workload [P18] and sensitivity of the crime data [P17] if providing an update to citizens. Although detailed information was preferred by the police, some police officers were also positive about anonymous reporting [P2]. Like PCSO P9 said: *"We'll always benefit from it* [Crimestoppers], *because having information is better than not having it at all."*

Findings show safeguarding the community as the primary motivation for citizen volunteers' self-policing, especially for building a safe environment for youth development. The Street Watch volunteer P23 mentioned: *"I'm giving back to my community, it's building community spirit and a presence, that people can see and join in with. And I want people to look after everybody, I want to be able to let my kids out and not be afraid that they're going to talk to the wrong person."* Parish councilors from the high-crime area initiated self-policing with similar motivations: *"We are safeguarding not only our friends and family, but the community as well. Because the kids are seeing the culture of seeing crime, seeing it as the norm, ignoring it, not talking to the police."* [P8] Citizen participants also reported that the experience of policing during their youth influenced their attitudes in later life. As P6 mentioned: *"I found that really hard when I first started working as a community worker, because I was brought up not to speak to the police"*.

Culture. Citizen participants valued the safety and the presence of police-related indicators. Findings indicate that citizens believed that a higher physical presence of uniformed police officers could increase reassurance [P3, P6, P11, P13, P23–24] and being informed about police work and updated status could promote police transparency [P12–13, P23–24]. Our citizen participants also highlighted the positive atmosphere in a community, as P24 suggested: *"I feel like we need to trust our communities, not to spread the fear... good news would really promote nice things in the community... things we've solved or things that didn't happen in some way, because of community involvement."*.

Although the police force has transformed to incorporate community policing and built collaborations with a wider range of external stakeholders, the traditional policing norms were still valued in the mindset of the police. The ideology of crime-fighting and law enforcement was seen as 'real' police work made sworn police officers more respected internally than civilian officers [P12], and most police officers treated petty crimes as a lower priority than 'serious' crimes. As police officer P18 pointed out: *"we're interested in stuff...have to be a proper crime... we have priority crime and non-priority crime."* This value is also reflected by citizen participants: *"I trust them* [the police] *to protect us in serious matters, but in daily life, it's not that helpful."*

Originality of Evidence. Findings indicate the police's preference for first-hand detailed evidence, to enable law enforcement to use it in a court case. The enforceable evidence was collected by police officers via making written notes on notebooks [P19], interviewing citizens in person [P21], copying or recording the CCTV screen by using the body-worn camera [P12], and archiving and recording every communication with the citizen [P19]. For example, the control room officer P24 mentioned: *"if I'm doing something for evidential value what I'll do is screenshot or get a video recording of what I'm looking at and then save that."* Another important finding that received little attention in previous work is that police treated the information from NGOs the same way as information from citizen witnesses, like police leader P21 claimed: *"...but it [Childline] is still third-party because something is coming into them from a source that can't be verified."* This reflects the police perspective on wanting enforceable evidence rather than information that could be construed as hearsay.

Infrastructure. Police forces in England provide services regionally, complemented by nationwide agencies and specialist units, such as the National Crime Agency. There are 43 separate police forces in England and Wales [45]. Each territorial police force has a slightly different policy on organizational structure, the responsibility of different roles, and shift work, etc. Different departments within a police force focus on different issues with one collective aim [P18]. For example, PCSOs complement the work of police officers by focusing on the lower-level crime and providing reassurance to the local community. Although our police participants were positive about technological artifacts, such as surveillance technologies, body-worn cameras, radios, digital note-taking devices, and ANPR (Automatic Number Plate Recognition) cars [P12], the real deployments of such equipment depend on each police force's financial infrastructure and situation. As police officer P18 explained: *"XX Police, as a force, is behind with technology compared to other forces. Like the mobile data terminals that my colleague has, that's just the norm for them. That's been around for ages. They can't believe that we're still writing on paper... it's all* [about] *money... and training...".*

Processes. We separate police practices from those of citizens and particularly focus on exploring the direct interaction between citizens and the police.

Police Practice. Police have adopted diverse tactics for interacting with citizens, such as foot, horse, bicycle, and car patrols; community meetings; community outreach programs; social media communication; encouraging the public to ring up for criminal activity [P11] and educating citizens via social media [P27]. However, the policing process was still mainly focused on reactive rather than proactive policing. The command-and-control strategy centralized public requests and triaged them to different departments. Police also collaborated with councils and third-party professionals or non-governmental organizations (NGOs) to interact with citizens. These collaborations allowed citizens to feel comfortable reporting certain issues to organizations that don't treat them as informants [P9]. For example, some police forces encouraged citizens to report through CrimeStoppers (an anonymous crime reporting charity) free landline or online form. Police also referred citizens to certain NGOs with professional expertise [P20], e.g., Victim Support.

Findings show the police identified the value of residents' local knowledge and voluntary work. Some police participants attended Community Forums on a regular basis [P16]. Police participants acknowledged the benefits of crime prevention programs involving residents, e.g., Street Watch and Speed Watch, because the neighborhoods knew their local area well and could participate out of police working hours, which also freed up police time. As PCSO P17 said: *"They* [residents] *know the best time when the speeding is happening, if it's at 7 o'clock in the morning, we don't start until 8. So they can be there at 7. They can be there later if it's the longer days, if it's happening after 5 or 6 o'clock. So we want to get them involved as much as possible"*.

Although police officers were trained to use the National Decision Model [74] to guide their engagement with the public and in problem-solving [P12], there were leadership decisions made at different levels and ranks depending on the cases, as police officer P18 said: *"It just goes up through the rank structure. We all know what we can make a decision on and what we can't"*. For serious crimes, police officers usually consulted with relevant legal authorities (CPS in the UK) to make decisions. The process was opaque to the public, which made the police-citizen relations worse, resulting in the public tending to blame the police [P1].

Citizen Practice. Citizens have traditionally communicated with the police by telephone or by visiting a police station. Our findings indicate that citizen engagement was enhanced by digital technologies, including police websites, emails, social media, mobile applications (Apps), etc. Witnesses and victims reported criminal activities mainly by dialing both emergency and non-emergency numbers, and citizens were guided by the police to send multimedia files via social media chat [P29] or email attachments [P28]. Our citizen participants believed that the younger generation was more confident and willing to use the technology than the older generation [P3, P14]. Some special groups, e.g., the LGBT community [P11], were more confident interacting with the police digitally compared to interacting face-to-face due to privacy concerns. Street Watch volunteers were trained by the police first, and they reported to the police via email or telephone rather than interfering in the ongoing criminal activity themselves. Additionally, volunteers kept their personal information private by meeting in a public area [P25]. Citizens could make complaints about police misconduct [P11, P18], often by going through a formal police complaint procedure. However, citizens were creative when commending police officers [P21], e.g., by sending thank-you note or gifts [P2].

All our citizen participants knew about Neighborhood Watch. However, people perceived there were confusing and inconsistent practice depending on geographic locations [P4] or needed to be improved [P5-P8] to get the younger people involved [P7]. Another disadvantage mentioned by citizens was overwhelming email notifications sent by Neighborhood Watch: *"They send out a lot of emails, but I don't read it because a lot of them are a bit scaremongering, so I don't really get involved that much. Rather I keep a general eye on my street."* [P24].

Technology. Our findings show that the digital transformation promoted police forces to shift from a traditional recording system to a more digital criminal justice system [P10], and digital technology also provided another potential channel for citizens who are willing to interact with the police in different ways.

Centralized Digital Presence of Police. The visibility of police work has been increased by using police websites, emails, TV programs, body cameras, cell phone videos, and social media. Most police websites enabled citizens to report crimes; some police forces provided social media communication on a 9-to-5 schedule but monitored it on a 24/7 basis, like P21 mentioned *"social media fills the gap due to changing lifestyles"*. The police branches have their own local social media accounts, but with no power of taking a crime report.

However, our findings indicate that only a few police officers could interact with citizens directly in the digital world. Police officers from the control room could interact with the citizens via the official website and central social media accounts, such as Single Online Home website, Facebook, Twitter, Instagram, Snapchat, and email [P28, P29]. As PCSO P11 said: "*the police force is trying to keep everything centralized, trying to keep corporate* [social media] *accounts.*" Police officers with special training could access police Facebook and Twitter accounts [P16, P18, P21, P28, P29], but updating on social media or police websites was still done by the media team based at the police force headquarters [P12], because "*everything needs to be redacted*" [P19] due to the sensitivity of cases. Even the control room officers had to get permission to post on social media: "*As things are updated whoever is on duty will get it and then write a little brief about it, so that it can be developed in the back office.*" [P28].

Findings also indicate that third-party mobile Apps and websites were increasingly adopted by both citizens and police. For instance, citizens used Nextdoor [P9] and Bright Sky [P9]; patrolling police officers used Google Translate to communicate with foreign residents immediately [P10]; IP/location tracking service [P28] and email tracking website [P18] were used by police for work, and some police officers also created Nextdoor account for personal use to know about community [P16]. The police educated citizens by referring them to the official police resource website [P29], e.g., *Ask the Police* [75] and *fearless.org* [76].

Police Set Boundary of Social Media Use. Findings indicate the boundary between the working and personal lives of police officers [P21]. Police officers were not allowed to access the policing system on their work devices for personal purposes [P9, P11–12]. There are rules from the College of Policing around the personal use of social media: "*you shouldn't identify yourself as a police officer*" [P21]. For instance, police officers were advised not to use their real names and profile photos on their private social media accounts [P20]. Police were very cautious about the balance between confidentiality and disclosure details, as police officer P20 said "*the freedom of speech, we don't really have in the police, because you've got to be very careful of the consequences.*" [P20].

Police leaders were deeply concerned about the police's capacity to adopt technology effectively. For example, a notable finding is that police forces set barriers to police officers when using social media: "*If I take pictures of a cadet session, I have to leave the session, email the pictures to my email account and then send it via the main PC in the office to Twitter. I can't just go like that and tweet it out anymore, I could do that three weeks ago. It's changed again... They want us to use technology, and then they put barriers in the way, because they get scared about us using the technology, like we can't be trusted.*" [P13].

Digital Citizen-Initiated Crime Vigilance Groups. The self-organized local social media groups were popular among residents. Other than mundane activities such as selling 2nd hand stuff, local Facebook groups also discuss and share information to directly support crime prevention and those affected by crime [P24]. As PCSO P11 reflected: "*it is all information that comes to and from the police. There are missing people on there..., road closures, burglaries that had happened in the local area to watch out for*" [P11]. Whereas

WhatsApp groups were more private [P4, P14, P23], which set boundaries between different groups [P3–4, P25], e.g., community worker groups [P14], Street Watch volunteer groups [P25], self-organized minority ethnicity-based communities [P23]. One victim P3 showed concerns related to privacy and safety about using Facebook: *"the criminals sometimes are on them, so you have to be careful because then they're finding out."*

4.2 Socio-Technical Challenges

The primary aim of using the socio-technical systems framework is to analyze and identify the potential problems and key challenges, which could be important contributions based on an empirical understanding of current police-citizen interactions. We now describe both social challenges and technological challenges, some of which are intertwined.

Social Challenges

Lack of Funding for Police. Findings highlight that lack of funding was quoted by police participants as the main reason why police forces could not fully be engaged with citizens. It directly led to a lack of police officers and a lack of devices, and some police forces adjusted the cost by combining the use of multiple systems [P18] and removing the costly but useful devices such as computers in police vehicles [P9, P12]. The frontline police officers believed that obsolete technologies put barriers to communicating with citizens and their routine work. For example, some police officers on patrols had to go back to the police station to make a record in the system and then go out again [P9–10, P16, P18], which causes frustrations [P19] and missing information [P16].

Findings show that citizens perceived either the absence of or a decreasing number of PCSOs/police officers patrolling in their community areas [P3–4, P6, P8]. Due to a lack of police officers, PCSOs sometimes were asked to attend emergency cases [P2]. And citizens also complained about the police's non-timely responses to non-emergency calls, which is costly [P5]. As police leader P21 said: *"The reality of today's policing and austerity is that we just don't have the number of officers we had in the past. Demands also have changed. Unfortunately, we don't have the luxury of people going out on foot patrol as they possibly did 15 or 20 years ago."*

Divergent Viewpoints between Citizen and Police. We also identified several divergent viewpoints between the police and citizens, as well as among police departments. Firstly, the police encouraged community engagement, but they perceived that the efficacy of citizen participants and the quality of community work required improvements. For example, police only sent a warning letter to the speeding vehicle reported by a Speed Watch volunteer, as police officer P18 explained *"they [volunteers] are not trained enough to speeding [issues]. So we don't enforce it, because they are not trained enough for prosecution purposes."* Our findings also indicate that police officers perceived that citizens could not differentiate between emergency and non-emergency issues [P2, P29], which may increase police workloads unnecessarily.

Secondly, public perception of the police was a big issue for the police. Policing was a black box for citizens, who perceived that the police only investigate serious crimes [P4, P23]. Moreover, residents in high-crime areas tended to lose trust in the police. They thought the police were unresponsive to their reports or needs, so they stated that the police were useless [P5]. These factors led to a reduced willingness to report suspicious activity [P8]. Furthermore, the public often overestimated the crime levels of their local areas, and these perceptions were difficult to change, even with police and city council reassurances [P21].

Finally, although police departments aimed to solve the problem collectively, there was a lack of communication and mutual understanding among police departments [P19]. As police officer P18 said: *"We're quite segregated. Sometimes it's hard trying to build those relationships. Paths don't always cross and when it does, it's not for very long...each team always says the other team is lazy...that's common. They don't know what that team does, I think that's normal"*.

Technological Challenges. Findings indicate that the police used multiple, but unlinked, internal systems [P18], which cause repeated input work and inconsistencies in reference numbers used for a reported case [P27]. For example, when citizens reported using the Single Online Home website, police officers received an email and they had to manually create a record on the police force's internal system and send the new reference number back to the reporters by email.

Low Uptake of New Policing System. There are several barriers to technology adoption: costs, policy, human-associated issues such as technology literacy [P13] and technology adoption laggard [P24], and privacy concerns. Findings indicate the failure of some previous applications due to a low uptake rate. One example is First Evidence, a private charity-run crime reporting App mentioned by police officer P27: *"it was a non-mandated app, but all police forces were encouraged to take it. In five years, we got one report because there weren't enough followings, and people just didn't take it."* Our findings show that citizens may not install and keep the App on their phones for just occasional use. Embedded digital evidence [P11–12] (e.g., GPSs) was helpful for the police to locate criminals more easily, but as it consumes battery power significantly and citizens tended to turn it off [P23].

Low Quality CCTV Footage. Apart from the local authority's CCTV cameras, such as CityWatch, there were private, non-commercial CCTV cameras used by residents. Findings show that police officers emphasized the challenges of utilizing privately owned CCTV footage, due to poor quality [P9, P19], or police not having the relevant technical skills for the various brands of systems [P11]. As P9 put it: *"not every household has CCTV, it's not necessarily always working, or they may not necessarily want to assist the police... they [the footage] will show that an incident has happened, but in terms of evidence in some situations they are not great. Trying to identify particular individuals or particular vehicles, it can sometimes be quite difficult"*.

Two Sides of Social Media. Findings indicate that social media is a double-edged sword. As a supplement to current channels of police-citizen communication, our findings show police participants were very positive about social media. However, police officers emphasized the careful use of social media [P16, P18, P21], as P18 suggested: *"social media's been amazing. There are positives and negatives for it, but I think we'd struggle even more than we do now to engage with our community if we don't have social media. Because it's the new thing, everyone is on social media"*. On the other hand, citizens showed frustrations over the erratic pattern of police use of social media because citizens may not know that police forces had multiple accounts but only the central account could take the citizens' crime reporting; secondly, citizens expected the police's response on social media [P20]. Thus, the police *"had to put out a strong message: we are not responding to this as quickly"* [P28]. Some citizens were concerned about the fear spread by social media [P23-P24]. The abusive comments [P15, P20], especially to the police officers, and misinformation [P20] could bring substantial harm and mental health issues.

5 Discussion

Our exploration of police-citizen interactions with a socio-technical perspective extends HCI insights into socio-technical infrastructure in a policing context. Our work highlights several unaddressed socio-technical challenges faced by the stakeholders when interacting with each other. The police-citizen interactions can be viewed as a complex socio-technical system, with some aspects clearly social (e.g., police patrols); some aspects clearly technological (e.g., CCTV). We argue that both social and technological elements are fundamentally entwined [53], technology has impacts on the process and people's awareness and its use is also affected by the organizational policy and goals. The interplay between social and technological challenges is also emphasized. For instance, due to a lack of funding, police forces have reduced the number of useful technologies or have to use multiple unlinked systems repeatedly to achieve their goals, which causes low efficiency of police work (e.g., PCSOs going back to the station to create a record; repeated input) and directly affect police's community engagement and citizens' perceptions of police presence and efficacy. The socio-technical challenges become more complex with dynamic interactions among people, between people and technology, and between people and the physical infrastructure. We propose several implications for both practice and design based on key socio-technical challenges (Table 2).

A key finding is that police and citizens had different viewpoints and expectations of police-citizen interactions, which leads to requirement conflicts between different stakeholders. As suggested by previous research [56], this is a crucial challenge when designing for community policing. The **hybrid online-offline presence and response** of police are highlighted by citizens; while the police, overwhelmed by massive workloads, expect first-hand, clear evidence and non-trivial suspicious activity with detailed information reported by citizens [19, 56]. It is suggested that the police should provide a set of ground rules and set their expectations clearly for citizens to participate, apart from supporting community capacity building [30] and training to raise awareness of law enforcement. With the social factors in mind, we argue that technologies need to be configured to support the interaction expectations of citizens and the police with a balanced consideration. The co-design activities involving stakeholders with different needs together could be one approach to achieve this.

Findings indicate that current digital technologies utilized by citizens to collaborate with the police are useful but limited. We found that the younger generation, people who fear bureaucracy, and vulnerable communities (e.g., LGBT, sex assault victims) tend

Table 2. Implications for both practice and design.

Police-citizen interaction challenges	Practical implications	Design implications
Divergent viewpoints and expectations of police-citizen interactions	• The police provide clear rules and expectations for citizen participation • The police offer training and community capacity building to citizens	• Technology needs to be configured to support the interaction expectations of citizens and the police • Co-design activities involving different stakeholders
Useful but insufficient digital technology for police-citizen collaborations		• Need for crowdsourcing technology with different levels of citizen engagement [54]
Safety and privacy issues on social media	• Law enforcement practitioners and technology designers work together to help users to build online ethics	
Imbalance of power and access to information between citizens and the police	• Police keep citizens in the loop to update the process regularly	• Allow citizens anonymous reporting and limited personal information disclosure [55]
Lack of police officer's autonomy	• Bespoke training for improving police officers' proficiency in digital technologies • Empower the front-line police officers to self-serve community	
Boundary of technology use		• Call for further research and practical experience to further engage with this design space
Low uptake of new systems	• Establish information sharing protocols among multiple stakeholders	• Design for integrating the police and other active collaborators

to interact with the police online, but cumbersome online crime reporting and erratic patterns of police online cause frustrations. Citizens are referred to as the *'eyes and ears'* of the police [30], and current technologies only enable citizens to play the role of *'citizens as sensors'* [57]. It suggests that crowdsourcing technologies [58] taking advantage of human intelligence, have the potential to optimize the configuration of citizen-police interactions. One promising direction is designing technology and policy that can facilitate richer citizen-led interventions at different levels from crime reporting, distributed analysis, and co-investigation to collective self-investigation, as described by Bandara et al.'s Citizen Forensics model [54]. Future work should investigate approaches to better design technologies to empower the mutually beneficial collaborations between the police, citizens, and other stakeholders in the field of community policing.

Our research supports the previous research on social media, as one of the socio-technical infrastructures [59], which has enabled and fostered interactions between the police and citizens in an alternative way. The capacity of social media in revitalizing neighborhood ties and civic engagement has been found in previous research [36, 38, 59, 60]. However, the social media engagement between the police and citizens tends to be limited due to the redacted collection and dissemination of information [23]. Moreover, there are concerns around the safety and privacy issues on social media, such as cyber harassment, misinformation, and fear spreading embodied via digital communications. We argue that it is the responsibility of both law enforcement practitioners and technology designers to help users to build appropriate ethics in the online communication space. HCI researchers and technology designers should work together to ensure that technology creates a positive atmosphere in the community.

Our findings also indicate the imbalance of power and access to information [61] between the police and citizens. Citizens could provide intimate knowledge of localized or specific communities online; however, they could not be able to check the results of reported cases online, and they perceived that they must give their contact details to the police. Police officers, vested with the coercive power of the state, are not just crime fighters [62], but also civil servants aiming to improve the quality of life for the community. Crime is a community problem, not a police problem. We acknowledge that some inequalities are necessary for the functioning of the social system [17], however, it is necessary for the police to update their progress regularly and keep citizens in the loop, which also increases transparency and trust [63]. We suggest that digital evidence collection with limited disclosure [55] could protect users' privacy as well as support building digital trust between citizens and the police.

Findings also suggest a lack of autonomy for police officers. Specifically, hierarchically organized, and centralized bureaucracies and policies create barriers for police officers (especially at the bottom level) in their daily work. For instance, front-line police officers heavily relied on the control room and centralized social media team to get or post the information online, and this might be due to the organizational nature of the police force [64]. And there are different levels of decision-making and approval needed from those higher up in the police's internal rank structure. The technical barrier of internal technology is another challenge, especially for older police officers. Autonomy is necessary to develop more intimate ties with their community [65]. We recommend providing bespoke training to help improve the officer's proficiency in using technologies (e.g., CCTV footage access skills) and to permit front-line officers to use the technology that they are comfortable with to self-serve the community.

In our view, community policing is desirable, because the nature of neighborhood crime and disorder requires collaboration among multiple stakeholders. The low uptake of third-party systems is because interaction with the police is not a must-have for some citizens. However, others (e.g., StreetWatch volunteers, and parish councilors) are self-motivated to actively safeguard their local community. In other words, citizens only want to be able to connect with the police when needed. Apart from designing citizen engagement incentive mechanisms, socio-technical design in community policing should focus on enhancing integration between the police, NGOs, councils, private security companies, and residents who voluntarily participate actively to address crime issues in their locality. Findings indicate that the police deal with NGO reports in the same way as citizen reports and contact police officers face heavy workloads to re-input the reported cases into internal police systems. It is suggested that establishing information-sharing protocols between different stakeholders, which effectively integrate information reported by the community and distribute it to the police for joint problem-solving, is vital for cross-organization collaborations.

Like physical spaces, digital interaction spaces should preserve some characteristics such as boundary and visibility, to avoid privacy violations. The public has become extremely sensitive to issues of privacy in our connected world, particularly when it comes to law enforcement. Understanding the boundaries set in technology use is necessary to empower citizens to act confidently and appropriately. For example, anonymous reporting is appreciated by citizens as an important feature, because citizens are concerned about being labeled as informants or fear reprisal especially if they report their neighbors [63]. The socio-technical design could assure sensitive victims in reporting without exposing them to potential harm (e.g., domestic violence). It is imperative to call for rigorous academic research and practical experience to further engage with this design space.

Finally, we believe the socio-technical systems approach has several potential benefits. First, STSs facilitate analyzing and understanding complex systems from a more holistic view. Second, they help identify what needs to improve for both practice and design. Third, STSs emphasize the joint optimization between social and technological elements [66], which guides HCI researchers to focus on a systems perspective rather than individual users. We argue that technology designers need to find a balance between social and technological requirements.

6   Limitations

Our interviews included participants from different locations and varying degrees of experience, including victims, witnesses, parish councilors, and StreetWatch volunteers. However, our sample is limited because we did not interview members of the public who had not ever interacted with the police and those who have been impacted by law enforcement actions by the police such as being taken into police custody [24]. Also, the police participants recruited were all White police officers from two England-based police forces, because police officers across England and Wales are mostly hired from the White ethnic group (93.1% at the end of March 2019) [1]. In addition, as evidence in psychology shows, it is possible that there were gaps between participants' actual experience and behavior and socially desirable answers [67]. However, our study still provides valuable socio-technical insights and empirical understandings of routine police-citizen interactions. It is acknowledged that our study was conducted prior to the COVID-19 pandemic, however, we think our findings are still valid as the nature of citizen-police interactions has not changed significantly since then [68]. Being aware of these limitations, future work could include the public and other ethnographic methods to reach stronger conclusions.

7 Conclusion

This empirical work investigates current police-citizen interactions from a socio-technical perspective, based on multi-sited interviews with 29 participants in England. This research provides a contribution of knowledge on both social and technological spheres of police-citizen interactions and key socio-technical challenges, followed by the practical and design implications, from which law enforcement practitioners and policymakers could seek requirements for improvements. Our findings highlight some of the key challenges in achieving effective citizen-police interactions, ranging from the need to deal with divergent viewpoints together with imbalances in power and information held by different parties. Addressing these challenges requires technology that is designed to support the interaction expectations of citizens and the police and enables flexibility in the level of interaction between citizens and the police, including the ability to adapt the level of anonymity provided to citizens. Our work also extends the HCI recent insights on socio-technical infrastructure in a policing context. It is imperative to call for rigorous HCI research and practice to take a holistic view of social and ICT infrastructure for potential crowdsourcing technology solutions, also to explore the associated organizational, human, and technological challenges.

Acknowledgements. This work was supported by the UK Engineering and Physical Sciences Research Council [grants EP/R033862/1, EP/R013144/1] and Science Foundation Ireland [grant 13/RC/2094_P2]. We also thank all the participants in our study.

References

1. Roché, S., Oberwittler, D.: Towards a broader view of police-citizen relations how societal cleavages and political contexts shape trust and distrust, legitimacy and illegitimacy. In: Oberwittler, D., Roché, S. (eds.) Police-Citizen Relations Across the World: Comparing sources and Contexts of Trust and Legitimacy (2007)
2. U.S. Department of Justice: Importance of Police-Community Relationships and Resources for Further Reading (2015)
3. National Police Chief's Council: Policing Vision 2025, 12 (2016)
4. WikiPedia: Community Policing. https://en.wikipedia.org/wiki/Community_policing#History. Accessed 15 Jan 2020
5. Meyer, M., van Graan, J.: Effective community policing in practice: the roodekrans neighbourhood watch case study, west rand. Acta Criminologica: South Afr. J. Criminol. **24**, 130–143 (2011)
6. Pala, E., Balcioglu, E.: Community policing in England, wales, and European union: past, present and future (2017). https://doi.org/10.1501/avraras_0000000232
7. Dietrich, O., Roché, S.: Police–Citizen Relations Across the World: Comparing Sources and Context of Trust and Legitimacy. Routledge (2019)
8. Famosaya, P.: Police-citizen interactions in Nigeria: the 'ordinary' aspects. Policing Soc. **31**(8), 936–949 (2020). https://doi.org/10.1080/10439463.2020.1798953

9. Rozin, P., Royzman, E.B.: Negativity bias, negativity dominance, and contagion. Pers. Soc. Psychol. Rev. **5**, 296–320 (2001). https://doi.org/10.1207/S15327957PSPR0504_2

10. Li, Y., Ren, L., Luo, F.: Is bad stronger than good? The impact of police-citizen encounters on public satisfaction with police. Policing **39**, 109–126 (2016). https://doi.org/10.1108/PIJ PSM-05-2015-0058

11. Trist, E.: The evolution of socio-technical systems: a conceptual framework and an action research program (1981)

12. Davis, M.C., Challenger, R., Jayewardene, D.N.W., Clegg, C.W.: Advancing socio-technical systems thinking: a call for bravery. JERG **45**, 171–180 (2014). https://doi.org/10.1016/j.ape rgo.2013.02.009

13. Oosthuizen, R., Pretorius, L.: Modelling methodology for engineering of complex sociotechnical systems. INCOSE Int. Symp. **24**, 268–281 (2014). https://doi.org/10.1002/j.2334-5837. 2014.00021.x

14. Baxter, G., Sommerville, I.: Socio-technical systems: from design methods to systems engineering. Interact. Comput. **23**, 4–17 (2011). https://doi.org/10.1016/j.intcom.2010.07.003

15. Hardin, D.A.: Public-Police Relations: Officers' Interpretations of Citizen Contacts (2015)

16. Radburn, M., Savigar-Shaw, L., Stott, C., Tallent, D., Kyprianides, A.: How do police officers talk about their encounters with 'the public'? Group interaction, procedural justice and officer constructions of policing identities. Criminol. Crim. Just. **22**, 59–77 (2022). https://doi.org/ 10.1177/1748895820933912

17. Chriss, J.: Beyond Community Policing: From Early American Beginnings to the 21st Century. Taylor & Francis (2011)

18. Ariel, B., Weinborn, C., Sherman, L.W.: "Soft" policing at hot spots—do police community support officers work? A randomized controlled trial. J. Exp. Criminol. **12**, 277–317 (2016). https://doi.org/10.1007/s11292-016-9260-4

19. Terpstra, J.: Community policing in practice: ambitions and realization. Policing **4**, 64–72 (2010). https://doi.org/10.1093/police/pap029

20. Dickson, G.: Bridging the gap? Police volunteering and community policing in Scotland. Policing: J. Policy Pract. **15**(4), 2070–2082 (2019). https://doi.org/10.1093/police/paz070

21. van Steden, R., Mehlbaum, S.M.: Police volunteers in the Netherlands: a study on policy and practice. Policing Soc. **29**, 420–433 (2019). https://doi.org/10.1080/10439463.2018.1523165

22. StreetWatch. http://www.street-watch.org/. Accessed 24 Dec 2019

23. Nhan, J., Huey, L., Broll, R.: Digilantism: an analysis of crowdsourcing and the Boston marathon bombings. Br. J. Criminol. **57**, 341–361 (2017). https://doi.org/10.1093/bjc/azv118

24. Savigar-Shaw, L., Radburn, M., Stott, C., Kyprianides, A., Tallent, D.: Procedural justice as a reward to the compliant: an ethnography of police–citizen interaction in police custody. Policing Soc. **32**, 778–793 (2022). https://doi.org/10.1080/10439463.2021.1960332

25. Wozniak, K.H., Drakulich, K.M., Calfano, B.R.: Do photos of police-civilian interactions influence public opinion about the police? A multimethod test of media effects. J. Exp. Criminol. **17**(2), 1–27 (2020). https://doi.org/10.1007/s11292-020-09415-0

26. Koster, N.S.N., Kuijpers, K.F., Kunst, M.J.J., van der Leun, J.P.: Crime victims' perceptions of police behavior, legitimacy, and cooperation: a review of the literature. Vict. Offender. **11**, 392–435 (2016). https://doi.org/10.1080/15564886.2015.1065532

27. Bottoms, A., Tankebe, J.: Beyond procedural justice: a dialogic approach to legitimacy in criminal justice. J. Crim. Law Criminol. **102**, 119–170 (2012)

28. Radburn, M., Stott, C.: The social psychological processes of 'procedural justice': concepts, critiques and opportunities. Criminol. Crim. Just. **19**, 421–438 (2019). https://doi.org/10. 1177/1748895818780200

29. Moose, C.: The Theory and Practice of Community Policing: An Evaluation of the Iris Court Demonstration Project (1993). https://doi.org/10.15760/etd.1330

30. Myhill, A.: Community Engagement in Policing: Lessons from the Literature (2012)
31. Brainard, L., Edlins, M.: Top 10 U.S. municipal police departments and their social media usage. Am. Rev. Publ. Adm. 45(6), 728–745 (2015). https://doi.org/10.1177/027507401452 4478
32. Jackson, B.A., Greenfield, V.A., Morral, A.R., Hollywood, J.S.: Police Department Investments in Information Technology Systems: Challenges Assessing Their Payoff (2011)
33. Nutsugah, N., Essandoh, M., Kuranchie, P., Kuupuolo, E.: Police-citizen Communication in the Digital Age: Evidence from Ghana
34. Kadar, C., Cvijikj, I.P.: CityWatch: the personalized crime prevention assistant. In: Proceedings of the 13th International Conference on Mobile and Ubiquitous Multimedia - MUM '14, pp. 260–261. ACM Press, New York, New York, USA (2014). https://doi.org/10.1145/267 7972.2678008
35. Kadar, C., Te, Y.-F., Rosés Brüngger, R., Pletikosa Cvijikj, I.: Digital neighborhood watch: to share or not to share? In: Proceedings of the 2016 CHI Conference Extended Abstracts on Human Factors in Computing Systems - CHI EA '16, pp. 2148–2155. ACM Press, New York, New York, USA (2016). https://doi.org/10.1145/2851581.2892400
36. Pridmore, J., Mols, A., Wang, Y., Holleman, F.: Keeping an eye on the neighbours: police, citizens, and communication within mobile neighbourhood crime prevention groups. Police J. Theor. Pract. Principles. 92, 97–120 (2019). https://doi.org/10.1177/0032258X18768397
37. Hattingh, M.J.: The use of Facebook by a community policing forum to combat crime. In: Proceedings of the 2015 Annual Research Conference on South African Institute of Computer Scientists and Information Technologists - SAICSIT '15, pp. 1–10. ACM Press, New York, New York, USA (2015). https://doi.org/10.1145/2815782.2815811
38. Erete, S.L.: Engaging around neighborhood issues. In: Proceedings of the 18th ACM Conference on Computer Supported Cooperative Work & Social Computing, pp. 1590–1601. ACM (2015). https://doi.org/10.1145/2675133.2675182
39. Brush, A.J.B., Jung, J., Mahajan, R., Martinez, F., Way, O.M.: Digital neighborhood watch: investigating the sharing of camera data amongst neighbors. In: 2013 Conference on Computer Supported Cooperative Work (CSCW '13), pp. 693–700 (2013). https://doi.org/10.1145/244 1776.2441853
40. Skogan, W.G.: Police and Community in Chicago: A Tale of Three Cities. Oxford University Press (2006)
41. Erete, S., Dickinson, J., Gonzalez, A.C., Rankin, Y.A.: Unpacking the complexities of community-led violence prevention work. In: Conference on Human Factors in Computing Systems - Proceedings. Association for Computing Machinery (2022). https://doi.org/10. 1145/3491102.3502122
42. Brewster, B., Gibson, H., Gunning, M.: Policing the community together: the impact of technology on citizen engagement. In: Societal Implications of Community-Oriented Policing and Technology, pp. 91–102 (2018). https://doi.org/10.1007/978-3-319-89297-9
43. Gill, C., Weisburd, D., Telep, C.W., Vitter, Z., Bennett, T.: Community-oriented policing to reduce crime, disorder and fear and increase satisfaction and legitimacy among citizens: a systematic review. J. Exp. Criminol. 10, 399–428 (2014). https://doi.org/10.1007/s11292-014-9210-y
44. Schanzer, D., Kurzman, C., Miller, E., Toliver, J.: The Challenge and Promise of Using Community Policing Strategies to Prevent Violent Extremism: A Call for Community Partnerships with Law Enforcement to Enhance Public Safety (2016)
45. Ottens, M., Franssen, M., Kroes, P., Van De Poel, I.: Modelling infrastructures as socio-technical systems. Int. J. Crit. Infrastruct. 2, 133–145 (2006)
46. Leavitt, H.J.: Applied organizational change in industry: structural, technological and humanistic approaches. Carnegie Institute of Technology, Graduate School of Industrial Administration (1962)

47. Challenger, R., Clegg, C.W.: Crowd disasters: a socio-technical systems perspective. Contemp. Soc. Sci. **6**, 343–360 (2011). https://doi.org/10.1080/21582041.2011.619862

48. Challenger, R., Clegg, C.W., Robinson, M.A., Leigh, M.: Understanding Crowd Behaviours: Volume 1 – Practical Guidance and Lessons Identified. London (2010). https://doi.org/10.1080/02722018109480726

49. Münch, C., Marx, E., Benz, L., Hartmann, E., Matzner, M.: Capabilities of digital servitization: evidence from the socio-technical systems theory. Technol. Forecast. Soc. Chang. **176**, 121361 (2022). https://doi.org/10.1016/j.techfore.2021.121361

50. Frers, L., Meier, L.: Hierarchy and inequality in research: practices, ethics and experiences. Qual. Res. **22**, 655–667 (2022). https://doi.org/10.1177/14687941221098920

51. Schön, D.A.: Designing as reflective conversation with the materials of a design situation. Knowl. Based Syst. **5**, 3–14 (1992). https://doi.org/10.1016/0950-7051(92)90020-G

52. Fereday, J., Muir-Cochrane, E.: Demonstrating rigor using thematic analysis: a hybrid approach of inductive and deductive coding and theme development. Int. J. Qual. Methods **5**, 80–92 (2006). https://doi.org/10.1177/160940690600500107

53. Taylor-smith, E.: Participation Space Studies : a Socio-technical Exploration of Activist and Community Groups ' Use of Online and Offline Spaces to Support their Work (2016)

54. Bandara, A., et al.: Towards citizen forensics: improving citizen-police collaboration. In: Workshop on Crime and/or Punishment: Joining the Dots between Crime, Legality and HCI, CHi'20 (2020)

55. Tun, T., Price, B., Bandara, A., Yu, Y., Nuseibeh, B.: Verifiable limited disclosure: reporting and handling digital evidence in police investigations. In: Proceedings - 2016 IEEE 24th International Requirements Engineering Conference Workshops, REW 2016, pp. 102–105 (2016). https://doi.org/10.1109/REW.2016.43

56. Zhang, M., et al.: Designing technologies for community policing. In: Extended Abstracts of the 2020 CHI Conference on Human Factors in Computing Systems, pp. 1–9. ACM, New York, NY, USA (2020). https://doi.org/10.1145/3334480.3383021

57. Haklay, M.: Citizen science and volunteered geographic information: overview and typology of participation. In: Sui, D., Elwood, S., Goodchild, M. (eds.) Crowdsourcing Geographic Knowledge: Volunteered Geographic Information (VGI) in Theory and Practice, pp. 105–122. Springer Netherlands, Dordrecht (2013). https://doi.org/10.1007/978-94-007-4587-2_7

58. Vera, A., Salge, T.O.: Crowdsourcing and policing : opportunities for research and practice, 143–154

59. Mosconi, G., Korn, M., Reuter, C., Tolmie, P., Teli, M., Pipek, V.: From Facebook to the neighbourhood: infrastructuring of hybrid community engagement. Comput. Support Coop Work. **26**, 959–1003 (2017). https://doi.org/10.1007/s10606-017-9291-z

60. Keane, N.J.: Police Use of Social Media to Support Community Engagement - Its Rise in Police Practice in the UK (2013)

61. Haklay, M.: Volunteered geographic information and citizen science. In: Understanding Spatial Media, pp. 127–135. SAGE Publications Ltd, 1 Oliver's Yard, 55 City Road London EC1Y 1SP (2017). https://doi.org/10.4135/9781526425850.n12

62. Neyroud, P., Loader, I., Brown, J.: Policing for a better Britain: Report of the Independent Police Commission (2016)

63. Bullock, K.: The police use of social media: transformation or normalisation? Soc. Policy Soc. **17**, 245–258 (2018). https://doi.org/10.1017/S1474746417000112

64. Dekker, R., van den Brink, P., Meijer, A.: Social media adoption in the police: barriers and strategies. Gov. Inf. Quart. **37**(2), 101441 (2020). https://doi.org/10.1016/j.giq.2019.101441

65. Corsianos, M.: The Complexities of Police Corruption: Gender, Identity, and Misconduct. Rowman & Littlefield Publishers (2012)

66. Meyer, E.T.: Examining the hyphen: the value of social informatics for research and teaching. In: Fichman, P., Rosenbaum, F. (eds.) Social Informatics: Past, Present and Future. pp. 56–72 (2014). https://doi.org/10.13140/2.1.4993.3441
67. Dang, J., King, K.M., Inzlicht, M.: Why are self-report and behavioral measures weakly correlated? Trends Cogn. Sci. **24**, 267–269 (2020). https://doi.org/10.1016/j.tics.2020.01.007
68. Peyton, K., Sierra-Arévalo, M., Rand, D.G.: A field experiment on community policing and police legitimacy. Proc. Natl. Acad. Sci. **116**(40), 19894–19898 (2019). https://doi.org/10.1073/pnas.1910157116

A Survey of Computer-Supported Remote Collaboration on Physical Objects

Maximilian Letter[1]([⊠]), Ceenu George[2,3], and Katrin Wolf[1]

[1] Berlin University of Applied Sciences and Technologies (BHT), Berlin, Germany
`{maximilian.letter,katrin.wolf}@bht-berlin.de`
[2] Technische Universität Berlin, Berlin, Germany
`ceenu.george@tu-berlin.de`
[3] University of Augsburg, Augsburg, Germany
`ceenu.george@uni-a.de`

Abstract. The need for remote collaborative work is constantly increasing. Collaboratively adapting digital content, such as documents and images, has come to a stage where it is part of our daily lives. In comparison, remote collaboration on *physical* objects has matured at a slower pace, even though this is a possible step towards location-independent cooperation and therefore equality in work. In this paper, we present a structured literature review on computer-supported remote collaboration on physical objects from the last 23 years. Our contribution is three-fold: First, we provide a comprehensive analysis of the current state of research on the topic of remote collaboration on physical objects. Second, we identify multiple research gaps, such as inclusion of haptic sense, mutual collaboration, and asynchronous collaboration. Third, we analyze code relationships in the selected publications and provide directions for future work in the form of exploratory research questions.

Keywords: Literature Review · Remote Collaboration · Physical Objects

1 Introduction and Background

Traditionally, collaborative work on physical objects is done by people in the same place at the same time. As companies are increasingly dependent on a global workforce, remote teams are becoming the norm. Currently, there are two ways to support remote teams that are working on physical objects: (1) They can either travel to each other, which results in high monetary and environmental costs [55]. Additionally, employees are strained by off-rhythm work schedules and jet lag [19,62]. (2) Alternatively, they can make use of collaborative tools for working remotely. For example, by prototyping with virtual abstractions of physical objects on 2D screens such as Figma [22] or 3D modeling in the form of Computer Aided Design (CAD) software, for example AutoCAD [7],

Supplementary Information The online version contains supplementary material available at https://doi.org/10.1007/978-3-031-42286-7_19.

Solidworks [18], or Blender [23]. While these approaches have the benefit of enabling remote collaboration through a fully digital workflow and allow for accurate fabrication, they detach the physical object from the physical world.

We see numerous reasons for emphasizing *physical* objects and reviewing research in this area to date. First, the naturalness of interaction that drives people to work with physical content, despite the advantages of digital workflows. An example for this is the creative domain, such as arts, product design, and craftsmanship, in which traditional painting as well as sculpturing are common practices despite the existence of drawing programs and 3D modeling tools [54]. The second reason is that our everyday lives are first and foremost rooted in the physical reality. Regardless of how digitization will shape the nature of productive work, the world we live in is physical and our daily needs will be physical and then only virtual. To this date, physical objects are by nature bound to space and therefore strongly limited in flexibility, compared to virtual objects that allow for replication, modification, and instant transfer. However, as novel technologies, like Augmented Reality (AR) and Mixed Reality (MR), grow more mature, new possibilities for collaborating on physical objects arise. These developments have the potential to overcome the fundamental disconnection between the physical world and digital information [81], thereby enabling better cooperation on physical objects independent of location, increasing equality in work.

In the context of this paper, the term *physical object* refers to content that is part of the real world and can be either a single artifact or an environment. We further specify physical objects as three-dimensional to exclude quasi two-dimensional artifacts like printed text documents or images. Since co-located work on physical artifacts most times does not require technical support, our work only examines remote collaboration.

A plethora of reviews has been conducted that touch on collaboration with physical objects [9,10,53,59,60,67,79,87,95]. Contrary to prior work, we present a structured literature review that amalgamates technology-focused surveys *and* Computer-Supported CooperativeWork (CSCW) literature, focusing on the current state and possibilities of remote collaboration on physical objects, rather than on the sole use of a technology or the social properties of a collaboration. In the following, we provide an overview of prior work to highlight specific gaps that we aim to fill with our structured literature review.

In 2018, Limbu et al. conducted a Structured Literature Review (SLR) of publications between 2014 and 2016 on AR for training [59]. They concluded with a promising outlook towards the development of AR and sensor technology. As a research gap, the use of sensors for capturing cognitive aspects of expert performance was identified. Opposed to the work of Limbu et al., we aim to investigate all possible collaboration scenarios and technologies, while scoping to works that actually include physical objects.

A systematic review on collaborative MR technologies was done in 2019 by Belen et al., including publications from 2013 to 2018 [10]. In their conclusion, Belen et al. pointed to potential research gaps in systems that support both co-located and remote collaboration, as well as in asynchronous collaboration. The work was limited to MR technologies and did not highlight the role of physical objects as the subject of collaboration.

In their work from 2020, Wang et al. provided a comprehensive survey of AR/MR-based co-design in manufacturing [95]. Analyzing publications from 1990 to 2017, they assessed the suitability and benefits of AR/MR environments for co-design. Their selected literature regarded manufacturing purposes and included co-located and remote interactions. While the use of AR has physical aspects by design, the examined applications rather utilized virtual object representations, similar to CAD programs. The authors concluded with the potential to establish an empathic co-design system and suggested the integration of AR/MR in commonly used CAD programs. In our approach, we elaborate on the role of physical objects and the activities that form around them in remote setups. The examined spectrum of application areas in our survey is not limited to manufacturing and technology-open.

Lapointe et al. reviewed the literature on AR-based remote guidance tasks in their work from 2020 [53]. They concluded with AR-based remote guidance being usable in variable application areas. As the scope of the survey was on the scenario of a remote expert helper guiding a local novice worker, other collaboration scenarios were not regarded. We aim to address this aspect of remote collaboration while including scenarios that go beyond guidance, as well as reviewing all available technologies.

In year 2020, Pidel and Ackermann presented a systematic overview on the collaboration in Virtual Reality (VR) and AR [79]. As a main finding, the underrepresentation of asynchronous collaboration was named. Our approach focuses more on the aspects of remote collaborations that form around physical objects, while Pidel and Ackermann provided a more general overview, as their research objective were not physical tasks.

Schäfer et al. conducted a survey on synchronous AR, VR, and MR remote collaboration systems in 2021 [87]. While some selected publications overlap with our selection, the work by Schäfer et al. mostly examined purely virtual content, such as meetings and digital design. The authors concluded with audiovisual systems being the default setup and guidance scenarios being the main use case for AR and MR, while in comparison, VR is more often suitable for equal involvement of collaborators. In comparison, our survey is technology-open but requires the collaboration to evolve around a physical artifact. Also, our work includes all collaboration types, including asynchronous collaboration.

Furthermore, numerous literature reviews have been published that investigate either related technologies [12,63,75] or collaboration aspects [52,60,99], without regarding the interaction between the two areas. Similarly, works of Hassenzahl et al. [32] and Li et al. [58] provide insights in the transfer of physicality across distance, but do not study the collaboration on physical objects.

The presented works show similarities in the collection of selected papers, as authors systematically searched through mostly same libraries (ACM DL [1], SpringerLink [5], IEEE Xplore [35] being used most often) using similar query keywords (collaboration, collaborative being used most often in combination with technologies like AR and MR). While there have been numerous literature reviews on computer-supported collaboration [10,53,59,79,87,95], limited research has been done concentrating the collaboration on physical real-world objects. The related surveys presented either give a general overview on the collaboration in MR or AR [10,79,87] or target specific collaboration scenarios, namely co-design [95], guidance [53], and training [59]. To the best of our knowledge, there has not been a systematic review of literature on the remote collaboration on physical objects.

To fill the above-mentioned gaps in prior work, we conducted a SLR, which sets out to gain a deeper understanding of the current state of remote collaboration on physical objects. A SLR is a systematic approach for evaluating all available research to a topic of interest [48]. We make the following contributions: (1) Comprehensive overview of the current state of research on the topic of remote collaboration on physical objects; (2) Identification of research gaps; (3) Analysis of code relationships and provision of exploratory research directions.

Our findings will help scientists that plan to participate in research on remote collaboration on physical objects. Developers and researchers working in overlapping research areas will also find the results useful in understanding how their contributions may affect research on remote collaboration on physical objects.

2   Method

The goal of this SLR is to gain an overview of existing work that addresses computer-supported remote collaboration on physical objects. Similar to prior SLRs [8,60,69], we follow the guidelines defined by Kitchenham's work "Procedures for Performing Systematic Reviews" [48] as described in the following.

We formulate the research question for this survey as: "What aspects of remote collaboration on physical objects have been explored in scientific literature?". The research question will be answered by reviewing work in this field of research using an unbiased approach [48].

For the extraction of publications, the ACM digital library [1], Springer-Link [5], and IEEE Xplore [35] were selected as databases, since they are the databases used most frequently by related literature surveys as well as most relevant to HCI research. The query chosen for extraction of work was: *(cscw OR "computer supported collaborative work" OR "tele-collaboration" OR "distributed collaboration" OR "remote cooperation" OR "remote collaboration") AND ("physical task" OR "physical object" OR "tangible object" OR "physical artifact" OR "physical computing").*

The total of 1093 search results were composed of 317 results for the ACM digital library, 771 results for SpringerLink, and 5 results for IEEE Xplore. The search was performed in late 2020 and refreshed mid 2021. Of the 1093 entries, a filtering process reduced the amount to 80 publications in the end. A history of the selection process is presented in supplementary material.

The final iteration of our coding process overlapped with the release of the CHI program in 2021. To the best of our knowledge, this was the only conference program that was released at the time of coding - from the list of relevant conferences that we had already synthesized during earlier coding rounds. Due to the high confidence we had, at this point in the coding process, on what relevant conference venues were for our literature review, we decided to include the papers from the CHI conference that matched with our search query keywords. This resulted in the inclusion of 4 additional papers in the last coding stage.

A more comprehensive report of the search and filtering process, including explanation of filtering criteria, can be found in the supplementary material.

3   Results

Our results consist of a list of the codes/codebook that were created during an open coding process by two researchers. Their numbers of appearance can be found in Table 1. The number of retrieved papers, broken down by publication date, is visualized in the top of Fig. 1, which shows a constant increase of works in that field. Codes that represent a category of codes and are indicated by an uppercase letter at the beginning, while in-text codes are written with a lowercase letter at the beginning.

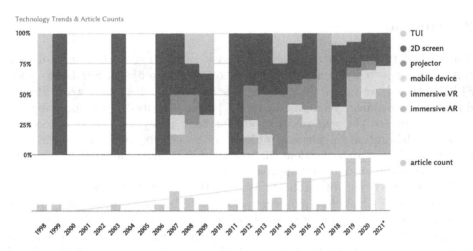

Fig. 1. Work on remote collaboration on physical objects by publication date. Top: Technologies in relation to the total amount of publications in a year, scaled to 100% for each year. The most common technologies and devices in the *Technology* code are selected. A trend towards technology diversification can be identified. Bottom: Amount of publications per year. An increasing amount of publications is visualized by a trendline. However, multiple increases and drops of publication numbers can be identified. 2021* only until June of the year, see Sect. 2.

Application Area describes the field of application or professional domain which is considered or at least named as an exemplary use case by a publication. We differentiate between five fields of work: *health* (n = 14); *scientific* (n = 2); *industrial* (n = 34); *educational* (n = 10); and *entertainment* (n = 6). It should

Table 1. Codebook. The 94 codes, their total number of appearances, and appearance ratio in comparison to the total amount of works (total 80 works, ratio rounded to 2 digits). Codes in bold represent parent codes that were added to categorize results.

Code	Count	Ratio	Code	Count	Ratio
Research Focus			**Prototype Setup**		
physical object	8	10%	symmetric system	22	28%
object interaction	8	10%	asymmetric system	60	75%
environment	8	10%	static	39	49%
device setup	4	5%	portable	41	51%
concepts and theory	3	4%	large scale	29	36%
User			small scale	50	62%
collaboration	15	19%	**Collaboration Type**		
Viewpoint			mutual	17	21%
viewpoint control	7	9%	training	3	4%
viewpoint independence	4	5%	guidance	62	78%
shared perspective	4	5%	synchronous	79	99%
Communication			asynchronous	6	8%
annotations	6	8%	dyadic	79	99%
gestures	16	20%	multiuser	1	1%
gaze	6	8%	**Targeted Senses**		
Application Area			auditory (only)	5	6%
industrial	34	42%	auditory + visual	71	89%
entertainment	6	8%	auditory + visual + haptics	9	11%
educational	10	12%	**Technologies**		
health	14	18%	2D screen	55	69%
scientific	2	2%	projector	21	26%
Study Design			2D video	52	65%
Study			monocular camera	47	59%
field study	2	2%	depth camera	19	24%
lab study	61	76%	SLAM	3	4%
Data Types			photogammetry	1	1%
task performance	39	49%	RFID	2	2%
behavioral measure	18	22%	360 degrees video	4	5%
perceptual measure	31	39%	mobile device	19	24%
presence	11	14%	spatial AR	9	11%
workload	8	10%	immersive AR	19	24%
Method			immersive VR	17	21%
questionnaire	42	52%	mobile device AR	4	5%
interview	27	34%	tabletop	3	4%
conversation record	31	39%	TUI	8	10%
quantitative tracking	15	19%	robotic device	7	9%
heuristics	14	18%	rapid prototyping	2	3%
Task			head-up display	5	6%
assembly	36	45%	LED Lights	3	4%
placement	12	15%	actuators	3	4%
operation	9	11%	shutter glasses	1	1%
repair	7	9%	machine learning	1	1%
search	10	12%	**Tracking**		
playing	5	6%	2D-marker-based	9	11%
design	5	6%	marker-less	2	2%
functionality test	8	10%	hand / fingers	10	12%
Materials			head	10	12%
dummy material	46	58%	eye gaze	7	9%
realistic material	27	34%	object	8	10%
continuous material	2	2%	**Input Devices**		
Recommendations			mouse + keyboard	13	16%
design	46	58%	touchscreen	11	14%
research	10	12%	pen	7	9%
hardware	7	9%	glove	3	4%
methodology	3	4%	controller	6	8%

be noted, that many of the studied works do not specify any *Application Area*, while others name several. We did not code an *Application Area* for works that might be associated with a field of application when it is never named.

Research Focus describes the main topic the work investigates. Publications are usually coded with a single *Research Focus*, in some cases with two. Notably, each of the selected works explores remote collaboration on physical objects, even if the research focus is not on the object itself. We differentiate between six different focus topics: *physical object* (n = 8), *environment* (n = 8), *object interaction* (n = 8), *device setup* (n = 4), *concepts and theory* (n = 3), and *User* (n = 58). Because of the high amount of *User*-focused works, we divided this code in multiple sub-codes. Besides a focus on *collaboration* (n = 15) between users, we identified two larger fields that can be further differentiated: *Viewpoint* (n = 15) and *Communication* (n = 28). *Viewpoint* is divided into *viewpoint control* (n = 7), *viewpoint independence* (n = 4), and *shared perspective* (n = 4). The code *Communication* has the sub-codes *gestures* (n = 16), *annotations* (n = 6), and *gaze* (n = 6) (Fig. 2).

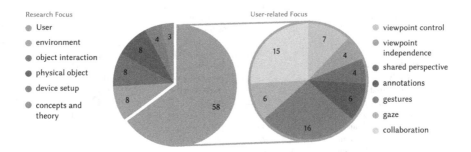

Fig. 2. Left: Comparison of *Research Focus* codes against each other, most works focus on *User*-related themes (divided by gap for clarity). Right: Distribution of sub-codes in the *User*-focus segment (total 58 works). Intermediate code layers regarding *User-Focus* are not visualized; *viewpoint control*, *viewpoint independence*, and *shared perspective* are categorized under the code *Viewpoint*; *annotations*, *free-form gestures*, *gestures pointing*, and *gaze pointing* belong to the parent code *Communication*.

Prototype Setup describes the properties of a proposed technical setup. We identify three properties that each can be separated into two states. The first property is the scale a prototype supports, divided into *small scale* (n = 50) and *large scale* (n = 29). If a prototype supports *large scale*, it can usually also be used in a *small scale* setup. The setup movement capabilities are further differentiated as *portable* (n = 41) or *static* (n = 39). If a prototype is *portable*, it can usually also be used in a static scenario. Lastly, we distinguish between *symmetric* (n = 22) and *asymmetric* (n = 60) systems, depending on how similar the systems in use are (in line with the definition by Heldal et al. for collaborative virtual environments [33]). In some cases, a prototype system can be used both in a *symmetric* and an *asymmetric* variant.

Collaboration Type describes the relationship between collaborators and how the collaboration takes place. The types of collaboration are coded as *training* (n = 3), *guidance* (n = 62), and *mutual* (n = 17). As a reference, mutual collaboration is in line with how Feld and Weyers describe a symmetric environment, while guidance and training are collaborations in an asymmetric environment [21]. Furthermore, we differentiate between *synchronous* (n = 79) and *asynchronous* (n = 6) collaboration. A work can support both *synchronous* and *asynchronous* collaboration. Lastly, a publication can regard a *dyadic* (n = 79) collaboration or a *multiuser* (n = 1) scenario (Fig. 3).

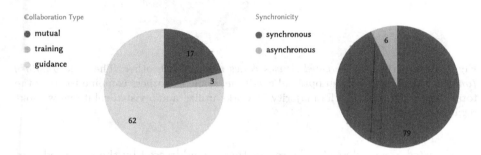

Fig. 3. Comparison of *Collaboration Type* codes against each other. Codes regarding the synchronicity are displayed separately. *Guidance* is the most often used type of collaboration, while *mutual* and *training* scenarios are rarer. Regarding the synchronicity of a collaboration, almost every work regards a *synchronous* but very rarely an *asynchronous* collaboration.

Technologies describe both hardware and software solutions that are used in a prototype and were observed throughout the reviewed works. While there is no need for further segregation, we sort the sub-codes in the order of input technologies, mixed technologies, and output technologies for convenience. For input technologies, we coded *monocular camera* (n = 47), *depth camera* (n = 19), and *RFID* (n = 2). Besides, the following *Input Devices* were identified: *mouse + keyboard* (n = 13), *touch screen* (n = 11), *pen* (n = 7), *glove* (n = 3), and *controller* (n = 6). One group of technologies processing the input content are *Tracking* technologies. *Tracking* is divided into *marker-based* (n = 9); *marker-less* (n = 2); *hand/fingers* (n = 10); *head* (n = 10); *eye gaze* (n = 7); and the tracking of *objects* (n = 8). As mixed technologies, that can serve as both, input and output, or have other processing uses, we identified the following codes: *2D video* (n = 52), *360° video* (n = 4), *mobile device* (n = 19), *mobile device AR* (n = 4), *spatial AR* (n = 9), *immersive AR* (n = 19), *immersive VR* (n = 17), *tabletop* (n = 3), *tangible user interface* (n = 8), *robotic device* (n = 7), *SLAM* (n = 3), *photogrammetry* (n = 1), and *machine learning* (n = 1). We point out that the codes *2D video* and *2D screen* correlate with the vast area of video-mediated collaboration, that is extensively studied in CSCW literature. The section of works analyzed in this SLR, that regard physical tasks or physical objects, is only a small part of video-mediated collaboration. As output technologies, we coded *2D screen* (n = 55), *projector* (n = 21), *head-up display* (n = 5), *rapid prototyping* (n = 2), *LED lights* (n = 3), *actuators* (n = 3), and *shutter glasses* (n = 1) (Fig. 4).

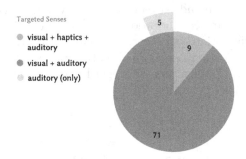

Fig. 4. Comparison of *Targeted Senses* codes against each other. The code *auditory (only)* is overlaid, as it is an optional condition, while the others combine to 80 as the total amount of papers. The majority of works utilize audio-visual solutions without regarding haptics.

Targeted Senses describe the senses that are addressed by the proposed prototype in a work. We differentiate between *auditory (only)* (n = 5), *auditory + visual* (n = 71), and *auditory + visual + haptics* (n = 9). In every presented prototype application, at least the *auditory + visual* senses are targeted. The *auditory (only)* condition serves as a control condition, as there is no work in which the auditory sense alone is targeted, given to our inclusion criteria. The code *auditory (only)* was not given to works in which the input of one of the collaborators is only voice while observing their partner's actions, as this term is used in multiple works, e.g. [44,47,73]. A work coded as targeting the senses *auditory + visual + haptics* cannot be simultaneously be coded as *auditory + visual*, as it already includes these senses.

Study Design describes the methodology as well as tasks used for measuring and acquisition of data in a conducted study. The *Study Design* is divided into *Setup*, *Data Types*, *Method*, and *Task*. We distinguish between the types of study *Setups* as *lab study* (n = 61) and *field study* (n = 2). The *Tasks* are divided into seven task types: *assembly* (n = 36); *placement* (n = 12); *operation* (n = 9); *repair* (n = 7); *search* (n = 10); *playing* (n = 5); *design* (n = 5); and *functionality test* (n = 8), which represents small tasks that test a specific functionality of the prototype. In addition to the different tasks, we coded the used *Materials* in a task. The identified material codes are *dummy material* (n = 46); *realistic material* (n = 27); and *continuous material* (n = 2), which refers to a material that does not have a discrete size as it can be seamlessly modified in all dimensions. For methods in the study design we identified the use of *questionnaires* (n = 42), *interviews* (n = 27), *conversation records* (n = 31), *quantitative tracking* (n = 15), and *heuristics* (n = 14). Lastly, the measured *Data Types* are split in *task performance* (n = 39), *behavioral measure* (n = 18), *perceptual measure* (n = 31), as well as *presence* (n = 11) and *workload* (n = 8) as a specific types of *perceptual measure*. None of these codes is exclusive, as a work can conduct multiple studies and measure different *Data Types*, using different *Tasks* and *Methods*.

Recommendations describes the kind of recommendations or takeaways a work gives for future researchers. A work can give recommendations of different types at the same time, or none at all. We differentiate between four recommendation types: *hardware recommendation* (n = 7); *design recommendation*; *research recommendation* (n = 10); and *methodology recommendation* (n = 3).

4   Discussion

In the following, we discuss our results and the current state of research in the field of remote collaboration on physical objects. Therefore, we highlight the research and technology trends derived from our survey. Second, codes that hint to research gaps are reviewed and condensed in Table 2. Lastly, the relationships between codes are analyzed. We complement notable findings with exemplary research questions that could conclude from our analysis. This is not an exhaustive set of questions, but rather a first step in the direction of future work.

4.1   Research Trends and Technologies

In order to identify trends in our selected publications, works were first analyzed in respect to their publication date.

Relationship Between Publication Counts and Introduction of Technologies. A constant increase in research on remote collaboration on physical objects can be observed, which is visualized by a trendline in the upper part of Fig. 1. However, we note that until 2006 very little work did happen in this field of research, possibly because of limited technological feasibility of capturing, augmenting, and transmitting physical content in a reasonable quality. While the overall publication count increased afterwards, the years 2010, 2014, and 2017 strike for low amount of works in comparison to the adjacent years. One explanation could be the introduction phase of novel technologies, where they are adapted in prototypes and evaluated with user studies, leading to publications 1–2 years later. Notable increases of publication counts happened around the years 2007 (the first batch of multiple works), 2012 (after the drop in 2010), and 2018 (after the drop in 2017), which could be tied to upcoming devices at that time. A constant in the technologies is the 2D screen.

The batch of works emerging in the years 2005 to 2009 shows the first introduction of mobile devices [76], projectors [36,76], immersive AR [17,56,98], and (TUIs) coupled with AR [56,98]. Most of the other research was done using 2D screen setups, especially on gesture supported collaboration in the context of guidance, studied extensively by Kirk et al. [44–47]. The ARToolkit [34], a marker-based tracking approach first presented in 1999 and released as an open source variant in 2005, came up in this timeframe and was used for early collaborative AR works [17,56]. The increase of publications from 2012 to 2016 appears to be related to the introduction of the Kinect camera by Microsoft

[65], which was first released in 2010 and found its way into academia around between 2011 and 2012 [100]. Especially from 2012 to 2014, 8 out of 18 publications utilized the Kinect [2,3,11,57,85,86,88,90]. In addition, depth-sensing systems were coupled with projector systems to enable a seamless interaction with physical content [2,3,11,85,86]. Technology use between the years 2015 and 2016 was more fragmented, but notable is the use of immersive VR headsets [6,25,72]. A prominent example of VR headsets of that time is the developer kit 2 of the Oculus Rift, released one year prior (2014 [71]) and used by Gao et al. [25] and Amores et al. [6]. The latest increase in publication counts, starting from 2018, may be related to the rise of Head-mounted Displays (HMDs), especially the HoloLens AR headset [64], which was first released in 2016. It was used in numerous works published since then [28,31,37,38,61,84,91,92,94]. The high amount of publications is currently lasting, possibly related to the hardware trend of combining VR and AR that can be observed in multiple works from 2020 and 2021 [28,37,43,93,94].

It can be stated that the research community usually rather adapts off-the-shelf devices than developing costly novel technical prototypes. We understand the traceability of publication numbers to hardware launches as a sign that research on remote collaboration on physical objects is still highly dependent on new technologies, which are yet to open many opportunities in that field.

Prominence in Technologies. We were able to identify a diversification of device use, correlating with publication counts, visualized in Fig. 1. The most prominent technology found in this survey is the 2D screen, as it is embedded into commercially available and long-time established technologies, such as laptops and mobile devices. Its widespread use could come from the maturity of the technology, as well as from its relevance for both personal and professional use in the form of video assistance. The different applications of video technology are studied extensively in CSCW literature as video-mediated collaboration, regarding visibility as a crucial aspect of collaboration. While we anticipate the high relevance of 2D video and 2D screens, the technological trends observed in this survey hint towards more immersive 3D representations of spatial content. Even though their fidelity is yet limited, they allow for a more natural experience, better understanding of spatial relationships, and free perspective, as highlighted by multiple publications [11,25,26,89,90]. However, researching a new technology in a collaborative scenario requires the technology to mature, which can lead to a temporal shift in research. Accordingly, it remains to be explored how novel technologies can be quickly embedded in prototype environments, so that they can be used to explore collaborative scenarios.

AR appears like an obvious choice for adding collaborative features to the real world and is used in 19 works (24%). In our selection of publications, we found AR plus VR setups [25,26,28,43,89,92], AR plus desktop setups [38,42, 61,84], and AR plus AR setups [31,98]. Optical see-through HMDs and video see-through AR/VR HMDs are equally in use. Overall, the research field seems to keep on adopting and experimenting with novel technologies. In its cause, we see multiple research topics related to collaboration being studied repeatedly under different technological conditions. This leads to the question if existing problems of remote collaboration on physical objects are being solved by novel technologies, or them being merely explored anew in the context of another technology. An example is the independence of viewpoints, that was investigated with projector setups [2, 30] as well as with immersive AR [42, 89].

Similar to our work, Wang et al. studied the use of immersive displays in their work on AR/MR-based co-design from 2020, in which they further differentiated the type of immersive HMDs and presented a diverse view on available technologies [95]. Unlike our results, their analysis showed a decline of head mounted displays in favor of desktop, handheld, and projector-based solutions. However, in the field of remote collaboration on physical objects, we can state a decline of projector-based solutions after year 2016 and a current increase in head-mounted displays. The exploration of suitable technologies is in line with the findings by Wang et al., who state that 37 percent of their reviewed works were dedicated to comparing AR/MR technologies [95]. The low number of 7 *hardware recommendations* (9%) made throughout our publications further indicates that authors are hesitant to present a technology as a potential solution.

To summarize properties of relevant technologies, the technologies highlighted in Fig. 1 and their most common use in the investigated literature are condensed in the following. The 2D screen provides video-based collaboration at a high resolution [13, 24, 70]. Its limitations are reached for depth perception and providing tangible experiences. Mobile devices as a variant of 2D screens allow for more flexible video-based collaborations [15, 39, 66]. Projectors can merge their output with physical content, thereby bringing remote places closer together [4, 41, 76], but are prone to light influences and complex in their setup. Immersive VR allows for real depth perception and more natural inputs [26, 37, 94]. Related to VR, immersive AR provides information directly in conjunction with the physical content [31, 89, 91]. Both, VR and AR are currently limited in their capabilities of streaming and representing remote physical environments at a high fidelity [2, 26, 50]. Lastly, TUIs are built on haptic in- and output, but are comparably niche to this date. They can be combined with other technologies to present more information [56, 57, 80].

4.2   Identified Research Gaps

Regarding this paper's research question of "what aspects of remote collaboration on physical objects have been explored in scientific literature", we review the codes obtained from our literature selection for striking numbers. While an infrequently occurring code does not necessarily indicate a research gap, it can serve as an indicator of under-researched areas, especially when accompanied by a highly represented counterpart. At first, codes that did not hint towards a research gap and showed expected occurrences are named without further elaboration. *Application Area* showed similar results to thematically adjacent literature reviews [60, 75]. For the *Study Design*, most codes returned expected numbers, like *assembly* tasks being used most often [75] and *task performance* as well as *perceptual measure* being the prime measurements in conducted studies. Lastly, the determined tracking technologies, such as *marker-based tracking*, *eye gaze tracking*, and *head tracking*, were mostly in line with expected outcomes [12,75,95]. Beside code appearances aligning with related work, some of the codes we recorded showed little significance and are therefore not further discussed. Among these codes are *Input Devices*, *static* and *portable Prototype Setups*, as well as prototypes capable of capturing *large scale* or *small scale* environments. In the following, potential research gaps are presented in thematically related combinations, as described in Sect. 4.3.

Physical Properties of Objects in Collaborative Settings. Regarding *Research Focus* and its sub-codes, it becomes apparent that with 58 works (73%) most of the research is *User*-targeted, thereby addressing potential user-related challenges during collaboration. An example is the management of different viewpoints and the correlating effects, e.g. [24,30,42,70,83,89]. While a research focus on the collaborating user is valuable, it does not address the existing challenges of representing and interacting with physical objects over distance. In contrast to the *User*-focus, only 8 works (10%) focus on the *physical object* as a part of collaboration. When taking works into account that regard the *object interaction* and eliminating document intersections, still only a limited amount of 13 publications (16%) can be found. While an *environment*-focus regards the physicality of the world, it is most often dedicated to challenges that are tied to scene capturing, transmission, and reconstruction of bigger surroundings [2,26,91]. Therefore, we interpret this as an alternative research direction compared to a focus on physical objects. Regarding the difficulties in both, representation and interaction with remote physical objects, our results indicate physical object focus being a research gap in remote collaboration. It remains to be seen, how the research focus can be moved onto the physicality of objects, in order to diminish the barrier between co-located and remote work.

We further investigated the sensory channels of collaborators that are addressed by a publication's prototype. It is apparent, that in contrast to the visual sense, haptics, as the main sensory complement provided by physical content through its tangibility, is only regarded in 9 publications (11%). This is in line with the lack of focus on physical objects, discussed in Sect. 4.3, as well as with the findings of Schäfer et al., who conclude that the majority of works in the field of VR, AR, and MR utilizes the audiovisual senses with tangibility only being rarely addressed by AR systems in case of applied markers [87]. The question rises, how research can be encouraged to study the tangibility of physical objects as part of a collaboration, since it is the sensual perception physical objects provide compared to digital ones. One explanation for the low representation of haptics is the use of established technologies, such as video conferencing [24,61,68], which rely on the visual sense in combination with audio without being capable of supporting haptics. Accordingly, haptics-simulating technologies, e.g. force-feedback gloves [77], are still highly experimental and were not found in our literature survey. Instead, we identified 8 TUIs (10%) [14,27,31,56,57,78,80,98] as ways of seamlessly merging physical with digital content while providing passive haptic feedback. This approach could become increasingly relevant for remote collaboration on physical objects in the future. We further justify this expectation by the trends of technologies, discussed in Sect. 4.1, that allow the interweaving of real and digital content, e.g. MR coupled with a TUI [31].

Another code that emerged is the kind of physical *Material* used in study tasks conducted with prototype systems. Both *dummy* and *realistic materials* were used in similar amounts. In contrast, *continuous materials* such as clay, that differ from part-based discrete materials like LEGO bricks, occurred only twice (3%) [50, 70] (clay and foam carving respectively). While many prototype systems could also support continuous materials, their use could result in different outcomes in some cases. It could be of interest to research into the use of continuous and flexible materials in remote collaborations in the future, as they seem to be the most challenging materials besides the fluids.

Mutual, Multiuser and Asynchronous Collaborations are Underrepresented. An apparent imbalance of codes can be found in the codes *dyadic* and *multiuser*, parented under *Collaboration Type*. Only a single publication exists that explicitly researches the case of more than two remote parties collaborating [74]. While other prototypes and systems might be able to support a multiuser collaboration with adjustments, its use and resulting consequences are usually not studied. This is in contrast to everyday practices, where work on physical objects is often done by more than two people simultaneously, for example if we think of a car being repaired in a workshop.

Regarding *Collaboration Type*, it can be stated that the majority of works examine a *guidance* scenario, adding up to 62 works (77%). In most of these expert-worker scenarios, the prototypes consist of *asymmetric* systems (*Prototype Setup*), which add up to 60 publications (75%). When comparing the amount of guidance scenarios to the 17 *mutual* collaborations (21%), it can be concluded that the latter is a rather underrepresented scenario. This possibly results from the nature of physical content being present in one place and therefore difficult to share, manipulate, and access from remote, while the use case of one person observing and guiding another person to do a task is much easier to accomplish. While the related literature surveys do not state a similar finding, the existence of dedicated literature on training [59] and guidance [53] in MR environments indicates bigger amounts of research in these areas. We conclude that there appears to be a research gap on the mutual collaboration on remote physical content. In line with that, further research could investigate how to equip remote collaborators with equal access rights to physical objects, to allow for mutual collaboration regardless of the objects' location.

Even though training is a unidirectional collaboration type similar to guidance, only 3 papers (4%) delved into this scenario [50, 92, 94]. This is in contrast to fully virtual setups, such as used in VR, where training is one of the main use cases [82, 97]. We assume, that the process of teaching and learning is difficult when the required physical content is not available on both locations, as the trainer or the trainee might not be able to perform an action due to missing artifacts. Alternatively, when physical objects are available, the fidelity of a presentation might not be high enough to emulate co-located training, in which case additional video might be necessary [50]. This assumption is similar to the findings of Limbu et al. in their literature review from 2018, in which they point out the missing sensors for capturing parts of the expert's performance [59]. Complementing their conclusion, we consider training with shared physical objects to be an interesting area of research.

Lastly, a notable discrepancy between *synchronous* and *asynchronous* collaboration was found. While asynchronous collaboration dominates our professional practice, it becomes apparent that asynchronous remote collaboration on physical objects is a research field that is strongly underrepresented and that synchronous collaboration is taken as the default case. It remains to be explored in what context asynchronous collaboration on physical objects is preferred. Only a total of 6 works (8%) [16,27,49,50,78,96] dealt with an asynchronous collaboration scenario. While many approaches of synchronous work might be transferable to asynchronous collaboration with some adjustments, we report the asynchronous remote collaboration on physical objects as a promising research field to be explored. Since synchronous collaboration on physical objects is so prevalent, the question rises how we can adapt existing findings to asynchronous collaboration. This is in line with the findings of Pidel and Ackermann, who also stated the under-representation of asynchronous collaboration in their survey on VR and AR [79], as well as with the recommendations of Belen et al., who attribute potential for research on asynchronous collaboration [10]. While these two literature surveys assess the need for research on asynchronous collaboration in regard to MR technologies, we further emphasize the challenges of implementing asynchronous collaboration with physical objects that are manifested in a non-dynamic state. We conclude that most reviewed publications regard a synchronous collaboration, while the asynchronous collaboration on physical objects appears to remain a research gap.

4.3   Code Relationships

Besides the identification of research gaps in Sect. 4.2, we analyzed co-appearances of codes. This analysis is visualized as an alluvial diagram, which is shown in Fig. 5 and discussed along it.

Support for Tangibility is Influenced by Research Focus. We detected co-appearances between the codes *Research Focus* and the human senses a system addresses. The code *auditory (only)* was stripped, as it is used as a control condition in addition to visual information, instead of being an independent condition. The most common research focus is the collaborating *User*, which results in targeting the *auditory and visual* senses without regarding the haptic sense in all works but one. In comparison, if the *physical object* or *object interaction* are the research objective, the haptic sense is addressed in more than half of the works. It surprises, that works researching the collaboration on an *environment* also do not regard the haptic sense. This could be attributed to the fact that most of these publications are concerned with challenges such as the reconstruction and

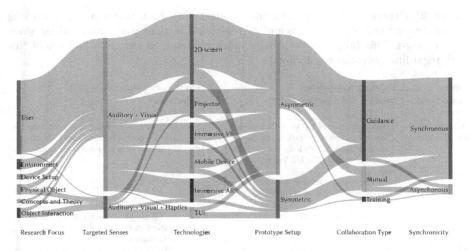

Fig. 5. The alluvial diagram highlights the relationship between prominent codes that stand out due to notable occurrence numbers and are part of this paper's discussion. The codes on the x-axis are abstracted categories from the detailed codes on the y-axis. It highlights, for example, that in most works that utilize an asymmetric prototype setup a guidance scenario is regarded, while symmetric prototype setups are rather used for mutual collaborations. It also reveals that this relation is not exclusive, meaning that asymmetric setups are also used in mutual collaboration and vice versa.

transfer of 3D environments [2,25,50,88]. As a research focus on users usually does not regard the haptic sense during a collaboration, it appears to be even more important to put the focus on the artifact itself to support tangibility in remote collaborations on physical objects.

When taking a look at how the *Targeted Senses* are connected to the used *Technology*, it becomes apparent that neither *immersive VR* nor *mobile devices* are used in systems that address the haptic sense for both collaborators. This does not mean that there are no prototypes using immersive VR or mobile devices that have a high proportion of physical interaction [29,39,80], but that the topic of allowing a remote collaborator to experience a haptic sensation through these technologies is not regarded. In comparison, the technologies *2D screen*, *projector*, and *immersive AR* are often used as a supplement technology to systems that allow for haptic interaction [31,56,57]. A promising research direction appears to be how existing technologies, such as mobile devices and VR, can be enhanced to support remote tangibility.

Prototype Setup and Collaboration Type are Related, But not Dependent on Each Other. Technology does not dictate whether a prototype system is set up as an *asymmetric* or a *symmetric* system. Each technology is used in similar proportions in both constellations, according to the distribution of asymmetric and symmetric systems, with a large tendency towards asymmetric setups. However, it can be stated that in the case of TUI, the proportional distribution between asymmetric and symmetric differs from the average distribution, as TUIs are

Table 2. Overview of underrepresented codes hinting at research gaps, existing approaches in these areas, and exemplary research directions that could address these research gaps. This table can be used as quick reference to the main findings of this work regarding potential research gaps.

Codes that are under-represented	Existing Approaches based on search query	Exemplary Research Questions to address research gaps
Asynchronous Collaboration	· Documentation of physical work steps [12] · Trace-based steps in TUI environments [21] · Tangible interface with digital access [61] · Spatial capture of a MR telepresence system [42] · Asynchronous audio/video-conferencing [40] · Using commonly available physical proxies [77]	In what context is asynchronous collaboration on physical objects preferred over the current default use case of synchronous collaboration?
Multi User Collaboration	· Switching between novices in video-training [74]	How can existing findings for synchronous collaboration on physical objects be adapted to asynchronous collaboration?
Mutual Collaboration	· Bi-directional gaze cues [37] · Distributed teams build physical components [13] · Open source documentation to rebuild an object [16] · Shared or independent view on shared object [42] · Physical proxy objects can be shared and exchanged [56,96,98] · Simulating, mirroring, and synchronizing physicality of two places [11,14,20,31,41,57,70] · Bidirectional Mixed Reality telepresence [50] · Mutually managed video-stream usage [40] · Managing access rights to distributed TUI artifacts [27]	How to equip remote collaborators with equal access rights to physical objects, to allow for mutual collaboration regardless of the objects' location?
Focus on Physical Object	· Capturing and projecting physical objects [36, 41] · Augmenting physical proxy objects [56,98] · Synchronize physical distributed twins [14] · Physical LEDs for collaborative highlighting [51] · Lightfields for object representation [66] · Version control for physical objects [78]	How can the research focus be moved onto the physicality of objects, in order to diminish the barrier between co-located and remote work?
Haptic sense targeted	· Proxy objects providing passive haptics [56,98] · Passive haptics due direct interaction with synchronized actuated objects [14,20] · Distributed physical objects providing passive haptics [13,96] · Tangible input for both collaborators [31] · Tangible output that can be interacted with [57] · Distributed tangible surfaces [27]	How can research be encouraged to study the tangibility of physical objects as part of a collaboration, since it is the sensual perception physical objects provide compared to digital ones?
Continuous material support	· Capturing continuous material via video [70] · Representing continuous material through 3D capture and video [50]	How is remote collaboration on physical objects influenced by continuous and flexible materials instead of discrete parts?

used in symmetric systems in half of their implementations. Besides this exception, asymmetric setups are highly favored, which is in line with the findings of

Schäfer et al., who state that MR setups are usually asymmetric since the input modalities are often not symmetric [87].

When comparing *Prototype Setup* and *Collaboration Type*, asymmetric systems are favored in *guidance* tasks, as expected. Similarly, *symmetric* systems are rather used for *mutual* collaborations. We note that nevertheless, both, asymmetric and symmetric setups, can be used to support the opposite collaboration type as these combinations can be found in 20 works (25%). This proposes the question, which properties of a system lead to it becoming an asymmetric system supporting mutual collaboration, or it becoming a symmetric system supporting a guidance scenario. Regarding the *training* code, there is no tendency in using an asymmetric or symmetric setup, as the amount of occurrences is too small to identify a clear relation.

Finally, we split up the code *Collaboration Type* into the collaborative action and the synchronicity of collaboration. It can be stated that all three collaborative actions: guidance, training, and mutual, are supported in synchronous and asynchronous collaborations. We cannot confirm any further relations, other than the low amount of publications regarding asynchronous collaboration consisting of guidance and mutual collaboration types to equal parts.

5   Conclusion

In this paper, we studied 80 publications in the field of remote collaboration on physical objects in the form of a structured literature review. The publications were coded in an open coding approach. Regarding technology trends, a diversification of technologies can be observed, with immersive head-mounted-displays being currently on the rise. By analyzing the created codes, we made the following findings about existing research gaps in that field: There is a general lack of research focus on the physical object as a component of collaboration. Further, the physicality of the object and the haptic sense of collaborators are identified as research gaps. We found a low amount of symmetric prototype systems and training scenarios utilizing shared physical artifacts. Mutual collaboration, multiuser collaboration as well as asynchronous collaboration were found to be poorly represented, posing many opportunities for further research. By analyzing code relations, we confirmed the relation between the lack of research focus on physical objects or object interaction and a low amount of works regarding haptic senses. We also found that the research gap of asynchronous collaboration is neither related to the design of the prototype nor the technologies used, but rather due to a lack of work in that field. Lastly, we reviewed the current state of research on remote collaboration on physical objects in the context of computer-supported cooperative work. Besides an overview of existing literature and research gaps worth to investigate, we provide a set of potential research questions for future work. Additionally, we emphasize the need for further research and discussion in the area of remote collaboration on physical objects.

References

1. ACM: ACM Digital Library (2023). https://dl.acm.org/
2. Adcock, M., Anderson, S., Thomas, B.: RemoteFusion: real time depth camera fusion for remote collaboration on physical tasks. In: SIGGRAPH VRCAI 2013 (2013)
3. Adcock, M., Feng, D., Thomas, B.: Visualization of off-surface 3D viewpoint locations in spatial augmented reality. In: SUI 2013 (2013)
4. Adcock, M., Gunn, C.: Using projected light for mobile remote guidance. CSCW **24**, 591–611 (2015)
5. AG, S.N.S.: SpringerLink. https://link.springer.com/ (2023)
6. Amores, J., Benavides, X., Maes, P.: ShowMe: a remote collaboration system that supports immersive gestural communication. In: EA CHI 2015 (2015)
7. Autodesk Inc.: AutoCAD. https://www.autodesk.com/solutions/cad-software (2023 (initial 1982))
8. Bacca Acosta, J.L., Baldiris Navarro, S.M., Fabregat Gesa, R., Graf, S., et al.: Augmented reality trends in education: a systematic review of research and applications. Int. Forum Educ. Technol. Soc. **17**, 133–149 (2014)
9. Baykal, G.E., Van Mechelen, M., Eriksson, E.: Collaborative technologies for children with special needs: a systematic literature review. In: CHI 2020 (2020)
10. Belen, R.A., Nguyen, H., Filonik, D., Favero, D.D., Bednarz, T.: A systematic review of the current state of collaborative mixed reality technologies: 2013–2018. AIMS Electron. Electr. Eng. **3**, 181–223 (2019)
11. Benko, H., Jota, R., Wilson, A.: MirageTable: freehand interaction on a projected augmented reality tabletop. In: CHI 2012 (2012)
12. Boboc, R.G., Gîrbacia, F., Butilă, E.V.: The application of augmented reality in the automotive industry: a systematic literature review. Appl. Sci. **10**, 4259 (2020)
13. Bonneau, C., Bourdeau, S.: Computer-supported collaboration: simulation-based training using LEGO®. Educ. Tech. Res. Dev. **67**, 1507–1527 (2019)
14. Brave, S., Ishii, H., Dahley, A.: Tangible interfaces for remote collaboration and communication. In: CSCW 1998 (1998)
15. Burnett, G.M., Calvo, A., Finomore, V., Funke, G.: The effects of multimodal mobile communications on cooperative team interactions executing distributed tasks. In: Streitz, N., Stephanidis, C. (eds.) DAPI 2013. LNCS, vol. 8028, pp. 358–367. Springer, Heidelberg (2013). https://doi.org/10.1007/978-3-642-39351-8_39
16. Calegario, F., Tragtenberg, J., Wang, J., Franco, I., Meneses, E., Wanderley, M.M.: Open source DMIs: towards a replication certification for online shared projects of digital musical instruments. In: Stephanidis, C., Marcus, A., Rosenzweig, E., Rau, P.-L.P., Moallem, A., Rauterberg, M. (eds.) HCII 2020. LNCS, vol. 12423, pp. 84–97. Springer, Cham (2020). https://doi.org/10.1007/978-3-030-60114-0_5
17. Chastine, J.W., Nagel, K., Zhu, Y., Yearsovich, L.: Understanding the design space of referencing in collaborative augmented reality environments. In: GI 2007 (2007)
18. Corporation, D.S.S.: Solidworks (2023 (initial 1995)). https://www.solidworks.com/
19. Dimitrova, M.: Of discovery and dread: Unpacking the complex effects of international business travel frequency. In: Academy of Management, Manor, NY 10510. Academy of Management Briarcliff (2019)

20. Feick, M., Tang, A., Bateman, S.: Mixed-reality for object-focused remote collaboration. In: UIST 2018 (2018)
21. Feld, N., Weyers, B.: Overview of collaborative virtual environments using augmented reality. Mensch und Computer 2019 - Workshopband (2019)
22. Figma, I.: Figma (2023 (initial 2016)). https://www.figma.com/
23. Foundation, B.: Blender. https://www.blender.org/ (2023 (initial 1994))
24. Fussell, S.R., Setlock, L.D., Kraut, R.E.: Effects of head-mounted and scene-oriented video systems on remote collaboration on physical tasks. In: SIGCHI 2003 (2003)
25. Gao, L., Bai, H., Lee, G., Billinghurst, M.: An oriented point-cloud view for MR remote collaboration. In: SA 2016 (2016)
26. Gao, L., Bai, H., Lindeman, R., Billinghurst, M.: Static local environment capturing and sharing for MR remote collaboration. In: SIGGRAPH Asia 2017 Mobile Graphics & Interactive Applications on - SA 2017 (2017)
27. Garbay, C., Badeig, F., Caelen, J.: Normative multi-agent approach to support collaborative work in distributed tangible environments. In: CSCW 2012 (2012)
28. Gasques, D., et al.: Artemis: a collaborative mixed-reality system for immersive surgical telementoring. In: CHI 2021 (2021)
29. Gauglitz, S., Lee, C., Turk, M., Höllerer, T.: Integrating the physical environment into mobile remote collaboration. In: MobileHCI 2012 (2012)
30. Gurevich, P., Lanir, J., Cohen, B., Stone, R.: TeleAdvisor: a versatile augmented reality tool for remote assistance. In: CHI 2012 (2012)
31. Günther, S., et al.: CheckMate: exploring a tangible augmented reality interface for remote interaction. In: EA CHI 2018 (2018)
32. Hassenzahl, M., Heidecker, S., Eckoldt, K., Diefenbach, S., Hillmann, U.: All you need is love: current strategies of mediating intimate relationships through technology. In: TOCHI 2012 (2012)
33. Heldal, I., Schroeder, R., Steed, A., Axelsson, A.S., Spant, M., Widestrom, J.: Immersiveness and symmetry in copresent scenarios. In: IEEE Proceedings. VR 2005. Virtual Reality 2005, pp. 171–178. IEEE (2005)
34. Kato, H., Mark Billinghurst, I.P.: AR ToolKit. http://artoolkit.sourceforge.net (2023)
35. IEEE: IEEE Xplore. ieeexplore.ieee.org/ (2023)
36. Iyoda, T., et al.: LightCollabo: distant collaboration support system for manufacturers. In: Satoh, S., Nack, F., Etoh, M. (eds.) MMM 2008. LNCS, vol. 4903, pp. 369–379. Springer, Heidelberg (2008). https://doi.org/10.1007/978-3-540-77409-9_35
37. Jing, A., May, K.W., Naeem, M., Lee, G., Billinghurst, M.: Eyemr-vis: using bi-directional gaze behavioural cues to improve mixed reality remote collaboration. In: EA CHI 2021 (2021)
38. Johnson, J.G., Gasques, D., Sharkey, T., Schmitz, E., Weibel, N.: Do you really need to know where "that" is? Enhancing support for referencing in collaborative mixed reality environments (2021)
39. Johnson, S., Gibson, M., Mutlu, B.: Handheld or handsfree? Remote collaboration via lightweight head-mounted displays and handheld devices. In: CSCW 2015 (2015)
40. Jones, B., Witcraft, A., Bateman, S., Neustaedter, C., Tang, A.: Mechanics of camera work in mobile video collaboration. In: CHI 2015 (2015)
41. Junuzovic, S., Inkpen, K., Blank, T., Gupta, A.: IllumiShare: sharing any surface. In: CHI 2012 (2012)

42. Kim, S., Billinghurst, M., Lee, G.: The effect of collaboration styles and view independence on video-mediated remote collaboration. In: CSCW 2018 (2018)

43. Kim, S., Lee, G., Billinghurst, M., Huang, W.: The combination of visual communication cues in mixed reality remote collaboration. J. Multimodal User Interfaces **14**, 321–335 (2020)

44. Kirk, D., Crabtree, A., Rodden, T.: Ways of the hands. In: Gellersen, H., Schmidt, K., Beaudouin-Lafon, M., Mackay, W. (eds.) ECSCW 2005. Springer, Dordrecht (2005). https://doi.org/10.1007/1-4020-4023-7_1

45. Kirk, D., Fraser, D.S.: The effects of remote gesturing on distance instruction. In: Computer Supported Collaborative Learning 2005: The Next 10 Years! (2005)

46. Kirk, D., Fraser, D.S.: Comparing remote gesture technologies for supporting collaborative physical tasks. In: SIGCHI 2006 (2006)

47. Kirk, D., Rodden, T., Fraser, D.S.: Turn it this way: grounding collaborative action with remote gestures. In: SIGCHI 2007 (2007)

48. Kitchenham, B.: Procedures for Performing Systematic Reviews. Keele University, Keele (2004)

49. Kortuem, G., Bauer, M., Segall, Z.: NETMAN: the design of a collaborative wearable computer system. Mob. Networks Appl. **4**, 49–58 (1999)

50. Kumaravel, B.T., Anderson, F., Fitzmaurice, G., Hartmann, B., Grossman, T.: Loki: facilitating remote instruction of physical tasks using bi-directional mixed-reality telepresence. In: UIST 2019 (2019)

51. Ladwig, P., Dewitz, B., Preu, H., Säger, M.: Remote guidance for machine maintenance supported by physical LEDs and virtual reality. In: MuC 2019 (2019)

52. Lai, E.R.: Collaboration: A Literature Review. Pearson Publisher, London (2011)

53. Lapointe, J.-F., Molyneaux, H., Allili, M.S.: A literature review of AR-based remote guidance tasks with user studies. In: Chen, J.Y.C., Fragomeni, G. (eds.) HCII 2020. LNCS, vol. 12191, pp. 111–120. Springer, Cham (2020). https://doi.org/10.1007/978-3-030-49698-2_8

54. Laviole, J., Hachet, M.: Spatial augmented reality to enhance physical artistic creation. In: Adjunct 25th Annual ACM Symposium on User Interface Software and Technology (2012)

55. Lee, D.S., et al.: Aviation and global climate change in the 21st century. Atmos. Environ. **43**, 3520–3537 (2009)

56. Lee, J.Y., Rhee, G.W., Park, H.: AR/RP-based tangible interactions for collaborative design evaluation of digital products. Int. J. Adv. Manuf. Technol. **45**, 649–665 (2009)

57. Leithinger, D., Follmer, S., Olwal, A., Ishii, H.: Physical telepresence: shape capture and display for embodied, computer-mediated remote collaboration. In: UIST 2014 (2014)

58. Li, H., Häkkilä, J., Väänänen, K.: Review of unconventional user interfaces for emotional communication between long-distance partners. In: MobileHCI 2018 (2018)

59. Limbu, B.H., Jarodzka, H., Klemke, R., Specht, M.: Using sensors and augmented reality to train apprentices using recorded expert performance: a systematic literature review. Educ. Res. Rev. **25**, 1–22 (2018)

60. Lopez, G., Guerrero, L.A.: Awareness supporting technologies used in collaborative systems: a systematic literature review. In: CSCW 2017 (2017)

61. Ludwig, T., Stickel, O., Tolmie, P., Sellmer, M.: shARe-IT: ad hoc remote troubleshooting through augmented reality. CSCW **30**, 119–167 (2021)

62. Mäkelä, L., Tanskanen, J., Kangas, H., Heikkilä, M.: International business travelers' job exhaustion: effects of travel days spent in short-haul and long-haul destinations and the moderating role of leader-member exchange. J Global Mob. Home Expatriate Manag. Res. **9**, 434–455 (2021)
63. Merino, L., Schwarzl, M., Kraus, M., Sedlmair, M., Schmalstieg, D., Weiskopf, D.: Evaluating mixed and augmented reality: a systematic literature review (2009–2019). In: ISMAR 2020 (2020)
64. Microsoft: HoloLens (2023). https://www.microsoft.com/en-us/hololens
65. Microsoft: Kinect (2023). https://developer.microsoft.com/en-us/windows/kinect/
66. Mohr, P., Mori, S., Langlotz, T., Thomas, B.H., Schmalstieg, D., Kalkofen, D.: Mixed reality light fields for interactive remote assistance. In: CHI 2020 (2020)
67. Neale, D., C, D., Carroll, J., M, J., Rosson, M.B., Rosson, M.B.: Evaluating computer-supported cooperative work: models and frameworks. In: CSCW 2004 (2004)
68. Neiva, F.W., Bittencourt, V., Ugulino, W., Borges, M.R.S., Vivacqua, A.S.: Remote collaboration support on physical tasks: exploring handheld and hands-free setups. In: Yuizono, T., Ogata, H., Hoppe, U., Vassileva, J. (eds.) CRIWG 2016. LNCS, vol. 9848, pp. 65–80. Springer, Cham (2016). https://doi.org/10.1007/978-3-319-44799-5_6
69. Noll, J., Beecham, S., Richardson, I.: Global software development and collaboration: barriers and solutions. ACM Inroads **1**, 66–78 (2011)
70. Norris, J., Schnädelbach, H.M., Luff, P.K.: Putting things in focus: establishing co-orientation through video in context. In: SIGCHI 2013 (2013)
71. Oculus: Oculus Developer Kit 2 (2023). https://www.roadtovr.com/oculus-rift-developer-kit-2-dk2-pre-order-release-date-specs-gdc-2014/
72. Oda, O., Elvezio, C., Sukan, M., Feiner, S., Tversky, B.: Virtual replicas for remote assistance in virtual and augmented reality. In: UIST 2015 (2015)
73. Ou, J., Fussell, S.R., Chen, X., Setlock, L.D., Yang, J.: Gestural communication over video stream: supporting multimodal interaction for remote collaborative physical tasks. In: ICMI 2003 (2003)
74. Ou, J., Shi, Y., Wong, J., Fussell, S.R., Yang, J.: Combining audio and video to predict helpers' focus of attention in multiparty remote collaboration on physical tasks. In: ICMI 2006 (2006)
75. Palmarini, R., Erkoyuncu, J.A., Roy, R., Torabmostaedi, H.: A systematic review of augmented reality applications in maintenance. Robot. Comput.-Integrated Manuf. **49**, 215–228 (2018)
76. Palmer, D., et al.: Annotating with light for remote guidance. In: OZCHI 2007 (2007)
77. Perret, J., Vander Poorten, E.: Touching virtual reality: a review of haptic gloves. In: ACTUATOR 2018. VDE (2018)
78. Perteneder, F., Grossauer, E.M., Xu, Y., Haller, M.: Catch-Up 360: digital benefits for physical artifacts. In: TEI 2015 (2015)
79. Pidel, C., Ackermann, P.: Collaboration in virtual and augmented reality: a systematic overview. In: De Paolis, L.T., Bourdot, P. (eds.) AVR 2020. LNCS, vol. 12242, pp. 141–156. Springer, Cham (2020). https://doi.org/10.1007/978-3-030-58465-8_10
80. Piumsomboon, T., et al.: On the shoulder of the giant: a multi-scale mixed reality collaboration with 360 video sharing and tangible interaction. In: CHI 2019 (2019)
81. Porter, M.E., Heppelmann, J.E.: Why every organization needs an augmented reality strategy. HBR'S 10 MUST (2017)

82. Radianti, J., Majchrzak, T.A., Fromm, J., Wohlgenannt, I.: A systematic review of immersive virtual reality applications for higher education: design elements, lessons learned, and research agenda. Comput. Educ. **147**, 103778 (2020)

83. Ranjan, A., Birnholtz, J.P., Balakrishnan, R.: An exploratory analysis of partner action and camera control in a video-mediated collaborative task. In: CSCW 2006 (2006)

84. Rasmussen, T.A., Huang, W.: SceneCam: using AR to improve multi-camera remote collaboration. In: SIGGRAPH Asia XR 2019 (2019)

85. Sakata, N., Kobayashi, T., Nishida, S.: Communication analysis of remote collaboration system with arm scaling function. In: Kurosu, M. (ed.) HCI 2013. LNCS, vol. 8007, pp. 378–387. Springer, Heidelberg (2013). https://doi.org/10.1007/978-3-642-39330-3_40

86. Sakata, N., Takano, Y., Nishida, S.: Remote collaboration with spatial AR support. In: Kurosu, M. (ed.) HCI 2014. LNCS, vol. 8511, pp. 148–157. Springer, Cham (2014). https://doi.org/10.1007/978-3-319-07230-2_15

87. Schäfer, A., Reis, G., Stricker, D.: A survey on synchronous augmented, virtual and mixed reality remote collaboration systems. ACM Comput. Surv. **55**, 1–27 (2021)

88. Sodhi, R.S., Jones, B.R., Forsyth, D., Bailey, B.P., Maciocci, G.: BeThere: 3D mobile collaboration with spatial input. In: SIGCHI 2013 (2013)

89. Tait, M., Billinghurst, M.: The effect of view independence in a collaborative AR system. CSCW **24**, 563–589 (2015)

90. Tecchia, F., Alem, L., Huang, W.: 3D helping hands: a gesture based MR system for remote collaboration. In: VRCAI 2012 (2012)

91. Teo, T., Lawrence, L., Lee, G.A., Billinghurst, M., Adcock, M.: Mixed reality remote collaboration combining 360 video and 3D reconstruction. In: CHI 2019 (2019)

92. Wang, P., et al.: I'm tired of demos: an adaptive MR remote collaborative platform. In: SA 2018 (2019)

93. Wang, P., et al.: Using a head pointer or eye gaze: the effect of gaze on spatial AR remote collaboration for physical tasks. Interact. Comput. **32**, 153–169 (2020)

94. Wang, P., et al.: 3DGAM: using 3D gesture and CAD models for training on mixed reality remote collaboration. Multimedia Tools Appl. **80**, 31059–31084 (2020)

95. Wang, P., et al.: A comprehensive survey of AR/MR-based co-design in manufacturing. Eng. Comput. **36**, 1715–1738 (2020)

96. Wu, T.Y., Gong, J., Seyed, T., Yang, X.D.: Proxino: enabling prototyping of virtual circuits with physical proxies. In: UIST 2019 (2019)

97. Xie, B., et al.: A review on virtual reality skill training applications. Front. Virtual Real. **2**, 645153 (2021)

98. Yamamoto, S., Tamaki, H., Okajima, Y., Okada, K., Bannai, Y.: Symmetric model of remote collaborative mr using tangible replicas. In: IEEE Virtual Reality Conference (2008)

99. Yusoff, N.M., Salim, S.S.: A systematic review of shared visualisation to achieve common ground. J. Visual Lang. Comput. **28**, 83–99 (2015)

100. Zhang, Z.: Microsoft Kinect sensor and its effect. IEEE MultiMedia **19**, 4–10 (2012)

Collaborative TV Control: Towards Co-experience and Social Connectedness

Melanie Berger[1,2](✉) , Rutger Verstegen[1] , Bahareh Barati[1] , Harm van Essen[1] , and Regina Bernhaupt[1,2]

[1] Eindhoven University of Technology, Eindhoven, The Netherlands
{m.berger,b.barati,h.a.v.essen,r.bernhaupt}@tue.nl
[2] Ruwido Austria GmbH, Neumarkt, Austria
r.verstegen@student.tue.nl

Abstract. Consuming media together is enjoyable and lets people connect with one another. However, the control of a TV, for instance, is still restricted to one user. This limits individual participation in group decision-making, particularly in the home context which can cause frustration and impact social interaction negatively. In this paper, we explore how we can support users in the living room to collaboratively interact with the TV in order to enhance social interaction and support the selection of a movie everyone is up for watching. Therefore, we investigate three collaborative approaches to movie selection: *Consensual*, *Hierarchical*, and *Autocratic*. We empirically validated the approaches' effect on perceived co-experience, social connectedness, and team performance as indicators for social interaction. Therefore, we conducted a mixed-subject experiment (N = 30, 10 groups) inside a living room in groups of three choosing a movie together. Results show that the collaborative approach to movie selection has an influence on collaboration and social interaction. Promoting consensual decision-making or enabling users to provide movie recommendations under the hierarchical approach empowers individuals, supports involvement, and is perceived as fair while also enabling a higher chance of picking a movie everyone enjoys watching. Letting only one user interact with the TV, stimulates communication, yet, it enhances the chance of excluding group members. Founded on these insights, we discuss suggestions for the future design of collaborative, interactive media systems toward co-experience and social connectedness.

Keywords: Collaboration · Interactive media · Social connectedness · Co-experience · Movie selection

1 Introduction

The living room is one of the central gathering places for social activities at home [23]. Particularly watching movies together generates a shared experience

J. Abdelnour Nocera et al. (Eds.): INTERACT 2023, LNCS 14144, pp. 369–392, 2023.
https://doi.org/10.1007/978-3-031-42286-7_20

which can enhance social engagement and enrich the overall viewing experience [25]. While streaming services have made it easy to access a wide variety of content, users spend almost an hour a day deciding on what content to watch [13]. In addition to the challenging and daunting task of making a choice, a traditional TV allows for single user input only [4]. However, research outlines that neglecting individual participation in group decision-making can cause a feeling of exclusion [11] due to limiting expression of needs [9] and lack of intervention in control if necessary [11]. This in turn impacts social interaction and belongingness negatively [16] which can cause interpersonal conflicts and frustration [24]. To overcome this, research on collaborative, interactive system design empathizes to balance individuals' contribution in order to enhance social interaction [15,33]. A promising approach, therefore, lies in the introduction of so-called coordination policies to distribute control over functions to multiple users at once [33]. Moreover, promoting perceived social connectedness (belongingness, connectedness, affiliation, companionship towards the group [2,28]) and team performance (team cohesion [37]) among group members and supporting co-experience (user experience, social experience [3]) play a major role in enhanced social interaction and successful group collaboration [2,28,29].

Previous work built upon these coordination policies and investigated a democratic voting system for movie selection in the living room using individuals' smartphones to encourage participation [32]. However, results show that it induces a high mental workload and impacts user experience negatively [32]. Promoting a democratic selection of music content in public spaces in turn increases social value, is entertaining, and supports fairness, even though it is time-consuming to initiate changes [36]. A recent study by Berger et al. outlines, that a democratic creation of a music playlist in the car among passengers enhances social connectedness, especially perceived belongingness and affiliation, while it also encourages communication [5]. In turn, providing users with different levels of control strengthens power games, induces dependency on others, and is perceived as unfair [5]. Nonetheless, it supports structured collaboration due to dedicated responsibilities [38].

Whilst previous research concerning collaborative movie services in the home provides a clear overview of the impact of coordination policies on technical feasibility [32,33], and mental workload [32] or investigated the usability of novel interaction mechanisms to promote collaboration (e.g., smartphones, gesture [32,38]), little is known about how to design for a higher level of social interaction when selecting a movie together. Since prior research from other none-home related contexts shows promising results of coordination policies' promoting social interaction [1,5], we thus see the need to investigate how the multi-user coordination policies, in combination with prior work concerning collaborative media system design (e.g., [8,32]) can be applied to support perceived social connectedness, team performance, and co-experience of a group selecting a movie together. In this paper, we focus on answering the following research question (RQ): *How does collaborative movie content selection among co-located users in the living room affect social interaction in terms of social connectedness, team performance, and co-experience?*

We designed three different types of collaborative approaches (*Consensual, Hierarchical, Autocratic*; details see Sect. 3) to support co-located users in the living room with the selection of a movie using several remote controls to interact with a single TV. To evaluate their effect on users' perceived co-experience, team performance, and social connectedness, we conducted a mixed-design lab experiment in groups of three (N = 30, 10 groups).

Contribution Statement: Our contribution is three-fold: First, we contribute to the exploration of implementing shared control of a TV using several remote controls. Secondly, with the experimental assessment of the three collaborative movie-selection approaches, we provide evidence-based insights on users' perceptions of co-experience, team performance, and social connectedness. Third, based on these insights we discuss proposals to conquer social interaction when designing interactive media systems for co-located users.

2   Background and Related Work

According to recent statistics, 76% of household members are open to sharing devices with one another in the home [27] or to use them simultaneously, especially for leisure or family bonding activities [17]. However, not all devices/systems enable joint interactions which limit the possibilities of collaboration [16]. In the following, we provide an overview of the important social aspects of collaboration, the design of collaborative media systems, and outline technological requirements to facilitate group collaboration in the home context.

2.1   Collaborative, Interactive Systems in the Home and Beyond

The design of collaborative, interactive systems for co-located users focuses on supporting communication, collaboration, and coordination of tasks [26] to achieve a common goal. The collaborative aspects can lie in regulating authority and responsibility [15] over functions by introducing coordination policies [33,34] to enable group work either at the same time (time-synchronously) or sequentially (time-asynchronously) [18]. Those policies balance decision making i.e., among co-located users in a shared environment by enabling them to vote for changes, providing users with different access levels, assigning dedicated functions to specific users, or having one key user who decides on behalf of the group [33,38]. McGill et al. [32] investigated a voting system for movie selection in the home using smartphones to encourage participation [32]. Their results show that it induces a high level of frustration, and high mental workload, while resulting in a low perceived usability [32]. Current research reports that using personal devices, such as smartphones to collaborate in a shared environment, detaches users despite being physically close [29]. Based on an online survey and the scenario of controlling the TV simultaneously in a group using gesture interaction, Plaumann et al. [38] report that users perceive voting as time-consuming.

However, democratically selecting music, e.g., in the car, is entertaining, stimulates discussion, and encourages communication, while indeed requiring more time [5]. Nevertheless, voting has the potential to increase social engagement and interaction [5,36]. Having a single key user instead who controls on behalf of others shows high usability and low frustration [32]. It is described as not ambiguous, encouraging storytelling, and ensuring conversations [1]. Even though this notion is the easiest to implement from a technological perspective [38], it generates high dependency on a single user and is perceived as unfair because it limits interventions which increases conflicts in case the key user does not want to perform changes requested by others [5]. Overall, the most common approach refers to providing different access levels to users [33,38] or switching key users from time to time (e.g., by means of a rotting access token [1,32]). While especially hierarchical levels sound promising in involving all users actively, it can provoke unbalanced power dynamics and has the potential to increase interpersonal conflicts [38]. Switching key users instead induces waiting times which lowers communication. However, it promotes fairness since everyone gets the chance to contribute [5]. While the various coordination policies seem to have both advantages and disadvantages in designing collaborative systems, it is essential that the system provides high usability [32]. Particularly when supporting collaboration in the home, the system or service should facilitate convenience [47], and promote workspace/change awareness [8,19] to best foster collaboration, mediated through technology.

2.2   Social Interaction and Its Design

Socially interacting, exchanging thoughts and visions are fundamental for humans, especially when collaborating together to achieve a goal. To feel comfortable expressing oneself in a collaborative setting, research outlines that the individual's perceived social connectedness (which incorporates feelings of belongingness, affiliation, companionship, and connectedness) [2,28], co-experience (social experience [3], user experience [44,45]), team performance(team cohesion [37]) play a significant role in enriching social interaction [3]. Especially a high level of companionship supports well-being, helps to reduce stress, and enhances social satisfaction [40]. Affiliation supports social interaction [46] and is important to establish self-esteem and maintain a social bond [28]. A high team cohesion affects the performance of the team and makes collaboration more efficient and effective [37]. Particularly when collaborating on media-oriented tasks, the co-experience which gets influenced by others' interactions, has a strong impact on the group dynamics [3]. Overall, social interaction can be supported by encouraging direct communication [14] and enabling a fair contribution of individuals [5]. Especially social connectedness gets established by providing the possibility to easily opt-in and opt-out and not forcing users to participate in decision-making [5].

Summed up, consuming media is a social activity. The collaborative selection of media content has the potential to stimulate social interaction and enhance individuals' experiences. To design interactive media systems for co-located users, the system needs to be created around the users [39] and promote any user to participate actively [5,26,31]. While research highlights the importance of balancing individual access to control possibilities by applying coordination policies [15,32,38] and outlines how collaboration impacts social interaction in other contexts [5], little is known about how to best design for shared control of a TV to enhance, particularly individuals' perceived social connectedness, team performance, and co-experience.

3   Designing for Collaborative Movie Selection

With the design of collaborative movie selection, we aim to support co-located users in the home to interact with one another and stimulate social interaction. Our spotlight lies in investigating how the distribution of control among co-located users affects social connectedness, team performance, and co-experience. Since the average European household compromises 2.2 people [12], we focused on the exemplary use case of three users selecting a movie together in the living room. To investigate movie selection under a familiar setting, we focused on the shared interaction with a single TV screen using (multiple) remote controls.

3.1   Collaborative Approaches to Movie Selection

To best support collaborative movie selection among three co-located users, we considered several key factors. First, we aimed to provide every user with a remote to lower the barrier to participating in the decision-making process and enable the continuous contribution of any user [18,33]. Moreover, literature shows that introducing coordination policies to coordinate decision-makers can minimize interpersonal conflicts [2,31,33,38]. Prior research indicates that the policies of enabling to vote for changes or providing different levels of control support continuous contribution best while also promoting social interaction and engagement [5,36]. Furthermore, having a key-user (for certain functions) can facilitate structured decision-making and avoid chaos [5,32]. Thus, we considered the approaches concerning *equal control possibilities* [15] and *limited/different control possibilities* [33] to define two initial types of collaborative movie selection. We combined them with the current standard of one user selecting a movie on behalf of the group (baseline) for comparison reasons. All concepts are in detail described below.

The **Consensual movie selection** is about all users having equal control possibilities [15] when it comes to movie selection. Thus decisions on what movie to watch can only be made jointly [31] based on democracy [32,33,38]. This means a movie can only be picked when every group member agrees and actively selects the movie to be watched (voted for it). **The Hierarchical movie selection** implies different levels of control possibilities [38]. This means that not every user has the possibility to perform every available task [15,34].

The **Autocratic movie selection** is added for completeness and reflects a single decision-maker [31] or a so-called master/key-user [32,38]. This concept is the current standard using a single remote to control the TV. Thus, the group relies on the key-user when it comes to making control decisions (restricted access for non-key-users) [15,34].

3.2 Choice of Interaction Concept and Interface Design

To enable controlling the TV by multiple remotes at once, we decided to explore this with absolute indirect touch-based (AIT) remote controls to ensure high usability [6] and workspace awareness [19]. These design choices are made independent of the collaborative concepts described above.

Absolute Indirect Touch-Based Remote Controls: A TV gets controlled over a distance (indirect interaction), usually via a single remote that provides a navigation grid (up, down, left, right, ok) to browse/navigate through content. However, promoting users to interact with the TV using absolutely indirect touch (AIT) with haptic marks for landmark-based target selection (for the demonstration of AIT see Fig. 1a) improves eyes-free tapping and accuracy [10]. It also improves usability and user experience (UX) [6], compared to standard, navigation-based remote controls [6]. Thus, we decided on AIT with a 3×3 landmark-based grid (see Fig. 1b) for the TV interaction. A grid position can be touched and the corresponding UI element gets highlighted, to ensure workspace awareness [19]. Pressing a grid position executes the underlying function/enters a menu.

User Interface for AIT Interaction: To map the 3×3 AIT grid of the remote control with the TV user interface (UI), we designed an app-based TV UI with the same dimensions. We took existing TV UIs (Apple TV, Android

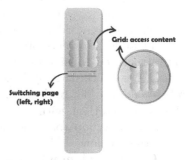

(a) Illustration of the mapping between the 3x3 remote grid and the TV UI. The user touches the right lower grid element which gets highlighted on the UI - represented in green.

(b) Key-user (left) and non-key-user remote (right). Both have the 3x3 AIT grid to access the content. The key-user remote in addition has two interactive dots below the grid to switch pages (picture by ruwido).

Fig. 1. Demonstration of the remotes which enable an active, indirect touch interaction (AIT) with the TV user interface.

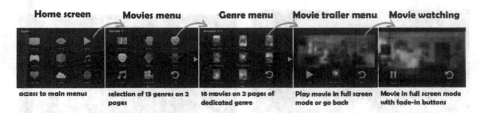

Fig. 2. Representation of the different menus and underlying layers of the movie library user interface (icons partly by Icons8.com).

TV) as inspiration to make the UI visually appealing and engaging. The UI provides access to TV channels, TV guides, an online movie library, games, an offline library, radio, favorites, the weather, and settings (see Fig. 2). Since the focus lies on collaborative movie selection, we provided the users with access to the 13 most prominent genres from the year 2022 [43] through the movie menu. Every genre had a variety of the 16 most prominent movies, derived from IMDB[1], demonstrated on two pages. With this extensive list, we ensured a large assortment of movies while best covering the preferences of each user. The available movies were static throughout the research presented in this paper. Once one movie got selected, the UI played the trailer and provided options to watch the full movie in full-screen mode or to go back to the movie overview page (for the UI layers see Fig. 2).

3.3 Implementation of the Collaborative Concepts to Movie Selection

We demonstrate how we implemented the three collaborative concepts using AIT-based remotes in combination with the dedicated TV UI. To provide every user with a remote and to ensure that individual TV interactions can be distinguished from one another, the backside of the remotes had different colors (white, gray, green). Additionally, we decided on two differently shaped AIT-based remotes (Fig. 1b) - a rectangular key-user remote and two circular non-key-user remotes. The reasons, therefore, are high-level TV functions (e.g., volume, on/off, paging/scrolling) which will induce chaos and confusion if performed by several users while having only one screen. Thus, to support a structured decision-making process [5] the key-user remote permits switching pages while the non-key-user remotes do not. To make the group aware of who is currently selecting/focusing on what element [8,19], user icons in the corresponding color of the remote are presented in the right lower corner of the UI. Additionally, all interactions are highlighted on the TV in the same color (see Fig. 3).

The Consensual movie selection provides every user with a dedicated remote control to vote for genres and movies. While all can vote, only the key-user-remote allows to enter the menu (collaboration was only active on a sub-menu level) and to switch pages. To establish workspace awareness in the UI,

---

[1] https://www.imdb.com/, last accessed 2022-12-23.

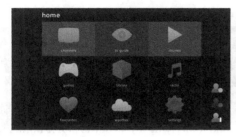

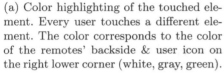

(a) Color highlighting of the touched element. Every user touches a different element. The color corresponds to the color of the remotes' backside & user icon on the right lower corner (white, gray, green).

(b) Left: Consensual control - votes are displayed as text in combination with colored user icons. Right: Hierarchical control - colored user icon gets visible when suggestions are placed.

Fig. 3. The developed user interface that can be controlled by three remotes simultaneously (icons partly by Icons8.com). (Color figure online)

every button/element gets highlighted with the current number of votes "x/3" including the colored user icon corresponding to the remote color (see Fig. 3b). A vote is made or retracted by pressing a grid element of the remote. The UI allows voting for an indefinite amount of elements. Once everyone votes for the same element (3/3), the underlying function gets executed automatically, and the voting of this particular element resets.

The Hierarchical movie selection demonstrates two different control levels: The key user, owning the key-user remote that can execute all functions directly (incl. paging), and the non-key-users having the non-key-user remotes who can indicate suggestions for movies. While the key-user can directly select any movie, independent of the suggestions provided, non-key-users are not able to start a movie. However, the suggestions enable users to express their interests more direct. Suggestions can be positioned/retracted by pressing a grid element on the remote. On the UI, the suggestions are visualized at the corresponding element by the user icon in the corresponding remote color (Fig. 3b).

The Autocratic movie selection provides only one user - the key-user with the key-user remote. The other two users do not have a remote available. The user interface stays in the standard mode without additional adjustments.

4   Research Question and Hypotheses

Literature outlines, that individuals' perceived social connectedness [2, 28], team performance (team cohesion [37]) and co-experience (social experience [3], user experience [44, 45]) are an indicator of social interaction in a group setting. Thus, we focused initially on investigating *What type of collaborative approach to movie selection supports social connectedness, team performance, and co-experience best?*

Since this is to our knowledge the first investigation of these concepts supporting collaborative movie selection using multiple remotes, we focus on users' impressions and experiences by gathering qualitative insights. We are particularly interested in how users perceive the decision-making process to achieve the goal of selecting a movie jointly. In addition, we want to investigate if there is a measurable effect on perceived social interaction. According to literature, enabling every user to interact with the system supports social connectedness and enhances the feeling of belongingness towards the group [5]. Thus, we speculate that both *Consensual & Hierarchical movie selection* support social connectedness best.

H1 *The perceived social connectedness in terms of belongingness, connectedness, affiliation, and companionship is higher for Consensual and Hierarchical movie selection compared to Autocratic movie selection (baseline).*

Secondly, promoting interaction with media content for all users at once enhances individuals' experience and enables exploring others' preferences and needs [5,38]. Thus we speculate that *Consensual & Hierarchical movie selection* generate a higher co-experience as well as team performance.

H2 *The perceived co-experience in terms of UX and social experience is higher for Consensual and Hierarchical movie selection compared to Autocratic movie selection (baseline).*

H3 *The perceived team performance in terms of team cohesion is higher for Consensual and Hierarchical movie selection compared to Autocratic movie selection (baseline).*

5   Comparative Study of the Collaborative Concepts

We conducted a mixed-subject experiment in a living room lab with groups of three to answer our research question and investigate the hypothesis.

5.1   Experimental Set-Up

Independent Variables: The concepts (*Consensual, Hierarchical, Autocratic*) were the within-subject variable and the type of control (key-user, non-key-user) was the between-subject variable. The between-subject variable was mapped to the users' sitting position: the key-remote user had the middle position, and the non-key-users were sitting at the key-users left and right sides to ensure verbal communication.

Dependent Variables/Measurements: To gather qualitative feedback, we conducted semi-structured group interviews after each concept round and at the end of the experiment. We particularly focused on how users experienced the decision-making process and what they liked/disliked. We assessed each user's perceived social connectedness in terms of connectedness, companionship,

Fig. 4. Experimental set-up in the living room lab.

and affiliation using the Social Connectedness Scale [28] and belongingness by applying the Inclusion of Community in Self-Scale [30]. We also measured the perceived team cohesion using the Team Performance questionnaire [37] and the social experience using the questions related to social experience from the *GAMEFULQUEST* [20]. For the User Experience (UX) (hedonic, pragmatic, and overall UX), we applied the short user experience questionnaire (UEQ-short) [41]. Moreover, we measured the decision-making time (in seconds) and used subjective ranking to investigate users' preferences among the concepts. After each concept round, we also asked about their interest in the movie and their personal preference for the selected movie. To control possible influences due to the TV UI and remote controls, we examined the evoked usability by employing the System Usability Scale (SUS) [7] after the trial round.

5.2 Participants

We recruited participants by convenience sampling in groups of three. Since watching a movie jointly is a typical family/friendship activity, we explicitly recruited groups of friends to reduce bias that might come from collaborating with strangers [29]. Overall, we recruited N = 30 participants (10 groups), 12 males, and 18 females, living in a country in Europe (blinded). Their age ranged from 22 to 42 ($M = 27.4$ years, $SD = 4.6$ years). All participants own a laptop and a smartphone while 20 out of 30 own also a TV. Besides, 20 out of 30 reported owning at least one subscription to an over-the-top media service (e.g., Netflix, Amazon Prime). When it comes to movie watching, 24 participants (80%) mentioned watching a movie at least several times a month, 2 (6.7%) do so only once a month, and 4 (13.3%) less than once a month. Additionally, 18 out of 30 watch movies together with others at least 5 out of 10 times. None of the participants had prior experience using an AIT-based remote.

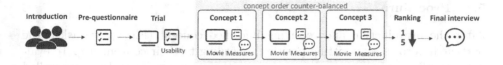

Fig. 5. Visual representation of the study procedure (Bootstrap icons).

Table 1. Experimental tasks of the trial round and the scenario description of the concept test rounds.

Trial tasks		Concept test round scenario
Task key-remote user	Please start the movie "Finding Nemo" from your favorites list in full-screen mode. And then go back to the home screen	Make it yourself comfortable. Try to feel at home and imagine it is Friday and you are having a cozy evening together. You want to chill, relax and therefore you want to watch a movie together. Your goal is to watch a movie everyone will enjoy watching. Therefore, you collaborate with the selection of the movie.
Task circular remote user (green)	Please start the movie "King Kong" from your favorites list in full-screen mode. And then go back to home screen	
Task circular remote user (gray)	Please start the Movie "Wonder Woman" from your favorites list in full-screen mode. And then go back to home screen	

5.3 Technical Set-Up

We implemented the TV UI as an Android TV app (Fig. 3) in Full HD (1920 × 1080) using Unity 3D. The remote controls have been produced by an industry partner (blinded). To enable the control of the TV UI simultaneously by three remotes, we used the NVidia SHIELD TV-Streaming Mediaplayer as a gateway to handle the Bluetooth input signals of multiple remotes. To generate a convenient TV-watching experience, we set up a living room in an empty lab with a couch, a small living room table, and a 49-inch smart TV (see Fig. 4).

5.4 Procedure

After the introduction and receiving informed consent (Fig. 5), we asked the participants to select a sitting position according to their convenience. To evaluate the effects of the concepts on social interaction, we aimed for a controlled social situation in our living room lab. Since we were interested in how the concepts evoke social interaction, we did not introduce the purpose of the concepts. We only presented a social scenario of having a movie night together with the goal of collaboratively selecting a movie everyone feels comfortable watching. We clarified that discussions are allowed and as many movie trailers as desired can be watched before making a final decision. Overall, the group had a maximum of 15 min per concept to decide on a movie. To avoid bias of the time constraints on the decision-making process, we did not share the time limit with participants. The experimenter reminded the group to find a movie in the next 5 min in case 10 min passed already. The groups had to select a different movie per concept to ensure ongoing decision-making. The experiment started with a trial round to familiarize each participant individually with the remotes and the TV UI (Table 1). After the trial task, we assessed the usability of the setup. This was followed by a counterbalanced set of the three concepts based on Latin square. For each concept, the group had to decide on a movie together (see Table 1). Exchanging or handing over remotes to others was forbidden. At the end of each concept condition, the participants filled out the questionnaires related to social connectedness, team cohesion, user experience, and social experience. In addition, the experimenter asked about their collaborative experiences and positive/negative impressions after each concept. The experiment concluded with a subjective ranking of the concepts and a semi-structured group interview about decision-making experiences and what they liked/disliked. The study was approved by the ethics committee of the researcher's institution and lasted on average an hour. Participants were not compensated for their participation.

6 Results

We report on concepts' effect on social connectedness, team cohesion, social experience, and UX. Due to technical problems, we had to omit the responses of one group resulting in a total of 27 data sets per concept. With the qualitative data, we conduct a thematic analysis based on inductive, free coding [22]. The quantitative data from the *Inclusion of Community in Self Scale* [30], the *Social Connectedness Scale* [28], team cohesion [37], social experience [20] use Likert scales. Due to the ordinal nature, we applied non-parametric Friedman tests to assess concept differences with Bonferroni-corrected Wilcoxon signed-rank tests for post-hoc comparisons. To investigate differences in time efficiency (normally distributed data assessed by Kolmogorov-Smirnov tests), we conducted a one-way repeated-measures ANOVA.

General: Selection Process and Usability. The usability score, as assessed after the trial task, resulted in an average score of 68.5, which indicates OK usability [7]. Besides, all groups could make a decision within the time limit of 15 min. The ANOVA revealed (sphericity not violated - Mauchly's test - $\chi^2(2) = 3.35, p = .187$) that there is a significant effect of the concepts on movie selection time, $F(1,8) = 87.57, p < .001, \eta^2 = .916$, while Bonferroni-corrected post-hoc tests did not unveil further insights. The concepts equally allowed participants to select a movie of interest ($\chi^2(2) = 1.605, p = .448$), indicated by a median score of $Mdn = 2$ for *Consensual & Hierarchical control* and $Mdn = 3$ for *Autocratic control* (most interesting $= 1$; least interesting $= 7$). Participants also reported that under all concepts they selected the movie considering their own preferences ($\chi^2(2) = 0.9, p = .956$). The *Consensual control* ($Mdn = 2$) lets users select a movie slightly more related to individual preferences, compared to *Hierarchical & Autocratic control* ($Mdn = 3$) (most preferred $= 1$; least preferred $= 7$).

6.1   Social Connectedness - H1

Group Belongingness: A Friedman test outlines no significant effect of the concepts on users' perceived group belongingness ($\chi^2(2) = 0.026, p = .987$, Fig. 6a). The median belongingness score is highest for *Consensual control* ($Mdn = e$) followed by *Hierarchical & Autocratic control* ($Mdn = d$) which indicates that all concepts let users belong to one another positively (original scale ranges from a $=$ no group belongingness to g $=$ max belongingness).

Connectedness: According to a Friedman test (Fig. 6d), the concepts do not evoke a significantly different perception of connectedness ($\chi^2(2) = 2.95, p = .228$). The media perceived connectedness lies above average for all three concepts, *Consensual control* ($Mdn = 5$), *Autocratic control* ($Mdn = 4.75$), and *Hierarchical control* ($Mdn = 5$).

Affiliation: A Friedman test shows no significant effect of the concepts on affiliation ($\chi^2(2) = 3.81, p = .149$; Fig. 6c). Median scores show an above average evoked affiliation for all concepts, *Consensual control* ($Mdn = 5$), *Autocratic control* ($Mdn = 4.67$), *Hierarchical control* ($Mdn = 4.67$).

Companionship: The companionship is not significantly different among the concepts, as outlined by a Friedman test ($\chi^2(2) = 0.03, p = .985$, Fig. 6b). The median companionship lies above average ($Mdn = 5$) for *Consensual, Hierarchical* as well as *Autocratic control.*

Taken together, all concepts evoke a high social connectedness, indicated by an above-average belongingness, companionship, affiliation, and connectedness rating. Since the concepts did not evoke significant differences in any of the social connectedness factors, we reject *H1*.

6.2   Co-Experience - H2

Social Experience: The evoked social experience is highest for *Consensual control* ($Mdn = 2.5$), followed by *Autocratic control* ($Mdn = 2.88$), and *Hierarchical control* ($Mdn = 3$) (Fig. 8a). However, there is no significant difference between the concepts as outlined by a Friedman test ($\chi^2(2) = 2.3, p = .317$).

Belongingness $\chi 2\ (2) = 0.026,\ p = .987$

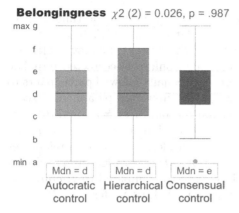

(a) Distribution of the measured group belongingness of each concept [30]. (g=max belongingness, a = no group belongingness)

Companionship $\chi 2\ (2) = 0.03,\ p = .985$

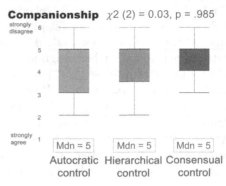

(b) Distribution of the measured companionship of each concept [28]. Q: Even around people I know, I don't feel that I really belong.

Affiliation $\chi 2\ (2) = 3.81,\ p = .149$

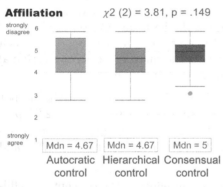

(c) Distribution of the average measured affiliation of each concept [28]. Q1: I don't feel I participate with anyone or any group; Q2: I have no sense of togetherness with my peers.; Q3: Even among my peers, there is no sense of brother/sisterhood.

Connectedness $\chi 2\ (2) = 2.95,\ p = .228$

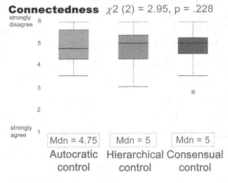

(d) Distribution of the average measured connectedness of each concept [28]. Q1: I feel so distant from the other people; Q2: I feel disconnected from the world around me; Q3: I don't feel related to anyone; Q4: I catch myself losing all sense of connectedness.

Fig. 6. Friedman tests for social connectedness measurements across the different collaborative movie selection concepts (significant at $p < .05$.)

User Experience: The overall UX (Fig. 7) is highest for *Consensual* (good), followed by *Hierarchical* (above average) and *Autocratic control* (below average). Our results indicate, that all concepts are equally practical, simple, and pleasant - indicated by an above-average score of pragmatic quality. Concerning hedonic quality (satisfactory, creative, original), *Consensual control* scored best (excellent), followed by *Hierarchical control* (good), and *Autocratic control* (bad). A Friedman test outlines a significant effect of the three concepts on perceived hedonic quality ($\chi^2(2) = 16.42, p < .001$). Post-hoc comparisons show a significantly lower hedonic quality for *Autocratic* compared to *Consensual control* ($Z = -3.81, p < .001$) and *Hierarchical control* ($Z = -2.93, p = .01$). An effect

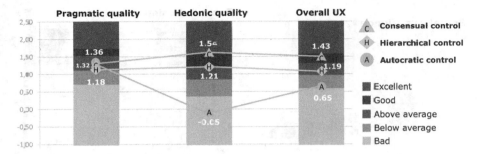

Fig. 7. The mean values of the measured pragmatic (left) & hedonic quality (middle), as well as the overall UX (right) score per concept The colors of the bars represent the UX scale, ranging from excellent (light green) to bad (light blue). The scale in general ranges from -3 (horribly bad UX) to +3 (extremely good UX), while values above 0.8 represent a positive evaluation [41]. (Color figure online)

of the concepts on pragmatic quality ($\chi^2(2) = 0.74, p = .964$) and overall UX ($\chi^2(2) = 5.15, p = .076$) was not observed.

Taken together, the *Hierarchical & Consensual concept* evoke a significantly higher hedonic quality which indicates high originality, creativity, and satisfaction. However, the pragmatic quality and overall UX did not result in differences among the concepts. Furthermore, all concepts evoke an equally high social experience. This leads us to reject *H2*.

6.3   Team Performance - H3

Team Cohesion: Our insights do not show a significant effect on team cohesion ($\chi^2(2) = 1.09, p = .850$). Nonetheless, all three concepts evoke a high team cohesion with a median score of $Mdn = 6$ (Fig. 8b). All concepts are promoting high perceived team cohesion with no observed differences. Thus, we also reject *H3*.

6.4   Qualitative Insights

Subjective Ranking: A Friedman test outlines a statistically significant order of preference for the concepts ($\chi_2(2) = 8.3, p = .016$). Post-hoc comparisons show significantly higher preferences for *Consensual* compared to *Hierarchical control* ($Z = 2.722, p = .019$). There is also a significantly higher preference for *Consensual* compared to *Autocratic control* ($Z = 2.177, p = .029$). Figure 9 outlines the ranking per concept with a median score of 1 for *Consensual*, and a media score of 2 for both *Hierarchical & Autocratic control*.

Qualitative Feedback from Interviews: We conducted a thematic analysis with the responses to the open-ended questions concerning each concept individually and the final interview. Sentences were iteratively assigned to themes and themes were clustered in overarching groups. The overview of the final themes

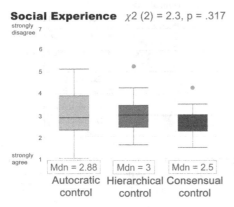

Social Experience $\chi 2\,(2) = 2.3,\ p = .317$

(a) Distribution of the measured Social Experience [20] - average score of the eight questions.

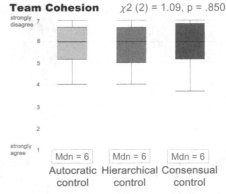

Team Cohesion $\chi 2\,(2) = 1.09,\ p = .850$

(b) Distribution of the average measured Team Cohesion [37] per concept. Q1: Dealing with the members of the team often left me feeling irritated and frustrated. Q2: I had unpleasant experiences with the team. Q3: Negative feelings between me and the team tended to pull us apart.

Fig. 8. Perceived social experience and team cohesion across the three concepts with pairwise comparisons. Friedman tests are significant at $p < .05$.

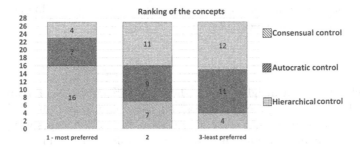

Fig. 9. The subjective ranking of the collaborative control concepts.

of the thematic analysis, and how they relate to one another, particularly to the three concepts can be found in Fig. 10.

The Autocratic movie selection provides the traditional, most *familiar way* of decision-making. Users perceive it as *efficient* and particularly *suitable for smaller groups*. However, it can happen that the *key-user performs actions without prior group discussion* or actions that are not in line with the discussion which is perceived as *exclusion* (e.g., *"[Key user] was just doing whatever he wanted"*, P#4.2; *"It was not clear to me if the [Key user] just want to check it or if it was of interest"*, P#3.1). It introduces unique social dynamics particularly *power roles* and *dependency* - primarily due to one remote only which *prevents interventions and impact on the final decision* by others. Besides, those users not in charge over the remote mentioned that the autocratic way of selecting a movie *encourages them to talk* with one another in order to express their wishes and interests which feels very *social*. However, particularly for introverts, it provides

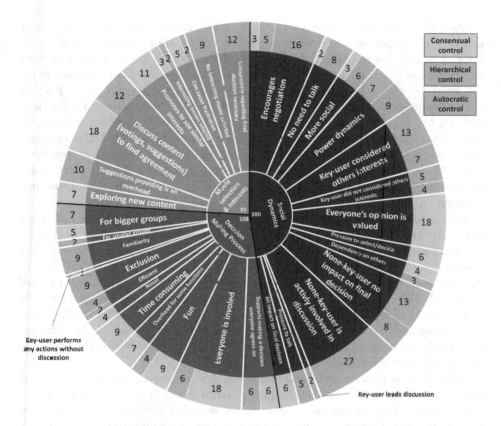

Fig. 10. Representation of the qualitative analysis. The inner circle shows the overarching groups. The middle circle presents the sub-groups of the overarching groups while the outer circle shows to which concept(s) the sub-groups are connected. The numbers refer to the total amount of mentions.

pressure to talk (e.g., *"It gives me more pressure because you got to talk with each other"*, P#9.2). Nevertheless, a few participants report that the key user *takes on the lead of discussions* and tries as best as possible to *consider others' interests* (e.g., *"[Key user] was more attentive to us"*, P#9.3). However, in some groups, the key-user did *not consider others' interests* at all (e.g., *"It did not feel [the Key user] was selecting the movie for and with us"*, P#4.3). Concerning the movie selection and interests, mainly those not in control reported that they had to make a *compromise* regarding the movie choice (e.g., *"Someone will give up their interests"*, P#10.3). This, according to user feedback, guides to a final movie selection that is most likely *not in line with everyone's interest* which can cause *frustration* (e.g., *"We felt OK watching it but no one had a strong feeling for that movie"*, P#3.2; *"It's a movie I least preferred to watch"*, P#10.3).

The Hierarchical movie selection is a *fun* (e.g., *"That is fun for me"*, P#9.3) and *efficient* way to make decisions together. Besides, users point out the fact that *everyone is involved* and can express themselves which is perceived as *active participation in the discussions* (e.g., *"I am allowed to have some opinions"*, P#2.1). Participants highlight that providing *suggestions helps in making decisions together*, and supports the *discussion around the final selection* (e.g., *"It helps because you can see what other people do and want to see"*, P#8.2) with a higher chance of *selecting a movie that everyone* is interested in. Particularly for the key-user, it is easy to check others' interests (e.g., *"I saw everyone's opinions"*, P#9.1). However, a few participants mentioned that the key-user nevertheless prioritized their own interests or *ignored the suggestions* provided (e.g., *"It is more like [the key user] makes the choice"*, P#6.2). Thus, some perceived the process of providing *suggestions as an overhead* to verbal communication and also stopped providing suggestions (e.g., *"I forgot about the remote because I could just talk and look"*, P#1.2). Others outline that they rather do not want a remote especially when the remote *does not have a direct impact on the final decision* (since it's only a suggestion) (e.g., *"They are useless to me since I don't have direct control"*, P#1.3). However, others like the possibility to position movie suggestions because they can express themselves *without the need to actively talk*/interrupt ongoing conversations or make a final decision (e.g., *"I can show my opinion but I don't need to make the final decision"*, P#9.2; *"I can give my opinion even if I don't have the courage to talk"*, P#4.3). The Hierarchical concept is seen particularly *suitable for bigger groups* where not everyone can be involved in verbal discussions.

The Consensual movie selection is a *fun* and *novel* way to decide on a movie together, even though it is more *time-consuming* until a decision is made. Due to consensual voting, users describe it as a fair decision-making process where *everyone is involved*, their *opinion is valued equally* and votes have an equal *impact on the final decision* (e.g., *"My opinions are actually being taken into consideration"*, P#2.3; *"Everyone's opinion is equally important"*, P#10.3). Besides, participants outline that the Consensual concept supports outlining similar interests and particularly promotes the *discussion of diverse interests* (e.g., *"We talk a lot more about the movies"*, P#8.2; *"It is nice to see who selected what"*, P#2.1). The voting also enables users to *explore new content together* which in turn provides a higher chance to *select a movie that everyone enjoys watching* (e.g., *"All three having to choose so we choose on a movie we really want to watch"*, P#8.2). Even though it was not experienced during the study, participants fear that too diverse interests can lead to *frustration* while too dominant personalities involved can impose pressure to vote for particular movies in order to proceed (e.g., *"If people are divided then it is difficult"*, P#2.1; *"It will somehow force me if there is an option and the others already select it"*, P#2.2). Both aspects thus can introduce a *dependency on other users*.

7   Discussion

In this paper, we presented how to design for collaborative movie selection among three co-located users by providing each with a remote control in order to enhance social interaction. We evaluated the multi-remote concepts of *Hierarchical control* and *Consensual control* in a controlled lab experiment against the baseline of the traditional *Autocratic* single-remote concept. Results show high social connectedness, team performance, and co-experience for all concepts. Qualitative insights outline that users prefer owning a dedicated remote because it promotes participation and thus creates a novel collaborative decision-making experience. In this section, we discuss the implications of our design decisions and results toward promoting social interaction among co-located users in the living room.

Implications of the Collaborative Approaches to Movie Selection on Social Connectedness, Team Performance and Co-experience: Despite being unable to validate our initial speculations, our findings indicate that various forms of collaborative movie selection promote social connectedness, well-being [40], and a sense of belonging among users [28]. Previous research has outlined the importance of social connectedness and co-experience in group decision-making processes [5,29,36]. In our study, we found that all concepts of collaborative movie selection evoked a high level of social connectedness, team cohesion, and co-experience, which ultimately supports well-being [40] and establishes a social bond among group members [28,46].

In particular, our study found that *Autocratic control* had a high level of social connectedness and co-experience, which can be attributed to the familiarity [48] of the concept and the amount of required verbal communication [5,14]. Despite the *Autocratic control* concept supporting a more efficient selection process [32], qualitative insights outline that it may not always result in a satisfying decision for all group members. Besides, it induces power dynamics and is also the user's least preferred choice. Promoting consensual decision-making or enabling users to provide movie recommendations under the hierarchical approach were found to promote the exploration of movie offerings because they provided the opportunity for group members to see the interests of others. This particularly stimulated richer, goal-related discussions. Additionally, both concepts support involvement, are perceived as fair, and thus provide a higher chance of picking a movie that everyone enjoys watching. The downside of *Consensual control*, however, relates to the fear of causing frustration [38] due to diverse interests that can hinder final decision-making. Yet, our research highlights that promoting direct involvement of every group member supports user experience and is a preferred solution when it comes to movie selection in the home.

Therefore, it is crucial for the design of future collaborative, interactive media systems to consider how users can feel empowered and included in the decision-making process, even if their input may not always directly influence the final decision. For example, providing opportunities for users to recommend movies or express their preferences can make them feel heard and valued, which can in turn enhance their overall experience. Additionally, providing clear guidance on how the collaborative decision-making process works and what role each user plays can promote a sense of fairness and inclusion among group members. Hence, the choice of the interaction mechanism and the design of the user interface [8], particularly the level of workspace awareness [19] have a crucial impact on the collaborative experience and outcome of the decision-making process. In conclusion, our study highlights the importance of understanding the role of user participation and empowerment in the design of collaborative media systems. While the specific approaches to control may vary, it is crucial to consider how users can feel included – beyond initiating conversations – and valued in the decision-making process to ultimately enhance social interaction and co-experience.

In our study, we introduced the concept of active-indirect-touch (AIT) TV interaction (details in Sect. 3.2) as an approach to enable collaborative movie selection. Our results showed that it is possible to apply this interaction concept to establish highly perceived social connectedness, team performance, and co-experience in group decision-making. Important to note is that we did not investigate the consequence of the interaction modality on social interaction. Consequently, we see the comparison of various ways of collaborative movie selection (e.g., voting smartphone app) as an interesting aspect of future research. Furthermore, users were only able to experience the concepts for a limited period of time under highly controlled circumstances. Thus a longitudinal study in the field is required to understand the long-term effects of the experience evoked and to increase the external validity of the diverse concepts of collaborative movie selection. Since the dynamics of a group changes with five or more users [21] due to social loafing (individuals reduce input because of e.g., a lack of responsibility or limited individual contributions [35]), our insights are limited to small group sizes of up to three users. We also need to acknowledge that our study was limited to Mid-European friends collaborating, hence it would be interesting to study diverse, social group settings, such as different types of relationships and different cultural backgrounds. Additionally, the personality of individuals may influence social interaction [42]. Therefore, future research is needed to understand how different personality types affect social connectedness and co-experience when selecting a movie together. Overall, our study provides valuable insights into the design of collaborative, interactive media systems, but further research is needed to understand long-term effects on social interaction and co-experience.

8   Conclusion

In this paper, we explored opportunities to design for a higher level of perceived social connectedness, team performance, and co-experience among co-located users when selecting a movie together on the TV. We, therefore, designed three collaborative approaches to movie selection (*Autocratic, Hierarchical, Consensual*) based on the distribution of control among users by providing several remote controls. Through an experimental assessment of these concepts in a living room lab environment in groups of three users, we looked into whether and how the type of collaborative concept has an influence on individuals' perceived social connectedness (H1), co-experience (H2), and team performance (H3). We found that the type of collaborative concept has no objective influence on any of the measurements performed (H1–H3). More precisely, our insights indicate that all collaborative approaches to movie selection, *Autocratic, Hierarchical*, and *Consensual*, evoke a high social connectedness, team performance, and co-experience, without quantitative significant difference observed. However, qualitative results show that users prefer owning a dedicated remote and being able to interact actively with the TV (*Hierarchical, Consensual*). The main reasons, therefore, refer to the support of fairness and having the opportunity to contribute towards the final movie selection. Furthermore, users perceive particularly *Consensual* movie selection as the possibility to find a movie everyone really enjoys watching. With this work, we contribute design opportunities on how to distribute control over a TV among co-located people, how they impact social collaboration and individuals' experience, and discuss aspects to support collaborative movie selection in future homes.

References

1. Ah Kun, L.M., Marsden, G.: Co-present photo sharing on mobile devices. In: Proceedings of the 9th International Conference on Human Computer Interaction with Mobile Devices and Services (MobileHCI 2007), New York, NY, USA, pp. 277–284. Association for Computing Machinery (2007). https://doi.org/10.1145/1377999.1378019

2. Ammarapala, V., Luxhøj, J.T.: A collaborative multi-criteria decision making technique for risk factor prioritization. J. Risk Res. **10**(4), 465–485 (2007). https://doi.org/10.1080/13669870701421563

3. Batterbee, K.: Defining co-experience. In: Proceedings of the 2003 International Conference on Designing Pleasurable Products and Interfaces (DPPI 2003), New York, NY, USA, pp. 109–113. Association for Computing Machinery (2003). https://doi.org/10.1145/782896.782923

4. Berger, M.: Social control interaction framework: design to technically support a group of users in making control decisions together. In: Extended Abstracts of the 2022 CHI Conference on Human Factors in Computing Systems (CHI EA 2022), New York, NY, USA, pp. 1–6. Association for Computing Machinery (2022). https://doi.org/10.1145/3491101.3503802

5. Berger, M., Barati, B., Pfleging, B., Bernhaupt, R.: Design for social control of shared media: a comparative study of five concepts. In: Nordic Human-Computer Interaction Conference (NordiCHI 2022), pp. 1–13, New York, NY, USA. Association for Computing Machinery (2022). https://doi.org/10.1145/3546155.3546694, Article 14

6. Bernhaupt, R., Drouet, D., Pirker, M.: Absolute indirect touch interaction: impact of haptic marks and animated visual feedback on usability and user experience. In: Bogdan, C., Kuusinen, K., Lárusdóttir, M.K., Palanque, P., Winckler, M. (eds.) HCSE 2018. LNCS, vol. 11262, pp. 251–269. Springer, Cham (2019). https://doi.org/10.1007/978-3-030-05909-5_15

7. Brook, J.: SUS: a "Quick and Dirty" usability scale. In: Jordan, P.W., Thomas, B., McClelland, I.L., Weerdmeester, B. (eds.) Usability Evaluation in Industry, pp. 189–194. Taylor & Francis, London (1996)

8. Cesar, P., Geerts, D.: Social interaction design for online video and television. In: Nakatsu, R., Rauterberg, M., Ciancarini, P. (eds.) Handbook of Digital Games and Entertainment Technologies, pp. 1157–1193. Springer, Singapore (2017). https://doi.org/10.1007/978-981-4560-50-4_39

9. Chuang, Y., Chen, L. L., Lee, Y.H.: Envisioning a smart home that can learn and negotiate the needs of multiple users. In: Adjunct Proceedings of the 2015

ACM International Joint Conference on Pervasive and Ubiquitous Computing and Proceedings of the 2015 ACM International Symposium on Wearable Computers (UbiComp/ISWC'15 Adjunct), New York, NY, USA, pp. 237–240. Association for Computing Machinery (2015). https://doi.org/10.1145/2800835.2800934

10. Corsten, C., Cherek, C., Karrer, T., Borchers, J.: HaptiCase: back-of-device tactile landmarks for eyes-free absolute indirect touch. In: Proceedings of the 33rd Annual ACM Conference on Human Factors in Computing Systems (CHI '15), New York, NY, USA, pp. 2171–2180. Association for Computing Machinery (2015). https://doi.org/10.1145/2702123.2702277

11. Dourish, P., Bellotti, V.: Awareness and coordination in shared workspaces. In: Proceedings of the 1992 ACM Conference on Computer-Supported Cooperative Work (Toronto, Ontario, Canada) (CSCW 1992), New York, NY, USA, pp. 107–114. Association for Computing Machinery (1992). https://doi.org/10.1145/143457.143468

12. Eurostat.   https://ec.europa.eu/eurostat/statistics-explained/index.php?title=Household_composition_statistics. Accessed 21 Jan 2023

13. Ericsson Consumer Lab, TV and Media 2017. https://www.ericsson.com/4ac627/assets/local/reports-papers/consumerlab/reports/2017/tv-media-2017-consumer-and-industry-insight-report.pdf. Accessed 22 Jan 2023

14. Fischer, U., Mosier, K.: The impact of communication delay and medium on team performance and communication in distributed teams. In: Proceedings of the Human Factors and Ergonomics Society Annual Meeting, vol. 58, no. 1, pp. 115–119 (2014). https://doi.org/10.1177/1541931214581025

15. Flemisch, F., Heesen, M., Hesse, T., Kelsch, J., Schieben, A., Beller, J.: Towards a dynamic balance between humans and automation: authority, ability, responsibility and control in shared and cooperative control situations. Cogn. Technol. Work **14**, 3–18 (2012). https://doi.org/10.1007/s10111-011-0191-6

16. Fogli, D., Lanzilotti, R., Piccinno, A., Tosi, P.: Am I@Home: a game-based collaborative system for smart home configuration. In: Proceedings of the International Working Conference on Advanced Visual Interfaces (AVI 2016), New York, NY, USA, pp. 308–309. Association for Computing Machinery (2016). https://doi.org/10.1145/2909132.2926083

17. Garg, R., Cui, H.: Social contexts, agency, and conflicts: exploring critical aspects of design for future smart home technologies. ACM Trans. Comput.-Hum. Interact. **29**(2) (2022). https://doi.org/10.1145/3485058

18. Grudin, J.: Computer-supported cooperative work: history and focus. Computer **27**(5), 19–26 (1994). https://doi.org/10.1109/2.291294

19. Gutwin, C., Greenberg, S.: A descriptive framework of workspace awareness for real-time groupware. Comput. Supp. Cooperat. Work (CSCW) **11**(3), 411–446 (2002). https://doi.org/10.1023/A:1021271517844

20. Hoegberg, J., Hamari, J., Wästlund, E.: Gameful experience questionnaire (GAMEFULQUEST): an instrument for measuring the perceived gamefulness of system use. User Model. User-Adap. Inter. **29**(3), 619–660 (2019). https://doi.org/10.1007/s11257-019-09223-w

21. Isaac, M.R., Walker, J.M.: Group size effects in public goods provision: the voluntary contributions mechanism. Q. J. Econ. **103**(1), 179–199 (1988). https://doi.org/10.2307/1882648

22. Joffe, H., Yardley, L.: Content and thematic analysis. In: Marks, D.F., Yardley, L. (eds.) Research Methods for Clinical and Health Psychology, pp. 56–68. SAGE Publications, London (2004). https://doi.org/10.4135/9781849209793

23. Kawsar, F., Brush, A.J.B.: Home computing unplugged: why, where and when people use different connected devices at home. In: Proceedings of the 2013 ACM International Joint Conference on Pervasive and Ubiquitous Computing (UbiComp 2013), New York, NY, USA, pp. 627–636. Association for Computing Machinery (2013). https://doi.org/10.1145/2493432.2493494

24. Kittur, A., Suh, B., Pendleton, B.A., Chi, E.H.: He says, she says: conflict and coordination in Wikipedia. In: Proceedings of the SIGCHI Conference on Human Factors in Computing Systems (CHI 2007), New York, NY, USA, pp. 453–462. Association for Computing Machinery (2007). https://doi.org/10.1145/1240624.1240698

25. Kim, H.S., Kim, M.: Viewing sports online together? Psychological consequences on social live streaming service usage. Sport Manag. Rev. **23**(5), 869–882 (2020). https://doi.org/10.1016/j.smr.2019.12.007

26. Koch, M., Gross, T.: Computer-supported cooperative work - concepts and trends, In: Feltz, F., Otjacques, B., Oberweis, A., Poussing, N. (ed.) AIM 2006 - Information Systems and Collaboration: State of the Art and Perspectives, Best Papers of the 11th International Conference of the Association Information and Management (AIM), pp. 165–172. Gesellschaft für Informatik e.V., Bonn (2006). https://dl.gi.de/20.500.12116/23754

27. Kraemer, M. J., Lyngs, U., Webb, H., Flechais, I.: Further exploring communal technology use in smart homes: social expectations. In: Extended Abstracts of the 2020 CHI Conference on Human Factors in Computing Systems (CHI EA 2020), New York, NY, USA, pp. 1–7. Association for Computing Machinery (2020). https://doi.org/10.1145/3334480.3382972

28. Lee, R., Robbins, S.: Measuring belongingness: the social connectedness and the social assurance scales. J. Couns. Psychol. **42**(2), 232–241 (1995). https://doi.org/10.1037/0022-0167.42.2.232

29. Liu, S., Smith, B.A., Vaish, R., Monroy-Hernández, A.: Understanding the role of context in creating enjoyable co-located interactions. Proc. ACM Hum.-Comput. Interact. **6**(CSCW1), 1–26 (2022). https://doi.org/10.1145/3512978

30. Mashek, D., Cannaday, L.W., Tangney, J.P.: Inclusion of community in self scale: a single-item pictorial measure of community connectedness. J. Community Psychol. **35**(2), 257–275 (2007). https://doi.org/10.1002/jcop.20146

31. Marakas, G.M.: Decision Support Systems in the 21st Century, 1st edn. Prentice Hall, Upper Saddle River (1998)

32. McGill, M., Williamson, J., Brewster, S.A.: How to lose friends & alienate people: sharing control of a single-user TV system. In: Proceedings of the ACM International Conference on Interactive Experiences for TV and Online Video (TVX 2014), New York, NY, USA, pp. 147–154. Association for Computing Machinery (2014). https://doi.org/10.1145/2602299.2602318

33. Morris, M.R., Ryall, K., Shen, C., Forlines, C., Vernier, F.: Beyond "social protocols": multi-user coordination policies for co-located groupware. In: Proceedings of the 2004 ACM conference on Computer supported cooperative work (CSCW 2004), New York, NY, USA, pp. 262–265. Association for Computing Machinery (2004). https://doi.org/10.1145/1031607.1031648

34. Neale, D.C., Carroll, J.M., Rosson, M.B.: Evaluating computer-supported cooperative work: models and frameworks. In: Proceedings of the 2004 ACM Conference on Computer Supported Cooperative Work (CSCW 2004), New York, NY, USA, pp. 112–121, Association for Computing Machinery (2004). DOI: https://doi.org/10.1145/1031607.1031626

35. North, A.C., Linley, P.A., Hargreaves, D.J.: Social loafing in a co-operative classroom task. J. Educ. Psychol. **20**(4), 389–392 (2000). https://doi.org/10.1080/01443410020016635
36. O'Hara, K., Lipson, M., Jansen, M., Unger, A., Jeffries, H., Macer, P.: Jukola: democratic music choice in a public space. In: Proceedings of the 5th Conference on Designing Interactive Systems: Processes, Practices, Methods, and Techniques (DIS 2004), New York, NY, USA, pp. 145–154. Association for Computing Machinery (2004). https://doi.org/10.1145/1013115.1013136
37. Paul, R., Drake, J.R., Liang, H.: Global virtual team performance: the effect of coordination effectiveness, trust, and team cohesion. IEEE Trans. Prof. Commun. **59**(3), 186–202 (2016). https://doi.org/10.1109/TPC.2016.2583319
38. Plaumann, K., Lehr, D., Rukzio, E.: Who has the force? Solving conflicts for multi user mid-air gestures for TVs. In: Proceedings of the ACM International Conference on Interactive Experiences for TV and Online Video (TVX 2016), New York, NY, USA, pp. 25–29. Association for Computing Machinery (2016). https://doi.org/10.1145/2932206.2932208
39. Rama, J., Bishop, J.: A survey and comparison of CSCW groupware applications. In: Proceedings of the 2006 Annual Research Conference of the South African Institute of Computer Scientists and Information Technologists on IT Research in Developing Countries (SAICSIT 2006), pp. 198–205. South African Institute for Computer Scientists and Information Technologists, ZAF (2006) 10.1145/1216262.1216284
40. Rock, K.S.: Social support versus companionship: effects on life stress, loneliness, and evaluations by others. J. Pers. Soc. Psychol. **52**(6), 1132–1147 (1987). https://doi.org/10.1037/0022-3514.52.6.1132
41. Schrepp, M., Hinderks, A., Thomaschewski, J.: Design and evaluation of a short version of the user experience questionnaire (UEQ-S). Int. J. Interact. Multimedia Artif. Intell. **4**(6), 103–108 (2017). https://doi.org/10.9781/ijimai.2017.09.001
42. Santos, R., Marreiros, G., Ramos, C., Neves, J., Bulas-Cruz, J.: Personality, emotion, and mood in agent-based group decision making. IEEE Intell. Syst. **26**(06), 58–66 (2011)
43. The Numbers: Market Share for Each Genre in 2022. https://www.the-numbers.com/market/2022/genres. Accessed 21 Mar 2023
44. Van Der Linden, J., Amadieu, F., Vayre, E., Van De Leemput, C.: User experience and social influence: a new perspective for UX theory. In: Marcus, A., Wang, W. (eds.) HCII 2019. LNCS, vol. 11583, pp. 98–112. Springer, Cham (2019). https://doi.org/10.1007/978-3-030-23570-3_9
45. Väänänen-Vainio-Mattila, K., Wäljas, M., Ojala, J., Segerstahl, K.: Identifying drivers and hindrances of social user experience in web services. In: Proceedings of the SIGCHI Conference on Human Factors in Computing Systems (CHI 2010), New York, NY, USA, pp. 2499–2502. Association for Computing Machinery (2010). https://doi.org/10.1145/1753326.1753704
46. Wongm, M.M., Csíkszentmihályi, M.: Affiliation motivation and daily experience: some issues on gender differences. J. Pers. Soc. Psychol. **60**, 154–164 (1991)
47. Zheng, S., Apthorpe, N., Chetty, M., Feamster, N.: User perceptions of smart home IoT privacy. Proc. ACM Hum.-Comput. Interact. **60**(CSCW) (2018). https://doi.org/10.1145/3274469
48. Zajonc, R.B.: Mere exposure: a gateway to the subliminal. Curr. Dir. Psychol. Sci. **10**(6), 224–228 (2001). https://doi.org/10.1111/1467-8721.00154

Introducing Sharemote: A Tangible Interface for Collaborative TV Control

Melanie Berger[1,2]([⊠]) [iD], Rutger Verstegen[1] [iD], Harm van Essen[1] [iD],
and Regina Bernhaupt[1,2] [iD]

[1] Eindhoven University of Technology, Eindhoven, The Netherlands
{m.berger,h.a.v.essen,r.bernhaupt}@tue.nl, r.verstegen@student.tue.nl
[2] ruwido austria GmbH, Neumarkt, Austria

Abstract. The TV is among the most favored devices to consume media together with others in shared living spaces. Yet, the interaction with a TV is still limited to one user. This likely causes frustration or leads to long decision-making processes which in turn can reduce belongingness and affiliation with one another and impact the overall TV-watching experience negatively. To overcome this, we investigate opportunities in designing tangible interfaces to support collaborative movie selection among co-located users. Therefore, we present Sharemote - a concept that provides physical genre-based tokens to explore group interests and to narrow down possible movies to select. We evaluated the effect of Sharemote on perceived social interaction in terms of social connectedness, team performance, and co-experience through a controlled mixed-subject lab experiment in groups of three (N = 30). Results show that providing genre-based tokens significantly promotes the overall user experience of jointly selecting a movie and is the users' preferred choice. Although Sharemote doesn't lead to a measurable increase in social connectedness and team performance compared to the current standard in homes using a single remote, it supports the investigation of shared interests and thus helps to select a movie everyone enjoys watching. With this work, we contribute toward the design of a novel entertainment experience and discuss the value of tangibles to promote collaborative movie selection.

Keywords: Collaborative Movie Selection · Tangible Interaction · Shared Control · Social Connectedness · Co-Experience

1 Introduction

The living room is a recreational area and the central place for social activities at home [8]. Statistics show that two-thirds of prime-time television is watched together [31]. Prevailing, watching movies jointly generates a shared experience that can enhance social engagement [36]. While the act of watching TV with others is considered a social activity, the selection of content, particularly the control of the TV, is often limited to one person at a time [5]. This

---

M. Berger and R. Verstegen—Contributed equally to this work.

J. Abdelnour Nocera et al. (Eds.): INTERACT 2023, LNCS 14144, pp. 393–416, 2023.
https://doi.org/10.1007/978-3-031-42286-7_21

can lead to conflicts and power struggles over movie selection [36], resulting in a choice that not everyone is satisfied with. Furthermore, limiting individuals from participating in the decision-making process can also cause conflicts and frustration [13], potentially harming the social bond among users [44]. To overcome this, research suggests designing interactive systems for co-located users in a way to promote collaboration by providing control over functions to various users at once (e.g., [6, 36, 37, 41]). Most prominent suggestions refer to designing TV interactions by enabling voting for elements [36, 37] or providing different levels of access to functions [18, 37]. Democratically selecting a movie notably encourages communication, and is also entertaining and fun. However, it induces dependency on others and it is less efficient [36], thus users fear it generates even more conflicts [41], particularly when used on a longer term. While different levels of access enable the involvement of everyone, it introduces power games and chaos [41]. Taken together, distributing or sharing control over the TV is technically feasible, and provides the opportunity to let everyone participate. However, previous research has not yet identified an overall successful approach for enhancing collaborative movie selection while also minimizing the risk of conflicts and promoting a high social bond among users.

To address this research gap, we see designing tangible interfaces - "physical objects to represent and manipulate digital data" [46] as a practicable solution since tangible interfaces have the potential to encourage discussion and foster collaboration in a subtle way [46]. Therefore, in this paper, we explore collaborative movie selection strategies through tangible interfaces in order to enhance the TV-watching experience and social interaction - particularly belongingness, affiliation, companionship, and connectedness among co-located users. To investigate this idea, we focus on movie genres as a tool for decision-making. Genres act as a classification system of movies [9] and are commonly used by online streaming services such as Netflix and Amazon Prime (e.g., [39,42]) to guide users through offerings [9]. Additionally, genres support finding a movie that fits certain moods or situations [9,27]. By utilizing genres as an initial decision-making process, we aim to guide a group toward a movie selection that everyone will enjoy more likely, while also promoting high levels of group experience and social interaction. In this paper, we focus on answering the following research question (RQ): *How can tangible interfaces, related to genres, support a group of users to collaboratively select a movie in the living room?*

To this end, we explore how physical, genre-based tokens help co-located users in selecting a movie together. Therefore, we designed the research artifact Sharemote. It incorporates tangibility while facilitating collaborative movie selection based on distributed TV control (final design in Sect. 3). For the initial exploration of Sharemote with regard to movie decision-making support and the encouragement of social interaction, we conducted a controlled mixed-design lab experiment in groups of three (N = 30, 10 groups). With this work, we contribute to the design of tangible, collaborative TV interfaces and provide empirical insights into how physicalized genres promote social interaction and movie selection among co-located users. Additionally, we discuss opportunities for future TV interfaces to support the group experience through tangibles when collaboratively picking a movie.

2   Background and Related Work

Watching movies together in the living room is among the most prominent social activities in the home [29]. However, not all devices or systems in the home support collaborative interactions and decision-making. In the following, we provide an overview of the qualities of tangible interfaces to support collaboration among co-located users, report on the design of collaborative media systems in general, and outline what constitutes social interaction in a group setting.

2.1   Designing and Qualities of Tangible Interfaces

Tangible interfaces are specified as *'physical objects to represent or manipulate digital data'* [46], in other words, its the design of *'physical metaphors which bridge physical and digital worlds'* [28]. Therefore, the meaning of the tangible artifact and its use needs to be easily understood by users [22] to ensure high usability and user experience [46]. Additionally, a tangible artifact should consider desired qualities such as being ergonomically pleasant to use, accessible, and practical [46]. The advantage of tangible interfaces in collaborative settings lies in the possibility to observe ongoing interactions from outside, supporting group awareness and coordination of tasks [25]. Moreover, tangible objects can be handed over more transparently to start discussions or engage deeply with one another [15,16]. Similarly, tangibles have the potential to provoke shared activities which in turn can impact and promote social interaction among users, particularly belongingness and affiliation with one another [3].

2.2   Shared Control of Media Systems

Enhancing collaboration and supporting group decision-making among co-located users, mediated by technology, lies on distributing control [18] over functions by introducing coordination policies [35,37,41]. Those policies balance decision-making i.e., by enabling users to vote for changes, providing users with different access levels, assigning dedicated functions to specific users, or having one key user who decides on behalf of the group [35,37,41]. Previous work explored how such policies support co-located collaboration on media in various domains including the living room (e.g. through smartphones [36] or via gesture [38,41]), dining area (e.g., [1]), the car (e.g., [6,7]), or public spaces (e.g., [30]). Insights show that introducing a democratic/voting system to facilitate the execution of functions, supports fairness [6,41], is perceived as entertaining [41], and increases social connectedness [6,7,30]. However, voting is time-consuming and, thus, users describe it as tedious when applied to frequently used tasks [41]. Particularly deployed to movie selection using several smartphones, it encourages participation [36] while inducing a high level of frustration and mental workload, and resulting in low usability [36]. The key-user approach is the most common one in day-to-day life of movie selection. It is not ambiguous, encourages storytelling [1], and ensures conversations [6]. Even though this approach prevents technical problems during simultaneous interactions [41], it is perceived as highly unfair [6], excluding, and generating dependency on others which particularly impacts belongingness and togetherness negatively [6]. The most typical approach directs to different access levels [37,41]. While this involves all users actively [6] and promotes structured collaboration [6], research shows that this can provoke unbalanced power dynamics and increase interpersonal conflicts [41]. Apart from introducing such policies, a collaborative system should provide a high usability [36] and a high level of workspace awareness [20] to outline individuals' contributions [11].

2.3   Social Aspects of Collaboration

Besides technology, social interaction, and in particular individuals' perceived social connectedness has a significant impact on group collaboration. Social connectedness (which incorporates feelings of belongingness, affiliation, companionship, and connectedness) notably defines how well users feel connected and appreciated in a group setting. Research shows that companionship has an influence on well-being, stress, and satisfaction [43] while a high affiliation can promote engagement [49] and establish self-esteem [32]. Primarily when collaborating on tasks together, the overall social experience [4], user experience evoked through products used [21] play a significant role towards co-experience – *the experience which is created in social interaction* [4]. Furthermore, the perceived team performance, particularly team cohesion can affect social interaction among co-located users [40]. Overall, social interaction can be supported by direct communication [17] and enabling a fair contribution of individuals [6]. Besides, social connectedness and team cohesion gets enhanced with continuous contribution by all group members [6].

While prior research outlines how coordination policies can be applied to enable collaborative decision-making on media in various domains, we see the potential to combine this knowledge with the design of tangible interfaces to enhance social interaction and promote collaborative movie selection among co-located users in the living room.

3   The Concept of Sharemote

With a design for collaborative movie selection supported by tangibles, we intend to enhance the decision-making process among co-located users toward social interaction and experience. More precisely, we want to assist users in the selection of a movie everyone is satisfied with while promoting group experience and a high feeling of belongingness, affiliation, connectedness, and companionship among group members. To explore this, we focused on the use-case of a group of three watching a movie together on TV in a living room, because the average European household comprises 2.2 people [14]. In the following, we present first the design decisions we made and then how they lead to Sharemote: a concept that enables collaborative movie selection supported by tangible genre tokens.

3.1 Design Decisions Considered

To promote collaborative movie selection through tangibles, we focused on movie genres, because they represent thematic movie categories and guide users through the available content [9]. To support a group of three in collaboratively selecting a movie, we split up the design for the decision-making process into two phases: First, the decision on genre(s), and second the selection of a movie from the specific genre(s).

Genre Selection – Tangible Tokens: To support the first decision-making phase of selecting genre(s), we designed physical tokens (Fig. 1) that represent the genres. The tokens come in a size of 75 mm × 12 mm × 12 mm (l × w × h), to take into account easy and ergonomic handling as well as visibility to other users even when held in hands [24]. The color of the tokens represents a dedicated genre. In our initial investigation, we concentrated on the five highest prevalence genres from the year 2022 [48] which are *Horror = red, Comedy = light blue, Action = yellow, Drama = blue, Adventure = cyan.* The colored genre tokens can then be grabbed and attached to a dedicated remote (on one of four sides, see Fig. 2b) in order to decide/vote on a specific genre(s). The remote, with its four sides, allows to select and attach up to four genre tokens (same genres or different genres), making use of its embodied constraints [25] to enable all users to attach an equal amount of tokens to their remote. Supporting movie selection through tangible tokens has the advantage, that groups' interests and choices made are continuously visible via the selected tokens attached to a remote which promotes workspace awareness [20]. Additionally, the attached genres can also be visualized e.g., digitally on the TV.

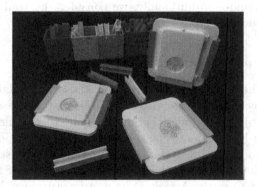

Fig. 1. The final set-up and design of Sharemote, showing the three remotes including the provided tangible genre tokens in their dedicated storage box. (Color figure online)

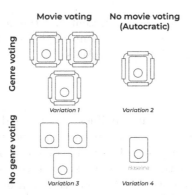
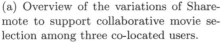

(a) Overview of the variations of Share-mote to support collaborative movie selection among three co-located users.

(b) Sharemote: the navigation-based remote where tokens can be attached to each side.

Fig. 2. Overview of the variations of Sharemote (left) and the general concept of Sharemote (right).

Movie Selection – Shared Control and Remote Controls: After the selection of genre(s), the group needs to interact with the TV to actively select a final movie. For the interaction with the TV in general (movie selection only), we decided on a standard smart TV remote that provides a navigation pad (up, down, left, right, ok). For the collaborative selection of the movie, prior work highlights that users strive for active participation [6]. Providing every user with equal control without having the possibility to overrule others promotes fairness and social connectedness [6]. However, having a key-user is the most established way of selecting a movie in current living rooms [5,36] and thus users are most familiar with it. Further, research shows that such an autocratic approach enforces communication which in turn enhances social interaction [6,36]. Thus, we focused on the democratic/consensual way of movie selection by providing everyone with a remote. Additionally, we consider the traditional, autocratic way, where only one user has a remote as the baseline mode.

3.2 Variations of Sharemote

With the idea of Sharemote we enable co-located users to collaboratively select a movie supported by tangible genre tokens. Sharemote presents a two-piece modular concept (Fig. 2b) that includes (1) tangible genre tokes which can be attached to (2) a navigation-based remote control. Therefore, the decision-making process is split up into two parts – first the decision on genre, and second the decision on a movie. For the decision on the genre(s), a maximum of four tokens out of five genres (Horror, Comedy, Action, Drama, Adventure) can be attached to the remote and confirmed by pressing ok (for the process of Sharemote see Fig. 3). To enable collaborative movie selection on the offerings that result from the (group) genre selection (more details on this in Sect. 3.2), we combined the collaborative

Fig. 3. Visual representation of Sharemotes' process of picking a movie together. Top: process of Genre-Voting variation. Bottom: process of Genre-Autocratic variation.

modes of *consensual* and *autocratic* (baseline) decision-making with the tangible genre-tokes. This resulted in a set of four different variations of Sharemote (Fig. 2a) which we describe in detail below.

(1) The Genre-Voting variation combines the genre selection process with a democratic way of selecting the movie [36,37] afterward. Therefore, every user has their own Sharemote and can first select up to four genres. Therefore, every user has their own Sharemote and can first select up to four genres by attaching the physical genre tokens to the individual base plate. During the movie selection, users can then vote for a movie using their own remote control. To support workspace awareness [20], every user/every remote has a dedicated colored cursor dot presented on the TV user interface (UI) (see Fig. 4a). However, the decision of what movie to watch can only be made jointly [35,37]. Thus, a movie can only be picked when every group member agrees and actively selects the movie to be watched. This means users can posit as many votes as they want. The movie that all voted on (3 out of 3 users) starts automatically.

(2) The Genre-Autocratic variation combines the genre selection process with an autocratic way of selecting a movie. In this variation, only one Sharemote is available for the group. The group can nevertheless jointly decide on up to four genre tokens. The active control of the TV to select a movie afterward, however, can only be performed by one single key-user [37].

The following two variations do not involve the genre selection process and are added for completeness to be able to investigate the impact of tangible genre tokens compared to no-tokens.

(3) The Voting variation is also about the democratic way of selecting a movie together [36,37]. Therefore, all users have the Sharemote remote part

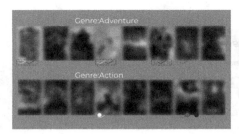
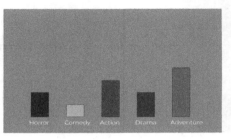

(a) Eight movies per genre genres with movie voting active. Positioned votes (colored checks) and focused movies (colored cursor dots) framed in red.

(b) Real-time visualization of the selected genre tokens. Bar colors match token colors.

Fig. 4. Developed user interface for the collaborative selection of a movie. Left: the movie library. Right: the real-time visualization of the selected genre tokens. (Color figure online)

available without the tokens. Thus, everyone can vote for movies. A movie gets only selected once every user votes for it.

(4) The Autocratic variation is about one key-user who decides on behalf of the group [37]. Therefore, only one user has the Sharemote remote part without tokens. The other users can only participate through verbal communication. This variation is the standard in current homes and thus represents the baseline.

TV User Interface and Movie Library: To support the decision-making process, we provide two UIs: First a real-time overview of the number of tokens attached to the remote(s) (Fig. 4b) to support workspace awareness [20]. Secondly, a movie library UI. Therefore, we created a database of the 16 most prominent movies per genre, derived from IMDB[1]. In the case of a Sharemote variation with genre tokens involved, the UI provides the users after acknowledging their genre selection with a total set of 16 movies. These movies derive from up to two most frequently selected genres (8 randomly selected movies per genre out of the database created). We are aware that there exist other concepts of providing movies. Since our focus lies on exploring the tangible aspect rather than the possibilities of group movie recommendations and UI variations, we argue that this is a viable approach for our investigation. In case no genre selection is involved, the UI provides the user with randomly picked 16 movies from the whole database (genre independent). To support workspace awareness [20] during the movie voting procedure, we highlight which user is focusing on which movie by displaying colored cursor dots (white, orange, green) at the bottom of the focused movie. Once a user votes for a movie, it shows a check icon in the

---

[1] https://www.imdb.com/, last accessed 2022-12-23.

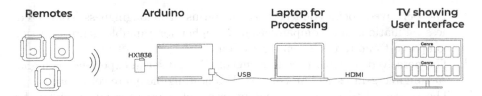

Fig. 5. Demonstration of the technical set-up of the implementation of Sharemote

corresponding cursor color (see Fig. 4a). Votes are made/retracted by pressing ok. The autocratic procedure shows only one cursor for the key-user remote.

Technical Implementation: We implemented the TV UI (Fig. 4a) with a resolution of Full HD (1920×1080) using Processing3 and hosted it on a Laptop that streamed to the TV. To enable the control of the UI by several remotes at once, we used infrared (IR) communication. For the remotes themselves, we re-modified existing IR-based remote controls to ensure diverse IR frequencies. The IR signals were received by an HX1838 IR sensor which was placed right under the TV and connected to an Arduino. The received signals were passed on to the laptop using serial communication. All incoming serial data was handled in the Processing UI application (Fig. 5). The colored genre tokens were 3D printed and provided to the users in dedicated laser-cutted storage boxes as presented in Fig. 1. Seven tokens per genre were available to ensure everyone can select the genre at least twice.

4   Research Question and Hypotheses

The experience of co-located users making decisions together gets influenced by the evoked social interaction, particularly by individuals' perceived social con-nectedness [2,6,32,43]. Additionally, the experience created in social interaction (co-experience) [4] can be influenced by the perceived social experience [4] and the user experience (UX) evoked through the products involved [21]. Addition-ally, perceived team cohesion can affect the way of social interaction in shared spaces [40]. Thus we want to explore how Sharemote supports social interac-tion by asking: *How does collaborative movie selection, supported by tangible interfaces influence social connectedness, team cohesion, social experience, and UX?* One of our goals lies in the qualitative exploration of how users perceive Sharemote, in particular the tangible tokens, and how they perceive the over-all decision-making process. Since tangible interactions tend to promote social interaction, we speculate that those variations with tangible aspects integrated (*Genre-Voting & Genre-Autocratic*) enhance social connectedness (H1), social experience (H2), team cohesion (H3) as well as UX (H4) compared to those variations without tangible interaction (*Voting & Autocratic*).

H1 The perceived social connectedness in terms of belongingness, connectedness, affiliation, and companionship is higher for tangible genre selection compared to no tangible genre selection.

H2 The perceived co-experience in terms of UX and social experience is higher for tangible genre selection compared to no tangible genre selection.

H3 The perceived team performance in terms of team cohesion is higher for tangible genre selection compared to no tangible genre selection.

5 Comparative Study of the Four Sharemote Variations

We performed a mixed-subject study in a living room lab setting, with groups of three participants, to examine the Sharemote variations' effect on collaborative movie selection.

5.1 Experimental Set-Up

We, therefore, had the variations (*Genre-Voting, Voting, Genre-Autocratic, Autocratic*) as **independent within-subject variable** and the owning of a remote (no-remote-owner, key-remote-owner - applicable for the *Autocratic* variations) as **independent between-subject variable**. We mapped the between-subject variable to the users' sitting position. Therefore, we assigned the key-remote-owner to the middle position, and the left and right positions as no-remote-owner to ensure verbal communication.

Dependent Variables and Measurements: As dependent variables, we assessed the user's individually perceived social connectedness in terms of connectedness, companionship, and group affiliation using the Social Connectedness Scale [32] and group belongingness by means of the Inclusion of Community in Self-Scale [34]. We evaluated their perceived team cohesion using the Team Performance questionnaire [40] and the social experience using the questions related to social experience from the *GAMEFULQUEST* [23]. Besides, we measured the user experience (UX) in terms of hedonic, pragmatic, and overall UX with the UEQ-short [45]. We then used participants' qualitative feedback to explore each variation's unique characteristics by conducting semi-structured group interviews after each variation and at the end of the experiment. Additionally, we assessed how long the decision-making process lasted (in seconds). To control for possible influences due to the TV user interface and Sharemote in general, we examined the evoked usability by employing the System Usability Scale (SUS) [10] after the trial round.

5.2 Participants

We used convenience sampling to recruit participants in groups of three. To limit bias that may be introduced by collaborating with strangers [33], we specifically aimed for groups of friends. Overall, we recruited N = 30 participants

(10 groups), 9 male, 20 female, and 1 non-binary living in a country in Europe (blinded for review). Their age ranged from 22 to 32 ($M = 23.93$ years, $SD = 2.36$ years). Their movie-watching frequency refers to 'Less than once a month' (1 out of 30), 'Once a month' (1) 'Several times a month' (12), 'Once a week' (6), 'Several times a week' (4), 'Once a day' (2), and 'Several times a day' (4). Participants on average watch a movie together with someone else 4.3 times out of 10 ($lowest = 0, highest = 9, SD = 3.443$).

5.3   Technical Set-Up

To create a comfortable TV viewing environment, we set up a cozy living room in an empty lab with a couch, a small living room table, and a 49-inch smart TV. To ensure easy access to Sharemote we place the remotes and tokens on the table in front of their seating position. The visualization of the selected tokens on the UI (Fig. 4b) is based on a Wizard of Oz method [12], handled by an independent research assistant (the Wizard of Oz functioning was not introduced to users).

5.4   Procedure

We introduced the goal of the study, collected informed consent, and handed out a demographic questionnaire. Afterward, we asked the participants to select a sitting position on the couch according to their convenience. To evaluate the effects of the variations on social interaction, we aimed for a controlled social situation in a living room lab. To evaluate how individual variations affect social interaction/experience, we did not introduce the functioning beforehand. We only introduced the participants orally to a social scenario of having a movie night with the goal of selecting a movie everyone enjoys watching (Table 1). Discussions with one another were allowed and appreciated. We also pointed out that there is no possibility to revoke the movie's decision made. Thus per variation round, the first movie selection was the final decision and the end of the test round. The group had a maximum of 15 min per variation to select a movie together. We did not communicate this time constraint to the participants in order to avoid influencing the decision-making. In case 10 min passed already, the experimenter reminded the group to make a decision in the upcoming 5 min. The group had to select a different movie per variation' test round to ensure (new) decision-making. The experiment started with a trial round to familiarize the group with the remotes, genre tokens, and TV UI (for tasks see Table 1). After the test round, we assessed the usability of the set-up by means of the SUS questionnaire. This was followed by a fully counterbalanced set of the four variations. For each variation, the group had to decide on a movie. Exchanging or handing over remotes to others was forbidden. At the end of each variation, participants filled out questionnaires related to social connectedness, team cohesion, user experience, and social experience. In addition, the experimenter asked about their collaborative experiences and positive/negative impressions after each variation. The experiment concluded with a subjective ranking of the four variations and a semi-structured group interview about their decision-making experience and what they liked/disliked. The experiment was approved by the Ethics Board of the researcher(s) institution(s) and lasted on average 1.5 h. Participants did not receive compensation.

Table 1. Trial round task and scenario description.

Trial task	Variation test round scenario
Select one Horror token and attach it to your remote. Then navigate to the right lower movie on the TV UI and press OK	Make it yourself comfortable. Try to feel at home and imagine it is Friday and you are having a cozy evening together. You want to chill, relax and therefore you want to watch a movie together. Your goal is to watch a movie everyone will enjoy watching. Therefore, you collaborate with the selection of the movie

6　Results and Findings

We report on how each variation affects users' perceived social interaction in terms of social connectedness, team cohesion, social experience, and UX. With the gathered qualitative data, we conducted a content analysis. For all the ordinal-scaled data collected via validated questionnaires, we used non-parametric Friedman Tests to assess group differences. For post-hoc comparisons, we executed Bonferroni-correction Wilcoxon signed-rank tests. In addition, we performed a repeated-measures ANOVA to investigate differences in time efficiency (normally distributed according to Kolmogorov-Smirnov test).

General Results Concerning Selection Process: The usability score, as assessed after the trial task (initial usage of the UI and remotes), resulted in an average score of 64.8, which indicates OK usability according to [10]. Additionally, all groups decided on a movie within the time limit of 15 min. The ANOVA revealed (sphericity violated as assessed by Mauchly's test, $\chi^2(5) = 11.7, p = .041$ – Greenhouse-Geisser correction applied, $\varepsilon = 0.673$) a statistically significant effect of the Sharemote variations on time needed to select a movie, $F(3, 27) = 10.178$, $p = .002$, $\eta^2 = .531$. Post-hoc tests show a significantly longer decision time for *Genre-Voting* compared to *Autocratic* (± 109.2 s, $p = .003$). Besides it took significantly longer to agree on a movie using *Genre-Autocratic* compared to *Voting* (± 139.1 s, $p = .004$) and *Autocratic* (± 125.1 s, $p = .018$).

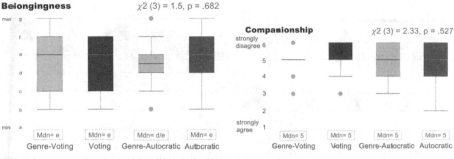

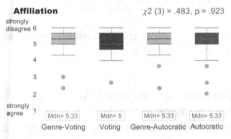

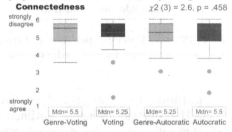

(a) Distribution of the measured group belongingness of each variation [37] (g=max belongingness, a = no group belongingness)

(b) Distribution of the measured companionship of each variation [35]. Q: Even around people I know, I don't feel that I really belong.

(c) Distribution of the average measured affiliation of each variation [35]. Q1: I don't feel I participate with anyone or any group; Q2: I have no sense of togetherness with my peers.; Q3: Even among my peers, there is no sense of brother/sisterhood.

(d) Distribution of the average measured connectedness of each variation [35]. Q1: I feel so distant from the other people; Q2: I feel disconnected from the world around me; Q3: I don't feel related to anyone; Q4: I catch myself losing all sense of connectedness.

Fig. 6. Social connectedness measurements across the different Sharemote variations with pairwise comparisons. Friedman tests are significant at $p < .05$.

6.1 Social Connectedness – H1

Group Belongingness: There is no significant difference between the four variations in their perceived group belongingness, as outlined by a Friedman test ($\chi^2(3) = 1.5, p = .682$, Fig. 6a). The median group belongingness score is equally high for *Genre-Voting*, *Voting*, and *Autocratic* ($Mdn = e$), followed by *Genre-Autocratic* ($Mdn = d$) (original scale ranges from a = no group belongingness to g = max belongingness).

Connectedness: A Friedman test shows, that the variations have no effect on Connectedness ($\chi^2(3) = 2.6, p = .458$, Fig. 6d). The average connectedness is highest for *Genre-Voting* and *Autocratic* ($Mdn = 5.5$) followed by *Voting* and *Genre-Autocratic* ($Mdn = 5.25$).

Affiliation: The variations do not have a significant effect on the perceived Affiliation as reported by a Friedman test ($\chi^2(3) = .483, p = .923$, Fig. 6c). *Genre-Voting, Genre-Autocratic & Autocratic* evoked a slightly higher average affiliation ($Mdn = 5.33$) than *Voting* ($Mdn = 5$).

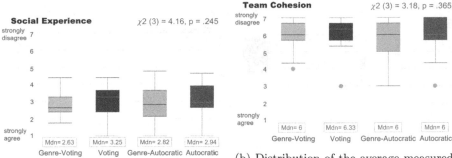

(a) Distribution of the measured Social Experience [25] per variation. The average score of the eight questions from [25].

(b) Distribution of the average measured Team Cohesion [43] per variation. Q1: Dealing with the members of the team often left me feeling irritated and frustrated. Q2: I had unpleasant experiences with the team. Q3: Negative feelings between me and the team tended to pull us apart.

Fig. 7. Perceived social experience and team cohesion across the Sharemote variations with pairwise comparisons. Friedman tests are significant at $p < .05$.

Companionship: The evoked companionship is not significantly different among the four variations, as outlined by a Friedman test ($\chi^2(3) = 2.23, p = .527$). Overall, the median companionship lies above average ($Mdn = 5$) for all four variations (Fig. 6b).

Taken together, all variations evoke a high social connectedness, indicated by an above-average belongingness, companionship, affiliation, and connectedness rating. Since the variations did not evoke significant differences in any of the social connectedness factors, we reject *H1*.

6.2   Co-experience – H2

Social Experience: The evoked social experience is highest for *Genre-Voting* ($Mdn = 2.63$), followed by *Genre-Autocratic* ($Mdn = 2.81$), *Autocratic* ($Mdn = 2.94$), and *Voting* ($Mdn = 3.25$) (Fig. 7a). However, there is no significant difference between the variations in terms of social experience as outlined by a Friedman test ($\chi^2(3) = 4.16, p = .245$), which let us reject *H2*.

User Experience: The overall UX (see Fig. 8) is highest for *Genre-Voting* (above average), followed by *Voting* (below average), *Genre-Autocratic* (bad), and *Autocratic* (bad). A Friedman test outlines a significant effect of the four variations on overall UX ($\chi^2(3) = 12.71, p = .005$). Post-hoc tests report a higher UX for *Genre-Voting* compared to *Autocratic* ($Z = 3.45, p = .003$). Looking into the UX in more detail, our results indicate, that all variations are equally practical, simple, and pleasant - indicated by an equal pragmatic quality ($\chi^2(3) = 1.98, p = .576$). Concerning hedonic quality (satisfactory, creative, original), *Genre-Voting* scored best (good), followed by the other three variations (bad). A Friedman test outlines a significant effect of the three variations on perceived hedonic quality ($\chi^2(3) = 40.98, p < .001$). Post-hoc pairwise comparison shows a significant higher hedonic quality for *Genre-Voting* compared to *Voting* ($Z = 3.2, p < .008$), *Genre-Autocratic* ($Z = 3.15, p = .01$), and *Autocratic* ($Z = 6.25, p < .001$). Besides, *Autocratic* has a significant lower hedonic quality than *Voting* ($Z = 3.05, p = .014$), and *Genre-Autocratic* ($Z = 3.1, p = .023$).

Summed up, there is no significant difference in terms of social experience. However, the UX shows a significant difference among the variations. Yet, group comparisons only outline a difference between *Genre-Consensual* and *Autocratic* which leads us to only partially accept *H2* - The perceived co-experience in terms of UX is higher for the tangible genre selection variation of *Genre-Consensual* compared to no tangible genre selection of *Autocratic*.

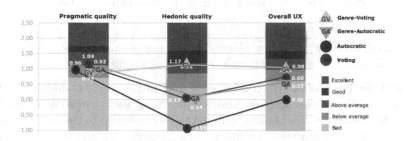

Fig. 8. Results from UEQ-short [45]. It shows the mean values of the measured pragmatic quality (left), hedonic quality (middle), as well as the overall UX (right) score per variation. The colors of the bars represent the UX scale, ranging from excellent (light green) to bad (light blue). The scale in general ranges from -3 (horribly bad UX) to +3 (extremely good UX), while values above 0.8 represent a positive evaluation [45]. (Color figure online)

6.3   Team Performance – H3

Team Cohesion: A Friedman test outlines no significant effect of the variations on perceived team cohesion ($\chi^2(3) = 3.18, p = .365$). Overall, *Voting* ($Mdn = 6.33$) resulted in a slightly higher average team cohesion than *Genre-Voting, Genre-Autocratic, & Autocratic* ($Mdn = 6$). Even though the variations evoke a high team cohesion, there is no evidence for differences among the variations. Thus, we need to reject *H3*.

6.4   Qualitative Insights

Subjective Ranking: There is a statistically, significant order of preferences among the four variations, as outlined by a Friedman test ($\chi^2(3) = 11.92, p = .008$). Post-hoc pairwise comparison shows a significantly higher preference for *Genre-Voting* compared to *Autocratic* ($Z = -3.4, p = .004$). Figure 9 outlines the ranking per variation, ranging from 1 = most preferred to 4 = least preferred

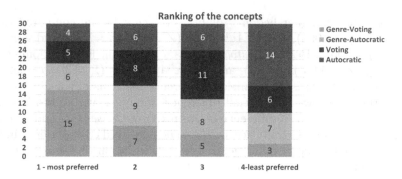

Fig. 9. The subjective ranking of the Sharemote variations.

with a median score of 1.5 for *Genre-Voting*, a median score of 2.5 for *Genre-Autocratic*, and a score of 3 for both *Voting & Autocratic*.

Qualitative Feedback: We conducted a qualitative content analysis with the responses to the open-ended questions concerning each variation individually and the final interview. Sentences were iteratively assigned to themes and themes were clustered in overarching groups by two researchers under a common agreement basis [19] (for an overview see Fig. 10).

The (1) **Genre-Voting variation** is described by participants as *playful* particularly because of the tokens involved (e.g. P#8.3; *"At the moment that is the fun part. Yeah, it's like playing some children's games"*). Further, this variation supports a more *focused selection* of movies in line with the group's preferences which also helps in initiating movie-related discussions (e.g. P#5.1; *"What I liked is that you have a good overview to start a discussion"*). Additionally, this variation allowed participants to be better involved, particularly through the possibility to *express* personal preferences through the genre tokens (e.g. P#2.3 *"I think it allows to pretty express like what you like"*). Participants also mention that it supported them in having an *overview of individuals' preferences* which required *less talking* in the early stage of decision-making (e.g. P#4.3; *"Like there's no discussion on the first part which did 'cause we did not get the double discussion. It's just put in what you like"*). Overall, the tokens enabled to *narrow down options* and to have a preference-oriented discussion which is perceived as being able to come up with a *movie everyone is more interested* in (e.g. P#10.1; *"Yeah but I like the feature of eliminating the choices to make it more focused"*). The feedback concerning *efficiency* was split up among the participants. Some perceived this variation as faster compared to the other variations (e.g. P#4.3 *"It went very quickly. It's nice, it's the first step for suggestions that works faster"*) while some mentioned that it takes notably more time (e.g., P#9.3 *"I think adding this wouldn't make this selection of movies more efficient than just talking"*). Mentioned downsides of this variation refer to the possibility of easily *losing the tokens* (e.g., P#1.3 *"I would actually lose all of the tokens"*). A few commented on the movie recommendations after the token selection, since they expected movies related to the *genre combination* instead of receiving offers from two separate genres (e.g. P#5.3 *"The options weren't overlapping or something. I assumed, we select action and comedy and that we would get action-comedy choices"*). Even though this variation might be particularly interesting for bigger groups, one participant had the feeling of being under pressure when it comes to the selection of genres/movies.

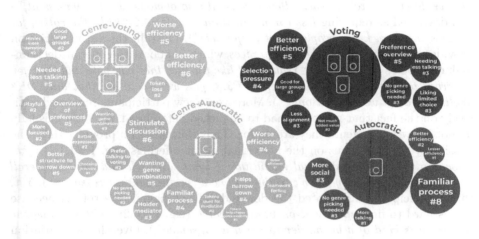

Fig. 10. Overview of the themes arrived from the qualitative analysis. Colors represent the Sharemote variations. The number refers to the times mentioned.

The (2) **Genre-Autocratic variation** *stimulates richer discussion* around both the genres and the movie (e.g., P#6.1 *"for me this one is better to share opinions with others"*). The key-user likely took on the *mediator* role and stimulated discussions around the genre selection as well as the movie selection (e.g. P#7.1 *"The one who gets the remote is still the most active one and authoritative about what we're going to watch"*). Particularly for two groups, the key-user encouraged others to grab tokens and discuss together which ones to attach to the remote (e.g. P#10.1; *"I think it's good to have the token here first, so you can - So it's very, very clear to see. The kind of genre the other people choose. And then we can start the conversation, based on the tokens."*). Users describe the token selection in this variation, particularly as supportive in terms of deciding on a *genre in advance* (e.g. P#2.1; *"I actually think that like having the genres physically in front of you makes it easier to choose, which one you want to take or something"*) to narrow down final movie decisions (e.g. P#1.2; *"Yeah, it takes away that ... you open Netflix you have like this ocean of choice. And it does help that it narrows it down"*). However, some participants also mentioned that they perceived this variation as time-consuming and that they rather prefer to talk to the key user without additional actions (*prefer talking to voting; no genre picking needed*) (e.g. P#1.1; *"I didn't really need to specify the genre"*; P#8.3; *"Because we have to wait and talk and wait and talk"*). Some even had the impression that it is already similar to the current situation in the living room (e.g. P#10.1; *"It's basically already what we do"*) while a few also mentioned here expecting movies related to *genre combinations* (e.g. P#4.2; *"It would be nice if there was a combination between two genres"*). Nevertheless, this variation was perceived as more social and as fostering teamwork (e.g. P#9.3 *"I kind of like the part of the whole team together"*).

The **(3) Voting variation** is perceived as efficient (e.g. P#8.3 *"It's super fast we don't even talk to each other because it's so obvious [what others want]"*) and described as requiring *less communication* (e.g. P#4.2 *"I like the voting for it. Like that you know people, what people like"*). Overall, the voting variation provides an *overview of other preferences* which supports the overall decision-making process (e.g. P#3.1; *"Yeah, but I like the idea that you vote and that you see what the other people vote like, oh P3.3, you wanted to see that one, OK? Well, why don't we see that one?"*). Moreover, a few participants remarked positively on the fact that no genres had to be picked beforehand, since they usually do not know which genre they are up for. Thus this variation provides them the possibility to more focus on the individual movie offerings (e.g. P#1.1; *"Yeah, I focus more on the individual movie that I want to watch and not the overall genre, because normally I don't really feel like a specific genre necessarily"*). Yet, three participants highlighted the downside of not having the tokens because it was hard to find *alignment on what to watch* (e.g. P#6.2; *"without choosing the genre is kind of a bit harder to reach a consensus"*). Overall, this variation is perceived as particularly suitable for *large groups* (e.g. P#1.2 *"In a bigger group it might be helpful to keep track of what everyone wants"*). While a few participants commented on the fact of having *limited choices* helped the overall selection of a movie, others felt under *pressure to select* movies (e.g. P#7.1*"I still got a feeling that we were pushing P7.3 to select a movie that he didn't have that much interest in"*).

The **(4) Autocratic variation** is described as the most familiar way of selecting a movie together (e.g. P#2.1 *"I don't know it was a bit conventional. I think it always goes like this. Same feelings as when choosing a movie normally at home"*). Thus some participants refer to an efficient movie selection process which is mainly connected to more conversations but for some participants also to the fact that no tokens were involved (e.g. P#9.3 *"I think it provides a chance for us to discuss a lot. [...] I think it's really good to elicit conversations and discussions"*).

7   Discussion

In this paper, we explored variations of Sharemote. More precisely, we investigated how tangible genre-based tokens support collaborative movie selection. In the following, we will delve deeper into the results of our controlled mixed-design lab experiment and explore the implications of our findings for the design of tangible, collaborative TV interfaces. We discuss the potential for tangibles to promote social connectedness, team performance, and co-experience to facilitate collaborative movie selection among co-located users.

Implications of Tangible Genre Tokens on Social Connectedness, Team Performance and Co-experience: Our results indicate, that the process of selecting a movie in a group setting is a general social activity that evokes high perceived social connectedness, team performance, and co-experience regardless of the structure of the decision-making process. Previous research has outlined the importance of social connectedness and co-experience in group decision-making processes [6,33]. In our study, we found that all Sharemote variations evoke a high level of social connectedness and co-experience, which ultimately supports well-being [43] and establishes a social bond among group members [32, 49]. Even though we could not validate all of our speculations, we found out that the Sharemote variations involving the tangible genre tokens stimulate a higher user experience, particularly when combined with movie voting. Overall, the genre tokens are associated with being original, creative, and satisfying, as indicated by high hedonic quality.

Moreover, the use of tangible genre tokens leads to narrowing down choices and provides a more inviting atmosphere for exploring individual preferences and daring to outline current moods. This, in turn, leads to more satisfying and creative decisions compared to traditional, autocratic movie selection methods. Additionally, the tokens encourage conversations about potential movies before browsing a list of options, which can be seen as a stimulating social activity [6]. Furthermore, the physicality of the genres enables users the possibility to actively participate in the decision-making process without feeling forced to provide input. This self-determination of participation generally improves social connectedness [6]. Despite the longer decision-making process when genre selection is involved, users did not necessarily perceive it as more time-consuming. A reason therefore can be the engagement and flow mode [47] that the tokens induce, which was found to aid in preventing conflicts and increasing belongingness and loyalty [26]. Even though participants expressed their preferences towards those Sharemote variations that incorporate tokens, it is important to note that the use of physical objects also has potential downsides. The tokens may induce overhead, particularly when the preferences of users are similar and a movie can be easily decided on. In such cases, autocratic decision-making, delegating a single user to select the verbally agreed-upon movie will be most convenient and efficient. Another downside is the physicality itself, which requires space to be stored and can be easily lost [46]. Moreover, the more users are involved, the more tokens and remotes are necessary which will certainly have an influence on whether or not users see the value in purchasing such or similar concepts. While this on the one hand is a downside, it can also be seen as an opportunity to easily welcome more users into the decision-making process of movie selection.

Overall, the insights show that physical genre tokens incorporated into the movie selection process are a novel and engaging method that evokes high user experience, promotes group satisfaction, and sustains social interaction. Our research emphasizes the value of introducing tangible interfaces to the collaborative process of movie selection to easily identify overarching interests and helps users to narrow down the list of possible movie choices. This prevents the tedious scrolling through a long list of none matching movie offerings. While it creates a novel user experience, it also provides the opportunity of using the genre selections to enhance group movie recommendations. Since genre preferences often correlate with users' moods and situations [27], it can be difficult for traditional recommender systems to accurately recommend movies that fit the diverse preferences and needs of several users at once [50]. Thus, we see the incorporation of genre preferences has a potential for future group-based movie recommendations.

We acknowledge the limitations of our study, such as the rather small movie library, as well as the choice of five genres only. Furthermore, users used the different Sharemote variations only once for a short period of time. This can have an influence on the measured social connectedness since differences in feelings might not be recognizable after an initial and short testing period. While we ensured internal validity through a lab experiment and by recruiting groups of friends, diverse, and dynamic social group settings such as natural in day-to-day life might evoke different experiences. Thus, as a next step, we plan a longitudinal, field study to investigate Sharemote under ecologically valid circumstances and to understand long-term experiences. Furthermore, we see the need to research whether and how Sharemote with movie voting via a remote control performs in comparison to a smartphone voting app or traditional hand raises. Also, future work is needed to investigate whether and how our insights are transferable to other societies as well as cultural contexts. Overall, our research work provides valuable insights into the interaction with tangible genre-based tokens in the process of collaborative movie selection, but additional investigation is needed to understand long-term effects on social interaction and group-experience.

8   Conclusion

In this paper, we presented the concept of Sharemote, a tangible interface that promotes social interaction among co-located users in the process of collaboratively selecting a movie. By using tangible genre-based tokens, users are able to vote for their genre preferences in order to narrow down movie choices. Results from our mixed-subject experiment in a living room lab setting have shown that having genre tokens enhances the overall user experience compared to traditional decision-making methods. The tokens were found to initiate conversations about personal choices and to stimulate discussions about overarching intentions. While the selection process may take longer, users prefer the pre-decision-making on genres in order to explore group interests and preferences to enhance the chance of finding a movie that everyone can enjoy. Our findings contribute to the design of interactive media systems and the role of tangible interfaces in facilitating decision-making among co-located users.

References

1. Ah Kun, L.M., Marsden, G.: Co-present photo sharing on mobile devices. In: Proceedings of the 9th international conference on Human computer interaction with mobile devices and services (MobileHCI 2007), pp. 277–284. Association for Computing Machinery, New York (2007). https://doi.org/10.1145/1377999.1378019
2. Ammarapala, V., Luxhøj, J.T.: A collaborative multi-criteria decision making technique for risk factor prioritization. J. Risk Res. **10**(4), 465–485 (2007). https://doi.org/10.1080/13669870701421563
3. Antle, A.N.: The CTI framework: informing the design of tangible systems for children. In: Proceedings of the 1st International Conference on Tangible and Embedded Interaction (TEI 2007), pp. 195–202, (2007). https://doi.org/10.1145/1226969.1227010
4. Batterbee, K.: Defining co-experience. In: Proceedings of the 2003 International Conference on Designing Pleasurable Products and Interfaces (DPPI 2003), pp. 109–113. Association for Computing Machinery, New York (2003). https://doi.org/10.1145/782896.782923
5. Berger, M.: Social control interaction framework: design to technically support a group of users in making control decisions together. In: Extended Abstracts of the 2022 CHI Conference on Human Factors in Computing Systems (CHI EA 2022), pp. 1–6. Association for Computing Machinery, New York (2022). https://doi.org/10.1145/3491101.3503802
6. Berger, M., Barati, B., Pfleging, B., Bernhaupt, R.: Design for social control of shared media: a comparative study of five concepts. In: Nordic Human-Computer Interaction Conference (NordiCHI 2022), pp. 1–13. Association for Computing Machinery, New York (2022). https://doi.org/10.1145/3546155.3546694
7. Berger, M., Dey, D., Dandekar, A., Barati, B., Bernhaupt, R., Pfleging, B.: Together in the car: a comparison of five concepts to support driver-passenger collaboration. In: Proceedings of the 14th International Conference on Automotive User Interfaces and Interactive Vehicular Applications (AutomotiveUI 2022), pp. 183–194. Association for Computing Machinery, New York (2022). https://doi.org/10.1145/3543174.3544940
8. Bernhaupt, R., Obrist, M., Weiss, A., Beck, E., Tscheligi, M.: Trends in the living room and beyond. In: Cesar, P., Chorianopoulos, K., Jensen, J.F. (eds.) EuroITV 2007. LNCS, vol. 4471, pp. 146–155. Springer, Heidelberg (2007). https://doi.org/10.1007/978-3-540-72559-6_16
9. Bondebjerg, I.: Film: genres and genre theory. Int. Encycl. Soc. Behav. Sci.: Second Edn. **2**(3), 160–164 (2015). https://doi.org/10.1016/B978-0-08-097086-8.95052-9
10. Brook, J.: SUS: a "quick and dirty" usability scale. In: Jordan, P.W., Thomas, B., McClelland, I.L., Weerdmeester, B. (eds.) Usability Evaluation in Industry, pp. 189–194. Taylor & Francis, London (1996)
11. Cesar, P., Geerts, D.: Social interaction design for online video and television. In: Nakatsu, R., Rauterberg, M., Ciancarini, P. (eds.) Handbook of Digital Games and Entertainment Technologies, pp. 1157–1193. Springer, Singapore (2017). https://doi.org/10.1007/978-981-4560-50-4_39
12. Dahlbäck, N., Jönsson, A., Ahrenberg, L.: Wizard of Oz studies-why and how. Knowl.-Based Syst. **6**(4), 258–266 (1993). https://doi.org/10.1016/0950-7051(93)90017-N

13. Dourish, P., Bellotti, V.: Awareness and coordination in shared workspaces. In: Proceedings of the 1992 ACM Conference on Computer-Supported Cooperative Work (Toronto, Ontario, Canada) (CSCW 1992), pp. 107–114. Association for Computing Machinery, New York (1992). https://doi.org/10.1145/143457.143468
14. Eurostat.   https://ec.europa.eu/eurostat/statistics-explained/index.php?title=Household_composition_statistics. Accessed 21 January 2023
15. Fernaeus, Y., Tholander, J: Finding design qualities in a tangible programming space. In: Proceedings of the SIGCHI Conference on Human Factors in Computing Systems (CHI 2006), pp 447–456. Association for Computing Machinery, New York (2006). https://doi.org/10.1145/1124772.1124839
16. Fernaeus, Y., Tholander, J., Jonsson, M.: Beyond representations: towards an action-centric perspective on tangible interaction. Int. J. Arts Technol. **1**(3–4), 249–267 (2008). https://doi.org/10.1504/IJART.2008.022362
17. Fischer, U., Mosier, K.: The impact of communication delay and medium on team performance and communication in distributed teams. In: Proceedings of the Human Factors and Ergonomics Society Annual Meeting, vol. 58, no. 1, pp. 115–119 (2014). https://doi.org/10.1177/1541931214581025
18. Flemisch, F., Heesen, M., Hesse, T., Kelsch, J., Schieben, A., Beller, J.: Towards a dynamic balance between humans and automation: authority, ability, responsibility and control in shared and cooperative control situations. Cogn. Technol. Work **14**, 3–18 (2012). https://doi.org/10.1007/s10111-011-0191-6
19. Graneheim, U.H., Lundman, B.: Qualitative content analysis in nursing research: concepts, procedures and measures to achieve trustworthiness. Nurse Educ. Toda **24**(2), 105–112 (2004). https://doi.org/10.1016/j.nedt.2003.10.001
20. Gutwin, C., Greenberg, S.: A descriptive framework of workspace awareness for real-time groupware. Comput. Supported Coop. Work (CSCW) **11**(3), 411–446 (2002). https://doi.org/10.1023/A:1021271517844
21. Hassenzahl, M.: User experience (UX): towards an experiential perspective on product quality. In Proceedings of the 20th Conference on l'Interaction Homme-Machine (IHM 2008), pp. 11–15. Association for Computing Machinery, New York (2008). https://doi.org/10.1145/1512714.1512717
22. Herstad, J., Holone, H.: What we talk about when we talk about co-creative tangibles. In: Proceedings of the 12th Participatory Design Conference: Exploratory Papers, Workshop Descriptions, Industry Cases, vol. 2, pp. 109–112. Association for Computing Machinery, New York (2008). https://doi.org/10.1145/2348144.2348179
23. Hoegberg, J., Hamari, J., Wästlund, E.: Gameful experience questionnaire (GAMEFULQUEST): an instrument for measuring the perceived gamefulness of system use. User Model. User-Adap. Inter. **29**(3), 619–660 (2019). https://doi.org/10.1007/s11257-019-09223-w
24. Holmquist, L.E., Redström, J., Ljungstrand, P.: Token-based access to digital information. In: Gellersen, H.-W. (ed.) HUC 1999. LNCS, vol. 1707, pp. 234–245. Springer, Heidelberg (1999). https://doi.org/10.1007/3-540-48157-5_22
25. Hornecker, E.: A design theme for tangible interaction: embodied facilitation. In: Gellersen, H., Schmidt, K., Beaudouin-Lafon, M., Mackay, W. (eds.) ECSCW 2005, pp. 23–43. Springer, Dordrecht (2005). https://doi.org/10.1007/1-4020-4023-7_2
26. Hussain, S., Qazi, S., Rizwan Raheem, A., Vveinhardt, J., Streimikiene, D.: Innovative user engagement and playfulness on adoption intentions of technological products: evidence from SEM-based multivariate approach. Econ. Res.-Ekon. istraživanja **32**(1), 555–577 (2019). https://doi.org/10.1080/1331677X.2018.1558086

27. Infortuna, C., et al.: The inner muses: How affective temperament traits, gender and age predict film genre preference. Pers. Individ. Differ. **178**(4) (2021). https://doi.org/10.1016/j.paid.2021.110877
28. Ishii, H., Ullmer, B.: Tangible bits: towards seamless interfaces between people, bits and atoms. In: Proceedings of the ACM SIGCHI Conference on Human Factors in Computing Systems, pp. 234–241. Association for Computing Machinery, New York (1997). https://doi.org/10.1145/258549.258715
29. Kawsar, F., Brush, A.J.B.: Home computing unplugged: why, where and when people use different connected devices at home. In: Proceedings of the 2013 ACM International Joint Conference on Pervasive and Ubiquitous Computing (UbiComp 2013), pp. 627–636. Association for Computing Machinery, New York (2013). https://doi.org/10.1145/2493432.2493494
30. O'Hara, K., Lipson, M., Jansen, M., Unger, A., Jeffries, H., Macer, P.: Jukola: democratic music choice in a public space. In Proceedings of the 5th Conference on Designing Interactive Systems: Processes, Practices, Methods, and Techniques (DIS 2004), pp. 145–154. Association for Computing Machinery, New York (2004). https://doi.org/10.1145/1013115.1013136
31. Lee, B., Lee, R.S.: How and why people watch TV: implications for the future of interactive television. J. Advert. Res. **35**(6), 9–19 (1995)
32. Lee, R., Robbins, S.: Measuring belongingness: the social connectedness and the social assurance scales. J. Couns. Psychol. **42**(2), 232–241 (1995). https://doi.org/10.1037/0022-0167.42.2.232
33. Liu, S., Smith, B.A., Vaish, R., Monroy-Hernández, A.: Understanding the role of context in creating enjoyable co-located interactions. Proc. ACM Hum.-Comput. Interact. **6**(CSCW1), 1–26 (2022). https://doi.org/10.1145/3512978
34. Mashek, D., Cannaday, L.W., Tangney, J.P.: Inclusion of community in self scale: a single-item pictorial measure of community connectedness. J. Community Psychol. **35**(2), 257–275 (2007). https://doi.org/10.1002/jcop.20146
35. Marakas, G.M.: Decision Support Systems in the 21st Century, 1st edn. Prentice Hall, Upper Saddle River (1998)
36. McGill, M., Williamson, J., Brewster, S.A.: How to lose friends & alienate people: sharing control of a single-user TV system. In: Proceedings of the ACM International Conference on Interactive Experiences for TV and Online Video (TVX 2014), pp. 147–154. Association for Computing Machinery, New York (2014). https://doi.org/10.1145/2602299.2602318
37. Morris, M.R., Ryall, K., Shen, C., Forlines, C., Vernier, F.: Beyond "social protocols": multi-user coordination policies for co-located groupware. In: Proceedings of the 2004 ACM Conference on Computer Supported Cooperative Work (CSCW 2004), pp. 262–265. Association for Computing Machinery, New York (2004). https://doi.org/10.1145/1031607.1031648
38. Morris, M.R., Huang, A., Paepcke, A., Winograd, T.: Cooperative gestures: multi-user gestural interactions for co-located groupware. In: Proceedings of the SIGCHI Conference on Human Factors in Computing Systems (CHI 2006), pp. 1201–1210. Association for Computing Machinery, New York (2006). https://doi.org/10.1145/1124772.1124952
39. Netflix, The Story Behind Netflix's Secret Category Codes. https://www.netflix.com/tudum/articles/netflix-secret-codes-guide. Accessed 25 Jan 2023
40. Paul, R., Drake, J.R., Liang, H.: Global virtual team performance: the effect of coordination effectiveness, trust, and team cohesion. IEEE Trans. Prof. Commun. **59**(3), 186–202 (2016). https://doi.org/10.1109/TPC.2016.2583319

41. Plaumann, K., Lehr, D., Rukzio, E.: Who has the force? Solving conflicts for multi user mid-air gestures for TVs. In Proceedings of the ACM International Conference on Interactive Experiences for TV and Online Video (TVX 2016), pp. 25–29. Association for Computing Machinery, New York (2016). https://doi.org/10.1145/2932206.2932208

42. Prime Video direct, Genre Definitions. https://videodirect.amazon.com/home/help?topicId=G202110120&ref_=avd_sup_G202110120. Accessed 25 Jan 2023

43. Rock, K.S.: Social support versus companionship: effects on life stress, loneliness, and evaluations by others. J. Pers. Soc. Psychol. **52**(6), 1132–1147 (1987). https://doi.org/10.1037/0022-3514.52.6.1132

44. Salvador, L. L.: Assimilation, imitation and the elementary social fact: towards a definition of social interactions. In Working notes of Socially Intelligent Agents Workshop, pp. 115–117. AAAI Press, AAAI Fall Symposium Serie (1997)

45. Schrepp, M., Hinderks, A., Thomaschewski, J.: Design and evaluation of a short version of the user experience questionnaire (UEQ-S). Int. J. Interact. Multimed. Artif. Intell. **4**(6), 103–108 (2017). https://doi.org/10.9781/ijimai.2017.09.001

46. Shaer, O., Hornecker, E.: Tangible user interfaces: past, present, and future directions. Found. Trends® Hum.-Comput. Interact. **3**(1–2), 4–137 (2010). https://doi.org/10.1561/1100000026

47. Sutcliffe, A.: Designing for user engagement: aesthetic and attractive user interfaces. Synthesis Lect. Hum.-Cent. Inform. **2**(1) (2009). https://doi.org/10.2200/S00210ED1V01Y200910HCI005

48. The Numbers: Market Share for Each Genre in 2022. https://www.the-numbers.com/market/2022/genres. Accessed 21 March 2023

49. Wongm, M.M., Csíkszentmihályi, M.: Affiliation motivation and daily experience: some issues on gender differences. J. Pers. Soc. Psychol. **60**, 154–164 (1991)

50. Yuan, Q., Cong, G., Lin, C. Y.: COM: a generative model for group recommendation. In: Proceedings of the 20th ACM SIGKDD International Conference on Knowledge Discovery and Data Mining (KDD 2014), pp. 163–172. Association for Computing Machinery, New York (2014). https://doi.org/10.1145/2623330.2623616

Social Media and Digital Learning

A Mixed-Methods Analysis of Women's Health Misinformation on Social Media

Lisa Mekioussa Malki[(✉)], Dilisha Patel, and Aneesha Singh

UCL Interaction Centre, University College London, London, UK
{lisa.malki.21,dilisha.patel,aneesha.singh}@ucl.ac.uk

Abstract. Propelled by the COVID-19 pandemic and recent overturning of Roe vs. Wade in the United States [21], concerns have grown around the proliferation of reproductive health misinformation online. While a body of work in HCI has explored female health and well-being from a socio-technical perspective, a knowledge gap relating to women's health misinformation and how it presents on social media remains. We report a mixed-methods content analysis of the ideological rhetoric, sources, and claims present in a sample of 202 officially fact-checked posts relating to female reproductive health. We found that reproductive health misinformation is diverse in its sources and represents a range of ideological standpoints, including pro-choice, feminist, and anti-authority rhetoric. We also found that claims are often tacit in nature, and rely on subtle manipulation and exaggerations to convey misleading narratives, as opposed to complete fabrications. In sum, we present a timely and nuanced analysis of the women's health misinformation ecosystem. Our findings may inform priorities for HCI interventions that abate health misinformation, and more broadly, support women in navigating a complex and polarised information landscape.

Keywords: Misinformation · Women's health · Social media

1 Introduction

Misinformation is increasingly recognised as a threat to public health, democracy, and trust in scientific authorities [12]. While health misinformation pre-dates the digital era, social media provides novel opportunities for this material to spread at scale and take root within vulnerable communities [26]. Accordingly, it is recognised that women face unique threats from online health misinformation arising from social inequalities such as increased childcare burden [5] and medical discrimination [28]. Misinformation related to women's health has attracted greater public interest in recent years, owing to the COVID-19 pandemic which saw widespread vaccine hesitancy among expectant mothers [7], and the landmark overturning of Roe vs. Wade in the United States. These highly disruptive events have caused concerns about a looming reproductive health infodemic,

J. Abdelnour Nocera et al. (Eds.): INTERACT 2023, LNCS 14144, pp. 419–428, 2023.
https://doi.org/10.1007/978-3-031-42286-7_22

exacerbated by a lack of moderation on social media, and structural barriers to accessing evidence-based health information [21].

Now, more than ever, is a focused and targeted response to women's health misinformation needed, to support vulnerable communities as they navigate some of the most trying public health events in recent history. It is well-established that factors such as information sources, ideological frames, and media formats can influence how users engage with information on social media, and impact how trustworthy or compelling they find certain material [23,25]. Understanding these attributes therefore, is key to developing a user-centered model for fostering information literacy among social media users [17]. However, we currently know very little about these characteristics with respect to women's health, as existing studies of misinformation typically overlook the element of gender [2].

Motivated to explore the major themes, ideological framing, and sources of women's health misinformation online, we collated and analysed a sample of 202 fact-checked posts from a range of social media platforms. We also explored the geographical distribution of fact-checking organisations, and tracked changes in the topical focus of posts over time. We contribute a baseline for understanding women's health misinformation across the social media ecosystem, and identify common rhetorical techniques used to promote misinformative health narratives, such as appealing to female empowerment, or fostering distrust towards authority. Insights from our study may inform interventions aimed at inoculating users against these narratives, and developing information literacy among women.

2   Related Work

Over the last several decades, the women's health movement has addressed inequalities in the medical treatment of women across a wide range of health concerns, including reproductive health, sexuality, and mental health [9]. Though there has been a growing HCI interest in exploring women's health [1, 29], little work focuses specifically on misinformation. Nonetheless, it is known that gender can bear on how individuals engage with misinformation [2] and that women, particularly new and expectant mothers, are at increased risk of harm, since anti-vaccine misinformation often strategically appeals to maternal identity to undermine trust in medical authorities [5]. The overturning of Roe vs. Wade has introduced additional threats: almost overnight, social media was flooded with dangerous at-home methods for inducing miscarriages, which many users perceived as credible alternatives to medical abortion [26]. It is feared that an 'abortion infodemic' may worsen rates of maternal mortality across the United States, in particular, for Black women who face medical discrimination and structural barriers to reproductive care [21,28]. Concerns have been voiced elsewhere around the world, such as in India, where menstrual stigma compounds the harmful impacts of low health literacy [18].

In recent years, social media platforms have begun working with independent fact-checking organisations to "identify and correct provably false claims that are timely, trending and consequential" [19]. Along with content removal and down-ranking, fact-check labelling constitutes one of the most prominent responses to misinformation [26]. While the intervention can potentially increase media literacy [12], user responses to content labelling are complex in practice and depend on baseline trust towards information authorities, as well as the broader cultural and political climates in which misinformation is embedded [3,23]. Therefore, fact-checking interventions on their own, may fail to address the psychological and affective drivers of misinformation belief [11]. We argue that effectively combating misinformation requires familiarity with the ideological space that it occupies. Our aim is to explore the themes and nuances of this content as it exists in the wild, to understand the phenomenon in greater depth, and inform priorities for design interventions. We now describe our methods for conducting an analysis of existing reproductive health misinformation on social media.

3 Methodology

3.1 Sample

Our sample consisted of social media posts which have been identified as misinformation by official fact-checking organisations. Despite the limited resources of fact-checkers, this approach is scalable, accurate, and eliminates the time-consuming and subjective task of determining whether a post is misinformation [24]. In line with work by Simon et al. [27], we used the Google Fact Check Explorer API [13] to collect credible fact-check articles from across the Internet.

3.2 Data Collection and Screening

We queried the API at the end of March 2023, with a set of keywords relating to female reproductive health. Though women's health covers a broad range of health topics and themes, we narrowed our focus to reproductive health as this is the timeliest and most widely explored component of women's health research [9]. Our keywords were informed by scholarly literature [1,9], online medical databases [20], and iterative testing using the Fact Check Explorer tool. The following set of finalised keywords were used to query the database: *reproductive health, women's health, menstruation, period, abortion, miscarriage, birth control, contraception, fertility, pregnancy*.

We collected all English-language articles returned by the API, and extracted a description of each claim being debunked, the fact-checking verdict (e.g., *False* or *Misleading*), the full text of the article and where available, a link to the original social media post. We automatically excluded duplicates (n = 673), articles over two years old (n = 358), and articles assigned a *True* or *Mostly True* verdict (n = 9), to ensure that only recently circulating misinformation was included in the sample. We then manually screened the remaining 278 articles for eligibility. We included articles which were both relevant to female reproductive health issues, and made a provably inaccurate claim about health. This left a total of 202 fact-check articles for further analysis.

3.3 Coding Instrument

A codebook for reproductive health misinformation was developed, tested, and used for our study. The codebook consisted of several factual characteristics such as the post's creation date and the name of the fact-checker, as well as variables capturing different types of claims, sources, and levels of falsity. Our coding frame was broadly adapted from previous content analyses of COVID-19 misinformation [24, 27] and women's weight loss material [10].

Claims and Rhetoric. Our typology of claims was constructed inductively, due to the lack of scholarly work taxonomising reproductive health misinformation. We drafted an initial set of claims by reading each article and post in full, and capturing the overarching focus of the misinformation. Our first iteration of coding produced three broad categories, relating to menstruation and fertility, the COVID-19 vaccination, and reproductive politics. On our second iteration, we re-read and compared posts across categories, to capture more fine-grained nuances in the material. For example, posts relating to reproductive politics were assigned to sub-categories of *governmental surveillance* or *criminalisation*. This process yielded a final taxonomy of nine sub-codes, organised under the three major categories described previously. We coded for ideological rhetoric deductively, in line with previous research which suggests that distrust of medical authority, female empowerment, and appeals to parental identity feature heavily in women's health misinformation [5, 16]. We re-reviewed posts with a focus on their underlying rhetoric, and noted whether these sentiments were present.

Sources. The articles in our sample typically dealt with a single claim, but included multiple examples of social media posts containing it. As such, we recorded the social media, news, or information websites mentioned in each article, to get a broad sense of the platforms focused on by fact-checkers. In addition, we sought information about the authors, to provide additional context about the specific individuals or organisations responsible for creating misinformation. If publicly available, we used the claimant's profile information and a sample of recent posts to classify users under four categories: unverified users (members of the public), mainstream public figures, online influencers, and news outlets.

Level of Falsity. We analysed the falsity rating of each article in line with methods by Shahi et al. [24]. We reviewed each fact-checker's rating system, collected similar verdicts, and mapped them to a single label based on the post's level of falsity. Verdicts relating to totally false or fabricated information were coded under *False*, whereas more nuanced verdicts such as *Misleading* and *Missing Context* were unified under the *Partially False* category.

3.4 Data Analysis

The first iteration of our codebook was developed using a subset of 50 posts, then piloted within the research team. Coding discrepancies were resolved through discussion. In line with standard practices for social media content analysis [10], we re-coded the full dataset with the finalised codebook, and performed a simple descriptive analysis to derive the prevalence of different claims, sources, and types of misinformation in the sample.

3.5   Ethical Considerations

Ethical concerns associated with using social media data include participant re-identification and a lack of informed consent from users [4]. As such, we only processed material that was publicly available, and maintained strict anonymity of social media users by collecting high-level codes and metadata, and paraphrasing quotes. The study was approved by our institutional ethical board.

Reflexivity Statement. As UK-based researchers at the intersection of HCI and women's health, we view media literacy and access to evidence-based information as critical dimensions of wellbeing in the digital age. Our work is situated within feminist HCI practice [1,29], and is framed by our desire to embed social justice into the design of interventions [6].

4   Results

Our study aimed to understand the major themes, ideological framing, and sources of fact-checked women's health misinformation on social media. We analysed 202 unique fact-check articles published between 2nd April 2021 and 23rd March 2023. The major topical themes included COVID-19 vaccination, fertility and menstruation health myths, and reproductive politics. The majority of posts in the sample (64.9%, n = 131) contained tacit misinformation, where facts had been skewed or misrepresented, as opposed to totally fabricated information, which comprised just under a third of the sample (29.2%, n = 59).

4.1   Fact-Checking Trends

Temporal. The articles in our sample were published over two years, with Fig. 1 illustrating the number of articles published per-quarter over this period. The shape of the graph suggests several peaks and troughs over the two years, with the highest point observed during the summer of 2022: a total number of 79 articles (39.1% of the total sample) were published during Q2 and Q3 of 2022. We note that this period correlates with the overturning of Roe vs. Wade in the United States, and indeed, of the articles published in this period, approximately two-thirds (n = 53) relate directly to abortion and reproductive care in post-Roe America. This is in contrast to previous periods, which were dominated by misinformation relating to the COVID-19 vaccine, or general female wellbeing.

Geographical. A total of 21 fact-checking organisations were present in our sample. As shown in Fig. 2, the most commonly occurring source was *FullFact* (12.9%, n = 26), a UK-based independent fact-checking organisation. Many fact-checkers were location-specific, and broadly prioritised information relevant to

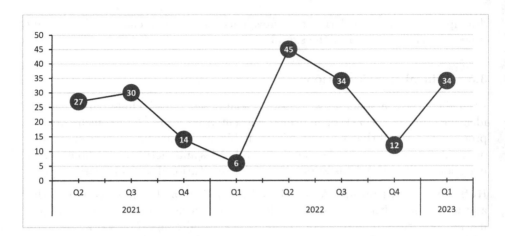

Fig. 1. Articles published per-quarter between the start of April 2021 and the end of March 2023.

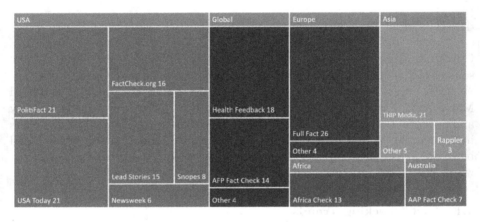

Fig. 2. Overview of the fact-checkers represented in our sample and their geographic locations. Organisations with fewer than 3 articles are collapsed into the *Other* category.

specific countries or national interests. The largest share of articles were published by US-oriented fact-checkers (43.1%, n = 87), and the second-largest by global organisations which covered multiple countries and territories (17.8%, n = 36). Fact-checkers based in Europe (14.9%, n = 30) and Asia (14.3%, n = 29) were also common, comprising a similar share of the sample. The least-covered regions were Africa (6.4%, n = 13) and Oceania (3.5%, n = 7).

4.2   Platforms and Sources

The most commonly occurring platform was Facebook, which appeared in 45.5% of articles (n = 92). Also frequently observed were Twitter (26.2%, n = 53)

Instagram (22.3%, n = 45), and TikTok (4.0%, n = 8). In addition to social media sites, a sizeable number of claims originated on digital news platforms (13.9%, n = 28) such as the Mail Online, Fox News, and The Express. The largest category of posts were created by unverified members of the public on social media (32.1%, n = 65). Of the posts originating from public figures (29.7%, n = 60), approximately half could be attributed to political activists (n = 29), and the other half to elected officials or medical professionals. Thirty posts were associated with news outlets, mostly conspiratorial networks, though (n = 9) originated from quality or mainstream news sources. Less common categories included health influencers (7.9%, n = 16), cases where the claimant could not be reliably identified (8.4%, n = 17), and other sources, such as meme pages and a personal blog (6.9%, n = 14).

4.3   Claims and Rhetoric

The largest share of articles in the sample related to the COVID-19 vaccination (39.1%, n = 79). Just under two-thirds of posts in this category stated that taking the Pfizer vaccine would lead to miscarriages, using skewed statistics or out-of-date government documents to substantiate the claim. Themes of distrust towards the government and pharmaceutical industry featured heavily in this category, with several posts referring to global vaccination campaigns as 'mass murder', and targeting women with conspiratorial narratives: *"[the men] at big pharma don't have your back."*

Several other posts spread inaccuracies about menstruation or fertility (32.6%, n = 66). Many contained ineffective home remedies: most were harmless, but fact-checkers identified others as potentially toxic to health. For instance, a handful of posts described dangerous herbal methods for inducing miscarriage. Whilst they often had the disclaimer *"avoid these herbs if pregnant"*, the timing (soon after Roe vs. Wade), could suggest that they were intended as an alternative method for abortion [22]. Posts relating to fertility and menstruation often appealed to female empowerment and bodily exploration. For example, a popular video on 'menstrual masking', in which menstrual blood is used as a skin treatment [15], used hashtags such as *#SmashThePatriarchy*, and encouraged viewers to post their own videos as a way to break menstrual taboos.

Lastly, a quarter of the misinformation in our sample related to reproductive care in the United States following the overturning of Roe vs. Wade. Fear of criminalisation was a common theme in this category, with posts inaccurately describing instances of women and girls being jailed for procuring abortions, or fabricating governmental surveillance policies. Posts in this category were overwhelmingly pro-choice in rhetoric, and conveyed fear, frustration, and unease alongside politicised anti-republican[1] sentiments: *"GOP'Alpha Males' are more afraid of our vaginas than they are of weapons of war."*

---

[1] Refers to the mainstream Republican political party in the United States, otherwise known as the GOP.

5   Discussion and Conclusion

We conducted an exploratory study of reproductive health misinformation on social media by analysing a sample of officially fact-checked posts. Our results illustrate a great diversity in the focus, rhetoric, and origins of online misinformation, with a number of implications for future interventions.

First, we found that women's health misinformation can originate from 'unusual suspects' such as reputable news outlets, individuals with legitimate medical credentials, and elected officials. In a similar vein, we found that the material in our sample was most likely to be tacit and subtly misleading, rather than altogether false. Thus, we highlight the value in educating users of the diversity in misinformation, and developing their psychological resistance against misinformation that is subtle, and likely to bypass their credibility judgement strategies. One existing approach involves implementing digital nudges, which visually draw a user's attention to common credibility cues through highlighting or context-aware prompting [8]. Our findings show that reproductive health misinformation employs a range of visual and rhetorical techniques, which are inextricably tied to social and medical contexts. For example, COVID-19 vaccine misinformation was more likely to rely on misreadings of official data, whereas content posted after the overturning of Roe vs. Wade tended to exploit fears of criminalisation. As such, a customisable nudging system designed to facilitate reflection on a broad range of media characteristics and rhetorical techniques may support women in navigating tacit and challenging material.

In a departure from studies which report that abortion misinformation is more likely to be anti- than pro-choice [14], almost all of the posts relating to abortion in our sample represented pro-choice standpoints; a trend which the overturning of Roe vs. Wade may explain. Many posts conveyed a message of liberation from medical oppression, which has been identified as a common dimension of both reproductive health misinformation, and alternative health narratives more widely [16,17,27]. Moreover, previous HCI research has identified that users are less critical towards information consistent with their ideologies and fears [25], suggesting that women, particularly those belonging to minority or disenfranchised groups, may be at particular risk from misinformation which appeals to past and current medical discrimination [28]. Therefore, our findings raise questions about how interventions may be tailored to specific communities of users, and address differential vulnerabilities which arise from misinformation exposure. In particular, we encourage fully recognising the role played by structural inequalities on how marginalised individuals process health information, and grounding design practice in addressing the feelings of disillusionment and uncertainty that drive engagement with misinformative health narratives [23].

We recognise limitations in our study. Firstly, our sample comprised of English-language content relating to female reproductive health. Though this ensured a focused sample, women's health encapsulates more holistic markers of wellness such as nutrition, physical, and mental health [9]. Future work could explore misinformation beyond the Anglosphere, and investigate a greater range of topics, including dieting, which is known to attract a great deal of misinformation [10]. Furthermore, though we provide a strong snapshot of the ecosystem of women's health misinformation, we did not explore users' lived experiences. Therefore, a key priority for future work is to conduct observational research on how women engage with health misinformation in-situ, to contextualise and validate the current study. Overall, our analysis provides a conceptual baseline for understanding the shades of grey inherent in reproductive health misinformation, and offers directions for culturally sensitive interventions which address users' holistic needs to promote health literacy.

References

1. Almeida, T., Comber, R., Balaam, M.: HCI and intimate care as an agenda for change in women's health. In: Proceedings of the CHI Conference on Human Factors in Computing Systems, pp. 2599–2611. ACM, San Jose (2016). https://doi.org/10.1145/2858036.2858187

2. Almenar, E., Aran-Ramspott, S., Suau, J., Masip, P.: Gender differences in tackling fake news: different degrees of concern, but same problems. Media Commun. **9**(1), 229–238 (2021). https://doi.org/10.17645/mac.v9i1.3523

3. Appling, S., Bruckman, A., De Choudhury, M.: Reactions to Fact Checking. Proc. ACM Hum.-Comput. Interact. (2022). https://doi.org/10.1145/3555128. CSCW, Association for Computing Machinery, New York

4. Ayers, J.W., Caputi, T.L., Nebeker, C., Dredze, M.: Don't quote me: reverse identification of research participants in social media studies. NPJ Digit. Med. **1**(1), 30 (2018). https://doi.org/10.1038/s41746-018-0036-2

5. Baker, S.A., Walsh, M.J.: 'A mother's intuition: it's real and we have to believe in it': how the maternal is used to promote vaccine refusal on Instagram. Inf. Commun. Soc., 1–18 (2022). https://doi.org/10.1080/1369118X.2021.2021269

6. Bardzell, S.: Feminist HCI: taking stock and outlining an agenda for design. In: Proceedings of the SIGCHI Conference on Human Factors in Computing Systems, CHI '10, pp. 1301–1310. Association for Computing Machinery, New York (2010). https://doi.org/10.1145/1753326.1753521

7. Bhattacharya, O., Siddiquea, B.N., Shetty, A., Afroz, A., Billah, B.: COVID-19 vaccine hesitancy among pregnant women: a systematic review and meta-analysis. BMJ Open **12**(8), e061477 (2022). https://doi.org/10.1136/bmjopen-2022-061477

8. Bhuiyan, M.M., Horning, M., Lee, S.W., Mitra, T.: NudgeCred: supporting news credibility assessment on social media through nudges. Proc. ACM Hum.-Comput. Interact. **5**(CSCW2), 1–30 (2021). https://doi.org/10.1145/3479571

9. Cohen, M.: Towards a framework for women's health. Patient Educ. Couns. **33**(3), 187–196 (1998). https://doi.org/10.1016/S0738-3991(98)00018-4

10. Dedrick, A., Merten, J.W., Adams, T., Wheeler, M., Kassie, T., King, J.L.: A content analysis of Pinterest belly fat loss exercises: unrealistic expectations and misinformation. Am. J. Health Educ. **51**(5), 328–337 (2020). https://doi.org/10.1080/19325037.2020.1795754

11. Ecker, U.K.H., et al.: The psychological drivers of misinformation belief and its resistance to correction. Nat. Rev. Psychol. **1**(1), 13–29 (2022). https://doi.org/10.1038/s44159-021-00006-y, https://www.nature.com/articles/s44159-021-00006-y

12. Flintham, M., Karner, C., Bachour, K., Creswick, H., Gupta, N., Moran, S.: Falling for fake news: investigating the consumption of news via social media. In: Proceedings of the CHI Conference on Human Factors in Computing Systems, pp. 1–10. Association for Computing Machinery, New York (2018). https://doi.org/10.1145/3173574.3173950

13. Google: Google Fact Check Explorer - About (2023). https://toolbox.google.com/factcheck/about#fce

14. Han, L., Boniface, E.R., Han, L.Y., Albright, J., Doty, N., Darney, B.G.: The abortion web ecosystem: cross-sectional analysis of trustworthiness and bias. J. Med. Internet Res. **22**(10), e20619 (2020). https://doi.org/10.2196/20619

15. HealthNews: period-blood face mask: why gynecologists disapprove? (2023). https://healthnews.com/beauty/skin-care/is-period-blood-good-for-skin-care/

16. Jolly, N.: Why are women buying GOOP? Women's health and the wellness movement. Birth **47**(3), 254–256 (2020). https://doi.org/10.1111/birt.12495

17. Lewandowsky, S., van der Linden, S.: Countering misinformation and fake news through inoculation and Prebunking. Eur. Rev. Soc. Psychol. **32**, 348–384 (2021). https://doi.org/10.1080/10463283.2021.1876983

18. McCammon, E., Bansal, S., Hebert, L.E., Yan, S., Menendez, A., Gilliam, M.: Exploring young women's menstruation-related challenges in Uttar Pradesh, India, using the socio-ecological framework. Sex. Reprod. Health Matters **28**(1), 1749342 (2020). https://doi.org/10.1080/26410397.2020.1749342

19. Meta: how Meta's third-party fact-checking program works (2021). https://www.facebook.com/formedia/blog/third-party-fact-checking-how-it-works

20. OASH: A-Z Health Topics. https://www.womenshealth.gov/a-z-topics

21. Pagoto, S.L., Palmer, L., Horwitz-Willis, N.: The next Infodemic: abortion misinformation. J. Med. Internet Res. **25**, e42582 (2023). https://doi.org/10.2196/42582, https://www.jmir.org/2023/1/e42582

22. Rougerie, P.: Abortifacient plants are dangerous, and ineffective as an abortion method (2022). https://healthfeedback.org/claimreview/abortifacient-plants-dangerous-and-ineffective-as-abortion-method/

23. Saltz, E., Leibowicz, C.R., Wardle, C.: Encounters with visual misinformation and labels across platforms: an interview and diary study to inform ecosystem approaches to misinformation interventions. In: Extended Abstracts of the 2021 CHI Conference on Human Factors in Computing Systems, pp. 1–6. ACM, Yokohama (2021). https://doi.org/10.1145/3411763.3451807

24. Shahi, G.K., Dirkson, A., Majchrzak, T.A.: An exploratory study of COVID-19 misinformation on Twitter. Online Soc. Netw. Media **22**, 100104 (2021). https://doi.org/10.1016/j.osnem.2020.100104

25. Shahid, F., Kamath, S., Sidotam, A., Jiang, V., Batino, A., Vashistha, A.: "It Matches My Worldview": examining perceptions and attitudes around fake videos. In: CHI Conference on Human Factors in Computing Systems, pp. 1–15. ACM, New Orleans (2022). https://doi.org/10.1145/3491102.3517646

26. Sharevski, F., Loop, J.V., Jachim, P., Devine, A., Pieroni, E.: Abortion misinformation on TikTok: rampant content, lax moderation, and vivid user experiences (2023). http://arxiv.org/abs/2301.05128

27. Simon, F., Howard, P.N., Nielsen, R.K.: Types, sources, and claims of COVID-19 misinformation. Technical report, Reuters Institute (2022)

28. Thomas, S.P.: Trust also means centering black women's reproductive health narratives. Hastings Cent. Rep. **52**(S1), S18–S21 (2022). https://doi.org/10.1002/hast.1362

29. Tuli, A., Chopra, S., Kumar, N., Singh, P.: Learning from and with Menstrupedia: towards menstrual health education in India. Proc. ACM Hum.-Comput. Interact. **2**(CSCW), 1–20 (2018). https://doi.org/10.1145/3274443

Evaluating the Effects of Culture and Relationship Strength on Misinformation Challenging Behaviours Within the UK

Lauren Scott[1]([✉])[iD], Marta E. Cecchinato[1][iD], Lynne Coventry[2][iD], and Mark Warner[3][iD]

[1] Northumbria University, Newcastle upon Tyne, Tyne and Wear, UK
lauren5.scott@northumbria.ac.uk
[2] Abertay University, Dundee, UK
[3] University College London, London, UK

Abstract. Misinformation has proliferated throughout our digital ecosystem, through social media feeds and group chats with friends and family members. However, a gap exists in the current literature on how individuals challenge misinformed views outside of social media platforms. Through an online survey, we exposed multi ($n = 50$) and mono-cultural ($n = 50$) participants to misinformation scenarios involving close and weak relationship ties, to understand how tie strength and cultural background affects people's behavioural responses. We found that both the tie strength between the misinformed individual and the cultural background of the challenger has a significant effect on the barriers that individuals foresee affecting their discussions about misinformation, and in the misinformed challenging behaviours. Our findings offer new insights into how relationship tie strength and culture affect misinformation challenging behaviours.

Keywords: Misinformation · Relationship · Culture

1 Introduction

Misinformation has many different definitions, but can broadly be defined as *"incorrect information shared without harmful intent"* [11] which is categorised as false *"based on the opinion of relevant experts at the time"* [22], and is something individuals encounter regularly, such as in messaging platforms where families and friends connect [15]. Misinformation poses particular dangers where there is low public trust in institutions [14,18,19] and can have a significant effect on individuals' health, well-being and identity [20,21], something that was experienced worldwide during the COVID-19 pandemic with the rise of vaccine hesitancy and anti-vaccination movements due to misinformation [8]. Due to its dangers, misinformation correction is an area currently being explored by HCI

© The Author(s), under exclusive license to Springer Nature Switzerland AG 2023
J. Abdelnour Nocera et al. (Eds.): INTERACT 2023, LNCS 14144, pp. 429–438, 2023.
https://doi.org/10.1007/978-3-031-42286-7_23

researchers [12,16] covering many areas; including preventative and cure-type digital interventions. Misinformation correction is often shared online, in publicly visible spaces; however, there is less work exploring corrections when it is taken from this public forum, and shared in a private (and sometimes offline) channel. Additionally, little research exists investigating misinformation correction where a personal tie is shared (such as friends or family), although there is an increased expectation for users of private, more intimate messaging spaces to correct the misinformed beliefs of friends and family members [12], or for those where misinformation is spread offline to correct the misinformed views in a conversation. This paper will cover related work and motivation for this study, followed by the method and sample descriptions, results and discussion, followed by future implications, limitations and conclusions.

2   Motivation

Information that aligns with an individual's identity is more likely to be believed [5], information that comes from a strong tie such as a friend or family member is also viewed with an increased level of trust [3,19]. This can result in strong ties being placed in a unique position to curb misinformation beliefs. However, research has shown that, when discussing misinformation on social media with strong ties, it can cause the same disconnect and potential conflict as is seen with political conversations [4,9], and that when faced with misinformation spread, the potential conflict that can arise can discourage individuals from correcting misinformed beliefs [16,20].

Prior research provided insight into how misinformation conversations are practically undertaken where ties are shared. Research has identified multiple reasons individuals choose to challenge misinformation, including educating or trying to change the views of the misinformed person [16]. However, prior literature has also identified a range of barriers that impact misinformation challenging behaviours, both within families and online. These include the personality of the individual, lack of a preferred communication method, and the difference in the type of conversation in comparison to a regular chat [16]. As well as their potential reaction, their role within the family [13,16], and their pre-existing views or identity [5,16]. It is therefore important to understand how relationship strength impacts misinformation challenge behaviour. To address this gap, this study asked the following research question: *(RQ1) Does the tie strength between an individual and the misinformed person affect the individual's experience when encountering a misinformed person?* To answer RQ1 we test the following hypotheses:

H1: The tie strength between two individuals affects the actions an individual takes when exposed to a misinformed person.

H2: The tie strength between two individuals affects the barriers perceived to have an impact on discussions about misinformation.

Malhotra and Pearce have investigated misinformation challenging in the context of younger adults challenging older family members in India [12,13].

However, in these studies the core cultural values of respect for elders may have had an impact on willingness to challenge misinformation, and the strategies and barriers that they used or experienced during the challenge. Similar behaviours have been shown within Kenyan culture, where elders also play a vital role in family dynamics [17]. As there is little further research investigating the impact of culture when addressing misinformation where an existing tie is shared, our work builds upon this and provides insights on mono- and multi-cultural individuals living within the UK; offering insights into a range of cultures. To address this gap, we pose the following research question *(RQ2): Does cultural background affect the actions individuals would take when encountering a misinformed person?* To answer RQ2, we test the following hypotheses:

H3: The cultural background of an individual affects the actions they would take when exposed to a misinformed person.

H4: The cultural background of an individual affects the barriers perceived to have an impact on discussions about misinformation.

In summary, prior research has highlighted that misinformation correction where a personal tie is shared has the potential to result in more effective misinformation challenging, and that cultural values and backgrounds can have an impact on experiences and behaviours relating to misinformation challenging. However, the difference between challenging behaviours for strong and weak ties, and how culture affects misinformation correction requires more investigation. To explore this further, and address the research questions above, we designed and deployed an online survey with mono ($n = 50$) and multi ($n = 50$) cultural UK residents to investigate the different strategies individuals would take and barriers they would encounter if exposed to a misinformed individual where a prior personal tie was shared. We contribute to misinformation literature by finding that both culture and relationship tie strength play a role in the actions individuals would choose to take when exposed to a misinformed individual, and in the number of barriers that individuals foresee impacting/preventing their discussions about misinformed views.

3   Method

We designed and deployed an online survey with mono ($n = 50$) and multi ($n = 50$) cultural UK participants comparing experiences with strong and weak relationship ties, using a mixed factorial 2×2 design. This method was used as it allowed large volumes of data to be obtained in a short time frame [7], and it would not be limited by region, which could be used to investigate the gaps in literature. The online study was developed using Qualtrics[1], with recruitment facilitated via the academic recruitment portal Prolific[2] and participants were remunerated for their time ($\approx £10/ph$). We received ethical approval from Northumbria University (ref: 43163) and all participants provided informed consent. In this paper we report only on the quantitative findings.

---

[1] https://www.qualtrics.com/.
[2] http://prolific.ac.uk/.

3.1 Independent Variables

To address our research questions and test hypotheses, we defined two independent variables: (1) cultural background (mono vs multi), and (2) tie strength (close vs weak).

Culture (Between-Subject). Within our sample, we defined the culture variable as either mono- or multi-cultural, which was determined at recruitment, based on preferences self-identified by participants on their Prolific accounts. Culture can be defined in a number of ways, and within our sample we observed a number of different interpretations used. For example, a mono-cultural participant identified as "British", a multi-cultural participant identified as "Japanese & Western European", but another identified as "Christian, European". Although cultural values such as power-distance, masculinity/femininity, uncertainty avoidance, long-term orientation and individualism were measured using the CVScale [23], when conducting an Independent Samples Mann-Whitney U Test to establish differences in these values for the two groups, the only score showing a statistically significant difference between these groups was individualism ($U = 903; z = -2.406; p = .016$). Throughout the analysis of this work, the self-identified categories are utilised for separating different cultural groups, as individuals' identities have a large role in both misinformation belief and subsequent correction [20].

Relationship Tie-Strength (Within-Subject). To determine the strongest and weakest tie for each participant from a pre-determined list (Mother, Father, Grandmother, Grandfather, Child, Romantic Partner, Colleague at work, friend, and strongest friend), we utilised the 'We Scale' [6], 'Inclusion of the Other Self' scale [1], and 'Subjective Closeness Index' [2,6] to calculate their strongest and weakest ties. This was to compare participants' potential behaviours towards individuals with whom they share a strong tie, and a weak tie.

3.2 Dependent Variables

Following the tie-strength questionnaires, participants were then shown two scenarios (presented randomly to prevent order bias), one involved the individual with the strongest tie and the other the individual with the weakest tie (based on the above calculations). The scenarios suggested the individual believed some form of health misinformation, and read as follows: *"You find out that your [strongest/weakest tie] believes some false information which could negatively impact their health. They have since started to share harmful articles and advice on social media"*. These scenarios explored whether the same behaviours and barriers shown in prior literature were utilised, and whether there were more common barriers and behaviours seen in different cultures or whether behaviours differed between individuals with a perceived strong or weak tie. Prior to being presented the scenarios, participants were informed of the following *"In this section you will be provided with a scenario related to a member of your family, a friend, or a work colleague that you should carefully read and consider. You will then be asked a series of questions related to this scenario."*

The two dependent variables that we tested were (1) actions taken when encountering a misinformed individual (Actions Taken) and (2) barriers to discussing beliefs with a misinformed individual (Barrier Count).

Actions Taken When Encountering a Misinformed Individual. For each scenario, participants were asked *"Faced with this scenario, how would you respond? (Please choose from the following options)"*, and were presented 6 options, all derived from prior literature [16]: (i) talk to them and agree with their misinformed beliefs; (ii) avoid talking to them about their misinformed beliefs; (iii) talk to them to find out why they hold these misinformed views and beliefs, but do not agree or disagree with them; (iv) talk to them and disagree with their misinformed views and beliefs, but do not try and change their views or beliefs; (v) talk to them and disagree with their views and beliefs and try to persuade them that they are wrong; (vi) none of these. Participants could select one option, and if they selected 'none of these' they were prompted to explain what they would do instead.

Barriers to Discussing Beliefs with a Misinformed Individual. Individuals were then asked what barriers they believed they would experience when discussing the misinformed individual's views, or that would prevent them from having a discussion about misinformation with this individual. They were asked the following, dependent on their response to the actions question (above): *"Are there any barriers that you would face whilst having this conversation? (Please tick all that apply)"* (if they had selected 'none of these'), *"Why would you choose not to address their misinformed beliefs? (Please tick all that apply)"* (if they chose not to discuss the misinformation), or *"Would any of these options pose a potential barrier to your strategy? (Please tick all that apply)"* (for other responses). We presented all participants with the following options, derived from prior literature [5,13,16], as potential barriers: (i) an aspect of their personality; (ii) their reaction; (iii) the effort required; (iv) the lack of possible consensus; (v) the lack of a preferred communication method; (vi) their pre-existing views; (vii) the difference in the type of conversation as opposed to a regular chat; (viii) the role within their family; (ix) that the individual would not have appeared misinformed from the behaviour described; and (x) other. Participants were able to select multiple responses, and if they selected 'other' were prompted to enter any additional barriers they foresaw with the conversation.

3.3   Participant Information

A total of 100 UK residents participated in this study, made up of two groups: 50 self-identified mono-cultural individuals, and 50 self-identified multi-cultural individuals. Of the 100 participants, 54 identified as female, 43 identified as male, and 3 identified as non-binary. Ages ranged from 18–60+, with the most common age being 18–29 ($n = 35$), and the next common being 30–39 ($n = 33$). Data such as employment status and socio-economic status were not collected.

4   Results

To address our hypotheses two repeated measures mixed ANOVAs were run to determine the effect of culture and tie-strength on both the perceived number of barriers and the actions taken when exposed to the misinformed individual. For both tests, we checked the 7 main assumptions associated with this test [10] in that: the dependent variables were measured at the continuous level, the within-subjects factor consisted of two categorical, related groups, whereas the between-subjects factor consists of two categorical "independent groups", there are no significant outliers in the independent groups, the data was normally distributed, there was homogeneity of covariances, as assessed by Box's test of equality of covariance matrices (actions: $p = .160$; barriers: $p = .230$). and the data passed Mauchly's test of Sphericity, as there were only two levels of repeated measures.

For the perceived number of barriers participants foresaw affecting their conversations, there was no statistically significant two-way interaction between relationship and culture ($F(1, 97) = .897, p > 0.05$), whereas for the actions an individual would take when exposed to a misinformed individual, there was a statistically significant two-way interaction between relationship and culture ($F(1, 98) = 7.541, P < 0.05$). To explore this in more detail, simple main effects were run.

4.1   RQ1: Does the Tie Strength Between an Individual and the Misinformed Person Affect the Individual's Experience When Encountering a Misinformed Person?

Actions Taken When Encountering a Misinformed Individual. The main effect of relationship showed a statistically significant difference in the actions an individual would take when exposed to the misinformed person ($F(1, 98) = 42.778, p < 0.05$), supporting H1. For those encounters where there was a strong tie, individuals preferred to talk about the misinformation and try to persuade the misinformed individual that they were wrong ($n = 70$), whereas with individuals where there was a weak tie, although the preference was still to address the misinformed belief ($n = 30$), behaviours were significantly more mixed.

Barriers to Discussing Beliefs with a Misinformed Individual. The main effect of relationship showed a statistically significant difference in the number of perceived barriers that individuals foresee ($F(1, 97) = 27.683, p < 0.001$), supporting H2. Participants believed that the most common barrier that would impact/prevent a discussion about misinformed views where a weak tie was shared would be the personality of the individual and how they would respond ($n = 41$), whereas with individuals who shared a strong tie, participants thought that there would be no barriers ($n = 44$). The second most popular foreseen barrier for both groups was the potential reaction of the individual when the challenge took place (weak: $n = 36$, strong: $n = 36$).

4.2   RQ2: Does Cultural Background Affect the Actions Individuals would Take when Encountering a Misinformed Person?

Actions Taken When Encountering a Misinformed Individual. The main effect of culture showed a statistically significant difference in the actions an individual would take when exposed to the misinformed person ($F(1, 98) = 4.073, p < 0.05$), supporting H3. For both groups, there was a preference to talk to the misinformed individual and try and persuade them that they were wrong. However, for individuals that identified as mono-cultural, a greater number of participants would choose to avoid the discussion completely compared to those who identified as multi-cultural.

Barriers to Discussing Beliefs with a Misinformed Individual. The main effect of culture showed a statistically significant difference in the number of perceived barriers that individuals foresee ($F(1, 97) = 6.768, p < 0.05$), supporting H4. The most common foreseen barrier for both groups was the potential reaction of the misinformed person. With the second most common for both groups being that there would be no barriers to the discussion.

5   Discussion

This study identifies actions individuals would take when exposed to a misinformed individual with whom they already share an existing personal tie, and the barriers they would foresee affecting these conversations. We describe the impact that both relationship tie strength and culture has on actions taken when exposed to a misinformed individual, and the number of barriers that individuals foresee impacting conversations that challenge misinformation. It is already understood that where individuals with strong ties share misinformation on social media, disagreement on the legitimacy of the information can cause conflicts, frustrations, and arguments [9], and that individuals correcting misinformation who already share a tie with misinformed individuals have a better chance of success [21]. This study adds to prior literature by demonstrating that, although concerns surrounding these conversations exist [9], individuals are more likely to choose to discuss the misinformed person's views and explain they are wrong when a strong tie is shared, and foresee fewer potential barriers when having the conversation with a strong tie compared to a weak tie.

This study expands on prior knowledge regarding the impacts of cultural background when challenging misinformation. Prior research has identified that these can affect both willingness to challenge misinformation, but also the strategies used for the challenge [12,17]. This study has also shown that cultural background affects the actions individuals take when exposed to a misinformed person. Prior work that also took a culturally informed approach to exploring misinformation correction within families has established that both concerns about maintaining politeness to reduce negative reactions [13] and the role of the family hierarchy [12] are barriers that have directly influenced conversations around misinformation. Our results show that across both cultural groups the knowledge of the personality combined with their potential reaction, was of a high concern to participants. However, the role within the family, although shown to participants as an optional barrier, was not a priority within this space. This suggests that concerns surrounding family hierarchy may be specific to some cultures, rather than a generalised observation.

6   Limitations and Future Work

This work is not without limitations. Firstly, the sample is skewed towards younger individuals. Due to this, the data could be more indicative to behaviours that would be taken from younger individuals challenging older individuals (e.g. mother, father etc.), a common limitation of work in this space (e.g. [12,16]). Secondly, we have translated culture into a binary variable, self-identified by participants, due to the role that identity holds in relation to misinformation [20,21]. Related literature may consider culture as a series of dimensions, such as those investigated by Yoo et al. [23]. Although within our work the individualism dimension indicated a statistically significant effect between our categories, future work should explore the role that specific cultural dimensions/values can have on misinformation challenging behaviours, as each can effect behaviour differently. Finally, due to the abstracted nature of the scenarios potentially prompting 'ideal world' thinking rather than reflections on real experiences, and additional limitations that come from the use of self-reporting Likert scale responses, participants may have provided insights into how individuals would like to act rather than how they would act in reality. More research to investigate misinformation challenging in practice from a cultural and relationship perspective would further address the research gap identified in this paper.

7   Conclusions

We investigated individuals' potential actions and concerns associated with exposure to misinformed individuals. Findings indicate that both tie strength and culture can have an impact on the actions an individual would take when exposed to a misinformed individual, and that the tie strength with the misinformed individual can have an impact on potential barriers that individuals foresaw affecting conversations with the misinformed individual, or barriers that would prevent them from conversing at all. This study expands on prior literature surrounding misinformation correction and provides grounds for future research to expand on the findings of this paper.

References

1. Aron, A., Aron, E.N., Smollan, D.: Inclusion of other in the self scale and the structure of interpersonal closeness. J. Pers. Soc. Psychol. **63**(4), 596–612 (1992). https://doi.org/10.1037/0022-3514.63.4.596, pp. 596–612. American Psychological Association (US), Washington, US
2. Berscheid, E., Snyder, M., Omoto, A.M.: The relationship closeness inventory: assessing the closeness of interpersonal relationships. J. Pers. Soc. Psychol. **57**(5), 792–807 (1989). https://doi.org/10.1037/0022-3514.57.5.792, pp. 792–807. American Psychological Association (US), Washington US
3. Bode, L., Vraga, E.K.: See something, say something: correction of global health misinformation on social media. Health Commun. **33**(9), 1131–1140 (2018). https://doi.org/10.1080/10410236.2017.1331312
4. Davies, K.: Sticking together in 'divided Britain': talking Brexit in everyday family relationships. Sociology **56**(1), 97–113 (2021). https://doi.org/10.1177/00380385211011569, SAGE Publications Ltd
5. Dawson, A., Oyserman, D.: Your fake news, our facts: identity-based motivation shapes what we believe, share and accept. In: The Psychology of Fake News: Accepting, Sharing, and Correcting Misinformation. Routledge, London, United Kingdom (2020)
6. Gächter, S., Starmer, C., Tufano, F.: Measuring the closeness of relationships: a comprehensive evaluation of the 'inclusion of the other in the self' scale. PLoS ONE **10**(6), e0129478 (2015). https://doi.org/10.1371/journal.pone.0129478, www.ncbi.nlm.nih.gov/pmc/articles/PMC4466912/
7. Hanington, B., Martin, B.: Universal methods of design expanded and revised. Quarto Publishing Group USA, Minneapolis, UNITED STATES (2019). www.ebookcentral.proquest.com/lib/northumbria/detail.action?docID=6039458
8. Kricorian, K., Civen, R., Equils, O.: COVID-19 vaccine hesitancy: misinformation and perceptions of vaccine safety. Hum. Vaccines Immunotherapeutics **18**(1), 1950504 (2022). https://doi.org/10.1080/21645515.2021.1950504
9. Leung, J., et al.: Concerns over the spread of misinformation and fake news on social media—challenges amid the coronavirus pandemic. Med. Sci. Forum **4**(1), 39 (2021). https://doi.org/10.3390/ECERPH-3-09078, www.mdpi.com/2673-9992/4/1/39
10. Lund Research Ltd.: How to perform a Mixed ANOVA in SPSS Statistics — Laerd Statistics (2018). www.statistics.laerd.com/spss-tutorials/mixed-anova-using-spss-statistics.php
11. Madraki, G., Grasso, I., M. Otala, J., Liu, Y., Matthews, J.: Characterizing and comparing COVID-19 misinformation across languages, countries and platforms. In: Companion Proceedings of the Web Conference 2021, pp. 213–223. ACM, Ljubljana Slovenia (2021). https://doi.org/10.1145/3442442.3452304
12. Malhotra, P.: A relationship-centered and culturally informed approach to studying misinformation on COVID-19. Soc. Med. + Soc. **6**(3), 2056305120948224 (2020). https://doi.org/10.1177/2056305120948224, SAGE Publications Ltd
13. Malhotra, P., Pearce, K.: Facing falsehoods: strategies for polite misinformation correction. Int. J. Commun. **16**(0), 22 (2022). www.ijoc.org/index.php/ijoc/article/view/18361

14. Rawlinson, F.: How Press Propaganda Paved the Way to Brexit. Springer, Berlin (2020). google-Books-ID: J2vLDwAAQBAJ
15. Resende, G., et al.: (Mis)Information dissemination in WhatsApp: gathering, analyzing and countermeasures. In: The World Wide Web Conference, pp. 818–828. WWW 2019, Association for Computing Machinery, New York, NY, USA (2019). https://doi.org/10.1145/3308558.3313688
16. Scott, L., Coventry, L., Cecchinato, M., Warner, M.: I figured her feeling a little bit bad was worth it not to spread that kind of hate: exploring how UK families discuss and challenge misinformation. In: Proceedings of the 2023 CHI Conference on Human Factors in Computing Systems. CHI EA 2023, ACM, Hamburg, Germany (2023)
17. Tully, M.: Everyday news use and misinformation in Kenya. Digit. Journal. **10**, 1–19 (2021). https://doi.org/10.1080/21670811.2021.1912625
18. Van Raemdonck, N., Meyer, T.: Why disinformation is here to stay. a sociotechnical analysis of disinformation as a hybrid threat. In: Lonardo, L. (ed.) Addressing Hybrid Threats: European Law and Policies. Edward Elgar (2022)
19. Vidgen, B., Taylor, H., Pantazi, M., Anastasiou, Z., Inkster, B., Margetts, H.: Understanding vulnerability to online misinformation. Technical report, The Alan Turing Institute (Mar (2021)
20. Vraga, E.K., Bode, L.: Using expert sources to correct health misinformation in social media. Sci. Commun. **39**(5), 621–645 (2017) https://doi.org/10.1177/1075547017731776, SAGE Publications Inc
21. Vraga, E.K., Bode, L.: Correction as a solution for health misinformation on social media. Am. J. Public Health **110**(S3), S278–S280 (2020). https://doi.org/10.2105/AJPH.2020.305916, publisher: American Public Health Association
22. Vraga, E.K., Bode, L.: Defining misinformation and understanding its bounded nature: using expertise and evidence for describing misinformation. Politic. Commun. **37**(1), 136–144 (2020). https://doi.org/10.1080/10584609.2020.1716500, publisher: Routledge _eprint
23. Yoo, B., Donthu, N., Lenartowicz, T.: Measuring Hofstede's five dimensions of cultural values at the individual level: development and validation of CVSCALE. J. Int. Consum. Mark. **23**(3–4), 193–210 (2011). https://doi.org/10.1080/08961530.2011.578059

Exploring Indigenous Knowledge Through Virtual Reality: A Co-Design Approach with the Penan Community of Long Lamai

Bram Kreuger[1]($\boxtimes$) and Tariq Zaman[2]

[1] Vrije Universiteit Amsterdam, Amsterdam, The Netherlands
bramkreuger@gmail.com
[2] University of Technology Sarawak, Sarawak, Malaysia

Abstract. This study aims to explore the design process of a virtual reality (VR) application to preserve indigenous knowledge (IK). Leveraging the community's preference for visual means of communication, a VR application was designed. The process involved working with the local Penan community in the forests of Borneo to co-design a VR application for a traditional hunting game called Nelikit and the mythological origin story associated with the game. Our methodology ensures that the application accurately represents the traditional game by community-led ownership of the design process and the final result. The findings of this study confirms that the use of VR can be an effective tool for cultural preservation and education, and that collaboration with the local indigenous community and designers is essential in the design process. Future research will further investigate the development, deployment and testing of the VR application.

Keywords: Co-design · Virtual Reality · Indigenous Knowledge · Penan

1 Introduction

It is important for game developers not to ignore the historical fact that Indigenous people (IP) have often been denied the power, status and authority to tell their own stories. Game players will get the most powerful and authentic experiences of Indigenous insights when Indigenous are involved in the games' design and development. It is a vital act of self-determination for us to be the ones determining how our people are portrayed and our stories are told [2].

Indigenous knowledge is highly valued by various indigenous communities around the world and is often passed down through generations. These communities struggle to preserve their traditional knowledge in the face of increasing industrialisation and globalisation. Therefore we found there is an increase in interest in researching how technology may be used to conserve and reinvigorate

J. Abdelnour Nocera et al. (Eds.): INTERACT 2023, LNCS 14144, pp. 439–448, 2023.
https://doi.org/10.1007/978-3-031-42286-7_24

IK. One such technology is VR, which has the potential to offer a distinctive and immersive experience for conserving traditional knowledge. There has been various research on the importance of visual arts and multi modality education with IP's, such as with the Aboriginal communities in Australia [3]. Here cross-cultural, participatory community research was conducted with indigenous elementary students to analyze the significance of indigenous visual arts in relation to trans generational indigenous Lore. Another demonstration of the effectiveness of using visual methods within an indigenous framework to facilitate social change and preserve IK, is exemplified in the Komuniti Tok Piksa project in Papua New Guinea, which involves local communities in narrating their experiences of HIV and AIDS through designing and recording their own messages [7]. Indigenous communities now have the opportunity to present their culture, history, and way of life through the creation of interactive and realistic virtual worlds.

Our study examines how VR technology could be used in collaboration with the Penan village of Long Lamai in Sarawak, Malaysia, to preserve and reinvigorate IK. The Penan people are traditionally a hunter-gatherer group with strong ties to Borneo's forests and waterways. Their traditional wisdom has been passed down through the years and they have a rich culture. Visual means of communication are of importance to the Penan community due to their close relation to the nature surrounding them [13]. Working together with researchers, the Penan community can design and create VR material that is representative of its culture and expertise. This strategy ensures that the community has active ownership over the process and that the final VR content will be relevant for the Penan community.

2   Related Studies

Over the years, there have been various studies that have used modern information and communication technologies to conserve and promote IK, VR being one of them. In this subsection, we briefly discuss a selection of these studies to better understand the task at hand.

In Zaman, Yeo and Jengan (2016) [11] the Oroo' language of the Penan is studied. This sign language is used in the rainforest to communicate between groups. It uses twigs, branches, and leaves attached to a signage stick to create different messages. The study then uses community-based research design to develop new IT solutions to preserve the Ooro' sign language. Two of the outcomes of this study were an adventure game, teaching the Ooro' sign language to Penan children [12] and custom made Ooro' short message signs (SMS) [10]. Both of these studies show that through participatory design methods, researchers can develop innovative solutions to conserve IK. VR applications have recently undergone significant developments, including hand gesture tracking, which presents new opportunities for creating immersive user experiences. Although there have been numerous studies on gesture elicitation, many lack validation and fail to include a diverse group of participants. This study addresses these limitations and explores the digitalisation of intangible cultural heritage in collaboration with San tribes in southern Africa [1]. Specifically, the researchers focus on incorporating gestures as embodied interactions in a VR implementation of a traditional San hunting story. The study includes an in situ elicitation of natural gestures, co-designed integration, and implementation of a VR story with grasping and gestures. The findings reveal the anthropological value of incorporating gestures determined by an indigenous community. Many of the challenges faced in this project resemble those of our research [6]. Another interesting example of VR and IP's is the fourth VR project [8]. The fourth VR is a database of VR cinema and games made by or with IP's. The study explores how indigenous creators utilise VR technology to tell their stories and resist colonial frameworks. Through case studies and analysis of the Fourth VR database, the authors identify a growing Indigenous-centred VR production framework.

3   Context

The village of Long Lamai is located in the interior of the Malaysian state of Sarawak on the island of Borneo. The village is not connected to the newly constructed logging road, a conscious decision that allows the community to have more control of the comings and goings of the village. The village is inhabited by the Penan people, who are attributed to be the last hunter gatherers of Borneo. The village was settled in the 1950s s and has grown to over 114 households [13]. The Long Lamai community has a long term relationship with the researchers from [university's name] and over the past decade has guided many researchers from all over the world to conduct research in collaboration with the community; which therefore has become accustomed to innovations. Since shedding its nomadic lifestyle, Penan society has gone through a whirlwind of modernisation. One of the effects of these developments is the loss of IK, which is not only an issue for the Penan, but a worrying trend around the world [4]. When new technologies and tools become more widely available, the younger generations are the first to embrace them. This leads to a generational gap in traditional knowledge, since interest in this knowledge differs between generations. The community recognises this issue and has a strong desire to design digital tools for the preservation of IK [9]. This project is the result of a collaboration between multiple partners. Through previous projects the community has become proficient in co-designing doigital tools for IK preservation [12]. They are experts with regards to knowledge from forest and also accustomed with co-design processes [5]. One of the researchers (the second author) is experienced in chairing the co-design sessions and working with the Long Lamai community. Finally, the technical components are to be developed by external collaborators (the first author). This project fits in the long term research collaboration between the UTS and the Long Lamai community to develop such technologies.

4   Research Approach

Our research approach is centred on the issue of loss of IK, a problem that many IP's around the world face. We believe that the Penan community can benefit from multimodal media, such as VR, which allows users to fully experience a virtual simulation. VR has the added advantage of being fully customisable, allowing applications to be modified according to the needs of users and customers. To ensure that the Penan community has full ownership over the process and content, we presented a prototype VR application to a panel from the Long Lamai community. Our approach is divided in four stages. Every stage has an input and an result. The four stages are as follows: 1) Exploration, 2) Ideation, 3) Documentation, and 4) Co-design. Each stage lasted around 1.5 h and the sessions were held on two different moments. These stages are loosely based on the similar successful approach used in [6].

4.1   Participants

We had the following seven participating co-designers: Two elders, two young men, two young women, and one teenage boy. One of the younger men was the village school teacher. The younger participants would help us translate between English and Penan language when there was any form of confusion. They had no previous experience with VR.

5   Stage 1: Exploration

5.1   Input: Prototype

In our study, we developed a prototype using the Unity Engine for mobile VR, with the purpose of showcasing some of the possibilities of VR. The decision to use mobile VR was made due to its cost-effectiveness and accessibility, as many community members already have smartphones [10] (Capable to run mobile VR). To achieve a feasible performance on lower-end devices, we adopted a stylised approach to the models rather than striving for realistic visuals. A screenshot of the demo can be seen in Fig. 1. The prototype consisted of two Penan character models set in a forest environment resembling Long Lamai's natural setting. Additionally, the prototype included various objects commonly used by the Penan in the jungle. To enhance the immersive experience, the prototype featured a boar that roamed around and produced sounds, accompanied by sape music in the background. The prototype also included several interactions, such as picking up and dropping items by gazing at them and using buttons floating in the air. The prototype aimed to provide a recognisable environment, with the goal of eliciting feedback.

Fig. 1. A screenshot from the prototype

5.2   Result

Visual. The participants provided valuable feedback on the prototype's visual elements. Here follows a list of the suggestions:

– The environment is acceptable, but the forest could be more lush.
– The colour of the sky would normally be blue. However, the coloration between the colour and the time of day was noted.
– The boar was well received, but there could be more animals.
– The characters' gender was identified; however, it was noted that the man should carry and wear more items to identify him as a man. (A parang/machette, blowpipe, etc.)
– The woman should wear different clothes then a T-shirt.
– The "typical" penan items were recognised; however, the basket was too large and the type of depicted basket in the prototype, specifically used by Penan women.

Interaction. All participants had the chance to interact with the scene's items while the prototype was being tested. After a quick explanation, the two younger men were able to engage with the items effortlessly and found it exciting. However, the other two participants found it to be a little more difficult. Both were able to engage effectively with the items after the successful participants helped them by explaining the interactions to them in the Penan language, which made it an enjoyable experience for them.

6   Stage 2: Ideation Session

6.1   Input: Video

To assist in the ideation we presented a video from the VR research project in namibia [1], which we discussed in the related studies. After getting accustomed to VR by using the prototype, this video would show what a fully developed VR application would be capable of. The hope was that this input would spark the imagination of the participants for applications specific to the Penan community.

6.2   Result

Following this demonstration, participants were asked if they thought a similar VR application would be of interest to the Long Lamai community. It was noted that children in the community would likely find such technology intriguing. Additionally, the researchers highlighted that VR technologies have been utilized for training purposes, such as in the field of surgery. The participants suggested that simulation activities, such as fishing or hunting, could be of interest to the community. Furthermore, the participants suggested that a simulation of the traditional game, Nelikit, could also be an interesting use case for VR technology as it's uniquely Penan. It was noted that one of the researchers was knowledgeable of this game, and therefore we collectively chose this game as the topic for our co-design session.

Inga' Telikit.[1] Nelikit is a traditional hunting game played by male Penan, in which players use a blowpipe to catch rattan rings of varying sizes that are thrown by other players Fig. 2. The Telikit, or rattan ring, serve as a representation of wild boar or other animals, and the game can be seen as a form of exercise. By using a blowpipe, the player must successfully catch the Telikit. It is usually played by teenagers, so they can practice their skills before the actual hunting. The players can choose between a number of "moves". There is an overhead throw, a side throw (left or right), or a low-front throw. The game itself is not usually being played by community members anymore, the younger generations now prefer to spend their leisure time differently.

Fig. 2. Playing Nelikit. The rattan ring is called Telikit

---

[1] Inga' means game in the Penan Language.

7   Stage 3: Documentation

7.1   Input: Collecting the Story

The origin of the game can be found in the mythological story of Nelikit. The genesis of Nelikit is at risk of becoming permanently lost. The story was first manually documented in 2013, during a visit of a researcher (second author). The initial script of the story was written by Garen Jengan, a community elder. However, due to his lack of recollection of the details, it was necessary to locate the source of the story. Tamin Pitah, a 97-year-old Penan elder, was identified as the original storyteller, and efforts were made to record his oral account. The narrative was captured through both video and audio recordings, which were later transcribed and translated from the Penan language into English.

7.2   Result

The following text is the collected and translated story of Nelikit, it connects the origin of the story with the game: *Once upon a time, there were two giant spirits named Aka and Gugak who were searching for a place where they could live forever. Aka decided to search the skies, while Gugak searched the earth. After some time, they reunited to share what they had found. Aka had discovered a beautiful place in the skies, while Gugak had found a challenging place to live on Earth. Aka's home was a river, teeming with fish and resources. The river had a mystic nature, and if someone caught a fish and threw its bones back into the river, they would come back to life as a new fish. Aka and Gugak were thrilled with their respective homes, and Aka began taking care of the skies and Gugak the land and its creatures. Whenever the people on earth faced a challenge, Aka and Gugak were always there to help and protect them. As the years went by, Aka and Gugak grew old. They noticed that the people on earth were afraid of thunderstorms, so they made a promise to help them even after they were gone. They told the people that if they ever needed their assistance, they could call their names in "Balei Padéng" and throw the Telikit in the air. They would use rattan to tie up the thunderstorm and bring it away from the people.*

8   Stage 4: Co-Design

8.1   Input: The Story

The last session in our process was the co-design session; here we walked through the details of the proposed VR-Nelikit game, together with local designers. As input we started the session by showing a video recording of the story, narrated by Taman Pitah. This story was not known to any of the participants of the session. The participants were asked how the (VR) game should be played and whenever something should be visualized (such as the characters or the scene) they were asked to draw their ideas, which later could be turned into a 3D environment. The approach is similar to [11]. These sketches can be in seen in Fig. 3.

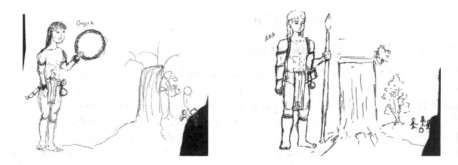

Fig. 3. Two of the sketches the panel made, depicting their vision for the game.

8.2   Result

The most interesting results of the co-design session are as follows:

- It was proposed to tell the story through a book. This is interesting given the oral tradition of these stories. This could be seen as a metaphor for modern storytelling.
- The giants: Aka and Gugak, should be very large and see through to indicate they are not mere men.
- It should be in a small village, surrounded by nature.
- The game should be bilingual, in Penan and English.
- Girls can play too, even though in real life, only boys play the game; as women are not allowed to hold a blowpipe.
- One question that came up, was how to prevent the thrower from playing unfair and throwing the Telikit far from the catcher. This did not seem a problem to the panel, who would not consider playing unfair; thus showing some of the cultural attributes of the community.

9   Discussion and Future Works

This study shows process to develop innovative ways to preserve IK. The usefulness of multimodal media is highlighted by making use of VR technology. Through extensive discussions with the community, giving them a free hand in designing and evaluating applications, we showed that it is possible to design a VR application where the community members have full ownership in the process and the end product. We realise that it would be beneficial for other members in the design panel to see what the wearer of the VR headset is seeing. In a future project, we would like to mirror the app to a projector. The next stage of the research project is to develop a functional VR application, where Nelikit can be played in virtual environment, preserved and, we hope, revived.

Acknowledgement. We thank the community of Long Lamai for their engagement, UTS for local research funding (2/2020/03 Crowdsourcing for Cultural Resource Mapping).

References

1. Arendttorp, E.M.N.: Grab it, while you can: a VR gesture evaluation of a co-designed traditional narrative by indigenous people (2023)
2. LaPensée, E.: Video games encourage Indigenous cultural expression. www.theconversation.com/video-games-encourage-indigenous-cultural-expression-74138
3. Mills, K.A., Doyle, K.: Visual arts: a multimodal language for Indigenous education. Lang. Educ. **33**(6), 521–543 (2019). https://doi.org/10.1080/09500782.2019.1635618. ISSN 0950–0782, 1747–7581. www.tandfonline.com/doi/full/10.1080/09500782.2019.1635618
4. Ramirez, Carlos R.: Ethnobotany and the Loss of Traditional Knowledge in the 21st Century. Ethnobot. Res. Appl. **5**, 245–247 (2007). ISSN 1547–3465. www.ethnobotanyjournal.org/index.php/era/article/view/134
5. Reitsma, L., Light, A., Zaman, T., Rodgers, P.: A Respectful Design Framework. Incorporating indigenous knowledge in the design process. Des. J. **22**(sup1), 1555–1570 (2019). ISSN 1460–6925, 1756–3062. https://doi.org/10.1080/14606925.2019.1594991. URL www.tandfonline.com/doi/full/10.1080/14606925.2019.1594991
6. Rodil, K., Maasz, D., Winschiers-Theophilus, H.: Moving Virtual reality out of its comfort zone and into the African Kalahari desert field: experiences from technological co-exploration with an indigenous san community in Namibia. In: 26th ACM Symposium on Virtual Reality Software and Technology, pages 1–10, Virtual Event Canada, November 2020. ACM (2020). ISBN 978-1-4503-7619-8. https://doi.org/10.1145/3385956.3418955. URL www.dl.acm.org/doi/10.1145/3385956.3418955
7. Thomas, V., Eggins, J., Papoutsaki, E.: Relational accountability in indigenizing visual research for participatory communication. SAGE Open **6**(1), 2158244015626493 (2016). ISSN 2158–2440. https://doi.org/10.1177/2158244015626493. URL https://doi.org/10.1177/2158244015626493. Publisher: SAGE Publications
8. Wallis, K., Ross, M.: Fourth VR: indigenous virtual reality practice. Convergence: Int. J. Res. New Media Technol. **27**(2), 313–329 (2021). ISSN 1354–8565, 1748–7382. https://doi.org/10.1177/1354856520943083. URL www.journals.sagepub.com/doi/10.1177/1354856520943083
9. Winschiers-Theophilus, H., Zaman, T., Stanley, C.: A classification of cultural engagements in community technology design: introducing a transcultural approach. AI Soc. **34**(3), 419–435 (2019). ISSN 0951–5666, 1435–5655. https://doi.org/10.1007/s00146-017-0739-y. URL www.link.springer.com/10.1007/s00146-017-0739-y
10. Zaman, T., Winschiers-Theophilus, H.: Penan's Oroo' short message signs (PO-SMS): co-design of a digital jungle sign language application. In: Abascal, J., Barbosa, S., Fetter, M., Gross, T., Palanque, P., Winckler, M. (eds.) INTERACT 2015. LNCS, vol. 9297, pp. 489–504. Springer, Cham (2015). https://doi.org/10.1007/978-3-319-22668-2_38 IIBN: 978-3-319-22667-5
11. Zaman, T., Yeo, A.W., Jengan, G.: Designing digital solutions for preserving penan sign language: a reflective study. Adv. Hum.-Comput. Interact. **2016**, 1–9 (2016). ISSN 1687–5893, 1687–5907, https://doi.org/10.1155/2016/4174795. URL www.hindawi.com/journals/ahci/2016/4174795/
12. Zaman, T., Winschiers-Theophilus, H., Yeo, A.W., Ting, L.C., Jengan, G.: Reviving an indigenous rainforest sign language: digital Oroo' adventure game. In: Proceedings of the Seventh International Conference on Information and Communication Technologies and Development, pp. 1–4, Singapore Singapore, May 2015.

ACM (2015). ISBN 978-1-4503-3163-0. https://doi.org/10.1145/2737856.2737885. URL www.dl.acm.org/doi/10.1145/2737856.2737885

13. Zaman,T., Winschiers-Theophilus, H., George, F., Wee, A.Y., Falak, H., Goagoses, N.: Using sketches to communicate interaction protocols of an indigenous community. In: Proceedings of the 14th Participatory Design Conference: Short Papers, Interactive Exhibitions, Workshops - Volume 2, pp. 13–16, Aarhus Denmark, August 2016. ACM (2016). ISBN 978-1-4503-4136-3. https://doi.org/10.1145/2948076.2948088. URL www.dl.acm.org/doi/10.1145/2948076.2948088

Factors Influencing Social Media Forgiveness Behavior and Cyber Violence Tendency Among Chinese Youth: Moderating Effects of Forgiveness Climate and Risk Perception

Zhirui Chen[1]($\boxtimes$) , Wenchen Guo[2] , and Qingxiang Zeng[3]

[1] University of Chinese Academy of Social Sciences, Beijing 102488, China
chenzhirui@ucass.edu.cn
[2] Peking University, Beijing 102600, China
[3] Chinese Academy of Social Sciences, Beijing 100021, China

Abstract. Over the past years, the issue of cyber violence has gradually become a key focus of social media studies. Most previous studies of cyber violence in social media have focused on superficial behaviors, with less attention given to implicit psychological factors, particularly on forgiveness behaviors and their effects. Based on the Unified Theory of Acceptance and Use of Technology (UTAUT), this study selects Chinese youth as the subject of analysis, and specifically examines the factors influencing their social media use forgiveness behaviors and cyber violence tendency. The study finds that empathy, trust, commitment, and anger rumination all positively influence forgiveness intention, and forgiveness intention significantly predicts forgiveness behavior, with forgiveness climate and risk perception playing a positive moderating role. In addition, the end of the structural equation modeling demonstrates that forgiveness behavior significantly predicts the tendency for cyber violence, which is the evidence of the importance of forgiveness behavior on cyber violence that cannot be ignored. This study provides a new path for understanding the causes of social media forgiveness behaviors among Chinese youth, and also provides a reference for emerging variables to mitigate cyber violence.

Keywords: Forgiveness Behavior · Cyber Violence · Social Media · Risk Perception · Anger Rumination · UTAUT

1 Introduction

Social conflict is a growing issue that continues to threaten the security and well-being of global society [1]. At the same time, with the rapid development of information technology, more and more social conflicts are being "uploaded" to the global Internet [2], and as a result, conflicts on social media are increasingly aligned with real social conflicts. Specifically, innovative applications and diffusion of social media have changed the ability of humans to perform complex tasks [3, 4], and the social perspectives and behaviors associated with them have also changed.

J. Abdelnour Nocera et al. (Eds.): INTERACT 2023, LNCS 14144, pp. 449–468, 2023.
https://doi.org/10.1007/978-3-031-42286-7_25

Recent years have seen an increase in the number of research topics focused on cyber violence, and the investigation of various psychological elements related to cyber violence has become a popular direction within the field of social media research [5–7], where the concept of forgiveness as opposed to cyber violence has also gained some attention in the academy [8]. However, such studies have taken forgiveness as a given behavior, and overall have not fully investigated the formation process of forgiveness behavior during social media use, and empirical studies on the relationship between forgiveness behavior and cyber violence are scarce, and need to be measured and explored by scholars in the social media field.

China is the first country to be affected by the COVID-19 and has gradually moved from being the "exception" to becoming the "norm" in online interactions [9]; at the same time, China also has a large number of social media users and is one of the global leaders in the innovation of social media applications. This has given rise to issues such as social media cyber violence, which need to be addressed through multi-level research [10]. Therefore, based on an in-depth analysis of forgiveness intention and forgiveness behavior, combining moderating variables such as forgiveness climate [11–13] and risk perception [14], the cyber violence tendency in China [15] has theoretical as well as practical value.

It is clear from the above analysis that studying the relationship between forgiveness intention and forgiveness behavior in social media use needs to focus more on the implicit attributes and social factors of people, which further provides richer empirical support for the study of cyber violence tendency. Taking into account factors such as sample collection and the Chinese context, this study takes young Chinese youth group as the research subject and measures them through a revised Unified Theory of Acceptance and Use of Technology (UTAUT) [16, 17], because the scale in this study is a distillation and aggregation of multiple studies, the analysis process in this study the analysis of this study was primarily exploratory, focusing on the examination and analysis of the overall structure of the model.

This study attempts to examine the implicit psychological factors such as empathy, trust, and commitment, and to link these variables to forgiveness intention. After examining the interplay of each dimension in a comprehensive manner, this study provides an in-depth understanding of the generative logic of forgiveness behavior used in social media in China, and explores its close relationship with the intensity of cyber violence. The elements of human emotion and cognition in the field of human-computer interaction have become important areas of exploration in recent years [18, 19]. Social media itself is one of the core subjects of HCI research, in which the various human emotional and cognitive elements of concern need to be addressed through interdisciplinary knowledge and methods. This study explores new perspectives on HCI from the user's perspective, incorporating perspectives from communication, cognitive and developmental psychology into the field of HCI, and building structural equation modeling to analyse the implicit psychological elements and motivations hidden behind the user's behaviour. In addition, this study's analysis of forgiveness and cyber violence in social media will further enrich the understanding of human behaviour and perception in the field of HCI, and provide empirical support for the design of good-oriented social media interaction systems.

Overall, this study contributes to the understanding of user and human behaviour in social media in two major ways:

On the one hand, based on empirical investigations, we have uncovered the links and interactions between implicit psychological factors (e.g. empathy, trust and commitment) and forgiveness intentions, and explored the logic of generating forgiveness behaviour in Chinese social media.

On the other hand, this work provides new ideas for the study and governance of online violence in the social media domain. This understanding is crucial for the design and management of future social platforms that take into account variables related to violence or forgiveness and their interactions (e.g. comment sections, forums, multiplayer games, etc.) in order to facilitate social media interactions in a more positive direction.

2 Literature Review

Forgiveness is a historical concept that can be traced back to the study of religion, philosophy, and other fields [20], and has gained a sudden development in recent modern times in the fields of psychology, law, and management [21–24]. At the same time, forgiveness is a complex structure without a consensus definition [25], and researchers have defined forgiveness in different ways, but defining forgiveness as a process is the current consensus among most researchers [26].

As Enright & Fitzgibbons [27] argue, forgiveness is a process that involves cognitive, emotional, and behavioral changes for the offender. In particular, it refers to the change from "negative cognitions, emotions, and behaviors" to "positive cognitions, emotions, and behaviors". In addition, Zhang & Fu [28] further pointed out that there are three main types of forgiveness, namely, trait forgiveness, situational forgiveness, and forgiveness in specific relationships, which together constitute the basic structure for understanding the causes of forgiveness behavior. It should be noted that the development of information and communication technology has provided a solid foundation for the emergence and popularity of social media, and the psychological research on social media around the logic of information technology has become a key direction of academic and industrial attention [29, 30]. Forgiveness in social media use is a concept of "suspension" that needs urgent attention in the context of increasing multi-subject conflict (violence) on the Internet.

Based on the initial focus on social media forgiveness, this study measured and tested it using a revised Unified Theory of Acceptance and Use of Technology (UTAUT.) In the original version of this model, Venkatesh et al. [17] used performance expectancy, effort expectancy, social influence, and auxiliary context as the main variables to predict people's intention and behavior toward the use of specific media technologies. In contrast, this study used empathy, commitment, trust, and anger rumination as predictors of forgiveness intentions and, in turn, forgiveness intentions as predictors of forgiveness behaviors. Finally, the influence degree of forgiveness behavior on the intensity of cyber violence is measured. The research reviews and hypotheses in this section will follow this logic of retrospection, dialogue, and construction.

The following are the 9 hypotheses proposed in this study, which are all from the authoritative literature of various disciplines, thus framing the theoretical model of this study (Fig. 1).

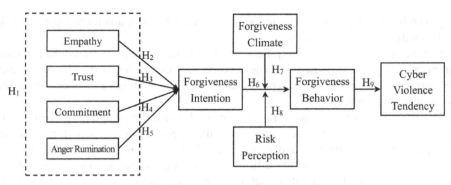

Fig. 1. Conceptual model and research hypotheses.

Forgiveness intention is influenced by many factors of different natures, some of which are social and cognitive, such as empathy [31], while others are related to the offense itself (e.g., anger rumination) or the relationship between the offender and the victim (e.g., trust, commitment) [32]. Regardless of the type of factor, some factors were found to be more influential than others [33]. In accordance with the literature base, this study focuses on the most influential factors, namely the victim's empathy, his or her commitment to the offender, his or her trust in the offender, and his or her anger rumination after being offended [3]. Based on the above four components, while including social media engagement as a contextual antecedent, this study hypothesizes that:

Hypothesis 1 (H1): Social media participation has a positive impact on empathy, trust, commitment and anger rumination.

Empathy refers to an individual's ability to understand and respond to the unique experience of another person, and empathy is prominently characterized by the development of empathy and altruistic behavior [34]. Fehr et al. [11] conducted a meta-analysis of 22 constructs related to forgiveness, which clearly indicated that state empathy was the only variable that showed a strong correlation with forgiveness (R = 0.53). Fincham [33] argues that empathy contributes to positive motivational change, while Wade & Worthington [35] go further and suggest that the development of empathy may enhance forgiveness because it allows the perception of aggression to be more easily understood. Therefore, this study hypothesizes that:

Hypothesis 2 (H2): Empathy has a positive impact on forgiveness intention for social media use.

On the basis of empathy, commitment and trust are also important predictors of forgiveness intention in social media use [36]. Numerous researchers have examined the effects of commitment and trust on forgiveness and found that both increase pro-social motivation, which is necessary to maintain relationships after wrongdoing [37, 38]. In a study on the mechanism of consumer forgiveness formation, Sun & Li [39] pointed out that after the outbreak of a functional crisis, pre-crisis consumer trust has a significant positive effect on post-crisis consumer willingness to forgive. And the study of Qiu et al. [40] also proved that interpersonal trust and forgiveness of high school students were positively related. Overall, this part of the study mainly explored the predictive effects of commitment and trust on forgiveness intentions in offline interactions or consumption scenarios, and there is a relative gap in the exploration of relationships in social media environments. Therefore, this study hypothesizes that:

Hypothesis 3 (H3): Commitment has a positive impact on forgiveness intention for social media use.

Hypothesis 4 (H4): Trust has a positive impact on forgiveness intention for social media use.

Forgiveness intention is closely related to anger behavior, which as a relatively external variable, where implicit motivational factors are an important aspect of measuring anger levels and emotional development, and there is now partial research demonstrating the relationship between anger and rumination [41], that anger and rumination, as more proximal social cognitive factors, also have an impact on forgiveness [42]. Anger rumination refers to an individual's immersive perception of angry emotions, consciously or unconsciously recalling past offensive experiences and envisioning possible consequences, and previous research has found a significant negative association between anger rumination and forgiveness [42]. Therefore, the study incorporates anger rumination into the measurement and proposes the following hypothesis:

Hypothesis 5 (H5): Anger rumination has a negative impact on forgiveness intention for social media use.

At present, most of the studies on "the influence of forgiveness intention on forgiveness behavior in social media use" focus on corporate crisis communication, in which the independent and dependent variables are mostly consumer forgiveness intention and forgiveness behavior, and are closely related to corporate response plans [43]. North [44] emphasized the motivational aspect of forgiveness, defining forgiveness behavior as "a change of will-an active effort to replace bad thoughts with kindness, pain and anger, and to replace them with compassion, which actually expresses the positive process from forgiveness intention to forgiveness behavior. Therefore, this study proposes hypothesis that in the process of social media use:

Hypothesis 6 (H6): Forgiveness intention has a positive impact on forgiveness behavior.

At the macro level, Fehr & Gelfand [45] wrote a thought-provoking paper on the process of forgiveness climate and its effects, and noted that forgiveness climate can have a significant impact on employees' interpersonal citizenship behavior. At the micro level, risk in the modern world has two paths: perception and response, where risk perception refers to our instinctive and intuitive response to danger, based on which risk analysis brings logical, rational and scientific considerations to risk assessment and decision-making [14]. Therefore, this study proposes hypothesis that during social media use:

Hypothesis 7 (H7): Forgiveness climate has a positive moderating effect on the relationship between forgiveness intention and forgiveness behavior.

Hypothesis 8 (H8): Risk perception has a positive moderating effect on the relationship between forgiveness intention and forgiveness behavior.

Cyber violence is a form of harassment and humiliation through the virtual world, as well as a form of violence in which real space interacts with cyberspace [46]. Cyberbullying is a type of cyber violence, specifically repetitive, deliberate and harmful online violence. Compared to cyber violence, Cyberbullying is more insidious and everyday. In a study of cyber violence among Saudi youth, it was further confirmed that cyber violence positively affects students' academic performance and their suicide attempts [47]. The strength of forgiveness behaviors reflects the overall level of tolerance in cyberspace, a level that may have a positive impact on cyber violence tendency. Therefore, this study hypothesizes that:

Hypothesis 9 (H9): Forgiveness behavior has a positive impact on the cyber violence tendency.

3   Methodology and Measurement Design

3.1   Objective and Data Collection

This study focuses on the effect of forgiveness intentions on forgiveness behavior and forgiveness behavior on the tendency of cyber violence among Chinese youth. With reference to the previous studies, the study population selected in this paper fits the age range of 18–40 years old for the youth group. This paper specifically constructs the structural equation modeling for this study, using the Unified Theory of Acceptance and Use of Technology (UTAUT) as a blueprint, so as to further explore the relationship between multiple dimensions. This study uses a web-based questionnaire (Wenjuanxing platform) to collect questionnaires on major social media platforms (Weibo, Zhihu, WeChat, Douban, etc.) for the Chinese youth group, and a total of 705 scale questionnaires are collected, and after eliminating invalid questionnaires, the number of valid copies are 520, and according to Alexandra [48], the sample size of this study meets the requirement of a minimum of 122 copies. The reasons for using self-report questionnaires in this study are twofold: firstly, self-report questionnaires collect cross-sectional data and are able to measure relatively fixed human cognitive and behavioural tendencies, and secondly, the anonymity of self-report questionnaires better simulates a natural measurement environment and reduces the interference caused by multiple confounding effects on the study. Among the Chinese youth group surveyed, 54.615% are male and 45.385% are female; the age distribution is 39.038% for 18–25 years old, 35.385% for 26–30 years old, and 25.577% for 31–40 years old (Table 1).

Table 1. Measurement of demographic variables

Variable	Item	Frequency	Percentage (%)
Gender	Male	284	54.615
	Female	236	45.385
Age	18–25	203	39.038
	26–30	184	35.385

(*continued*)

Table 1. (*continued*)

Variable	Item	Frequency	Percentage (%)
	31–40	133	25.577
Education	Undergraduate	248	47.692
	Junior college	219	42.115
	Master	36	6.923
	Doctor	10	1.923
	High School and below	7	1.346
Total		520	100.000

3.2 Conceptual Model

This paper mainly utilizes structural equation modeling (SEM) as the research method and uses AMOS 24.0 with SPSS 23.0's Process 4.0 plug-in for analysis and model testing of the research data. Based on the results of the literature review, this study includes variables such as social media participation, empathy, trust, commitment, anger rumination, forgiveness intention, forgiveness climate, risk perception, forgiveness behavior, and tendency to cyber violence, which led to the construction of a conceptual model from which subsequent reliability tests and relationship analysis are conducted. Structural equation modeling is used because it allows the combination of validating factor analysis (CFA) and regression analysis in the same model in order to test and analyze the relationship between the underlying constructs and their measured variables. In the final model, only items with reasonably high loadings are included in the model to achieve acceptable structural reliability and variance explained by the structure.

3.3 Variable Measurement

The scale is first developed by combining a review of the existing literature, from which this study summarized 10 dimensions measuring social media participation, forgiveness intention, forgiveness climate, risk perception, forgiveness behavior, and cyber violence tendency. The scale design of this study mainly consists of 10 sections with a total of 63 questions, and after statistical analysis to eliminate invalid items, the total number of questions was 57 (For questionnaire items, see supplementary materials at the end of the article). The questionnaires selected for this study are validated versions that have been verified by several studies and are able to measure the study variables relatively accurately. At the same time, this study takes into account the specificities of Chinese users and eliminates questions that do not adequately reflect the content of the variables (factor loadings below a critical value) after data collection and analysis to ensure the accuracy of this study. The basic demographic variables are also set, totaling 4 questions, including gender, age, education and occupation. In addition, the scales in this study are all based on a 5-point Likert scale. In this study, internal consistency was analysed for all ten dimensions, measured using the Cronbach's alpha coefficient. The results of the analysis were shown in the table below, and the Cronbach's alpha coefficients for all dimensions were above 0.8, indicating that all dimensions in this study had internal consistency (Table 2).

Table 2. Scale reliability tests of the study variables and the literature base

Variable	Cronbach's α	Literature base
Social Media Participation	0.933	[3]
Empathy	0.861	[3]
Trust	0.934	[3]
Commitment	0.883	[3]
Forgiveness Intention	0.902	[49]
Forgiveness Behavior	0.917	[50]
Forgiveness Climate	0.909	[49]
Risk Perception	0.916	[51]
Anger Rumination	0.923	[52]
Cyber Violence Tendency	0.919	[53]

4 Findings and Hypothesis Testing

4.1 Descriptive Analysis

"Forgiveness intention" (M = 3.0737, SD = 0.62180) has the most consistent internal topic structure; "Trust" (M = 3.0199, SD = 1.08308) and "Risk perception" (M = 3.0150, SD = 1.06481) structures are generally consistent with the mean. "Anger rumination" (M = 3.1673, SD = 1.09357) is the most divergent structure, but the actual differences between it and the other variables are smaller and the overall scale structure remains largely consistent. " Forgiveness behavior" (M = 2.5354, SD = .66467), on the other hand, shows a more stable performance and is the most negative structure for overall attitudes (Table 3).

Table 3. Basic statistics and distribution of the measurement model (scale 1 = completely disagree, 5 = completely agree)

Dimensions	Mean	SD	Kurtosis
Social Media Participation(SOC, 6 items)	3.1320	1.07504	−.908
Empathy(EM, 3 items)	3.0560	1.06472	−.882

(continued)

Table 3. (*continued*)

Dimensions	Mean	SD	Kurtosis
Trust(TRU, 6 items)	3.0199	1.08308	−1.001
Commitment(COM, 4 items)	2.9613	1.02816	−.950
Forgiveness Intention(INT, 6 items)	3.0737	.62180	1.316
Forgiveness Behavior(ACT, 7 items)	2.5354	.66467	1.362
Forgiveness Climate(ATM, 4 items)	3.1029	1.09275	−1.046
Risk Perception(RIS, 5 items)	3.0150	1.06481	−.853
Anger Rumination(ANG, 5 items)	3.1673	1.09357	−1.027
Cyber Violence Tendency(VIO, 7 items)	3.3900	.64766	1.628

4.2 Overall Fitness of the Structural Equation Modeling

The test of convergent validity and discriminant validity has been carried out in this study. In this study, confirmatory factor analysis is conducted for all dimensions, and the factor loadings of all dimensions ranged from 0.5 to 0.9 and are statistically tested significant. This study have significant convergent validity. We use the method of comparing the mean variance extracted (AVE) with the correlation coefficient, and judge the discriminant validity by constructing the correlation coefficient between dimensions and the average variance extracted. There is significant discriminant validity among the 10 dimensions in this study at 95% confidence level.

In the process of validation of structural equation modeling, a model fitness that meets the criteria is necessary for further analysis, and a better fitness means that the model matrix is closer to the sample matrix. In this study, the fitness indicators are selected from Schreiber [54] and Boomsma [55] for the overall model fitness evaluation, including RMSEA, GFI, CFI, NNFI, $\chi2$, and the ratio of $\chi2$ to degrees of freedom. According to the calculated results, all the measures are close to the ideal values and the overall model fitness is good (Table 4).

Table 4. Model fitness profile

Fitness indicators	Ideal requirement index	Model actual indicators
$\chi2$	Smaller the better	3447.591 (p = .000)
$\chi2$/df	<3	2.693(df = 1280)
GFI	>0.8	.843
CFI	>0.8	.894
NNFI	>0.8	.886
RMSEA	<0.09	.057

4.3 Path Coefficient Analysis of the Structural Equation Modeling

Based on the analysis of convergent and discriminant validity, it is clear that the model expectation covariance matrix of this study does not differ significantly from the sample covariance matrix, and the model fitness is satisfactory (in line with the expectation) (Fig. 2).

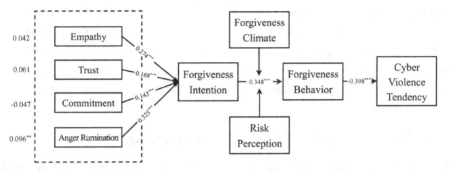

Fig. 2. Structural equation modeling with path coefficients.

According to the structural model coefficients (Table 5), social media participation of the Chinese youth group is not significant for empathy, trust, and commitment (p >0.05), but is significant for anger rumination with p = 0.044, which is less than 0.05, so H1 is partially supported. Other than that, the results of the analysis between the other dimensions show significance (p <0.05), which allows for further hypothesis testing and analysis.

In the path coefficient test (Table 5), the standardized regression coefficients β that meet the significance criteria are all in the range of values from 0.1 to 0.4, the significance among the variables is consistent, and the overall structure of the model is satisfactory. Empathy, commitment, trust, and anger rumination as predictors of forgiveness intention all possess statistical significance (p <0.05), which is consistent with the theoretical model of this study. However, anger rumination shows a positive predictive effect on forgiveness intention (β = 0.325, p = 0.000 <0.05), which is inconsistent with the study hypothesis, which may stem from the fact that rational thinking from anger rumination increases forgiveness intention, which is a new finding of this study that distinguishes it from previous studies [42]. In conclusion, H2, H3, and H4 are supported and H5 is not supported.

In addition, the standardized regression coefficient β for " forgiveness intention -> forgiveness behavior" is 0.348 (p <0.05), and the relationship is statistically significant to demonstrate the positive effect of forgiveness intention on forgiveness behavior, so H6 is supported. The standardized regression coefficient β of "forgiveness behavior -> cyber violence tendency" reaches −0.398 (p <0.05), which proves that forgiveness behavior of social media use has a significant negative effect on cyber violence tendency, such that H9 is supported.

Table 5. Path coefficients of the structural equation modeling

Model Path	Std.	Unstd.	t-value	P
Social Media Participation -> Empathy	0.042	0.04	0.874	0.382
Social Media Participation -> Trust	0.061	0.066	1.305	0.192
Social Media Participation -> Commitment	−0.047	−0.043	−0.98	0.327
Social Media Participation -> Anger Rumination	0.096	0.106	2.035	0.042
Empathy -> Forgiveness Intention	0.274	0.181	5.913	***
Trust -> Forgiveness Intention	0.168	0.098	3.858	***
Commitment -> Forgiveness Intention	0.143	0.099	3.205	***
Anger Rumination -> Forgiveness Intention	0.325	0.183	7.177	***
Forgiveness Intention- > forgiveness behavior	0.348	0.334	7.135	***
Forgiveness Behavior -> Cyber Violence Tendency	−0.398	−0.407	−8.116	***

Note: * $P < 0.1$ ** $p < 0.05$ *** $p < 0.01$

4.4 Analysis of Moderating Effects

In the moderating effect test, this study follows the calculation method of Wen et al. (2005), firstly, the independent variable forgiveness willingness is centralized, and the variables are controlled and analyzed by using stratified regression. Stratified regression is the normative method for conducting moderating effect analysis in psychology, allowing for the introduction of a hierarchy of independent variables, moderating variables and interaction terms to discover whether the moderating variable acts as a moderator between the independent and dependent variables, and to measure the magnitude of the moderating effect. Secondly, this study separately tests the significance of forgiveness intention, forgiveness climate, risk perception and forgiveness behavior, and finds that forgiveness intention ($\beta = 0.314$, $p = 0.000 <0.05$), forgiveness climate ($\beta = 0.265$, $p = 0.000<0.05$) and risk perception ($\beta = 0.253$, $p = 0.000<0.05$) have significant predictive effect to forgiveness behavior.

Finally, the interaction terms "forgiveness intention × forgiveness climate" and "forgiveness intention × risk perception" are placed in the forgiveness intention and forgiveness behavior. It is found that the interaction terms " forgiveness intention × forgiveness climate" ($\beta = 0.161$, $p = 0.000<0.05$, $\triangle R2 = 0.137$), "forgiveness intention × risk perception" ($\beta = 0.155$, $p = 0.000<0.05$, $\triangle R2 = 0.137$), and "forgiveness intention × risk perception" ($\beta = 0.155$, $p = 0.000<0.05$, $\triangle R2 = 0.158$) are significant predictors of forgiveness behavior, which also indicates that the positive moderating effect of forgiveness climate (Table 6) and risk perception (Table 7) on the relationship between forgiveness intention and forgiveness behavior is significant, so that H7 and H8 are supported.

Table 6. The moderating effect of forgiveness climate on the relationship between forgiveness intention and forgiveness behavior

	Model 1	Model 2	Model 3
Const	2.482***	2.348***	3.814***
	(17.609)	(16.195)	(10.307)
INT	0.314***	0.091***	−0.218*
	(6.996)	(3.399)	(−1.794)
ATM		0.265***	−0.409***
		(5.679)	(−3.42)
INT*ATM			0.161***
			(4.292)
Sample size	520	520	520
R^2	0.086	0.106	0.137
Adjusted R^2	0.085	0.103	0.132
F	F (520,1) = 48.871	F (2,517) = 30.704	F (3,516) = 27.266
	p = 0.000	p = 0.000	p = 0.000
ΔR^2	0.086	0.106	0.137
ΔF	F (1,520) = 48.941	F (1,517) = 11.556	F (1,516) = 50.2
	p = 0.000	p = 0.001	p = 0.000

Dependent variable: ACT

Note: *P < 0.1 ** p < 0.05 *** p < 0.01

Table 7. The moderating effect of risk perception on the relationship between forgiveness intention and forgiveness behavior

	Model 4	Model 5	Model 6
Const	2.482***	2.242***	3.646***
	(17.609)	(15.476)	(9.517)
INT	0.314***	0.142***	−0.204***
	(6.991)	(5.272)	(−1.645)
RIS		0.253***	−0.344***
		(5.586)	(−2.736)
INT*RIS			0.155***
			(3.951)

(*continued*)

Table 7. (*continued*)

	Model 4	Model 5	Model 6
Sample size	520	520	520
R^2	0.086	0.133	0.158
Adjusted R^2	0.085	0.130	0.154
F	$F(520,1) = 48.941$ $p = 0.000$	$F(2,517) = 39.634$ $p = 0.000$	$F(3,516) = 32.373$ $p = 0.000$
ΔR^2	0.086	0.133	0.158
ΔF	$F(1,520) = 48.941$ $p = 0.000$	$F(1,517) = 27.796$ $p = 0.000$	$F(1,516) = 56.365$ $p = 0.000$

Dependent variable: ACT

Note: *P <0.1 ** p <0.05 *** p <0.01

4.5 Summary of Hypothesis Testing Results

Based on the above explanation of the data analysis results, most of the hypotheses of this study are strongly proved, and the Table 8 is a summary of whether the study hypotheses are supported.

Table 8. Summary of study hypothesis results

Hypothesis	Result
H1: Social media participation has a positive impact on empathy, trust, commitment and anger rumination	Partially supported
H2: Empathy has a positive impact on forgiveness intention for social media use	Supported
H3: Commitment has a positive impact on forgiveness intention for social media use	Supported
H4: Trust has a positive impact on forgiveness intention for social media use	Supported
H5: Anger rumination has a negative impact on forgiveness intention for social media use	Not supported
H6: Forgiveness intention has a positive impact on forgiveness behavior	Supported
H7: Forgiveness climate has a positive moderating effect on the relationship between forgiveness intention and forgiveness behavior	Supported
H8: Risk perception has a positive moderating effect on the relationship between forgiveness intention and forgiveness behavior	Supported
H9: Forgiveness behavior has a positive impact on the cyber violence tendency	Supported

5 Conclusions

With the rapid advancement of social media, there have been positive changes in society as well as hidden concerns and thoughts. This study uses the Unified Theory of Acceptance and Use of Technology (UTAUT) as a blueprint to construct a structural equation modeling from the forgiveness intention to forgiveness behavior of social media use, and derives from this to test and explore the cyber violence tendency. In sum, this study originates from reflections and alerts on online social conflicts, and ultimately acts on the micro-research level of online social conflicts, forming a logical closure loop of empirical research with a first-to-last link.

5.1 Conclusion 1: High-Intensity Cyber Violence is Becoming the Norm, and Social Media Forgiveness Provides a Psychological Solution to Alleviate It

Cyber violence seems to be more prevalent than traditional violence and bullying because it can happen at any time [56]. Some scholars noted in earlier years that the prevalence of cyberbullying ranges from 10% to 35% [57]. Furthermore, since cyber violence is a broader term, it is reasonable to accept its broader prevalence range, for example, some studies have also found the prevalence of cyber attacks to be over 50% [58]. It can be found that previous studies of cyber violence have mostly measured its scope and prevalence, and slightly under-measured the cyber violence tendency.

The study associates the tendency of cyber violence with the intensity of cyber violence among the youth group, on the one hand, because of the activeness and representativeness of this group, and also because this group is the main force of the in-depth use of social media. On the other hand, it is also because the propensity to engage in cyber violence represents the possibility of the group to engage in cyber violence. When the cyber violence tendency of a certain group is much higher than the normal value of other indicators, it is reasonable to infer that the intensity of cyber violence will also show high values.

In the findings of this study, the cyber violence tendency among the Chinese youth group reaches a high value of 3.39, which is the highest among all measured dimensions. Although other relevant reference factors are not examined, they do provide a perspective that there is a possible relationship between the gradual increase in cyber violence in China and the cyber violence tendency among the youth group, which needs to be scientifically tested by subsequent empirical studies. The basic hypothesis of this study is that forgiveness behaviors have an implicit psychological antecedent of forgiveness intention, and these antecedents have a positive and significant impact on the actual implementation of forgiveness behaviors.

The empirical data in this study have provided preliminary evidence of the existence of a partial propensity for cyber violence among the Chinese youth group, and have also proposed an empirical-level path to alleviate, i.e., social media forgiveness influenced by the combination of empathy, trust, and commitment, which will provide a psychological-level direction for exploration, while the previous governance path from cyber violence itself can be shifted to a governance path from the psychological motivation itself.

5.2   Conclusion 2: Social Media Participation Hardly Interferes with Cognitive Sedimentation, and Forgiveness Intention Stems from Pro-social Motivation

The argument that social media brings about dramatic changes in user participation and their behaviors due to the collective cultural acceptance of social media. Among them, one study found that Facebook users have 10% more intimate relationships than ordinary Internet users [59], which is an intuitive empirical result brought by social media participation.

Moreover, it is also this logic of argument and empirical results that suggest that current research on social media forgiveness is trapped in a technology-driven framework in which social media represents a powerful influence of technological development [60]. Therefore, social media participation is not examined for deeper implicit psychological motivations in the study of social media forgiveness and other similar concepts, but rather introduce and highlight the impact of social media engagement as a natural context.

Van Dijck [61], for example, has pointed out that the spread of social media logic transforms network communication into platform-based social communication, which is profoundly changing the nature of our connection, creation and interaction. Although this view clearly points out the profound influence of social media logic on the logic of communication behavior, it also ignores the influence of implicit psychological motivation.

Therefore, in constructing a structural equation modeling, this study explores the degree of importance of social media participation in social media forgiveness by referring to the basic structure of the Unified Theory of Acceptance and Use of Technology (UTAUT) on the one hand, and also introducing social media participation into the model by testing it as an independent variable of empathy, trust, commitment, and anger rumination on the other hand.

After data collection and model testing, this study found that social media participation is not significant for empathy, trust, and commitment. From this perspective, empathy, trust, and commitment, as deep implicit psychological motivations at the cognitive level, are not influenced by social media participation. Therefore, if this study is directly focused on social media participation as the main factor that influences social media forgiveness, it will produce a large systematic bias from the beginning of the structure.

This study distills empathy, trust, and commitment into cognitive sedimentation, which denotes the overall elements that are latent deep in the psyche, difficult to change, and permeate culture, and social media participation is difficult to interfere with cognitive sedimentation, a concept that is also partially similar to the concept of culture genes [62]. Since it is difficult for social media participation to intervene in cognitive sedimentation, and also since the effect of social media participation on forgiveness intention is not significant ($\beta = 0.121$, $p = 0.06$) according to the results of the out-of-model regression analysis, the source of social media forgiveness intention becomes a matter for discussion. Therefore, the elements of empathy, trust, commitment, and anger rumination proposed in this study become empirical support for exploring the significance of social media forgiveness intention.

In addition, as a component of pro-social behavior, the pro-social motivation of forgiveness may provide some insights. Pro-social behavior refers to all behaviors that benefit others and society, including cooperation, sharing, helping, forgiveness, and comfort, etc. Its cognitive processes include concern for others, social information processing, reward expectations for outcomes, social norm representation, self-control, and information integration and value calculation.

On the basis of conceptual combing, the four components of empathy, trust, commitment, and anger rumination can all be found to be specific manifestations of pro-social motivation, and social media forgiveness intention, as external psychological motivation, is initially confirmed to originate from empathy, trust, commitment, and anger rumination in the model construction and testing. While these four dependent variables may not cover all the predictors, the results of the analysis of these factors have at least demonstrated that social media forgiveness intention mainly originates from pro-social motives, which in turn originate from the immutable human sedimentation of humans. Social media participation has difficulty interfering with this cognitive process of occurrence.

6 Discussions and Limitations

After careful and comprehensive empirical testing, the present study has largely proved the association of the social media forgiveness and cyber violence model structured in this paper, and justified the research hypotheses, which supports previous studies [63, 64]. Although previous studies have pointed out the importance of forgiveness behavior, the understanding of its importance remains at the level of basic psychological elements [8].

In light of the aforementioned state of research, the value of this study lies firstly in proposing a model for measuring forgiveness behavior in social media and organically linking it to elements of cyber violence, thus forming a comprehensive set of measurement and governance models that serve the development of real social networks.

Secondly, it raises the importance of forgiveness behavior in social media use to a new position. And along with the introduction of moderating variables such as forgiveness climate and risk perception, the model of this study shows a layer-by-layer convergence in the measurement of forgiveness intention to forgiveness behavior. This measurement process is meaningful for the detection of the intensity of cyber violence. It has been pointed out that the main reason for the occurrence of cyber violence is retaliation [6]. Therefore, the low revenge character of forgiveness itself is relevant to address the problem of cyber violence.

Since the outbreak of the COVID-19, the social distance between people has continued to increase, and the "net-to-net" mode of communication has gradually become the everyday landscape of interpersonal communication, which has also been called the "Untact" era. In the face of this situation, social media will see a new wave of rapid development, but at the same time, the development of cyber violence may also become more and more unfavorable. In this regard, the forgiveness behavior of social media use may gradually play a significant role in the future.

For demographic variables, the research questions or hypotheses in this paper do not focus on demographic factors, and we prefer to examine overall cyber violence and human behavior from implicit psychological perspectives. In addition, we have added demographic variables as control variables to the statistical analysis of this study, and the results of the statistical analysis have not resulted in significant changes that would affect the validity of the results. Therefore, after considering all aspects, we have not included demographic factors in the presentation of our results.

The limitation of this study is the use of self-reported behavioral measures rather than observed behaviors. Further research on the relationship between social media forgiveness behaviors and cyber violence could be facilitated by incorporating more influential factors into structural equation modeling in future studies.

References

1. Ho, M.Y., Fung, H.H.: A dynamic process model of forgiveness: a cross-cultural perspective. Rev. Gen. Psychol. **15**, 77–84 (2011). https://doi.org/10.1037/a0022605
2. Bliuc, A.-M., Betts, J., Vergani, M., Iqbal, M., Dunn, K.: Collective identity changes in far-right online communities: the role of offline intergroup conflict. New Media Soc. **21**, 1770–1786 (2019). https://doi.org/10.1177/1461444819831779
3. Laifa, M., Akrouf, S., Mammeri, R.: Forgiveness and trust dynamics on social networks. Adapt. Behav. **26**, 65–83 (2018). https://doi.org/10.1177/1059712318762733
4. Sun, P., Zhao, G., Liu, Z., Li, X., Zhao, Y.: Toward discourse involution within China's internet: class, voice, and social media. New Media Soc. **24**, 1033–1052 (2022). https://doi.org/10.1177/1461444820966753
5. Turan, N., Polat, O., Karapirli, M., Uysal, C., Turan, S.G.: The new violence type of the era: cyber bullying among university students: violence among university students. Neurol. Psychiatry Brain Res. **17**, 21–26 (2011). https://doi.org/10.1016/j.npbr.2011.02.005
6. Peterson, J., Densley, J.: Cyber violence: what do we know and where do we go from here? Aggress. Violent. Beh. **34**, 193–200 (2017). https://doi.org/10.1016/j.avb.2017.01.012
7. Rebollo-Catalan, A., Mayor-Buzon, V.: Adolescent bystanders witnessing cyber violence against women and girls: what they observe and how they respond. Violence Against Women **26**, 2024–2040 (2020). https://doi.org/10.1177/1077801219888025
8. Safaria, T., Tentama, F., Suyono, H.: Cyberbully, cybervictim, and Forgiveness among Indonesian high school students. Turk. Online J. Educ. Technol.-TOJET **15**, 40–48 (2016)
9. Lan, J.: Biopolitics and political ecology in post-pandemic era. J. Nantong Univ. (Soc. Sci. Ed.) **38**, 1–9 (2022)
10. Feng, G., Huang, Y.: The Cause and Symptoms of the Group Polarization of College Students' Public Sentiment on the Internet. Studies in Ideological Education (2021)
11. Fehr, R., Gelfand, M.J., Nag, M.: The road to forgiveness: a meta-analytic synthesis of its situational and dispositional correlates. Psychol. Bull. **136**, 894 (2010). https://doi.org/10.1037/a0019993
12. Zhang, J., Long, L.: The impact of servant leadership on employees' interpersonal citizenship behavior: the role of forgiveness climate and middle-of-the-road thinking. J. Ind. Eng. Eng. Manage. **30**, 43–51 (2016). https://doi.org/10.13587/j.cnki.jieem.2016.01.006
13. Khan, M.S., Elahi, N.S., Abid, G.: Workplace incivility and job satisfaction: mediation of subjective well-being and moderation of forgiveness climate in health care sector. Eur. J. Invest. Health, Psychol. Educ. **11**, 1107–1119 (2021). https://doi.org/10.3390/ejihpe11040082
14. Slovic, P., Peters, E.: Risk perception and affect. Curr. Dir. Psychol. Sci. **15**, 322–325 (2006). https://doi.org/10.1111/j.1467-8721.2006.00461.x
15. Huang, C., Hu, B., Jiang, G., Yang, R.: Modeling of agent-based complex network under cyber-violence. Physica A **458**, 399–411 (2016). https://doi.org/10.1016/j.physa.2016.03.066

16. Davis, F.D.: Perceived usefulness, perceived ease of use, and user acceptance of information technology. MIS Q. **13**(3), 319–340 (1989). https://doi.org/10.2307/249008
17. Venkatesh, V., Davis, F.D.: A theoretical extension of the technology acceptance model: four longitudinal field studies. Manage. Sci. **46**, 186–204 (2000). https://doi.org/10.1287/mnsc.46.2.186.11926
18. Guo, W., et al.: A "magic world" for children: design and development of a serious game to improve spatial ability. Computer Animation and Virtual Worlds, e2181 (2023). https://doi.org/10.1002/cav.2171
19. Guo, W., et al.: The "rebirth" of traditional musical instrument: an interactive installation based on augmented reality and somatosensory technology to empower the exhibition of chimes. Computer Animation and Virtual Worlds **34**(3–4), e2171 (2023). https://doi.org/10.1002/cav.2171
20. Fu, H.: Forgiveness: a new philosophical and psychological proposition. J. Nanjing Normal Univ. (Soc. Sci. Ed.), 80–87 (2002)
21. Hebl, J., Enright, R.D.: Forgiveness as a psychotherapeutic goal with elderly females. Psychother. Theor. Res. Pract. Training **30**(4), 658–667 (1993). https://doi.org/10.1037/0033-3204.30.4.658
22. Cameron, K.S.: Forgiveness in organizations. Positive Organ. Behav. **2**, 129–142 (2007). https://doi.org/10.4135/9781446212752.n10
23. Tsarenko, Y., Tojib, D.: Consumers' forgiveness after brand transgression: the effect of the firm's corporate social responsibility and response. J. Mark. Manag. **31**, 1851–1877 (2015). https://doi.org/10.1080/0267257X.2015.1069373
24. Zhou, Y., Liu, X., Zhao, L., Zhang, Y.: The Relationship between college students' self-esteem and forgiveness: a moderated mediating effect model. Psychol. Explor. **40**, 188–192 (2020)
25. Du, G., Huang, X.: Development of the Chinese community residents' forgiveness scale. J. Southwest Univ. (Soc. Sci. Ed.) **48**, 192–199 (2022)
26. Donovan, L.A.N., Priester, J.R.: Exploring the psychological processes that underlie interpersonal forgiveness: replication and extension of the model of motivated interpersonal forgiveness. Front. Psychol. **11**, 2107 (2020). https://doi.org/10.3389/fpsyg.2020.02107
27. Enright, R.D., Fitzgibbons, R.P.: Helping Clients Forgive: An Empirical Guide for Resolving Anger and Restoring Hope. American Psychological Association, Washington (2000). https://doi.org/10.1037/10381-000
28. Zhang, T., Fu, H.: The scale development and investigation of the courtship forgiveness for college students. Stud. Psychol. Behav. **12**, 220–225 (2014)
29. Han, B.: Social media burnout: definition, measurement instrument, and why we care. J. Comput. Inf. Syst. **58**, 122–130 (2018). https://doi.org/10.1080/08874417.2016.1208064
30. Huang, H.: Causes of social media burnout among youth groups and the impact on intention to disengage from online communities. Shanghai Journalism Rev. **11**, 38–53 (2020)
31. Cornish, M.A., Guyll, M., Wade, N.G., Lannin, D.G., Madon, S., Chason, K.C.: Does empathy promotion necessarily lead to greater forgiveness? An Experimental Examination. Curr. Psychol. **39**, 1001–1011 (2020). https://doi.org/10.1007/s12144-018-9816-8
32. Osterman, L.L., Hecmanczuk, T.A.: Parasocial forgiveness: the roles of parasocial closeness and offense perceptions. J. Soc. Pers. Relatsh. **37**, 800–820 (2020). https://doi.org/10.1177/0265407519879511
33. Fincham, F.D.: The kiss of the porcupines: from attributing responsibility to forgiving. Pers. Relat. **7**, 1–23 (2000). https://doi.org/10.1111/j.1475-6811.2000.tb00001.x
34. Wu, F.: An analysis on the theoretical foundation and practical approach of empathetic communication. Journalism Commun. **26**, 59–76+127 (2019)
35. Wade, N.G., Worthington, E.L.: In search of a common core: a content analysis of interventions to promote forgiveness. Psychother. Theor. Res. Pract. Training **42**(2), 160–177 (2005). https://doi.org/10.1037/0033-3204.42.2.160

36. Molden, D.C., Finkel, E.J.: Motivations for promotion and prevention and the role of trust and commitment in interpersonal forgiveness. J. Exp. Soc. Psychol. **46**, 255–268 (2010). https://doi.org/10.1016/j.jesp.2009.10.014

37. Finkel, E.J., Rusbult, C.E., Kumashiro, M., Hannon, P.A.: Dealing with betrayal in close relationships: does commitment promote forgiveness? J. Pers. Soc. Psychol. **82**, 956 (2002). https://doi.org/10.1037/0022-3514.82.6.956

38. Rusbult, C.E., Hannon, P.A., Stocker, S.L., Finkel, E.J.: Forgiveness and relational repair. In: Handbook of Forgiveness, pp. 209–230. Routledge (2007)

39. Sun, N., Li, H.: The formation mechanism of consumer forgiveness after clustered product crisis: the dynamic driving effect of customer participation. J. Central Univ. Financ. Econ., 101–109 (2017)

40. Qiu, S., Zhao, Z., Wang, Y., Lei, X.: Relationship among self-compassion, interpersonal trust and forgiveness qualities in high school students. Psychol. Res. **10**, 84–90 (2017)

41. Kong, F., et al.: Why do people with self-control forgive others easily? The role of rumination and anger. Front. Psychol. **11**, 129 (2020). https://doi.org/10.3389/fpsyg.2020.00129

42. Riek, B.M., Mania, E.W.: The antecedents and consequences of interpersonal forgiveness: a meta-analytic review. Pers. Relat. **19**, 304–325 (2012). https://doi.org/10.1111/j.1475-6811.2011.01363.x

43. Christodoulides, G., Gerrath, M.H., Siamagka, N.T.: Don't be rude! The effect of content moderation on consumer-brand forgiveness. Psychol. Mark. **38**, 1686–1699 (2021). https://doi.org/10.1002/mar.21458

44. North, J.: Wrongdoing and forgiveness. Philosophy **62**, 499–508 (1987). https://doi.org/10.1017/S003181910003905X

45. Fehr, R., Gelfand, M.J.: The forgiving organization: a multilevel model of forgiveness at work. Acad. Manag. Rev. **37**, 664–688 (2012). https://doi.org/10.5465/amr.2010.0497

46. Vandebosch, H., Van Cleemput, K.: Defining cyberbullying: a qualitative research into the perceptions of youngsters. Cyberpsychol. Behav. **11**, 499–503 (2008). https://doi.org/10.1089/cpb.2007.0042

47. Alotaibi, N.B., Mukred, M.: Factors affecting the cyber violence behavior among Saudi youth and its relation with the suiciding: a descriptive study on university students in Riyadh city of KSA. Technol. Soc. **68**, 101863 (2022). https://doi.org/10.1016/j.techsoc.2022.101863

48. Alexandra, V.: Predicting CQ development in the context of experiential cross-cultural training: the role of social dominance orientation and the propensity to change stereotypes. Acad. Manag. Learn. Educ. **17**, 62–78 (2018). https://doi.org/10.5465/amle.2015.0096

49. Cox, S.: A forgiving workplace: an investigation of forgiveness climate, individual differences and workplace outcomes. Louisiana Tech University (2008)

50. Rye, M.S., Loiacono, D.M., Folck, C.D., Olszewski, B.T., Heim, T.A., Madia, B.P.: Evaluation of the psychometric properties of two forgiveness scales. Curr. Psychol. **20**, 260–277 (2001). https://doi.org/10.1007/s12144-001-1011-6

51. Niu, J., Meng, X.: The impacts of social media trust on perceived privacy risk and self-disclosure: mediating effects of network interpersonal trust. Chin. J. Journalism Commun. **41**, 91–109 (2019). https://doi.org/10.13495/j.cnki.cjjc.2019.07.007

52. Sukhodolsky, D.G., Golub, A., Cromwell, E.N.: Development and validation of the anger rumination scale. Pers. Individ. Differ. **31**, 689–700 (2001). https://doi.org/10.1016/S0191-8869(00)00171-9

53. Zhao, F., Gao, W.: Reliability and validity of the adolescent online aggressive behavior scale. Chin. Ment. Health J. **26**, 439–444 (2012)

54. Schreiber, J.B.: Core reporting practices in structural equation modeling. Res. Social Adm. Pharm. **4**, 83–97 (2008). https://doi.org/10.1016/j.sapharm.2007.04.003

55. Boomsma, A.: Reporting analyses of covariance structures. Struct. Equ. Model. **7**, 461–483 (2000). https://doi.org/10.1207/S15328007SEM0703_6

56. Šincek, D., Duvnjak, I., Milić, M.: Psychological outcomes of cyber-violence on victims, perpetrators and perpetrators/victims. Hrvatska revija za rehabilitacijska istraživanja **53**(2), 98–110 (2017). https://doi.org/10.31299/hrri.53.2.8

57. Kowalski, R.M., Limber, S.P.: Electronic bullying among middle school students. J. Adolesc. Health **41**, S22–S30 (2007). https://doi.org/10.1016/j.jadohealth.2007.08.017

58. Pornari, C.D., Wood, J.: Peer and cyber aggression in secondary school students: the role of moral disengagement, hostile attribution bias, and outcome expectancies. Aggressive Behav. Official J. Int. Soc. Res. Aggression **36**, 81–94 (2010). https://doi.org/10.1002/ab.20336

59. Hampton, K.N., Sessions, L.F., Her, E.J., Rainie, L.: Social Isolation and New Technology. Pew Internet & American Life Project (2009)

60. Yin, Y., Xie, Z.: Playing platformized language games: social media logic and the mutation of participatory cultures in Chinese online fandom. New Media Soc., 14614448211059488 (2021). https://doi.org/10.1177/14614448211059489

61. van Dijck, J.: The Culture of Connectivity: A Critical History of Social Media. Oxford University Press (2013). https://doi.org/10.1093/acprof:oso/9780199970773.001.0001

62. Zeng, Q., Wu, X.: Cultural differences, culture genes and the expression of enigma - an example of Chinese and American sports loss and victory reporting. Mod. Commun. **42**, 34–39 (2020)

63. Watson, H., Rapee, R., Todorov, N.: Imagery rescripting of revenge, avoidance, and forgiveness for past bullying experiences in young adults. Cogn. Behav. Ther. **45**, 73–89 (2016). https://doi.org/10.1080/16506073.2015.1108360

64. Barcaccia, B., et al.: Forgiveness and friendship protect adolescent victims of bullying from emotional maladjustment. Psicothema (2018)

Gender and Racism: Considerations for Digital Learning Among Young Refugees and Asylum Seekers

Denise Lengyel[1]([✉]) [iD], Ahmed Kharrufa[1] [iD], James Stanfield[2] [iD], Haley Powers[3],
Bridget Lara Stratford[3], and Reem Talhouk[4] [iD]

[1] Open Lab, School of Computing, Newcastle University, Newcastle upon Tyne, UK
denise.lengyel@newcastle.ac.uk
[2] School of Education, Communication and Language Sciences, Newcastle University,
Newcastle upon Tyne, UK
[3] North East Solidarity and Teaching, Newcastle University, Newcastle upon Tyne, UK
[4] School of Design, Northumbria University, Newcastle upon Tyne, UK

Abstract. Young refugees and asylum seekers (RAS) in the UK face barriers related to language and accessing formal schooling. While HCI research has focused on migration, less work has been done with young RAS and less so on how digital platforms may be used to support young RAS during times in which they are unable to access schooling. Through co-design workshops with young RAS in the UK, we explored social and contextual factors influencing their engagement in and experiences with digital tools to learn and develop their learning skills outside of school. Our findings highlight and nuance gender, culture and racism as factors that need to be accounted for when designing digital education tools for this population. More specifically, we detail how accounting for the aforementioned factors may inform the: (1) learning approaches that may underpin such technologies, (2) the timing and duration of digitally facilitated learning activities and (3) the platforms through which learning activities may be mediated. We argue that not accounting for these factors may result in reduced engagement and in propagating existing gender inequities. As such, our research contributes to a growing body of work focused on HCI, migration and education.

Keywords: learning technologies · migration · youth · cultural norms · racism

1 Introduction and Related Work

The United Kingdom (UK)– where our research is conducted– is home to only 1% of the world's Refugee and Asylum Seeking (RAS) population [1]. Re-settling in new countries poses challenges to RAS as they encounter barriers related to language [2] and accessing services [3, 4]. In the UK, young RAS often spend a significant amount of time outside of formal schooling due to: (1) a lack of available spaces and resources to support RAS students, (2) the schools' hesitance to admit RAS students "due to fear of negatively influencing results profiles" and (3) RAS arriving outside the typical

J. Abdelnour Nocera et al. (Eds.): INTERACT 2023, LNCS 14144, pp. 469–478, 2023.
https://doi.org/10.1007/978-3-031-42286-7_26

school registration window [5]. Additionally, RAS are initially placed in temporary accommodation– usually overcrowded hotels– where they may enroll in nearby schools only to find themselves relocated to other parts of the country during the school year and thus disrupting their education. Due to such challenges, local councils and charities are encouraged to generate innovative programmes to support young RAS during the times in which they are excluded from formal schooling [5].

There has been over a decade of HCI research focused on migration [6] however, relatively less work has been conducted with young RAS. Nonetheless, existing research brings to the fore the specific technological considerations warranted when designing for and with this population. Tachtler et al. [3] highlight the need for mental health technologies to adapt to the constrained settings in which RAS youth might find themselves in. Research in Jordan indicated that young RAS often utilize internet services to overcome challenges they encounter as well as take on roles of information wayfarers supporting others within their community [7].

For RAS learning the language of the host country is paramount as language poses a major barrier to accessing services and building social capital [8]. Accordingly, Kharrufa et al. [9] developed a web app that promoted language and cultural learning through media authoring tasks. In Germany, Wiebert et al. [2] designed a digital tool to support RAS in accessing language courses in their locale. Dahya & Dryden-Peterson [10] demonstrate how RAS leverage social media platforms to construct pathways for accessing higher education. Lastly, Computer Clubs have been established as a means for providing ICT education for refugees with the support of volunteers. Such initiatives have highlighted the value of such spaces for learning digital skills and become spaces for intercultural learning [11], the building of social ties between refugees and volunteers [12, 13] and overcoming gender-related barriers to learning [14].

Our research is situated within the above-detailed context and literature. The project is being conducted in partnership with North East Solidarity and Teaching (N.E.S.T.). N.E.S.T. approached one of the research team members, who volunteers for the organization, to explore how digital platforms may be used to support young RAS during the time periods in which they find themselves unable to access schooling. The aim of the research was not to codesign digital educational platforms that would substitute formal education. Rather we aimed to codesign digital tools and/or approaches that enable young RAS to develop their learning skills (i.e. learning how to learn). In this paper we report on the first phase of our research, where we explore: *What social and contextual factors influence the ability of young RAS in the UK to engage with digital learning interactions?*

We explore our research question through codesign workshops with 10 young RAS. Participants are currently enrolled in schools after spending periods of time excluded from schooling and therefore were able to draw on their experience of using digital tools to develop their learning skills while outside of school and which strategies aided them in their transition back into formal education. Our findings highlight and nuance the need to account for gender, culture and experiences of racism when designing digital education tools, including tools that mediate and facilitate both online and offline learning. We discuss: (1) how gender differentials intersecting with culture and the occupying of carer roles complicate when and where young RAS who identify as girls may engage with digital learning interactions and (2) how wariness of racism influences the degree of online sharing participants are willing to engage in when undergoing online learning activities. The research contributes to a growing body of work focused on HCI, migration and education by nuancing how gender-related factors and racism may be accounted for when designing digital tools for learning.

2 Methods

We adopted a codesign approach informed by research on creating a safe space for RAS youth and mitigating unequal participation during the design process [15]. In addition, our choices of data collection tools and activities drew on research documenting codesigning with young individuals, e.g. co-constructing a code of conduct [16], storytelling as a research tool, e.g. use of scenarios and storyboards [17, 18], and educational research, e.g. use of Pupil View Templates (PVTs) [19]. The research received ethical approval from Northumbria University and was conducted over a series of 3 workshops with 10 young RAS in the Northeast of England. All the researchers attained a Disclosure and Barring Service check and attended Childhood Trauma training.

Recruitment and Participants. Recruitment was done through N.E.S.T. A meeting with potential participants was held, where the research team introduced the project and participants' rights were communicated. Informed consent was attained from participants and their parents/guardians. We made sure to highlight that participation was voluntary and the choice not to participate would not impact their relationship with N.E.S.T. and any services they access. Participants' ages ranged between 11–15 years. 5 of the participants were siblings from Eritrea who spoke Tigrinya and Arabic; another 3 were from El Salvador and spoke Spanish (2 of whom were siblings); and another 2 were from Turkey and Kurdistan, speaking Turkish and Kurdish respectively. All participants also have a working knowledge of the English language and were therefore able to participate in English. Some participants were not as confident in speaking and writing English at times; however, they were supported by participants who spoke their mother tongue and/or by two members of the research team who spoke Arabic.

Co-creating a Safe Space. At the first workshop, we drew on Duarte et al.'s [15] work on the utilisation of iterative ethics when engaging with young RAS, and as they suggest, we revisited the research project with the participants, discussing how data is going to be collected as well as their rights within the project and its activities. The 'project revisiting' was subsequently repeated at the beginning of each workshop. Furthermore, at the start of each workshop, participants (and all workshop facilitators) were asked to draw a quick self-portrait and write down their favorite food to be used as a pseudonym. Both, the use of pseudonyms connected via a common theme (here: food) and the self-portraits, aimed to ease-in the days' activities and establish a sense of togetherness/community and protection [20]. Furthermore, in order to create a safe space for participation, we engaged in a reflective process [15] on how we want to treat one another, which was facilitated through the co-creation of a code of conduct. Using post-it notes, elements such as 'respect', 'empathy', and 'listening' were placed on a flipchart paper that was then hung up on a wall in the room. The code of conduct was revisited and added at the beginning of each workshop and as the need arose during the workshops. After the code of conduct creation/revision, each workshop continued with the main activities (see Table 1) and ended with a feedback round, in which the participants could share their day's reflections, insights and suggestions.

Table 1. Table detailing workshop aims, activities and methods used

Activities	Methods *and Participation*
Workshop 1 *(WS1)* Aim: Exploring how participants learn to learn something new	
Describe how you learn(ed) something new while (not) enrolled in school	Draw-Write-Tell *individually* (with sentence completion for Tell)
Workshop 2 (WS2) *Aim: Explore participants' existing digital ecosystem*	
Tell the story of someone who just arrived in the UK and is not in school. What do they want to learn, with whom, where, with which technology? Choose a scene, re-tell or re-enact it. Discuss it in the group	Visual Storytelling *in groups* (with drawing and card facilitation) Roleplay *in groups* Discussion *all*
Workshop 3 (WS3) *Aim: Explore benefits and challenges of online technologies*	
What do you/others say and think about the online technologies you use? Discuss what is good and bad about them (benefits and dangers)	Pupil View Templates (PVTs) *individually* Discussion *groups, then all*

Workshops. The workshop series aimed to interrogate how participants learn how to learn, how they use/may use digital technologies to do so and their perspectives on the safety, benefits and challenges to using technologies as part of their learning strategies (See Table 1). The technologies identified and further reflected on were varied, but mainly focused on WhatsApp, Snapchat, TikTok, YouTube, Spotify and digital games. Activities and facilitation were structured in a manner that enabled continuous interrogation of the social and contextual factors that interplay with their use of technologies for learning. Audio recordings and the artefacts made by participants were collected from the workshops.

Data Analysis. Through initial exploration of the data– transcription of audio recordings, multiple readings of the transcripts and joint reflection on the data by the research team– the following challenge areas were identified for follow-up analysis: gender, racism, access and sustainability. This paper focuses on the first two and analysis is limited to the audio transcriptions from the workshops. Data was thematically analyzed [21] using an inductive approach within each theme. After data familiarization through joint transcription and individual (re-)reading of the data, (semantic) coding of the whole data set was undertaken individually, with one researcher focusing on gender, the other on racism. Thereafter, the researchers jointly worked on identifying, reviewing and describing themes, thus fleshing out the challenge areas and setting the stage for the collaborative write-up.

3 Findings

English language learning was a prevalent topic repeatedly chosen by the participants. Our findings illustrate ways in which gender and racism are interrelated with the participants' use of technologies for offline and online learning. Gender and its interplay with culture and caring roles was a factor in availability and choice of (safe) platforms and physical spaces for learning. Racism was a factor in the (un)willingness to engage on publicly accessible platforms.

3.1 Gender and Cultural Considerations for Online and Offline Learning

The issue of gender as it relates to learning with one another, and online/offline learning was prominent throughout the workshops. This was especially true for participants who identified as girls from Eritrea, who followed culturally based gender roles. Within the code of conduct, participants demonstrated a sensitivity to issues of gender by indicating that we should not discriminate against each other based on gender and sexuality: *"respecting different sexualities" [Chow Mein, WS1]*.

However, when engaging in activities participants tended to want to work with peers of the same perceived gender. In Workshop 2, participants requested that they be divided into groups based on gender. The boys formed a group and generated the character of a boy named Lionel– after Lionel Messi– and those identifying as girls formed the second group and developed a girl character named Suleyfa. The research team conceded to this grouping with the intention of respecting participants' agency within the codesign process. Furthermore, the division of groups based on gender allowed us to identify nuanced gender related distinctions regarding the use of digital tools for learning and subsequent design considerations primarily as they relate to culture, caring roles and physical/digital places of learning.

Places for Engaging in Learning. Interestingly, in the first scene the boy's group situated their character Lionel in a summer camp being run by N.E.S.T., whereas the girl's group placed Suleyfa in her bedroom at home with each group citing the aforementioned places as ideal for online and offline learning. Upon further discussion participants highlighted that there are gendered differences regarding where they can engage in offline and online learning pointing to how boys are more likely to go to public spaces to learn things like speaking English: *"You know, boys they are asking to go outside. Not girls" [Noodles, WS2]*.

Furthermore, participants indicated that *"learning English for boys and girls is different" [Noodles, WS2]* and attributed it to boys' use of body language: *"they [boys] use gestures", [Injera, WS2]*. These sentiments were broadly shared by all participants. After further discussion, facilitated by the research team, participants highlighted that the root of this gender inequality is not necessarily related to how they use technologies and the use of body language but rather stems from their gendered social experiences in the U.K: *"Technology is not a reason, boys they, like, they can play football together" [Pizza, WS2]; "boys are always trying to have friends. And when you come to England, the British boys, they are friendly with you." [Chow Mein, WS2]*.

Participants who identified as girls from Eritrea also attributed this distinction to the cultural norms they hold and are held to: *"yes, especially in our culture girls stay at home" [Noodles, WS2]*. Additionally, participants who identified as girls from Eritrea indicated they, unlike those who identified as boys, do not feel safe in public spaces such as parks but rather, if they were to engage in learning in a public space, it would more likely be in a shop where there are members of staff. Indeed, in another scene participants in the girls group situated their character, 'Suleyfa', in Primark – a clothes retailer– where she comfortably interacted with staff members, handing over her phone to a member of staff: *"I give to the staff my phone for them to write down what they are saying and I translate it" [Noodles after conferring in Tigrinya with group, WS2]*.

The gendered difference regarding the ability to go to public spaces had implications on ways to access technologies. Participants highlighted that during the times in which they did not have access to Wi-Fi at home, the boys would go into the town center and use publicly available Wi-Fi in restaurants (e.g. McDonalds) and the local college. However, the girls tended to rely on hot spotting from their parent's phone and on visiting relatives in the area that have Wi-Fi. This further highlighted the gendered and cultural consideration needed when designing education technologies for both online and offline learning.

Platforms for Engaging in Learning. Another issue that arose from the girl's group that was not apparent within the work and discussions held in the boy's group was the gendered preferences of the use of social media platforms. Indeed, participants in the girl group (WS2) indicated that they would rather use Snapchat for learning rather than WhatsApp as with Snapchat they do not have to share their phone number: *"[On WhatsApp] you must know the person you are talking to" [Noodles, WS2]*.

Instead, they said that if 'Suleyfa' was to use WhatsApp to learn it should be to only speak with a 'trusted friend'. Additionally, participants in the girls group elaborated that girls have less time to use social media platforms for learning due to the gendered and cultural nature of the responsibilities that they hold: *"in our culture girls needs to be in their home and doing stuff like cleaning and making food for the boys. But the boys can watch phone more than the girls so they have more chance to learn" [Noodles, WS2]; "like when she wakes up in the morning she has to do breakfast and she has to clean after people eat and make lunch and eat lunch…she maybe use her phone in the evening before she goes to bed." [Noodles translating for Fish, WS2]*.

Here it is important to note that this particular group of girls are the carers of their ill mother and therefore the responsibility of caring for their siblings has fallen to them.

3.2 Experiences of Racism Influencing Online Sharing

Participants instigated several discussions related to racism and how it impacts their interactions online and in turn would impact their willingness to generate and share content, such as videos and comments, as part of online learning. As one participant indicated it is common for their presence in UK (online) spaces to be questioned: *"some people make fun of your race…they say 'explain the reason why you've come [here]' [Chow Mein, WS3]"*.

Their sensitivity to issues of race was exemplified during the co-creation of the code of conduct where participants made it a point to include: (1) Not being racist; (2) Don't make fun of each other's appearance and (3) No discrimination. While at first glance,

'Don't make fun of each other's appearance' may not have any relationship to race, however, in further discussions among participant's they highlighted how they are wary of being made fun of due to their and/or parent's non-White appearance:

> Cheeseburger: *"like if you make a video [...] when you show your appearance"*
>
> Researcher: *"You get racism there?"*
>
> *"Cheeseburger: yes and discrimination as well"* [from WS3]

Another participant iterated on this point by highlighting how the comments they may make online are usually viewed by others through the lens of race: *"if you make a comment like 'OMG Argentina won [in football] and I think that is the best thing'...someone will say 'oh you like Argentina because you are brown'"* [Chow Mein, WS3].

Such wariness to engage online due to expectations held among participants of experiencing racism was not only restricted to appearances and/or making online comments. For example, Chow Mein then continued to elaborate that wanting to avoid racism deters him from sharing videos in which his accent might be picked on: *"basically if you make a video and you are speaking in English...there will always be one stupid British man making fun of your accent and that actually hurts."* [Chow Mein, WS3]. Our findings highlight that digital means of engaging with learning, such as tasking young people to take videos and share them on social media platforms in response to a question and/or prompt, need to consider the visibility of such content and how potential exposure to online racism may dissuade young refugees and asylum seekers from completing such tasks.

4 Discussion and Conclusion

Our findings highlight issues of gender, and its inter-relatedness to culture, and of racism as social and contextual factors that impact how young RAS engage with technologies and envision their use for learning.

Considerations for Gender and Culture. The workshops with young RAS of diverse genders and cultural backgrounds bring to the fore how gender and cultural norms intersect in a manner that interplay with where and for how long RAS who identify as girls from specific cultural backgrounds can engage with technologies for learning. Furthermore, we identified that gender and culture play a role in influencing what social media applications they would be willing to use to learn. This complicates the transferability of previous digital education interventions that appropriate social media technologies for coordinating participation in learning [22, 23]. Similarly, while recent research has advocated for the use of place-based learning approaches mediated through online technologies [24], the gender differences identified in this study complicates the use of digital learning tools that leverage public spaces such as parks for learning. Furthermore, the gender divide regarding the ability to access the internet among RAS poses a challenge similar to that previously identified by Yafi et al. [7]. Our research highlights constraints to where and when participants that identified as girls from a specific cultural background may access the internet. Not accounting for such constraints may result in digital learning tools propagating existing gender inequities. This is further compounded by the caring responsibilities held by some of the participants that Dahya & Dryden-Peterson [10] point to as heightening factors of gender inequalities during conflict and migration. Collectively, our findings prompt us to consider when designing learning technologies how the timing, duration and location of learning activities, as well as the activities they prompt, and platforms used might disproportionally exclude those who identify as girls from specific cultural backgrounds and young RAS who have caring responsibilities. As such, there is a need to design technologies for learning that account for and adapt to the everyday gendered constraints experienced by young RAS. Given that the majority of RAS are migrating from non-Western contexts, there is a need for technological design within this space to explore and work with non-Western feminist theories and views [25] to address the above-mentioned gender disparities while also avoiding the imposition of Western feminist values that might be in tension with the cultures held by young RAS.

Considerations for Racism. Recent research has highlighted how online sharing encourages and enables learning through content creation [26, 27]. However, online technologies have been identified as a resource for RAS while also being spaces in which they are exposed to racism [4]. Our findings indicate that wariness of online racism discourages young RAS from publicly sharing on social media platforms as part of their learning activities. Therefore, nuanced consideration regarding online safety and racism are warranted when designing for online learning interactions for this population. Our research further stresses the importance of codesigning protective measures in the realm of online safety together with adolescents [28] and extending such measures to designing learning technologies to be used by young RAS. Furthermore, there is a need for learning technologies to integrate knowledge on supporting the coping mechanisms of targets of interpersonal racism through social technologies [29] and to create inclusive spaces and counter-narratives encouraging communities subject to racism to engage in learning [30].

In sum, the research presented in this paper brings to the fore issues of gender, race and culture that need to be accounted for when designing technologies to support young RAS in learning and developing their learning skills. We highlight the ways in which these factors interplay and may disproportionally exclude young RAS who identify as girls from non-Western cultural backgrounds and those with caring responsibilities from engaging in technologically mediated learning activities that leverage existing social media platforms and place-based learning pedagogies. Furthermore, we show how wariness of online racism discourages young RAS from engaging in online learning activities. We discuss ways forward when designing learning technologies for this population.

Limitations. While the participant group is culturally heterogenous, the majority of girls was from Eritrea. More research is needed to further explore cultural factors and their interplay with gender.

Acknowledgements. The research was funded by Northumbria University and the Center for Digital Citizens (EP/T022582/1). For the purpose of Open Access, the authors applied a CC BY public copyright license to any Author Accepted Manuscript (AAM) version arising from this submission. We also want to thank N.E.S.T. and our participants for their support and contribution to this project.

References

1. Refugee Council: The truth about asylum. https://www.refugeecouncil.org.uk/inform ation/refugee-asylum-facts/the-truth-about-asylum/?gclid=Cj0KCQjwla-hBhD7ARIsAM9 tQKv5IuAp2cNc4YgmpNG2ZfbZ-QZVGjYrf-BngiBgWbKgmkJEtMkvLH0aAgq9EALw _wcB
2. Weibert, A., et al.: Finding language classes: designing a digital language wizard with refugees and migrants. In: Proceedings of the ACM on Human-Computer Interaction (2019)
3. Tachtler, F., Talhouk, R., Michel, T., Slovak, P., Fitzpatrick, G.: Unaccompanied migrant youth and mental health technologies: a social-ecological approach to understanding and designing. In: In Proceedings of CHI 2021 Conference on Human Factors in Computing Systems, pp. 1–19 (2021)
4. Almohammed, A., Talhouk, R., Vyas, D.: Towards a Conceptual Framework for Understanding the Challenges in Refugee Re-settlement 4 (2021)
5. Gladwell, C., Chetwynd, G.: Education for Refugee and Asylum Seeking Children: Access and Equality in England, Scotland and Wales (2018)
6. Sabie, D., et al.: Migration and mobility in HCI : rethinking boundaries, methods , and impact. In: In Extended Abstracts of the 2021 CHI Conference on Human Factors in Computing Systems (CHI EA'21). p. Article 97, pp. 1–6 (2021)
7. Yafi, E., Yefimova, K., Fisher, K.E.: Young Hackers : Hacking technology at Za'atari syrian refugee camp. In: In Proceedings of the CHI Conference on Human Factors in Computing Systems (CHI'18). p. CS21. ACM, Montreal, CA (2018)
8. Almohamed, A., Vyas, D.: Rebuilding social capital in refugees and asylum seekers. ACM Trans. Comput. Interact 26 (2019). https://doi.org/10.1145/3364996
9. Kharrufa, A., Satar, M., Dodds, C.B., Seedhouse, P.: Supporting non-expert users in authoring tasks for learning language and culture. Int. J. Comput. Lang. Learn. Teach. 12, 1–22 (2022). https://doi.org/10.4018/ijcallt.315278
10. Dahya, N., Dryden-Peterson, S.: Tracing pathways to higher education for refugees: the role of virtual support networks and mobile phones for women in refugee camps. Comp. Educ. 53, 284–301 (2017). https://doi.org/10.1080/03050068.2016.1259877
11. Arawjo, I., Mogos, A., Jackson, S.J., Parikh, T., Toyama, K.: Computing education for intercultural learning: lessons from the Nairobi play project. Proc. ACM Human-Computer Interact 3 (2019). https://doi.org/10.1145/3359154
12. Aal, K., Yerousis, G., Schubert, K., Hornung, D., Stickel, O., Wulf, V.: Come_IN@Palestine: adapting a German computer club concept to a palestinian refugee camp. In: In Proceedings of the 5th ACM international conference on Collaboration across boundaries: culture, distance & technology (CABS'14), pp. 111–120 (2014)
13. Yerousis, G., Aal, K., von Rekowski, T., Randall, D.W., Rohde, M., Wulf, V.: Computer-enabled project spaces. In: In Proceedings of the CHI Conference on Human Factors in Computing Systems (CHI'15), pp. 3749–3758 (2015)
14. Aal, K., von Rekowski, T., Yerousis, G., Wulf, V., Weibert, A.: Bridging (Gender-Related) Barriers. In: In Proceedings of the Conference on GenderIT (GenderIT'15), pp. 17–23 (2015)
15. Bustamante Duarte, A.M., Ataei, M., Degbelo, A., Brendel, N., Kray, C.: Safe spaces in participatory design with young forced migrants. CoDesign 17, 188–210 (2021). https://doi. org/10.1080/15710882.2019.1654523
16. Gupta, A., Fulfagar, L., Upadhyay, P.: Co-designing with visually Impaired Children. Smart Innov. Syst. Technol. 222, 429–439 (2021). https://doi.org/10.1007/978-981-16-0119-4_35/ COVER
17. Haigh, C., Hardy, P.: Tell me a story - a conceptual exploration of storytelling in healthcare education. Nurse Educ. Today. 31, 408–411 (2011). https://doi.org/10.1016/j.nedt.2010. 08.001

18. Lupton, D., Leahy, D.: Reimagining digital health education: reflections on the possibilities of the storyboarding method. Health Educ. J. **78**, 633–646 (2019). https://doi.org/10.1177/0017896919841413
19. Wall, K.: Understanding metacognition through the use of pupil views templates: pupil views of Learning to Learn. Think. Ski. Creat. **3**, 23–33 (2008). https://doi.org/10.1016/j.tsc.2008.03.004
20. Barry, L.: Syllabus: Notes from an accidental professor. Draw. Q (2014)
21. Braun, V., Clarke, V.: Successful Qualitative Research: A Practical Guide for Beginners. SAGE (2013)
22. Lambton-Howard, D., Olivier, P., Vlachokyriakos, V., Celina, H., Kharrufa, A.: Unplatformed design: a model for appropriating social media technologies for coordinated participation. In: Proceedings of the 2020 CHI Conference on Human Factors in Computing Systems (CHI'20). p. Paper 52, pp. 1–13. ACM, New York, NY (2020)
23. Lambton-Howard, D., Kiaer, J., Kharrufa, A.: 'Social Media is Their Space': Student and Teacher Use and Perception of Features of Social Media in Language Education. **40**, 1700–1715 (2020). https://doi.org/10.1080/0144929X.2020.1774653
24. Richardson, D., Crivellaro, C., Kharrufa, A., Montague, K.: Exploring public places as infrastructures for civic m-learning. In: In Proceedings of the 8th International Conference on Communities and Technologies, pp. 222–231. Association for Computing Machinery, Troyes (2017)
25. Rabaan, H., Young, A.L., Dombrowski, L.: Daughters of men: Saudi women's sociotechnical agency practices in addressing domestic abuse. Proc. ACM Human-Computer Interact, **4** (2021). https://doi.org/10.1145/3432923
26. Sarangapani, V., Kharrufa, A., Balaam, M., Leat, D., Wright, P.: Virtual.cultural.collaboration - mobile phones, video technology, and cross-cultural learning. In: Proceedings of the 18th International Conference on Human-Computer Interaction with Mobile Devices and Services (MobileHCI 2016), pp. 341–352. Association for Computing Machinery, New York (2016)
27. Sarangapani, V., Kharrufa, A., Leat, D., Wright, P.: Fostering deep learning in cross-cultural education through use of content-creation tools. In: Proceedings of the 10th Indian Conference on Human-Computer Interaction (IndiaHCI'19). p. Article 7, pp. 1–11. Association for Computing Machinery, New York (2019)
28. Badillo-Urquiola, K.: A social ecological approach to empowering foster youth to be safer online. Proc. ACM Conf. Comput. Support. Coop. Work. CSCW, pp. 75–79 (2020). https://doi.org/10.1145/3406865.3418365
29. To, A., Sweeney, W., Hammer, J., Kaufman, G.: "they Just Don't Get It": towards social technologies for coping with interpersonal racism. Proc. ACM Human-Computer Interact. **4** (2020). https://doi.org/10.1145/3392828
30. Erete, S., Thomas, K., Nacu, D., Dickinson, J., Thompson, N., Pinkard, N.: Applying a transformative justice approach to encourage the participation of black and latina girls in computing. ACM Trans. Comput. Educ. **21** (2021). https://doi.org/10.1145/3451345

Understanding Users and Privacy Issues

Concerns of Saudi Higher Education Students About Security and Privacy of Online Digital Technologies During the Coronavirus Pandemic

Basmah Almekhled[1,2] (ID) and Helen Petrie[1(✉)] (ID)

[1] Department of Computer Science, University of York, Heslington East, York, U.K.
helen.petrie@york.ac.uk

[2] College of Computing and Informatics, Saudi Electronic University, Riyadh, Saudi Arabia

Abstract. Due to COVID-19, higher education institutions worldwide shifted rapidly to online learning. While a number of studies have examined students' attitudes towards online learning in general, little research has focused on students' concerns about security and privacy. A survey of 62 Saudi higher education students to explore their views on privacy and security concerns, particularly about using video conferencing and online chat technologies in online teaching during the pandemic. Students rated their concerns about using video conferencing for teaching, studying with other students, and using chat technologies for studying with other students as moderate. In contrast, they did not express significant concerns about using chat technologies for teaching. Open-ended responses revealed a range of concerns, including unauthorized people entering and disrupting online sessions, leaked personal information and being recorded without permission. Students did not turn on their webcams often during online teaching, indicating that they may not feel the need to do so unless the instructor requests them to do so. Most students reported that their instructors also rarely turn on their webcams while teaching. The results suggest that students are only somewhat aware of the potential privacy and security risks associated with online communication technologies. Going forward, it is important of ensuring that appropriate measures are in place to protect students' privacy and security during online teaching.

Keywords: Online higher education · Privacy and security concerns · Videoconferencing technologies · Online chat technologies · COVID pandemic

1 Introduction

Higher Education institutions (HEIs) across the globe witnessed substantial transformations as a result of the coronavirus pandemic, particularly due to the rapid shift to teaching online. The pandemic led to a surge in the use of video conferencing tools, both for live sessions and recordings, as a substitute for in-person learning [22]. Studies of HEI educators' experiences of the pandemic have highlighted privacy and security issues in such online teaching, including the challenges of monitoring student participation and engagement in online sessions [14], the use of microphones and webcams

© The Author(s), under exclusive license to Springer Nature Switzerland AG 2023
J. Abdelnour Nocera et al. (Eds.): INTERACT 2023, LNCS 14144, pp. 481–490, 2023.
https://doi.org/10.1007/978-3-031-42286-7_27

[12, 23], as well as how to monitor online assessments and examinations for collusion and cheating [20]. Several studies have also explored the experiences of HEI students with digital technologies during the pandemic across various countries and contexts [1, 2, 21]. However, only one study was identified that specifically investigated students' privacy and security concerns about online teaching technologies. Kim [13] investigated the attitudes of South Korean HEI students in relation to online privacy and security and found their concerns related to online privacy and security had a negative impact on students' intentions to participate in live online teaching sessions.

Although not about online teaching specifically, a global survey conducted in the early months of the pandemic (May 2020) revealed that privacy and security were the most commonly cited concerns in the use of digital conferencing and communication tools [10]. Similarly, a large general survey conducted a few months prior to the pandemic [15] found that users were apprehensive about the security and privacy of group chat technologies, a concern that may also apply to the digital technologies employed by many HEIs for online teaching during the pandemic.

Several studies have investigated HEI students' attitudes to the use of webcams in online teaching and specifically why students do not want to have their webcams on during online teaching sessions [4, 6, 9, 12]. Conducted in a range of countries (Germany, the United States, the United Kingdom, and Romania respectively), all found reluctance on students' part to have webcams on during teaching sessions. A range of reasons was proposed including shyness, anxiety, and social norm but all studies highlighted privacy issues as major concerns. However, educators highlight the difficulty of engaging with students who cannot be seen at all [17, 23]. Research also shows that if students in online sessions cannot see one another or the instructor, they feel isolated and disengaged [16, 17].

Due to the limited amount of information available about HEI students' concerns about privacy and security issues in relation online teaching, which are likely to persist to some degree despite the return to face-to-face education since the pandemic has waned, we undertook a survey of HEI students in Saudi Arabia about these issues. The choice of one specific country was made for a number of reasons. Educational practices at HEI level can vary significantly between different countries. But most importantly, students from different cultures may have different attitudes to online privacy and security, and students in an Arab culture may have particular concerns about privacy and security in relation to their visibility in online teaching situations. There is already similar research conducted with UK students [3] which we built on (comparisons with that study will be made in a further publication.)

The research questions addressed in the study were:

RQ1: What are Saudi HEI students' concerns about privacy and security issues about using video conferencing and online chat technologies for online teaching?
RQ2: Do Saudi HEI students have their webcams on during online teaching and what are their attitudes to using webcams in these situations?
RQ3: Do Saudi HEI students find that their instructors typically have their webcams on during online teaching and what are the students' attitudes to their instructors using webcams in these situations?

2 Method

2.1 Participants

The inclusion criteria for participants were to be Saudi, studying at a Saudi HEI and to have been studying there since before the coronavirus pandemic started (i.e. to have started studying in the 2019 – 2020 academic year or earlier).

An invitation to participate in the study was posted on the first author's social media accounts and HEI student group accounts in Saudi Arabia. In addition, we emailed a number of educators at Saudi HEIs asking them to post the invitation on their social media accounts. 370 students responded, but 306 had not started studying before the pandemic, thus their data were deleted, and two participants failed attention check questions (see section 2.2, below) leaving a sample of 62 participants.

Table 1. Demographics of the participants

Age	
Range	19 – 44 years
Mean	24.9
Gender	
Men	18 (29.0%)
Women	38 (61.3%)
Prefer not to say	6 (9.7%)
Degree level	
Bachelor	50 (80.6%)
Masters	1 (1.6%)
PhD	9 (14.5%)
Other (e.g. Higher Diploma)	2 (3.22%)
Academic year started	
2019 – 2020	24 (38.7%)
2018 – 2019	13 (21.0%)
2017 – 2018	15 (24.2%)
Earlier	10 (16.1%)
Subject being studied	
Arts/Humanities	6 (9.6%)
Administrative and Financial sciences	7 (11.2%)
Computer science and Engineering	33 (53%)
Medical sciences and Health Science	14 (22%)
Social sciences (e.g. psychology, sociology)	2 (3.2%)

Participants' demographic details are summarized in Table 1. The age range of the participants was surprisingly wide (19-44 years), but 40 participants (64.5%) were 25 years or younger. Participants were studying at 20 different Saudi HEIs, representing every type of HEI in Saudi Arabia, from elite universities to newer HEIs. Most participants were studying at public HEIs (75.2%) and the remaining quarter were studying at private HEIs (25.8%). The distribution of degree levels is quite close to the overall Saudi higher education population, according to statistics from the General Authority of Statistics, Kingdom of Saudi Arabia [11]. Participants were studying a wide range of subjects in both the sciences and humanities.

Participants were entered into a prize draw to win one of 10 gift vouchers from Amazon worth 50 Saudi riyals (approximately USD 13.30).

2.2 Online Questionnaire

A questionnaire was developed to explore attitudes and concerns about privacy and security issues in online teaching and learning. The questionnaire asked about attitudes and concerns held before the pandemic and during the pandemic (only the latter are presented here).

At the outset the questionnaire a definition of the term of "online privacy and security" was provided: "that a person's data, including their identity, is not accessible to anyone other than themselves and others whom they have authorised and that their computing devices work properly and are free from unauthorised interference". This was to ensure that participants understood what was being asking about in subsequent sections. The questionnaire used a mixture of rating scales and open-ended questions.

The sections of the questionnaire relevant to this paper were:

Privacy and Security Concerns About Videoconferencing and Chat Technologies in Teaching: participants' experiences and concerns of online security and privacy specifically about videoconferencing and chat technologies in their teaching and learning. Questions also addressed concerns about security and privacy issues in relation to the different activities such as in teaching sessions or with other students.

Use of Webcams by Educators During Online Teaching: Questions whether students' educators had their webcams on or not during online teach and what students thought about this.

Demographics: asked basic questions about age, gender, and how knowledgeable participants rated themselves about online privacy and security issues and videoconference and chat technologies.

The online questionnaire was deployed using the Qualtrics survey software in December 2021. A pilot study with five students assessed the clarity of the questions and the time required to complete the questionnaire and some small adjustments were made as a result.

The survey was approved from Physical Sciences Ethics Committee at the University of York. The questionnaire was developed in English and then translated into Arabic with back translation to check accuracy. The questionnaire included two "attention check" questions at different locations in the survey to check whether participants read the questions carefully and did not respond randomly [7]. Two participants failed these questions, so were removed from the sample.

2.3 Data Preparation

The questionnaire used 7-point Likert items responses on which were heavily skewed towards the lower end of the scale and were therefore analyzed using non-parametric statistics. Thematic analysis was performed separately on each open-ended question using an inductive approach [5].

3 Results

What are Saudi HEI students' concerns about privacy and security issues about video conferencing and online chat technologies for online teaching (RQ1).

Participants were asked to rate their level of concern about security and privacy issues regarding the use of videoconferencing and online chat technologies for teaching sessions and for studying with other students (on 7-point Likert items, coded as 1 = not at all concerned to 7 = very concerned). Table 2 shows that the only rating which differed significantly from the midpoint of the scale was using chat technologies for teaching had a median rating of 2.90, which is significantly below the midpoint of the rating scale, meaning students were not particularly concerned about privacy and security issues of using chat technologies in online teaching.

In all other three cases, they rated their concern with a median rate of 3.40, which is significantly nearly to the midpoint of the scale, which indicates students had a moderate level of concern about privacy and security issues using videoconferencing for teaching and studying with other students and using chat technologies for studying with other students.

Table 2. Participants' level of concern about online privacy and security with videoconferencing and chat technologies

Activity	Median (SIQR)	z	P
Videoconferencing for teaching	3.40 (2.62)	−1.67	n.s
Chat technologies for teaching	2.90 (2.48)	−3.30	< .001
Videoconferencing for studying with other students	3.40 (2.61)	−1.84	n.s.
Chat technologies for studying with other students	3.40 (2.60)	−2.83	n.s.

However, in a follow-up open-ended question about any concerns on this topic, 14 (22.6%) of participants raised concerns. The small percentage of participants providing answers to the open-ended question, may suggest a general lack of concern about the issues, but we have found over a number of recent studies with Saudi participants that they seem much more reluctant to answer open-ended questions in online surveys than

British participants (a topic for another study), so one should be cautious in drawing that conclusion. A thematic analysis of these concerns is summarised in Table 3 (only concerns raised by more than one student are included). The most commonly mentioned concerns were about leaked personal information by unauthorized people entering online sessions. Less frequently mentioned concerns were about the ability to know and locate their location from their status on some online chat app (although it was not explicitly mentioned, this presumably related to the privacy concerns), videoconferencing sessions being recorded without permission, and interruptions by some students by making inappropriate racist or biased comments. A small number of concerns were about the lack of control of their camera or microphone being on or off, the lack of guarantee of the safety of other students' devices which may lead to the interruption of the secure connection in the video chat, and other students stealing ideas during discussions in online sessions.

Table 3. Participants' concerns about videoconferencing and online chat technologies (N = 14, number of participants mentioning, %)

Theme	Examples
Personal information leak 5 (35.7%)	The ability of unauthorized persons to know my personal information (P53) My phone number is known in online chat (P25)
Location leak 2 (14.3%)	Ability to know and locate my location if I used WhatsApp in online chat (P42)
Being recorded without permission 2 (14.3%)	As for making recordings …. The issue is worrying in terms of how these recordings will be and whether will they be published on social media (P40)
Inappropriate behaviour by other students 2 (14.3%)	The occurrence of interruptions by some students, sabotage, and throwing inappropriate words because there is no system to punish the person for it. (P37)

Do Saudi HEI students have their webcam on during online teaching and what are their attitudes to using webcams in these situations? (RQ2).

Participants were asked to rate often they turned on their webcam during different types of teaching sessions (see Table 4). In all cases, they rated their turned-on webcam as very low. In all five online teaching situations, the median is significantly below the midpoint of the rating scale.

In a follow-up, open-ended question, only four of the participants (6.5%) described how they decide to turn on their webcam during different teaching and study activities. Three of the participants mentioned that they turn on their webcam if their instructors ask them. The other participant mentioned that they had to turn on their webcam only if they had an online exam.

Table 4. Frequency with which participants turned on their webcam during different teaching situations (scored as 1 = Never to 7 = Very frequently)

Activity	Median (SIQR)	z	p
Online lectures	1.00 (2.04)	−4.55	< .001
Small group sessions/seminars	1.00 (2.16)	−4.51	< .001
Lab sessions (e.g. chemistry, biology, or computer labs)	1.00 (2.05)	−4.25	< .001
One-to-one sessions with your teachers	1.00 (2.48)	−3.28	< .001
Online study sessions with other students	1.00 (2.00)	−4.55	< .001

RQ3: Do Saudi HEI students find that their instructors typically have their webcams on during online teaching and what are the students' attitudes to their instructors using webcams in these situations?

Participants were asked to rate their instructors' typical frequency of having their webcam on during different teaching situations (see Table 5). In all four online teaching situations, the median is significantly below the midpoint of the rating scale.

In a follow up open-ended question, 11 participants (17.7%) expressed their opinion about whether instructors should have their webcams on or not. Three participants preferred their teachers to have their webcams on because they felt they understood the instructor better and it facilitated communication. Two participants preferred their instructors to have their webcams off because they felt distracted by looking at the instructor during online sessions. One participant mentioned that they considered this an aspect of their instructors' privacy and they did not like to infringe on this. Five participants (45.5%) stated that they do not care or are indifferent to whether their instructor has their webcam or not.

Table 5. Participants' ratings of their instructors typical frequency of having their webcams on during online teaching situations (scored as 1 = Never to 7 = Always)

Activities	Median (SIQR)	z	p
Online lectures	1.00 (2.23)	−2.76	< .001
Small group sessions/seminars	1.00 (2.43)	−2.96	< .001
Lab sessions (e.g. chemistry, biology, or computer labs)	1.00 (2.32)	−3.22	< .001
One-to-one sessions with other students	1.00 (2.25)	−3.50	< .001

4 Discussion and Conclusions

This study investigated Saudi HEI students' concerns and attitudes about privacy and security issues related to using video conferencing and online chat technologies for online teaching and studying during the coronavirus pandemic.

In relation to RQ1, the findings suggest that students have varying levels of concern about these technologies, depending on the technology and teaching situation. The results showed that students were not particularly concerned about using chat technologies for online teaching sessions. However, in the other three combinations, including using video conferencing for online teaching, studying with other students, and using chat technologies for studying with other students, students rated their level of concern as medium. One reason for this could be the differences in the type and level of communication and interaction involved in each situation. For instance, when using chat technologies for teaching, the communication may be limited to the exchange of course materials or assignment submissions, which may not involve sharing personal or sensitive information. In contrast, video conferencing for teaching or studying with other students may involve more personal interaction, including face-to-face conversations, which may increase the risk of privacy breaches or unauthorized access. Similarly, when using chat technologies for studying with other students, students may discuss personal or sensitive information, which could raise their concerns about the platform's security and privacy. In summary, levels of privacy and security concerns may depend on the degree of personal interaction and information sharing involved. When communication is more controlled and limited, such as when using chat technologies for teaching, the level of concern may be lower. However, when interaction and sharing are more personal, the level of concern may increase. The results suggest that students are somewhat aware of potential risks associated with online communication technologies. While the quantitative analysis showed that the majority of participants did not express high levels of concern, the open-ended question revealed that a considerable proportion of participants had some concerns. However, this shows the importance of not relying on quantitative data alone, which in this instance may have been susceptible to socially desirable answers (students not wanting to appear overly concerned).

However, this apparent moderate level of concern on the part of Saudi HEI students is similar to studies which have shown concerns amongst the working population about online privacy and security issues [10, 15]. The results are also similar to those from Rashidi et al. [19], whose results from before the pandemic, found that Saudi users are aware of privacy concerns when using chat technologies.

In relation to RQ2, the study found that the students rated their frequency of turning their webcams on as very low, regardless of the type of teaching session. This result shows that Saudi students strongly prefer not to use webcams during online classes. The follow-up open-ended question provided further insight into the reasons for this. The majority of participants stated that they only turn on their webcams if their instructors ask them to. One participant mentioned that they only turn on their webcam during online exams, which suggests that students may view webcam use as being monitored rather than a channel to interaction and engagement with the teaching. These results are consistent with previous research with students in other cultures that have found reluctance on the students' part to have their webcams on during online teaching sessions [4, 6, 9, 12].

In relation to RQ3, the study found that students think their instructors have their webcams off during online teaching, during different teaching situations. However, the open-ended responses revealed mixed opinions about whether teachers should have their webcams on or off. Some participants preferred their instructors have their webcams on as they felt this led to better understanding and communication. But this view was held only by a minority of students, although the finding aligns with previous research indicating that videoconferencing tools, particularly webcams, can facilitate communication and enhance social presence in online education [8]. A small number of participants actually preferred their instructors to have their webcams off, because they found it distracting to look at the instructor during online sessions. This finding is consistent with previous research indicating that webcams can be a source of distraction for some learners [18]. Additionally, one participant mentioned that the instructor's privacy should be respected, suggesting that students realise that instructors might have reasons for keeping their webcams off that go beyond instructional considerations. It does need to be borne in mind that nearly half the participants expressed indifference to whether the instructor had their webcam on or not. These findings highlight the need for further research on the use of webcams during online teaching sessions, as well as the importance of providing instructors with training on how to use webcams effectively. Ultimately, the goal should be to enhance students' engagement and motivation during online teaching sessions. A particular limitation of this study is that although a sample of 62 students from a range of Saudi HEIs is very adequate for the quantitative analysis and amount of data elicited in the open-ended questions was relatively small for the qualitative analysis.

It was necessary to make most of the open-ended questions optional – participants could not answer about concerns they did not have, but we also did not want to make the questionnaire too onerous to complete. Thus, some participants who may have concerns may not have written about them. More importantly, the number of students who expressed concerns was not large (e.g. 14 for RQ1). Thus, more data and different methods are needed to explore these issues further, but this study provides some initial pointers of interest.

As mentioned in the Introduction, we specifically sampled the population of Saudi students studying at Saudi HEIs. The attitudes and concerns of international students studying in Saudi Arabia may be different, and the attitudes and concerns of students studying at HEIs in other countries are very likely to be very different. That is a topic we will address in further research. In addition, the questionnaire also asked about students' attitudes and concerns before the coronavirus pandemic and how the pandemic had changed their attitudes. This will be the focus of further analysis of our data.

References

1. Adnan, M., Anwar, K.: Online learning amid the COVID-19 pandemic: students' perspectives. J. Pedagogical Sociology Psychol. 2(1), 45–51 (2020)
2. Agarwal, S., Kaushik, J.S.: Students' perception of online learning during COVID pandemic. Indian J. Pediatr. 87(7), 554 (2020)
3. Almekhled, B., Petrie, H.: UK students' concerns about security and privacy of online higher education digital technologies in the coronavirus pandemic. In Proceedings of the 15th International Conference on Computer Supported Education - Volume 2, pp. 483–492 (2023)
4. Bedenlier, S., et al.: "Generation invisible"?: higher education students' (non)use of webcams in synchronous online learning. Int. J. Educ. Res. Open 2, 100068 (2021)
5. Braun, V., Clarke, V.: Using thematic analysis in psychology. Qual. Res. Psychol. 3(2), 77–101 (2006)

6. Castelli, F.R., Sarvary, M.A.: Why students do not turn on their video cameras during online classes and an equitable and inclusive plan to encourage them to do so. Ecol. Evol. **11**(8), 3565–3576 (2021)
7. Curran, P.G., Hauser, K.: I'm paid biweekly, just not by leprechauns: evaluating valid-but-incorrect response rates to attention check items. J. Res. Pers. **82**, 103849 (2019)
8. Develotte, C., Guichon, N., Vincent, C.: The use of the webcam for teaching a foreign language in a desktop videoconferencing environment. ReCALL **22**(3), 293–312 (2010)
9. Dixon, M., Syred, K.: Factors influencing student engagement in online synchronous teaching sessions: student perceptions of using microphones, video, screen-share, and chat. In: 9th International Conference, LCT 2022, Held as Part of the 24th HCI International Conference, HCII 2022, Virtual Event, June 26 – July 1, 2022, Proceedings, Part I, pp. 209–227 (2022)
10. Emami-Naeini, P., Francisco, T., Kohno, T., Roesner, F.: Understanding privacy attitudes and concerns towards remote communications during the COVID-19 pandemic. In: Symposium on Usable Privacy and Security (SOUPS'21) USENIX (2021)
11. General Authority for Statistics, Kingdom of Saudi Arabia: Yearbook of 2019. Chapter 04 | Education and Training (2019). www.stats.gov.sa/en
12. Gherhes, V., Simon, S., Para, I.: Analysing students' reasons for keeping their webcams on or off during online classes. Sustainability **13**, 3203 (2021)
13. Kim, S.S.: Motivators and concerns for real-time online classes: focused on the security and privacy issues. Interactive Learning Environments (2021)
14. Müller, A.M., Goh, C., Lim, L.Z., Gao, X.: COVID-19 emergency elearning and beyond: experiences and perspectives of university educators. Education Sciences, 11, Art. 19 (2021)
15. Oesch, S., et al.: Understanding user perceptions of security and privacy for group chat: a survey of users in the US and UK. Proceedings of Annual Computer Security Applications Conference (ACSAC'20). ACM Press (2020)
16. Pallof, R.M., Pratt, K.: Building Online Learning Communities: Effective Strategies for the Virtual Classroom. John Wiley & Sons (2007)
17. Petchamé, J., Iriondo, I., Azanza, G.: "Seeing and Being Seen" or just "Seeing" in a smart classroom context when videoconferencing: a user experience-based qualitative research on the use of cameras. Int. J. Environ. Res. Public Health **19**(15), 9615 (2022)
18. Pham, A.T.: Engineering students' perception of using webcams in virtual english classes. Int. J. Eng. Pedagogy (IJEP) **12**(6), 115–127 (2022)
19. Rashidi, Y., Vaniea, K., Camp, L.J.: Understanding Saudis' privacy concerns when using WhatsApp. In: Proceedings of the Workshop on Usable Security (USEC'6) (2016)
20. Reedy, A., Pfitzner, D., Rook, L., Ellis, L.: Responding to the COVID-19 emergency: student and academic staff perceptions of academic integrity in the transition to online exams at three Australian universities. Int. J. Educ. Integr. **17**(1), 1–32 (2021)
21. Serhan, D.: Transitioning from face-to-face to remote learning: students' attitudes and perceptions of using Zoom during COVID-19 pandemic. International J. Technol. Education Sci. **4**(4), 335–342 (2020)
22. United Nations Educational, Scientific and Cultural Organization (UNESCO).: *COVID-19: reopening and reimagining universities, survey on higher education through the UNESCO National Commission* (2021). https://unesdoc.unesco.org/ark:/48223/pf0000378174/PDF/378174eng.pdf.multi
23. Yarmand, M., Solyst, J., Klemmer, S., Weibel, N.: It feels like I am talking into a void: understanding interaction gaps in synchronous online classrooms. In Proceedings of ACM Conference on Human Factors in Computing Systems (CHI'21), Yokohama, Japan. ACM Press: New York, NY, USA (2021)

Exploring the Experiences of People Who Inherited Digital Assets from Deceased Users: A Search for Better Computing Solutions

Maria Fernanda Lira[1]([✉]) [iD], Cristiano Maciel[1,2] [iD], Daniele Trevisan[2] [iD], Vinicius Carvalho Pereira[3] [iD], Simone Barbosa[4] [iD], and Flavia Beppu[5] [iD]

[1] Instituto de Computação, Universidade Federal de Mato Grosso, Cuiabá, MT, Brasil
nandalira57@gmail.com, cristiano.maciel@ufmt.br
[2] Instituto de Educação, Universidade Federal de Mato Grosso, Cuiabá, MT, Brasil
[3] Instituto de Linguagens, Universidade Federal de Mato Grosso, Cuiabá, MT, Brasil
[4] Departamento de Informática, Pontifícia Universidade Católica Do Rio de Janeiro, Gávea, RJ, Brasil
simone@inf.puc-rio.br
[5] Laboratório de Ambientes Virtuais Interativos, Universidade Federal de Mato Grosso, Cuiabá, MT, Brasil

Abstract. Users produce a significant amount of data in different internet spaces and, after their death, these data constitute part of their digital legacy, which can be managed by third parties. However, what are the perceptions of heirs and legacy managers when interacting with such systems? The aim of this research was to explore the experience of family members and others who inherited digital legacies from loved ones in systems that enable post-mortem digital legacy management. It also sought to understand how heirs interacted with these digital artifacts. To this end, the study was divided into two parts. Initially, a Systematic Literature Review was carried out in search of studies from 2015 to 2022 that addressed such issues. Next, we conducted an in-depth qualitative study with online interviews with people who had inherited digital assets and/or had turned a deceased person's profile into a digital memorial on Facebook. Based on our findings, we discuss how to enhance and improve aspects that affect interaction involving digital legacy.

Keywords: Post-mortem digital legacy · digital memorial · Facebook · Digital Legacy Management Systems

1 Introduction

As the Internet widens its scope, family members and friends from different places are drawn closer together through message exchanges, video and phone calls and, chiefly, by using social networks. Family members and friends logged into the same network can view and share photos, videos and information through smartphones, computers, laptops, tablets, etc., which constitutes a so-called generalized connection [16].

J. Abdelnour Nocera et al. (Eds.): INTERACT 2023, LNCS 14144, pp. 491–510, 2023.
https://doi.org/10.1007/978-3-031-42286-7_28

Plenty of data are produced throughout a lifespan; however, we do not always stop to think about what we want to happen to these data after we pass away [23]. According to Maciel and Pereira [20], people have different perceptions of what they want to happen to their digital assets when they die, such as: whether they want their accounts to be deleted; whether they want their social networks to be transformed into digital memorials; whether they want only loved ones to have access to images, videos, files and passwords. However, there is a gap in the literature: what are the perceptions of heirs and people who manage legacies when interacting with such systems?

The objective of this research was to explore the experience of people and family members who have inherited digital legacy from loved ones in systems that support post-death digital legacy management. Furthermore, we sought to understand how the heirs interacted with these digital artifacts, raising questions such as: whether they deleted any photos/videos; whether they still share those data, or whether they ever think of permanently deleting those data.

This study was divided into two parts. Initially, a Systematic Literature Review was carried out searching for studies that addressed these issues, published from 2015 to 2022. This time frame was determined because the functionality of memorializing Facebook profiles became available in Brazil in 2015 [9]. Subsequently, the authors looked for people who had inherited digital assets from Facebook and/or transformed the profile of a deceased person into a digital memorial on Facebook and invited them to participate in an interview. The invitation was made to Internet users through messages sent in study groups of educational institutions, through the WhatsApp instant messenger. It was also publicized on social networks such as Facebook and Instagram. Six in-depth interviews were conducted and analyzed in order to understand the experiences of users when interacting with such systems.

This is a research project from the DAVI - Dados Além da Vida [10] group, from the Institute of Computing at the Federal University of Mato Grosso, whose main goal is to develop research on postmortem digital legacy and propose improvements and solutions for computer systems engineering, so that heirs may protect digital assets, according to the will expressed by deceased users.

The paper is structured as follows: at first, the Literature Review covers concepts of digital memorials and presents their characteristics on Facebook. Next, we present the research method. Finally, we present and discuss the results in two sections: 1) Results of the Systematic Literature Review and 2) Partial results of the interviews with the volunteers.

2   Literature Review

According to Lopes et al. [19], digital memorials provide users with a new way of mourning and honoring those who have passed away. Memorials may produce considerable content that provides grief support, as they allow visitors to post letters, words of comfort, memories, etc., and thus comfort people who are suffering from the loss of a loved one.

Yamauchi et al. [31] carried out a systematic research analyzing DLMS (Digital Legacy Management Systems) from three points of view: theoretical, systemic, and user's. They typify those systems as dedicated (DDLMS) or integrated (IDLMS). The main difference between them is that IDLMS do not have digital legacy management as one of their main objectives, whereas the main purpose of DDLMS is to manage one's digital legacy.

Facebook is an integrated system that allows users to register a legacy contact to manage the user's account after their death. Additionally, the tool allows the account of a deceased user to be transformed into a digital memorial. Some authors address the situation of people who inherited digital assets on Facebook and/or people who decided to transform the profile of a deceased person into a digital memorial, such as: Bell and Kennedy [3]; Santos [24]; Ataguba [1]); Bassett [2]; Little [18]; Gach [13]; Yeager [32]. These works will be discussed in Sect. 4.1.

From a legal perspective, the discussion touches upon the right of succession or data protection. Patti and Bartolini (2019) carried out a study to analyze the Italian legislative reform from 2017, which regulated data protection and the succession of post-mortem digital data. They discussed the changes introduced in the Italian legislation to deal with the issue of digital inheritance, such as access to the digital data of the deceased, and the protection of the privacy of the deceased and his relatives. The authors pointed out that there were still some issues to be addressed, such as the harmonization of national and international laws and the need for an adequate balance between privacy and the rights of heirs.

In the context of Brazil, where our study was carried out, the country's Civil Code [7] addresses legitimate and testamentary succession [34]. The former refers to the hypotheses in which the legitimate heirs receive the inheritance, according to the order of succession (Article 1829, Brazil Civil Code) [7]. The latter, which deals with the institute of the legacy, concerns the will of the deceased person, who leaves, in a singular capacity, a certain and determined thing to a person, who may or may not be an heir [30].

There is no specific regulation for digital legacy in the Brazilian legal system, and the legislature for this purpose does not address the problem broadly. For example, nothing is mentioned about the protection of personality rights. These rights (such as the right to one's image, intimacy, honor, and freedom), albeit not subject to succession (transfer of ownership or possession), must also be protected, for they constitute pivotal interests of the deceased person's personality [4]. For Taveira Jr. [26], there may be, for example, violations that affect the identity of the person, "in its moral aspect, in the informational context".

Another point of divergence in relation to digital legacy lies in the terminology used. Sometimes we find, in legal works and in the field of ICT, the term "digital assets", defined by Taveira Jr [26] as "the set of files in binary format which constitute the digitized heritage of the person, natural or legal". However, the same author refutes the use of this expression, as it is not the most adherent to the Brazilian civil law. Instead, he adopts the term "digital heritage" when referring to the set of digital assets of a person, and "digital asset" or "digital goods" when referring to a digital object or to some objects in binary form [26].

As for the value of digital goods, we have goods of a pecuniary nature, and those considered "not economically relevant or immaterial" belonging to a person [26]. Taveira

Jr. Maintains that the classic paradigm of the Brazilian civil law must be overcome to include digital assets of a non-asset-related nature in the sphere of digital heritage[26].

Thus, the assets and digital artifacts left by the dead person to legal and/or testamentary heirs, or even those registered in applications as a kind of digital will, must be analyzed from two perspectives: (i) property rights and (ii) personality rights. These heirs, in a broad sense, will have encumbrances or rights, depending on what is covered in the digital inheritance (herein considered in a broad sense).

3   Methods and Materials

The research was conducted by initially performing a systematic literature review (SLR) of articles that address the subject of digital inheritance. The aim was to gather information about what has already been researched, what results were found, and how these research studies were conducted. Morandi and Camargo [22] define systematic literature review as secondary studies to "[...] *map, find, critically evaluate, consolidate and aggregate the results of relevant primary studies on a question or research topic as well as identifying gaps to be filled, resulting in a coherent report or synthesis*".

The SLR followed the guidelines proposed by Castro [8] in a seven-step process. The first six consist of: 1) formulation of the question(s); 2) location and selection of studies; 3) critical evaluation of studies; 4) data collection; 5) data analysis and representation; and 6) interpretation of results. The seventh stage concerns the improvement, updating, and continuity of the study.

First, the research protocol was developed by defining the objective of the study and the questions posed to guide the work. Our guiding question was: What are the backgrounds, motivations, and sentiments of users who inherited and/or transformed profiles of deceased people into a digital memorial on Facebook? This main issue unfolded into the following questions: What is the importance of transforming a profile into a digital memorial for friends and family? With regard to the analysis of the papers reviewed, we also sought to answer the following questions: What is the background of the participants involved in the studies? What methodologies were used in the research? If the study was related to digital heirs, we attempted to answer the following question: What did these users do with the inherited data? And, finally, if the study was about people who converted a profile into a digital memorial, our objective was to answer the following question: Why did users decide to transform these profiles into a digital memorial?

Then, in step 2, we mapped out studies published between 2015 and 2022, analyzing data of users who inherited or transformed the Facebook profile of a deceased person.

In order to find free-access online studies related to the questions above, the following search strings were used on Google Scholar: "Digital memorial" + Facebook. These terms should appear throughout the articles to be included in the review. Google Scholar was chosen because it allows searching for articles from different databases, such as ACM (Association for Computing Machinery), IEEE (Institute of Electrical and Electronics Engineers) and Springer. However, according to the inclusion and exclusion criteria mentioned below, only articles to which we had full and open access were considered.

The criteria for including papers in our sample were: studies published between 2015 and 2022; studies written in Portuguese or English; full or abridged articles; studies that focused on Facebook; studies published between 2015 and 2022; studies written in Portuguese or English; full or abridged articles; studies that focused on Facebook; studies that analyzed the experience of people who inherited digital goods from Facebook and/or had turned someone's profile into a digital memorial. Studies that mentioned the use of digital memorials. The criteria for excluding papers from our sample were: studies without free access in digital libraries; studies published before 2015; duplicate works and/or with a more recent or more complete version.

After the systematic review, we moved on to the second step of this research, which was to find volunteers who had inherited digital assets from deceased users and/or had transformed the profile of a deceased user on Facebook into a digital memorial. This social network was chosen because it was one of the first social media platforms to allow users to transform the profiles of deceased people into digital memorials, as presented by Trevisan et al. [27].

We publicized our call for volunteers through messages in groups of educational institutions in the WhatsApp instant communicator. The call was also publicized on social networks such as Facebook and Instagram. People who were interested in participating in this research filled out a form on Google Forms informing their name, telephone number and email. After this process, one of the researchers contacted the volunteers, so that the day and time for the interviews could be scheduled. Despite the various posts on social media and contacts with acquaintances who might help, as well as deadline extensions, we have only obtained six participants for this study. Although the number is small, it indicates in itself the difficulty of exploring this topic, as we discuss throughout this paper.

After signing the informed consent form, participants were interviewed online through Google Meet. Each interview lasted about 45 min, and they were all recorded and transcribed.

During the interview, each participant revealed whether they were heirs of a Facebook digital memorial, or whether they had transformed the profile of a loved one into a digital memorial. All participants were asked similar demographics questions, questions about the deceased and death, and about decisions about their own legacy. The remaining of the interview script varied depending on whether the participant was an heir or whether they turned their loved one's account into a digital memorial. Regarding the deceased and their death, heirs were asked about their relationship with the deceased; the deceased's cause of death; when the death occurred; how the friends reacted on social media; the heir's feelings and actions when first accessing the deceased's account after their death; and other digital goods the deceased had left them. The last group of questions for both groups asked participants about whether they had already defined their own digital legacy, their concerns and actions about the subject.

The specific group of questions for the heirs was related to the digital legacy management. They were asked about when and how they learned they would be heirs; their reasons for accepting this role; how and how frequently they interact with deceased's account and with the people who interact with that account; the main tasks they performed with the account; and their thoughts about deleting the account altogether.

For the digital memorialists, the specific group of questions were: whether Facebook had detected the death to transform the account into a digital memorial, or whether the memorialist had to ask; how long after the death the account was asked to be transformed into a memorial; how long it took for Facebook to effect the change; the difficulties involved in the process; the reasons for deciding to transform the account into a digital memorial; and, finally, the main changes they had perceived between the original account and the digital memorial.

The questions in both surveys were adapted from the work by Maciel and Pereira [35]. Considering the sensitive topic of the interview, the interviewer offered emotional support to participants when needed. Interviewees were also informed that, if they felt uncomfortable answering any question, they could skip it or interrupt or cancel the interview, as expressed in the consent form. Still concerning research ethics, this study is part of the DAVI [10] project, which is approved by the Research Ethics Committee of the Federal University of Mato Grosso (Brazil). The researchers have ensured ethical issues were respected, such as privacy over users' data and anonymization of interviewees and deceased users.

After the interviews, the respondents were grouped according to their profiles and attributions on the social network. The first group comprised a) those who requested the transformation of Facebook profiles of deceased loved ones into a digital memorial, and the second group consisted in b) those who were heirs of deceased profiles on the Facebook social network. In this text, the profiles are anonymized and identified with the letter P for participant, followed by a sequential number from 1 to 6 (e.g. P1 means participant 01). The analysis was based on reflection on the data collected in the interviews in comparison with the literature in the area.

4   Results

This section presents the results from the Systematic Literature Review and from the interviews with volunteers who transformed and/or inherited digital memorial profiles on Facebook.

4.1   Results of the Systematic Literature Review

Using the search string "Digital memorial" AND Facebook, Google Scholar found 307 articles. At this stage, 141 articles were excluded, for two reasons: either 1) there was no link available for the works in the virtual library; or 2) the research had not been conducted between 2015 and 2022. The remaining 165 articles were sorted by year of publication and moved on to the next stage of the study.

Titles and abstracts of the 165 articles were analyzed. If the abstract did not address users who had inherited digital assets on Facebook and/or transformed the profiles of deceased people into digital memorials on Facebook, the article was excluded. In total, 118 articles were excluded, leaving 46 to be read in full. After reading the articles, only nine dealt with digital inheritance and were selected for further analysis. These works were analyzed, and the following data were extracted: year of publication; functionalities on the Facebook tool; how people interacted with profiles of people who had passed away; the methodology used by the researchers; and the feeling of heirs of digital assets on Facebook and/or of people who transformed profiles of deceased users into digital memorials on Facebook.

In order to present the results, we organized the data according to the previously defined questions. The nine selected studies were identified numerically, as shown in Table 1.

Table 1. Related studies

Year	Authors	Title	Ref
2015	Bell, J., Bailey, L., and Kennedy, D.	"We do it to keep him alive': bereaved individuals' experiences of online suicide memorials and continuing bonds	[3]
2016	Santos, L.	Repositórios digitais na preservação da memória de clubes de futebol: a descrição arquivística na análise do Esporte Clube Vitória	[24]
2018	Ataguba, G.	Towards an evaluation of mobile life logging technologies and storytelling in socio-personal grieving spaces	[1]
2019	Bassett, D.	You Only Live Twice: A constructivist grounded theory study of the creation and inheritance of digital afterlives	[2]
	Little, N.	Rape-Related Mourning on a Social Network Site: Leah Parsons's "Facebooked" Grief and the Angel Rehtaeh Parsons Page	[18]
	Gach, K.	How to Delete the Dead: Honoring Affective Connections to Post-mortem Data	[13]
2021	Gach, K., and Brubaker, J.	Getting Your Facebook Affairs in Order: User Expectations in Post-mortem Profile Management	[12]
	Yeager, S.	Mourning practices on Facebook: Facebook shrines and other rituals of grieving in the digital age	[32]
2022	Lira et al.	Mine, yours, ours: family discussions on digital legacy	[17]

As can be observed in Table 1, in 2017 and 2020 there were no surveys with people reporting their experience in relation to digital heritage. In 2019 only 2 articles were published [2, 28] and in 2021 there was a modest growth of 3 studies on the subject of digital inheritance [12, 13, 32].

Eighteen percent (18%) of the studies (9 out of 46) analyzed the experiences of people who transformed deceased users' profiles into digital memorials, such as in Bell and Kennedy's [3], who analyzed the experiences of individuals in digital memorials on Facebook profiles of suicidals. Three men and eight women between the ages of 20 and 60 participated in this study. Participants were asked what motivated them to create their websites online; how they used the websites; how the websites helped them process their grieving; their views on the role of the Internet in understanding and coping with suicide bereavement; and any negative experiences encountered while interacting online for the purpose of managing their grief. Participants justified their objectives in memorializing those profiles to keep the deceased alive, to comfort family and friends, and to inform third parties about the death and dates of funeral ceremonies. Santos's [24] study analyzed the preservation of the memory of football clubs, based on the construction of a digital repository. The author carried out a digital repository study on Facebook and then elaborated a survey to find out the opinion of the fans of Esporte Clube Vitória (a soccer team from the Brazilian city of Salvador-BA) on data such as photos/videos etc. that were available at the memorial. The study was carried out with 18 fans, who reported what they thought of the data collection. Some participants liked that the club had preserved those memories in a non superficial way, and others wanted to share their own photos, news clips and memorabilia of the team as well.

Ataguba [1] presents an initial work based on the theory of continuous bonds. The theory explains how bereaved people are continually reminded of their lost loved ones when exposed to certain memory triggers, such as familiar sounds from the past, faces that resemble the deceased person, and places they once had visited together. There were 22 participants volunteering in the study, and the results showed that those people wanted to not only maintain personal spaces or share memories in social spaces, like Facebook, but also revisit old memories and reimagine the presence of the deceased person.

Bassett [2] talks about inheriting messages and profiles on social media platforms, including Facebook. By interviewing 48 people on this subject, the article sought to answer some questions, such as: "How do mourners experience the inheritance of digital memories and messages?". One of the participants reported that it had been five and a half years since her mother had passed away, but she still had voice messages on her phone from her mother, and listened to them on difficult days. Another participant reported that there were many videos on Facebook of her deceased brother and that she did not watch those videos because she did not want to hear his voice because it would make her suffer.

Yeager [32] examines how Facebook users use the social media platform to mourn beloved ones, process their own pain, and provide support to other people grieving. The author also explores how the experiences of death and loss shape bereaved people's religious beliefs and actions, and how social media impacts the experience of grief. He looks at the organically emerging mourning communities on deceased people's Facebook timelines and examines the social pressure to mourn in a public space. Finally, his paper questions how the interaction with these virtual memorials impacts participants' mental and social health.

Little [18] analyzes the digital memorial of Rehtaeh Parsons, who committed suicide after being sexually abused. Leah, Rehtaeh's mother, turned her profile into a memorial andbecame an activist, protesting against society's branding of Rehtaeh as a "suicidal whore". Her main objective in creating the profile was to clear Rehtaeh's reputation, to dispel false rumors and negativity, and furthermore, to redirect the blame for Rehtaeh's rape and death onto the rapists and abusers, as well as onto the system (police, doctors and justice) that, according to Leah, shared responsibility for her daughter's death. Leah reported that the memorial was a space in which she could articulate clear boundaries on how Rehtaeh's memory should be framed and treated, and in which she moderated the integrity of Rehtaeh's postmortem digital "body", by ensuring that it remains inviolable in death and the afterlife.

Gach [13] conducted a study with 28 participants to evaluate the experiences of managing the Facebook account of a deceased loved one. One of the conclusions of the study was that most participants accepted being heirs because it meant that they had been a very important person in the account owner's life. However, some did not discuss the matter with the account owner in advance. One of the participants reported that he used the profile to share with friends and family where his mother's funeral would be held, among other important information. Another participant reported that he accessed the profile to save messages from his mother, as that made him feel good, unlike another participant who said that, when entering his mother's profile, he felt lost because the space was a little messy. Furthermore, the study digs deeper into why these people were chosen to be the legacy contact, and it found that they were chosen for one reason only: the users trusted them.

Gach and Brubaker [12] evaluated the legacy contact configuration process and asked how users inform and communicate their expectations about what would be the responsibilities of a digital heir. The researchers interviewed 30 Facebook users who had configured their own digital legacy settings or were chosen by other users as digital heirs. The authors found that account holders chose the Facebook friend they felt closest to, and this was often reciprocated. Both account holders and legacy contacts felt confident that they had communicated (or could communicate) effectively about being the legacy contact, but their expectations did not align with the actual functionality of the legacy contact system.

Lira et al. [17] conducted a study with five families and analyzed different perceptions by family members regarding digital legacy. The study revealed that most participants understood the importance of thinking about the destination of digital goods, and they reflected on that during the study. They also reported that, during family discussions, some issues were raised concerning the lack of trust in the systems responsible for their digital assets and the emotional cost of participating in the study for the different generations of the family.

All nine works herein systematically reviewed have the same objective, that is, to analyze the perception of users who transformed the profile of a deceased person into a digital memorial and/or inherited digital assets from a deceased person on Facebook. And all participants showed the same reasons for doing so: honoring those who are gone. Considering that only nine papers out of our initial sample of 308 report studies related to people who inherited digital assets on Facebook and/or transformed the profile of users who have died on Facebook, we can conclude these are still understudied matters. In the Brazilian context, as well, there are very few studies that address these issues.

A social factor that may stimulate such studies is the worldwide movement of laws regulating the processing of personal data. Reference should be made to the General Data

Protection Regulation (GDPR), a European regulation that came into force in 2018 and inspired the publication of the General Law for the Protection of Personal Data (LGPD), a Brazilian regulatory instrument that came into full force in 2020 [4, 5]. Although neither law addresses digital legacy specifically, these legislations may contribute to greater interest in researching this topic and encourage a wider angle on the related debate. It is certainly an issue that should be monitored in future research.

On a related note, laws in several countries, such as Italy, France, and Bulgaria, have been edited to regulate the use of deceased persons' data. Some of these laws limit the use of personal data to family members, who can extend this possibility to third parties [21].

According to Beppu et al. [5], whereas the LGPD does not go into detail on the subject in Brazil, it contributes by providing orientation on how to address post-death digital legacy. This is also an issue to be monitored in future works.

4.2 Interviews

In this section, we present the results of the interviews with the participants.

4.2.1 Participants' Background

There were six volunteers from different Brazilian states: São Paulo (1 participant), Paraná (2 participants), and Mato Grosso (3 participants); 5 women and 1 man, all between 20 and 48 years old, all Facebook users. Participants were split between those who transformed a deceased user's profile into a digital memorial and those who inherited a digital memorial profile. The following table sums up these data (Table 2).

Table 2. Characterization of the participants.

Part	Age	Relationship with the deceased	Year of death	Participant's role
P1	33	Friend	2021	Heir
P2	48	Daughter in law	2020	Heir
P3	20	Grandson	2019	Transformed profile into digital memorial
P4	46	Spouse	2014	Heir
P5	22	Friend	2021	Transformed profile into digital memorial
P6	24	Daughter	2017	Transformed profile into digital memorial

We show below how the participants interacted with the digital memorial profiles on Facebook. Then we discuss the different perceptions of heirs of digital memorials and users who transformed a profile into a digital memorial.

4.2.2 Interaction with Digital Memorial Profiles on Facebook

The transformation of participants' accounts into digital memorials seeks to maintain a bonding interaction between the subject and deceased loved ones and to relive memories. In this sense, P1 reported that "the closest people left tributes, and many visited the profile to find out what had happened to her, and photos on her profile continue to receive likes even after her death". P4 reported: "Sometimes people cannot attend wakes, especially in this case: he was a person who had studied in different cities and also participated in projects with people from different universities, so many people could not attend. Some people used telegrams or sent condolences by email, but social media was my first choice".

Contemporary ways of showing emotion and offering condolences are common on social networks. Although, in the initial stages of grieving, the memories brought back by social networks can cause sadness. For P4, "it's another moment of the grieving process, it's reliving grieving. There are several moments in grief. I was with him in the hospital when he died, at the moment of the wake, after the farewell, and at the cremation. So, at all these moments I said farewell, and all these were stages of the process. I kept his profile active for a while. There were no resources to memorialize the profile when he passed away. The day I decided to memorialize him was approximately 5 years after his death. It is and.... (breathing) I experienced the mourning once again and it is as if it had never gone away, it felt as if you were giving away a little piece of the person again in a new dimension, a new dimension... It's a new moment, when you bury a little bit of the person's memory." This quote from the interview highlights the fact that for several years, even before the creation of the digital memorial functionality, Facebook users have been using other resources of the platform to honor the dead such as posting photos of the deceased or changing one's profile photo for images that refer to mourning practices. This kind of cultural practice is still widely use, especially in the case of users who do not know there is a digital memorial functionality, or who ignore how to use it.

P1 also said that "it's also a matter of maintaining the bond, you know, it's a way of keeping everything that the person lived here, keeping the memories alive. I think that having the person's profile available to look at makes the pain much smaller than it would be if the profile was no longer there". P2 said that he felt that "It seems that I was entering her account and I felt great (paused) sadness... But it also seemed as if I was invading her territory, because I was touching her things, but she wasn't there anymore, you know?" This shows an important element of many cultural practices concerning death: taboos of profanation of the deceased's body, image or possessions, which affect both users and designers when it comes to software related to death, dying and mortality.

Out of the total pool of participants, those who requested the memorialization of profiles reported that they could do no other change to those accounts because Facebook would not allow it (only heirs can change cover photos, accept friends etc.). Those profiles remain, thus, like offline-world uncared-for tombs. On the other hand, in the case of the heirs trying to make changes in the profile, P1 said she left a final message to honor the deceased, and P2 said she had changed the cover photo of the deceased to inform his friends that he had passed away, because in 2014 it was not possible to request a memorialized profile. P2 converted the account but did not know about its functionalities (such as accepting friend requests, deleting friends, modifying profile and cover photos, etc.). She found out about those possibilities during the interview and asked the following questions: "What do I do now? What if I accept a friend request, and scare the person? I don't know what to do... What if it renews the pain felt by their children and relatives again? I don't know what to do". This demonstrates some of the difficulties faced and a lack of knowledge about the tools available for those who manage the profile. It also shows a fear of people's reactions when interacting with a memorialized profile.

On other digital platforms, the deceased may also have left digital goods. During the interviews questions about the destination of these goods were made and we noticed that none of the participants tried to access any goods left on other digital platforms. P5 reported: "Instagram does not have the option to convert the profile into a memorial. If that option were available, I would try to convert the profile into a memorial because she was very active there".

4.2.3 From the Perspective of the Heirs

Nowadays, with passwords stored on mobile devices or saved in accounts for speedier access, many users can allow their accounts to be accessed after their death by family members who are in possession of these devices. In view of this, P2 and P4 reported that they registered as heirs by accessing the deceased's account through a device belonging to him, which was left with his account logged in. P2 justified this by arguing that she also tried to request the memorialization of her mother-in-law's account, but was not successful because of a problem related to the death certificate. She reported that "they would not accept it, and they said that the certificate was not valid, and I knew that her account was still logged into her cell phone, so I just went ahead and registered as a legacy contact". P4 said that the possibility of converting a regular profile into a memorial and registering someone as a legacy contact did not exist in the year her husband died. Because the participant did not know what the process was like, she registered her sister as her heir, and, years later, after a conversation with her daughters, she decided to register as her husband's heir, so she could manage his account.

Only P1 was chosen as an heir by the owner of the account. P1 reported the user's reasons for configuring an heir for her Facebook account: "So, to tell you the truth, she didn't want to disappear from the world and it's strange how people who leave this world early live very intensely. She was really concerned about not disappearing, she wanted to leave a trace and didn't want to be forgotten. She is here even though she's not here".

P1 also reported why she accepted to be a digital heir. "It is an act of trust: the person likes and trusts you. It is an honor for you to represent them, and that is why I accepted it. I think it is an opportunity to keep someone alive not only within you but present in everyone's lives, so it's hard to say no." This shows how caring for one's account after their death is a way to maintain strong bonding with that person and show respect and care even after their death. P1 and P4 also said that they accessed the deceased person's account on commemorative dates or dates that were important to the deceased person. P2 said that he only accessed the profile last year on his mother-in-law's birthday and has not accessed it since then. Some of the typical interactions of social media, such as posting birthday and anniversary messages, remain after the user's death, despite the fact that the addressee is no longer there to read those messages.

Participants were then asked about how they interacted with the account left by the deceased. P4 stated that she did not receive many friend requests after the death of her husband and that she did not modify his profile picture. Neither did P1 and P2. P1 said: "No, I changed nothing and I wouldn't even think about changing anything. It would feel like I was changing something she purposely decided on, so I wouldn't feel comfortable doing that". P1 also reported that there were many friend requests, but she only accepted requests if she knew who that person was, as she was afraid that someone in bad faith would post slanderous things about her friend.

As to posting on their loved one's profile, the participants were asked about what kind of information they published on the pages, or what final message they had left. P1 reported that she posted information about the funeral and, as a final message, she wrote a trajectory of her friend's life. P4, on the other hand, reported that, after her husband's death, she informed through his Facebook page the location where the requiem mass would be held, so that those who could not attend the funeral could attend the mass instead.

P1, P2, and P4 stated that they never tried to delete any publication, photo/video, or tried to remove friends from the owner's account. The participants said that they had no right to do such things, as they felt that it would go against the deceased person's will. Moreover, they reported that they did not make any attempt to download a copy of the deceased person's shared content on Facebook. However, P4 reported that she printed the screenshots taken from the messages that people left on her husband's profile and kept them. She explained that: "I am a person who likes physical things and I am also a very nostalgic person. So, in some moments, I like to revisit those messages. I did it because of my daughters: I was afraid that, when they grew up, they wouldn't be able to see the messages that people left on their father's profile".

P1, P2, and P4 said they have not considered deleting their loved one's account. P4 further stated: "No, I never thought about deleting their account. This is something I have never contemplated. I think it's because I don't consider myself the only heir. My daughters are also heirs and, for me to delete his account, I would have to consult them." P4's comment shows the sentimental value of the husband's legacy and the importance of discussing the future of digital goods within the family, especially in the case where there is more than one heir and conflict can arise, as it often happens when there is no will and inheritance has sentimental and/or financial value.

4.2.4 From the Perspective of the Users Who Requested the Conversion of a Profile into a Digital Memorial

All participants who requested the conversion of an account into a digital memorial profile initially sought to understand how the system could detect a user's death. P3, P5, and P6 reported that it was necessary to fill out an online form to request the conversion of the profile into a memorial.

P4 gives us an account of this procedure, stating that "Facebook has a page, I believe it is still a little hard to find, but there is a page to memorialize the profile. And to complete the memorialization, some information is needed. There was only one piece of information that I found unnecessary: the deceased's email address and the email he used to log into the account. How does anyone know this information? It's kind of complicated to find out which email was used to access the account. Another piece of information that was required was his name and death certificate, or something that certified that he had died. And also something that proved a connection with the loved one." P5 said about the same process that "I remember that I went into settings and had to fill out a form. I had to say what my connection to her was and send a certificate stating that she had really died. And I also had to give her email address. I found that rather pointless. But overall it was pretty straightforward."

We sought to understand how long after death they requested to memorialize the profiles on Facebook. P3 reported that it took about two and a half years for the request, P5 took about five months, and P6 one year. After the request, participants reported that there was a wait of about a week for Facebook to respond to the request. They did not experience difficulties in making the request.

They were also asked why they opted to convert the profiles into digital memorials. P3 reported: "It was in order not to leave his profile forgotten. Basically to leave it there as a memorial, to leave it as something eternal, to transform it into something more respectful than simply leaving it there abandoned, as if nobody cared, And there are a lot of people who leave messages for him. I don't know, I just did it." P5 said: "She was a person full of light. Right after her death, people left messages and everything and then I saw the possibility of memorializing the profile. I felt that it would be the right thing to do because I can tell if a profile was abandoned, you know? And the memorial is a way of letting her live on."

P3 and P4 reported that they didn't see much difference between a normal profile and a digital memorial profile. P3 added: "The memorial profile basically adds a message under the photo, the person's name, and adds the caption "remembering" to the person's name and also leaves a tribute to the person. Something like that, but that's all that changes; the profile is basically the same".

5 Discussions

In the studies analyzed in the SLR, people who converted the profile of a deceased person into a memorial and/or inherited these digital assets on Facebook demonstrate that memorialized profiles are a means to ease the pain of losing a loved one and that the messages left by friends and family on the deceased person's memorial helped ease the pain they were feeling. However, in studies by Bassett [2], some participants stated that they do not like to enter and look at the profile so as not to suffer when remembering a loved one. But in this research, we showed that memorial profiles served as a space for memories and tributes, which also contributed to the experience of mourning and the maintenance of the memory of the deceased.

The data from the interviews we carried out with heirs of digital legacy and people who requested the conversion of a dead user's profile into a memorial show that digital memorials are used as spaces for interacting with and maintaining an emotional bond with the deceased. Participants reported that many tributes are left even long after death. According to the data, memorials allow people who are physically distant to express their feelings, when unable to attend funeral processions. This demonstrates that new forms of interaction extend to social networks even when users are no longer present.

In this sense, networks take on meaning for relatives and friends who still access and experience reminiscing moments by viewing photographs and posted homages.

From the interviews, we also noticed that, although the conversion of the account into a memorial did not occur immediately after death, there was a need to maintain this space as a place to keep the memory of the deceased user alive. Participants referred to the pain experienced when looking for the profile of a deceased person, and not finding it there anymore. This reinforces digital memorial profiles are spaces for interaction and grief support.

Since the deceased users had not previously registered a legacy contact to their account, the solution found by some of the participants was accessing the account through the password left by the original user on a device, assigning themselves the role of heirs, and then requesting the memorialization. Although this is a strategy that contributes to caring for the profile and the family with some comfort, it does not match a will previously defined by the deceased. Also, the system only allows the registration of heirs who are already part of the system, which seems limiting, if we consider that the right of succession does not restrict who can be the legatee (heir) of a will [17].

With regard to the right of succession, some other aspects must be considered. The Brazilian Civil Code [7] addresses legitimate and testamentary succession. The former refers to the hypotheses in which the legitimate heirs receive an inheritance, according to the order of succession (Art. 1829, CC). The second concerns the will of the deceased person, who leaves a singular determined possession to a person, who may or may not be the heir [17, 29].

There is no specific regulation for digital legacy, and bills on related themes do not address this problem directly. For example, they do not concern the protection of personality rights. These rights (image, privacy, honor, freedom, among others), although not subject to succession (transfer of ownership or possession), must also be protected, as centers of personality interest of the deceased person [4]. For Taveira Jr. [26], there can be, for example, attacks that affect the person's identity, "in its moral aspect, in the informational context." The fact is that now a user can only allocate their accounts to any third party, without having a distinction between what could have financial value and should go to their legitimate heirs, and what has only emotional value [17].

Choosing an heir is an act of utmost responsibility since this person will be responsible for looking after the goods left by the user. Gach and Brubaker [12] conducted a study on this topic and emphasized that trust is the main reason for choosing a digital "heir". P1's comment corroborates with the authors' studies, as the participant states that she accepted her friend's invitation to become her legacy contact because she felt that her friend had placed a lot of trust in her.

No participant mentioned it was hard to find the option to turn the loved one's profile into a digital memorial; however, P2 reported that she had difficulty proving that her mother-in-law had died. As for the request for memorialization, the participants mentioned difficulties in gaining access to the deceased user's email, since this information is required. Although it is an important piece of data for the social network to go ahead with the process, many users who make the request may not know how to find out that email address. It would be necessary to find mechanisms that facilitate memorializing the digital profile of a deceased user.

In view of the functionality of the network upon registering a legacy contact, the tool automatically sends the following message to the legacy contact: "Since you know me well and I trust you, I chose you. Please let me know if you want to talk about this." [11]. P1 reported that the conversation about being a legacy contact was not a difficult one to have, but she did not approve that Facebook sends an automatic message that lacks sensitivity considering the delicate matter of death. The participant suggested that the person could write the invitation in their own words, as this would perhaps be less painful. From this point of view, it is important to design and evaluate the tool so that it does not harm relationships For example, the person inviting someone to be the legacy contact should be able to set a deadline for the answer, so that, if the user does not accept the invitation, the account owner would be notified of that and then select another legacy contact.

This study also revealed the taboo surrounding death, which imposes restrictions on the action of the heirs. When the participants report that they were afraid to accept new friend requests, as they were uncertain of how people would react upon receiving the confirmation, it demonstrates how poorly society deals with death. This requires the network to proceed differently with this confirmation so that the friend would know that the person who accepted the request was the legacy contact and not the deceased user. Or, along with the confirmation, there could be a sensitive message informing the death of the user. As presented by Trevisan et al. [27], there is a lack of transparency on Facebook regarding the management of memorialized profiles. It is not possible to know if a profile transformed into a digital memorial is being managed by someone or not. If there were such information, there would not be so much need for fear, as the deceased user's friends would know that the legacy contact is taking care of the memorial.

Regarding the actions carried out by participants who turned a deceased person's profile into a memorial, P1 said that she left a final message honoring her friend, P2 simply changed the cover photo of her mother-in-law to inform that the account user had passed away, P4 informed friends and family where the requiem mass would be held, and P6 informed his mother's friends where her funeral would take place. We can compare the data found in this study to the research by Gach [13], where participants also reported that they left final messages to friends and family to comfort those who remained, to inform them where the funeral would take place, or even to raise money for the funeral. In view of this, it is evident that posthumous messages are sent to relatives and friends through the profile of the deceased. Trevisan et al. [27] show that in the researched profiles, which reinforces the fact that there are cases of third parties using the deceased person's account, since the logins remain persistent on mobile devices or with passwords saved on desktops, allowing access to third parties without the need for a password. This possibility of continued use may discourage users from requesting the transformation of the profile into a memorial.

There is an evident lack of understanding of the possibilities brought by the network to the legacy contact and the changes arising from the transformation of a profile into a digital memorial. We emphasize, therefore, the need to pay attention to the data left by users and to design better ways to interact with these data. There is a need for tools to provide different options for the destination of digital goods and to reformulate the profile in a digital memorial, clearly explaining any change in its functionalities. That way, users can better understand legacy-related issues, consciously define a future for their digital legacy, and pay homage to those who are gone.

Even after dealing with the digital legacy or memorials of deceased friends and relatives, P2, P3, P5, and P6 reported that they had not devised a plan for their future digital legacy yet. P5 said that she did not post many things on her social networks, so she was doubtful about the destination of her goods. The other participants were unable to answer why they have not yet defined a future for their digital assets. Perhaps this happens because of society's taboos surrounding death and because we are not taught to deal with it. Therefore, we spend our lives in fear of death, as shown in the studies by Lira et al. [17].

Trevisan et al. [27] show that most of the interactions with these profiles occur shortly after death, on dates such as birthdays, or during moments of nostalgia. Thus, we reinforce the need for the system to promote changes that favor user interaction with the profile transformed into a digital memorial, so that it is not merely an account that remains stagnant in time, accessed only when there is a specific search for that profile.

Finally, we agree with Trevisan et al. [27], who state that "the digital culture in which we are involved offers new dilemmas while presenting us with new systemic possibilities for exploring existential themes. Questions concerning digital technologies are questions about human existence. In order to change the reality that surrounds us, it is necessary for everyone involved, both users and designers, to face the finitude of life. At this point, social interactions are essential for accepting death as part of life. In digital times, one must reflect on the social meaning of the objects we manipulate, giving them meaning in interactions".

6 Final Remarks

The objective of the systematic review was to seek different studies that would help answer the predefined questions in our research. We can see that the vast majority of studies are about people who transformed the profile of deceased users into digital memorials, and only a few address the experience of those who inherited digital assets from a dead person. We can hypothesize that this might be due to society's taboo of death. People shy away from thinking of death-related issues for fear or because of uncertainties related to the afterlife, among other issues.

Analyzing the papers reviewed and the interviews we carried out, we could observe that the loved ones of P2, P3, P4, P5, and P6 did not plan the future of their digital legacy, similarly to the participants of the research papers we reviewed. Furthermore, most of our respondents have yet to define a future for their digital legacy. P3 reported that he did not define a future destination for his digital legacy due to laziness. P5 said that they had not done it yet because of uncertainty or lack of knowledge about digital assets. Finally, most participants reported that they would leave their digital assets to someone in the family, such as their parents or children, as they believe that these assets possess sentimental value.

It was very difficult to find volunteers who inherited and/or transformed the profile of loved ones into a digital memorial on Facebook, which led to our small sample of interviewees. That might be the result of a lack of information about digital legacy and related tools and systems, but it could also be due to taboos of death and mortality, which discourage people from talking about these themes. Fostering that kind of discussion at school and other educational institutions might lead to a greater interest in the planning and organization of one's digital assets (both for owners and future legatees).

Some studies are being carried out to expand discussions on this topic in educational environments. Trevisan et al. [33] present the results from a pedagogical activity for Computer Science students that focused on software engineering for the web in the domain of postmortem digital legacy. The authors claim that the activity was positive both for students' learning about software engineering and for reflecting on the importance of computer systems for digital legacy management. It is paramount that software developers are aware of how complex this domain is, so that they can design solutions that properly meet users' needs.

In the field of digital legacy, other research perspectives are possible, since users have digital assets in different applications and devices, which may or may not be available after their death. For example, research on interaction with posthumous data on WhatsApp would allow exploring whether this data is animated and revisited, supports grief; is erased or even lost due to configurations or technological limitations. Other examples include searches on Facebook, on non-memorial pages to which individuals do not have access, on pages that remain static since they last left; or cases involving copyright and financial issues in apps like Apple's iTunes.

In conclusion, the challenges and perceptions of the participants in this experiment, regarding the treatment of deceased Internet users' posthumous data, may contribute to more adequate design practices and development of digital legacy management systems. This is a hot topic in the HCI community, with a demand that grows fast as the first generations of users of digital platforms grow older and die.

Acknowledgments. The authors thank the volunteers of the study for their time and insights. This research was partially funded by the Research Support Foundation of the State of Mato Grosso—Fapema and by the National Council for Scientific and Technological Development—CNPq: Cristiano thanks to CNPq (grant #310665/20220–1). Simone Barbosa thanks CNPq (grant #313049/2021–1) and CAPES (Finance Code 001). Vinicius thanks to CNPq (grant #302671/2021–8).

References

1. Ataguba, G.: Towards an evaluation of mobile life logging technologies and storytelling in socio-personal grieving spaces. In: Proceedings of the 2018 ACM International Joint Conference and 2018 International Symposium on Pervasive and Ubiquitous Computing and Wearable Computers (2018)
2. Basset, D.: You Only Live Twice: A Constructivist Grounded Theory Study of the Creation and Inheritance of Digital Afterlives (2019)
3. Bell, J., Bailey, L., Kennedy, D.: 'We do it to keep him alive': bereaved individuals' experiences of online suicide memorials and continuing bonds. Mortality **20**(4), 375–389 (2015)
4. Beppu, F, Maciel, C.: Perspectivas normativas para o legado digital pós-morte face à lei geral de proteção de dados pessoais. In: Anais do I Workshop sobre as Implicações da Computação na Sociedade. SBC, pp. 73–84 (2020)

5. Beppu, F., Maciel, C., Viterbo, J.: Contributions of the Brazilian act for the protection of personal data for treating digital legacy. Journal on Interactive Syst. **12**(1), 112–124 (2021)
6. Brasil: Constituição da República Federativa do Brasil de 1988 (1988). https://www.planalto. gov.br/ccivil_03/constituicao/constituicao.htm. Accessed 01 Feb 2023
7. Brasil: Projeto de Lei nº 4099, de 20 de junho de 2012. Altera o art. 1.788 da Lei nº 10.406, de 10 de janeiro de 2002, que "institui o Código Civil". Brasília: Câmara dos Deputados (2012). https://www.camara.leg.br/proposicoesWeb/prop_mostrarintegra?cod teor=1004679&filename=PL+4099/2012. Accessed 01 Feb 2023
8. Castro, A.: Cursos de revisão sistemática e metanálise. São Paulo: LEDDIS; Unifesp, 2001 (2001). http://www.usinadepesquisa.com/metodologia/wp-content/uploads/2010/08/meta1. pdf. Accessed 01 Feb 2023
9. Cousandier, C., Ribeiro, G., Carvalho, C.: O Luto e a Comunicação nas Redes Sociais: Um Estudo Sobre Perfil Póstumo no Facebook. In: 40º Congresso Brasileiro de Ciências da Comunicação. Anais (2017)
10. DAVI. Dados Além da Vida (2023). https://lavi.ic.ufmt.br/davi/en/. Accessed 12 June 2023
11. Facebook (2023). https://www.facebook.com/. Accessed 01 Feb 2023
12. Gach, K., Brubaker, J.: Getting your facebook affairs in order: user expectations in post-mortem profile management. Proceedings of the ACM on Human-Computer Interaction **5**(CSCW1), 1–29 (2021)
13. Gach, K.: How to Delete the Dead: Honoring Affective Connections to Post-mortem Data. University of Colorado at Boulder, Tese de Doutorado (2021)
14. Gagliano, P., Filho, R.: Novo curso de direito civil, volume 6: direito de família. 9.ed., São Paulo: Saraiva Educação. Edição Kindle (2019)
15. Houaiss, A., Villar, M., Franco, M.: Dicionário Houaiss da língua portuguesa. Dicionário Houaiss da língua portuguesa. lxxiii-2922 (2001)
16. Lemos, A.: Cibercultura. Porto Alegre: Sulina, **320** (2002)
17. Lira, M., Maciel, C., Trevisan, D., Barbosa, S., Bim, S.: Mine, yours, ours: family discussions on digital legacy. In Anais do XXI Simpósio Brasileiro sobre Fatores Humanos em Sistemas Computacionais. Porto Alegre: SBC (2022)
18. Little, N.: Rape-Related Mourning on a Social Network Site: Leah Parsons's "Facebooked" Grief and the Angel Rehtaeh Parsons Page (n.p)
19. Lopes, A., Maciel, C., Pereira, V.: Virtual homage to the dead an analysis of digital memorials in the social web. In: Proceedins of the International Conference on Social Computing and Social Media. Springer (2014). https://doi.org/10.1007/978-3-319-07632-4_7
20. Maciel, C., Pereira, V.: A morte como parte da vida digital: uma agenda de pesquisa em IHC. In: Proceedings of the 13th Brazilian Symposium on Human Factors in Computing Systems, pp. 441–444 (2014)
21. Martins, R., Guariento, D.: A herança digital e a tutela dos dados pessoais de titulares falecidos. Impressões Digitais (2021). https://www.migalhas.com.br/coluna/impressoes-digitais/347 956/a-heranca-digital-e-a-tutela-dos-dados-pessoais-de-titulares-falecidos. Accessed 1 Feb 2023
22. Morandi, M., Camargo, F.: Revisão sistemática da literatura. In: Dresch, A., Lacerda, D.P., Antunes, J.A.V.:. Design sciencie research: método e pesquisa para avanço da ciência e da tecnologia. Porto Alegre: Bookman (2015)
23. Riechers, A.: The persistence of memory online: digital memorials, fantasy, and grief as entertainment. Digital legacy and interaction: Post-mortem issues, Springer, pp. 49–61 (2013)
24. Santos, L.: Repositórios digitais na preservação da memória de clubes de futebol: a descrição arquivística na análise do Esporte Clube Vitória. Dissertação (Mestrado) – Universidade Federal da Bahia, Instituto de Ciência da Informação (2016)
25. Silva, A., Lima, I.: Herança digital (2013). www.arcos.org.br/download.php?codigoArquiv o=649

26. Taveira, F.: Bens digitais (digital assets) e a sua proteção pelos direitos da personalidade: um estudo sob a perspectiva da dogmática civil brasileira. Simplissimo Livros Ltda (2018)

27. Trevisan, D., Maciel, C., Pereira, V., Pereira, R.: Dead Users' Profiles on Facebook: Limited Interaction Beyond Human Existence, Interacting with Computers, 2023, iwad003 (2023). https://doi.org/10.1093/iwc/iwad003

28. Ueda, G.S., Maciel, C., Viterbo, J.: Analysis of the features of online tools in the post-mortem digital legacy domain Anais do IX Workshop sobre Aspectos da Interação Humano-Computador para a Web Social. SBC (2018)

29. Venosa, S.: Direito Civil: família e sucessões. 20.ed São Paulo: Atlas,. Edição Kindle (2020)

30. Verdan, T.: O Instituto do Legado no Direito Sucessório: Comentários Introdutórios Conteúdo Jurídico, Brasília-DF. https://conteudojuridico.com.br/consulta/Artigos/29390/o-instituto-do-legado-no-direito-sucessorio-comentarios-introdutorios. Accessed 01 Feb 2023

31. Yamauchi, E., Maciel, C., Mendes, F., Ueda, G., Pereira, V.: Digital legacy management systems: theoretical, systemic and user's perspective. In: ICEIS (2), pp. 41–53 (2021)

32. Yeager, S.: Mourning Practices on Facebook: Facebook Shrines and Other Rituals of Grieving in the Digital Age (2021)

33. Trevisan, D., Maciel, C., Bim, S.A.: Morte, educação e tecnologias: uma experiência formativa com estudantes da computação. Revista De Educação Pública, 31(jan/dez), pp. 1–20 (2022). https://doi.org/10.29286/rep.v31ijan/dez.13388

34. Maciel, C., Pereira, V.C., Sztern, M.: Internet users' legal and technical perspectives on digital legacy management for post-mortem interaction. In: Human Interface and the Management of Information. Information and Knowledge Design: 17th International Conference, HCI International 2015, Los Angeles, CA, USA, August 2–7, 2015, Proceedings, Part I 17 (pp. 627–639). Springer International Publishing (2015)

35. Maciel, C., Pereira, V.: The internet generation and its representation of death: considerations for posthumous interaction projects. In: Proceedings of the 11th Brazilian Symposium on Human Factors in Computing Systems, pp. 85–94 (2012)

"Hello, Fellow Villager!": Perceptions and Impact of Displaying Users' Locations on Weibo

Ying Ma[1]([✉]), Qiushi Zhou[1], Benjamin Tag[2], Zhanna Sarsenbayeva[3], Jarrod Knibbe[1], and Jorge Goncalves[1]

[1] School of Computing and Information Systems, University of Melbourne, Melbourne, Australia
{ying.ma3,qiushi.zhou,jarrod.knibbe,jorge.goncalves}@unimelb.edu.au
[2] Department of Human Centred Computing, Monash University, Melbourne, Australia
benjamin.tag@monash.edu
[3] School of Computer Science, University of Sydney, Sydney, Australia
zhanna.sarsenbayeva@sydney.edu.au

Abstract. In April 2022, Sina Weibo began to display users' coarse location for the stated purpose of regulating their online community. However, this raised concerns about location privacy. Through sentiment analysis and Latent Dirichlet Allocation (LDA), we analysed the users' attitudes and opinions on this topic across 20,162 related posts and comments. We labelled 300 users as either supportive, critical, or neutral towards the feature, and captured their posting behaviour two months prior and two months post the launch. Our analysis elicits three major themes in the public discussion: online community atmosphere, privacy issues, and equity in the application of the feature, and shows that most people expressed a negative attitude. We find a drop in activity by objectors during the first month after the launch of the feature before gradually resuming. This work provides a large-scale firsthand account of people's attitudes and opinions towards online location privacy on social media platforms.

Keywords: location privacy · social media mining · sentiment analysis · Latent Dirichlet Allocation · Weibo

1 Introduction

Social media has become an integral part of our daily lives as a means to share daily activities, experiences, interests, and opinions [39]. At an average of 2 h and 27 min per day, social media accounts for the largest single share (35%) of our online media time[1]. In China, one of the most popular social media platforms, Sina Weibo, reached 582 million monthly active users in the first quarter of 2022. However, the scale of the platform and the ease in which information can

---

[1] https://datareportal.com/reports/digital-2022-global-overview-report.

© The Author(s), under exclusive license to Springer Nature Switzerland AG 2023
J. Abdelnour Nocera et al. (Eds.): INTERACT 2023, LNCS 14144, pp. 511–532, 2023.
https://doi.org/10.1007/978-3-031-42286-7_29

be shared and propagated has also led to significant issues regarding information quality, disinformation, misinformation, and fake news [16].

Recently, in what was portrayed as an attempt to tackle these issues, many popular Chinese social media platforms including Sina Weibo, WeChat, Douyin, Little Red Book, and Zhihu, rolled out a new feature that displays users' coarse location. For Sina Weibo, this new feature shows the user's province or region in China, or name of country if overseas, on their profile page and next to their comments. This feature was touted by the platforms as a way to reduce the dissemination of malicious rumours, impersonation, and other negative behaviours, with the aim of increasing the authenticity and transparency of the disseminated content. However, the feature also raises significant concerns regarding the users' location privacy and self-presentation, and risks encouraging geographic discrimination and cyberbullying.

Previous studies have investigated users' perceptions towards location privacy on social media, exploring different platforms (e.g., MySpace, Yelp, Foursquare), genders [50], user groups [9,13] and scenarios [12,21,58]. However, the majority of these studies were conducted on location-based social media platforms (i.e., those whose core function is to provide location-based information and services). The impact of increased location transparency on non-location-based, general-purpose social media platforms, however, remains poorly understood. Furthermore, most of the existing studies were conducted in a western cultural context. We need a better understanding of how location privacy is perceived by non-western cultures – a participant population that is often overlooked in HCI research [49]. The recent implementation of the user location information feature on Weibo offers a unique opportunity to conduct an in-depth investigation of users' perception of location privacy, and the impacts on their participation, on a large non-western general-purpose social media platform that does not use location information for its normal operation.

Based on the research gaps identified above, in this work, we focus on two research questions:

- **RQ1**. How do users perceive and respond to the adoption of a location display feature on the Chinese social media platform – Weibo?
- **RQ2**. Based on users' different attitudes (negative, neutral, positive) towards location display on Weibo, how does this feature affect users' posting behaviours?

For RQ1, in order to understand users' attitudes and opinions towards this new feature, we collected 16,199 comments from 19 announcement posts published by verified accounts and 4,043 users' posts from the 16 most popular related hashtag topics. Then we analysed their sentiment trends and key opinion topics that were frequently discussed by users. For RQ2, to detect user behaviour change after the implementation of this feature, we collected posts published by 100 supporters, 100 objectors, and 100 neutral users in the four months surrounding this new feature's launch. We analysed the changes in the posting behaviour of each group during this time frame.

Our main findings are the following: (1) Most users hold a negative attitude toward this feature as they feel it can risk amplifying geographic discrimination and cyberbullying, while also questioning its usefulness and accuracy. (2) We identified three major themes in the public discussion: online community atmosphere, privacy issues, and equity in the application of the feature. (3) Furthermore, we found a decrease in activity from those that were critical of the feature for the month following its implementation and we also provide evidence of the existence of the location privacy paradox. Our research contributes to the growing body of work on the impact of location privacy in social media platforms by providing a large-scale investigation of this topic in a real-world scenario.

2   Related Work

Our work seeks to further our community's understanding of perceptions around online privacy and, more specifically, location privacy. In this section, we discuss the literature that our work builds upon.

2.1   Online Privacy and the Privacy Paradox

There are many online platforms or applications that involve the sharing of large amounts of personal information. This increased exposure has obvious privacy implications, which has been identified as a primary concern of citizens in the digital age [32]. Interestingly, the value people put on their online information can vary based on a number of different factors. For instance, users value interaction data on social media (e.g., browsing history, posting behaviours) higher (12 Euros) than search information (2 Euros) [6]. Along similar lines, Tsai et al. [55] conducted an experimental study on privacy information concerns on online shopping behaviour and found that participants were willing to pay extra to purchase from privacy-protective websites when privacy information is made more prominent and accessible.

Researchers have also investigated the impact of user demographics on proactiveness to safeguard personal information in online settings. For example, several studies have challenged the widespread belief that young people, the most active users on social media, do not sufficiently protect their personal information on social networking sites. Previous work has shown that young people are more likely to utilise different ways to protect their online information, such as not giving the right information or using pseudonyms [40]; opening the setting that only their friends can access their recent post [35]; deleting their names from images that friends have posted by untagging themselves [65]. Nevertheless, neglecting one's online privacy remains a pervasive challenge across all types of users [1].

Based on previous research, users are increasingly aware of the possibility of privacy violations on social media [28,64], even though they still post their real-time location information and personal information online and few of them take all the required precautions to protect their sensitive data [15]. The phenomenon of the difference between users' stated privacy concerns and their real behaviour is called the "privacy paradox" [42]. In other words, although users may claim they are concerned over their online privacy, they simultaneously are willing to provide important personal information through social media in order to gain a benefit [23]. Although the "privacy paradox" has been widely investigated, the findings remain contradictory and inconsistent [32]. Some studies indicate a widespread occurrence of this phenomenon [56,66] while other studies provide evidence against it [10,65].

In this paper, we explore people's reactions to online privacy in a naturalistic environment where we collect their organic attitudes, opinions and behaviours towards this highly-debated feature introduced by Weibo. In addition, we provide additional evidence towards the privacy paradox hypothesis, especially within the context of geographic information.

2.2 Perceptions on Online Location Privacy

With the rise of location-based games (LBGs) (e.g., Pokémon GO), versatile location-based applications (LBAs) and various location-based services (LBSs) (e.g., location-based advertisement) embedded in traditional social media platforms, users' geographical location information is more widely used than ever before. Unfortunately, the increased ease of sharing this information online can lead to breaches in location privacy, which in turn can have significant negative implications such as stalking, tracking people's movements, exposing a user's true identity or geographical discrimination [7]. Thus, understanding how users perceived the risk of location information and disclosure intentions is crucial.

Researchers have made a concerted effort in studying users' attitudes and behaviours towards location privacy from a variety of different angles. However, people's opinions on online location privacy has been shown to vary. Some are more concerned about the possible dangers of revealing their location data, while others are more tolerant when there are clear advantages offered by location-based services. For example, Gana and Thomas [19] studied consumers' perspectives regarding location-based advertising where they expressed concerns about disclosing personal data to unknown agencies and organisations which might be used without permission. Interestingly, the same consumers appreciated the ease of using their location information for travelling activities. This dichotomy showcases the importance of value proposition for the willingness of users to share their location information. Furthermore, through a study conducted by Fisher et al. [17], the researchers examined the use of location controls on iPhone devices and found users fall into different categories, including those who deny all apps access, those who allow all apps access, and those who selectively permit certain apps to access their location.

Other studies found that users tend to pay more attention to their own geographical location information compared with other types of information. Furini and Tamanini [18] investigated 122 participants' opinions after showing them the amount of personal and sensitive information that a simple application can access by browsing content publicly available on social media platforms. Their findings show that those who were originally unconcerned about privacy ended up being the most concerned about location privacy breaches. In another example, participants expressed that they were much more concerned about dynamic privacy (location-tagged) leaks when compared to their static private information on Facebook (e.g., personal information including real names, fan pages joined) [9]. Similarly, Hecht et al. [25] examined location field usage in Twitter user profiles and found that 34% of users provide inaccurate location information, and when accurate, location is often limited to the city level.

The previous examples showcase how location information raises important privacy concerns among online users due to its sensitive nature and the subsequent implications of having this information shared with malicious parties. As a result, many studies have explored different ways to alleviate users' concerns regarding their location information on LBAs. Existing research suggests that the LBAs with various levels of location granularities are more welcomed and accepted [11,54]. Similarly, researchers have proposed using more transparent and straightforward location privacy settings to mitigate users' concerns regarding their location information [3,30]. The authors also propose the use of interventions such as third-party seal programs provided by platforms to enable increased users' trust [63].

Despite the fact that substantial research has been conducted on user attitudes and behaviour towards location privacy, the majority of this work focuses on general views around location privacy, and self-reported intention to provide location information through a user study. The recent implementation of the location disclosure function by Sina Weibo provides a unique possibility to conduct an in-depth exploration of location privacy with a large user base in a naturalistic scenario, which will help us better understand social media users' perceptions and opinions on online location privacy. The generated insights can in turn be used to inform the design of social media platforms to better safeguard user's location privacy.

3   Methodology

We conducted an exploratory analysis of publicly available data on Weibo to better understand people's reactions to their coarse location being made visible on the platform. This included sentiment analysis, topic modelling and user behaviour analysis. Figure 1 shows the methodological framework of this work, which we explain in further detail next.

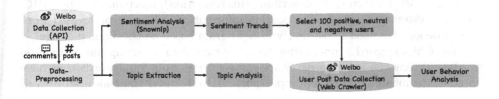

Fig. 1. Methodological framework of our work

3.1 Data Collection

On April 28th 2022, the official Sina Weibo account published a post regarding the rollout of the location display feature. To gather a wide variety of user's opinions on this matter, we employed two data collection mechanisms. First, we collected user comments through Weibo's API[2] from the original Weibo post that initially publicised the change. Then we carefully selected an additional 19 posts regarding this announcement published by different verified organizations (i.e., news outlets) that all have at least 1 million followers. These 19 posts paraphrased or repeated the original official announcement posts by the Sina Weibo administrator account, explaining the feature and its implementation, without any personal sentiment or bias.

Second, we collected users' original posts from relevant hashtags topics with a web crawler[3]. We crawled hashtags and filtered the results based on keywords, including "IP territorial", "IP address", and "IP". From all the hashtag topics we acquired, we chose 16 relevant hashtag topics that were established in response to this new feature in Sina Weibo and with a high number of occurrences (the lowest number of posts in these topics is greater than 100), such as "#Weibo fully open IP territorial function#", "#Weibo full open comments show IP territorial function#", "#the personal homepage of Weibo will display the IP territory#". It is important to note that hashtags on Weibo are often long and presented in sentence formats, and not restricted to a single word or short sentence as commonly seen on Twitter.

3.2 Data Pre-processing

As content originating from microblog platforms (e.g., Twitter, Weibo) are known to contain a large amount of noise and errors, we conducted data pre-processing before proceeding with our analysis. The following steps were used in our data pre-processing process.

The first step is duplication and noise removal. We manually deleted the posts or comments that were obviously irrelevant to the topic (e.g., advertisements and irrelevant news posts). In addition, we deleted redundant posts that were collected due to the use of multiple relevant hashtags. The next step is non-Chinese character filtering and conversion. We removed information from each individual post and comment that was not relevant to our analysis, such as hashtags (narrative sentences describing this transition), username handles, URL links, or system-generated GPS location information. Then we performed word segmentation. We used a custom Python program based on the Jieba package[4], a popular Chinese word segmentation tool. We split the text string into individual words and removed stop words. Stop words refer to functional words that have no concrete meaning, such as prepositions [61]. We used the Baidu stop word

---

[2] https://open.weibo.com/wiki/API/en.

[3] https://github.com/Python3Spiders/WeiboSuperSpider.

[4] https://github.com/fxsjy/jieba.

list[5] during this process. Finally, in order to protect users' privacy in the latter analysis, we omitted personal privacy information in our datasets like post ID or username. All posts involved in our analysis only contained textual contents that were posted publicly.

3.3   Sentiment Analysis

We used SnowNLP[6] to conduct text sentiment analysis. SnowNLP is a third-party Python package that can perform segmentation of Chinese words, part-of-speech tagging, sentiment analysis, text categorisation, pinyin conversion, simplification of traditional text, extraction of keywords, extraction of abstracts, segmentation of sentences, and text similarity calculation. It has been frequently and successfully used to analyse Chinese natural language in different fields [37,43,59,60]. We also leveraged emoticons present in the text for our sentiment analysis, as they have been shown to contain important sentiment information [33].

The original model of SnowNLP is based on a naive Bayesian classification method using Chinese E-commerce, book and movie reviews as the dataset for training and prediction. This particular dataset includes 16,548 positive and 18,574 negative sentiment sentence data [29]. For that reason, this dataset might not precisely reflect posts and comments appearing on Weibo. Therefore, we randomly selected 20% of the dataset as the training dataset and two native speakers manually annotated the posts/comments. The annotators worked independently and labelled the text into two categories: positive and negative. After finishing the annotation, we calculated the degree of inter-rater reliability ($\kappa = 0.93$), which indicates that there was a high level of agreement between the annotators. We then updated the data with the labelled information and trained it accordingly to achieve the new model.

3.4   Topic Modelling

We used Latent Dirichlet Allocation (LDA) – a common method of topic modelling to extract the underlying topics from text documents. It has been used broadly in previous HCI research. For example, to study privacy-related issues on Stack Overflow [53], to investigate working from home challenges differences between Weibo and Twitter users [20], and to analyse what parents discuss on Reddit [4].

LDA is an unsupervised method used to create generative probabilistic models, it estimates the chances for combinations of words (topics) to repeatedly appear together, and that are similar to each other using Bayesian inference [48]. A topic can be described as a combination of strongly related words that appear at a statistically significant rate in a text corpus [38]. Put differently, these words frequently appear together in the texts, i.e., comments and posts. Since different

---

[5] https://github.com/goto456/stopwords/blob/master/baidu_stopwords.txt.
[6] https://github.com/isnowfy/snownlp.

topics can appear in one piece of text and different texts can contain the same topic, topic modelling can theoretically produce two clusters: one presenting clusters of topics based on the similarity of words, and one presenting clusters of texts based on the similarity of topics [2]. The advantage of this model is that it allows us to analyse a larger dataset than is feasible with manual annotation.

To determine the optimal number of topics we looked at the topic quality. For this, we consider both the coherence score and the perplexity score. Topic coherence is a measure of semantic similarity of the words comprising the topics. High coherence scores indicate high topic quality. The perplexity score, on the other hand, describes the generalization of a topic model. In order to make sense of the perplexity score, different models have to be run to obtain different perplexity scores. A lower perplexity score describes a better model [5]. Deciding the optimal number of topics, therefore, does not only require a combination of high coherence and low perplexity scores, but also the intuition and domain expertise of the researchers. Once the optimal topic number was decided, we visualised the topic extraction result using the LDAvis[7] python package. The visualisation provides an overall view of the topics and how they differ and overlap from each other [48]. Finally, we used the words that are most indicative of each topic to interpret the topics identified by the model.

3.5 User Behaviour Analysis

To understand the change in user behaviour that may have been caused by the introduction of this feature, we randomly selected 100 users from each of these groups: supporters and objectors of this feature, and neutral users who neither expressed support or objection towards this feature. We collected the posts they published in the time period of two months before and after the location display feature was implemented on Sina Weibo.

Previous work has shown that the message volume of microblog users follows power-law distribution [46]: a small number of users tend to generate a large proportion of posts on social media, while the majority of users generate relatively few posts. This phenomenon is often referred to as the "long tail" of user activity. In particular, when examining the relationship between the social network of microblog users and their behaviours, the distribution exponent of message volume is shown to be inversely proportionate to the interaction exponent of each user [46]. First, to verify the reasonableness of our sampling, we fit the volume of posts of each user through power-law distribution. Furthermore, we produced a time-series graph of the original and retweeted posts of each of the three groups of users mentioned above. It is important to note that the frequency and time of users' usage of Weibo (i.e., how often they tweet) are affected by many factors (e.g., public events and holidays) and have a certain degree of randomness. Therefore, when analysing the sample data, we labelled important events in relevant peaks on the time series graph.

---

[7] https://github.com/bmabey/pyLDAvis.

4   Results

4.1   Sentiment Analysis

Dataset. The collected data for this analysis pertains to the period between 0:00 on April 28, 2022, and 23:59:59 on May 28, 2022 (Beijing time). A one-month time frame was chosen as previous work has shown that the active period for most microblog topics lasts for about a month, after which these topics are typically replaced by new topics [36]. The data included 16,799 comments originating from the 19 verified account posts and 4,624 posts with relevant hashtags. After data preprocessing, a total of 20,162 valid textual data were retained for our analysis. The metadata only contains text content attributes as we removed partial user attributes.

In order to further verify the validity and reliability of our collected dataset, we calculated the relationship between the number of responses we collected from all provinces in mainland China and current population figures. The Pearson correlation coefficient between these two datasets is 0.81, indicating that our dataset sufficiently reflects the characteristics of the Chinese population and can be used to draw valid conclusions about general Chinese social media users.

Sentiment Distribution. After manually annotating data and training it, the sentiment distribution of the posts/comments of our dataset is shown in Fig. 2. The sentiment analysis value outputs are in a range between 0 and 1, with 0 representing a negative sentiment, 0.5 representing a neutral sentiment, and 1 representing a positive sentiment. As shown in Fig. 2, the majority of posts/comments are negative towards the implemented feature, with a high prevalence of extremely negative opinions. We can also observe a similar number of neutral and positive posts/comments.

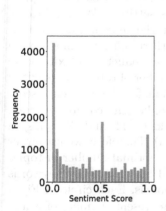

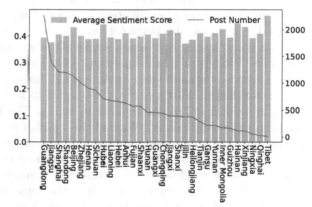

Fig. 2. Histogram of sentiment of posts/comments

Fig. 3. Average sentiment score and total post/comment number of each province

According to the general sentiment classification criterion used in previous research [34,44], we categorised all posts/comments into three categories based on their sentiment value: negative (0 to 0.3), neutral (0.3 to 0.7), and positive (0.7 to 1). This resulted in 4,834 (24%) positive posts/comments, 8,777 (43.5%) negative posts/comments, and 6,551 (32.5%) neutral posts/comments. By dividing the users into two categories based on their current location: those from mainland China and those from overseas. Among the 18,071 posts/comments made by users from mainland China, 4,333 (24%) were positive, 8,049 (44.5%) were negative and 5,689 (31.5%) were neutral. Regarding the overseas users', there were 2,091 posts/comments in total. Among these, 501 (24%) were positive; 728 (35%) were negative and 862 (41%) were neutral.

In addition, Fig. 3 illustrates the average sentiment score and number of posts/comments from 31 provinces in mainland China. The average score of all provinces ranged between 0.371 and 0.448. In general, we can observe that all provinces demonstrate a negative sentiment towards location display on Weibo. The four provinces with the highest sentiment scores are Hainan (0.448), Hubei (0.444), Xinjiang (0.434) and Beijing (0.433). The four provinces with the lowest sentiment scores include Jilin (0.371), Jiangsu (0.376), and Heilongjiang (0.386) and Henan (0.389). In our subsequent analysis, we only consider provinces with the number of posts/comments above 100.

4.2 Topic Analysis

Topic Number Choice Based on LDA Models. Before conducting topic analysis, an important step in LDA analysis is determining the appropriate number of topics to optimise the processing time and accuracy of the model [24]. We achieved this by using perplexity scores, coherence scores and model visualisation.

The results of perplexity and coherence scores for various numbers of topics are shown in Fig. 4(top) and Fig. 4(bottom). First, we calculated the perplexity scores with a range of different number of topics settings. As described in Sect. 3.4, the lower the perplexity score, the better the model. Figure 4(top) shows a continuously decreasing perplexity score until running the model with 19 topics. While a higher number of topics leads to a smaller perplexity score indicating a better model performance [62], a large number of topics can result in model over-fitting. Furthermore, it is crucial to account for the coherence score when choosing the optimal number of topics. The higher the coherence score, the better the topic quality. We find three global peaks (6, 11, and 17 topics) in the range of 1–19 topics, as presented in Fig. 4(bottom). Therefore, we use either 6, 11, or 17 topics to train our model. To choose the optimal number of topics among those three choices, we additionally inspected high-frequency keywords and visualisations generated for each of the topic models. Each circle in Fig. 5 represents a different topic and the size of the circle represents number of words in our corpus that belong to that topic. The distance between each topic roughly represents the semantic relationship (the closer the circles, the more words they have in common) between the topics, while the overlap of circles means the topic

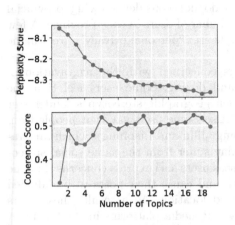

Fig. 4. Perplexity and Coherence scores with different settings of number of topics

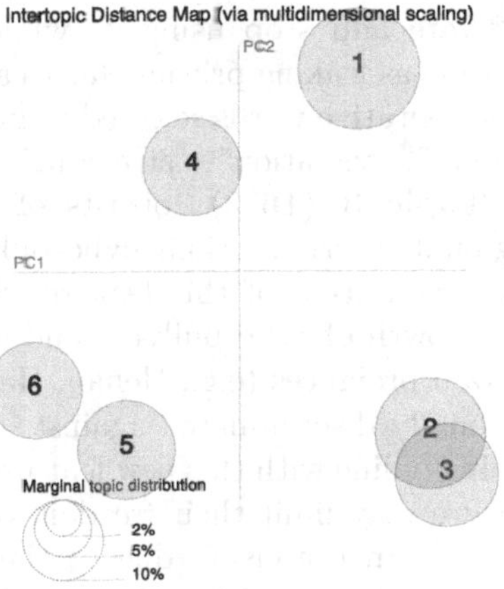

Fig. 5. LDA model visualization containing all six selected topics

shares some common words as opposed to non-overlapping topic. This enabled us to determine 6 as the optimal number of topics for our sample, based on the high distance between the topics and the absent overlap (except for topics 2 and 3).

Topic Clusters. In this section, we summarise the content of the six topics based on the most frequently used words generated from each topic. We note that these keywords are grouped together (based on their latent meanings) because they are commonly featured in the posts/comments clustered together. Consequently, words that seem unrelated to one another might be categorised together.

Topic 1 (22.4%) consists of postings that express curiosity and a desire to experiment with the new feature. Some posts just contain random short content without any meaning. As users can see the approximate location of other users through comments, some of them greet each other in their posts and try to engage with users from the same province. A few representative words/expressions selected from this topic are: "let me have a try" (users checking if their location would be displayed), "city", "Fellow Villager", "been to" (users stating they have been to the shown location).

Topic 2 (18.3%) consists of postings that contain concerns and involve discussion on privacy leaks and violations. These users feel uncomfortable about the platform showing their geographic location information without their consent, likening the experience to "streaking" (i.e., running naked) on social media. They also worry that more personal information might be shown in the future, such as more detailed location information and/or other privacy-related data. Nevertheless, the users did not have a unified opinion on privacy matters. Some view the feature as an invasion of personal privacy and would uninstall the software and stop using it, while others do not consider showing provincial address as leaking privacy due to a large number of users in each province. A few representative words selected from this topic are: "personal privacy", "real-name system", "violation", "streaking", "rights".

Topic 3 (16%) consists of postings concerned with the aggravation of regional discrimination, cyberbullying, and doxing. Some users feel that the implementation of this feature will deepen geographic stereotypes, and foster the growth of cyberbullying and doxing. Also, some users say that people from certain provinces (e.g., Henan, Heilongjiang, Jilin and Liaoning), which are traditionally discriminated against [8,45], may suffer from the same social stereotyping online with this new feature. Overseas users also express concerns that the feature may limit their freedom of speech and cause their posts to be labelled as "foreign criticism" due to the displayed location. As a result, these users may be more cautious when posting on social media platforms in the future. A few representative words selected from this topic are: "regional discrimination", "cyberbullying", "attacking", "exposure".

Topic 4 (14.8%) contains postings containing self-declarations and the questioning of the accuracy and usefulness of this feature. On the one hand, some users express that what they said on social media had nothing to do with their region and provinces, where they were born, received education and worked in totally different provinces. Some users even (jokingly) said "I hereby declare that I am not a well-mannered person, I am surfing online for fun and all my comments are unrelated to my real identity". On the other hand, some other users argue that location can easily be changed using virtual private network (VPN) tools so that they could hide their identities through proxy. Hence, this feature would not be effective in stopping those who try to spread rumours, as their locations would be fake. Nevertheless, others argue that this need of using VPN is still a hindrance for people who post with those purposes. Furthermore, many users have expressed dissatisfaction about the platform's low accuracy of displaying users' location information. A few representative words selected from this topic are: "speech", "VPN", "well-mannered", "proxy".

Topic 5 (14.6%) is related to the strong support of this new feature and the belief that it could make information on social media more authentic. These users believe this measure can help foster a better online community and is able to reduce rumours, cyberbullying, defamation, trolling, fake accounts, and will prevent the occurrence of other potentially harmful activities. They argue that Weibo users will treat the online community with more respect and will be mindful when publishing posts or comments that use offensive language. Furthermore, some users mention that this feature could effectively reduce the occurrence of malicious content and misinformation regarding the pandemic situation during the COVID-19 lockdowns, and increase bonding between users from affected cities. A few representative words selected from this topic are: "platform", "spreading rumours", "stir up", "no big deal", "responsibility".

Topic 6 (13.9%) discusses the theme related to celebrities, opinion leaders and social media influencers. Users of the platform raised an important point that many opinion leaders and influencers show geographic location of Hunan province; however, their posts show the content that has been created abroad (e.g., image or video taken in Europe, but location is shown as Hunan). The reason behind this phenomenon is that these accounts are managed by a number of Multi-Channel Network Companies in the Hunan province.

Another aspect that sparked discussion was that when the platform initially implemented this feature, verified celebrity accounts did not show their location information. As a result, users complained they feel treated differently–disadvantaged–as compared to verified account users. One more phenomenon users also mentioned is that through this feature they can know whether the celebrity's account is managed by themselves or by their agent company. This is similar to recent developments on Twitter (e.g. harsher stance on impersonation, charging users for the blue tick). A few representative words selected from this topic are: "celebrities", "Hunan", "influencer", "company", "ordinary people", "fake accounts".

4.3 User Behaviour Analysis

To investigate changes in user behaviour potentially caused by the introduction of this feature, we selected 100 users of the three user groups (supporters, neutrals, and objectors) and studied how their behaviour changed during the two-month period around the announcement and implementation of the location display feature in Weibo.

Power-Law Analysis. In Fig. 6, we present the cumulative complementary distribution function (CCDF) of the total number of posts per user and the percentage of users for selected three groups. As we can see in all the groups the distributions are skewed, demonstrating that the proportion of users who frequently publish posts is relatively small, while most users do not post often which aligns with the long-tail characteristic of power-law distributions.

We can observe from Fig. 6(a) that for the supporter group, the slope for posting behaviour before the feature's implementation is -0.54 ($R^2 = 0.72$); whereas the slope value for posting behaviour after the feature's implementation is -0.55 ($R^2 = 0.75$). The two values are close to each other indicating that the behaviour of this user group did not change significantly after the location display feature was introduced on Weibo.

A similar trend can be observed for the neutral group (Fig. 6(c)). To be precise, the slope of posting behaviour before the feature was implemented is -0.94 ($R^2 = 0.90$); whereas the slope for posting behaviour after feature's implementation is -0.90 ($R^2 = 0.87$). The two values are close to each other indicating that the behaviour of the neutral user group was not significantly affected after the location display feature was implemented on Weibo.

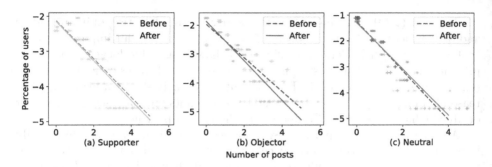

Fig. 6. CCDF of the number of posts per user group (log-log scale)

Interestingly, a slightly different trend can be observed for the objector user group. According to (Fig. 6(b)), the slope for posting behaviour before the location display was introduced is equal to -0.56 ($R^2 = 0.67$); whereas the slope value for posting behaviour was -0.65 ($R^2 = 0.85$) after the feature was implemented. In particular, the users who were against the implementation of displaying user coarse location, to some degree, decreased their activity on Weibo during the one month after the feature was introduced. From the power-law fitting result, the average $R^2 = 0.80$, which means our sample is well-suited for analysis.

User Posting Behaviour Analysis Based on Time Series. We looked at user posting behaviour in the time period of two months prior- and post-implementation of the feature. We collected user posts starting from February 28th until June 28th and analysed the average number of posts per user per day for the three user groups and smoothed the results using a moving average function with the window size of 7 (to account for any differences between days of the week). Since users' posting behaviour can potentially be affected by many other factors (e.g., public events, holidays, etc.), we took into account major events that took place around the time period used in our analysis and labelled these events on the graph (Fig. 7).

As can be seen from Fig. 7, in general, the behaviour of the supporter and neutral users did not exhibit a significant change in terms of the number of posts published per day prior- or post-implementation of the feature on April 28th. However, the behaviour of the objector user group did exhibit a change. Precisely, the objectors published fewer posts per day during the first month after the feature was implemented. Interestingly, in the second month after the feature was implemented the number of posts caught up with the values prior to implementation. This to some extent suggests that the impact of the location display feature on the posting behaviour of the objectors was temporary and the behaviour eventually returned to pre-implementation levels, while also noting the presence of a significant event around that period, which resulted in a flood of outrage on Chinese social media.

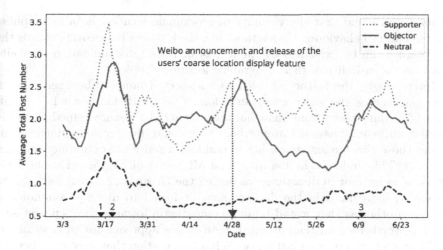

Fig. 7. Average total post number per user of the three selected groups. The dotted vertical line shows when the feature was announced and released. The first marker is China's Consumer Rights Day; the second marker is the China Eastern Airlines flight crash; and the third marker is the Tangshan restaurant attack incident.

5   Discussion

In this paper, we investigate people's attitudes, opinions and behaviours towards location privacy on social media in a naturalistic environment, following the widespread implementation of a coarse location display feature on Weibo. In this section, we discuss issues that arise due to the visibility of users' coarse location, including geographical discrimination and bonding, user self-presentation, change in user behaviour, and fairness within an online community.

5.1   Geographical Discrimination and Bonding

Our findings show that the overall sentiment towards this new feature was negative in all provinces. This indicates that, in general, Weibo users across China did not support the implementation of location visibility on the platform. Furthermore, we found that the three provinces with the lowest average sentiment scores are Jilin, Jiangsu and Heilongjiang—mostly located in North-Eastern China. This is an expected outcome as previous work has shown that there is widespread online regional discrimination against residents of North-Eastern China. For example, Sun and Liang [51] studied the reputation of North-Eastern Chinese social media users (from Liaoning, Jilin, and Heilongjiang) and found that users from those regions are often treated in a discriminatory and stereotypical manner. In addition, Henan, which exhibits an average sentiment score that ranks fourth from the bottom, also serves as an illustrative example of a province frequently subjected to geographical discrimination. Peng [45] analysed user comments under news related to regional discrimination against Henan citizens, and found that the visibility of geographic location notably amplified discriminatory behaviours. Understandably, the level of disapproval towards this new feature can be explained by the fear of increased discrimination on Weibo based on the visibility of their geographic location (Topic 3).

Interestingly, the feature also led to unexpected bonding between users in Shanghai during the strict two-month long COVID-19 lockdown in the city (Topic 5). Many users from Shanghai argued that the feature helped them distinguish authentic Shanghai users whom they could directly communicate with during those challenging times, hence building a sense of community amongst the users. This finding is in line with what Miyabe et al. [41] found about Twitter users' behaviour in disaster areas during the Great East Japan Earthquake. Generally, individuals in the disaster area preferred to directly communicate with each other as they would be more empathetic towards their current situation. Nevertheless, one can argue that an opt-in approach for such situations would be preferred over a platform-wide implementation that may yield benefits in specific situations.

The sensitivity of geolocation information seems to have expanded the gap between users from different provinces, expressed by their opposing points of view. However, more importantly, it amplifies the risk of discrimination on social media platform discussions, solely on the basis of geographical location [45]. Location disclosure creates a path for discrimination to be extended to the virtual world if it exists in the physical world. As such, social media platforms should be aware of these scenarios in order to be able to effectively and proactively tackle the propagation of geographical discrimination. Platforms could selectively display location information when it is deemed beneficial, such as during the Shanghai COVID-19 lockdown, when online social bonding may be enhanced. Conversely, a platform could automatically identify posts/comments that can potentially lead to instances of geographic discrimination, and subsequently hide location information or alert the user.

5.2   Erosion of User Self-presentation

Social media platforms should also be aware of the potential impact of displaying the location information with regards to user self-presentation. For instance, our data highlighted an intended disconnect between users' online personas and their real personas (Topic 4), similar to Goffman's concept of the public and private persona in the dramaturgical lens of human behaviour [22]. People use social media to share views, information, jokes, etc., beyond that which they would feel comfortable sharing in person, whether maliciously or idealised [26]. As such, their online identity is not a virtual manifestation of themselves and exists only on the platform. As a result of this, tagging this virtual persona with a physical location seems nonsensical to those users. This could, for example, lead to a preference for some 'online-only' tag for a user's location. In reality, however, it is still likely that the user's physical location and context informs their online persona, whether intentionally or not, so there may yet be useful information in providing that coarse physical location.

As suggested in previous research [14], exploring users' performative selves is important as it shows they adjust their presentation when engaging with locative media. Further exploring this relationship between online-only personas and the physical location of their creator remains an interesting avenue for future work.

5.3   Privacy Concerns on Social Media Behaviour

One interesting aspect we noticed is that people who have a more polarized view of this new platform feature tend to be more active on social media than people who have moderate views. This implies people with extreme views tend to be more passionate about their beliefs and are more likely to use social media to express their opinions and engage with like-minded or opposite people.

Our results also provide evidence regarding the relationship between privacy concerns and users' online behaviour in social networks. We found that the group of people who expressed strong concerns about coarse location privacy changed their posting behaviour by significantly reducing the number of their original posts and reposts in the first month after the implementation of the feature. Prior literature shows that the ability to express oneself is the main factor that influences both increase in time spent on Sina Weibo and in posting behaviour [67]. Nevertheless, our findings demonstrate that the concerns related to the visibility of geographical location will inhibit both self-expression and interactivity, leading to reduced activity within the platform.

Furthermore, many previous studies described the "privacy paradox" in social media, namely the discordance between attitudes and behaviour [47,52,57]. In line with previous studies, our results show that the location privacy paradox was present within the objector group. However, we note that they substantially increased their activity during the violent attack incident that happened in a restaurant in Tangshan. In addition, Sina Weibo is by far the biggest microblogging system in China, and other similar microblogging services (e.g., Tencent Weibo, NetEase Weibo, and Sohu Weibo) have ceased operation in the past few years. Consequently, it is challenging for users to switch to a different platform, which could also contribute towards disgruntled users eventually coming back to Sina Weibo.

5.4   Fair Enforcement of Social Media Platform Policies

Social media platforms provide a crucial means of communication between celebrities/influencers and their fans [27]. It also helps fans to build a closer relationship with their favourite celebrities by having access to more content regarding the celebrities' personal lives [27]. The launch of the coarse location display feature on Weibo led to many discussions regarding displaying the locations of celebrities (Topic 6). On the one hand, if fans discover that the celebrities' locations on social media do not match their actual locations, it becomes clear to them that the account is managed by third-party agencies. This might reduce fans' loyalty and interaction with the celebrity, as fans feel closer to the celebrity when they are able to interact with them directly (e.g., commenting their posts) [31].

Interestingly, in the initial days of the launch of this feature, Weibo did not reveal coarse location of celebrities and influencers. However, this led to heated debates among netizens indicating that the public had a strong desire for equality in the online community, and a waning tolerance for preferential treatment that is typically given to celebrities and influencers. These discussions offer valuable lessons regarding the fairness in implementing functions across different types of users. Given a long-standing debate of online communities matching up the standards of real communities, fair application of policies across an entire online community is the basic requirement that social media platforms should strive to provide to their users.

5.5   Limitations and Future Work

We acknowledge several limitations in our study. First, due to restrictions in Weibo's API, we were unable to collect the number of comments made by individual users in addition to the number of posts/reposts for our behavioural analysis. This new feature displays users' coarse location not only on the personal homepage but also from comments. Therefore, we lacked an additional indicator to measure user engagement before and after the implementation of the feature. Furthermore, our behavioural analysis is limited to a period of four months (2 months prior- or post-implementation of the feature). However, due to a commonly used Weibo feature that allows users to hide posts older than six months, we were unable to reliably collect older historical data, thus settling for a time period that would yield more robust data.

In future work, researchers could conduct user studies to gather additional insights into how users perceive the implementation of this feature and what they consider to be the way forward in this space.

6   Conclusion

In this paper, we present a comprehensive sentiment and opinion extraction analysis related to users' attitudes toward displaying their coarse location on a social media platform, using large-scale data from Sina Weibo. We found that the majority of users hold negative sentiments towards this feature with substantial privacy concerns, and revealed a potential risk of amplifying geographical discrimination and doxing. Moreover, our findings suggest that those users who voiced their disapproval about this feature decreased their activity on Weibo. Through data collection from a naturalistic environment and data analysis based on organic attitudes and opinions of real users, we provide a better understanding of social media users' attitudes toward location privacy, the impact of location visibility's on user engagement, and user sentiment towards fair enforcement of social media platform policies. We hope that our results can inform the development of novel technology that can help promote a more connected online community while respecting users' privacy and autonomy.

References

1. Aghasian, E., Garg, S., Gao, L., Yu, S., Montgomery, J.: Scoring users' privacy disclosure across multiple online social networks. IEEE Access **5**, 13118–13130 (2017)
2. Alamsyah, A., Rizkika, W., Nugroho, D.D.A., Renaldi, F., Saadah, S.: Dynamic large scale data on twitter using sentiment analysis and topic modeling. In: 2018 6th International Conference on Information and Communication Technology (ICoICT). pp. 254–258. IEEE (2018)
3. Alrayes, F., Abdelmoty, A.I.: Towards understanding location privacy awareness on geo-social networks. ISPRS Int. J. Geo-Inf. **6**(4), 109 (2017)
4. Ammari, T., Schoenebeck, S., Romero, D.M.: Pseudonymous parents: Comparing parenting roles and identities on the mommit and daddit subreddits. In: Proceedings of the 2018 CHI Conference on Human Factors in Computing Systems. pp. 1–13 (2018)
5. Blei, D.M., Ng, A.Y., Jordan, M.I.: Latent dirichlet allocation. J. Mach. Learn. Res. **3**, 993–1022 (2003)
6. Carrascal, J.P., Riederer, C., Erramilli, V., Cherubini, M., De Oliveira, R.: Your browsing behavior for a big mac: Economics of personal information online. In: Proceedings of the 22nd International Conference on World Wide Web. pp. 189–200 (2013)
7. Chen, J.C., Ha, Q.A.: Factors affecting the continuance to share location on social networking sites: the influence of privacy concern, trust, benefit and the moderating role of positive feedback and perceived promotion innovativeness. Contemp. Manag. Res. **15**(2), 89–121 (2019)
8. Chen, Y.: Exploring the Changing Portrayal of 'Henan People' by Web Media. Master's thesis, Central China Normal University (2016)
9. Chiang, S.L., Chang, C.Y.: An exploratory index for facebook users' privacy concerns: The relationship between attitude and behavior. (39), 135–165 (2020)
10. Christofides, E., Muise, A., Desmarais, S.: Information disclosure and control on facebook: are they two sides of the same coin or two different processes? Cyberpsychology Behav. **12**(3), 341–345 (2009)
11. Consolvo, S., Smith, I.E., Matthews, T., LaMarca, A., Tabert, J., Powledge, P.: Location disclosure to social relations: why, when, & what people want to share. In: Proceedings of the SIGCHI conference on Human factors in computing systems. pp. 81–90 (2005)
12. Debatin, B., Lovejoy, J.P., Horn, A.K., Hughes, B.N.: Facebook and online privacy: attitudes, behaviors, and unintended consequences. J. Comput. Med. Commun. **15**(1), 83–108 (2009)
13. Dhawan, S., Singh, K., Goel, S.: Impact of privacy attitude, concern and awareness on use of online social networking. In: 2014 5th International Conference-Confluence The Next Generation Information Technology Summit (Confluence). pp. 14–17. IEEE (2014)
14. Dunham, J., Xu, J., Papangelis, K., Schwartz, D.I.: Advertising in location-based games: An exploration in pokémon go. In: CHI Conference on Human Factors in Computing Systems Extended Abstracts. pp. 1–6 (2022)
15. Dwyer, C., Hiltz, S., Passerini, K.: Trust and privacy concern within social networking sites: A comparison of facebook and myspace. AMCIS 2007 proceedings p. 339 (2007)

16. Emamjome, F., Rabaa'i, A., Gable, G., Bandara, W.: Information quality in social media: a conceptual model. In: Proceedings of the 17th Pacific Asia Conference on Information Systems (PACIS). pp. 1–12. Association for Information Systems (AIS) (2013)

17. Fisher, D., Dorner, L., Wagner, D.: Short paper: location privacy: user behavior in the field. In: Proceedings of the second ACM workshop on Security and privacy in smartphones and mobile devices. pp. 51–56 (2012)

18. Furini, M., Tamanini, V.: Location privacy and public metadata in social media platforms: attitudes, behaviors and opinions. Multimedia Tool Appl. **74**(21), 9795–9825 (2015)

19. Gana, M.A., Thomas, T.K.: Consumers attitude towards location-based advertising: an exploratory study. J. Res. Mark. **6**(1), 390–396 (2016)

20. Gao, J., Ying, X., Cao, J., Yang, Y., Foong, P.S., Perrault, S.: Differences of challenges of working from home (wfh) between weibo and twitter users during COVID-19. In: CHI Conference on Human Factors in Computing Systems Extended Abstracts. pp. 1–7 (2022)

21. Goncalves, J., Kostakos, V., Venkatanathan, J.: Narrowcasting in social media: Effects and perceptions. In: 2013 IEEE/ACM International Conference on Advances in Social Networks Analysis and Mining (ASONAM 2013). pp. 502–509. IEEE (2013)

22. Gray, P.S., Williamson, J.B., Karp, D.A., Dalphin, J.R.: FEMINIST METHODS, p. 211–240. Cambridge University Press (2007)

23. Hargittai, E., Marwick, A.: "what can i really do?" explaining the privacy paradox with online apathy. Int. J. Commun. **10**, 21 (2016)

24. Hasan, M., Rahman, A., Karim, M.R., Khan, M.S.I., Islam, M.J.: Normalized Approach to Find Optimal Number of Topics in Latent Dirichlet Allocation (LDA). In: Kaiser, M.S., Bandyopadhyay, A., Mahmud, M., Ray, K. (eds.) Proceedings of International Conference on Trends in Computational and Cognitive Engineering. AISC, vol. 1309, pp. 341–354. Springer, Singapore (2021). https://doi.org/10.1007/978-981-33-4673-4_27

25. Hecht, B., Hong, L., Suh, B., Chi, E.H.: Tweets from justin bieber's heart: the dynamics of the location field in user profiles. In: Proceedings of the SIGCHI conference on human factors in computing systems. pp. 237–246 (2011)

26. Hollenbaugh, E.E.: Self-presentation in social media: review and research opportunities. Rev. Commun. Res. **9**, 80–98 (2021)

27. Hou, M.: Social media celebrity and the institutionalization of youtube. Convergence **25**(3), 534–553 (2019)

28. Hoy, M.G., Milne, G.: Gender differences in privacy-related measures for young adult facebook users. J. Interact. Advertising **10**(2), 28–45 (2010)

29. Jiang, Z., Di Troia, F., Stamp, M.: Sentiment analysis for troll detection on weibo. In: Malware Analysis Using Artificial Intelligence and Deep Learning, pp. 555–579. Springer, Cham (2021). https://doi.org/10.1007/978-3-030-62582-5_22

30. Kelley, P.G., Benisch, M., Cranor, L.F., Sadeh, N.: When are users comfortable sharing locations with advertisers? In: Proceedings of the SIGCHI Conference on Human Factors in Computing Systems. pp. 2449–2452 (2011)

31. Kim, M., Kim, J.: How does a celebrity make fans happy? interaction between celebrities and fans in the social media context. Comput. Hum. Behav. **111**, 106419 (2020)

32. Kokolakis, S.: Privacy attitudes and privacy behaviour: a review of current research on the privacy paradox phenomenon. Comput. Secur. **64**, 122–134 (2017)

33. Kralj Novak, P., Smailović, J., Sluban, B., Mozetič, I.: Sentiment of emojis. PloS one **10**(12), e0144296 (2015)
34. Lee, C.B., Io, H.N., Tang, H.: Sentiments and perceptions after a privacy breach incident. Cogent Bus. Manag. **9**(1), 2050018 (2022)
35. Lenhart, A., Madden, M., Smith, A., Purcell, K., Zickuhr, K., Rainie, L.: Teens, kindness and cruelty on social network sites: How american teens navigate the new world of" digital citizenship". Pew Internet & American Life Project (2011)
36. Li, L., Chen, X.: Extraction and analysis of chinese microblog topics from sina. In: 2012 Second International Conference on Cloud and Green Computing. pp. 571–577. IEEE (2012)
37. Lian, J., Zhang, F., Xie, X., Sun, G.: Restaurant survival analysis with heterogeneous information. In: Proceedings of the 26th International Conference on World Wide Web Companion. pp. 993–1002 (2017)
38. Liu, B.: Sentiment Analysis and Opinion Mining. Springer International Publishing, Cham (2012). https://doi.org/10.1007/978-3-031-02145-9
39. McCay-Peet, L., Quan-Haase, A.: What is social media and what questions can social media research help us answer. The SAGE handbook of social media research methods pp. 13–26 (2017)
40. Miltgen, C.L., Peyrat-Guillard, D.: Cultural and generational influences on privacy concerns: a qualitative study in seven European countries. Eur. J. Inf. Syst. **23**(2), 103–125 (2014)
41. Miyabe, M., Miura, A., Aramaki, E.: Use trend analysis of twitter after the great east japan earthquake. In: Proceedings of the ACM 2012 conference on Computer Supported Cooperative Work Companion. pp. 175–178 (2012)
42. Norberg, P.A., Horne, D.R., Horne, D.A.: The privacy paradox: personal information disclosure intentions versus behaviors. J. Consumer Affairs **41**(1), 100–126 (2007)
43. Ouyang, S., Li, C., Li, X.: A peek into the future: predicting the popularity of online videos. IEEE Access **4**, 3026–3033 (2016)
44. Parikh, S.B., Patil, V., Atrey, P.K.: On the origin, proliferation and tone of fake news. In: 2019 IEEE Conference on Multimedia Information Processing and Retrieval (MIPR). pp. 135–140. IEEE (2019)
45. Peng, A.Y.: Amplification of regional discrimination on Chinese news portals: an affective critical discourse analysis. Convergence **27**(5), 1343–1359 (2021)
46. Qiang, Y., Lianren, W., Lan, Z.: Research on user behavior characters and mechanism in microblog communities. J. Univ. Electron. Sci. Technol. China **42**(3), 328–333 (2013)
47. Reynolds, B., Venkatanathan, J., Gonçalves, J., Kostakos, V.: Sharing ephemeral information in online social networks: privacy perceptions and behaviours. In: Campos, P., Graham, N., Jorge, J., Nunes, N., Palanque, P., Winckler, M. (eds.) Human-Computer Interaction - INTERACT 2011, pp. 204–215. Springer, Berlin Heidelberg, Berlin, Heidelberg (2011)
48. Sievert, C., Shirley, K.: Ldavis: A method for visualizing and interpreting topics. In: Proceedings of the Workshop on Interactive Language Learning, Visualization, and Interfaces. pp. 63–70 (2014)
49. Sturm, C., Oh, A., Linxen, S., Abdelnour Nocera, J., Dray, S., Reinecke, K.: How weird is HCI? extending HCI principles to other countries and cultures. In: Proceedings of the 33rd Annual ACM Conference Extended Abstracts on Human Factors in Computing Systems. pp. 2425–2428 (2015)

50. Sun, Y., Wang, N., Shen, X.L., Zhang, J.X.: Location information disclosure in location-based social network services: Privacy calculus, benefit structure, and gender differences. Comput. Hum. Behav. **52**, 278–292 (2015)
51. Sun, Y., Liang, C.: "others" and social memory in regional prejudice: A study of the image of "north-easterners" in the we-media context. Journal of Communication and Sociology (52), 27–55 (Apr 2020). https://doi.org/10.30180/CS.202004_(52).0003
52. Taddicken, M.: The 'privacy paradox' in the social web: The impact of privacy concerns, individual characteristics, and the perceived social relevance on different forms of self-disclosure. J. Comput. Mediated Commun. **19**(2), 248–273 (2014)
53. Tahaei, M., Vaniea, K., Saphra, N.: Understanding privacy-related questions on stack overflow. In: Proceedings of the 2020 CHI conference on human factors in computing systems. pp. 1–14 (2020)
54. Tang, K., Hong, J., Siewiorek, D.: The implications of offering more disclosure choices for social location sharing. In: Proceedings of the SIGCHI Conference on Human Factors in Computing Systems. pp. 391–394 (2012)
55. Tsai, J.Y., Egelman, S., Cranor, L., Acquisti, A.: The effect of online privacy information on purchasing behavior: an experimental study. Inf. Syst. Res. **22**(2), 254–268 (2011)
56. Tufekci, Z.: Can you see me now? audience and disclosure regulation in online social network sites. Bull. Sci. Technol. Soc. **28**(1), 20–36 (2008)
57. Venkatanathan, J., Kostakos, V., Karapanos, E., Gonçalves, J.: Online Disclosure of Personally Identifiable Information with Strangers: Effects of Public and Private Sharing. Interacting Comput. **26**(6), 614–626 (2013). https://doi.org/10.1093/iwc/iwt058
58. Vu, H.Q., Law, R., Li, G.: Breach of traveller privacy in location-based social media. Current Issues Tourism **22**(15), 1825–1840 (2019)
59. Wang, Y., Lu, X., Tan, Y.: Impact of product attributes on customer satisfaction: an analysis of online reviews for washing machines. Electron. Commerce Res. Appl. **29**, 1–11 (2018)
60. Weng, H., Ji, S., Duan, F., Li, Z., Chen, J., He, Q., Wang, T.: Cats: cross-platform e-commerce fraud detection. In: 2019 IEEE 35th International Conference on Data Engineering (ICDE). pp. 1874–1885. IEEE (2019)
61. Xiao, Y., Li, B., Gong, Z.: Real-time identification of urban rainstorm waterlogging disasters based on weibo big data. Natural Hazards **94**(2), 833–842 (2018)
62. Xie, R., Chu, S.K.W., Chiu, D.K.W., Wang, Y.: Exploring public response to COVID-19 on weibo with lda topic modeling and sentiment analysis. Data Inf. Manag. **5**(1), 86–99 (2021)
63. Xu, H., Teo, H.H., Tan, B.: Predicting the adoption of location-based services: the role of trust and perceived privacy risk (2005)
64. Yao, M.Z.: Self-protection of online privacy: A behavioral approach. In: Privacy online, pp. 111–125. Springer (2011). https://doi.org/10.1007/978-3-642-21521-6_9
65. Young, A.L., Quan-Haase, A.: Privacy protection strategies on facebook: the internet privacy paradox revisited. Inf. Commun. Soc. **16**(4), 479–500 (2013)
66. Zafeiropoulou, A.M., Millard, D.E., Webber, C., O'Hara, K.: Unpicking the privacy paradox: can structuration theory help to explain location-based privacy decisions? In: Proceedings of the 5th Annual ACM Web Science Conference. pp. 463–472 (2013)
67. Zhang, L., Pentina, I.: Motivations and usage patterns of weibo. Cyberpsychology Behav. Soc. Netw. **15**(6), 312–317 (2012)

Intimate Data: Exploring Perceptions of Privacy and Privacy-Seeking Behaviors Through the Story Completion Method

Diana P. Moniz[1,4]([⊠]), Maryam Mehrnezhad[2], and Teresa Almeida[3,4]

[1] Instituto Superior Técnico, Lisbon, Portugal
[2] Royal Holloway University of London, Egham, UK
[3] Department of Informatics, Umeå University, Umeå, Sweden
[4] Interactive Technologies Institute/LARSyS, Lisbon, Portugal
dianamoniz@tecnico.ulisboa.pt

Abstract. Privacy is a fundamental human right in the digital age. With the proliferation of intimate health technologies, such as data-driven apps and connected devices that track bodily care and sensitive topics, privacy is increasingly critical. In this paper, we explore the complexity of intimate data and user perspectives and the choices they make to protect themselves. We introduce a story completion study with 27 participants to examine individuals' concerns about data privacy, their protective or avoidant actions, and the potential mismatches between privacy concerns and actual behaviors. We suggest future research that combines User-Tailored Privacy (UTP) and participatory threat modeling to create privacy solutions that account for users' needs and the potential risks and harms associated with the use of their data.

Keywords: Intimate Data · Digital Health · Privacy

1 Introduction

The digitalization of the human body has brought along a wide range of technologies that offer solutions in different areas of health, including **intimate health**. These technologies commonly involve the collection and storage of **intimate data**, which refers to information pertaining to one's sexual orientation and behavior, reproductive health, and well-being. In HCI, research in this sensitive area is growing and topics are as diverse as intimate anatomy [2], tech-enabled experiences of menstruation [30], menopause [5], or infertility [10], as well as the intersectional qualities that traverse the use of these technologies, such as the impact of religion on women's intimate health [23], or designing for trans and non-binary communities [16]. However, although these technologies offer innovative, affordable, and accessible resources and interventions, there is also a growing concern for their security and privacy. With *datafication* becoming an increasingly prevalent trend, people are sharing more personal and intimate

J. Abdelnour Nocera et al. (Eds.): INTERACT 2023, LNCS 14144, pp. 533–543, 2023.
https://doi.org/10.1007/978-3-031-42286-7_30

data than ever before. This information is collected, analyzed, and used for different purposes that inform decision-making, including targeted advertising, research, and the development of new products [26]. This model approaches data as a valuable resource that can be bought and sold [18] and can tend to leave human considerations behind, not accounting for people's diverse preferences and needs for security and privacy. Nevertheless, the number of intimate digital health users is at an all-time high [29], which leads us to inquire if there is a gap between what people claim to care about and their actual behaviors. Known as the *privacy paradox*, the notion that although people care about their online privacy, their behavior does not always reflect their stated privacy preferences [7]. This paradoxical behavior has been explained in previous studies [17, 25] through people's low understanding of how their data is collected, processed, and shared, and their level of privacy literacy. Nonetheless, "digital resignation" offers an alternative explanation to this inconsistent behavior, stating that people experience feelings of powerlessness as a response to what they consider to be "inescapable" monitoring and surveillance, translating then to their subsequent inaction or privacy-avoidant behaviors [11].

In this paper, we explore the perceptions of privacy and privacy-seeking behaviors of individuals using intimate digital health technologies. Privacy relates to a subjective understanding and beliefs about personal data protection, while privacy-seeking behaviors refer to the manifestation of strategies and actions adopted to preserve privacy. We seek to identify the potential mismatch between people's stated privacy (non)concerns and their subsequent privacy-seeking or avoidant behaviors. We aim to understand if people are digitally resigned, conformed to the normalization of their concerns, or if they actively care about protecting their most intimate private lives. We contribute to ongoing research in HCI and intimate health, data, and care.

2   Background and Related Work

There is a growing market of health apps, digital platforms, and wearables that have introduced solutions for a number of intimate health concerns [22]. This includes e.g. tracking fertility, managing menstruation, supporting pregnancy, and helping detect infections and diseases [13, 24], to offering remote care and support for medical abortion [12]. These technologies offer resources for intimate health needs that were commonly neglected and stigmatized [1, 20]. HCI research has also looked at digital tools that aim to provide help, guidance, and management of sexually transmitted infections and diseases [14, 15], or chronic conditions such as HIV [8]. Additionally, intimate digital health technologies deal with extremely sensitive, personal data that can put people at risk if and when misused or misappropriated by a number of threat actors, including (ex-)partners, family, employer and colleagues, insurance firms, cyber-criminals, advertising companies, governments, political and religious organizations [22]. Therefore, to reduce the complexities of risks and potential harms, it is of utmost importance to safeguard and improve the security and privacy of these systems.

Privacy and Security of Intimate Data. Research has gone into analyzing the security and privacy practices of women's mHealth (mobile health) apps [4,24], as well as into the security and privacy protection mechanisms of menstruation and fertility tracking apps, and their adherence to regulatory bodies such as the GDPR [20,27]. These studies found that applications share information even without the users' consent, do not comply with all regulations, and their security practices leave room for improvement according to security recommendations. Similarly, the IoT environment in intimate health technologies, such as wearable smart pumps or pelvic floor exercises, has introduced new security risks that can harm different communities [3,22]. In [22], the authors enquire if these risks could outweigh the benefits people expect from such products and services. We address the latter and set out to understand the degree of concern for privacy and data control, and how people balance their perceived risks and benefits when utilizing intimate digital health.

3   Study

We investigate how people understand intimate health data and their perceptions of privacy and privacy-seeking behaviors. We seek to explore the privacy-protective or avoidant behaviors that the participants resort to and how these align with their privacy concerns and preferences. We follow the design advanced in [21] to report the feelings and protective actions mentioned by the participants.

Method. We used the *Story Completion Method* (SCM), which consists of introducing hypothetical scenarios that contain the beginning of a story, prompting the participants to continue by answering questions of "What happens next?", "What does (the character) think?" [9]. When using this method, participants are invited to write a narrative by resorting to creative inquiry, whether by taking from their own experience or imagining themselves as the person in the story. The method encourages people to consider social problems in a way that does not involve personal or direct questioning [31]. Therefore, it allows more freedom because "any challenge could always be rebutted with 'it's just a story'" [9].

Design Approach. The SCM activity consisted of four scenarios. These were crafted around interactions with various types of intimate technologies, seeking to encompass different levels of intimacy and sensitivity pertaining to the type of data collected and the topic addressed. Our selection process for the topics of each story included one of the most commonly used self-tracking tools, a menstruation app; moving on to a fertility app; then to sexual health testing and digital records; and finally to the management of a sexually transmitted disease. Similarly to [21], the stories are based on common privacy and security concerns, namely in regard to user tracking and profiling, user surveillance, misinformation, and violations of users' privacy. The story prompts are presented in Table 1. All the characters were given gender-neutral names.

Table 1. Stories used in the SCM activity

Story 1: Menstrual app and advertisements

Alex has started using a mobile application for tracking their menstrual cycle. After having used it for a couple of days, they log-in to their Instagram or Facebook account, and begin to see advertisements for tampons and period pads on their feed.

Story 2: Fertility app and advertisements

Sam is using a Fertility tracking application for contraception (preventing pregnancy). Every time that they take the contraceptive pill, they log it into the app. One day, they are on a work Zoom call and are sharing their computer screen, and while clicking on some pages, an advertisement about contraception methods shows up.

Story 3: Digital medical records and sexual health

Charlie has not been feeling well after their last intimate encounter and wonders if they have been exposed to a Sexually Transmitted Infection (STI) or a Sexual Transmitted Disease (STD). They go online and find out that there are multiple ways to get tested and that this intimate data will be kept in their medical records.

Story 4: Digital health platform for HIV

Blake was diagnosed with HIV. They have been given a new treatment that needs to be taken at different times throughout the day. Knowing that HIV treatment is for life, it is important that they remember to take the medication and keep track of the side effects that they might experience over time. To help with this, Blake plans on using a digital health platform but that platform requests they reveal their personal identity.

Data Collection and Analysis. We used Google Forms to perform our study due to its user-friendly interface. The form contained the four scenarios presented in Table 1, followed by the questions *"How does (the character) feel?"* and *"What does (the character) do next?"*. The form was open from October until November 2022. We suggested participants spend ten minutes on each scenario. Each participant was required to complete the four scenarios, following the same order as presented in Table 1. The participants provided an average of 128 words for the sum of all scenarios, with a median of 92. The word count per participant for all scenarios ranged from a minimum of 12 to a maximum of 412. The average word count for the first three scenarios was 33 each, and 30 for the fourth, following the order in Table 1. Each scenario word count had medians of

19, 21, 26, and 21 words, respectively. Two researchers performed an inductive thematic analysis [6] to obtain the emerging themes amongst the collected data. We started by identifying and assigning initial codes. Then, we focused on finding similarities and patterns throughout the obtained narratives and grouping them together. Finally, we arrived at a final set of themes representing and interpreting the data. Table 2 shows that some participants were classified in more than one category for their reported feelings. Additionally, some participants did not indicate any protective action in their stories.

Participants. We shared the form via Social Media, mainly on the first author's personal accounts on Instagram, Facebook, and Twitter. The invitation posts contained a short explanation of the study and the link to the form, also encouraging people to share the link. We received a total of 27 responses through the study, of which 15 participants identified as male and 12 as female. The majority of the participants belonged to the 21–29 age range (25 participants), with only one participant for each age range of 19–20 and 50–59.

Limitations. Most participants were recruited through the first author's social media, which resulted in an incline toward their age group. Therefore, the findings might not represent the wider population. Our data set may be skewed due to people not wanting to participate, e.g. if privacy-conscious or advocates not using technologies that are conducive to data harvesting. However, this exploratory study provides valuable insights and a starting point for further research in this area.

4   Findings

Normalizing (Lack of) Privacy in Intimate Data. The normalization of privacy concerns and risks was a common element throughout the stories produced by the participants. Across all four scenarios, the story characters were described as either concerned about their data and privacy, or seemingly indifferent to it. However, in the narratives where indifference was depicted, participants conveyed a sense of powerlessness and a perceived inability to influence the technology and the issue that arose from its use. For instance, in the cases of Alex and Sam, the narratives indicated that they were *'just accepting it'*, *'used to it'*, and *'to just let it be'*, because there was *'not much they can do about it'*, and also that it is *'so normalized that I would ignore it'*. On another note, six participants recognized potential benefits from the targeted ads and weighed the trade-offs of not agreeing to third-party sharing in terms of app functionalities. The benefits included: the app can show better results, offer additional features, lead to the purchase of suggested products, and for Sam, seeing the ad could improve their knowledge about contraception methods. Nonetheless, almost all of the participants that weighed between risks and benefits gave two alternative scenarios for one specific story (which was not a part of the prompt): one where they embrace those perks and another where they stop using the app because they don't want

Table 2. Summary of feelings and protective actions reported by the participants in the stories (design based on [21]).

Story Prompt		Feelings (n°. of users)	Protective Action (n°. of users)
Alex	Menstrual app and ads	Negative(15), Neutral(8), Positive(3), Undefined(3)	Uninstall app/delete account(7), switch app(2), review/change settings(5), block/disable ads(2), request data removal(1), Use it less often(1)
Sam	Fertility app and ads	Negative(17), Neutral(6), Positive(1), Undefined(4)	Uninstall app or delete account(2), switch app(2), review/change settings(2), block/disable ads(2)
Charlie	Digital medical records and sexual health	Negative(7), Neutral(18), Positive(2), Undefined(1)	Request temporary medical record(1), testing center with best privacy(5), anonymous testing center(3)
Blake	Digital health platform for HIV	Negative(15), Neutral(10), Positive(0), Undefined(2)	Uninstall app or delete account(3), switch app(6), request or use anonymity (3), request policy change(1), set up alarms(6)

their data being shared. Participants appeared less worried about Charlie's privacy, likely due to a higher trust in the health centers' ability to handle the test results and their intimate data in a *'private and secure'* manner. From a majority of the participants that mentioned proceeding with testing (17 participants), one in particular gave the following explanation: *'they would feel and think there is already too much information out there for theirs to be a distinguished one, underestimating their own info'*. Participants were more concerned for Blake's privacy than the other story characters, showing more discomfort with giving away their personal identifiable information while using a tool to help manage HIV. Some participants, despite choosing to use the platform, were still concerned about the app potentially sharing their data.

Pressing (individual) Responsibility and Privacy-Seeking Behaviors. The stories show that when a person's privacy seemed to have been violated, there was a tendency to take action in response, hoping to alter the course of the situation, even in the cases where the stories indicated pessimism and cynicism over the success of said action. Many of the responsive actions for Alex and Sam had to do with stopping the use of the app, deleting it, looking for another one with different privacy policies, or closing the account down. Four participants mentioned downloading an add blocker and seven suggested blocking the ads through the app or phone settings. This is a privacy-seeking behavior that only addresses the visibility of ads, and not their implications of data collection by companies. For Blake, there were suggestions to find a different application or platform, wanting to ensure that they did not have to reveal their personal identity; otherwise, they would prefer not to use any digital tool if their privacy was at risk of being compromised since they would need to input sensitive information about the status and management of HIV. Across the four scenarios, only one participant showed awareness about *data rights*, mentioning Alex's *right to remove information* from the app. For Alex, there were two suggestions to change the privacy settings, while for Sam there were five. For Charlie, one participant suggested that the platform should change their policy, and another would like a mechanism of *negotiation* with the platform, where they would ask for an agreement to only keep the records for a short period of time. Other two participants mentioned the *'benefit of anonymity'*. These responses reflect that even if users are aware that each platform should be responsible for protecting their customers' data, when their privacy seems to be at risk, they turn to protective actions that shift that responsibility onto themselves and away from the application service.

Intimate (In)security and Surveillance. Throughout the stories, there was an atmosphere of apprehension, concern, and even fear of being tracked, observed, and surveilled. When the character in the story was described as feeling insecure, unprotected, or like their privacy had been compromised, they worried about *what* data was being seen, *who* could see it, and *why*. They worried about potential security leaks, hacks, privacy violations, and illegal access to their information. They showed concern about who gains access to their information, wondering if done by the application itself, developers, external entities, hackers, and even work colleagues. For Alex, most participants identified that their data is being sold and shared by the app to advertisers, claiming that *'info is being given away'* and wondering why *'such data is leaving the application and landing in the hands of such other companies'*. One participant said that *'sharing personal health data to numerous companies beyond their control is a step too far'*. They called this an *'invasion of privacy'*, reflecting *'how much phones know about people'*. They also mentioned that Alex feels *'like she is being watched or tracked'*, causing them to think *'about the power of big data'*. Similarly, in Sam's story, participants identified that advertising is targeted and it *'reveals something about their personal life'*. Sam feared that *'their coworkers will now make assumptions about their personal life, whether they are good, bad, or neutral'*, with two participants worrying about their reputation and future at work. For Charlie and Blake, the worry about information leakage or potential security issues was more prominent, mainly due to the information's sensitivity level, e.g. *'feel afraid of this information to be leaked, or used for other purposes'*, or *'a concern over the competing multiple ways of testing by data sharing companies that offer such a service'*. Several participants mentioned that the platforms needed to offer the *'most amount of security and privacy over data'*. Even though Charlie needed to get tested, some people decided to self-diagnose or avoid testing for fear of others having access to their data. For Blake, participants said that they *'will not want to use the app for fear of being hacked'* and being *'scared of leaking the personal data'* because *'it's something they want to have control of when it comes to sharing it with someone'*.

5 Discussion and Future Work

Our exploratory study found that the participants were concerned about their intimate data and privacy. They resorted to privacy-seeking behaviors even while seemingly pessimistic about the effectiveness of those actions, or "digitally resigned" [11]. In other situations, they worried about their privacy but did not take protective actions, aligning with the initial privacy paradoxical behavior [7]. Whether an individual is motivated to protect their privacy or has the knowledge to do so, they are still limited by the tools and mechanisms that are available to them. Therefore, it is critical to explore new approaches that provide users with 'know-how' mechanisms, making privacy protections more accessible and user-friendly while empowering them to take control of their data and protect their privacy. In the context of our research, this includes future work to *advance user-centered privacy* and for HCI researchers and developers to explore *User-Tailored Privacy* (UTP) and participatory threat modeling to improve privacy and security in intimate digital health.

User-Tailored Privacy. UTP is a method that aims to give individuals more control and agency over their privacy by allowing them to customize their privacy preferences and settings according to their needs [34]. It addresses the disadvantages of the different approaches to privacy and aims to maintain the advantages of each. First, *technical solutions* are not always feasible from an implementation standpoint and therefore need to be combined with user-centric approaches while still shifting part of the burden from the user to the system by leveraging computational power. Second, *Privacy by Design* can fall short when privacy and functionality conflict, but it strives to make privacy an effortless process. Third, the *notice and choice* approach places all of the responsibility on the user, which can be limited by their individual abilities, knowledge, or motivation; however, it encourages users to take control. Lastly, *privacy nudging* can assume a one-size-fits-all approach with general assumptions on the best privacy decisions but still acknowledges users' heuristic decision-making practices [34].

UTP attempts to find a balance between placing the responsibility for customizing privacy on the users and simplifying some of the privacy management responsibilities. Some examples of applications include making user-tailored recommendations through a profile-based personalized privacy assistant for app privacy permissions [19], leveraging different user profiles based on their privacy boundaries [33] and adapting the privacy settings interfaces with their most used functionalities [32]. In intimate digital health, it could help empower users by increasing their autonomy and control and addressing their privacy preferences while providing suggestions and personalized recommendations that prioritize their privacy. This approach can be combined with further research to identify the threats, harms, and risks arising from the misuse and misappropriation of intimate data [3]. *Participatory threat modeling* [28], which involves working collaboratively with users and including marginalized groups' experiences to identify potential threats to a system, can provide valuable insights into the specific privacy risks that different users may face. By embedding participatory threat modeling in the design process, UTP can provide users with privacy options that are tailored to their specific needs and concerns. In turn, this will help mitigate the risks associated with data misuse and misappropriation, contributing to more equal and (socially) just intimate data privacy.

Acknowledgments. This work benefited from the BIG ERAChair EU-funded project through Grant agreement ID: 952226. ITI/LARsyS is funded by FCT Project UIDB/50009/2020; LA/P/0083/2020 - ITI - IST-ID.

References

1. Almeida, T., Balaam, M., Bardzell, S., Hansen, L.K.: Introduction to the special issue on HCI and the body: reimagining women's health (2020). https://doi.org/10.1145/3406091
2. Almeida, T., Comber, R., Wood, G., Saraf, D., Balaam, M.: On looking at the vagina through labella. In: Proceedings of the 2016 CHI Conference on Human Factors in Computing Systems, pp. 1810–1821 (2016). https://doi.org/10.1145/2858036.2858119
3. Almeida, T., Shipp, L., Mehrnezhad, M., Toreini, E.: Bodies like yours: enquiring data privacy in femtech. In: Adjunct Proceedings of the 2022 Nordic Human-Computer Interaction Conference, pp. 1–5 (2022). https://doi.org/10.1145/3547522.3547674
4. Arora, S., Yttri, J., Nilsen, W.: Privacy and security in mobile health (mhealth) research. Alcohol Res. Curr. Rev. **36**(1), 143 (2014)
5. Bardzell, J., Bardzell, S., Lazar, A., Su, N.M.: (re-)framing menopause experiences for HCI and design. In: Proceedings of the 2019 CHI Conference on Human Factors in Computing Systems, pp. 1–13 (2019). https://doi.org/10.1145/3290605.3300345
6. Braun, V., Clarke, V.: Thematic analysis. American Psychological Association (2012)
7. Brown, B.: Studying the internet experience. HP laboratories technical report HPL 49 (2001)
8. Bussone, A., Stumpf, S., Wilson, S.: Designing for reflection on shared HIV health information. In: Proceedings of the 13th Biannual Conference of the Italian SIGCHI Chapter: Designing the next Interaction, CHItaly 2019. Association for Computing Machinery, New York (2019). https://doi.org/10.1145/3351995.3352036
9. Clarke, V., Braun, V., Frith, H., Moller, N.: Editorial introduction to the special issue: using story completion methods in qualitative research. Qual. Res. Psychol. **16**(1), 1–20 (2019)
10. Dilisha, P., Ann, B., Mark, W., Jill, S., Judith, S.: I feel like only half a man": Online forums as a resource for finding a" new normal" for men experiencing fertility issues. 3. Proc. ACMHum.-Comput. Interact 3 (2019)
11. Draper, N.A., Turow, J.: The corporate cultivation of digital resignation. New Media Soc. **21**(8), 1824–1839 (2019). https://doi.org/10.1177/1461444819833331

12. Endler, M., Lavelanet, A., Cleeve, A., Ganatra, B., Gomperts, R., Gemzell-Danielsson, K.: Telemedicine for medical abortion: a systematic review. BJOG: Int. J. Obstetrics Gynaecol. **126**(9), 1094–1102 (2019)
13. Erickson, J., Yuzon, J.Y., Bonaci, T.: What you don't expect when you're expecting: Privacy analysis of femtech. IEEE Trans. Technol. Soc. (2022). https://doi.org/10.1109/TTS.2022.3160928
14. Gibbs, A.S.J., Estcourt, C., Sonnenberg, P., Blandford, A.: Are hiv smartphone apps and online interventions fit for purpose? In: ACM International Conference Proceeding Series Part F128634 (2017)
15. Gkatzidou, V., et al.: A user-centred approach to inform the design of a mobile application for STI diagnosis and management. In: 27th International BCS Human Computer Interaction Conference (HCI 2013) 27, pp. 1–6 (2013)
16. Haimson, O.L., Gorrell, D., Starks, D.L., Weinger, Z.: Designing trans technology: defining challenges and envisioning community-centered solutions. In: Proceedings of the 2020 CHI Conference on Human Factors in Computing Systems, pp. 1–13 (2020). https://doi.org/10.1145/3313831.3376669
17. Kokolakis, S.: Privacy attitudes and privacy behaviour: a review of current research on the privacy paradox phenomenon. Comput. Secur. **64**, 122–134 (2017)
18. Levy, K.E.: Intimate surveillance. Idaho L. Rev. **51**, 679 (2014)
19. Liu, B., Lin, J., Sadeh, N.: Reconciling mobile app privacy and usability on smartphones: could user privacy profiles help? In: Proceedings of the 23rd International Conference on World Wide Web, pp. 201–212 (2014)
20. Mehrnezhad, M., Almeida, T.: Caring for intimate data in fertility technologies. In: CHI '21: Proceedings of the 2021 CHI Conference on Human Factors in Computing Systems, pp. 1–11. ACM (2021). https://doi.org/10.1145/3411764.3445132
21. Mehrnezhad, M., Almeida, T.: "My sex-related data is more sensitive than my financial data and i want the same level of security and privacy": user risk perceptions and protective actions in female-oriented technologies (2023). https://doi.org/10.48550/arXiv.2306.05956
22. Mehrnezhad, M., Shipp, L., Almeida, T., Toreini, E.: Vision: too little too late? do the risks of femtech already outweigh the benefits? In: EuroUSEC '22: Proceedings of the 2022 European Symposium on Usable Security, pp. 145–150 (2022). https://doi.org/10.1145/3549015.3554204
23. Mustafa, M., Zaman, K.T., Ahmad, T., Batool, A., Ghazali, M., Ahmed, N.: Religion and women's intimate health: towards an inclusive approach to healthcare. In: Proceedings of the 2021 CHI Conference on Human Factors in Computing Systems, pp. 1–13 (2021). https://doi.org/10.1145/3411764.3445605
24. Nurgalieva, L., O'Callaghan, D., Doherty, G.: Security and privacy of mhealth applications: a scoping review. IEEE Access **8**, 104247–104268 (2020)
25. Park, Y.J.: Digital literacy and privacy behavior online. Commun. Res. **40**(2), 215–236 (2013). https://doi.org/10.1177/0093650211418338
26. Sadowski, J.: When data is capital: datafication, accumulation, and extraction. Big Data Soc. **6**(1), 2053951718820549 (2019)
27. Shipp, L., Blasco, J.: How private is your period?: a systematic analysis of menstrual app privacy policies. Proc. Priv. Enhancing Technol. **2020**(4), 491–510 (2020)
28. Slupska, J., Dawson Duckworth, S.D., Ma, L., Neff, G.: Participatory threat modelling: exploring paths to reconfigure cybersecurity. In: Extended Abstracts of the 2021 CHI Conference on Human Factors in Computing Systems, pp. 1–6 (2021)
29. Statista: Digital health - worldwide (2023). www.statista.com/outlook/dmo/digital-health/worldwide. Accessed 20 April 2023

30. Tuli, A., Singh, S., Narula, R., Kumar, N., Singh, P.: Rethinking menstrual trackers towards period-positive ecologies. In: Proceedings of the 2022 CHI Conference on Human Factors in Computing Systems. CHI 2022. Association for Computing Machinery, New York (2022). https://doi.org/10.1145/3491102.3517662
31. Watson, A., Lupton, D.: Tactics, affects and agencies in digital privacy narratives: a story completion study. Online Information Review 45 (2021)
32. Wilkinson, D., et al.: User-tailored privacy by design. In: Proceedings of the Usable Security Mini Conference (2017)
33. Wisniewski, P.J., Knijnenburg, B.P., Lipford, H.R.: Making privacy personal: profiling social network users to inform privacy education and nudging. Int. J. Hum Comput Stud. **98**, 95–108 (2017)
34. Wisniewski, P.J., Page, X.: Privacy theories and frameworks. In: Modern Socio-Technical Perspectives on Privacy, pp. 15–41. Springer, Cham (2022). https://doi.org/10.1007/978-3-030-82786-1_2

User Movement and 3D Environments

Eyes on Teleporting: Comparing Locomotion Techniques in Virtual Reality with Respect to Presence, Sickness and Spatial Orientation

Ariel Caputo[1]([⊠]) [iD], Massimo Zancanaro[2,3] [iD], and Andrea Giachetti[1] [iD]

[1] Department of Engineering for Innovation Medicine, University of Verona, Verona, Italy
ariel.caputo@univr.it
[2] Department of Psychology and Cognitive Science, University of Trento, Trento, Italy
[3] Fondazione Bruno Kessler, FBK, Trento, Italy

Abstract. This work compares three locomotion techniques for an immersive VR environment: two different types of teleporting (with and without animation) and a manual (joystick-based) technique. We tested the effect of these techniques on visual motion sickness, spatial awareness, presence, subjective pleasantness, and perceived difficulty of operating the navigation. We collected eye tracking and head and body orientation data to investigate the relationships between motion, vection, and sickness. Our study confirms some results already discussed in the literature regarding the reduced invasiveness and the high usability of instant teleport while increasing the evidence against the hypothesis of reduced spatial awareness induced by this technique. We reinforce the evidence about the issues of extending teleporting with animation. Furthermore, we offer some new evidence of a benefit to the user experience of the manual technique and the correlation of the sickness felt in this condition with head movements. The findings of this study contribute to the ongoing debate on the development of guidelines on navigation interfaces in specific VR environments.

Keywords: virtual reality · locomotion in virtual environment · teleporting

1 Introduction

As immersive virtual reality applications are becoming widespread, a better understanding of the effects of different locomotion techniques on user experience is paramount. Although there is an increasing amount of research on this topic (see below for a short review, and Butussi & Chittaro [6] and Al Zayer and colleagues [2] for recent literature analysis), there is still a stringent need to collect and compare more studies in different contexts of usages and along different dimensions of user experience.

The term (virtual) locomotion technique refers to a control technique for allowing a person to move freely in a virtual environment while remaining within a small physical space [26]. It is well known that virtual movements in an immersive environment can induce sickness [7] and the specific locomotion technique can have an impact on that [6, 8, 11], together with other individual variables such as individual propensity to sickness [12, 25], and sex [19]. Furthermore, the choice of locomotion technique can impact the experience of presence, although the evidence for that is less clear [4–6, 11].

© The Author(s), under exclusive license to Springer Nature Switzerland AG 2023
J. Abdelnour Nocera et al. (Eds.): INTERACT 2023, LNCS 14144, pp. 547–566, 2023.
https://doi.org/10.1007/978-3-031-42286-7_31

Several locomotion techniques have been proposed in the literature, but manual movement and teleporting are the two most often investigated in research and employed in consumer applications [2, 6]. The manual locomotion technique involves using a joystick or a similar controller to move the viewport in the chosen direction and control the speed by operating the controller. Teleporting is more straightforward, requiring the user to select a destination point in the environment and confirm it to move the viewpoint to the target.

Teleporting can be implemented in two ways: instant teleporting that can reduce the sickness (as the visual motion perceived is removed) at the cost of losing spatial awareness or teleporting with animation (where the final position is reached by moving the viewport, typically at a constant speed on a straight path). Previous studies tried to assess both the advantages of teleporting to reduce sickness with respect to manual control [5], to compare manual control and teleporting with respect to both sickness and orientation [3, 4] or to evaluate the effects on orientation and sickness of continuous vs. discrete animation when using teleporting [1, 21].

However, none of these studies directly compare the manual control with both instant and animated teleporting in an active exploration task, which might be relevant since manual control (i.e. the use of a joystick to move the viewport) is the most simple and straightforward locomotion technique. In Rahimi et al. [21] the discrete animation is evaluated in a task featuring a passive viewport change, in [1] jumps are added to continuous viewpoint control and not to teleport.

Furthermore, even if most studies feature subjective and objective measurements quantifying sickness and orientation, they do not evaluate the relationships of these effects with head and eye movements, which can be relevant to understand the causes of the sickness and suggesting strategies to reduce it.

In this paper, we designed a user study that directly compare all the three locomotion approaches for navigation and orientation tasks also evaluating the behavior of the subjects in terms of eyes, head and body movements, and considering the experienced sickness and the susceptibility to sickness of the participants.

Specifically, we aimed to investigate the following research questions:

$Q1$: is there a relation between sickness and susceptibility to sickness, and do the specific locomotion methods affect this relation differently?

$Q2$: do the different locomotion techniques impact efficiency, spatial awareness, the perception of presence, difficulty, and pleasantness of the task?

$Q3$: do the behaviour (in terms of eyes and body movements) change among the different conditions, and do those changes explain presence, difficulty, or pleasantness?

The study involved 25 volunteer participants who had the task to navigate a virtual environment resembling a museum with each of the three locomotion techniques. The study was approved by the Person Research Approval Committee (CARP) of the University of Verona.

2   Related Works

There are many studies in the literature regarding the perception of discomfort while navigating in virtual reality and many techniques have been proposed to reduce this effect. Recent surveys [7, 27], however, pointed out that many findings of these studies are inconsistent. Chang and colleague [7] suggest that multiple factors of a VR system are related to users' discomfort, while Tian et al. [27] pointed out that there is a huge variability in the sickness effects in different users and it is necessary to profile individual susceptibility, and there is lack of proper validated physiological measurements.

The control of the navigation is an important factor affecting the perceived sickness. Several methods have been proposed to provide efficient ways of navigating VR without inducing VR sickness [2]. A method to avoid it is certainly the use of teleporting, as also shown in the work of Frommel et al. [11] and Bozgeyikli et al. [5]. Teleporting is considered a valid solution for in-place VR locomotion, as it is also more efficient and usable than other methods [6]. However, locomotion techniques that instantly teleport users to new locations may increase user disorientation [4].

If a user wants to navigate in an exploratory way while avoiding sickness and maintaining spatial orientation, it is not obvious whether to use teleportation or a method of reducing sickness by controlling navigation more freely.

A few recent studies address the simultaneous evaluation of sickness and spatial orientation for different sets of locomotion control methods and tasks, even if with some limitations. Langbehn et al. [18] compared joystick based control, similar to our manual technique, with instant teleport and redirected walking, but only for limited movements on pre-defined paths. They found that redirected walking provided a better understanding of the space and that joystick-based navigation did not provide better orientation while resulting in higher sickness.

In a work of Bhandari et al. [3], teleportation with a fast animation at a constant speed, similar to our teleporting with animation, is proposed as a possible solution to avoid disorientation. While the authors adopt this solution to limit the exposure to optical flow and found it effective, it must be noted, looking at the environment used for the tests, that the virtual environment used for the test presents limited texturing and no obstacles, so that the optical flow is not too relevant and this may have biased the results.

Rahimi and colleagues [21] compared three variations of teleporting (instant, animated and pulsed) evaluating effects in spatial awareness, in an object-tracking task involving three moving objects with a viewport transition not controlled by the user. They concluded that animation might improve spatial awareness, but it also worsens sickness. The results on the passive task are not necessarily the same that would have obtained in an active one.

Farmani and Theater [9] tested the effects of rotation and translation snapping, showing that discontinuous motion could result in reduced sickness with no disorientation effects. The effects of introducing the discontinuity, however, was studied separately for the different motion on simple tasks avoiding body motions.

Adhikari et al. [1] proposed to add iterative jumps (i.e. 'HyperJump') to continuous locomotion reaching faster navigation in large environments but without significant changes in orientation and sickness. The discontinuous animation was not, however, applied to teleport and/or compared with simple teleport. A similar idea was also proposed by Riecke [22], who merged continuous locomotion with jumps in a novel navigation control interface.

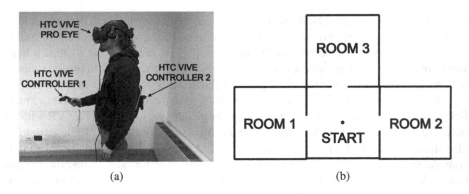

(a)   (b)

Fig. 1. (a) Hardware setup (HMD and Controller 1 for interaction and Controller 2 to track the torso orientation), (b) Map of the museum used in the orientation task

While all these studies provide useful ideas and insights on how to reduce sickness and maintain spatial awareness, we have seen that they presents some limitations making often not obvious to derive guidelines for the navigation control design in classic exploration tasks in VR applications. Furthermore, many studies are based on the assumption that the methods to reduce the sickness should be based on the reduction of the visual illusion of self-motion often referred to as *vection* [20], there is evidence of a decoupling of vection and motion sickness [17,29].

According to Webb et al., [29], vection is influenced by the peripheral vision, while visual-induced motion sickness seems to be influenced by central (foveal) visual stimulation or by eye movements, in particular, by the optokinetic response (e.g., the automatic movement of the eye following objects in motion when the head remains stationary) [28]. The relationships between sickness and vection are complex, and the outcomes of related studies are not always considered in the literature on methods to reduce motion sickness in immersive Virtual Reality.

Keshavarz et al., [16], tackled these issues and pointed out that *vection might be a necessary prerequisite for visual-induced motion sickness, but only in combination with other factors (e.g., sensory conflict, postural stability, eye movements, head movements, etc.*

This suggest that user studies aimed at assessing motion sickness in conjunction with other factors (e.g. orientation) should capture as much as possible fine-grained physiological measurements to understand the origin of the different symptoms. In general, there is a need for further studies to understand the complex relationships between locomotion control and user experience, as well as sickness, vection, and eye and body movements. This fact motivated us to design a novel experiment to investigate on them.

3   The Study

In order to assess the research questions outlined above, we designed a task to be performed in an immersive VR environment, and we asked the participants to experience it with each of the three locomotion techniques. The study had a within-subject design with 25 participants and it was exploratory in nature.

3.1 Materials and Task

We used the HTC Vive Pro Eye Head-Mounted Display for our experiments, as it allows the recording of gaze data and head movements. Subjects used an HTC Vive controller to guide the locomotion, while a second controller was positioned on the back of the user to automatically record the torso orientation data (Fig. 1a). The application was developed using the Unity framework and featured a Virtual Museum environment with 4 rooms arranged as shown in 1b. Each room contains 6 paintings distributed along the walls and 3 items, such as sculptures or other props, displaced around the room to create non-trivial navigation options (Fig. 2). Each item is associated with a plaque attached close to it on the wall or on the pedestal.

We used these plaques to define the navigation task. In fact, the plaque associated with each item displayed the instructions to reach the next one to be visited (for example, "Go visit painting with the lighting in Room 3" (Fig. 2f). These instructions are arranged such that the user visits all the items in the museum returning to the starting item and creating a looping path.

The task required the subjects to navigate for a fixed amount of time (5 min), and we counted the number of reached items to assess the locomotion efficiency.

To avoid order effects across different conditions for the same participant, we created three loops. Each loop starts from a different initial item, which is communicated to the user when the task begins.

As explained above, the application implemented 3 different locomotion techniques (which were the three conditions of the study):

- **Manual:** This technique implements a straightforward mapping of the movements captured by the Vive Controller's directional pad. On the vertical axis, we added the forward and backward directions of the movement while, on the horizontal axis, the left and right strafing can be used. The speed of movement, regardless of the direction, is 7 km/h. The forward direction is aligned with the camera direction, meaning the reference frame of the movement controls is the same as the camera's, projected on a plane parallel to the museum floor. In other words, the technique recreates the mechanics of the character's movements used in many popular video games featuring a first-person view.
- **Teleport:** our implementation of the instant Teleport locomotion control uses the tracked Vive Controller: when the user presses and holds the trigger button, a visible ray, directed along the device axis, appears to help the user to identify the target position (Fig. 2d). While the user can aim the device at any visible part of the environment, the viewport translation only takes place upon releasing the trigger button, provided that the ray points towards an empty spot on the floor. In order to provide feedback about the potential outcome of the teleport command, the ray is displayed as green if the target spot is valid (Fig. 3b) or red if not (Fig. 3a). If the button is released when the pointed target is valid, the viewport is then instantly translated to the x-y coordinates of the target.

Fig. 2. Navigation task in the virtual museum. (a) Starting position in front of room 3. The subject is asked to go in room 2 (b,c) find the painting with the Statue of Liberty (d) and read the plaque under it. The text asks to go in room 3 (e), find the painting with the lightning and follow the instructions there reported, iterating the procedure (f).

– **Teleport+animation:** This technique is a variation of the Teleport technique described above. The destination selection and visual feedback (the color of the ray) are the same. The difference is that, after the release of the trigger button, the viewport position is not instantly changed, but rather it is moved following a straight path towards the selected spot at a constant speed of 7 km/h. This value has been chosen because it is a realistic human walking speed, although slightly higher than the average [10]. Preliminary pilot tests confirmed that it resulted comfortable for users. In fact, we tested higher speeds like those proposed in [3], but they were not comfortable for users in our museum scenario. Both in the preliminary tests and the user study several participants reported slight discomfort in using the animated teleport because of the feeling of potential collisions with walls and statues.

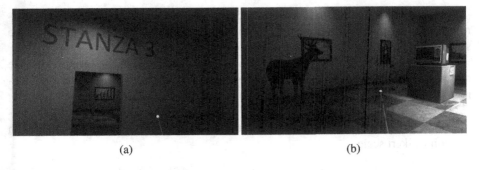

(a)   (b)

Fig. 3. (a) Teleport ray aimed at a not reachable position and colored in red. (b) When the ray is aimed at a reachable position the ray is colored in green and when the button is released the viewpoint is moved to the target. (Color figure online)

The main task assigned to the participants consisted of navigating the museum for a fixed amount of time (5 min) and visiting the different items. Each subject performed the task three times, each time with a different locomotion technique and following a different path. The paths started with the first instruction given by the experiment supervisor, asking to reach a particular item in a room, read the associated plate, go to the artwork indicated in the text, read its plate, and so on. To remove the biases due to the execution order with the different paths and locomotion techniques, the technique-path pair for each task was assigned following a Latin square arrangement. In this way, the same number of users had a particular path or technique in the first, second, and third trials.

We also assigned a secondary task, asking the subjects, at the end of each run, to indicate the position of 2 paintings and one sculpture on a map representing the museum's layout (shown in Fig. 1b). The paintings were chosen from the items the user had to visit, while the statue was just placed in one of the rooms and never mentioned in the instructions. We introduced this task to assess the effects of the different techniques on spatial orientation and awareness and eventually evaluate possible trade-offs with other effects, such as motion sickness.

3.2 Participants and Measures

We collected data with questionnaires (pre- and post-study) and automatically collected data from the VR application runs. In detail, the app recorded the head orientation, the torso orientation, and the eye movements captured by the Vive tracking systems. The app also counted the number of visited items for each navigation task.

We used Motion Sickness Susceptibility Questionnaire (MSSQ) for the pre-study measure of susceptibility to sickness, the scores were normalized in percentiles [12].

After each task performed in the different conditions, we administered a questionnaire to the subjects to assess the experienced sickness, the perceived presence, and task difficulty. The questions include those of the standard Simulator Sickness Questionnaire (SSQ) from which we estimated the scales for nausea, oculomotor, and disorientation

[15]. While we are aware that the use of SSQ to measure visual-induced motion sickness has been recently criticized [14], for this study, we decided to keep using it for the sake of comparison with the extant literature on the topic.

To evaluate the perceived presence, we used the questions of the igroup presence questionnaire (IPQ), and measured the scales of spatial presence, involvement, and realness, adding a single item about the sense of being in a place [23].

After the conclusion of all the tasks, we asked the subjects to fill out a final questionnaire, to have an overall assessment of the perceived difficulty and pleasantness on a 5-point Likert scale.

Table 1. Means and standard deviations for different measurements per navigation methods. Angles are reported in radians and eye movements were measured on the screen space plane with range $[-1,1]$ on both axis.

	Manual		Teleport		Teleport+anim	
	Mean	STD	Mean	STD	Mean	STD
SSQ Nausea	1.85	0.67	1.37	0.57	2.04	0.85
SSQ Oculomotor	1.35	0.51	1.35	0.54	1.80	0.53
SSQ Disorientation	2.77	0.85	2.02	0.79	2.79	0.81
IPQ Spatial Presence	4.18	0.85	4.12	1.02	3.88	0.87
IPQ Involvement	3.58	1.01	3.89	0.90	3.71	0.89
IPQ Realness	2.74	0.64	2.48	0.68	2.44	0.78
Post Difficulty	2.08	0.83	1.46	1.02	2.71	1.12
Post Pleasantness	3.67	1.09	4.17	0.96	1.96	1.00
Objects Visited	19.04	8.58	20.71	8.64	16.25	6.85
Objects Located	0.83	0.92	0.75	0.74	1.13	1.15
Cumulative Torso Angle	103.45	32.13	132.03	86.53	119.83	42.02
Cumulative Head Angle	173.15	39.76	298.54	63.54	216.04	41.28
Total Eye Movement	4643.82	1780.43	6264.48	1796.92	6126.62	1719.97

4   Results

Of the 25 participants, one has been excluded because of some errors in data collection. The remaining 24 subjects (14 males and 10 females) completed the required tasks. Most had no or few previous experiences with VR (respectively 9, and 10), while 4 participants declared some previous experience, and the remaining 1) had several previous experiences. Being recruited on the university campus, the large majority of the participants (21) were in the 20–35 years old age range.

In the following, we present the descriptive statistics for the collected data, including reliability analysis for the multi-items questionnaires and normality check for all the variables. The Mann-Whitney test (equivalent of a non-parametric t test) has been used to check the male vs female possible differences. The inferential analysis related to the research questions is presented in Subsect. 4.1.

We also controlled the possible effect of sex on the other measures because the extant literature has contradictory results ([19]. Although our study did not aim at investigating this difference, it was necessary to check its possible impact on the other measures.

The susceptibility to sickness collected with the MMSQ questionnaire was low (*mean* = 26.02, *std* = 27.91) and not normally distributed (Shapiro $s = 0.81$, $p < 0.01$). There was no difference between male and female participants (Mann-Whitney $w = 80$, $p = 0.576$).

Looking at the sickness experienced by the participants, all the three scales used from the SSQ questionnaire had good internal reliability (specifically, 0.803 for the nausea scale, 0.815) for the oculomotor scale and 0.66 for the disorientation scale. All the scales were not normally distributed (Shapiro, $s = 0.875$, $p < 0.01$ for nausea; $s = 0.907$, $p < 0.01$ for oculomotor; and $s = 0.901$, $p < 0.01$ for disorientation). There were no differences between males and females in either of the three scales (Mann-Whitney $w = 673$, $p = 0.621$ for nausea; Mann-Whitney $w = 702$, $p = 0.409$ for oculomotor; and, Mann-Whitney $w = 719$, $p = 0.303$ for disorientation).

For the IPQ questionnaire on presence, the reliability of the spatial presence scale was low (Cohen's $alpha = 0.154$) mainly because of one item that was consequently eliminated, the adjusted scale reached then the satisfactory alpha of 0.708. The reliability of the involvement scale was low too (Cohen's $alpha = 0.386$) and also in this case the elimination of one single item raised the reliability to a satisfactory alpha of 0.633. The reliability of the realness scale was low too but, in this case, all the items had low correlation among themselves: we, therefore, decided not to use this subscale. The scales of spatial presence and involvement were not normally distributed (Shapiro $s = 0.969$, $p = 0.077$ for spatial presence; $s = 0.972$, $p = 0.106$ for involvement). There were no statistical differences between males and females (Mann-Whitney $w = 644$, $p = 0.877$ for spatial presence; $w = 580.5$, $p = 0.574$ for involvement).

As objective measures, we first counted the number of artworks visited during each task and the number of objects correctly located in the post-task questionnaire. The count of the artworks visited in 5 min was normally distributed (Shapiro, $s = 0.924$, $p < 0.01$), with no statistical differences between males and females (Mann-Whitney $w = 728.0$, $p = 0.265$). as well as the correctly located query item count (Shapiro, $s = 0.801$, $p < 0.01$) with no statistical differences between males and females (Mann-Whitney $w = 564.0$, $p = 0.423$).

Concerning the eye, head, and body tracking data, we estimated the accumulated amount of eye movements and the orientation changes for both the torso and the head during the tasks in the three experimental conditions. For the torso, the measures of 6 subjects were missed in some conditions, therefore in the analysis below, the remaining 18 participants only are used for what concerns torso angle variations. The distribution of the eye movements was not normally distributed (Shapiro $s = 0.971$, $p = 0.094$) while both the distribution of the angles of torso and head were normally distributed (Shapiro $s = 0.95$, $p < 0.05$ for angle variations of the torso; and, $s = 0.952$, $p < 0.01$

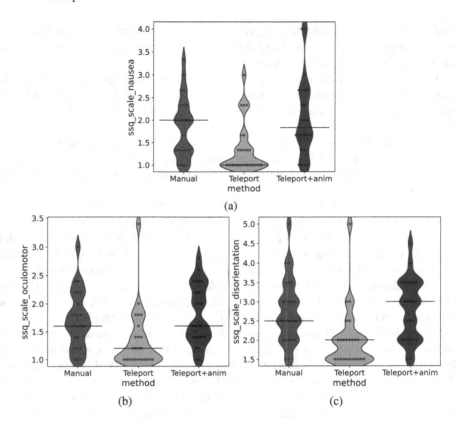

Fig. 4. Violin plot of the scales used to measure the effect of the sickness (nausea, oculomotor and disorientation) grouped by navigation method.

for the angle variations of the head). Yet, in both cases, there is a statistically significant difference in the variances (Bartlett's K-squared, $k = 17.415$, $p < 0.01$ for the torso and $k = 6.554$, $p < 0.05$ for the head), therefore we decided to use non-parametric statistics for these measures too. There were no statistical differences between males and females (Mann-Whitney $w = 467$, $p = 0.063$ for eye movements; $w = 480.5$, $p = 0.915$ for torso angle; and, $w = 537$, $p = 0.291$ for head angle).

Finally, for what concerns the post-study measures of perceived difficulty and perceived pleasantness, they were both not normally distributed (Shapiro $s = 0.837$, $p < 0.01$ for difficulty; and, $s = 0.881$, $p < 0.01$ for pleasantness). No statistical differences between males and females (Mann-Whitney $w = 733$, $p = 0.219$ for difficulty; and, $w = 651$, $p = 0.810$ for pleasantness).

The mean scores and standard deviations for all the measures are reported in Table 1.

4.1 Inferential Statistics

For the inferential statistics, we mainly used Friedman test as a non-parametric equivalent of the repeated measures ANOVA, since the data are usually not normally distributed. To assess correlations, we first employed linear mixed models and then, when significant, we used regression analysis to estimate the direction. As good practice in statistical analysis, we always reported non significant outcomes too.

With respect to $Q1$, all the three measures of sickness are different in the three conditions (Friedman $chi = 16.692$ $p < 0.01$ for nausea; $chi = 23.718$, $p < 0.01$ for disorientation; and, $chi = 17.452$, $p < 0.01$ for oculomotor). Pairwise comparisons using Conover's all-pairs test with Bonferroni correction reveal that the teleporting technique scores significantly lower with respect to the other two techniques, while there is no difference between manual and teleport+animation (Fig. 4).

We found that, among the correlations between each of the sickness measures and the susceptibility to sickness, the only one statistically different from zero is the oculomotor scale for the manual technique (Pearson's product-moment correlation $t = 2.144$, $p < 0.05$). Yet, a regression model between these variables demonstrates that the explained variance is relatively low (adjusted R squared 0.135) (Fig. 5).

Considering the research question $Q2$, for what concerns presence, there are no statistical differences on either the scale of spatial presence, or involvement (respectively, Friedman $chi = 5.448$, $p = 0.066$ for spatial presence; and, $chi = 0.026$, $p = 0.987$ for involvement). Yet, for the general presence (the sense of being in place [13]),

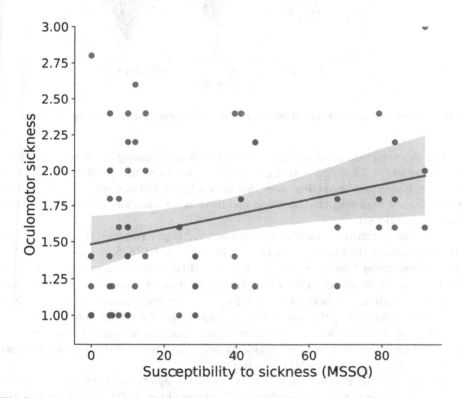

Fig. 5. Regression model for the oculomotor sickness (SSQ) and susceptibility to sickness (MSSQ).

there is a small but significant difference (Friedman chi = 12.299, $p < 0.01$). Pairwise comparisons using Conover's all-pairs test with Bonferroni correction show that teleport+animation is lower than manual ($p < 0.01$) but the other comparisons are not significant. In the perceived difficulty scores, there is a difference among the three conditions (Friedman chi = 16.892, $p < 0.01$). Pairwise comparisons using Conover's all-pairs test with Bonferroni correction show that teleport is perceived as less difficult than teleport+animation but the other comparisons do not reach significance.

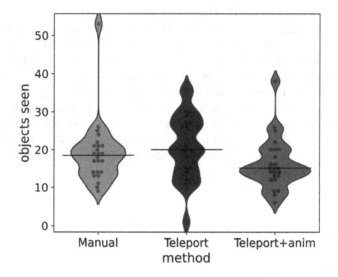

Fig. 6. Violin plot of the number of objects visited by the users grouped by navigation method.

For the perceived pleasantness, there is a difference among the three conditions (Friedman chi = 28.787, $p < 0.01$). Pairwise comparisons using Conover's all-pairs test with Bonferroni correction show that both teleport and manual are perceived as more pleasant than teleport+animation and there is no statistical difference between manual and teleport.

For what concerns the number of items reached (e.g. navigation speed), there is a difference among the three conditions (Friedman chi = 10.7826, $p < 0.01$). Pairwise comparisons using Conover's all-pairs test with Bonferroni correction show that the most significant difference is between teleport and teleport+animation ($p = 0.07$): in the latter condition, the participants ended up reaching fewer items. Yet, this result is most likely influenced by the movement speed that slowed down the whole visit (Fig. 6).

The analysis of the number of items correctly located by the users, to measure spatial awareness, (Fig. 7) showed no significant differences between the three locomotion technique (Friedman chi = 0.800, $p = 0.670$).

Considering the research question $Q3$, there are significant differences in all of the measures among the three conditions (Friedman chi = 19.083, $p < 0.01$, for eye movements; Friedman chi = 39.083, $p < 0.01$ for head angle variations; and, Friedman chi = 9.333, $p < 0.01$ for torso angle variations, in this last case, only the 18

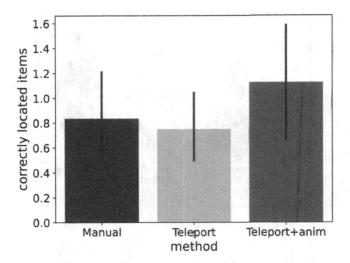

Fig. 7. Average number of objects correctly located on the map by the subjects at the end of each run, grouped by navigation method.

participants with full data has been used in the analysis). Pairwise comparisons using Conover's all-pairs test with Bonferroni correction show that the manual technique has significantly fewer eye movements than both teleport ($p < 0.01$) and teleport+animation ($p < 0.01$), while the two versions of teleport do not have differences (Fig. 8a).

The same post-hoc analysis shows that the manual technique has significantly fewer head movements than teleport ($p < 0.01$) and teleport+animation fewer than teleport ($p < 0.01$). The difference between manual and teleport+animation does not reach significance, but the tendency seems to be that manual is lower (although the standard deviation is pretty high) (Fig. 8b).

Finally post-hoc analysis for torso angle variations (Fig. 8c), the only significant difference is that manual is lower than teleport ($p < 0.05$) while there is no statistically significant difference for manual vs. teleport+animation and between the two versions of teleport.

Considering the possibility of explaining (part of) the variation of presence with behavior measures, we fitted a linear mixed model by maximum likelihood for each presence scale (general presence, spatial presence, and involvement) using both eyes movements and head variations (we did not use torso variation because of the missing participants). In order to account for the individual variations, the models included participants as random effects. The only significant model was the one for the general presence scale, and the only significant term was eye movements with a negative score: that is, higher eye movements mean a reduction in spatial presence. A further regression analysis for the three separate conditions (Fig. 9) reveals that the effect is significant for the manual condition only and that eye movements explain around 10% of the variance of the spatial presence in that condition.

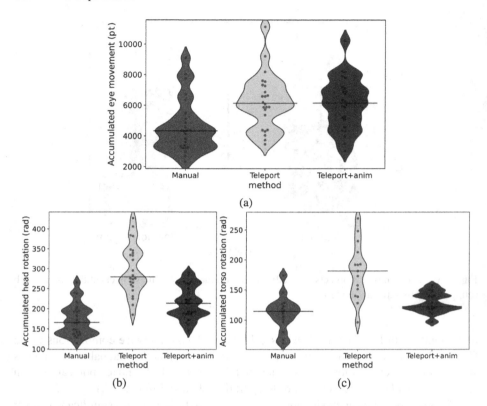

Fig. 8. Violin plots of the accumulated user's head rotation, torso rotation, and total eye movement. Eye movement was reported in points on the display screen space (range [−1,1] on both axes).

A similar approach with perceived difficulty and perceived pleasantness did not produce significant results. We also performed an analysis with all these measures by grouping users by gender; however, no significant difference was found.

Finally, for what concerns behavioural measures and sickness, we performed three separate correlation analyses, one for each technique. The analyses show that only for the manual condition there are significant positive correlations between the head movements and both oculomotor sickness (Pearsons's $r = 0.567$, $p < 0.05$) (Fig. 10), and disorientation sickness (Pearsons's $r = 0.484$, $p < 0.05$); the correlation with nausea sickness is closed to significance (Pearsons's $r = 0.375$, $p = 0.07$).

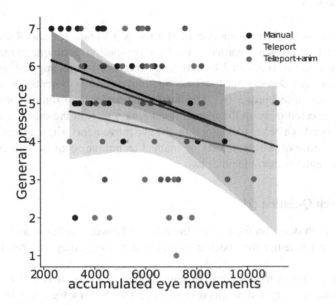

Fig. 9. Regression analysis for the three separate methods and the total eye movement on general presence.

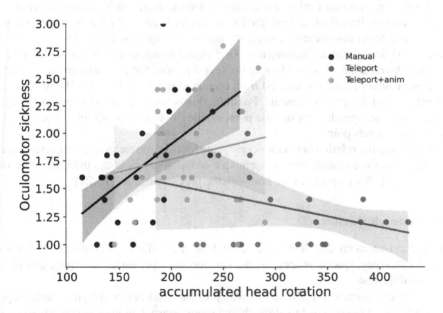

Fig. 10. Regression analysis (for the three separate methods) of head rotation vs oculomotor sickness.

5   Discussion

In several studies (see the discussion of Butussi & Chittaro [6] and Rahimi and colleagues [21]), teleport was regarded as the best locomotion technique in many respects. Although its value is confirmed by our study too, our results suggest some original insights that might deserve further investigation regarding potential benefits of the manual locomotion technique. In particular, (i) the oculomotor dimensions of sickness seems to be affected more in the manual locomotion than in the others and the movements of the head is a better indicator than the eye movements; (ii) it seems that it might give a higher sense of presence; (iii) the manual technique seems to induce fewer eyes and body movements than the other two.

5.1   Research Question $Q1$

Our first research question focused on the relation between sickness and susceptibility to sickness, and whether the specific locomotion methods may differently affect this relation.

For what concerns the relation between motion sickness in virtual reality and the (declared) susceptibility, our results do not suggest such a link for either instant teleport or teleport with animation, yet we found a small correlation with the manual technique for what concerns the specific oculomotor dimensions of sickness. This is apparently in contrast to some of the original studies on visual sickness (for example [12]), but it is worth noting that also a recent literature survey [27] raises some points of attention. Our results suggest that further studies might need to focus on locomotion techniques as a mediator of the effect. Indeed, the lower accumulated head rotation for the manual method and teleport+animation, suggests that users might be trying to minimize the effects of sickness with techniques involving virtual movement by looking forward and avoiding the creation of optical flow in the foveal region. Subjects who rotated the head more in manual navigation suffered from increased sickness (Fig. 10). We did not find a similar effect for eye movements. Possibly, this is because, in the point and teleport control, the user spends a lot of time pointing the ray toward a suitable target location and looking at this point.

Regarding the relation between sickness and locomotion technique, our results seem to suggest that the instant teleport technique induces less sickness than the other two techniques. In this respect, it is in line with the previous results [18, 21].

5.2   Research Question $Q2$

The second research question focused on how the different locomotion techniques impact efficiency, spatial awareness, the perception of presence, difficulty, and pleasantness of the task.

Our results seem to suggest, in line with previous studies (see [6]), that subjects perceive the instant teleport as less difficult and more pleasant, at least in comparison with teleport+animation. Nevertheless, the manual technique gives a higher general presence (the sense of being in a place) than teleport+animation, and the tendency suggests that it is higher than teleport (although the difference is not statistically significant). Furthermore, the manual technique is perceived as pleasant as teleport and not more difficult (in this respect, it might be different from the results of Butussi and Chittaro [6]).

We did not find a significant difference in the number of objects correctly located in the post-task questionnaire as this number was in general low with a high variance. However, the fact that the average count for the animated teleport is higher for the animated teleport (with a non-negligible difference) may suggest further investigation into spatial awareness as a function of visual feedback.

It is worth noting that, contrary to other studies (see [21]), we did not find differences in the spatial dimension of presence among the methods. In this respect, we can say that for the users, there's no trade-off between reduced sickness by using teleport and better mapping of the environment by using techniques featuring continuous viewpoint animation.

Our results may suggest that manual technique may be a valid alternative to teleporting in some cases. This was not found by Butussi and colleagus [6] where the authors did not measure differences in presence across the tested methods and possibly related to the different tasks proposed.

5.3 Research Question $Q3$

The third research questions was aimed at understanding whether the eyes and body movements are differed among the conditions, and whether those changes can explain presence, difficulty, or pleasantness.

Indeed, the manual technique seems to induce fewer eyes and body movements than the other two. Given the well-established relation between body and eye movements to sickness [19,24], these results seem to suggest that, at least in some situations, the manual technique might be preferred. Although we could not find any relation between body movements and sickness, there was a small but significant negative correlation between the variation of the head angle and all three measures of sickness: yet, in the manual condition only.

During the trials, we observed that many participants, while moving with either teleport method, preferred to only rotate their torso and head to aim the selection ray rather than turning on their feet to face the intended direction. This fact suggests that some other effect, such as the fear of moving in the real world while unable to see it, can influence the interaction and therefore needs further investigation. Yet, as a matter of speculation, the increased head and body movements for teleporting may be due to the necessity of recovering orientation after the viewpoint displacement. This recovery seems effective in keeping spatial awareness while not causing sickness, but we could not bring evidence in support, as the view is rotated but does not translate. On the other hand, the positive correlation between head rotation and sickness in the manual condition reveals that the sickness effects may be due to lateral optical flow in the foveal region while translating forward and suggests that potential solutions to reduce it can rely on specific training or visual feedback helping the user to avoid head rotation when moving. Rotations while translating forward are allowed in animated teleport as well, and the fact that it was not related to sickness in [3] is possibly due to the lack of scene texture creating the optical flow.

Although the evidence is still preliminary, an original result of our study is that, for the manual technique only, the amount of eye movements (but not of the movements of the head and body) seems correlated with decreased general presence. Nevertheless, for the other dimensions of experience, such as difficulty and pleasantness, we did not find any correlation, and this suggests that further studies are still needed.

Considering the goal of better understanding the relationship between vection and sickness [16], our results are inconclusive, and it is probably necessary to capture further information during the tasks, like camera motion, magnitude and localization of the optical flow on the image plane to have a better understanding of the phenomenon. In future studies, we also plan to extract additional information from the eye-tracking records (e.g., saccades) and estimate postural instability with external tracking.

Finally, it is worth noting that, contrary to other studies (for example, [19]), in our case, there is no difference between males and females in either susceptibility to sickness or the actual sickness experienced in the three conditions. We collected this data in order to prevent an impact of this variable on the analysis.

6   Conclusion

In this work, we presented the results of a within-subject study investigating the effects of three locomotion techniques on the quality of an immersive VR experience, including presence, spatial awareness, and sickness. We also tried to find correlations between those measures and the behavior in terms of eyes, head, and body movements.

Our study confirms some results already discussed in the literature regarding the reduced invasiveness and the high usability of instant teleport [6] and some of the issues related to teleporting with animation [21]. Contrary to the results of Bowman and colleagues [4] and Rahimi et al. [21], and in accordance with Bhandari et al. [3], and Langbehn et al. [18], we did not find that teleporting increase disorientation in terms of spatial awareness or reduced spatial presence.

Also, contrary to what seems to be suggested by Langbehn et al. [18] our study suggests that the manual locomotion technique might have benefits of both instant and animated teleporting with less problematic aspects.

An original result worth further investigation is that, for what concerns the user experience (i.e. general presence, at least pleasantness, and perceived difficulty of the task), both the manual and the instant teleport techniques score better than teleport with animation and, although there are no significant differences among them, the tendency appears to favor the manual technique.

We plan to further investigate these effects in future works and to further exploit the additional data acquired from subjects' behavior and physical response.

Acknowledgments. This study was partially partially carried out within the PNRR research activities of the consortium iNEST (Interconnected North-Est Innovation Ecosystem) funded by the European Union Next-GenerationEU (Piano Nazionale di Ripresa e Resilienza (PNRR) - Missione 4 Componente 2, Investimento 1.5 - D.D. 1058 23/06/2022, ECS00000043).

References

1. Adhikari, A., et al.: Integrating continuous and teleporting VR locomotion into a seamless 'hyperjump' paradigm. IEEE Trans. Vis. Comput. Graph. (2022)
2. Al Zayer, M., MacNeilage, P., Folmer, E.: Virtual locomotion: a survey. IEEE Trans. Vis. Comput. Graph. **26**(6), 2315–2334 (2018)
3. Bhandari, J., MacNeilage, P.R., Folmer, E.: Teleportation without spatial disorientation using optical flow cues. In: Graphics Interface, pp. 162–167 (2018)
4. Bowman, D.A., Koller, D., Hodges, L.F.: Travel in immersive virtual environments: an evaluation of viewpoint motion control techniques. In: Proceedings of IEEE 1997 Annual International Symposium on Virtual Reality, pp. 45–52. IEEE (1997)
5. Bozgeyikli, E., Raij, A., Katkoori, S., Dubey, R.: Point & teleport locomotion technique for virtual reality. In: Proceedings of the 2016 Annual Symposium on Computer-human Interaction in Play, pp. 205–216 (2016)
6. Buttussi, F., Chittaro, L.: Locomotion in place in virtual reality: a comparative evaluation of joystick, teleport, and leaning. IEEE Trans. Visual Comput. Graphics **27**(1), 12 (2021)
7. Chang, E., Kim, H.T., Yoo, B.: Virtual reality sickness: a review of causes and measurements. Int. J. Hum.-Comput. Interact. **36**(17), 1658–1682 (2020)
8. Dong, X., Yoshida, K., Stoffregen, T.A.: Control of a virtual vehicle influences postural activity and motion sickness. J. Exp. Psychol. Appl. **17**(2), 128 (2011)
9. Farmani, Y., Teather, R.J.: Evaluating discrete viewpoint control to reduce cybersickness in virtual reality. Virtual Reality **24**(4), 645–664 (2020)
10. Fitzpatrick, K., Brewer, M.A., Turner, S.: Another look at pedestrian walking speed. Transp. Res. Rec. **1982**(1), 21–29 (2006)
11. Frommel, J., Sonntag, S., Weber, M.: Effects of controller-based locomotion on player experience in a virtual reality exploration game. In: Proceedings of the 12th International Conference on the Foundations of Digital Games, pp. 1–6 (2017)
12. Golding, J.F.: Motion sickness susceptibility questionnaire revised and its relationship to other forms of sickness. Brain Res. Bull. **47**, 5070516 (1998)
13. Heeter, C.: Being there: the subjective experience of presence. Presence Teleoperators Virtual Environ. **1**(2), 262–271 (1992)
14. Hirzle, T., Cordts, M., Rukzio, E., Gugenheimer, J., Bulling, A.: A critical assessment of the use of SSQ as a measure of general discomfort in VR head-mounted displays. In: Proceedings of the 2021 CHI Conference on Human Factors in Computing Systems, pp. 1–14 (2021)
15. Kennedy, R.S., Lane, N.E., Berbaum, K.S., Lilienthal, M.G.: Simulator sickness questionnaire: an enhanced method for quantifying simulator sickness. Int. J. Aviat. Psychol. **3**(3), 203–220 (1993)
16. Keshavarz, B., Riecke, B.E., Hettinger, L.J., Campos, J.L.: Vection and visually induced motion sickness: how are they related? Front. Psychol. **6**, 472 (2015)
17. Kuiper, O.X., Bos, J.E., Diels, C.: Vection does not necessitate visually induced motion sickness. Displays **58**, 82–87 (2019)
18. Langbehn, E., Lubos, P., Steinicke, F.: Evaluation of locomotion techniques for room-scale VR: joystick, teleportation, and redirected walking. In: Proceedings of the Virtual Reality International Conference-Laval Virtual, pp. 1–9 (2018)
19. Munafo, J., Diedrick, M., Stoffregen, T.A.: The virtual reality head-mounted display Oculus Rift induces motion sickness and is sexist in its effects. Exp. Brain Res. **235**(3), 889–901 (2017) https://doi.org/10.1007/s00221-016-4846-7, www.link.springer.com/10.1007/s00221-016-4846-7

20. Palmisano, S., Allison, R.S., Schira, M.M., Barry, R.J.: Future challenges for vection research: definitions, functional significance, measures, and neural bases. Front. Psychol. **6**, 193 (2015)
21. Rahimi, K., Banigan, C., Ragan, E.D.: Scene transitions and teleportation in virtual reality and the implications for spatial awareness and sickness. IEEE Trans. Visual Comput. Graphics **26**(6), 2273–2287 (2018)
22. Riecke, B.E., Clement, D., Adhikari, A., Quesnel, D., Zielasko, D., von der Heyde, M.: HyperJumping in virtual Vancouver: combating motion sickness by merging teleporting and continuous VR locomotion in an embodied hands-free VR flying paradigm. In: ACM SIG-GRAPH 2022 Immersive Pavilion, pp. 1–2 (2022)
23. Schubert, T., Friedmann, F., Regenbrecht, H.: The experience of presence: factor analytic insights. Presence: Teleoperators Virtual Environ. **10**(3), 266–281 (2001). https://doi.org/10.1162/105474601300343603
24. Smart, L.J., Stoffregen, T.A., Bardy, B.G.: Visually induced motion sickness predicted by postural instability. Hum. Factors: J. Hum. Factors Ergonomics Soc. **44**(3), 451–465 (2002). https://doi.org/10.1518/0018720024497745
25. Stanney, K.M., Kennedy, R.S., Drexler, J.M., Harm, D.L.: Motion sickness and proprioceptive aftereffects following virtual environment exposure. Appl. Ergon. **30**(1), 27–38 (1999)
26. Templeman, J.N., Denbrook, P.S., Sibert, L.E.: Virtual locomotion: walking in place through virtual environments. Presence **8**(6), 598–617 (1999)
27. Tian, N., Lopes, P., Boulic, R.: A review of cybersickness in head-mounted displays: raising attention to individual susceptibility. Virtual Reality, 1–33 (2022)
28. Webb, N.A., Griffin, M.J.: Optokinetic stimuli: motion sickness, visual acuity and eye movements. Aviat. Space Environ. Med. **73**(4), 351–358 (2002)
29. Webb, N.A., Griffin, M.J.: Eye movement, vection, and motion sickness with foveal and peripheral vision. Aviat. Space Environ. Med. **74**(6), 622–625 (2003)

Sample-Based Human Movement Detection for Interactive Videos Applied to Performing Arts

Rui Rodrigues[1,2], João Diogo[1], Stephan Jurgens[3], Carla Fernandes[4,5], and Nuno Correia[1(✉)]

[1] NOVA LINCS, NOVA School of Science and Technology, NOVA University Lisbon, Lisbon, Portugal
`rui.rodrigues@estsetubal.ips.pt, jp.diogo@campus.fct.unl.pt, nmc@fct.unl.pt`
[2] SUSTAIN.RD, Escola Superior de Tecnologia de Setúbal, Instituto Politécnico de Setúbal, Setúbal, Portugal
[3] ITI/LARSYS, Funchal, Portugal
[4] ICNOVA, FCSH, NOVA University of Lisboa, Lisbon, Portugal
`carla.fernandes@fcsh.unl.pt`
[5] CITUR, Instituto Politécnico de Leiria, Leiria, Portugal

Abstract. In the performing arts context, video analysis plays a significant role in analyzing the artists' movement in educational and professional artistic environments. However, current research lacks user-centered systems for artists to directly engage with movement detection in their respective practice recordings. Our framework presents an annotation tool capable of automatically analyzing human poses of individual examples in real-time and presenting motion data in the form of simple reports.

At the core of this system, augmenting multimedia content by manually adding different types of annotations to the intended video segment is possible. Therefore, we developed novel features that combine automatic intelligent movement analysis with manual annotation capabilities for a more rewarding and efficient user experience. We demonstrate how pose estimation techniques can be employed to set up customized sets of human poses that can be automatically identified in videos. In addition, this paper discusses the results obtained from two system evaluation phases, where we report our findings based on expert feedback.

Keywords: Video Augmentation and Annotation · Human Pose Estimation · Movement Detection · intelligent tools · HCI

1 Introduction

Video visualization and interaction have become a constant component of our everyday lives with visible applications in our personal and professional spheres. With the growth of streaming technologies, online communication platforms and video-distribution websites such as YouTube, freely accessing, sharing and creating videos is a natural recurring

J. Abdelnour Nocera et al. (Eds.): INTERACT 2023, LNCS 14144, pp. 567–587, 2023.
https://doi.org/10.1007/978-3-031-42286-7_32

process in our ubiquitous environments. Thus, a subsequent natural need exists for mechanisms capable of supporting additional video interactions, for instance, by creating notes and comments.

Video annotation and augmentation are valuable techniques for highlighting specific moments and increasing the information and knowledge contained in videos [1]. Several annotation tools often employ these techniques in the form of different annotation types (e.g., text and drawing annotations) as is the case with the system we present. In this paper, these and additional mechanisms are the primary focus since it is here that we look for improvements regarding existing technologies employed in the performing arts context.

Performers are often subject to time constraints inherent to their rehearsal practices that, in turn, rely upon the availability of practice spaces [2]. Annotation tools can thereby present a viable solution to optimize the feedback and analysis given to artists independently of their established work sessions. Dance artists often review their work to improve performance, leading to situations where human pose and movement analysis are key.

Consequently, noteworthy research strives to optimize this process and enable artists to analyze their work based on recorded video content [3, 4]. However, adding specific information types and manually creating potential notes when working with human movement recordings can be time-consuming.

To partially tackle such issues, some systems create specific ontologies to help guide the annotation process [5] in which pre-defined concepts (e.g., body parts and their relative position) outline what can be added as annotations. This method presents a very limited approach from an expandability standpoint since creating notes relies mostly on the system's existing ontology.

Thus, to obtain further human motion data from videos, other systems rely on using external devices (e.g., depth sensors) [6] in order to extract human pose information and help direct the manual annotation features towards the movements present in videos [7, 8]. However, the set-up requirements can present an obstacle for artists trying to use those systems, since incorporating this additional equipment in rehearsal areas may prove to be impractical due to the spatial limitations of these systems.

The recent advances in AI-based algorithms for motion capture create novel possibilities for human movement analysis and identification, namely through the use of pose estimation frameworks [9, 10]. Human pose estimation now relies primarily on machine learning to identify the spatial location of a person's body parts/joints, also known as *keypoints*. Through this technique, our system enables extracting human movement data directly from a monocular video without needing extra devices [11, 12].

We present an annotation system that integrates the OpenPose library [13] to retrieve human motion data from videos. There are several examples of tools using OpenPose to aid human movement analysis in the performing arts world and similar contexts [14, 15]. However, our work emphasizes the need for dynamic mechanisms capable of supporting movement analysis when applied to educational and professional artistic contemporary practice and performance. Thus, we assert that empowering choreographers, dancers and instructors to create their own databases of movements using minimal equipment, i.e., monocular videos, is essential for this goal. Our approach is not solely reliant on the ML model but rather on its integration and subsequent new interaction possibilities.

Moreover, our human motion software module communicates with OpenPose using standard technologies with a loose coupling interface, enabling effortlessly switching to other pose models. Ongoing research in the computer vision field has led to new developments in algorithms for human action recognition [16–18]. Notably, as previously mentioned, the OpenPose model remains a reliable tool for accurately detecting human motion while presenting additional perks (e.g., detailed documentation and customizable output) [19]. For the annotation system, pose estimation enables users to easily visualize their poses by automatically displaying a simple skeletal representation on top of each respective person throughout a video. This type of visual content enables users to quickly review a person's overall pose and then further analyze each body part's relative motion. The movement and shapes performed by dancers can be meticulously perfected through systematic practice and coaching where even a slight deviation from the ideal form is susceptible to professional criticism and impact the performance of these artists. Additionally, new movement material created in improvisational situations can be analyzed and developed in choreographic and dramaturgical contexts.

Pose estimation visualization can thus enhance the assessment of dance practitioners' motion by simplifying the process of observing a person's body structure and positioning. However, some factors may hinder this process, most notably body part obstruction, distracting moving elements and strenuous movement identification. To address some of these challenges in the initial stage, we extended the existing pose estimation features by expanding the current interface to include individual selective pose estimation and automatic (pre-defined) motion recognition, which are further discussed ahead. To test the impact of these features on the annotation system, we organized a preliminary system evaluation aimed at a less specialized audience. The subsequent results were positive with great interest in these functionalities and their applications in specific fields of work such as education, sports and creation in performing arts. Our findings motivated the further development of this pose estimation software module, with some participants often mentioning recurring suggestions to address other possible needs. Thus, we identify the following main contributions:

- The architecture and implementation of a web-based annotation tool's pose estimation module; novel motion detection by extending from static to dynamic gesture recognition and movement report generation.
- Results from two empirical user studies in the performing arts; findings regarding the examined user interaction.
- Design implications on the effect of movement detection modules in the proposed system and how it can guide the future development of similar systems.

This paper has the following structure: We start by presenting the research problem and respective motivation in the first two sections. The work methods and interaction techniques are introduced in Sect. 3, followed by the technological description in Sect. 4. Afterward, Sects. 5 and 6 present the preliminary and main user studies with the respective results achieved. Finally, we draw our conclusions and suggestions for future work in Sect. 7.

2 Related Work

Analyzing and reflecting upon multimedia resources such as video recordings positively supports the learning of multiple activities in different areas [20–23]. Moreover, using annotations is a common practice in several daily tasks since taking notes is essential to retaining important information and helping our memory. Currently, recording and sharing videos is easy and inexpensive, rendering video annotation an easy and affordable solution for providing better feedback [24–26]. Therefore, over the last few years, we have witnessed the development of several annotation tools targeting a wide range of application areas.

2.1 Motivation

In the Performing Arts, video analysis of movement can serve different purposes. In education and training, annotated movement content can be used to learn new movements or to assess filmed execution of movement to improve performance [20]. Furthermore, such techniques can also be used for movement analysis from a more theoretical viewpoint, such as in performing arts history. An instance of an annotated movement can also be analyzed as a singled-out movement or be examined in its semantic context to look at its function and relation in a given choreographic or dramaturgical context [27].

Beyond the technical perspective of training in movement techniques, other important fields exist in performing arts education and training such as improvisation, composition and dramaturgy. In these contexts, annotation can support creative work through recognition, retrieval and analysis of important moments in rehearsal or performed work [28]. The same use cases of multimodal video annotation mentioned here also apply to professional artistic work and production to support the creative process.

For both educational and professional artistic use cases, a user-centered approach with regards to movement descriptions and building a database for retrieval and analysis of the annotations is highly beneficial. Particularly in the contemporary performing arts, there is a growing emphasis on unique collaborative creative processes and the use of improvisational techniques [29, 30]. As a result, the vocabulary (e.g., movement descriptions) developed and shared by collaborating artists is often idiosyncratic and context-dependent [31]. Thus, educators and artists benefit from a user-centered approach, which enables the annotator to define ontologies, keywords and search terms by themselves.

As mentioned above, the instances that comprise such user-centered databases and ontologies can be used individually and in relation to other instances, enabling a wide range of use cases including to teach or learn a movement; to perfect the performance of a movement; to identify new and unique movements; to understand the semantic context of the movement; and to improvise and compose movement based on its semantic context. Last but not least, the entirety of the user-centered database and ontology can serve to better understand and transmit a specific artistic oeuvre, style or genre.

2.2 Related Projects and Tools

Many representative examples of annotation systems exist; one of the pioneers was the Microsoft Research Annotation System (MRAS) [32]. This tool was initially developed to support work performed on video archives where users could interact collaboratively and asynchronously, targeting mainly academic environments. This application served as a valuable reference for future annotation systems.

ELAN [33] is one of the most well-known tools for manually annotating video content (text-based). ELAN is predominantly used for conversational analysis, the study of human interaction/communication, and is also employed in gesture studies.

In medical contexts, students, doctors and healthcare personnel can also take advantage of video content for practical applications [34]. Similarity, A. Pless et al. [35] describe how using annotations in such scenarios can improve the communication and comprehension of information in this environment.

In most sports, the training quality depends on the movements to be executed precisely to achieve the desired result and decrease the injury risk. For instance, the EventAnchor framework [36] supports data annotation of racket sports videos. This framework uses events recognized by computer vision algorithms as anchors to help users locate, analyze and annotate objects more efficiently.

With the Collaborative Lecture Annotation System (CLAS) [37], students work on pre-recorded videos by selecting relevant moments and annotating accordingly. After, the system gathers the collective data and combines it into a group graph representing the crucial points identified by all the students, thus enabling students to opt between using their personal sets of annotations and the group's resulting notes.

Besides academic, sports and medical settings, the performing arts are another excellent example where annotation systems can become an invaluable resource throughout the creative process. One of the main objectives of the TKB (Transmedia Knowledge Base) project was the research into the annotation process as part of the creative process for dance [38]. As a result, the team developed the "Creation Tool," which enabled its users to create multimodal annotations, including the standard text and drawing "digital ink" annotations in real-time. Later, as part of the BlackBox research project, a Virtual Reality Annotator prototype was developed to experiment with annotations in a virtual reality environment using Microsoft Kinect [39].

The Choreographer's Notebook [4] application enables choreographers and fellow partners to use the resources at their disposal more efficiently. Similarly to the Creation Tool, annotations using text and ink strokes are available, enabling the user to combine them when working on videos.

PM2GO [40], developed under the Motion Bank project, is a video annotation tool for dance analysis using text as the main annotation type. The annotation process consists of note-taking for choreographic reflection and scoring video recordings of dance and theatrical pieces.

The WholoDance project uses technology to preserve European dance cultural heritage [41]. A mechanism for working with dance motion was developed (WML - WholoDancE movement library). The WML uses descriptors for dance movements that were categorized into Action, Movement Principle and Movement Quality. This tool is available online and enables working with video recordings and annotating them.

Another recent example of a web-based tool that uses ontologies is TDAT [42]. This tool was developed to annotate intangible cultural heritage dance videos, enabling users to switch between different pre-built ontologies to better adapt to the different dance styles.

Riviere et al. [43] explored the decomposition of choreography into segments in order to support reflection on contemporary dance, learning and teaching. This software was developed to target individual dance practice and development rather than a classroom or collaborative scope. Their application (MoveOn) was developed for Apple's iPad.

MotionNotes[1] [44, 45] can assist both professional and amateur users working in any creative and exploratory setting where human performance analysis is essential. The available annotation types are text notes, ink strokes, short audio instructions, user-configured marks and URL hyperlinking. Sample-based human movement detection has been developed for this version, and the details will be described in the following chapters.

3   Methodology Description

Our methodology was designed with one major objective: to enable end users to easily create their database of movements without technical help. The goal is to enable users to process their performance videos against their database and automatically receive reports about the periods where those movements are performed.

3.1   Working with the Tool

Following the previous experiments and reflecting on the feedback received, an updated version of this MotionNotes was developed. The previous version of the tool enabled users to describe their goals using different annotation types and observe human motion through the integration of a machine-learning technique [46]. This new prototype extends this technology with different features, enabling the end user to process and identify movement without technical help.

Fig. 1. MotionNotes' working environment.   Fig. 2. Movements' database.

In order to better understand the interaction, we describe a fictitious scenario, in which "Anna" interacts with MotionNotes' new features. Anna starts by opening MotionNotes

---
[1] A version of the annotation tool is available at https://motion-notes.di.fct.unl.pt/.

in her web browser. She wants to upload the video from her last rehearsal, which is about one hour. She clicks on the "file menu" and selects the "import video" option. Anna browses her computer folders and selects the correct video file. Once done, she clicks "play" and watches several minutes of her performance (Fig. 1). Anna wants to seek, review and annotate a moment in which a given movement has been executed in the video. She starts by recording the movement and adds it to the movement database. To do that, she clicks on "settings menu" and then selects the pose option. A popup with the list of movements added before, and the option to add new ones, is shown (Fig. 2). Fields with the movement's name, description and a 3–5 s video sample are needed to save the new record. MotionNotes saves this new information in the server and processes movement information. Anna submits this form with the required data, returns to the rehearsal video and clicks on the trigger with the skeleton icon, which activates the human detection feature. A load panel is displayed for a few seconds; after that, the panel is hidden; two new visual components are added to the work environment (Fig. 3).

1. A layer with the human skeleton is drawn over the video.
2. The auxiliary popup "Motion UI" is activated.

She immediately selects the "Motion UI" popup and chooses the "report" option. Inside this option, Anna finds the information that the selected movement is performed three times in the video and the respective starting time stamps. After that, she jumps to the required video timestamp and annotates the movement with draw/text annotations in order to improve it with new ideas. Finally, she shares the new annotations and thoughts with her colleagues, using the MotionNotes' collaborative features with a direct link for the annotation work.

Fig. 3. Right: Regular video playing; Left: Video playing with human skeleton layer and auxiliary motion UI popup.

3.2 Technological Overview

MotionNotes is a single-page application (SPA), meaning that it was developed using a client-server architecture enabling users to share their videos and respective annotation work. No specific software needs to be installed to use this tool; the user's device only needs to have a web browser, which was selected as the application client due to its wide availability and compatibility with all operating systems.

Regarding the programming technologies employed, this software was implemented using HTML5, CSS3 and JavaScript (ES6) for the client side. The video streaming between the client and server uses WebRTC technologies. On the server side, Node.js, Express.js framework and MongoDB database were used for development (Fig. 4).

While the accuracy of the deep learning model is essential, our primary focus was on selecting a model that could facilitate the intended interaction mechanisms, rather than the model itself being the end goal. To achieve flexibility in changing the model when needed, we adopted a software development approach with loose coupling, which also enabled us to utilize standard technologies such as JSON for data transfers. This approach enables us to seamlessly swap out the pose model, while simultaneously taking full advantage of its subsequent interaction possibilities.

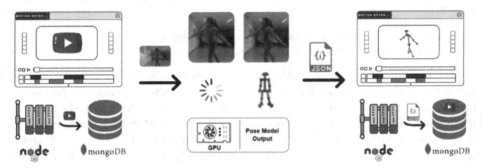

Fig. 4. System architecture. Left: video upload, storage and display. Center: pose processing unit and keypoints JSON generation. Right: JSON storage and keypoint display.

4   Preliminary Lab Experiment

At an earlier stage of the development of our system, the pose estimation module was adapted to include functionalities other than simple keypoint visualization displayed on top of each human figure throughout a video. In this preliminary user evaluation, the analysis target was entirely centered around the following pose estimation functionalities:

a) Base pose estimation: the skeletal images for each person in the selected video are generated and drawn over each frame.
b) Dynamic annotations: annotations such as drawings and text can be anchored in a keypoint, thereby following the movement of that individual body part.
c) Selective pose estimation: the isolated skeletal image of each person can be duplicated at an auxiliary interface with the option of selecting the intended human pose per frame.
d) Static gesture recognition: using pre-defined rules (e.g., feet distance > shoulder distance), the system determines whether or not a movement is executed throughout the duration of the video.

A total of 30 volunteers ranging from 18 to 52 years old (mean: ~26, standard deviation: ~8) participated in this study with a gender distribution of 18 males and 12 females. The participants reported variable professional and academic backgrounds. They also expressed that they often interact with video content as well as having an overall reasonable (semi-experienced) comfort level with video interactions.

Following a brief demonstration of MotionNotes' capabilities, the participants engaged with each of the mentioned functionalities using the provided materials to see each feature in a practical example (e.g., dance and sports). In order to evaluate the system from a usability standpoint and retrieve valuable feedback, the volunteers proceeded to answer a final set of questions containing the SUS standard questionnaire complemented by additional statements and questions in regard to the approached features. The empirical values show that user acceptance was very high, achieving a near-excellent acceptability score. Moreover, as it pertains to the integration of these new features into an existing intricate system, the respondents revealed that the efforts made toward a smooth integration of the development functionalities was perceived as rather successful.

This information reinforces the potential of these developmental processes in addition to positively validating this system's pose estimation module. In the complementary section containing module-specific questions, participants were encouraged to add personal comments on their experience. Some relevant recurring impressions of the system caused the following discussion topics to move forward:

– The movement recognition section relied on pre-defined rules, which limits the identification of new movements or poses without creating new rules manually.
– Automatic generation of movement reports present a feasible path for development, as users can receive a visual summary detailing the movement execution, which can be viewed in real-time.
– There is potential in the possibility of directing the system towards a movement-oriented context such as sports or performing arts.

The latter statement is in line with what had already motivated the creation of a workshop session applied to the basketball sports setting, which initially explored the application of these concepts in a specialized environment [46]. Similarly, the notion of generating reports was a topic of debate since it was deemed a possibly valuable resource. The experience gathered from the user-guided evaluation sessions deeply influenced the subsequent features and improvements, which are now the topic of examination. Overall, this preliminary evaluation provided initial evidence that the approached possibilities in movement analysis using pose estimation-based functionalities is a valid route of development.

5 Movement Recognition Implementation

The OpenPose library proved to be a reliable pose estimation model for accurately detecting human keypoints when compared to prior experiments with the system [46] and works well with known occlusion and multi-person overlap problems. Therefore, in our pose estimation module, the first layer of computation relies on OpenPose to output the location of each person and their respective body parts throughout the video. Understanding that some limitations inherent to the algorithm's behavior deeply influence the developmental process as a whole is essential. For each frame that exists in a video, the OpenPose framework infers keypoint data as if each image is independent from the previous and subsequent frames. As a result, even though humans are identified with a high accuracy rate, no explicit information is provided regarding whether the order of identified people in a given frame will be coherent with other frames, even if no visible differences exist (e.g., successive frames with only two people have switched indexes in the outputted data). Nevertheless, this isolated knowledge of how many humans appear in the video and their respective body part locations is enough to display a simple visual representation of their skeletal image. However, since the objective of this system module is to optimize the analysis of human movement throughout a video, retaining individual information regarding where each person is from a temporal standpoint is crucial.

5.1 Solving People Tracking Across Multiple Frames

Pose estimation frameworks are often characterized by this behavior of blindly finding human keypoints without keeping identification consistent throughout time due to it being able to drastically increase the algorithm's computational complexity. OpenPose addresses this problem by restricting the number of people that can be tracked to one, while also reducing the number of people that can be found using the standard algorithm to the same number. This significantly limits the ability to actually track people.

To solve this problem without generating unnecessary computational complexity, we assume that for scenarios when a given person in a video moves along a continuous path (i.e., does not teleport or instantly move to another location), then they can be tracked. This is achieved by preserving keypoint data from one frame to another, thereby enabling us to know the prior location of each person and propagate its similarity to the subsequent frames. Intuitively, this means that no assurances are made in cases with sudden changes in the video's elements in which individuals instantaneously exchange positions (possibly with different people). Even so, during a performance or practice, the recording device is often placed in a fixed position, meaning that even if some editing is performed on the video, those instances only represent a small fraction of time compared to the full video duration (Fig. 5).

Consistent temporal information about human positioning throughout a video enables us to isolate people individually and identify movement patterns that could only be achieved on a frame-by-frame basis. In contexts where movement analysis is a central goal, separating a given person from a group is often vital in order to provide personalized feedback (e.g., athletes and dance performers). Thus, the initial features explored in the preliminary lab experiment that go beyond general pose estimation tackle the following envisioned needs: isolating individual poses, emphasizing movement annotation and automatic gesture identification. Each need is materialized into a feature in the pose estimation module that can be accessed with an interactive control available beside the main video section (Fig. 6).

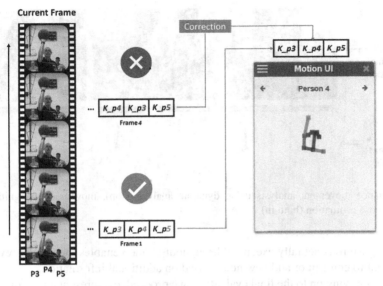

Fig. 5. Keypoints tracking across multiple frames.

5.2 Individual Pose

To individually analyze each person's movements, the interface displays selective pose estimation on a neutral background, i.e., users are able to toggle which individual pose they want to focus on in the range of the number of people currently present in the video frame. Since these features exist within an annotation system, movement correction and identification in this context are usually solved by manually adding annotations to the video to provide the intended feedback. However, movements, by nature, occur over time and with variable positions.

5.3 Dynamic Annotation

With tracking implemented, a novel annotation mechanism now enables users to anchor annotations onto a given body part and follow its movement for a specified duration. Moreover, following a given body part can help improve the attention span of the people receiving such feedback via annotations, since the conveyed message is transmitted more dynamically, which was further confirmed in the basketball preliminary case study.

5.4 Simple Movement Identification

Some recurring context-specific movements are often analyzed to improve the execution of technical gestures (e.g., *relevée* in ballet). Since subsequent technical analysis after a practice session may include several students or athletes, automatically identifying a specific movement transversal to all of the analyzed people involved in the recording can positively impact the observation process. Having a visual cue detailing whether a

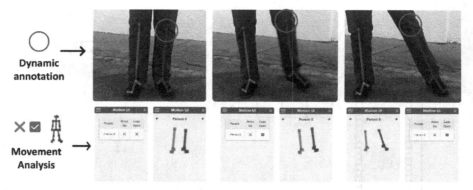

Fig. 6. Dance movement analysis using dynamic analysis (top), movement recognition and selective pose estimation (bottom).

specified gesture is actually executed throughout a video enables the person reviewing the content to confirm or add new notes based on additional information.

Before moving on to the final evaluation, we proceeded to present a version of these functionalities applied both to a general and to a more specific context (basketball practice and competition). The features were positively reviewed by both groups of participants, complemented by relevant remarks that guided the following development phases. Other than calibrating minor visual details, two noteworthy observations significantly impacted the ensuing work:

a) the lack of generated reports or summaries of the executed gestures and the movement recognition relying on static rule-based decisions - pre-defined by the system (e.g., are arms raised) - and therefore not being easily expandable to context-specific movement recognition.

b) human motion is complex and can be differently characterized depending on the environment in which it is applied. Consequently, dynamically adding a target (sample) gesture that can later be automatically identified in another video provides significant flexibility regardless of the intended context.

5.5 Sample-Based Human Movement Detection

To expand the movement identification feature, we proceeded to convert the raw keypoint data received from the OpenPose's inference into a layered object containing additional information other than simple keypoint locations throughout the video. For each frame, the resulting structure includes data that holds the IDs for each person as well as their body part locations and stores the comparison factor used to compare movement execution (e.g., body part distances and angles). Then, to conduct movement recognition, our system receives sample videos containing specific human motion, which are then attributed an ID and a name.

In the previously mentioned interface, said motion is visible as a dynamic movement with a visual representation portraying if it is currently happening in the chosen video. At first, the distance between keypoints in the sample and final video was used as the comparison factor to determine if the sample movement was being executed. However, despite serving its purpose for the initial testing, this metric was deeply influenced by other aspects, such as different movements resulting in similar overall distances and people executing the same movement but performing it in different initial positions, which could lead to false positive examples often due to the mitigation of the actual motion distances.

To solve this, we compare the differences in the keypoint angles between the people's themselves (sample video), which are then cross-checked for each person appearing in the final video. Therefore, only the actual movement differences with each human body as a reference are considered, thus nullifying possible positional bias. In cases where a close match exists in the similarity between such differences, the created movement is deemed as a positive (is executed) or a negative (not executed) example otherwise during that period. Moreover, when analyzing the proper execution of a movement based on a sample, a temporal tolerance or threshold is applied. This means that sample movements have the possibility of occurring in the video during a different timeframe (e.g., movement is executed faster) then in the initial sample and must thus be given a set tolerance (e.g., 2 s), considering aspects such as pose matching accuracy, timeframe discrepancy and noticeable pose variations.

Additionally, the need for generalized reports for the executed movements was reinforced in both preliminary studies, since it can present a valuable resource for retrieving a summary of each person's specified gestures, for instance, during a practice session. Given that temporal information always exists about a given movement's execution, as well as the person responsible for it, we display information regarding standard motion execution, namely: movement name, start time, duration and respective person.

6 User Study

The study was created and designed to understand two different perspectives regarding the movement recognition feature in the annotation tool. First, we will focus on usability, interaction, acceptance and respective user feedback. After that, we will discuss MotionNotes' performance by analyzing the results collected during the test with each participant.

For this second user study, we decided to contact a group of participants with higher expertise in a specific area due to our need for volunteers sensitive to human movement performance which could possibly benefit from the new features we propose with this work. Potential candidates were sports modalities like basketball, healthcare such as physiotherapy and performing arts with dance. After evaluating each of these scenarios, we decided to advance with contemporary dance. This decision was supported by informal interviews with several dance instructors, whose experience told them that our solution could be very useful in assisting the rehearsal periods.

6.1 Participants and Procedure

We invited 7 participants, all female, from a contemporary dance company. The participants' ages were between 14 and 27 years old. Participants had similar levels of technological expertise when using web browsers and video players - more than 85% self-reported having high experience with this type of software. Regarding dancing, the group also reported high levels of expertise: 29% over 20 years, 14% between 10–20 years, 43% between 5–10 years and 14% between 1–5 years.

Each participant had a half-hour session with our team. The testing sessions always started by demonstrating the tool and providing basic training on how to use it. First, the essential features, e.g., import video, play video and add annotations were explained. Next were the pose estimation features, followed by an introduction to the new movement detection feature. Afterward, the participants were asked to work freely for several minutes, record a specific movement into their database and test this information against a longer rehearsal video (this will be discussed in the next section). During that time, our team provided support whenever required. The participants were asked to comment on their thoughts while using MotionNotes and to offer new insights and constructive criticism about the experiment. These sessions all ended with a questionnaire to collect feedback about the tool, its new features and the quality of the presented solution (Fig. 7).

The questionnaire consisted of a demographic section, professional background and the following group of questions:

1. SUS standard questionnaire
2. Pose Estimation Integration
3. Movement Detection Feature

Questions consisted of 5-point Likert scales, ranging from 1- "strongly disagree" to 5- "strongly agree." The last question was open-ended so that the participants could express their suggestions.

Fig. 7. Participants performing movement tasks in the testing session.

6.2 Qualitative Results

Under the first group, the ten standard SUS questions, we obtained a SUS score of 81.78 (Fig. 10). This value is above the usual threshold (68), suggesting that this tool has an acceptable level of usability. This score indicates that after using our application for a few moments, users quickly gain confidence that the system is solid and could be recommended to others. Nonetheless, we must proceed carefully, even with this SUS score, given the limited scope of our tests.

The second group had the four following statements (Fig. 8):

1- *I found that the pose estimation features are a good complement to the annotation system.*

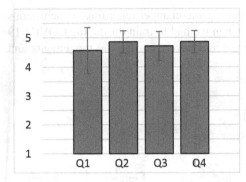

Fig. 8. Group 2 items' summary.   **Fig. 9.** Group 3 items' summary.

2- *I felt that it was intuitive to visualize the estimated pose through the skeletal figure.*
3- *I think that having dynamic annotations is a useful complement to the base pose estimation feature.*
4- *I found the skeletal view available on the Motion UI to be relevant in the system's context.*

In statement one the participants were asked to rate if they thought pose estimation could be of value for annotation work. The scores demonstrate clearly that all the participants are receptive to this feature. The answers to statements 2 and 4 tell us that the use of a skeleton layer over the person and the possibility of analyzing the movements on a neutral background was well received. Regarding statement 3, associating an annotation with a specific body part, the participants also had high scores and positive comments.

Concerning the last group of statements/questions about the new movement detection feature, we approach the following topics (Fig. 9):

1- *I thought that the automatic gesture identification feature has a lot of potential.*
2- *I believe that having dynamic movement identification can be useful in the performing arts context.*
3- *How often would you employ these functionalities when analyzing a video?*
4- *I find the report generation functionality to be of value in the performing arts context*
5- *How would you classify your experience with the MotionNotes interaction?*

All participants recognized a significant potential in this movement recognition technique, as we can see from the high scores concerning statements 1 and 2. In question 3, the scores were just acceptable. From the participant feedback and comments, we can conclude that they want to use this technique often, but not always. Regarding the report feature, question 4, the acceptance was good, but some comments about improving the report format were obtained. The answers to the last question about overall interaction during the test session were also positive.

User satisfaction while learning and using MotionNotes' new features was mostly positive, highlighted in several moments. One user (U3) said: "Really liked the idea and the software itself; anyway, I recommend a design a little bit more similar to Adobe." Another user (U1) suggested expanding the testing to other fields: "I'm also a P.E. teacher, and I think I could benefit from this software in my classes." Feedback from an additional user (U4) said that MotionNotes is a game-changer regarding asynchronous training. "I remember the huge difficulties when we had to train during the COVID-19 lockdown; with a tool like this, our teacher could have recorded the movements and shared them with us easily."

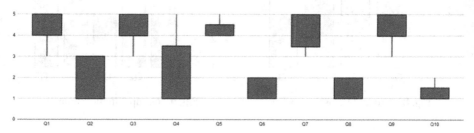

Fig. 10. Boxplot chart with System Usability Scale.

6.3 Performance Results

A key moment in each testing session was when we asked the participants to record a random performance from one of the last shows for approximately 20 s. Every one of these recordings had more than a dozen movements between jumping, rotations and the floor. The next task was for the participants to select a specific movement from their recordings and add it to their database of movements.

Then they could run the automatic movement identification feature without help from the researchers, read the reports and jump to the specific moments to confirm if the software was working as expected. Table 1 summarizes, for each session, the duration, the number of movements, precision and recall metrics.

Overall, the system's performance was positive, as we can see by the precision and recall values obtained. We started to analyze the false positive cases from P2, and the problem was related to a very similar movement, in which over half of the body was in the same pose. Regarding the false negatives, the software's internal scores were high in both cases and very close to detecting these movements. These issues could be mitigated later with a fine-tuning procedure that consists of adding a threshold applied to the body-part angles and distances.

Table 1. Movement detection performance.

	Duration	# Movements	Target Movement	Precision	Recall
P1	16s	15	Jump with crossed legs	1	0.67
P2	14s	14	Arms and legs open at the same time	0.33	1
P3	16s	16	Lift legs while on the floor	1	1
P4	29s	27	Body rotation from left to right	1	1
P5	36s	24	Knees on the floor and lift the right arm	1	1
P6	35s	23	Lift the left heel behind the body	1	0.5
P7	22s	14	All body rotation twice	1	0.5
	148s	118		0.904	0.809

7 Conclusions

This paper presents a web-based video annotation tool that enables users to create their own database of movements, process them to understand human poses better and query them against other performance videos. This innovation resulted from several discussions and suggestions obtained from our collaboration with users having expertise in diverse fields such as sports and dance.

Technical developments enabled implementing the required interaction while taking advantage of novel machine-learning techniques for human-pose estimation. The MotionNotes' movement module architecture successfully processes movement by using human pose information about body parts in each video frame. Inherent to these technical advancements, the subsequent design choices led to the development of two complementary UI components. The motion UI to display detailed movement data (e.g., individual selective poses) and the movement database's interface to store and analyze movement samples.

We propose a user-centered interaction methodology with an interface that enables users to work on their own movement examples and structure without external help. MotionNotes can automatically find the movements of interest, which provide many possibilities, 1) to analyze them in order to learn and perfect future performances; 2) to understand the different contexts where the movement is used to foster creativity. While working with movement features, users can still annotate the video and share their thoughts with colleagues. So far, our system has successfully enabled users in our case study to compare and annotate movement, which can be automatically detected and retrieved. In the future, we aim to develop this technique in order to isolate the movement of single body parts. For annotators in the performing arts, this could open up a variety of new possibilities. Particularly in dance, the movement of different body parts is frequently coordinated and (re-)combined, sometimes even across different genres and styles. Hence, the possibility to isolate and annotate the movement of different body parts could help to better analyze, teach and perform complex and unique combinations of movements. Additionally, in filmed records of dance improvisations, creatively intriguing and unique movements can be annotated, retrieved and choreographically explored in novel ways.

Lastly, this study's results highlight the importance and need for technology-supported strategies to achieve better creativity and productivity in application areas where human movement analysis is key.

Acknowledgments. This work is funded by Fundação para a Ciência e Tecnologia through Studentship grants: 2020.09417.BD (Ph.D.), UIDB/04516/2020/BIM/11 (MSc). It was supported by the project WEAVE, Grant Agreement Number: INEA/CEF/ICT/A2020/ 2288018. It is also supported by NOVA LINCS (UIDB/04516/2020) with the financial support of FCT.IP. Lastly, we would like to thank Virgínia Gonçalves, Ana Carvalho, Alina Teles, Bárbara Salvador, Berta Berton, Carolina Ramalho, Inês Costa and Mariana Colaço from Centro Cultural e Recreativo do Alto do Moinho for their feedback.

References

1. Torre, I., Galluccio, I., Coccoli, M.: Video augmentation to support video-based learning. In: ACM International Conference Proceeding Series (2022)
2. Dias Pereira Dos, A., Loke, L., Martinez-Maldonado, R.: Exploring video annotation as a tool to support dance teaching. In: ACM International Conference Proceeding Series, pp. 448–452 (2018)
3. Paul, S., Saha, R., Padhi, S., Majumdar, S., Das, P.P., Rao, S.: NrityaManch: an annotation and retrieval system for bharatanatyam dance ACM reference format. Proceedings of the 14th Annual Meeting of the Forum for Information Retrieval Evaluation, p. 22 (2022). https://doi.org/10.1145/3574318
4. Singh, V., Latulipe, C., Carroll, E., Lottridge, D.: The choreographer's notebook-a video annotation system for dancers and choreographers. C and C 2011 - Proceedings of the 8th ACM Conference on Creativity and Cognition, pp. 197–206 (2011). https://doi.org/10.1145/2069618.2069653
5. Lagrue, S., et al.: An ontology web application-based annotation tool for intangible culture heritage dance videos. SUMAC 2019 - Proceedings of the 1st Workshop on Structuring and Understanding of Multimedia heritAge Contents, co-located with MM 2019, pp. 75–81 (2019). https://doi.org/10.1145/3347317.3357245
6. Chen, K., Zhang, D., Yao, L., Guo, B., Yu, Z., Liu, Y.: Deep learning for sensor-based human activity recognition. ACM Computing Surveys (CSUR), p. 54 (2021). https://doi.org/10.1145/3447744
7. Kuffner dos Anjos, R., Ribeiro, C., Fernandes, C., Sartor, J.B.: Three-Dimensional Visualization of Movement Qualities in Contemporary Dance (2018). https://doi.org/10.1145/3212721.3212812
8. Ho, C., Tsai, W.T., Lin, K.S., Chen, H.H.: Extraction and alignment evaluation of motion beats for street dance. ICASSP, IEEE International Conference on Acoustics, Speech and Signal Processing – Proceedings, pp. 2429–2433 (2013). https://doi.org/10.1109/ICASSP.2013.6638091
9. Ashwin, T.S., Prakash, V., Rajendran, R.: A systematic review of intelligent tutoring sys-tems based on Gross body movement detected using computer vision. Computers and Education: Artificial Intell. **4**, 100125 (2023). https://doi.org/10.1016/J.CAEAI.2023.100125

10. Kong, Y., Fu, Y.: Human action recognition and prediction: a survey. Int J Comput Vis. **130**, 1366–1401 (2022). https://doi.org/10.1007/S11263-022-01594-9

11. Munea, T.L., Jembre, Y.Z., Weldegebriel, H.T., Chen, L., Huang, C., Yang, C.: The progress of human pose estimation: a survey and taxonomy of models applied in 2D human pose estimation. IEEE Access. **8**, 133330–133348 (2020). https://doi.org/10.1109/ACCESS.2020.3010248

12. Difini, G.M., Martins, M.G., Barbosa, J.L.V.: Human pose estimation for training assistance: a systematic literature review. ACM International Conference Proceeding Series, pp.189–196 (2021). https://doi.org/10.1145/3470482.3479633

13. Cao, Z., Simon, T., Wei, S.E., Sheikh, Y.: Realtime multi-person 2D pose estimation using part affinity fields. In: Proceedings - 30th IEEE Conference on Computer Vision and Pattern Recognition, CVPR 2017 (2017)

14. Li, Y.C., Chang, C.T., Cheng, C.C., Huang, Y.L.: Baseball swing pose estimation using openpose. 2021 IEEE International Conference on Robotics, Automation and Artificial Intelligence, RAAI 2021, pp. 6–9 (2021). https://doi.org/10.1109/RAAI52226.2021.9507807

15. Potempski, F., Sabo, A., Patterson, K.K.: Technical note: quantifying music-dance synchrony during salsa dancing with a deep learning-based 2D pose estimator. J Biomech **141**, 111178 (2022). https://doi.org/10.1016/J.JBIOMECH.2022.111178

16. Muhammad, K., et al.: Human action recognition using attention based LSTM network with dilated CNN features. Future Generation Computer Syst. **125**, 820–830 (2021). https://doi.org/10.1016/J.FUTURE.2021.06.045

17. Yen, C.C., Pin, T., Xu, H.: Bilateral pose transformer for human pose estimation. ACM International Conference Proceeding Series. Par F180473, pp. 21–29 (2022). https://doi.org/10.1145/3532342.3532346

18. Xia, H., Zhang, Q.: VitPose: multi-view 3D human pose estimation with vision transformer. 2022 IEEE 8th International Conference on Computer and Communications, ICCC 2022, pp. 1922–1927 (2022). https://doi.org/10.1109/ICCC56324.2022.10065997

19. Janardhanan, J., Umamaheswari, S.: A comprehensive study on human pose estimation. 8th International Conference on Advanced Computing and Communication Systems, ICACCS 2022, pp. 535–541 (2022). https://doi.org/10.1109/ICACCS54159.2022.9784965

20. Raheb, K.E., Stergiou, M., Katifori, A., Ioannidis, Y.: Dance interactive learning systems. ACM Comput Surv. **52**, 1–37 (2020). https://doi.org/10.1145/3323335

21. Towey, D., et al.: Students as partners in a multi-media note-taking app development: best practices. In: Proceedings - 2017 IEEE/ACM 39th International Conference on Software Engineering Companion, ICSE-C, pp. 334–335. Institute of Electrical and Electronics Engineers Inc. (2017)

22. Rodrigues, R., Neves Madeira, R.: Studying natural user interfaces for smart video annotation towards ubiquitous environments. In: 20th International Conference on Mobile and Ubiquitous Multimedia (MUM 2021), pp. 1–18. ACM, New York, NY, USA, Leuven, Belgium (2021)

23. de Sousa, L., Richter, B., Nel, C.: The effect of multimedia use on the teaching and learning of Social Sciences at tertiary level: a case study. Yesterday and Today, pp. 1–22 (2017). https://doi.org/10.17159/2223-0386/2017/n17a1

24. Sidi, Y., Blau, I., Shamir-Inbal, T.: Mapping active and collaborative learning in higher education through annotations in hyper-video by learning analytics. J. Comput. Assist Learn. **38**, 1752–1764 (2022). https://doi.org/10.1111/JCAL.12714

25. Tseng, S.S.: The influence of teacher annotations on student learning engagement and video watching behaviors. Int. J. Educ. Technol. High. Educ. **18**, 1–17 (2021). https://doi.org/10.1186/S41239-021-00242-5/FIGURES/5

26. Mirriahi, N., Jovanović, J., Lim, L.A., Lodge, J.M.: Two sides of the same coin: video annotations and in-video questions for active learning. Education Tech. Research Dev. **69**, 2571–2588 (2021). https://doi.org/10.1007/S11423-021-10041-4/TABLES/3

27. Rijmer, S.: Negotiating deliberate choice-making: Insights from an interdisciplinary and multimodal encounter during the making of a new contemporary dance. In: Dance Data, Cognition, and Multimodal Communication, pp. 15–37. Routledge, London (2022)

28. Jurgens, S.: Three methods of designing a workflow with multimodal video annotation in interdisciplinary choreographic processes. Multimodality and Performance, Fernandes, C. (Ed.). Cambridge Scholars Publishing, Newcastle upon Tyne, pp. 159–178 (2016)

29. Butterworth, J., Wildschut, L.: Contemporary Choreography: A Critical Reader. Routledge (2009)

30. Harvie, J., Lavender, A.: Making Contemporary Theatre: International Rehearsal Processes, p. 252 (2010)

31. Jürgens, S., Fernandes, C.: Choreographic practice-as-research. In: Performance as Research, pp. 249–274. Routledge, First edition. Routledge, New York (2017)

32. Bargeron, D., Gupta, A., Grudin, J., Sanocki, E.: Annotations for streaming video on the web. Conference on Human Factors in Computing Systems – Proceedings, pp. 278–279 (1999). https://doi.org/10.1145/632716.632887

33. Wittenburg, P., Brugman, H., Russel, A., Klassmann, A., Sloetjes, H.: ELAN: a professional framework for multimodality research. In: Proceedings of the 5th International Conference on Language Resources and Evaluation, LREC 2006, pp. 1556–1559 (2006)

34. Buono, P., Desolda, G., Lanzilotti, R.: Scenes extraction from videos of telementored surgeries. Proceedings: DMS 2013 - 19th International Conference on Distributed Multimedia Systems, pp. 106–111 (2013)

35. Pless, A., Hari, R., Brem, B., Woermamm, U., Schnabel, K.P.: Using self and peer video annotations of simulated patient encounters in communication training to facilitate the reflection of communication skills: an implementation study. GMS J Med Educ. **38** (2021). https://doi.org/10.3205/ZMA001451

36. Deng, D., et al.: EventAnchor: reducing Human Interactions in Event Annotation of Racket Sports Videos KEYWORDS. https://doi.org/10.1145/3411764.3445431

37. Risko, E.F., Foulsham, T., Dawson, S., Kingstone, A.: The collaborative lecture annotation system (CLAS): a new TOOL for distributed learning. IEEE Trans. Learn. Technol. **6**, 4–13 (2013). https://doi.org/10.1109/TLT.2012.15

38. Cabral, D., Valente, J., Silva, J., Aragão, U., Fernandes, C., Correia, N.: A creation-tool for contemporary dance using multimodal video annotation. MM'11 - Proceedings of the 2011 ACM Multimedia Conference and Co-Located Workshops, pp. 905–908 (2011). https://doi.org/10.1145/2072298.2071899

39. Ribeiro, C., Kuffner, R., Fernandes, C., Pereira, J.: 3D annotation in contemporary dance. In: Proceedings of the 3rd International Symposium on Movement and Computing, pp. 1–4. ACM, New York, NY, USA (2016)

40. de Lahunta, S., Jenett, F.: Making digital choreographic objects interrelate. In: Performing the Digital, pp. 63–80. transcript Verlag (2016)

41. Rizzo, A., et al.: WhoLoDancE: whole-body interaction learning for dance education. In: CEUR Workshop Proceedings, pp. 41–50 (2018)

42. Lagrue, S., et al.: An Ontology Web Application-based Annotation Tool for Intangible Culture Heritage Dance Videos (2019). https://doi.org/10.1145/3347317.3357245

43. Rivière, J.P., Alaoui, S.F., Caramiaux, B., Mackay, W.E.: Capturing movement decomposition to support learning and teaching in contemporary dance. Proc ACM Hum Comput Interact. **3** (2019). https://doi.org/10.1145/3359188

44. Rodrigues, R., Madeira, R.N., Correia, N.: Exploring the user interaction with a multimodal web-based video annotator. Lecture Notes of the Institute for Computer Sciences, Social-Informatics and Telecommunications Engineering, LNICST. 429 LNICST, pp. 13–22 (2022). https://doi.org/10.1007/978-3-030-99188-3_2/COVER
45. Rodrigues, R., Madeira, R.N., Correia, N., Fernandes, C., Ribeiro, S.: Multimodal web based video annotator with real-time human pose estimation. Lecture Notes in Comput-er Science (including subseries Lecture Notes in Artificial Intelligence and Lecture Notes in Bioin-formatics). 11872 LNCS, pp. 23–30 (2019). https://doi.org/10.1007/978-3-030-33617-2_3/COVER
46. Diogo, J., Rodrigues, R., Madeira, R., Correia, N.: Video annotation tool using human pose estimation for sports training. ACM International Conference Proceeding Series, pp. 262–265 (2022). https://doi.org/10.1145/3568444.3570592

Skillab - A Multimodal Augmented Reality Environment for Learning Manual Tasks

Ambika Shahu[1]([envelope]), Sonja Dorfbauer[1], Philipp Wintersberger[2], and Florian Michahelles[1]

[1] TU Wien, Vienna, Austria
{ambika.shahu,sonja.dorfbauer,florian.michahelles}@tuwien.ac.at
[2] FH Hagenberg, Hagenberg, Austria
philipp.wintersberger@fh-hagenberg.at

Abstract. The paper investigates the usage of AR-based systems in teaching manual skills. We propose Skillab, a novel AR-based scaffolding system. It aids in the learning of manual work and functions as a multimodal immersive tool for feedback, including muscle actuation. As our initial investigation, we made a floor lamination tutorial. We evaluated our system's performance and user experience in comparison to traditional paper instructions. With 20 participants, we conducted a between-group user study and obtained both qualitative and quantitative data. In terms of task performance, learnability, and overall user experience, Skillab significantly outperformed conventional paper instructions. In contrast to learning from paper instructions, Skillab training demonstrated a significant improvement in the systematic rating on the quality of the performed task. We believe that by demonstrating the potential of immersive multi-modal feedback technology for skill-building, researchers would be motivated to explore this area further.

Keywords: Augmented Reality · Immersiveness · Skill Building · Muscle Actuation

1 Introduction

Augmented reality (AR) can be considered as an interactive, reality-based display environment that integrates actual and computer-based scenes and images to create a seamless yet improved perspective of the world [2, 3, 36, 39]. Recent developments in AR have a great deal of promise to be influential in many industries, particularly education and training. Chang indicates that various researchers have proposed that AR can help learners improve their educational realism-based practices and increase their eagerness to learn [4]. Implementing AR in education and training is still quite difficult due to problems with its

Supplementary Information The online version contains supplementary material available at https://doi.org/10.1007/978-3-031-42286-7_33.

integration with conventional learning methods, the expense of developing and maintaining the AR system, and a general aversion to new technologies [20].

Pan and colleagues investigated how a virtual learning environment (VLE) could be used in education to facilitate collaboration on learning, training, and entertainment [27]. The findings showed that the suggested VLE could improve, inspire, and stimulate learners' comprehension of certain events that the conventional learning strategy could not readily do. Under a virtually enjoyable environment, users can learn quickly and with interest. Similarly, AR can be used to expand the user's range of understanding while simultaneously presenting facts and information in a real-world context [17]. Wang and colleagues examined the most recent advances and innovations in the field of AR technologies in formal and informal learning [40]. They categorized the benefits of adopting AR in training and education into the following three groups: a) Learner outcomes-improved academic performance, higher drive for learning, better comprehension, a good attitude toward learning, and increased satisfaction; b) Pedagogical contributions and interactions—improved enjoyment, boosted learner engagement, encouraged curiosity, offered chances for collaboration and encouraged self-learning; and c) Other—enables the visualization of oblique or abstract ideas, is simple for learners to use, and requires less material. Similar research has been done by Tang, but the effectiveness of learning compared to conventional methods has not been thoroughly examined [38].

With the recent COVID-19 pandemic, when people have limited access to and contact with in-person learning facilities, systems based on AR offer the flexibility to pick up new skills without depending on an expert. This makes learning increasingly hands-free and immersive. Users are able to do the activity using both hands while still paying attention to the task instructions. This technology has the potential to offer audio and visual feedback at the appropriate points in the learning process. Also, the tangibility dimension is necessary to fully appreciate skill-building in digital systems. For example, in order to simulate the sensation of blending paint with a finger, [35] built a special tangible display that resembles liquid for mobile, digital color mixing. Electrical muscle stimulation (EMS) has been used to collaborate on the creation of visual art pieces. Authors used EMS to simulate the process of painting, allowing the audience to direct the artist's brushstrokes [5].

To contribute to the field of AR education and learning, we introduce Skillab, an "AR-based craft-work learning system". It enables learners to follow a step-by-step tutorial for learning and developing floor lamination skills while using real-world tools and objects to promote learning and playful experiences. Utilizing computer vision to examine their progress, Skillab uses AR to deliver in-situ feedback. Using Skillab, we also demonstrate how muscle actuation methods can be leveraged to offer haptic assistance for guiding motoric action. We used a simple hammering demonstration to gauge people's initial impressions of on-body actuation technology. Thus, our multimodel system includes visual, auditory, and haptic components in its distinct learning processes. We compared it to the printed manuals as many toolkits on the market still come with a lengthy and complex printed manual of instructions. To learn the skill, users are expected to read through the illustrated instruction manual and make sense of it. In order to further enhance our AR-based solution, we compared the advantages and disadvantages of print instructions with AR. Our research questions are exploratory in nature: **(1) What are the key advantages and challenges of the "AR-based craft-work learning system" approach to skill-building compared to traditional instructions? (2) What aspects of Skillab seem to assist and encourage learning? (3) What impact do multimodal feedback interactions have on the user experience?**

To evaluate Skillab, we implemented floor lamination as the craft in a between-group study with 20 participants. While one group followed traditional paper instructions, the other group completed the tutorial using the Skillab application. We calculated multiple performance indicators and discovered that participants using Skillab made fever errors when re-creating the task. Participants using Skillab reported a better user experience, based on the evaluation of video recordings and a post-experiment survey. However, some participants reported issues with the Skillab tutorial and provided valuable feedback for improving the system.

In this paper, we contribute with: a) the concept for a novel AR-based application incorporating muscle actuation technology to learn craft-work; The research's novelty resides in its ability to deliver muscle actuation feedback without sacrificing user agency; b) user study results that show how users can interact with our application and what kind of feedback was found to be useful; c) insights on how people can be encouraged and inspired to learn new skills by utilizing immersive environments. As a result of their improved user experience and engagement with the AR-based system, our participants expressed a greater interest in using it to learn new skills.

2   Related Work

Through immersive experiences and multi-modal feedback including muscle actuation, our work aims to teach users how to laminate a floor. We draw upon the following theoretical constructs [16]:

- *Structure-Behavior-Function framework (SBF)*: SBF divides complex systems into three categories: structure, which consists of the fundamental parts and their connections; behavior, which describes how each element of the structure behaves both individually and collectively; and function, which describes the goal of the system as a whole or its parts [13]. With this three-pronged strategy, the SBF framework may methodically draw users' attention to essential elements of the craftwork and assist them in dissecting and visualizing the relationships that are often difficult to understand [10]. The SBF framework is put into practice by Skillab. It explains each component's role in relation to the others clearly and step by step.
- *Constructionism*: According to this learning theory, learning occurs "felicitously" when learners create and tinker with tangible objects [28,34]. We employed AR technology because it allows users to interact with real tools and objects.

– *Scaffolding*: Scaffolding can come in a variety of ways, from suggestions for task breakdowns to coaching and prompts, all of which aid learners in completing work that might otherwise be too difficult [30]. We offered users AR-mediated scaffolds that make conceptual understanding and craft design simpler.

2.1 Skill-Building and AR

The most common method of learning a craft is through an apprenticeship, which involves observing an expert craftsperson and getting feedback as the skills are repeatedly practiced [9]. Undoubtedly, having an expert present provides for professional demonstration and personalized comments. Nevertheless, the current traditional approach has a number of drawbacks. The apprentice has a high level of dependence on the instructor because the majority of learning is done through observation [6]. A skilled practitioner might have to repeat something multiple times because a learner might not be able to comprehend and remember it [26]. The COVID-19 pandemic has shown that physical presence is not always possible. In the conventional learning process, it takes a while for a student to finish each task or activity. This makes the actual learning process dull and uninteresting. The traditional method's constrained viewing angle can lead to learning difficulties. Additionally, learners find it difficult to visualize bodily motion in its entirety. Nawahdah and Inoue created a system that interactively modifies the learner's point of view and displays the instructor's mobility in a 3D virtual environment, suggesting that the system increases the effectiveness of learning [25]. Anderson introduced a system that shows the difference between learners' motion and instructed motion by employing an augmented reality mirror to teach full-body motion. When compared to traditional video learning, the system performed better in terms of learner performance [1].

Iyobe described and assessed a mobile virtual traditional crafting presentation system that consists of a Content Browsing Mobile Application and a content management web application [14]. The former offers a wide range of conventional craft information and a strong sense of immersion through AR content. The latter controls how the Content Browsing Mobile Application handles information on traditional crafts and techniques. Hiyama approached with the intention of skill transmission and preservation, but in a more integrated manner using a variety of sensors, giving the numerical tacit knowledge of professionals a closer look [12]. They developed a comprehensive framework for artisanship's digital preservation. For Kamisuki (Japanese traditional craftworks), they employed projection-based augmented reality displays that superimposed expert motion on the wooden tool. The quality of the paper produced by learners and the performance of the coaching expert were both enhanced by quantized motion data presentation. Thus, interactive simulation systems show potential in improving learners' conceptual understandings [31,41]. Drawing from all of these strategies, Skillab stands out due to its emphasis on user experience, muscle actuation technology, and step-by-step real-time scaffolding.

2.2   Electrical Muscle Stimulation

EMS mimics the body's natural electrical impulses by introducing a small electrical current into the muscles, which can cause muscle contraction and, as a result, movement of the body [19,29]. A calibration procedure is necessary to ensure pain-free functioning because the amount of force needed to activate a muscle varies between body parts and users [18]. Due to the fact that EMS directly writes to the muscles creating motor movements, it can offer a variety of unique interaction scenarios. It can be used to offer haptic feedback [24] by varying stimulus parameters (i.e., amplitudes, pulse widths, frequencies). In an augmented reality tennis game, Jain and colleagues used EMS on the wrist muscles to simulate the impact of a ball striking a racket [15]. Impacto used EMS in conjunction with tactile feedback (a solenoid tapping the skin) to replicate the feeling of striking or being hit in VR boxing [22]. Lopes showcased a mobile device that uses EMS to provide mid-air force feedback for Mixed Reality games and experiences [23]. Their solution was centered on the HoloLens headset, which frees users' hands and enables them to interact fully with both virtual and real-world objects, including furniture, appliances, and props.

EMS was also used for assistance and training. Ebisu and team, for instance, regulated users' movements by actuating both their arms and legs to teach users how to play percussion instruments [7]. Even though there were no professional percussionists present, the students were nevertheless able to pick up the rhythm. One hand's beat and the rhythm of both hands can be taught to students at the same time. It was possible to play drum beats that required both arm and foot motion. Unfortunately, there is a trade-off between the sense of agency and haptic support [37]. Shahu brought attention to the significance of maintaining user control. The study's findings imply that users should always be in charge. To avoid being taken off guard, they should be psychologically and physically prepared. Hence, based on the literature, it was crucial that we keep the user's sense of agency intact when they engage in activities with Skillab in order to provide them with a more authentic experience [8,32,33]. We adopted a wake-word activation method in our study, for users to have the upper hand and control over the system.

3   Skillab

We introduce the AR-based learning application "Skillab", a Unity 3D-based program that includes the Vuforia Engine 10.8 as well as the Microsoft Mixed Reality Toolkit MRTK. It utilizes Microsoft Hololens 2 as the digital eyewear for the prototype development.

3.1   Development

AR-Based System. The AR environment displays step-by-step explanations including a textual summary, an illustration, and a recorded voice-over. An exemplary step with its description can be seen in Fig. 1. Four sections make up the instruction panel. First, there is a progress bar at the top that displays how far you have progressed, followed by a text description on the left of the panel. On the right, there are graphics that illustrate the task at hand and the tool needed.

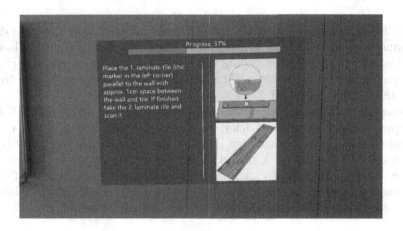

Fig. 1. Instructions board with step-wise descriptions. Example: "Place the 1. laminate tile (with the marker in the left corner) parallel to the wall with approx. 1cm space between the wall and tile. If finished, take the 2. laminate tile and scan it."

The primary functionality of the AR Guide, the detection of actual objects in the real environment, is made possible by the Vuforia Engine. The framework offers a marker-based detection called *VuMarks*. *VuMarks* are completely self-customizable markers that encode a variety of unique IDs into one marker design, comparable to QR-Codes. In our scenario, there are nine separate tools and items with individual *VuMarks*. Detecting a *VuMark* is rather easy; all that is required is for the user to hold the object and look directly at the marker through the Hololens at a distance of approx. 20 to 30 cm. When the marker is successfully detected, an event is triggered, a sound indicates that the scanning was successful, and the appropriate task instructions are displayed.

The user can interact with the visualization and holograms via touch or speech in addition to seeing them through Microsoft's Mixed Reality Toolkit MRTK 2. Importantly, the *Interactable* component, which capsules the input and event handling, was employed[1]. An example of how it is employed is the voice command that participants used to start the guide. Following a brief explanation of the craft, users must speak "Vumarks" in order to start the application. It creates the impression that someone is observing them and understanding what they are doing. The *Manipulation handler*, which makes it possible to move, scale, or rotate a hologram, is another crucial component. In our case, this makes it

---

[1] https://docs.microsoft.com/en-us/windows/mixed-reality/mrtk-unity/mrtk2/features/ux-building-blocks/interactable?view=mrtkunity-2022-05, accessed on 14.07.2022.

possible to move the screen, which displays the instructions for the current work at hand, to the user's desired location for looking up the information[2]. The AR Environment incorporates both functional software and simulated functionality through a Wizard of Oz methodology, further described in Sect. 4.

EMS. The hardware for the EMS is an off-the-shelf, medically approved device we connected with Adafruit Feather 32u4 Bluefruit. Additionally, it has two channels, with channel 1 controlling the contraction of the biceps and channel 2 the contraction of the triceps. With the help of relays, it was feasible to turn the EMS channel on and off.

Using the Arduino software IDE for programming, we first set pins 6 and 9 to output. Following a 1000ms delay, we toggle both pins high and low, causing the arm to move upward when high (Fig. 2a) and downward when low (Fig. 2b). The muscle is actuated for a period of 1000ms, either lifting or dropping the arm up or down. Since this is a subjective parameter, it can be altered for each participant if they are unable to work at this pace during calibration. This time period was found to be the ideal time for the majority of people.

3.2   Design

When the AR software is first launched, users enter the Instruction mode, where they see an instruction screen and hear a voiceover outlining the goal and subsequent steps. After uttering "VuMarks", the users enter the Demo mode, where the basic controls, such as moving and understanding the layout of the instruction panel (Fig. 1), are described. Only 35% of the participants in our study (see Sect. 4.2) have experimented with augmented reality using digital eyeglasses like the Hololens, it was crucial to give the participants adequate time to become familiar with the controls and the technology. The demo mode instructs the user to scan the first required object after explaining how to scan things to fetch further details. After selecting the appropriate tool, a transition that the user cannot see occurs, and the main guide, which gives a detailed explanation of the process starts.

Since individuals complete tasks at a different paces - some people may need more time to review the task, whereas others may finish it faster by merely listening to the voiceovers. Therefore, automated skipping, for instance, depending on the time is impractical. Therefore, the Wizard of Oz technique is chosen for some parts. It offers the user a wide range of benefits, including the freedom to work unhindered throughout the creation of the craft and smooth transactions between processes. The participant is given instructions to grab the new object, scan and use it till the final step. The EMS tool is activated over a Wizard of Oz voice command if it is the final step, the step when the user must use a hammer to fix the tiles. This guarantees that users have control over when they wish to

---

[2] https://docs.microsoft.com/en-us/windows/mixed-reality/mrtk-unity/mrtk2/
features/ux-building-blocks/manipulation-handler?view=mrtkunity-2022-05,
accessed on 14.07.2022.

begin and stop allowing the system to actuate their muscles. Therefore, to start or stop EMS, the user must say "Start EMS" or "Stop EMS" respectively. In the final step of the guide, where the laminate tiles must be secured so they are not simply clicked but settled together, the EMS system aids the participants. As shown in Fig. 2a and b, the fixing is done by pounding on a woodblock that is positioned at the short side of a laminate row. Two muscles, the biceps, and triceps must be alternately activated to replicate the arm movement of hammering. Consequently, two electrode patches are each placed on both muscles.

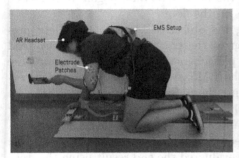 

(a) EMS supporting the arm up   (b) EMS supporting the arm down

Fig. 2. Participant receiving EMS assistance in the last tutorial stage

4   User Study

A portion of the study used the Wizard of Oz technique, due to the fact that every person requires a varied amount of time to finish a task. VuMarks were used to automate the scanning and consequently the identification of the tools and objects. Whereas the wizard pressed the key once the user had finished a step to display the next step using an obscured keyboard, it gave the impression that the system had fully understood the user's actions. By moving on to the next segment of the guide at the appropriate point, the Wizard assisted the participants. The Wizard of Oz technique creates the idea that the AR Environment is responsive in nature. Because of this, the participants get a good guided laminating experience, allowing them to completely concentrate on the craft. The process of laminating the floor was condensed into 10 basic steps with 4 tools and 8 pieces of material (Fig. 3a). The primary goal was to gradually introduce the fundamental procedures for this craft so that one can later effectively recreate the laminating process on their own. As seen in Fig. 3b, the finished product of the guide is a small space where the participant learned how to prepare the floor, laminate, and fix four tiles.

4.1   Procedure

We divided the participants into two groups (between-subjects experimental design). In order to maintain an even distribution of sample sizes between the two groups, we used block randomization to divide the participants. One group received the AR guide with EMS, while another received paper instructions with identical textual descriptions and graphics in the same exact order. We made sure that the environment was set up uniformly for each participant, so we put all of the equipment and materials that came with the VuMarks on a table next to the area where they would laminate the floor. Everyone began at the same location, which was marked with a cross on the floor.

A brief oral introduction explaining the objectives, tasks, and safety precautions for muscle actuation was given to the participants. Next, they read and signed the consent form. For the participants in the Skillab group, the study started with the calibration of the EMS system, which comprised setting the electrodes in place and calibrating the pulse rate and pulse width. The last two parameters fell between 170-180us and 45-50hz respectively. The study proceeded with Hololens built-in eye calibration. Following this, the program was started and the participants were requested to follow the instructions. The moderator served as both the judge who evaluated the end result using the well-defined and structured rating schema (see Sect. 4.3) and the wizard who ensured that the guide continued at the proper time.

After finishing the guide, the participants filled out the User Experience Questionnaire (UEQ) while the laminate is taken apart and placed back on the table. The participants re-did the lamination in an evaluation round without any instruction after a 10-minute break. The judge evaluated this round as well. Participants in both the Skillab vs. paper instructions groups completed the same surveys and underwent the same two-round process. Both rounds of the lamination process were evaluated and graded using a rating schema for both groups.

(a) All tools arranged on a table.   (b) Space for testing out the lamination

Fig. 3. User Study Setup

4.2   Participants

We had a total of 20 participants (10 female, 10 male) ranging in age from 21 to 32 (M = 23.7, SD = 2.3) years. We found them through word-of-mouth and online forums via our university courses. 16 out of the 20 participants reported having no prior experience at all of laminating the floor, whereas 4 had some passive experience. These 4 people had merely observed as someone installed laminate flooring. In addition, 7 people have used digital eyewear to experience augmented reality. None of the 20 participants have ever engaged with EMS in any way.

4.3   Measurements

Both quantitative and qualitative measurements were computed throughout the user study. Every floor lamination round was video-taped, and the interviews were audio-taped.

Quantitative. As a quantitative measurement, we recorded participants' completion time for each round (first round: *learning time*, second round: *evaluation time*). In order to compare and evaluate the final outcomes and the accuracy of the processes, we built a scoring rating schema. First, we simply determined whether or not each step had been applied correctly. If it wasn't correct, we took note of what went wrong, which advice was required, and how many pieces of advice, so that one error wouldn't affect the entire subsequent craft. There were a total of 9 steps that might be either correct or incorrect.

(a) Craft with a score of 19 out of 21 points.   (b) Craft with a score of 14 out of 21 points.

Fig. 4. Sample craftwork from the study participants

Next, we evaluated two components that were critical to the overall aesthetic and level of craftsmanship. First, the grading of the clamps; these were the spaces between the laminate tiles and the wall where a toeboard would eventually be mounted. Each participant in this stage was supposed to set a stack of clamps every 20 cm, at least 4 stacks of clamps. The clamps must then be turned correctly, that is, horizontally rather than vertically. For instance, if a participant adds at least four clamps in the proper direction, they received a maximum score of 7 (Fig. 4a). As shown in 4b, the participant used fewer clamps and turned them in the wrong direction, hence the rating was low. The laminate tiles could simply be clicked together while laminating the floor, but hammering was required to secure them so that there is a seamless integration between them. Therefore, we gave it a maximum of 7 points if all of the tiles have been hammered and clicked into place (see Fig. 4a), and only 3 points, for instance, if there are still tiny gaps. The rating of the craft's overall appearance came last; it considered the ratings of the clamps and the tiles as well as the alignment of all the tiles, including whether or not the ends are parallel. Again, the process was performed in both rounds (first round: *learning rating*, second round: *evaluation rating*).

Qualitative. The following topics were covered in our final semi-structured interviews: (1) General impressions (2) Learning-enhancing parameters (3) Experience with EMS (4) Pros and cons of the overall system covering the assistance or guidance they preferred; (5) Recommendations. We used the thematic analysis method to categorize and sort interview data. The core team consisted of four researchers (three females, and one male) with experience in HCI research. We used an online whiteboard tool (Miro) to facilitate discussion and categorization. Together, the four of us coded all of the interview transcripts. In accordance with various codes, we highlighted specific phrases using colors. We examined the codes we generated, searched for patterns among them, and developed themes. We got back to the data set and cross-verified our themes to make sure they accurately reflect the data and are valuable.

5   Results

We present a detailed evaluation of the obtained results. Statistical comparisons were carried out using IBM SPSS Version 27, and the results are reported as statistically significant at $p < .05$. Based on Shapiro-Wilk test, all data was following a normal distribution. We conducted an independent sample t-test for the two conditions, Skillab vs. paper instructions. We also conducted a pairwise t-test between the training and the evaluation phase for both conditions. For the qualitative data, we categorized and sorted information using an affinity diagram. We sought to make sense of all the notes, observations, and discoveries we had recorded via the interviews by using themes to categorize the data and build throughlines.

5.1   Quantitative Data: Timing and Accuracy

In the Skillab tutorial, participants spent more time following every step of the instructions compared to the paper manual, where some parts were skipped or combined. Participants could complete the evaluation round considerably rapidly than the learning round in both conditions because we chose a task that was reasonably simple. For Skillab and paper instructions, total learning time vs. total evaluation time scores are strongly and positively correlated ($r = 0.654$, $p = 0.020$), ($r = 0.583$, $p = 0.039$) respectively. There was a significant mean difference between total learning time and total evaluation time scores for both Skillab ($t = 17.533$, $p < 0.001$) and paper instructions ($t = 7.194$, $p < 0.001$) tutorials. The task's repeatability following the learning phase was quicker, demonstrating reasonable levels of learning. A paired-sample t-test was conducted to compare the task performance score in the evaluation phase of Skillab and paper instruction conditions. There was a significant difference in the overall rating scores for Skillab condition [$t(9)=-2.805$, $p = 0.021$]. There was not a significant difference in the overall rating scores for the paper instructions condition [$t(9)=-.474$, $p = 0.647$]. For Skillab participants, the recreated craft work was of higher quality than the paper instructions (Fig. 5a and b). An independent-samples t-test was conducted to compare UEQ scores between the two conditions. There was a significant difference in the scores for both pragmatic items ($t(18)=$, $p=0.034$) and hedonic items ($t(18)=$, $p=0.030$) conditions. The pragmatic and hedonic item's values are higher for Skillab [(M=0.925, SD= 0.457), (M= 2.7, SD= 0.346)] compared to paper instructions [(M=0.525, SD= 0.463), (M= 2.4, SD= 0.316)] respectively. Overall ratings of the UEQ score was also significant ($t(18)=$, $p=0.015$). The overall item's value was higher for Skillab (M = 1.812, SD= 0.307) than paper instructions (M = 1.462, SD= 0.358). This demonstrated that the immersive multi-modal setting and playful learning style did have a substantial impact on the user experience. A two-sample t-test was performed to compare the total time taken in Skillab and paper instructions conditions. There was a significant difference in the training phase between Skillab (M = 10:52, SD = 1:30) and paper instructions (M = 8:44, SD = 2:25); t(18) = -2.364, p = 0.015.

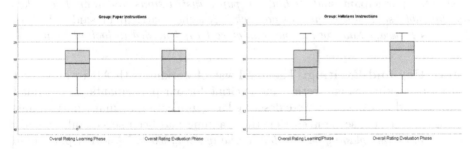

(a) Learning and Evaluation phase score for paper instructions   (b) Learning and Evaluation phase score for Skillab

Fig. 5. Comparison of the overall task performance for Skillab and the Paper instructions

In a nutshell, Skillab requires more time investment from participants than paper instructions. The negative t-value and low p-value for the comparison of means suggest that this difference is unlikely to be due to chance. The positive correlations between learning and evaluation times in both conditions provide evidence of the consistency of the task across participants and the fact that participants who spent more time learning the task also tended to perform better in the evaluation phase. The paired t-test comparing overall rating scores in the evaluation phase between Skillab and paper instructions shows that participants who used Skillab had significantly higher ratings than those who used paper instructions. The negative t-value and low p-value suggest that this difference is also unlikely to be due to chance. The independent-sample t-test comparing UEQ scores between conditions shows significant differences in both pragmatic and hedonic items, as well as overall ratings. While these findings support Skillab's effectiveness, practical significance, and generalizability should be considered. The findings are based on a specific task and a specific group of participants, so one should be cautious when applying them to other contexts or populations.

5.2   Qualitative Findings

Post learning and evaluation sessions, we conducted a brief interview with all the participants. We were interested in knowing what interaction helped them learn and what didn't. The following are the themes that emerged from the analysis:

Convenience with Hololens: Skillab enabled hands-free tool interaction. Paper instructions required a lot of back-and-forth reading of the step-by-step instructions. One could position the panel on the Hololens however one choose in the field of view or according to convenience. This improved the user experience overall by providing a more fluid and unhindered transition from one step to the next. One participant said *"I had the paper instructions and then I left them on the table so I always had to go back."* Another participant said *"With the Hololens I always had the instructions close by if I needed to look at them."*

Interesting and Exciting: The novel way of working with AR technology to learn a new skill was interesting and exciting for our participants. The Vumark scanning and identification were described as gamification by many participants. An auditory response signaled that the scanning had been successful. One said *"It was more like playing games than actually doing work."* Another participant said *"Especially when laminating the floor, which is I think not so a fun task. Actually, it was just a lot more fun to do it with the Hololens."*

Interactivity: Users had the impression that the system understood them and responded to them because they received confirmation after each step. The system provided ideas for error rectification when users picked up the wrong object and scanned it. One participant mentioned *"I couldn't choose the wrong thing.*

So it prevents doing some mistakes and also you have this Learning by Doing and getting rewards feeling." Some participants described having a companion who "has your back" so that they are not left to complete the activity alone. Some people claimed that receiving visual, audio, and tactile feedback at various stages aided in greater comprehension.

Paper is More Flexible and Self-paced: Some reported when compared to the print-out guide, the tutorial's step-by-step breakdown through Skillab makes it easier and more beginner-friendly. This was not only presented as a pro argument but also as a con argument for those who favor skipping steps and doing them all at once. The printable instruction allows for customization by skipping or combining steps, however, the Skillab session does not. Some people said they wanted complete control over the process. One participant said *"I think the step-by-step guide is nice because you can't skip a step that easily like when you have to place these little markers (clamps). For example, I almost forgot it in my first round."* On the other hand, one mentioned *"I think this was the main difference for me so in the printout version I always looked like two or three steps ahead which I couldn't do with the Hololens."*

EMS Helpful in a Foreign Context: Participants highlighted the significance of using muscle actuation techniques when performing unfamiliar movements that are crucial to the job. Some participants reported it helpful to use EMS as a support system for an entirely new interaction. They reported no compromise of the sense of agency. A participant reported *"If someone doesn't know how to make the movement, it really helps to learn it too, because it gives cues and you can then start yourself like amplifying these moves, but it gives you a very good hint how to do things."*

Assistance with Power-Demanding Tasks: Some participants stated that when it comes to craftwork that needs higher power and heavier lifting, muscle actuation technology could be useful. It can therefore be employed as a method for supporting and strengthening muscles rather than just nudging the user in the right direction. One said *"I also think that this could greatly improve motor skills for elderly people, maybe because they can't just throw the hammer up and down. Maybe that's also for them."*.

Experiencing a Sense of Overload: Some participants initially found it difficult to understand how to accomplish some sub-tasks, but this changed as they became more accustomed to using Hololens. One participant said *"I mean at the beginning it was a little bit overwhelming, so because everything was new and never worked with, one of those things. And at the start of the exercise, it was a little bit difficult for me to look at the charts here and listen to what it was saying and also do it."* Some people worried that if the technology fails, they won't be able to fix the problem and will have nothing left to complete the job.

A participant showed concerns by saying *"Maybe if there are technical issues with the Hololens that maybe some people rely on the Hololens and do not know how to do it without it and they cannot work without it."*

6   Discussion

We have endeavored to understand the primary advantages and challenges of the "AR-based craft-work learning system" approach to skill development throughout this study. We discovered that learning occurred for the floor lamination activity using both Skillab application and paper instructions. In the following, we discuss our results in relation to our research questions.

6.1   Skillab vs. Traditional Paper Instructions

Using Skillab, participants took longer to finish the floor lamination task during the learning phase (*learning time*) compared to paper instructions. There could be multiple reasons for this observation. First, participants using Skillab had to frequently "scan" objects which took some time. Second, Skillab used the SBF framework, where participants were introduced to the tools, parts, and steps required for floor lamination. According to the Constructionism theory [11], when learners construct and interact with physical objects, learning happens "felicitously". However, during the evaluation phase (*evaluation time*), both groups were able to repeat the task more quickly, demonstrating optimal levels of learning. According to the systematic rating score (*learning vs. evaluation rating*), the Skillab training showed a significant improvement, in contrast to the paper instructions learning. Despite no differences have been found when solely looking at the accuracy of the individual steps (a high number of steps have been carried out correctly in both conditions, i.e. *learning vs. evaluation correct*), this indicates that Skillab provided them with a deeper and more thorough level of learning to reproduce a high-quality craft work. AR-mediated scaffolds may be accountable for this. Every object and tool included both visual and audio instructions that described how the work was broken down and led users to the next step.

6.2   Advantages of Multimodal AR Learning Environments

Despite the lack of statistically significant differences for some of the obtained parameters (in particular, *learning and evaluation time and correctness*), the learning process with Skillab was more controlled – participants using paper instructions used different strategies on how they approached the task. For example, some participants skipped some steps, and others combined steps and performed multiple at once. For floor lamination, this might not per se be a problem, but for learning more sensitive tasks like maintenance of Airplane engines, environments such as Skillab provide more fine-grained control over the process. This could help to reduce the effort of teachers in such areas as they would need less time monitoring their trainees while being able to focus on other aspects of training. Furthermore, Skillab offered participants an improved overall user experience than paper instructions, based on UEQ scores and follow-up interviews. Because AR enables hands-free interaction, our participants found it convenient to use in parallel with the floor lamination task. They were not required to alternate between reading and work completion. They also stated that the auditory feedback was quite helpful. Overall, they described the experience as enjoyable and fascinating; they felt as though they had a partner who helped them through the entire lamination process, who understood them, and who responded in accordance with their actions and needs. The Skillab system's steadily immersive and interactive features appear to support and promote learning. This is in line with the previous research work [31,41].

The majority of the individuals responded favorably to EMS. None of our participants who used the EMS system mentioned feeling a loss of agency. It might be because we only turned the system on and off in response to voice commands from users. It is consistent with earlier research on the importance of preserving user control by Shahu and colleagues [32]. Participants believed that because they were already accustomed to hammering, the novelty of the system would be greater for an altogether unfamiliar motor movement. Despite the fact that Skillab provided a better overall experience, some participants emphasized that paper instructions are more adaptable. They are simpler to customize. Instead of following the process step-by-step, they might skip or combine some parts and study the entire instruction set first before even starting with the hands-on work. Due to their lack of experience with the Hololens setup, some participants first felt overwhelmed. However, they said that they quickly grew accustomed to it. Overall, Skillab acts as a good place to start when thinking about developing powerful immersive skill-building tools that promote craftsmanship.

6.3   Limitations and Future Work

For this paper, we had to deal with various limitations. First, concerning the technical setup. Skillab has limited accuracy and range as given by the used Hololens device and development frameworks. Additionally, calibration is needed for both the integrated EMS components and AR vision. Future research is needed to improve and partly automate such calibration steps. Also, the subsequent steps were triggered by a Wizard-of-Oz, while a real system would need to detect not only individual objects but also task boundaries and crafting quality to be able to switch between different "learning paths". Second, some limitations concern the user study. We did only compare Skillab to paper instructions. Previous research has already shown the advantage of AR over video tutorials in assembly tasks [21]. In future studies, we aim for improving Skillab according to the provided interview statements and perform an extensive cross-comparison between different learning methods, including videos, paper manuals, and human teachers. Further, our study included a well-defined sample of relatively homogeneous young participants, many with a technical background. It would be fascinating to see how various age groups respond to our prototype. Ultimately, it will be interesting to see how Skillab is perceived by DIY'ers of all ages and backgrounds.

7   Conclusion

In this paper, we introduce Skillab, an AR-based scaffolding system to support craftwork learning with immersive and multimodal feedback. We implemented this concept by combining AR and EMS. The evaluation of the Skillab application revealed participants' interactions with AR scaffolds, challenges in learning, preferences, and overall user experience. The immersiveness and multimodality of the AR-based system's feedback were its main benefits. Skillab users were encouraged to participate in each step of the process, which made it more understandable and simple to remember. As a result, the laminate work they created was of higher quality overall. Users appreciated the auditory input to advance to the next step and the auditory feedback regarding how well the step worked. The gamified learning aspects were enjoyable and engaging. These features of Skillab appear to support and promote learning and a positive user experience. The sense of agency was preserved by using the wake word to initiate and terminate EMS. The study's results indicate that skills acquisition platforms could provide a superior and captivating learning environment compared to traditional methods, particularly if combined with an immersive multimodal feedback system that enables task replication and learning while acknowledging the need for further research to validate these findings in broader contexts. The main challenge was that the prototype didn't provide them the freedom to modify specific steps in accordance with participant preferences. Steps should be adaptable for the user based on their preferences and past knowledge. Potentially, our work will inspire researchers to further delve into this avenue of applying immersive multi-modality feedback technologies for craftwork. We believe there are several ways that researchers can further expand on our work. Possible future investigations include exploring: a) interactions with eye-tracking and visual gaze redirection b) providing varying levels of customization c) improved object detection. Researchers can use the foundation provided by our work to investigate issues and expand on our system or findings in fresh ways.

References

1. Anderson, F., Grossman, T., Matejka, J., Fitzmaurice, G.: YouMove: enhancing movement training with an augmented reality mirror. In: Proceedings of the 26th Annual ACM Symposium on User Interface Software and Technology, pp. 311–320 (2013)
2. Azuma, R.T.: A Survey of Augmented Reality. Presence: Teleoperators Virtual Environ. **6**(4), 355–385 (1997). https://doi.org/10.1162/pres.1997.6.4.355
3. Barfield, W.: Fundamentals of Wearable Computers and Augmented Reality. CRC Press (2015)

4. Chang, G., Morreale, P., Medicherla, P.: Applications of augmented reality systems in education. In: Society for Information Technology & Teacher Education International Conference, pp. 1380–1385. Association for the Advancement of Computing in Education (AACE) (2010)

5. Colley, A., Leinonen, A., Forsman, M.T., Häkkilä, J.: Ems painter: co-creating visual art using electrical muscle stimulation. In: Proceedings of the Twelfth International Conference on Tangible, Embedded, and Embodied Interaction, pp. 266–270 (2018)

6. Collins, A., Brown, J.S., Newman, S.E.: Cognitive apprenticeship: teaching the crafts of reading, writing, and mathematics. In: Knowing, Learning, and Instruction, pp. 453–494. Routledge (2018)

7. Ebisu, A., Hashizume, S., Ochiai, Y.: Building a feedback loop between electrical stimulation and percussion learning. In: ACM SIGGRAPH 2018 Studio, pp. 1–2 (2018)

8. Faltaous, S., Koelle, M., Schneegass, S.: From perception to action: a review and taxonomy on electrical muscle stimulation in HCI. In: Proceedings of the 21st International Conference on Mobile and Ubiquitous Multimedia, pp. 159–171 (2022)

9. Gamble, J.: Modelling the invisible: the pedagogy of craft apprenticeship. Stud. Contin. Educ. 23(2), 185–200 (2001)

10. Goel, A., et al.: Learning functional and causal abstractions of classroom aquaria. In: Proceedings of the Annual Meeting of the Cognitive Science Society, vol. 32 (2010)

11. Hinchliffe, G.: Situating skills. J. Philos. Educ. 36(2), 187–205 (2002)

12. Hiyama, A., Onimaru, H., Miyashita, M., Ebuchi, E., Seki, M., Hirose, M.: Augmented reality system for measuring and learning tacit artisan skills. In: Yamamoto, S. (ed.) HIMI 2013. LNCS, vol. 8017, pp. 85–91. Springer, Heidelberg (2013). https://doi.org/10.1007/978-3-642-39215-3_10

13. Hmelo-Silver, C.E., Marathe, S., Liu, L.: Fish swim, rocks sit, and lungs breathe: expert-novice understanding of complex systems. J. Learn. Sci. 16(3), 307–331 (2007)

14. Iyobe, M., Ishida, T., Miyakawa, A., Uchida, N., Sugita, K., Shibata, Y.: Development of a mobile virtual traditional crafting presentation system using augmented reality technology. Int. J. Space-Based and Situated Comput. 6(4), 239–251 (2016)

15. Jain, S., Sharma, S., Babbar, D.: Star-force: a playful implementation of the jedi-force. In: Proceedings of the Eleventh International Conference on Tangible, Embedded, and Embodied Interaction, pp. 761–766 (2017)

16. Kang, S., Norooz, L., Bonsignore, E., Byrne, V., Clegg, T., Froehlich, J.E.: PrototypAR: prototyping and simulating complex systems with paper craft and augmented reality. In: Proceedings of the 18th ACM International Conference on Interaction Design and Children, pp. 253–266 (2019)

17. Khan, W.A., Raouf, A., Cheng, K.: Augmented reality for manufacturing. In: Virtual Manufacturing. Springer Series in Advanced Manufacturing. Springer, London (2011). https://doi.org/10.1007/978-0-85729-186-8_1

18. Knibbe, J., Alsmith, A., Hornbæk, K.: Experiencing electrical muscle stimulation. Proc. ACM Interact. Mob. Wear. Ubiquitous Technol. 2(3), 1–14 (2018)

19. Kono, M., Ishiguro, Y., Miyaki, T., Rekimoto, J.: Design and study of a multi-channel electrical muscle stimulation toolkit for human augmentation. In: Proceedings of the 9th Augmented Human International Conference, pp. 1–8 (2018)

20. Lee, K.: Augmented reality in education and training. TechTrends 56(2), 13–21 (2012)

21. Loch, F., Quint, F., Brishtel, I.: Comparing video and augmented reality assistance in manual assembly. In: 2016 12th International Conference on Intelligent Environments (IE), pp. 147–150 (2016). https://doi.org/10.1109/IE.2016.31

22. Lopes, P., Ion, A., Baudisch, P.: Impacto: simulating physical impact by combining tactile stimulation with electrical muscle stimulation. In: Proceedings of the 28th Annual ACM Symposium on User Interface Software and Technology, pp. 11–19 (2015)

23. Lopes, P., You, S., Ion, A., Baudisch, P.: Adding force feedback to mixed reality experiences and games using electrical muscle stimulation. In: Proceedings of the 2018 chi conference on human factors in computing systems. pp. 1–13 (2018)

24. Lu, K., Brombacher, A.: Haptic feedback in running: is it possible for information transfer through electrical muscle signalling? In: Proceedings of the Fourteenth International Conference on Tangible, Embedded, and Embodied Interaction, pp. 479–485 (2020)

25. Nawahdah, M., Inoue, T.: Motion adaptive orientation adjustment of a virtual teacher to support physical task learning. Inf. Media Technol. **7**(1), 506–515 (2012)

26. Osman, S., Zin, N.A.H.M.: Proposed model for courseware development of virtual teaching and learning traditional craft. In: 2010 International Symposium on Information Technology, vol. 1, pp. 1–6. IEEE (2010)

27. Pan, Z., Cheok, A.D., Yang, H., Zhu, J., Shi, J.: Virtual reality and mixed reality for virtual learning environments. Comput. graph. **30**(1), 20–28 (2006)

28. Papert, S., Harel, I.: Situating constructionism. Constructionism **36**(2), 1–11 (1991)

29. Pfeiffer, M., Duente, T., Rohs, M.: Let your body move: a prototyping toolkit for wearable force feedback with electrical muscle stimulation. In: Proceedings of the 18th International Conference on Human-Computer Interaction with Mobile Devices and Services, pp. 418–427 (2016)

30. Quintana, C., Reiser, B.J., Davis, E.A., Krajcik, J., Fretz, E., Duncan, R.G., Kyza, E., Edelson, D., Soloway, E.: A scaffolding design framework for software to support science inquiry. In: Scaffolding, pp. 337–386. Psychology Press (2018)

31. Repenning, A., Ioannidou, A., Phillips, J.: Collaborative use & design of interactive simulations (1999)

32. Shahu, A., Wintersberger, P., Michahelles, F.: Scenario-based investigation of acceptance of electric muscle stimulation. In: Proceedings of the Augmented Humans International Conference 2022, pp. 184–194 (2022)

33. Shahu, A., Wintersberger, P., Michahelles, F.: Would users accept electric muscle stimulation controlling their body? insights from a scenario-based investigation. In: CHI Conference on Human Factors in Computing Systems Extended Abstracts, pp. 1–7 (2022)

34. Stager, G.: Papertian constructionism and the design of productive contexts for learning. In: Proceedings of the EuroLogo, pp. 43–53. Citeseer (2005)

35. Steer, C., Robinson, S., Pearson, J., Sahoo, D., Mabbett, I., Jones, M.: A liquid tangible display for mobile colour mixing. In: Proceedings of the 20th International Conference on Human-Computer Interaction with Mobile Devices and Services, pp. 1–7 (2018)

36. Syberfeldt, A., Danielsson, O., Gustavsson, P.: Augmented reality smart glasses in the smart factory: product evaluation guidelines and review of available products. IEEE Access **5**, 9118–9130 (2017)

37. Tajima, D., Nishida, J., Lopes, P., Kasahara, S.: Whose touch is this?: understanding the agency trade-off between user-driven touch vs. computer-driven touch. ACM Trans. Comput.-Hum. Interact. **29**(3), 1–27 (2022). https://doi.org/10.1145/3489608

38. Tang, Y., Au, K., Leung, Y.: Comprehending products with mixed reality: geometric relationships and creativity. Int. J. Eng. Bus. Manage. **10**, 1847979018809599 (2018)

39. Thomas, P., David, W.: Augmented reality: an application of heads-up display technology to manual manufacturing processes. In: Hawaii International Conference on System Sciences, vol. **2**. ACM SIGCHI Bulletin (1992)

40. Wang, M., Callaghan, V., Bernhardt, J., White, K., Peña-Rios, A.: Augmented reality in education and training: pedagogical approaches and illustrative case studies. J. Ambient. Intell. Humaniz. Comput. **9**(5), 1391–1402 (2018)

41. Zacharia, Z., Anderson, O.R.: The effects of an interactive computer-based simulation prior to performing a laboratory inquiry-based experiment on students' conceptual understanding of physics. Am. J. Phys. **71**(6), 618–629 (2003)

User Self-Report

A Longitudinal Analysis of Real-World Self-report Data

Niels van Berkel[1]([✉]), Sujay Shalawadi[1], Madeleine R. Evans[2], Aku Visuri[3],
and Simo Hosio[3]

[1] Aalborg University, Aalborg, Denmark
{nielsvanberkel,sujaybs}@cs.aau.dk
[2] Levell, London, UK
madeleine@levell.io
[3] University of Oulu, Oulu, Finland
{aku.visuri,simo.hosio}@oulu.fi

Abstract. While self-report studies are common in Human-Computer
Interaction research, few evaluations have assessed their long term use. We
present a longitudinal analysis of a web-based workplace application that
collects well-being assessments and offers suggestions to improve individual, team, and organisational performance. Our dataset covers 219 users.
We assess their first year of application use, focusing on their usage patterns, well-being evaluations, and behaviour towards notifications. Our
results highlight that the drop-off in use was the steepest in the first week
(-24.2%). However, substantial breaks in usage were common and did not
necessarily result in dropout. We found that latency periods of eight days
or more predicted a stronger intention to drop out than stay engaged and
that reminder notifications did not result in more completed self-reports
but significantly prolonged the usage period. Our work strengthens findings related to high drop out rates, but also provides counter-evidence by
showing that despite individuals appearing to drop-off in short-term studies, individuals can and do return to self-report applications after extensive
breaks. We contribute an analysis of usage behaviour drivers in the area
of technology-enabled well-being measurement, responding to the call for
longer-term research to extend the growing literature on self-report studies.

Keywords: Self-report · well-being · longitudinal · diary study ·
experience sampling

1 Introduction

The collection and analysis of self-report data has a long history in Human-
Computer Interaction (HCI), particularly in subjective well-being research. Well-
known examples of self-report-based studies are diary studies [41] and experience sampling studies [2,30], in which researchers provide participants with a
self-report application (desktop or mobile) or device to regularly report on the

---

The original version of the chapter has been revised. A footnote has been added indicating that the label *'Anonymised Company'* was revised to "Levell" for the published
version. A correction to this chapter can be found at
https://doi.org/10.1007/978-3-031-42286-7_38

© The Author(s), under exclusive license to Springer Nature Switzerland AG 2023, corrected publication 2024
J. Abdelnour Nocera et al. (Eds.): INTERACT 2023, LNCS 14144, pp. 611–632, 2023.
https://doi.org/10.1007/978-3-031-42286-7_34

experiences or aspect(s) of their lives that are being studied. For example, self-report applications have been utilised to gather insightful and valuable data as to what drives the states of e.g. happiness, calm, pain, or peacefulness [22], as well as helped HCI researchers to understand aspects of digital interactions, such as usage patterns [19] and user experiences [8] among many others. In recent years, the Quantified Self (QS) movement has popularised the value of self-report data for personal use [10, 29, 33], driving popular interest in self-tracking applications [31]. Much in the manner that academic well-being researchers seek to pair self-report data on affective experience with contextual data such as activity logs, QS users seek to review the logs of self-report data for health, performance, or wider well-being insights that they can then use to improve their lives [29, 32, 46].

Prior work has highlighted the typically limited duration of self-report studies as a limitation in identifying persistent changes in use, self-reported affect, and real-world outcomes over time [17, 24]. Kjaerup et al. analysed longitudinal studies published in CHI between 1982–2019 and found only 56 studies with a duration of more than one month [27]. A recent review by Caraban et al. on nudging technologies, *i.e.* technology that promotes subtle behaviour changes, finds that just 18 out of the analysed 50 studies had a duration longer than a day, with seven studies being over one month in duration [7]. The lack of longitudinal data in such studies can result in skewed insights into participant motivation, engagement, usage, as well as real-world experience and outcomes patterns, in particular in relation to the long-term usage of self-report applications. A lack of longitudinal research data can also lead researchers to draw unreliable conclusions. Bias due to the characteristics of individuals that participate in academic studies is another major concern, as individuals that opt to participate in research evaluations may not necessarily behave similarly to average users along the parameters of motivation and usage behaviour, limiting the insights drawn to that sample rather than to a wider population [35]. This 'participation bias' is a widely recognised research participation effect, perhaps most well-known to the reader in the context of course evaluations. In such evaluations, motivation to take part is highest among those with strong positive or negative sentiments toward the stated potential outcome or topic of the study at hand—thereby creating an effect of self-selection among the studied population [13].

In this paper we present an analysis of one year of usage data of a self-report application designed to enable individual users, teams and companies to track and improve experienced well-being in the context of work. Specifically, our application offers a web-based platform and is designed to be integrated in a professional context to inform and support employees and team leaders. Users of the application can track four dimensions of their subjective well-being, add and share ideas to improve well-being in the context of work, and report 'blockers' they experience in work or home life which negatively impact their subjective well-being, and thus their health, productivity, or job satisfaction. The application provides users with a historical overview of these collected self-reports and an opportunity to safely share their data with their team, generating an aggregated and anonymised well-being data stream (group-level summary statistics and trends) that is visible on shared team and company-level dashboards.

To improve our understanding of the long-term use of well-being applications truly 'in the wild' and outside the context of a controlled academic study, we present an analysis of one year of application use data. We deployed the application to two organizations, one in the recruitment services industry and the other in the healthcare services industry. Our analysis spans a total of 219 users, is informed by prior research findings within the HCI community, and allows us to quantify changes in application use, well-being, and configuration settings in a longitudinal setting. Concretely, our work aims to answer the following research questions:

- How does usage and non-usage behaviour change over time?
- How do self-reports of both well-being dimensions and challenges fluctuate as the result of temporal aspects such as time of day or day of week?
- Using a long-term data set, can we identify new insights as to what types of usage behaviour may predict drop out vs. long-term use?

Our analysis shows that the steepest drop in usage over an entire year of use is already found in the first week of use, totalling 24.2% of our entire user sample. In contrast to prior work analysing shorter usage periods, we find that users do return to use the application even after week-long breaks in application use. We compare and contrast our results with earlier findings on *e.g.*, dropout rates, collection of self-report data, and well-being evaluations, contributing to the HCI literature by demonstrating the new insights that can be obtained by taking a long-term view on user behaviour.

2 Background

A recent review by Sanches et al. highlights the increasing interest within the HCI community towards the study and support of affective health [43]. Workshops organised in relation to the topic of mental health and well-being, for example at DIS 2020 [44], highlight that many questions concerning the methods and tools to study well-being are still unanswered. We motivate our work and analysis by building on prior work focused on subjective well-being measurement and understanding as the research goal and longitudinal research as a method and form of data collection.

2.1 Collecting Longitudinal Well-Being Insights

The HCI community has long shown an interest in studying user experience and other aspects of interaction with technology over longer periods of time. Wilson highlights the challenges often encountered in longitudinal research, *"Longitudinal studies, which involve repeated sessions spread out over multiple days [...] are expensive and time-consuming. As a result, many interactive sensing-based systems come with few convincing quantitative user studies that prove their utility."* [50]. One of the earliest reviews on longitudinal HCI research analysed the research methods employed in the mobile HCI community [26]. Among the 144 published research papers considered, 79% of them used some form of field study as a validation scheme. However, Kjeldskov et al. comment that these studies lack the depth and duration to provide an accurate picture of mobile devices and their relationships to real-world scenarios. As aforementioned, a recent review of longitudinal studies published at CHI found only 56 studies that extend over one month in duration.

A number of studies have tried to overcome the challenges of conducting longitudinal studies in the use of self-tracking experience data for well-being research. For example, Isaacs et al. demonstrate a smartphone application called *Echo* which supports technology-mediated reflection, studying usage for durations of both one month and four years [20]. Using the data from the initial one month, Issac et al. showed that reflections improved actions and lessons learnt for future behaviour. Using data collected over four years, the researchers discovered new insights, including the surprising attenuation of affect bias (*i.e.,* observing that negative emotions associated with past reflective moments faded quicker than positive emotions). The 'Tesserae Project' is another recent example of a longitudinal study with data collection covering up to one year [34]. In this project, participants' use of social media was logged and stored by the researchers to obtain insights into workplace performance—allowing for fully passive participation by the study participants. The authors state that the high retention rates of the study (95% of participants are still enrolled over halfway through the study duration), are due to strict privacy efforts, compensation schemes, unobtrusive nature of the data collection, and the perceived potential value of the study outcomes for the participants [34]. In contrast to the passive collection of data found in the Tesserae Project, we are specifically interested in measuring subjective well-being of individuals in work which, by definition, requires collecting active data contributions. Active data contributions, as for example found in experience sampling-based studies in which participants provide multiple contributions throughout the day [2,30], allow for the collection of insights into the participants' experiences, thoughts, and feelings in a way that is not possible to capture through researcher observation, wearable data collection, or passive monitoring. Furthermore, the literature suggests that the moment of reflection generated by active tracking can provide benefits: prompting the individual to more clearly attend to and evaluate their in-work experiences, leading to the potential for performance-improving and self-corrective behaviour off the back of immediate insight generated by the act of reflection itself [45].

One prominent example of such a study is the 'StudentLife' study [48]. In this study, a total of 48 participants regularly reported on various aspects of their life (including dimensions of experienced well-being) over ten weeks. Combined with passive sensing on mobile devices, the researchers uncover several correlations between the active and passive sensing data. For example, sleep duration, conversation frequency, and co-location with others all correlate significantly with the PHQ-9 depression scale. Furthermore, the authors highlight how the active data contributions on participant mood and other variables provide insight into a trend among participants, with positive affect and low stress levels at the start of semester followed by increased stress and a drop in positive affect towards the end of the semester due to increased workload [48]. Such insights can only be uncovered through deployments that cover an extensive period. Another example is found in the work by Fritz et al., who study long term usage of activity-tracking devices in the context of exercise [14]. Through a study involving 30 participants, the researchers investigated usage behaviour across periods ranging from 3 to 54 months. Results highlighted how obtaining a long streak of tracking exercise positively affected participants' experienced well-being and acted as an accountability tool in completing exercises and earning digital rewards through gamification. Finally, within the domain of digital health Yeager et al. present a two-week study of an internet intervention for trauma recovery [51]. While the intervention was found to be effective across a two week period, the researchers highlight the absence of longitudinal studies as a limiting factor in designing and evaluating the effect of self-guided intervention during patient relapse.

Within the broader HCI community, various researchers have explicitly expressed the need for longitudinal studies, arguing that short deployments do not provide insight into long-term engagement, data patterns and real-world outcomes, and possibly conceal a novelty effect driving initial engagement with new technologies [17,24]. Following this call for more longitudinal studies and deeper insights into the drivers of technology usage and patterns in user reported data over time [24,27], we set out to analyse usage behaviour and user subjective (experienced) well-being data as collected by a self-report application deployed in a real-world context.

2.2   Self-tracking Applications

Self-tracking, the process of *"turning everyday experience into data"* [37], has expanded from physical activity tracking (*e.g.*, step counters) towards the goal of capturing and presenting a holistic overview of a person's physical condition, mental state, or overall well-being. Those using Quantified Self applications primarily use self-tracking to gain knowledge about themselves, such as their behaviours, affect patterns, and habits, which allows them to derive meaningful insights to incorporate positive changes [4,10]. Schön distinguishes between 'reflection in action', which takes place during the activity, and 'reflection on action', which occurs after the activity with the user analysing the captured data [45]. With reference to the domain of HCI, self-report applications typically focus on 'reflection on action' by providing users with the possibility to observe changes over time.

Whether as a study participant or to collect data for one's own interests, adherence to self-tracking is a widely recognised challenge. Several papers provide suggestions to reduce end-user strain in logging data, with the goal of reducing dropout rates. For example, Zhang et al. present 'unlock journaling', in which users can log mood data while unlocking their smartphone [52]. An evaluation of this system highlights that the presented technique of unlock journaling was experienced as less intrusive than a traditional notification-driven approach while resulting in a higher frequency of data journaling. A recent study by Cherubini et al. on daily step counts showed a detrimental effect on long term engagement after notification frequency and monetary compensation was increased, as participants' intrinsic motivation decreased as a result [9]. Another method of integrating self-tracking into everyday life can rely on the principle of affordances (properties of objects which show users the actions they can take) that users have developed during their lifetime to make the data acquisition seamless. Rapp and Cena suggest that everyday physical objects (*e.g.*, bracelets, t-shirts) are highly suitable for self-tracking as they integrate easily into the day-to-day activities of the wearer [40]. Kim et al. present a self-tracking application that allows users to more easily interact with visualisations of their self-tracking data in order to make the collection of data itself more meaningful [25].

With most affect tracking applications focused on the individual, the study of affect tracking at a group level has been relatively sparse. A notable exception to this research gap is the work by Pelayo et al. [42]. In their study, Pelayo et al. collaboratively engaged with call centres to assess whether mood self-tracking can improve work performance, emotional awareness, and team communication. The authors conducted a four-week study in which participants collected mood data through a desktop application. Pelayo et al. identify that participants generally had a positive attitude towards using the application, primarily based on the hope that interpretation of the data by the user's management will improve the working conditions.

Among the spectrum of self-tracking applications, long-term usage is a particularly common problem. Blandford, in discussing the challenges and opportunities in HCI for health and well-being, suggests that meaningful steps forward can be made by collaborating with technology developers in evaluating technologies [6]. Such an approach can empower users to reflect on their data and eventually improve data quality and reduce user effort to acquire self tracking data [36]. In this paper, we set out to do precisely this. Through a collaboration with a well-being measurement start-up, we generate a year-long stream of data comprised of individual subjective well-being self-reports as well as usage data. This allows us to expand the HCI literature with a substantially longer-than-average study length, from which we derive novel insights into patterns in individual well-being as well as into the patterns and drivers of long-term user adherence to self-report applications.

3   Method

Our analysis is based on a collaboration with *Levell. Levell* offers an application for regular assessments of experienced affective well-being across a company by enabling individual employees to report their experienced well-being, showing individual employees their own data and insights, and offering aggregate team- and company-level insights through shared dashboards. Users of the application can report their well-being levels (detailed below, see Fig. 1), anonymously capture and share specific 'blockers' that may stagnate their progress at work, or anonymously share ideas with their team or company management (Fig. 2). Blockers can represent a variety of issues that can arise at a workplace or in an individual's personal life, such as work relationships (e.g., difficulties in interacting with management), work environment (e.g., interruptions, air quality), or struggles with health, sleep, or exercise. In this analysis we focus on engagement with the application to actively input self-reports, the reported well-being and blockers data itself, as well as a potential moderator of short and long-term usage. *Levell* offers the same features through both a mobile and web-based application that allow for the exact same data collection input. However, given the recent release of the mobile application, the large majority of the collected data originates from web-based input. We therefore solely focus on the analysis of data from the web-based application.

Fig. 1. Self-report component of the online application.

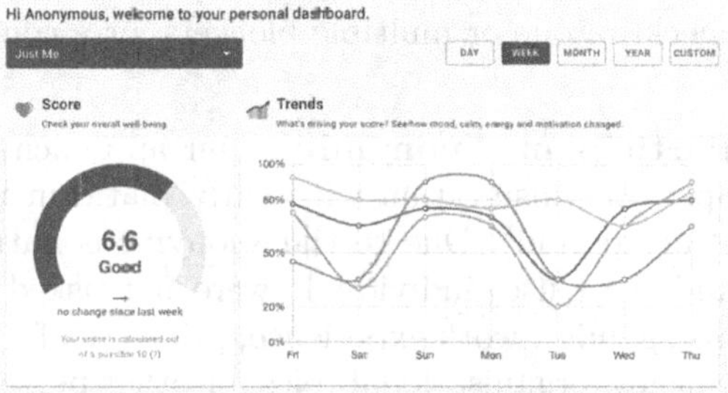

Fig. 2. Dashboard, displaying changes in self-reported well-being values over time (day, week, month, year).

3.1   Participant Recruitment

The target population for our study was the entire population of two organizations, including all employees, managers, and leadership of the firms. All participants were sent email-based invitations inviting them to sign-up, along with contextual information as to the purpose and potential benefit for them, along with information designed to inform individuals of how their data would or would not be used, and the expected time-cost of the self-report 'check-in'. The sample assessed in this paper reflects the characteristics of the individuals who received the email and decided to download and subsequently use the application at least once.

We introduced the application to each organization through a predesigned roll-out process. This process started with a kick-off and induction for the leadership team, followed by the individuals in each team, consisting of specific training on the overarching problem (*i.e.*, poor or varied employee well-being that impacts performance at work), the application's well-being measurement concept, the features of the application, and how the data would be analysed and used. Emphasis was placed on the collective and participatory nature of the well-being tracking for the joint benefit of both individuals and the group. Furthermore, we highlighted the fact that the individual user was in control of how their data was shared, something reinforced by the users' ability to see their data aggregates on the team and company dashboards. In all cases it was stressed to users that participation was voluntary, and they were free to cease usage if they wished to do so. In addition, in both organization A and B, team leaders and company leaders were trained to use the dashboards to identify how well-being has changed, respond to blockers submitted by employees within the application, and use the data and insights to inform their organisational strategies.

Participants were not instructed or required to complete any minimum number of self-reports, and were not compensated for their participation, thus limiting the bias that could come from extrinsic incentives or a sense of obligation. Within the application, participants could provide either a personal well-being check-in, one or multiple blockers, or a combination of both.

Participant Anonymity. Our approach to participant anonymity was developed in consultation with early platform users during beta tests (prior to the study period). Due to the anonymous nature of the platform's data collection and data use, individuals were not asked to provide information about their age, gender, work experience, prior use of well-being tracking or technology, self-efficacy, organisational roles, or other personal information. Further, the leaders of the organizations in which the application is deployed were kept unaware of which individuals use or do not use the application. Critically, team dashboards were accessible to both team leaders as well as all members of the team. By opening up the team dashboards to every member of the team, we sought to head-on address issues and concerns with anonymity. By viewing the dashboards themselves, individuals could see what was meant by the analysis of the team data and presentation 'on average and in aggregate', and also see where their blockers and ideas feedback appeared, and therefore make their own judgement about whether the structure of these features in the app afforded them sufficient flexibility in anonymity. Our study aligns with our University's regulation on research ethics and data management.

3.2   Dataset

The specific variables represented in the dataset are as follows;

- **Well-being check-ins.** Self-reported experiences on the four dimensions 'Mood', 'Calm', 'Energy', and 'Motivation', as captured through four horizontal sliders in response to the question 'How are you feeling?'. The interface allows the user to independently capture positive versus negative states, with a single line capturing the conjoin of a 0–50 positive affect scale (neutral to the right) and an 0–50 negative affect scale (neutral to the left). For all sliders, the default position is in the middle 'neutral' state.

- **Blockers.** Self-reported issues negatively impacting well-being. Categorised as either personal or work related.
- **Timestamp of self-reports.** For each self-report on well-being or blockers, a timestamp is recorded. Reporting of well-being check-ins and blockers can be completed independently from one another.
- **Reminder notification configuration.** The application offers users the ability to send up to one reminder email per day at a timepoint set by the user. The email consists of one question 'How did it go today?' and suggest to 'check in', which takes the user directly to the self-report screen in the application. Further, users are able to select the days at which they receive a reminder—ranging anywhere from zero (no reminders at all) to seven days.

In order to allow for a longitudinal analysis of the presented results, we exclude any user whose account was created less than one year before the last available data dump (July 2021). Following this exclusion criteria, we conduct our analysis on the first year of application usage of the remaining total of 219 individual users.

4 Results

Our analysis focuses on an assessment on an analysis of long-term usage behaviour, a review of the self-reported well-being check-ins and blockers, and an investigation into user preferences into reminder notifications and their effect on completed self-reports. In order to ensure comparability in our analysis, we solely consider the first year of data that we have available on each user of the application. As our dataset consists of users that commence usage of the application at different times, we ensure a relative calculation of usage duration (*i.e.*, we consider a user's first day of use as the starting point of application usage). This analysed dataset consists of a total of 2968 completed self-reports and 515 blockers. The data are provided by a total of 219 unique users, 192 of which work at organization A and 27 users which work at Organization B.

4.1 Application Usage

We first present the overall drop-off rate among users over a one year period in Fig. 3. Here, we define the drop-off week as the last week in which a check-in (*i.e.*, a full well-being report) is provided following their initial check-in. Overall, we find the steepest drop-off of users within the first week of usage (dropping 24.2% of users). A total of 43 users, 19.6%, only provide one check-in. The number of users dropping out increases throughout the year, with the increase in dropouts becoming more gradual following the initial month. The distribution of the users' check-ins over time is shown in Fig. 4 (day of the week) and Fig. 9 (time of day). The fact that most check-ins are on weekdays rather than weekends reflects the strong focus of the application on the workplace context. Assessing the time of check-in, we observe that most users check in at the end of their (work)day or later in the evening.

We furthermore assess whether and how usage of the application changes over time. Figure 5 shows the average number of check-ins made and blockers reported among active users of the application per week. This highlights that the average number of weekly check-ins decreases rapidly from an average of 1.7 in the first week of use to 1.0 in one month of usage, after which the decrease slows down and stabilises around 0.3 check-ins per week. The visualisation of Fig. 5 furthermore highlights that the most long-term users (over 40 weeks of use) provide a higher average of check-ins per week, hovering around 0.75.

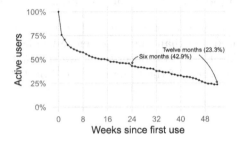

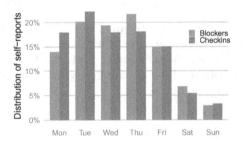

Fig. 3. Overall drop-off of rate across a one-year period.

Fig. 4. Distribution of check-ins and blockers across the week.

To better understand usage differences between short-term and long-term users of the application, we divide users into quartiles as based on their dropout week. We report these characteristics in Table 1. Our overview on these usage characteristics highlights that users belonging to Q4 (those with the longest usage duration) not only have the longest usage duration but also provide the highest number of check-ins (an average of 30 check-ins over the analysed usage duration). The information on median breaks among users (*i.e.*, days in-between two provided self-reports) highlights that extended breaks in usage of the application are common. Users with the longest usage duration have a median break in usage duration of three weeks.

Breaks in application usage may be indicative of a user quitting an application. Being able to predict which user will return to an application would be worthwhile information for application developers, as users can be reminded or incentivised to continue their usage of an application. Therefore, we next assess whether a relationship exists between gaps in usage duration and a user's final application usage. Figure 6 shows the distribution of usage gaps in the days leading up to a subsequent usage of the application (*i.e.*, non-final application usage) or the final usage of the application. We find a median value of a two-day break for a check-in that is eventually followed by a next check-in. For a check-in

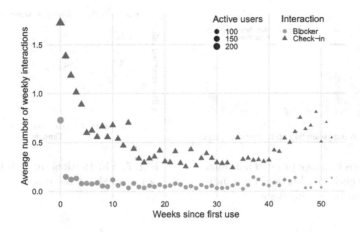

Fig. 5. Average number of interactions among active users.

Table 1. Usage characteristics as grouped by quartiles of usage duration.

Quartile	Weeks till dropout	Avg no. check-ins	Median break (days)
Q1	0–0	1.4 (SD = 0.6)	0
Q2	0–10	5.9 (SD = 4.7)	4.5
Q3	11–41	17.1 (SD = 14.5)	13.7
Q4	43–52>	30.1 (SD = 32.7)	21.1
All	0–52>	13.6 (SD = 21.0)	6.5

which is not followed by any further usage (*i.e.*, the final check-in), we find a median break in usage of five days leading up to this final check-in. A Mann Whitney U (non-parametric equivalent to the two sample *t*-test) indicates that the distributions between the two groups differed significantly (Mann-Whitney $U = 248312$, $n1 = 2749$, $n2 = 219$, $p < 0.01$ two-tailed). As indicated in Fig. 6, after a break in participant usage of eight days, the likelihood of the participant quitting usage of the application is larger than future usage of the application.

4.2 Well-Being and Challenges

On each check-in, users reported their mood, calmness, energy, and motivation levels on a scale from −50–50 (see Fig. 1), translated in this paper to 0–100 for analysis and reporting purposes. Assessing fluctuations in participant well-being, we identify the start of the working day (08:00–12:00) and end of the working day (16:00–18:00) as the timeslots with the most positive well-being check-ins reported. Well-being check-ins are consistently lowest in the early afternoon (13:00–15:00) and dip again toward the late evening (19:00–22:00).

Next, we analyse the blockers as reported by application users. Across the dataset, a total of 515 blockers were reported. On average, users report one

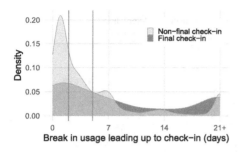

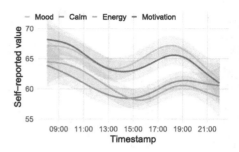

Fig. 6. Gaps in usage prior to non-final and final check-ins. Vertical lines indicate median breaks in usage.

Fig. 7. Fluctuations in well-being values throughout the day.

blocker for every 5.8 well-being reports. Assessed by category, roughly 60% of the blockers are work-related blockers (314, of which 180 on work and resources and 70 on work processes, among smaller categories) and 40% of blockers are of personal nature (201 blockers). Figure 4 shows the frequency of blockers per day of the week. Unsurprisingly, and in line with the well-being reports, we find that users are reporting the fewest number of blockers on the weekends. Across the working days, we find the least number of blockers to be reported on Monday.

4.3   Reminder Notifications

As a final element of analysis, we assess user preferences towards reminder notifications and their effect on completed self-reports. The application provides users the opportunity to change the default notification schedule, which is set to trigger at 08:00 at every workday (Mon–Fri). Our dataset contains information solely on the user's final configuration, *i.e.* any changes throughout use are not considered in this description. The majority of users change away from the default time of notification (77.6%). However, significantly fewer users change the default days of notification (37.0%). In changing the reminder notification time, participants primarily shift to a later time in the day, either towards the end of the working day or later in the evening (see Fig. 8 for an overview). In their preference of notification days, next to the default option of Mon–Fri (63.0%), the most popular option is to disable notifications altogether (23.3%), followed by a long tail of combinations with fewer notification days. Contrasting the time at which reminder notifications arrive (Fig. 8) with the time of check-ins being completed (Fig. 9), we observe a temporal correlation between the reminders and the actual check-ins—especially when disregarding the default reminder time.

Perhaps the most critical in terms of reminder notifications is whether they help in the collection of self-report data. Our dataset allows us to assess both whether users without notifications provide fewer self-reports, and whether they are more prone to stop using the application altogether. We calculate the average number of submitted self-reports among those with notifications enabled and

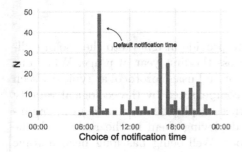

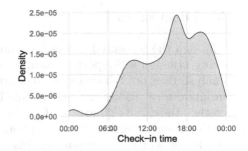

Fig. 8. Distribution of preferred reminder time.

Fig. 9. Distribution of check-in times across time of day.

those with notifications disabled. Users with notifications enabled completed an average of 13.4 self-reports, with users without notifications completing an average of 14.1 self-reports. A t-test did not find a significant difference between these two groups ($t(106.39) = 0.234$, $p = 0.815$). In terms of usage duration, we find a significant difference between those with notifications enabled (average of 21.3 weeks of active usage) as compared to those with notifications disabled (an average of 13.1 weeks), $t(106.58) = 2.957$, $p = 0.004$. We visualise this difference in Fig. 10. While this highlights that participants with notifications enabled make use of the application for a significantly longer period of time, we are unable to establish a causal relationship (*i.e.*, reminder notifications could lead to sustained usage, or those that disabled notifications were simply less interested from the beginning and therefore disabled notifications early on).

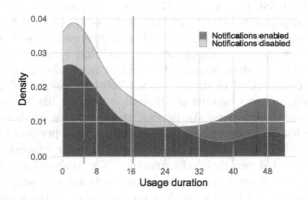

Fig. 10. Distribution of usage duration as split between those with notifications disabled and enabled.

5   Discussion

Through the presented analysis we aim to provide insights into the use of well-being oriented self-report application across the first year of usage. While our analysis does not follow a strict recruitment and usage protocol as typically seen in laboratory studies, we believe this is compensated by the ecological validity of the study. It is impossible to study these deployments in a team or organisational environment without actually deploying them in the real-world, the results of which we present in this paper. Well-being has long been a topic of interest within the broader HCI community [6], as well as one of the main topics of interest within Quantified Self research [18, 28]. Our data on participants' self-reported well-being levels align closely with the existing literature. Widely reported phenomena of shifts in well-being, including high well-being values in the morning, followed by a dip in the early afternoon, and a subsequent increase after working-hours [15], are closely matched (see Fig. 7). Our findings further indicate a close alignment between the self-reported well-being variables of mood, calmness, energy, and motivation when aggregated across users, albeit with different intra-daily fluctuations in these. Given the large overlap in construct measured, the collection of these four well-being parameters may be an unnecessary burden to participants. Especially in the light of widely reported participant strain in Experience Sampling-based studies, potentially resulting in fewer completed self-reports or earlier dropout rates [3, 12].

5.1   Considering Dropout

Within the HCI community, and among Quantified Self researchers in particular, attrition of users (or participants in the context of a study) is a well-known phenomenon [1, 21, 38]. For example, Gouveia et al. found that only 14% of the users of their app-based activity tracker used the application for longer than two weeks, despite implementing a number of literature-based design strategies to promote long-term engagement [16]. Such low numbers are no outliers, with application usage often being highly exploratory and quickly removed once installed [39]. Comparison of dropout rates between different deployments is, however, challenging, as a number of different factors are likely to influence participants' usage commitments. We provide three possible explanations for our relatively high level of observed engagement over a long period of time.

First, our analysis is based on a deployment within the context of two organizations and embedded into their infrastructure. The analysed application allows teams to assess and monitor their well-being levels anonymously and in aggregate, share blockers and ideas with their teams. This sets the application apart from other well-being tracking applications, as the end user (*i.e.*, employee) is aware that their contribution is not solely of use to themselves but might be picked up as part of a larger trend within the organisation. This highlights the potential positive impact on engagement rates of operationalising (well-being) self-reports beyond the scale of the individual. Along this line, Berrocal et al. studied 'Peer-ceived Momentary Assessment', in which an individual's self-reports are further complemented with peer-reports as provided by family members or friends [5]. The findings from Berrocal et al.'s study highlight how the assessments provided by peers align with self-reports across a number of constructs (observable behaviours and states). The involvement of peers, especially in an inherently hierarchical setting such as the workplace, may add additional pressure on individuals to join in participating in active self-reported data collection. While the current study focused solely on well-being reports as perceived by the user, future work may explore how the collection of well-being in the context of work can affect workplace dynamics and support the optimisation of work for experienced well-being.

Second, in addition to collecting self-report data, our application also provides users with a dashboard through which they can observe changes in their well-being reports across different timespans (day, week, month, year). This allows users to generate personal value from the application over the long term, by deriving their own insights. Furthermore, the application provides a way for users to respond to blockers and ideas shared within the app, which may lead to user expectations that self-reporting will generate a novel response. This aligns with earlier recommendations by Gouveia et al. to maintain engagement with users [16]. While Gouveia et al.'s work focused primarily on the use of activity trackers, their suggestion to sustain engagement by providing a novel message in response may be applicable also in the scenario of self-report studies.

Third, our evaluation indicates that users can and do return to using the application even after extended periods of dropout. This behaviour is not captured in deployments restrained to a shorter time period.

5.2   Check-in Settings and Behaviour

While our results show that having notifications enabled did not result in more completed self-reports, they do highlight that those with notifications enabled are more likely to use the application for a longer period of time. Prior work suggests that users rarely change the default notification settings of applications [49], although it does not provide any concrete numbers on how many users do change away from system defaults. Our results highlight that, although the default notification time is the most popular time for notifications (see Fig. 8), a large majority of 78% of our users did change away from the default notification time. Contrasting the insights on default notification time in Fig. 8 with the distribution of check-in times across the day in Fig. 9 furthermore highlights that while 08:00 is the most common time for notifications to arrive, it is not the most common time for users to provide their self-reports. Instead, we see an obvious temporal correlation between participant check-in time and their choice of notification time among those that have adjusted the default notification time. This indicates that, at least for studies in which one daily notification is common (*e.g.*, diary studies), allowing participants to customise the time of incoming notification could increase participant responsiveness. While this increased flexibility in study design was already suggested in 2003 by Consolvo and Walker [11], it is still rather uncommon to allow study participants to choose their time of notification in diary/Experience Sampling Method studies. Whether or not providing a default notification time in the first place, as compared to forcing users to pick a time of their own, affects subsequent response rate and response time to notifications is an interesting avenue for future work.

Our results highlight that active users provide less than one well-being self-report on average per week. The reporting of blockers is rare, with blockers making up close to 15% of the entire dataset. How do we interpret these numbers in light of the aforementioned discussion on attrition and dropout rates? A relevant study on well-being in the workplace was conducted by Pelayo et al. [42], who investigated mood self-tracking in call centres over four weeks across 71 participants. Their results highlight an average of 17 moods reported per team member, or just over four per week. The setup of this study relied on regular meetings with team managers and coaches to motivate and support managers and coaches of the call centre teams in the evaluation. This stands in stark contrast with our study, in which we minimised research contact with the application's users and therefore obtain a better understanding of the users' natural behaviour and interaction with the application.

5.3   Implications for Research

By investigating the long-term usage of a self-report application deployed in a real-world company environment, we uncovered novel insights into using self-report applications. Several of our findings contradict existing work or raise new questions regarding the use of self-tracking applications. Simultaneously, we acknowledge the limitations of interpreting results from individual deployments. As such, we present the following implications primarily as an opportunity for future research to better inform researchers and practitioners of real-world application usage.

Long-term Deployments Reveal Varying Usage Patterns. Contrary to our expectations, we found that users that had seemingly given up on using the application returned to use the application after relatively long usage breaks (up to three weeks for the top 25% of long-term users – Table 1). This behaviour would not be captured during typical study deployments and may require the research community to revisit some of the existing beliefs regarding long-term application usage. One factor that may cause such behaviour is that our users are surrounded by individuals who still retain the use of the tracking application, thus reminding of the option to continue their self-tracking.

Usage Patterns may Indicate Future Application Abandonment. Our results highlight a significant difference in the length of usage breaks between continuing and final application usage, indicating that the length of usage breaks can be used to predict future abandonment (see Fig. 6). While additional investigation of this phenomenon is required to confirm the generalisability of this finding, the possible implications are numerous. Applications within ubiquitous computing, Quantified Self, and self-report studies, among others, could directly benefit from knowing when users may quit – providing the opportunity to incentivise continued application usage or support alternative forms of usage [47]. We, therefore, consider further identification and the possible prediction of future application abandonment as a valuable opportunity for the research community.

Industry Collaboration can Produce Rich Longitudinal Insights. While *in situ* evaluations are often recognised for their high external validity, they have also been described as *"costly and often technically challenging"* [23]. This may, in part, explain the relatively low number of longitudinal deployments that have been conducted within our research community [27]. While not a silver bullet to resolve these challenges, we highlight that collaboration with industry provides opportunities for data collection that overcome some of the constraints academic researchers face. Furthermore, we stress that such collaborations should not impact researcher impartiality. The limitations of assessing such datasets, such as sample bias, should be explicit in the published work.

5.4   Limitations

We highlight several limitations in our work that should be considered when interpreting the presented results. First, our analysis focuses on one specific application and may therefore not generalise to other well-being oriented self-report applications. While the primary elements of the application closely align with existing applications in Quantified Self and self-report research (*e.g.*, reminders, logbook of past activities), individual aspects of an application may significantly affect end-user motivation and willingness to provide data input [16]. Second, users of the application may have left the organisation during data collection. As such, they have stopped using the application as a result of their employment situation rather than other factors that might affect application usage. We are unable to incorporate this aspect into our analysis due to the anonymity of user data. While we expect the effect to be relatively limited, this may have resulted in a slight overestimation of the users' dropout rate. Finally, our analysis is focused on the deployment across two individual organizations. Given this limited sample of organizations, we are unable to assess the effect that different organisational cultures or leadership advocacy patterns have on the usage of such an application. We suggest this as a potential avenue for future research.

6   Conclusion

We present an analysis of one year of well-being self-report data. This longitudinal analysis, involving over two hundred individual users, provides insights into real-world usage behaviour. Our findings highlight that while dropout rates of self-report applications are high, we also find that, contrary to prior work, a short-term break in usage does not necessarily signal a dropout, with a cohort of users returning to the application in the long term after extended intervals in use. In terms of well-being values, we find the application's well-being reports are consistent with prior findings regarding the changing patterns of well-being self-reports during the day at various times. Regarding notifications, we find that a large majority of users change their default notification time and that those with notifications enabled have a significantly longer average usage duration compared to those with notifications disabled. Based on our findings, we highlight recommendations for future studies involving active participant contributions, including the use of contextual feedback features to increase long-term engagement rates; the impact of presenting not only individual but also the self-report data of peers; and the effect of organisational culture on long-term self-report behaviour and retention.

References

1. Attig, C., Franke, T.: Abandonment of personal quantification: A review and empirical study investigating reasons for wearable activity tracking attrition. Comput. Hum. Behav. **102**, 223–237 (2020). https://doi.org/10.1016/j.chb.2019.08.025
2. van Berkel, N., Ferreira, D., Kostakos, V.: The experience sampling method on mobile devices. ACM Comput. Surv. **50**(6), 1–40 (2017). https://doi.org/10.1145/3123988
3. van Berkel, N., Kostakos, V.: Recommendations for conducting longitudinal experience sampling studies. In: Karapanos, E., Gerken, J., Kjeldskov, J., Skov, M.B. (eds.) Advances in Longitudinal HCI Research. HIS, pp. 59–78. Springer, Cham (2021). https://doi.org/10.1007/978-3-030-67322-2_4
4. van Berkel, N., Luo, C., Ferreira, D., Goncalves, J., Kostakos, V.: The curse of quantified-self: an endless quest for answers. In: Adjunct Proceedings of the 2015 ACM International Joint Conference on Pervasive and Ubiquitous Computing and Proceedings of the 2015 ACM International Symposium on Wearable Computers, pp. 973–978. UbiComp/ISWC 2015 Adjunct (2015). https://doi.org/10.1145/2800835.2800946
5. Berrocal, A., Concepcion, W., De Dominicis, S., Wac, K.: Complementing human behavior assessment by leveraging personal ubiquitous devices and social links: an evaluation of the peer-ceived momentary assessment method. JMIR Mhealth Uhealth **8**(8), e15947 (2020). https://doi.org/10.2196/15947
6. Blandford, A.: HCI for health and wellbeing: challenges and opportunities. Int. J. Hum Comput Stud. **131**, 41–51 (2019). https://doi.org/10.1016/j.ijhcs.2019.06.007
7. Caraban, A., Karapanos, E., Gonçalves, D., Campos, P.: 23 Ways to Nudge: A Review of Technology-Mediated Nudging in Human-Computer Interaction. In: Proceeding of the 2019 CHI Conference, pp. 1–15 (2019). https://doi.org/10.1145/3290605.3300733
8. Chalhoub, G., Kraemer, M.J., Nthala, N., Flechais, I.: "it did not give me an option to decline": a longitudinal analysis of the user experience of security and privacy in smart home products. In: Proceedings of the 2021 CHI Conference on Human Factors in Computing Systems (2021). https://doi.org/10.1145/3411764.3445691

9. Cherubini, M., Villalobos-Zuñiga, G., Boldi, M.O., Bonazzi, R.: The unexpected downside of paying or sending messages to people to make them walk: Comparing tangible rewards and motivational messages to improve physical activity. ACM Trans. Comput.-Hum. Interact. **27**(2), 1–44 (2020). https://doi.org/10.1145/3365665

10. Choe, E.K., Lee, N.B., Lee, B., Pratt, W., Kientz, J.A.: Understanding quantified-selfers' practices in collecting and exploring personal data. In: Proceedings of the SIGCHI Conference on Human Factors in Computing Systems, pp. 1143–1152 (2014). https://doi.org/10.1145/2556288.2557372

11. Consolvo, S., Walker, M.: Using the experience sampling method to evaluate ubicomp applications. IEEE Pervasive Comput. **2**(2), 24–31 (2003). https://doi.org/10.1109/MPRV.2003.1203750

12. Eisele, G., et al.: The effects of sampling frequency and questionnaire length on perceived burden, compliance, and careless responding in experience sampling data in a student population. Assessment (2020). https://doi.org/10.1177/1073191120957102

13. Fowler, F.: Survey Research Methods. Thousand Oaks, California, 4th edn. (2009). https://doi.org/10.4135/9781452230184

14. Fritz, T., Huang, E.M., Murphy, G.C., Zimmermann, T.: Persuasive technology in the real world: A study of long-term use of activity sensing devices for fitness. In: Proceedings of the SIGCHI Conference on Human Factors in Computing Systems, pp. 487–496. CHI 2014 (2014). https://doi.org/10.1145/2556288.2557383

15. Golder, S.A., Macy, M.W.: Diurnal and seasonal mood vary with work, sleep, and daylength across diverse cultures. Science **333**(6051), 1878–1881 (2011). https://doi.org/10.1126/science.1202775

16. Gouveia, R., Karapanos, E., Hassenzahl, M.: How do we engage with activity trackers? a longitudinal study of habito. In: Proceedings of the 2015 ACM International Joint Conference on Pervasive and Ubiquitous Computing, pp. 1305–1316. UbiComp 2015 (2015). https://doi.org/10.1145/2750858.2804290

17. Grudin, J.: Why CSCW applications fail: Problems in the design and evaluation of organizational interfaces. In: Proceedings of the 1988 ACM Conference on Computer-Supported Cooperative Work, pp. 85–93. CSCW 1988 (1988). https://doi.org/10.1145/62266.62273

18. Hollis, V., Konrad, A., Whittaker, S.: Change of Heart: Emotion Tracking to Promote Behavior Change. In: Proceedings of the 33rd Annual ACM Conference on Human Factors in Computing Systems, pp. 2643–2652 (2015). https://doi.org/10.1145/2702123.2702196

19. Horvitz, E., Koch, P., Apacible, J.: Busybody: Creating and fielding personalized models of the cost of interruption. In: Proceedings of the 2004 ACM Conference on Computer Supported Cooperative Work, pp. 507–510. CSCW 2004 (2004). https://doi.org/10.1145/1031607.1031690

20. Isaacs, E., Konrad, A., Walendowski, A., Lennig, T., Hollis, V., Whittaker, S.: Echoes from the past: How technology mediated reflection improves well-being. In: Proceedings of the SIGCHI Conference on Human Factors in Computing Systems, pp. 1071–1080. CHI 2013 (2013). https://doi.org/10.1145/2470654.2466137

21. Jun, E., Hsieh, G., Reinecke, K.: Types of motivation affect study selection, attention, and dropouts in online experiments. Proc. ACM Hum.-Comput. Interact. **1**(CSCW), 1–15 (2017). https://doi.org/10.1145/3134691

22. Kahneman, D., Krueger, A.B.: Developments in the measurement of subjective well-being. J. Econ. Perspect. **20**(1), 3–24 (2006). https://doi.org/10.1257/089533006776526030

23. Kaptein, M.: Experiments, longitudinal studies, and sequential experimentation: how using "intermediate" results can help design experiments. In: Karapanos, E., Gerken, J., Kjeldskov, J., Skov, M.B. (eds.) Advances in Longitudinal HCI Research. HIS, pp. 121–149. Springer, Cham (2021). https://doi.org/10.1007/978-3-030-67322-2_7

24. Karapanos, E., Zimmerman, J., Forlizzi, J., Martens, J.B.: User experience over time: An initial framework. In: Proceedings of the SIGCHI Conference on Human Factors in Computing Systems, pp. 729–738 (2009). https://doi.org/10.1145/1518701.1518814

25. Kim, Y.H., Lee, B., Srinivasan, A., Choe, E.K.: Data@hand: Fostering visual exploration of personal data on smartphones leveraging speech and touch interaction. In: Proceedings of the 2021 CHI Conference on Human Factors in Computing Systems. CHI 2021 (2021). https://doi.org/10.1145/3411764.3445421

26. Kjeldskov, J., Paay, J.: A longitudinal review of mobile HCI research methods. In: Proceedings of the 14th International Conference on Human-Computer Interaction with Mobile Devices and Services, pp. 69–78 (2012). https://doi.org/10.1145/2371574.2371586

27. Kjærup, M., Skov, M.B., Nielsen, P.A., Kjeldskov, J., Gerken, J., Reiterer, H.: Longitudinal studies in HCI research: a review of CHI publications from 1982–2019. In: Karapanos, E., Gerken, J., Kjeldskov, J., Skov, M.B. (eds.) Advances in Longitudinal HCI Research. HIS, pp. 11–39. Springer, Cham (2021). https://doi.org/10.1007/978-3-030-67322-2_2

28. Klasnja, P., Consolvo, S., Pratt, W.: How to Evaluate Technologies for Health Behavior Change in HCI Research. In: Proceedings of the SIGCHI Conference on Human Factors in Computing Systems, pp. 3063–3072 (2011). https://doi.org/10.1145/1978942.1979396

29. Kuosmanen, E., et al.: How does sleep tracking influence your life? experiences from a longitudinal field study with a wearable ring. Proc. ACM Hum.-Comput. Interact. 6(MHCI), 1–19 (2022). https://doi.org/10.1145/3546720

30. Larson, R., Csikszentmihalyi, M.: The experience sampling method. In: Flow and the Foundations of Positive Psychology, pp. 21–34. Springer, Dordrecht (2014). https://doi.org/10.1007/978-94-017-9088-8_2

31. Lee, J.H., Schroeder, J., Epstein, D.A.: Understanding and supporting self-tracking app selection. Proc. ACM Interact. Mob. Wearable Ubiquitous Technol. 5(4), 1–25 (2021). https://doi.org/10.1145/3494980

32. Lukoff, K., Yu, C., Kientz, J., Hiniker, A.: What makes smartphone use meaningful or meaningless? Proc. ACM Interact. Mob. Wearable Ubiquitous Technol. 2(1), 1–26 (2018). https://doi.org/10.1145/3191754

33. Lupton, D.: The Quantified Self. Wiley (2016)

34. Mattingly, S.M., et al.: The tesserae project: Large-scale, longitudinal, in situ, multimodal sensing of information workers. In: Extended Abstracts of the 2019 CHI Conference on Human Factors in Computing Systems, pp. 1–8 (2019). https://doi.org/10.1145/3290607.3299041

35. McCambridge, J., Kypri, K., Elbourne, D.: Research participation effects: a skeleton in the methodological cupboard. J. Clin. Epidemiol. 67(8), 845–849 (2014). https://doi.org/10.1016/j.jclinepi.2014.03.002

36. Meyer, J., Simske, S., Siek, K.A., Gurrin, C.G., Hermens, H.: Beyond quantified self: data for wellbeing. In: CHI 2014 Extended Abstracts on Human Factors in Computing Systems, pp. 95–98. CHI EA 2014 (2014). https://doi.org/10.1145/2559206.2560469

37. Neff, G., Nafus, D.: Self-tracking. MIT Press (2016)
38. Rabbi, M., Li, K., Yan, H.Y., Hall, K., Klasnja, P., Murphy, S.: ReVibe: a context-assisted evening recall approach to improve self-report adherence. Proc. ACM Interact. Mob. Wearable Ubiquitous Technol. **3**(4), 1–27 (2019). https://doi.org/10.1145/3369806
39. Rahmati, A., Tossell, C., Shepard, C., Kortum, P., Zhong, L.: Exploring iphone usage: the influence of socioeconomic differences on smartphone adoption, usage and usability. In: Proceedings of the 14th International Conference on Human-Computer Interaction with Mobile Devices and Services, pp. 11–20. MobileHCI 2012 (2012). https://doi.org/10.1145/2371574.2371577
40. Rapp, A., Cena, F.: Affordances for self-tracking wearable devices. In: Proceedings of the 2015 ACM International Symposium on Wearable Computers, pp. 141–142. ISWC 2015 (2015). https://doi.org/10.1145/2802083.2802090
41. Rieman, J.: The diary study: A workplace-oriented research tool to guide laboratory efforts. In: Proceedings of the INTERACT 1993 and CHI 1993 Conference on Human Factors in Computing Systems, pp. 321–326. CHI 1993 (1993). https://doi.org/10.1145/169059.169255
42. Rivera-Pelayo, V., Fessl, A., Müller, L., Pammer, V.: Introducing mood self-tracking at work: empirical insights from call centers. ACM Trans. Comput.-Hum. Interact. **24**(1), 1–28 (2017). https://doi.org/10.1145/3014058
43. Sanches, P., et al.: HCI and Affective Health: Taking Stock of a Decade of Studies and Charting Future Research Directions. In: Proceedings of the ACM Conference on Human Factors in Computing Systems (CHI 2019), pp. 1–17 (2019). https://doi.org/10.1145/3290605.3300475
44. Sas, C., Höök, K., Doherty, G., Sanches, P., Leufkens, T., Westerink, J.: Mental wellbeing: future agenda drawing from design, HCI and big data. In: Companion Publication of the 2020 ACM Designing Interactive Systems Conference, pp. 425–428. DIS 2020 Companion (2020). https://doi.org/10.1145/3393914.3395920
45. Schön, D.A.: The reflective practitioner: How professionals think in action. Routledge (2017)
46. Thieme, A., Wallace, J., Meyer, T.D., Olivier, P.: Designing for mental wellbeing: towards a more holistic approach in the treatment and prevention of mental illness. In: Proceedings of the 2015 British HCI Conference, pp. 1–10. British HCI 2015 (2015). https://doi.org/10.1145/2783446.2783586
47. Visuri, A., van Berkel, N., Goncalves, J., Rawassizadeh, R., Ferreira, D., Kostakos, V.: Understanding usage style transformation during long-term smartwatch use. Pers. Ubiquit. Comput. **25**(3), 535–549 (2021). https://doi.org/10.1007/s00779-020-01511-2
48. Wang, R., et al.: StudentLife: assessing mental health, academic performance and behavioral trends of college students using smartphones. In: Proceedings of the 2014 ACM International Joint Conference on Pervasive and Ubiquitous Computing, pp. 3–14 (2014). https://doi.org/10.1145/2632048.2632054
49. Westermann, T., Möller, S., Wechsung, I.: Assessing the relationship between technical affinity, stress and notifications on smartphones. In: Proceedings of the 17th International Conference on Human-Computer Interaction with Mobile Devices and Services Adjunct, pp. 652–659. MobileHCI 2015 (2015). https://doi.org/10.1145/2786567.2793684
50. Wilson, A.: Sensor- and Recognition-Based Input for Interaction, chap. 10, pp. 153–176. CRC Press (2009). https://doi.org/10.1201/b10368-13

51. Yeager, C.M., Shoji, K., Luszczynska, A., Benight, C.C.: Engagement with a trauma recovery internet intervention explained with the health action process approach (HAPA): longitudinal study. JMIR Ment. Health 5(2), e9449 (2018)
52. Zhang, X., Pina, L.R., Fogarty, J.: Examining unlock journaling with diaries and reminders for in situ self-report in health and wellness. In: Proceedings of the 2016 CHI Conference on Human Factors in Computing Systems, pp. 5658–5664 (2016). https://doi.org/10.1145/2858036.2858360

Awareness, Control and Impact in Digital Wellbeing - Results from Explorative Self-experiments

Yavuz Inal[1] (✉) (iD), Frode Guribye[2] (iD), Lee Taber[3] (iD), and Steve Whittaker[3] (iD)

[1] Department of Design, Norwegian University of Science and Technology, Gjøvik, Norway
yavuz.inal@ntnu.no
[2] Department of Information Science and Media Studies, University of Bergen, Bergen, Norway
[3] Computational Media Department, University of California, Santa Cruz, USA

Abstract. Research and design for digital wellbeing commonly focus on a single device, and time spent is the most common indicator of digital wellbeing. In this paper, we examine digital wellbeing along three dimensions: awareness, control, and impact, including positive and negative aspects. We report from two-week explorative self-experiments with 29 participants that made diary entries and reflection reports. The study discusses how digital wellbeing can be seen across devices and tasks to understand the usage patterns that can be used to identify possible interventions and problematic use that can be addressed by new designs. The impact of computers and smartphones differed among participants, with laptops receiving a more positive evaluation than smartphones. While the choice of the device itself may not be the primary factor in understanding digital well-being, further research efforts should identify different usage patterns - across devices and over the three dimensions of awareness, control, and impact.

Keywords: Digital Wellbeing · Self-experiment · Multi-device · Self-monitoring · Technology Overuse

1 Introduction

Digital wellbeing concerns how comfortable people are with their use of their digital devices and how that use affects their physical health, mental health, and overall life satisfaction. Ongoing debates about digital wellbeing adopt different perspectives within human-computer interaction. There is a clear need to understand the measurable impacts of digital devices on wellbeing, and this concern is shared with psychological research [2, 17]. Much clinically-oriented research frames current usage as potentially harmful and pathological, characterizing specific patterns of smartphone [7], game [10], and social media [1] usage as addictions. Research conducted within this framework has produced scales that aim to measure the negative impact of interactions with these digital devices and assess whether usage needs to be treated clinically. There is a similarly influential narrative within HCI, where the notion of 'overuse' is often assumed as a starting point for the research [14, 17], and screen-time is seen as a proxy measure of digital wellbeing.

J. Abdelnour Nocera et al. (Eds.): INTERACT 2023, LNCS 14144, pp. 633–642, 2023.
https://doi.org/10.1007/978-3-031-42286-7_35

Often, screen-time is used as the dependent variable as well as a target for behavior change. Nevertheless, others have taken a more critical stance towards the debate on addiction [8]. One problem with the addiction narrative is that it focuses on overuse while de-emphasizing the benefits of using digital devices. Nor does it identify different, positive motives for device usage. For example, certain types of information work would be impossible without digital devices. Social media and communication technologies represent important ways to maintain vital social ties with friends and family.

In contrast with the addiction narrative, Cecchinato et al. [4] take a more analytical and balanced stance. They argue that digital wellbeing can be framed from multiple perspectives, including medical, user-oriented, or design perspectives. A recent analysis of the effects of social media [13] found a very small but significant negative correlation between the use of social media and mental health. Similarly, Przybylski et al. [15] suggest a weak negative effect on mental health for overuse - measured as screen-time. Still, Meier and Reinecke [13] further claim that the finding varies according to what mental health indicators are used, and the diverse approaches to conceptualizing, framing, and measuring the problem make it hard to reach conclusive evidence, suggesting that research on digital wellbeing should move beyond a focus on screen-time as the indicator of use.

The ability to control the use of digital devices has been linked to the notion of self-regulation [12] and can be considered fundamental for digital wellbeing [11]. This ability to exert control over digital devices is crucial for how you can align use with your own goals. Still, using control as the only aspect of digital wellbeing could take away focus from how different usage patterns can have different impacts on overall wellbeing and give a too-narrow understanding of the different facets of digital wellbeing.

Meier and Reinecke [13] characterize the research on the relation between computer-mediated communication, including social and mobile media, and mental health as conceptually diverse. They identify various indicators of technological use and a similar diversity in how to conceptualize mental health. In mental health, the two main approaches are psychopathology and psychological well-being. In this paper, we focus on the latter. Psychological well-being refers to how an individual experiences and functions in everyday life. Digital well-being can then be seen as a way of conceptualizing how digital devices play a role in the overall psychological well-being of an individual.

To this end, this paper explores the relationship between how digital devices are used and how they impact users' wellbeing. To examine these questions, we devised an exploratory self-experiment with 29 participants. We focused on smartphone use and examined other devices, such as computers, tablets, interactive TVs, and gaming consoles. Seeing digital wellbeing as dependent on an ecology of tools [3] counters a sole focus on a single device, which has been a focus of much of the research on digital wellbeing, which has targeted smartphone use [14]. Focusing on digital wellbeing across devices [9] can help us identify use patterns and how different applications and tasks are allocated across and between different devices. Tools for time-tracking, such as Apple's Screen Time and Google's digital wellbeing tools, also consider this cross-device use and enable tracking across devices. This study's contributions are results from exploratory self-experiments and a questionnaire for measuring digital wellbeing with three dimensions: awareness, control, and impact.

2 Methods

We explored digital well-being using both self-experiments and a questionnaire. Self-experiments investigate how people identify a habit or behavior for change, enact a plan to change that behavior, and experience the results [5]. The participants analyze their behavior, interventions, and outcomes in such self-experiments, where tracking and systematic note-taking are key analytic tools. The method's strengths are that it is based on reflections and a contextualized understanding of how the incurred changes fit into daily routines and the particulars of each participant's life situation. Self-experiments are exploratory as each participant documents and reflects on the impact of digital devices on their wellbeing to discover a habit or behavior they want to change. They also reflect on the process of monitoring and experiencing the impact of the chosen variable when they implement their intervention.

A total of 29 master's students carried out individual self-experiments as a mandatory task as part of a master's course. Over two weeks, they filled out a daily diary according to a template provided by the researchers, where they documented how much and for what purpose they used their digital devices. They were encouraged to actively use the time-tracking tools that come with their devices (such as Apple screen time or Google's digital wellbeing tools). Each day they also wrote a short reflection note. After the first week, the participants were tasked with identifying one habit or usage pattern they wanted to change based on the first week of logging and reflection. They attempted to change that behavior for the second week, keeping track of their successes and failures. When the two weeks were over, the participants wrote a longer reflection note, analyzing if it was easy to change their habit, if they were surprised by their usage, if they found the tracking tools useful, and whether they perceived that their modified use of digital tools impacted their wellbeing. These reflection documents and daily diaries were subsequently anonymized and then analyzed for patterns and themes by the researchers.

We also had the students answer a questionnaire on digital well-being. The questionnaire has three primary constructs concerning awareness, control, and impact. The questions on impact addressed both eudaimonic and hedonic [10] aspects of digital well-being and their impact on health and social connectivity. We determined the Cronbach Alpha score to be .618, indicating an acceptable level of reliability of the items. Only parts of the results from the survey are reported in this paper. The Institutional review board for research ethics approved the study, and anonymized data was used for the analysis.

3 Results

Participating students were enrolled in a master-level human–computer interaction course. Of the participants, 15 (52%) were female, 13 (45%) were male, and one did not state their gender. Their mean age was 25.1 years (SD = 3.14). The questionnaire showed that overall time online was high: a significant proportion (31%) reported that they spent 9–10 h per day on their digital devices, followed by 11–12 h (24%), 5–6 h (17%), and 7–8 h (17%). Participants ranked which devices were necessary. Smartphones (69%) and computers/laptops (31%) were rated as the most important digital devices the participants used, while interactive TV, game consoles, and wearables were rated as the least important digital devices. Participants also ranked the importance of how they used their devices. Entertainment/media streaming and communication were the most important ways the participants used their digital devices, followed by school/work tasks, social media, time management, games, information seeking, and finance/business. We next explored the well-being constructs by analyzing participants' self-experiment reflections.

3.1 Awareness

Awareness Level. Reflections indicated that most participants (n = 19) felt they had a clear picture of their use of digital devices. "I am pretty adamant about not letting digital devices and social media take over too many aspects of my life." [ID8] As part of their diary entries, the participants kept a record of their screen-time, and many chose to use the built-in tools in their devices and received daily or weekly notifications, so they could easily keep track of their usage. "I am very aware of how much time I spend in front of screens. I use digital wellbeing tools, so I feel I have the use under control." [ID11].

Another 6 participants were somewhat aware of using digital devices in everyday life. "I wouldn't say accurate, but neither was I surprised. I'm aware that I spend much time with digital devices, as work and hobbies depend on them." [ID7] Although they reported being somewhat aware of their use, some expressed being surprised by the screen-time measures. "I realize that I spend much more time on my phone than I thought. It was not really shocking to me, but it was definitely interesting." [ID28] There were only four participants who did not have a precise picture. "I also have never thought of my Apple TV as screen-time, so I was a bit shocked at how many hours I look at a screen." [ID9] They had never checked screen-time features in the settings of their digital devices. "I thought I was not using my phone that much. Then when I enabled the digital wellbeing features on my phone, I was surprised to see that I was still using my phone around 2 to 3 h a day." [ID27].

Temporal and Device Usage Patterns. The participants mostly used their mobile phones in the morning (n = 5), in the evening (n = 5), during the daytime (n = 1), or the whole day (n = 2). They used their computers/laptops in the middle of the day (n = 3) or evenings (n = 2). The participants used their mobile phones for social media (n = 11) and communication (n = 6), followed by entertainment (n = 5), banking (n = 3), and productivity (n = 2). Productive tasks (e.g., schoolwork) (n = 14), streaming (n = 5), digital games (n = 3), and entertainment (n = 3) were major activities performed on a computer/laptop. Fewer participants reported using a tablet device during the study period. They reported using their tablet device for productivity (n = 3), news (n = 1), streaming (n = 1), and games (n = 1). The participants also reported multitasking, such as listening to music/audiobooks (n = 3) or watching videos (n = 3) while doing another task (e.g., doing laundry, eating meals, cooking, cleaning).

Impression of Digital Time-tracking Tools. The participants used time-tracking tools more on mobile phones than computer/laptop and tablet devices. In-built screen-time applications were the most popular tools, with 19 participants on mobile phones, five on computers/laptops, and two on tablet devices. Some participants used different time-tracking tools such as Action Dash, PostBox, Google Digital Wellbeing, Appblock, Rescue Time, and Webtime Tracker.

Most participants (n = 21) considered digital time-tracking tools useful for increasing awareness. "Very useful to see what parts of the day I spend most on my phone. I got more aware of my phone usage because of the weekly reports you get, which tell you how much time you spent on your phone compared to last week." [ID15] Digital time-tracking tools gave the participants more control over how much time they spent on leisure time activities. "It gives me a choice to either put it down and do something else, or I have to choose to continue the mindless scrolling." [ID24] Of those participants, some (n = 3) reported using digital time-tracking tools before but cut out using them due to the pandemic. "During the pandemic, I ignored both apps to improve my mental health. I think I will get back to that from now on." [ID1] Besides, three participants preferred to keep track by themselves. "The digital time tracking tools felt pointless to me as I already know exactly what I get up to on my phone." [ID19].

Seven participants considered digital time-tracking tools to be useless. Three of them reported that these tools did not affect their usage habits. "I don't think it made me significantly more aware of my use of digital devices." [ID18] Justifying this, one felt that they didn't overuse their digital devices, another considered their personal information, another was not interested in how much time spent or setting limitations, and one didn't want to spend less time on digital devices. Three participants reported that digital time-tracking tools didn't work well. Hence, they were annoying. "It tracks every open application. For example, one day, I used "finder" for 5 h, but it was just because it was not closed. So, it should rather track the ones you are using." [ID20].

3.2 Control

Regulation Level. More than half of the participants (n = 19) reported that it was hard to regulate and control their use of digital devices. "The hardest part was to get started and find something to replace my phone as a source of entertainment." [ID18] The participants found it very challenging to break their habit of using their digital devices. "My problem was that it was way too easy to just extend the time limit set. This made it hard to change the behavior as I could click a button to keep scrolling." [ID21] Furthermore, the participants found it difficult to separate leisure and work. "It's all bundled together in a bit of hot mess where the result is that I'll spend time worrying about school when I'm supposed to have time off, and then go and spend 50% of the time on procrastination when I'm supposed to be doing schoolwork." [ID19].

Only 9 participants reported that it was easy to regulate and control the use of their digital devices. Most of these participants reported that they could prioritize productive tasks, communication, and leisure activities. "I don't have the urge to answer a text message immediately; my only exception is if it is from my mom, dad, or boyfriend." [ID20] One participant reported no need to regulate and control the use of their digital devices, and one reported it varied. "If I have had a good and productive day watching shows or scrolling on Instagram feels more justified and more like a treat." [ID4].

Barriers to Changing Digital Behaviors. Five participants identified the pandemic as a barrier to changing their digital behaviors. Digital devices seemed to dominate their lives, especially since the pandemic. "I use my phone and computer a lot, and after corona hit even more, I have tried to cut down before, but with no real social options other than online, it is tough." [ID17] Pandemic restrictions made participants less likely to socialize face to face, relying more on their digital devices to talk to friends or meet fellow students. "I am fully aware of my bad habits, and if it were not for the pandemic, I would maybe even consider changing them." [ID1].

These social and communication needs provided strong incentives that kept participants (n = 4) tethered to their digital devices. "As I live literally on the other side of the country from my family at the moment, I also love my phone because it allows me to stay in touch with family and friends back home." [ID24] Three participants reported that it depended on their school workload and how much it demanded digital devices. "Most things I do on my devices are necessary, and hence not controllable (such as attending class, necessary contact with, i.e., work, e-mails, etc.). "Mandatory use" is a barrier to change habits." [ID12].

Three participants reported that the most significant barrier to changing their habits is the thought of missing out. They felt they had to be digitally available at all times. "I chat a lot with my friends, even more now due to Corona, and I always respond to messages when I see them. This is probably one reason why I kept wanting to open Instagram." [ID22] Furthermore, unchangeable daily habits (n = 2) and easy access to social media accounts (n = 1) using different digital devices were other barriers reported by the participants to changing their habits.

3.3 Impact

Habit or Behavior to Change. Many participants chose to stop or reduce phone use before going to sleep at night (n = 9) or after just waking up before getting up (n = 1). "I tend to watch videos in bed. And studies have shown that this is a bad habit as it hurts your sleep. I have also noticed that my eyes get sorer and more strained when I watch a screen in a dark room, even if the brightness is on the lowest setting." [ID4] This intervention made participants fall asleep earlier than usual, which enhanced productivity, suggesting that increasing sleep impacted wellbeing. "Putting the phone down before midnight allowed me to get more sleep. Some differences were noticeable. More productivity and less time spent on entertainment. The biggest difference would be that I went to bed earlier." [ID13].

Six participants chose to reduce the time spent on their mobile phones during the day. "I tried to spend less time watching a series by setting a cap on a maximum of two episodes per day." [ID5] They reduced the time spent on their mobile phone just procrastinating, especially for social media use. Overall, this helped them feel less stressed and focus more on productive tasks. "I feel less stressed and like I don't check apps when I am supposed to do school, etc." [ID26] Some participants chose to leave their mobile phones in another room (n = 3) when they were going to bed at night (n = 2). "I left my phone for charging in another room on day five of the first week of this experience. I experienced that I could concentrate well now that my phone was out of sight." [ID15].

To handle excessive use, three participants deleted an app such as Instagram or TikTok that they tend to get most distracted by. "I noticed that when I picked up my phone to distract myself while doing schoolwork, the first thing I would do was go on Instagram." [ID3] Two participants chose to turn off notifications on social media so as not to be distracted by their mobile phones during the daytime or when working on a productive task. "My phone was next to me all day, but I forgot it was there. It was liberating to control my day without the constant notifications from my phone. I will not change it back." [ID9] Some participants chose not to use their mobile phones and computer/laptop at the same time (n = 1), to read a book instead of reading on the internet (n = 1), and to spend their time studying (n = 1). Most participants (n = 18) reported that changing the variable they chose was easy. Only 6 participants reported it to be complicated initially and getting more challenging as the week passed (n = 2) and easy to start but possibly harder to maintain over time (n = 1).

Impact of the Use of Digital Devices on Wellbeing. A significant number of participants (n = 12) reported that using mobile phones affected their wellbeing negatively. "It is a real time-thief, and it is easy to get distracted by it when doing other things." [ID21] There were only five participants who reported that the use of mobile phones had a positive influence on their wellbeing. "Being able to socialize through messenger/Snapchat is something I truly appreciate." [ID19] However, this depended on the device, as 13 participants reported that using their computer/laptop positively impacted their wellbeing because they mostly use them for productive tasks such as schoolwork. "Using my computer mostly makes me feel productive and doesn't negatively affect my wellbeing." [ID3] There was only one participant who reported that the use of a computer/laptop affected their wellbeing negatively. "I've struggled to separate leisure and work. I used to browse memes, watch tv-series, or mindlessly surf the internet." [ID19] Seven participants reported mixed benefits, i.e., that digital devices (in general) positively and negatively affected their wellbeing. "It can keep me from being active by distracting me and keeping me sitting on the couch, or it can inspire me to be more active with exercises and inspirational people." [ID25] They believed a fine line existed between using digital devices in moderation and excessively.

4   Discussion and Conclusion

Our study analyzed digital device use as part of an artifact ecology, with participants reporting on digital wellbeing across devices. This holistic approach points to the multiple purposes for which devices are used, which is central to digital wellbeing. Many participants reported different impacts when comparing computers and smartphones, with laptops judged more positively than smartphones. However, cross-device usage patterns suggest that it is not the particular device that is the key to understanding wellbeing; instead, usage patterns are critical. Laptops are generally used for work tasks, while smartphones are used more for entertainment and social media. These latter tasks gave rise to behaviors that participants thought were problematic. These complex heterogeneous forms of usage across devices and tasks also make it difficult for participants to analyze their behaviors if they wish to intervene, suggesting design opportunities we discuss below.

Awareness: Most participants reported a clear picture of their use, and few were surprised by how much time they spent. Higher awareness was correlated with higher scores on the digital wellbeing scale, while the reported time spent did not show such correlations. While the data is inconclusive, we can ask whether time spent does not necessarily affect digital wellbeing (as measured). Several digital wellbeing tools are focused on tracking how much time you spend to increase user awareness. Most participants struggled to manage their actions, particularly when using their phones, which was the primary source of their difficulties. However, they were positive about using a self-monitoring tool to increase their awareness and cut down on use. This aligns with previous research that individuals desire to use personal tracking devices to increase their productivity and reduce screen-time [6, 16]. When proposing and identifying interventions, it is clear that they can be something other than digital and can be as simple as leaving the phone in another room. There might also be opportunities for designs that allow people to create new habits and track these. Our findings also suggest that while these are useful tools for increasing awareness, more than general awareness is needed and that there might be a need for breaking down the usage by task and device as a step towards understanding certain usage patterns.

Control: Most participants reported finding it hard to control their behaviors, with most problems arising from phone usage. The ability to regulate the use depends on the patterns of use across devices and the different tasks users engage in when using these devices. This difficulty in controlling use shows how a singular focus on self-control as the most important barrier can be too narrow when researching digital wellbeing. Participants identified control as one of the main barriers to changing their behavior. They referred to their mixed usage of devices and their situation where they were reliant on their digital devices for doing work tasks and being in a situation due to the regulation of social distancing during the pandemic, where the digital devices were their primary tool for keeping in touch with others. An issue with digital device use is that there is a thin line between controlled and disorganized use. Our participants described needing to use their devices for various reasons, opening the door for unrestricted use.

Impact: When discussing digital wellbeing, an essential part is understanding its impact on daily life. The participants reported positive and negative effects in their reflection notes, but most reported negative consequences, such as impacting sleep. Again, many of them saw different impacts according to different devices. Participants reported a typical pattern of watching YouTube on the phone before going to sleep and being caught in an endless stream of new content. Too much YouTube at night before bed was an example of a habit that should be possible to change, and the participants, when tasked with changing a habit or behavior, were able to propose something that they wanted to change. Furthermore, most were able to propose a concrete way to change that habit or behavior, indicating that they could potentially change that behavior at any time.

In the paper, we have argued that a narrow focus on time-tracking or self-regulation can overlook important aspects of use, such as use across devices, and that a path forward could be to look at usage patterns across tasks and devices when designing for wellbeing and interventions for changing digital habits and behavior. In future work, we plan to further explore the three dimensions of digital wellbeing and develop the digital wellbeing questionnaire to examine how we can measure digital wellbeing across different devices and tasks, including impacts on social connectivity, productivity, and eudaimonic and hedonic well-being.

References

1. Andreassen, C.S., Pallesen, S., Griffiths, M.D.: The relationship between addictive use of social media, narcissism, and self-esteem: findings from a large national survey. Addict. Behav. **64**, 287–293 (2017). https://doi.org/10.1016/j.addbeh.2016.03.006
2. Bauer, M., et al.: Smartphones in mental health: a critical review of background issues, current status and future concerns. Int. J. Bipolar Disorders **8**, 1–19 (2020). https://doi.org/10.1186/s40345-019-0164-x
3. Bødker, S., Klokmose, C.N.: The human-artifact model: an activity theoretical approach to artifact ecologies. Human-Computer Interaction **26**(4), 315–371 (2011). https://doi.org/10.1080/07370024.2011.626709
4. Cecchinato, M.E., et al..: Designing for digital wellbeing: a research & practice agenda. In: Extended Abstracts of the 2019 CHI Conference on Human Factors in Computing Systems, pp. 1–8. ACM (2019). https://doi.org/10.1145/3290607.3298998
5. Daskalova, N., Desingh, K., Papoutsaki, A., Schulze, D., Sha, H., Huang, J.: Lessons learned from two cohorts of personal informatics self-experiments. In: Proceedings of the ACM on Interactive, Mobile, Wearable and Ubiquitous Technologies, **1**(3), pp. 1–22. ACM (2017). https://doi.org/10.1145/3130911
6. Hiniker, A., Hong, S., Kohno, T., Kientz, J.A.: MyTime: designing and evaluating an intervention for smartphone non-use. In: Proceedings of the 2016 CHI Conference on Human Factors in Computing Systems, pp. 4746–4757. ACM (2016). https://doi.org/10.1145/2858036.2858403
7. Kwon, M., Kim, D.J., Cho, H., Yang, S.: The smartphone addiction scale: development and validation of a short version for adolescents. PLoS ONE **8**(12), e83558 (2013). https://doi.org/10.1371/journal.pone.0083558
8. Lanette, S., Chua, P.K., Hayes, G., Mazmanian, M.: How much is' too much'? the role of a smartphone addiction narrative in individuals' experience of use. In: Proceedings of the ACM on Human-Computer Interaction, 2(CSCW), pp. 1–22. ACM (2018). https://doi.org/10.1145/3274370
9. Lascau, L., Wong, N.G.O.I., Brumby, D., Cox, A.: Why are cross-device interactions important when it comes to digital wellbeing? In: CHI 2019 Workshop "Designing for Digital Wellbeing: A Research Practice Agenda". ACM (2019)
10. Lemmens, J.S., Valkenburg, P.M., Peter, J.: Development and validation of a game addiction scale for adolescents. Media Psychol. **12**(1), 77–95 (2009). https://doi.org/10.1080/15213260802669458
11. Lyngs, U.: Putting self-control at the centre of digital wellbeing. In: CHI 2019 Workshop "Designing for Digital Wellbeing: A Research Practice Agenda". ACM (2019)
12. Lyngs, U., et al.: Self-control in cyberspace: applying dual systems theory to a review of digital self-control tools. In: Proceedings of the 2019 CHI Conference on Human Factors in Computing Systems, pp. 1–18. ACM (2019) https://doi.org/10.1145/3290605.3300361
13. Meier, A., Reinecke, L.: Computer-mediated communication, social media, and mental health: a conceptual and empirical meta-review. Commun. Res. **48**(8), 1182–1209 (2021). https://doi.org/10.1177/0093650220958224

14. Monge Roffarello, A., De Russis, L.: The race towards digital wellbeing: issues and opportunities. In: Proceedings of the 2019 CHI Conference on Human Factors in Computing Systems, pp. 1–14. ACM (2019) https://doi.org/10.1145/3290605.3300616
15. Przybylski, A.K., Orben, A., Weinstein, N.: How much is too much? examining the relationship between digital screen engagement and psychosocial functioning in a confirmatory cohort study. J. Am. Acad. Child Adolesc. Psychiatry **59**(9), 1080–1088 (2020). https://doi.org/10.1016/j.jaac.2019.06.017
16. Rooksby, J., Asadzadeh, P., Rost, M., Morrison, A., Chalmers, M.: Personal tracking of screen time on digital devices. In: Proceedings of the 2016 CHI Conference on Human Factors in Computing Systems, pp. 284–296. ACM (2016). https://doi.org/10.1145/2858036.2858055
17. Zheng, X., Lee, M.K.O.: Excessive use of mobile social networking sites: negative consequences on individuals. Comput. Hum. Behav. **65**, 65–76 (2016). https://doi.org/10.1016/j.chb.2016.08.011

Eliciting Meaningful Collaboration Metrics: Design Implications for Self-Tracking Technologies at Work

Alina Lushnikova[1]([✉])[iD], Kerstin Bongard-Blanchy[1][iD], Vincent Koenig[1][iD], and Carine Lallemand[1,2][iD]

[1] University of Luxembourg, 2, Avenue de l'Université,
4366 Esch-sur-Alzette, Luxembourg
{alina.lushnikova,kerstin.bongard-blanchy,
vincent.koenig,carine.lallemand}@uni.lu
[2] Eindhoven University of Technology, 5600 MB Eindhoven, The Netherlands
c.e.lallemand@tue.nl

Abstract. As the workplace collaboration software market is booming, there is an opportunity to design tools to support reflection and self-regulation of collaboration practices. Building on approaches from personal informatics (PI), we aim to understand and promote the use of data to enable employees to explore their work practices, specifically collaboration. Focused on the preparation stage of PI (deciding to track and tools selection), we invited office workers (N=15, knowledge workers in academia) to identify meaningful aspects of their collaboration experience and report them in a logbook for two weeks. We then conducted semi-structured interviews with participants to identify and reflect on metrics related to collaboration experience. We contribute new insights into employees' motivations and envisioned metrics reflecting their collaboration, including the personal, social, and organizational considerations for collecting and sharing this data. We derive design implications for self-tracking technologies for collaboration.

Keywords: Collaboration · Self-tracking · Group-tracking · Personal informatics · Computer-Supported Cooperative Work

1 Introduction

The recent COVID-19 pandemic and the need to work remotely spiked an already present interest in collaborative tools. A 2020 report by Gartner [22] predicted the worldwide market for social software and collaboration in the workplace to grow from \$2.7 billion in 2018 to \$5.1 billion by 2022. Despite most people working collaboratively and an ever-growing offer of software tools to support collaborative work, there is a shared impression that subjective collaboration experiences and non-instrumental goals are still insufficiently accounted for in the design of collaboration technology [7].

© The Author(s), under exclusive license to Springer Nature Switzerland AG 2023
J. Abdelnour Nocera et al. (Eds.): INTERACT 2023, LNCS 14144, pp. 643–664, 2023.
https://doi.org/10.1007/978-3-031-42286-7_36

Personal informatics (PI) provides opportunities to collect and reflect on meaningful data [16]. This approach is also referred to as 'self-tracking' or 'quantified-self' and consists of collecting and reflecting on personal information. It starts with the preparation stage where the person decides what and how to track. The practice of self-tracking has gained popularity in the past decade and is now widely spread in the private sphere, where smartphone applications and wearable devices (e.g., smartwatches, fitness trackers) support self-tracking in well-being [28] and health management [11] contexts. However, it remains under-explored in the work environment [16], mainly limited to self-reflection on productivity [25], emotions at the workplace [32,44], or organization stress [50].

While personal informatics puts the emphasis on tracking as an individual activity, recent research initiatives explore less individualistic approaches with an increasing interest in studying and designing for more collective PI practices [37]. Among these, we see a focus on groups of individuals tracking data, described as a valuable opportunity for collective sense-making [9]. Family informatics [41, 42] is such an example where family members track and visualize elements of interest together [41]. Professional informatics (Pro-I) refers to personalized, data-driven professional development [39].

With this exploratory empirical study, we expand the body of knowledge on the application of a personal informatics approach in the work context, with the goal of investigating the value of a user-driven implementation of self-tracking tools. Our research questions are: (RQ1) What aspects of collaboration are elicited as meaningful during the preparation stage of PI? (RQ2) What impact does preparing to self-track collaboration have? (RQ3) What risks and opportunities of data tracking and sharing are perceived during preparation to self-track collaboration? We contribute insights into how HCI researchers envision metrics for reflecting their collaboration experience, including the personal, social, and organizational considerations for collecting and sharing this data. We discuss how these insights inform the design of self-tracking technologies for collaboration, with the main focus on the preparation stage of personal informatics [17,29], one of the least supported in the current technological landscape [15].

2   Related Work

2.1   Understanding Collaboration Experiences

Vast literature from organizational behavior, business management, environmental science, education, and other fields seeks to comprehend the concept of collaboration, often focusing on specific collaboration settings such as meetings [5]. However, most of that research follows a business-centric approach [7], even though the effectiveness of collaboration - "joint effort towards a group goal" - is not only defined by people's satisfaction with the outcome but also with the process [5]. In this regard, the notion of user experience and specifically experience at work [7,30] has gained momentum with the focus on the fulfillment of users' psychological needs [21,26] and well-being [7].

Beyond the individual level, collaboration is a social activity [7] happening in an organizational setting that should foster and stimulate a collaborative spirit via a clear vision [2], supportive processes [3], and a shared concern for the task [2,7]. To this end, workspace awareness," up-to-the-moment understanding of another person's interaction with a shared workspace", is beneficial to collaboration, and its support is a traditional concern for technologies used by groups [2,7,19]. The relevance of time and space as contextual factors is growing, with an increasing number of people collaborating remotely or in a hybrid fashion over different time zones. Below we present the approach of personal informatics, whose sense-making and empowering potential makes it appropriate to the work context [6,16].

2.2 Personal Informatics at the Workplace

The field of personal informatics focuses on systems that "help people collect personally relevant information for self-reflection and gaining self-knowledge" [29]. The benefits of self-tracking are numerous. Thanks to knowledge about oneself, individuals discover insights into their activities, reflect on them, and perhaps even make changes [1,10,17]. While self-tracking expands into mainstream practice in the domain of health and well-being, the office environment remains a relatively under-explored area of study [6,24,38]. Among the most frequent domains of investigation and metrics in the personal informatics literature, only productivity refers explicitly to the workplace in the review by Epstein et al. [16] (representing 27 out of 523 publications). Prior work [24,38] investigated the acceptance of quantified-self trackers at work and described specific challenges linked to privacy and ethics. Yet these concerns remain largely unexplored [16]. Other authors have designed and deployed open-ended sensor kits aimed at empowering office workers to investigate their working habits [6]. The authors advocate for a dissenting voice to existing system-driven technologies for office health and well-being [6].

As personal informatics is inherently about the individual, studies documenting group tracking are scarce. For example, family informatics is a family-centered approach to tracking where "all family members participate in and benefit from tracking" [41]. These studies show that group tracking allows spreading the burden of collecting data, facilitating support and curiosity but also awareness and coordination between group members [41,42]. These systems also support gaining insights into the relationship between the experiences of individuals in the group. An example is the DreamCatcher project [41] where parents wanted to learn about the relationship between their children's sleep and their own. Once placed in a social context and made visible (e.g. through wearables), self-tracking becomes social and triggers changes in social dynamics and communication, as observed by Häkkilä et al. [20] where individual busyness level was represented in a necklace worn in the workplace. To this end, social self-tracking serves as awareness support [33].

2.3   Identification of Collaboration Aspects to Self-Track

Epstein et al.'s [17] model distinguishes consecutive stages in the tracking process: deciding to track and selecting tools (preparation stage in Li et al.'s [29] model), tracking and acting, integration and reflection, and lapsing of tracking (that may later be resumed). Each stage entails specific opportunities and challenges. The initial preparation stage [29] focuses on identifying relevant tracking aspects (what to track?) and the tools used for tracking these (how to track?), guided by the motivation for collecting the data (why tracking?). As well as other stages, preparation can be user-driven in case the responsibility for the choices is on the user, or system-driven, which provides user guidance [29]. Motivation for tracking is not limited to behavioral change but may also stem from curiosity, desire to learn about others or desire for awards [17]. Only a few studies in the field of personal informatics focus on this foundational stage (60 out of 523 publications in the review by Epstein et al. [16]). Existing literature mostly addresses the barriers related to the choice of the self-tracking tool. There is limited knowledge on design opportunities in this stage beyond the flexibility of the tools configuration [15,16]. Kim et al. [25] have addressed these barriers by inviting participants to freely define a phenomena (productivity) in a diary study. This approach allows to inductively identify what constitutes the phenomena of interest. Authors indicate high variability in terms of entry numbers, yet challenges and participants' perceptions related to the metrics selection are not reported. Another approach to facilitate the start of self-tracking is self-experimentation, a specific form of self-tracking that consists of creating and testing hypotheses on the effect of small behavior change [13]. Individuals are invited to think of causal relations between variables, looking at a specific goal for self-improvement. For example, can they imagine factors that influence their productivity and make progressive variations in these factors?

Overall, why would one want to promote the practice of self-tracking collaboration at work? Similar to reflection-in-action, self-trackers "learn about their behavior and make changes to their practices while they collect and integrate data" [17]. Tracking collaboration can contribute to enhancing the collaboration experience and promote self-regulation within a team. Designing self-tracking technologies for collaboration is, however, challenging when it is unclear which types of data are relevant to individuals and work teams and what is relevant and acceptable to display on a group level. In this paper, we contribute insights into how knowledge workers envision metrics for their collaboration experience, what personal, social, and organizational considerations surround collecting and sharing this data. We discuss how these insights inform the design of self-tracking technologies for collaboration.

3   Method

This study examines what aspects of collaboration are meaningful to office workers. To explore their collaboration experiences, we conducted a qualitative study focusing on the preparation stage in Li et al.'s [29] 5-stages model of personal informatics (Epstein et al. [17] refer to it as'deciding to track and selecting tools'), which occurs before people start collecting information.

3.1 Participants

Fifteen participants (six men, nine women, aged 25 to 41, with eight different nationalities) from a single HCI research team participated in this study in March 2022. They were recruited via convenience sampling. All participants hold a university degree and work in an office environment, 2-3 persons share an office. Their work is highly collaborative and interdisciplinary by nature (e.g., planning, study execution, designing solutions, publications and grant proposals, teaching and organizing team life). The team had 5 main projects during data collection. Remote work is common for 1-2 days per week, and the days are not synchronized within the team. Remote, hybrid, and face-to-face interactions are equally frequent. All participants provided informed consent, and the study has been conducted in compliance with the ethics guidelines of the authors' host institution.

3.2 Procedure

Each participant received a notebook (Fig. 1) with these instructions: *Some people track their step count to improve their level of physical activity. Some people track their sleeping time and quality to improve their health. Some people track their spending to improve their financial security. These are just a few examples of self-tracking activities aimed at improving one's life. What if you aim at improving teamwork with your colleagues? What could you self-track to inform your collaboration experience? This is your collaboration notebook. Write down any element that you deem meaningful to understand the experience of collaboration. There is no right or wrong answer. Do not worry about the feasibility of actually tracking them so far. You can, of course, start writing down elements right away, yet we advise you to take your time and come up with elements during the week as you reflect on teamwork and interactions. P.S. Nobody will read what you write here - even the researcher.*

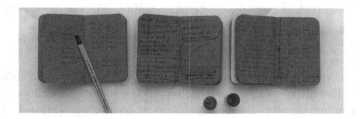

Fig. 1. Examples of collaboration notebooks shared with the participants' consent.

Literature indicates that many people engage in self-tracking with a particular goal in mind (e.g., increasing physical activity, keeping a budget) [17]. For our study, we intended to recruit people independently of any goal; we did thus not recruit people who specifically intended to improve their collaborations. Goal orientation was mentioned in the instructions under the form of several examples.

We conducted individual 1-hour long semi-structured interviews two weeks after the distribution of the notebooks. To pursue an experience-centered perspective on these meaningful metrics, we purposefully chose to seclude data collection from the social dynamics and ensure a private and confidential setting. The interview explored the following topics: (a) the entry points into the selected elements of collaboration, (b) the meaningful elements and the narratives that inspired them, (c) implications of tracking such as privacy and the impact of such practice on the participants and their collaborations.

3.3 Data Analysis

We invited participants to verbally share the meaningful elements from their notebooks. We transcribed the interviews. The codebook deductively builds on the collaboration elements identified by Anderson [2], Patel et al. [40], Marek et al. [34]. The other themes were identified deductively following the interview questions but inductively coded regarding their content. Three coders independently coded 4 out of 15 interviews and met to discuss and merge codes into a common codebook. To test how clearly the categories were distinct from each other, the coders applied this codebook to a proportion of interviews. Disagreements led to refined definitions of codes, merging codes into higher level categories or addition of new codes. A last round of double-coding led to a finalized codebook. Codebook and interview guide are provided on OSF [31].

4 Results

This section addresses our research questions. We present the analysis of the collaboration elements elicited by the participants and which entry point they used (RQ1). We describe participants' reflections on collaboration triggered by the activity (RQ2). Last, we present their perspectives on sharing and receiving tracked data and their overall reflections on self-tracking at work (RQ3).

4.1 Collaboration Experience Elements

The exercise invited the participants to record elements of their collaboration experience. The fifteen participants elicited 136 elements (117 unique ones) they deemed meaningful; nine elements per person on average (Min=4, Max=21). Most of the elements (73%) at this preparatory stage of self-tracking can be qualified as qualitative (non-quantifiable), 27% as quantifiable. Examples of qualitative elements are trust to delegate, flow, personal expectations, mood.

Examples of quantifiable elements are: the number of projects successfully finished, the number of interactions, the number of opinions shared, the number of eye contacts. Participants identified elements that fell into five topical groups (Table 1). The most prominent categories of the elements elicited in the study are task-oriented, individual-oriented, and relation-oriented. Spatial and temporal elements were also evoked, revealing the impact of synchronicity and the work environment on collaboration experiences.

Table 1. Meaningful collaboration aspects elicited in the study

Group	Subgroup	Examples of collaboration aspects elicited in the study
Task-orientation	Contribution to task	Speaking time during a meeting, N of mistakes found by a teammate
	Outcome of the task	N of projects successfully finished, KPI (N of articles published), result quality
	Productivity/Efficiency	Flow, focus on planned tasks, improvements, meeting efficiency, N of meetings useless/relevant, N of people in a meeting
Relation-orientation	Interdependency of collaborators	Learning from each other, trust to delegate, reciprocity of help
	Values, norms, attitudes	Impact of hierarchy, transparency, discrimination, inequalities, the required level of diplomacy
Individual-orientation	Emotions and feelings	Mood, emotions, hormones, level of tiredness, frustration, regret, feeling overwhelmed, stress/physical state, level of fun, N of laughs, impact of personality, awkwardness
	Psychological needs	Feeling useless, belonging, feeling in sync, connectedness, level of competence, level of autonomy
Time-orientation		Deadlines respected, scheduling, time spent efficiently, time pressure, time spent collaborating/availability for collaboration, time overlap, time spent preparing a meeting, (a)synchronicity of work
Space-orientation		Space connection (door open/closed), space structure, impact of space (informal collaboration vs focused work)

Task-Oriented Elements. Task-oriented elements refer to the process, productivity, and outcome of collaboration. They include quantifiable achievements (e.g., performance indicators specific to the work field) and less tangible factors such as (perceived) efficiency and focus on the goals to achieve. Among these elements, a participant mentioned how collaboration improved the quality of outputs (*"It increased the quality [...] of what we created"*, P10). Another participant elicited this quality as a trackable element in terms of *"evaluation of the result, improvements I could bring to improve collaboration"* (P7).

Relation-Oriented Elements. Participants elicited several metrics referring to interpersonal relations. The value of mutual learning in collaboration and the importance of complementary contributions was mentioned as a potential element to self-track, *"I enjoyed that I get to learn from her, she gets to learn from me"* (P5). Another meaningful element mentioned was the impact of hierarchy on collaboration. It was evoked as impacting the processes (*"X is my manager and some things need his approval"* (P8), and also as a factor potentially hindering collaboration: *"ideally, whether you have a certain position or a certain gender or age, [it] would not matter about the role that you have in the collaboration"* (P8).

Individual-Oriented Elements. Elements of this group cover personal aspects of experience. Emotions, positive or negative, were frequent indicators mentioned by the participants. Fun and frustration were both deemed meaningful to track, and also used as entry point into eliciting elements. Participants for instance reflected on frustration by linking it to its source: *"I think it was a point of frustration that led me to writing this down: an optimal way of contacting each team member seems different [laughs]"* (P15). Certain elements evoke the psychological needs of collaborators, such as feeling competent or vice versa (*"when in a collaboration situation, I don't see how I can contribute anything useful"*, P1) or connectedness when realizing *"we have the same problems"* (P2).

Temporal-Oriented and Spatial-Oriented Elements. As the study focuses on a specific human experience, no surprise that the elements identified as time-oriented also fall into other categories, mainly adding a temporal axis to the experience measurement. For example, "time spent preparing a meeting" is a time investment to work on a task (*"If I prepare a meeting, the fact that I do it, just 5 min, makes the meeting feel more productive"*, P3). The ratio of time invested as compared to the outputs generated or synchronicity between team members are key representatives of this temporal orientation: *"it was asynchronous and made me waste time"*, P2; *"A meeting that lasts two hours and doesn't bring much to the table - the ratio isn't great in terms of efficiency. You have very short but very productive meetings too. The ratio of time spent - [we should] try to optimize as much as possible"*, P7.

Space-related elements reveal the impact of the environment on the collaboration experience. It was mentioned as having the potential to improve team availability (*"the office doors that we open so that everyone can come and ask for things"*, P11), facilitate collaboration (*"IT department has 10 people in the common space. When I ask them to fix my laptop, [...] they are having this direct collaboration to solve my problem"*, P4) or focused work mode (*"space rules or how we just separate the focus task where we don't need to collaborate and the task where we need to collaborate. On the other hand, living together in the shared office triggers a lot of jokes"* (P2).

Mapping Causal Assumptions. When eliciting elements of collaboration, participants spontaneously drew causal relations between some of them. Several elements were repeatedly connected with others, namely: (a) organizational alignment (of roles, processes, outcomes), (b) disposition to collaborate, (c) (meeting) efficiency, (d) shared feeling, (e) (a)synchronicity of work. For instance, *clarity of expectations, roles, deliverables, timeline, and vision,* as well as *shared feelings* foster *alignment.* However, *asynchronous work* on collaborative tasks may hinder it: it is easier to deviate from goals established together; *efficiency* is thus decreased. Meanwhile, *coordination* efforts positively impact *efficiency*. We represent the connections in a network graph published on OSF [31].

Elements Viewed as Unique and Common. Out of all elicited elements, we prompted participants to identify those they imagined were common to other participants versus those they thought were unique (elicited only by them). Elements deemed unique include the number of work interruptions, the trust to delegate tasks, the cultural diversity within a team, or the autonomy given to others in a collaboration. Elements identified as common within the team refer to emotional aspects (number of laughs, frustration), communication aspects (number of interactions, conflict management), and organizational or task-related aspects (performance objectives and outcomes). Having analyzed the data from all participants, we could see whether elements identified as unique or common were indeed so. Many participants elicited the same elements (e.g., frustration, performance objectives, outcomes, uncertainty). Some "unique" elements were elicited once (e.g., autonomy given to others, cultural diversity). Yet, others were shared by more respondents (e.g., number of work interruptions, results of collaboration).

4.2   Entry Points to Collaboration Elements

As they received only one generic reminder, participants relied on intrinsic triggers to elicit elements. Findings show three main strategies adopted by the participants to define the meaningful elements they would track: (a) conceptual-based (i.e., the participant selected a metric a priori, based on their conceptualization of collaboration, N=8), (b) event-based (i.e., something happened that caused the participant to elicit a metric, N=13), and (c) time-based (i.e., the participant decided to track something at regular intervals, N=2).

Many expressed that it was challenging to start the elicitation (*"at the beginning, I had a hard time thinking about what is collaboration and what is not?"*, P11). Therefore, in most cases they started with conceptual questions about meaningful collaboration experiences. Unsurprisingly, a very common reflection was "What is (good) collaboration?". Vocabulary also played a role: although some participants used concepts like "coordination", "cooperation", or "collaboration" interchangeably, others made a finer distinction: e.g. *"Cooperating is helping someone to achieve their goal. Whereas in collaboration first of all - a common goal and everyone contributes more or less equally"* (P7).

Second, emotions were often indicators of a *"critical incident"* (P2) and a point of an event-based entry. Addressing what caused a specific emotion allowed participants to identify meaningful elements at the root:*"Anytime I felt an emotion, I was like 'ok, it has to be meaningful because it makes me react emotionally'"* (P2). The feeling of being unproductive is another event-based entry point: *"What did I just do during the time [I collaborated] that made me feel unproductive?"* (P3). Interactions with colleagues incited our participants to reflect on the task: "*It was interactions. I think each time we had something in the office, I was like 'oh maybe this is a moment to write something'*" (P5). Finally, participants also tried a more formal time-based approach: "*I tried to use a formal approach, how many minutes or how many interactions we had. I can't say I was very strict on that*" (P6). Routines also played a temporal role in writing down collaboration elements: "*This little tool [the notebook] actually helped a lot, because it's quite a unique design on my desk. I have a habit of cleaning my desk every day. When I clean, I pick it up to see the things that I write, and then I add something*" (P4). Writing attitudes varied. For instance, P4 was writing once per day or more often, while P14 wrote 2 times - once a week after a work meeting. Many participants highlighted that they carried the notebook with them during the work hours.

4.3   Preparing to Track as a Trigger to Reflection

Participants described how privately taking notes of their experiences led to in-depth reflections about their role and perspective on collaboration. Most participants shared that the exercise made them more reflective of how they collaborate. It led to introspection, illustrated by quotes such as: "*How do I feel and how do I make others feel during the collaboration, how does it impact the results?*", P15; "*What do I do at work - do I collaborate or do I cooperate?*", P7. One person was surprised by how many negative incidents they noted and how much their mood impacted their collaboration. Another participant spoke about their awakened sense of agency: "*Before, I was passively accepting collaboration, as natural. [With the notebook] I asked myself: what is my role in collaboration?*", P4. One person shared how the notebook exercise led them to actively address their frustration:"*I wrote down "frustration" and "uncertainty". And by writing down those words [...] I thought: well, you have to act*" (P2). Over the course of the interviews, the participants spontaneously verbalized what they perceive as good or bad collaboration ("*For a good collaboration, it definitely should be a set of rules, at least partly mutually understandable*", P6), what are the conditions for optimal collaboration ("*For me, the best collaboration is always just with one other person*", P1), what is their priority in collaboration (e.g., outcome: "*Whether you like it or not, whether it's frustrating or not, you just have to suffer through it*", P5) or what it means to be a good collaborator ("*If you want to be a really good collaborator, it's also being more sensitive to everybody else in the room. [...] Then ideally you can adapt a little bit your behavior so that people feel better*", P1). Some conflicting outlooks on collaboration transpired: while one participant voiced a preference for synchronous work (P11), another stated that they consider asynchronous work more efficient and they make efforts to reduce meetings (P10). However, these participants did not work on the same project.

Participants spoke about the importance of accounting for factors indirectly related to collaboration, like mood or fatigue: "*If you haven't slept the whole week and then you're trying to work on the project with someone, whatever they say will annoy you*", P5; "*I had a little clash with [my partner], and it put me in a bad mood. It followed me the whole day and I could feel that in all the collaborative situations. I was very critical, I was criticizing everything*", P1.

Besides pragmatic considerations, participants also reflected on how to improve collaboration, e.g., by taking distance (*"an emotion is an indicator if the collaboration works, but it wouldn't help find the solution. Taking distance and understanding why I felt that way - this is what would help"*, P11), empathizing (*"By enhancing empathy towards each other, because that would create a better-shared goal and vision"*, P9), being attentive to diverse interests (*"We should be careful that we don't forget about different needs in our team. If we are aware of these biases, that's already a big step ahead"*, P8).

Some reflections indicate that when measuring experience, one should be mindful of the desired outcomes. For example, while "shared values" is frequently elicited as a desirable element of collaboration, participant P6 questions the extent to which this should be achieved: *"Should every collaboration finish with united feelings towards something or not?"* (P6). Furthermore, constancy of performance as a potential metric is questioned: *"In collaboration, you can't feel engaged equally at all times with everything"* (P15).

4.4   Sharing and Receiving Data About Collaboration

Despite collaboration being a highly interpersonal topic, many of the elements elicited by participants were personal. We asked the participants about their attitude towards sharing the tracked information with their teammates. Most of them expressed an initial reservation about sharing their data and some questioned the value of doing so, *"I can but I can't see any added value"* (P6) and the shortcoming of self-tracking to reflect collaboration comprehensively, *"the monitoring aspect is unlikely to reflect the complexity of collaboration"* (P10). Sharing is, however, also perceived as a way to *"understand the team better"* (P12), check the alignment around shared values (*"It could be a way to see if we all value the same things or see moments as collaborative"*, P12) and eventually improve the collaboration experience for all. On several occasions our participants expressed their interest in comparing their notes with those of their teammates: *"I think it would help me to learn better to read how other people live the situation"*, P1, *"it would be nice to check in with people that I collaborated with to see if we have similarity in our notes, how their collaboration with me felt. So I would understand better what I can do to work better with them"*, P15. Tracked data from others can also serve as a source of self-regulation: *"I'd like to know from people who worked with me how they think we're working together. I'm thinking of me as being this organized person but maybe I'm disorganized and it's a mess"*, P5. Emotions were considered sensitive, and participants thought of curating what could be shared: *"I would not share strong emotions and something a person cannot change"*, P1, *"I would not share frustration parts, to not create bad feelings in the team"*, P5. On the positive side, sharing and receiving tracked information was perceived as a less confrontational way of giving feedback to a teammate (*"I'd like to know because definitely there's something bad to fix"*, P13) or even avoiding group pressure (*"If they follow because it's the group effect, or are they really in agreement with the decisions that were chosen"*, P14). It is also seen as an opportunity to re-calibrate the collaboration, identify imbalances, and achieve better goal alignment. Our participants envision data sharing as a prompt to speak up about negative aspects and encourage positive feedback (*"Tracking compliments I receive from colleagues, I realized the impact of small acts of kindness and gave more compliments in return"*, P2). They believe the data would reveal how present people are in a collaborative situation and thus revise their involvement. Last, participants pointed out that such data may support healthy group dynamics by revising the social graph of interactions.

Among the disadvantages, the participants evoked risks of misinterpretation of their inputs within the group (*"people are always taking things personally [laughs]. It could really create tension"*, P6). They emphasized the difficulty of receiving and processing critique: *"On the one hand, I think it would be something important for each of us to know, on the other hand, it's very painful to be criticized. To find a way that's not insulting, that just helps you grow without feeling bad, that would be quite nice, because you want people's feedback, but at the same time, you're afraid of it"* (P1). Besides, factors out of the collaborators' control may impact the metrics. This might lead to situations in which it is unclear what exactly is measured (*"Do the people look at each other to enrich this moment of collaboration or just because they don't like each other?"*, P12). Sharing negative experiences also raised concerns about repercussions (*"I would consider sharing only if there is a realistic chance to change [the situation]"*, P10), which is why some participants stated that they would *"maybe not share the exact experience, but come up with a suggestion on how to make it better or at least make another person aware that something is not working out for me"* (P15). According to a participant, if tracked data is made available to everyone, it may turn into an inappropriate performance objective. The relations between positive feeling and collaboration experience (*"collaboration doesn't necessarily need to give the most positive feelings to everyone involved for it to be good"*, P10) or the consequence of fostering comparison (*"it was a little bit of pressure. If you compare yourself to the others, that's not really the point"*, P14; *"People will force themselves to do many things to prove that they have collaborated a lot"*, P12) were challenged. Sharing data about group members' experiences can be perceived as a burden if it calls for an over-personalized approach to collaboration: *"If everyone does this [shares the data], so what? Are we going to have a tailored approach to work with everyone?"*, P5.

4.5   Reflections on Self-Tracking at Work

We asked the participants to envision how they could track the identified collaboration elements. While selecting these elements, some showed concern about the feasibility of tracking them. They emphasized the importance of external and contextual factors (*"tracking some aspects not related to collaboration but to me in order to learn more about correlation/causality"*, P2, *"I would track how tired I am to control why I feel frustrated while collaborating"*, P5). The participants concluded that some elements could be tracked automatically (e.g., number of messages exchanged, distributed tasks, clues of synchronicity in agendas). Yet, several team members raised doubts about automated tracking from an accuracy or validity perspective (*"sensors might be misleading"*, P9), but also for social dynamics (*"If someone perceives something that is relevant to me, I trust them to share it with me, I don't want my work reduced to these types of metrics"*, P10). Moreover, since power and hierarchy too play a role in the work context, they may challenge the implications for data tracking and sharing (*"lack of transparency annoys me and creates some problems about expectation management"*, P2, *"you cannot say that because they are the bosses"*, P13).

Participants identified opportunities for semi-automated tracking, imagining how technology would support collaboration improvement: *"a sort of button, the more you turn one way, the more you feel positive, the other way - negative, something that is not too present"*, P7. Such measures with regular self (or group) evaluation would allow the group to see trends over time and take action if improvement is needed. Envisioned tracking frequency varied from hourly measurements (to *"see the reality that is closer to truth"*, P2) to once a day or event-based. The granularity of the tracking frequency was highly dependent on the element tracked. Another requirement highlighted by our participants was the unobtrusive nature of experience tracking (*"It doesn't interrupt you, it's in the environment but lets you collaborate"*, P7).

Participants identified several advantages and limitations related to the free paper format: portability, physical presence acting as a reminder, and flexibility. Criticism was mostly related to the lack of onboarding potential or effort that would be needed to format it for systematic tracking. Among technological mediators, one participant envisioned *"an app in line with your calendar. For each meeting, the app will automatically start and give you an alert - what you think of that? It might be annoying, but it can get a lot of data rigorously"*, P9. Another participant imagined an ephemeral data visualization that the team would access after collaboration: *"We have this shared pop-up. We write our feedback, and then it disappears forever. So no one else can read it. It's just you and me or a group project. You would have to think more about the format: who can read what I said about you? Who can read what I said about the group?"*, P5. Another idea was a tracking artifact, for example, to measure frustration level, *"every time you get frustrated, you tap on it, and you distort it. Finally, you look with your colleagues if today you have all deformed it a lot, then perhaps you have the same experience of collaboration. Whereas if there's one all dented, the other one is all clean, you can say, we may not have experienced things in the same way"*, P14. Comparing the app with the notebook, multiple participants saw potential in prompting, *"The app can be smart and give regular updates. It can remind me that I need to do something to make this collaboration better, and this thing [notebook] cannot"*, P9.

5   Discussion

In this contribution, we explored what aspects of collaboration are meaningful to a team of office workers via a qualitative study focusing on the preparation stage in Li et al.'s [29] model of personal informatics. The main categories of elements distinguished are in line with prior literature, supporting the opportunities to differentiate between individual, relational, and task-oriented levels, as well as map them on space and time axes [2,34,40]. Our findings emphasize a prevalence of task-related aspects in the collaboration elements elicited by participants, with nonetheless a significant proportion of individual and relational elements deemed essential to understand and reflect on collaboration experiences. Most of the elements were qualitative and hence harder to quantify and track, especially in an automated fashion. In practice, this implies a user-driven data collection [29] which has the advantage of empowering and stimulating but can also be a burden to report frequent events. It is worth looking at how tracking devices can support hybrid scenarios combining user-driven and system-driven data collection.

5.1   Onboarding to Self-Tracking

Our findings highlighted opportunities and challenges related to tracking collaboration experiences. Participants described how privately taking notes of their experiences already led to deep reflections about their role and perspective on teamwork. This is a known benefit of self-tracking [17]. However, it can also be a source of negativity [1]: in some cases, it exacerbated friction as negative feelings were now on paper rather than fading from memory.

The entry points and the vagueness of some metrics selected by the participants indicate that most people require support to guide their thought process from collaboration experiences or behaviors to operational metrics that can be self-tracked. In this process, the type of metrics to track (what to track?), the number of metrics to track (how many to track?), the temporality of reporting an entry (when to track?), and the triangulation (how to combine metrics to uncover causality links and make sense of the data?) enter into play. With his CoSensUs framework, Toebosch [48] proposes a guided way to operationalize collaboration experiences into metrics (that can be tracked by sensors). As a potential entry point, the framework prompts participants to define experiences, translate them into "observable" behaviors or events before selecting relevant tracking devices. This prevents unsuccessful onboarding to self-tracking and cascading barriers in subsequent stages [29]. In our study, the conceptual-based onboarding could be conducted within a team, deciding together what is meaningful in their collaboration and what scope to adopt. Some elements elicited as meaningful do not stem from collaboration directly. However, beyond accounting for the contextual factors, tracking them will make participants more engaged in the practice of self-tracking and enable them to benefit from it [36]. Many participants spontaneously shared their assumptions of causality between the elicited metrics. This reveals the opportunity to develop this study with a self-experimenting outlook [13,23] and allow participants to test their hypotheses about connections. Some of the connections assumed by our participants are supported by existing literature (e.g., the impact of uncertainty on collaboration [4]).

5.2   Implications for Sharing Tracked Data Within a Team

Given the social nature of collaboration, multiple actors shape the experience of the collaborating group. Sharing individual members' experience data might help the group improve their collaboration. Among the elements suggested by the participants, many were rather personal. Participants had mixed feelings about sharing their data. They imagined that tracking and disclosing data could support awareness and problem-solving within the team, echoing the results of [20, 44]. It can also be an opportunity to share information with others indirectly (e.g., when one does not dare to speak up). This observation resonates with a study on family informatics [41] where "children appreciated being able to self-report through (the device) and share information with others without having an explicit conversation." Sharing information was described as "uncomfortable but providing opportunities of shared accountability." While the context is different, the family and workplace environments share a group focus with interdependencies (see "ripple effect" in [42]) and power relations between individuals. In this regard, data can enter into play as a mediator of relations [20], serve as a support for one's point of view, and facilitate collaborative tracking [37]. Moreover, self-reflection promoted through self-tracking may lead to better group awareness ('we-awareness' in Tenenberg et al. [47]): a group may achieve a clearer outlook on shared intentionality and decode each other's actions to support collaborative behavior. Group awareness, in turn, guides the collaboration process and can stimulate members to regulate their behaviors and adjust their strategies [8]. Conversely, our participants also voiced concerns about the possible adverse consequences of sharing information at work, which calls for special attention when designing tracking technologies [38]. A work environment is a place where surveillance can present risks for individuals. It is thus important to account for potential self-censoring (i.e. not reporting unwanted data - similar to the concern [32] about reporting emotions inappropriate to the workspace) or alienation from oneself in the event of self-disclosure [27]. Collectively defining what to track may mitigate these risks. Additionally, sharing the data on a group level as same/different from one's own and moving from prescriptive visualization may be a discreet way to handle the risk of disclosing sensitive data. Previous work highlighted the direct influence of privacy concerns on the intention to use tracking devices [24, 38]. While the social perspective of personal informatics is often seen as a motivating space to proudly share achievements in the private sphere [17], data tracking at work is a different case, however able to stimulate discussions [20].

Besides the risks of the data dissemination itself, quantification of behavior at the workplace from the perspective of group-tracking may introduce negative consequences. Metrics diverted from their primary use can lead to work pressure or detrimental organizational / performance standards or social norms. Researchers in the community, therefore, advocate for a focus on the qualitative

("qualitative self"), whose insights would benefit sense-making and behavioral change over time [9].

5.3   Towards Group-Tracking

Although our study focused on individuals reflecting on collaborative practices, we also gained insights into group-tracking compared to the widespread practice of self-tracking. Certain aspects of people's experiences and behaviors are impacted by other people in the private sphere [42] and in the professional one. Group tracking is an emerging trend in PI in recent years [16,42] and is a valuable opportunity for collective sense-making [9] in interpersonal contexts such as collaboration. On the one hand, an aggregated cohort data sharing may promote social discovery of common experiences [18], which were deemed essential for several participants. On the other hand, group-tracking would ideally differ from the simple aggregation of data from individuals, but adequate trackable group elements remain to be identified. This is both to avoid the aforementioned risks and to yield shared accountability and reflection on collaboration. Making privacy-sensitive design choices is a way forward: the most straightforward approach is to aggregate the data or show high-level visualizations. More elaborated tracking strategies could focus on the group as an entity. A challenge here is that group-level data can be harder to understand, especially when presented as an overlay of individual data [41].

Our study showed much diversity in the participants' outlooks. Some appeared less convinced of the usefulness and benefits of tracking collaboration. Co-design methods can unveil the values and needs of people prior to the tracking [14,41]. Open-ended tracking kits [6,14,49] might bring advantages over solutions supporting one scenario only. Another concrete design implication, aligned with Pina et al.'s [41] study on family tracking, is that tracking devices should support the non-involvement or disengagement of a team member while "avoiding disruptions for the rest of the group."

Finally, two key challenges relate to collaboration as an area of investigation. First, the elements elicited seem more complex and multi-faceted than the variables commonly tracked in the personal informatics literature. Designing technologies to track collaboration would involve reducing the complexity of these experiences to simpler measurable units. Not enclosing ourselves in a self-tracking approach, future research could explore other design solutions than data tracking. Second, tracked data in personal informatics often have a short-term use [45], whereas collaboration processes have a long time-span.

5.4   Tracking Collaboration Experiences: Design Implications

The insights gathered through our study are preliminary steps to identify design requirements for self-tracking collaboration tools and methods. Building on our data and prior work, we summarize implications for design, particularly relevant to improve the - currently under-researched - way personal informatics technologies support the self-tracking preparation stage [15,17,29].

- Supporting onboarding into the practice of tracking by providing a framework or method for participants to transform experience goals into operational measures that can realistically be tracked [48].
- Moving from self-tracking to group-tracking. To reflect the social nature of collaboration, participants together identify and negotiate meaningful and operational metrics providing relevant insights into the collaboration. Technologies for group-tracking are currently under-explored [8].
- Supporting participants in selecting metrics and tracking devices that are non-obtrusive to the work activities and collaboration flow (see 4.5).
- Respecting consent and privacy: obtaining opt-in consent by all participants before starting a tracking initiative (also see data proportionality in awareness systems [35]); supporting ways of sharing and visualizing the data that accounts for participants' privacy concerns [20].
- Integrating the iterative nature of tracking within self-tracking technologies. This enables teams to learn from and re-calibrate their metrics [17] during their collaboration journey.
- Supporting collaborative sense-making as a socially embedded practice to facilitate mutual awareness [37] and heading towards qualitative-focused approaches, aka the qualitative-self [9].
- Supporting perception of the data as secondary to the lived experience: tracked data is not absolute truth, support the user to trust their experience. See "beautiful seems" in awareness systems [35].

5.5   Limitations and Future Work

Our study entails some limitations. First, we sampled a single team from a unique work domain and with a high level of education, limiting our results' generalizability. Despite mitigation precautions, the use of convenience sampling involving participants known to the researchers could impact the results. An opportunity is to extend the research to professional teams in a variety of fields. Second, we focused purposefully on the preparation stage (i.e., getting ready to track data [29] and identifying tracking elements [12]). While this narrow scope allows an in-depth inquiry, there are logical intricacies between identifying tracking elements and the actual act of self-tracking, which the present study does not account for. Individuals gain awareness of their data needs and adjust their tracking aspects continuously by tracking and reflecting on their data [43]. Third, by choosing to distribute individual booklets to participants and inviting them to note their meaningful collaboration elements, we collected mostly individual perspectives on a shared experience.

A follow-up study will invite participants to define and negotiate collaboration elements to track within their team, thus elevating the group as the primary level of analysis. To explore how privacy boundaries are redefined via self-tracking practice in the work context, we will conduct a co-design workshop using an open-ended sensor kit as a research probe. Finally, we will explore existing tensions surrounding the ethics of tracking technologies at the office [46] through design fiction and open the design space by exploring possible solutions for measuring collaboration experiences beyond self/group tracking.

6 Conclusion

We conducted a study focusing on the preparation stage of self-tracking with fifteen knowledge workers. We invited participants to manually elicit meaningful collaboration elements over a 2-weeks period, before conducting semi-structured interviews about their experience. As emphasized by Li et al. [29], "effective personal informatics systems help users collect the necessary personal information for insightful reflection." Our empirical study contributes insights into how employees envision metrics for reflecting their collaboration experience; and what personal, social, and organizational considerations are involved when collecting and sharing this data. Identified metrics fall into topical categories (individual-, relational-, task-related and space/time). Most metrics at this stage are hard to quantify, which calls for onboarding support and user-driven approach to tracking. Knowing which aspects of collaboration are meaningful and how this information should be shared, contributes valuable insights to designing self-tracking technologies for the work context. Our design implications concern the preparation stage of PI [17,29], one of the least supported in the current technological landscape [15]. We invite the community to pursue this timely research on the opportunities, challenges, and risks of (self-)tracking technologies for collaboration, in order to support employees' needs and values in an ethical way.

Acknowledgements. This research has been supported by the Luxembourg National Research Fund (FNR) IPBG2020/IS/14839977/C21.

References

1. Abtahi, P., et al.: Understanding physical practices and the role of technology in manual self-tracking. Proc. ACM on Inter. Mob. Wear. Ubiq. Technol. **4**(4), 1–24 (2020). https://doi.org/10.1145/3432236
2. Anderson, N.R., West, M.A.: Measuring climate for work group innovation: development and validation of the team climate inventory. Journ. of Org. Behav. **19**, 235–258 (1998). https://doi.org/10.1002/(SICI)1099-1379(199805)19:3⟨235::AID-JOB837⟩3.0.CO;2-C
3. Bedwell, W.L., Wildman, J.L., DiazGranados, D., Salazar, M., Kramer, W.S., Salas, E.: Collaboration at work: an integrative multilevel conceptualization. Hum. Res. Manag. Review **22**, 128–145 (2012). https://doi.org/10.1016/j.hrmr.2011.11.007
4. Bowler, R.D., Bach, B., Pschetz, L.: Exploring uncertainty in digital scheduling, and the wider implications of unrepresented temporalities in HCI. In: Proceedings of the 2022 CHI Conference on Human Factors in Computing Systems. CHI 2022, ACM, New York (2022). https://doi.org/10.1145/3491102.3502107
5. Briggs, R.O., Reinig, B.A., Vreede, G.J.D.: Meeting satisfaction for technology-supported groups: an empirical validation of a goal-attainment model. Small Group Res. **37**, 585–611 (2006). https://doi.org/10.1177/1046496406294320

6. van Bussel, T., van den Heuvel, R., Lallemand, C.: Habilyzer: Empowering office workers to investigate their working habits using an open-ended sensor kit. In: 2022 CHI Conference on Human Factors in Computing Systems Extended Abstracts, pp. 1–8. ACM, New York (2022). https://doi.org/10.1145/3491101.3519849

7. Simsek Caglar, P., Roto, V., Vainio, T.: User experience research in the work context: maps, gaps and Agenda. Proc. ACM Hum.-Comput. Interact. 6(CSCW1), 1–28 (2022). https://doi.org/10.1145/3512979

8. Chen, D., Zhang, Y., Lin, Y.: Group awareness and group awareness tools in computer-supported collaborative learning: A literature review. In: 2022 International Symposium on Educational Technology (ISET), pp. 18–22 (2022). https://doi.org/10.1109/ISET55194.2022.00013

9. Cho, J., Xu, T., Zimmermann-Niefield, A., Voida, S.: Reflection in theory and reflection in practice: An exploration of the gaps in reflection support among personal informatics apps. In: Proceedings of the 2022 CHI Conference on Human Factors in Computing Systems, CHI 2022, ACM, New York (2022). https://doi.org/10.1145/3491102.3501991

10. Choe, E.K., Lee, N.B., Lee, B., Pratt, W., Kientz, J.A.: Understanding quantified-selfers' practices in collecting and exploring personal data. In: Proceedings of the SIGCHI Conference on Human Factors in Computing Systems, pp. 1143–1152. ACM, New York (2014). https://doi.org/10.1145/2556288.2557372

11. Chung, C.F., Dew, K., Cole, A., Zia, J., Fogarty, J., et al.: Boundary negotiating artifacts in personal informatics: patient-provider collaboration with patient-generated data. In: Proceedings of the 19th ACM Conference on Computer-supported Cooperative Work and Social Computing, pp. 770–786. CSCW 2016, ACM, New York (2016). https://doi.org/10.1145/2818048.2819926

12. Coşkun, A., Karahanoğlu, A.: Data sensemaking in self-tracking: towards a new generation of self-tracking tools. Int. Journ. of Hum.-Comp. Inter. 0(0), 1–22 (2022). https://doi.org/10.1080/10447318.2022.2075637

13. Daskalova, N., Desingh, K., Papoutsaki, A., Schulze, D., Sha, H., Huang, J.: Lessons learned from two cohorts of personal informatics self-experiments. Proc. ACM on Inter. Mob. Wear. Ubiq. Technol. 1(3), 1–22 (2017)

14. Denefleh, T., Berger, A., Kurze, A., Bischof, A., Frauenberger, C.: Sensorstation: exploring simple sensor data in the context of a shared apartment. In: Proceedings of the 2019 on Designing Interactive Systems Conference, pp. 683–695. ACM, New York (2019). https://doi.org/10.1145/3322276.3322309

15. van Dijk, E.T.K., Westerink, J.H., Beute, F., IJsselsteijn, W.A.: Personal informatics, self-insight, and behavior change: A critical review of current literature. Hum.-Comp. Inter. 32, 268–296 (2017). https://doi.org/10.1080/07370024.2016.1276456, https://doi.org/10.1080/07370024.2016.1276456

16. Epstein, D.A., Caldeira, C., Figueiredo, M.C., Lu, X., Silva, L.M., et al.: Mapping and taking stock of the personal informatics literature. Proc. ACM on Interact. Mob. Wearable Ubiq. Technol. 4(4), 1–38 (2020)

17. Epstein, D.A., Ping, A., Fogarty, J., Munson, S.A.: A lived informatics model of personal informatics. In: Proceedings of the 2015 ACM International Joint Conference on Pervasive and Ubiquitous Computing, pp. 731–742. ACM, New York (2015). https://doi.org/10.1145/2750858.2804250

18. Feustel, C., Aggarwal, S., Lee, B., Wilcox, L.: People like me: designing for reflection on aggregate cohort data in personal informatics systems. Proc. ACM on Inter. Mob. Wear. Ubiq. Technol. 2(3), 1–21 (2018)

19. Gutwin, C., Greenberg, S.: A descriptive framework of workspace awareness for real-time groupware. Comput. Support. Coop. Work (CSCW) **11**(3), 411–446 (2002)
20. Häkkilä, J., Poguntke, R., Harjuniemi, E., Hakala, L., Colley, A., Schmidt, A.: Businec - studying the effects of a busyness signifying necklace in the wild. In: Proceedings of the 2020 ACM Designing Interactive Systems Conference, pp. 2177–2188. DIS 2020, ACM, New York (2020). https://doi.org/10.1145/3357236.3395455
21. Hassenzahl, M.: The thing and i: understanding the relationship between user and product. In: Blythe, M.A., Monk, A.F., Overbeeke, K., Wright, P.C. (eds.) Funology: From Usability to Enjoyment. Kluwer Academic Publishers, Dordrecht, Netherlands (2003)
22. Inc., G.: Gartner forecasts worldwide social software and collaboration market to grow 17% in 2021 (3 2020), www.tinyurl.com/fj92t8na
23. Karkar, R., Fogarty, J., Kientz, J.A., Munson, S.A., Vilardaga, R., Zia, J.: Opportunities and challenges for self-experimentation in self-tracking. In: Adjunct Proceedings of the 2015 ACM International Joint Conference on Pervasive and Ubiquitous Computing and Proceedings of the 2015 ACM International Symposium on Wearable Computers, pp. 991–996. ACM, New York (2015). https://doi.org/10.1145/2800835.2800949
24. Khakurel, J., Immonen, M., Porras, J., Knutas, A.: Understanding the adoption of quantified self-tracking wearable devices in the organization environment: an empirical case study. In: Proceedings of the 12th ACM International Conference on PErvasive Technologies Related to Assistive Environments, pp. 119–128. PETRA 2019, ACM, New York (2019)
25. Kim, Y.H., Choe, E.K., Lee, B., Seo, J.: Understanding personal productivity: How knowledge workers define, evaluate, and reflect on their productivity. In: Proceedings of the 2019 CHI Conference on Human Factors in Computing Systems, pp. 1–12. ACM, New York (2019). https://doi.org/10.1145/3290605.3300845
26. Lallemand, C., Gronier, G., Koenig, V.: User experience: a concept without consensus? exploring practitioners' perspectives through an international survey. Comp. Hum. Behav. **43**, 35–48 (2015). https://doi.org/10.1016/j.chb.2014.10.048
27. Lanzing, Marjolein: The transparent self. Ethics Inf. Technol. **18**(1), 9–16 (2016). https://doi.org/10.1007/s10676-016-9396-y
28. Lee, K., Hong, H.: Designing for self-tracking of emotion and experience with tangible modality. In: Proceedings of the 2017 Conference on Designing Interactive Systems, pp. 465–475. DIS 2017, ACM, New York (2017). https://doi.org/10.1145/3064663.3064697
29. Li, I., Dey, A., Forlizzi, J.: A stage-based model of personal informatics systems. In: Proceedings of the SIGCHI Conference on Human Factors in Computing Systems, vol. 1, pp. 557–566. ACM, New York (2010). https://doi.org/10.1145/1753326.1753409
30. Lu, Y., Roto, V.: Evoking meaningful experiences at work - a positive design framework for work tools. J. Eng. Design **26**(4–6), 99–120 (2015). https://doi.org/10.1080/09544828.2015.1041461
31. Lushnikova, A.: Eliciting meaningful collaboration metrics. www.osf.io/z2qfg
32. Lutchyn, Y., Johns, P., Roseway, A., Czerwinski, M.: MoodTracker: monitoring collective emotions in the workplace. In: 2015 International Conference on Affective Computing and Intelligent Interaction (ACII), pp. 295–301. IEEE (2015). https://doi.org/10.1109/ACII.2015.7344586

33. Mantau, M.J., Barreto Vavassori Benitti, F.: Awareness support in collaborative system: reviewing last 10 years of CSCW research. In: 2022 IEEE 25th International Conference on Computer Supported Cooperative Work in Design (CSCWD), pp. 564–569 (2022). https://doi.org/10.1109/CSCWD54268.2022.9776091

34. Marek, L., Brock, D., Savla, J.: Evaluating collaboration for effectiveness. Amer. Journ. of Eval. **36** (2014). https://doi.org/10.1177/1098214014531068

35. Markopoulos, P.: A design framework for awareness systems. In: Markopoulos, P., De Ruyter, B., Mackay, W. (eds.) Awareness Systems. Hum.-Comp. Inter. Ser, Springer, London (2009)

36. McKillop, M., Mamykina, L., Elhadad, N.: Designing in the dark: Eliciting self-tracking dimensions for understanding enigmatic disease. In: Proceedings of the 2018 CHI Conference on Human Factors in Computing Systems, pp. 1–15. CHI 2018, ACM, New York (2018). https://doi.org/10.1145/3173574.3174139

37. Murnane, E.L., Walker, T.G., Tench, B., Voida, S., Snyder, J.: Personal informatics in interpersonal contexts: towards the design of technology that supports the social ecologies of long-term mental health management. Proc. ACM Hum. Comput. Interact. **2**(CSCW), 1–27 (2018)

38. Møller, N.H., Neff, G., Simonsen, J.G., Villumsen, J.C., Bjørn, P.: Can workplace tracking ever empower? collective sensemaking for the responsible use of sensor data at work. Proc. ACM Hum. Comp. Inter. **5**, 1–21 (2021). https://doi.org/10.1145/3463931

39. Ngoon, T.J., Patidar, P., Ogan, A., Harrison, C., Agarwal, Y.: Professional informatics: Personalized, data-driven professional development (2022)

40. Patel, H., Pettitt, M., Wilson, J.R.: Factors of collaborative working: a framework for a collaboration model. Appl. Ergon. **43**(1), 1–26 (2012). https://doi.org/10.1016/j.apergo.2011.04.009

41. Pina, L., Sien, S.W., Song, C., Ward, T.M., Fogarty, J., et al.: Dreamcatcher: exploring how parents and school-age children can track and review sleep information together. Proc. ACM Hum.-Comp. Inter. **4**, 1–25 (2020). https://doi.org/10.1145/3392882

42. Pina, L.R., et al.: From personal informatics to family informatics: Understanding family practices around health monitoring. In: Proceedings of the 2017 ACM Conference on Computer Supported Cooperative Work and Social Computing, pp. 2300–2315. ACM, Portland (2017). https://doi.org/10.1145/2998181.2998362

43. Raj, S., Lee, J.M., Garrity, A., Newman, M.W.: Clinical data in context: towards sensemaking tools for interpreting personal health data. Proc. ACM on Inter. Mob. Wear. Ubiq. Technol. **3**(1), 1–20 (2019)

44. Rivera-Pelayo, V., Fessl, A., Müller, L., Pammer, V.: Introducing mood self-tracking at work: empirical insights from call centers. ACM Trans. Comput. Hum. Interact. (TOCHI) **24**(1), 1–28 (2017)

45. Rooksby, J., Rost, M., Morrison, A., Chalmers, M.: Personal tracking as lived informatics. In: Proceedings of the SIGCHI Conference on Human Factors in Computing Systems, pp. 1163–1172. CHI 2014, ACM, New York (2014). https://doi.org/10.1145/2556288.2557039

46. Stamhuis, S., Brombacher, H., Vos, S., Lallemand, C.: Office agents: Personal office vitality sensors with intent. In: Extended Abstracts of the 2021 CHI Conference on Human Factors in Computing Systems, pp. 1–5. ACM, New York (2021). https://doi.org/10.1145/3411763.3451559

47. Tenenberg, J., Roth, W.M., Socha, D.: From i-awareness to we-awareness in CSCW **25**,(4–5) (2016)

48. Toebosch, R.: Improving collaboration experiences and skills: An open-ended, user-driven self-tracking approach for education. In: Proceedings of the Seventeenth International Conference on Tangible, Embedded, and Embodied Interaction, pp. 1–4. ACM, New York (2023). https://doi.org/10.1145/3569009.3576220

49. Wannamaker, K.A., Kollannur, S.Z.G., Dörk, M., Willett, W.: I/o bits: User-driven, situated, and dedicated self-tracking. In: Proc. 2021 ACM Design. Inter. Sys. Conf.: Nowhere and Everywhere, pp. 523–537. ACM, New York (2021). https://doi.org/10.1145/3461778.3462138

50. Xue, M., Liang, R.H., Hu, J., Yu, B., Feijs, L.: Understanding how group workers reflect on organizational stress with a shared, anonymous heart rate variability data visualization. In: 2022 CHI Conf. on Hum. Fact. in Comp. Sys. ACM, New York (2022). https://doi.org/10.1145/3491101.3503576

Perception Versus Reality: How User Self-reflections Compare to Actual Data

Hannah R. Nolasco[1]([⊠]) [iD], Andrew Vargo[2] [iD], Yusuke Komatsu[2] [iD],
Motoi Iwata[2] [iD], and Koichi Kise[2] [iD]

[1] Osaka Prefecture University, 599–8531 Sakai,Osaka, Japan
df104001@st.osakafu-u.ac.jp
[2] Osaka Metropolitan University, 599–8531 Sakai, Osaka, Japan
{awv,imotoi,kise}@omu.ac.jp, sb22947a@st.omu.ac.jp

Abstract. One of the main promises of wearable sensing devices capable of physiological tracking is the potential that users can leverage the technology to make positive life changes. Now that these devices have sufficient accuracy, it is feasible that users could make decisions based on feedback from the device to change their habits and improve their well-being. A potential challenge to this, however, is whether users are able to recognize actual changes in their behavior compared to perceived changes. In this work, we look at participants who used the Oura ring as part of an in-the-wild study. Based on data analysis following 10–12 months of usage, we find that users who had positive perceptions of habit change towards sleep failed to show long-term improvement in their sleep quality, indicating a gap between perceived success and real-world impact. This work is important to informing the future design and implementation of health-tracking wearables.

Keywords: Wearable devices · In-the-wild · Self-tracking · Self-reflection

1 Introduction

Extensive research has been conducted on wearable abandonment and the many challenges faced by users when attempting to integrate the technology into their daily lives. Some of the major concerns described by users have to do with the data that these devices collect: Users report being disinterested in the type of information that they receive [11] or they lose motivation or a sense of purpose in the act of self-tracking [2]. Many users also perceive inaccuracies in the data when comparing it to their actual feelings and experiences [2,15], while others find difficulties interpreting and contextualizing their visual data [8,15]. Despite efforts to encourage self-reflection or display visual data in ways that are easy to translate into action, many users struggle with maximizing the use of their data. One of the leading reasons users abandon their device is because they do not know what to do with the information it provides [4,5,9,11,12,15].

Wearable devices offer a detailed glimpse into one's personal data and can assist in meeting goals for self-improvement through quantification of the self.

J. Abdelnour Nocera et al. (Eds.): INTERACT 2023, LNCS 14144, pp. 665–674, 2023.
https://doi.org/10.1007/978-3-031-42286-7_37

However, simply obtaining this information is not enough to encourage changes in habits and behaviors-active and intentional self-reflection is necessary to gain useful insight on the self [3]. There have been many conversations on self-reflection in the realm of personal informatics [16] and studies exist comparing users' self-reflections and their actual data [3,6,10,14]. However, these studies were conducted in controlled environments and laboratory settings where users were prompted or guided to self-reflect. In this study, we examine participants from an in-the-wild setup and look at how these participants evaluate themselves when they are given no prompts or instructions on how to do so.

This study compares the self-reflections of a sample of 22 Japanese young adults and their actual data in an in-the-wild setting where they were not prompted to assess themselves nor explicitly told how to interact with their data. Participants were given a physiological sensing device to wear called the Oura ring, which they used over the course of a year. We found that declared positive changes in habits did not align with the data produced by the wearable. This is important because it indicates another potential problem for the consumers and producers of wearables: Users may be getting false positive results from their engagement with their device. This would indicate that work needs to be done to optimize these devices for users in the real world.

Fig. 1. The interface of Oura ring's mobile application.

1.1 The Oura Ring's Sleep Data

The Oura ring is a wearable device with research-grade sensors. It is primarily designed for tracking sleep. Everyday, the application reports a **Sleep Score** out of 100 that is calculated using the many sleep contributors that the device measures (i.e. total sleep, sleep efficiency, restfulness, percentage of rapid eye movement sleep, resting heart rate, etc.) (Fig. 1). This score gives the user an idea of how well they slept the previous evening. The application breaks the score down into suggestions on how the user can improve their sleep (e.g. by sleeping earlier, sleeping longer hours, or by matching their wake time to certain sleep stages). Several studies have confirmed the accuracy of the Oura ring's ability to detect sleep stages [1] and predict sleep quality [13]. Apart from the mobile application, a web-based dashboard is available for users to view their long-term sleep trends and examine their data more closely. Oura's applications are available in both English and Japanese, therefore no users had language issues when navigating the platform.

2   User Study

2.1   Experiment Background

This investigation into user behavior and wearables is part of a larger project which uses the Oura ring. 140 graduate and undergraduate university students volunteered to wear Oura rings as part of this setup. The participants do not receive remuneration for wearing the ring itself, but may receive remuneration for taking part in experiments. Participants experience the ring in an in-the-wild setting. There are no restrictions on their usage and no penalties for intermittent use or the cessation of use. This project and all related studies were approved by the institution's ethics committee.

2.2   Participants

In the summer of 2021, we recruited participants for a long-term in-the-wild study with the Oura ring. The participants were graduate and undergraduate university students from a graduate school of engineering at a large public Japanese university. Potential participants were given an Oura ring at no personal cost. 37 participants joined in the second half of 2021 and received either Generation 2 or Generation 3 Oura rings depending on when they joined. Oura switched from delivering the Generation 2 ring at the end of September 2021 and started delivering the Generation 3 ring in November 2021.

The project leaders gave all participants an orientation session where the features and capabilities of the device were explained, including details on how the mobile application, web cloud services, and API worked. The project leaders also shared research on the Oura Ring's use in early detection of COVID-19 cases [7]. Additionally, participants received information on what type of data was to be collected and how the data from the ring could be used to make health decisions by sharing case studies. Special care was also made to guarantee that users' privacy would be enforced.

In late 2022, 35 of the 37 participants were asked to reaffirm their participation in the project as well as answer a survey about their usage of the ring.

The two missing participants were unavailable due to having dropped the study after graduation. The participants were paid 3000 JPY (approximately 20 USD) for completing the survey and completing several tasks related to raw data collection. The survey took about 15 min to complete (the entire session took one hour) and asked a wide range of questions, including questions about habits and changes in lifestyle due to ring usage.

3   Analysis and Results

Table 1. Survey Responses of Users Who Declared Changes in Sleep Habits

ID	Reported Lifestyle Changes
001	I became more concerned about sleep duration and sleep quality.
002	I checked the amount of sleep I was getting, and when I felt I was not getting enough, I tried to sleep longer, etc.
003	I made a conscious effort to sleep in the beginning.
004	I've become more conscious of maintaining a consistent sleep schedule.
005	When I'm on, I try to improve the quality of my sleep by going to bed early and getting up early, etc.
006	I started to pay more attention to sleep. I go to bed earlier, don't touch electronic devices before bed, etc.
007	I tried to go to bed early.
008	I became more aware of the efficiency of sleep.
009	I began to decide when to go to bed for the day according to my condition. I also became more conscious of my condition in my life.
010	I have become more careful about the amount of exercise and the amount of sleep I get.
011	I started to pay more attention to my sleep schedule.
012	I started to pay attention to the amount of sleep I was getting.
013	I started going to bed earlier on days when I was tired or sleep deprived.
014	Being aware of sleep scores and other factors made it easier to manage my lifestyle. Better control of sleep onset time and sleep duration.
015	I started paying attention to my sleep score

The majority of participants had 1 year's worth of ring data, although some joined the experiment later and had been participating for a little less than a year. We decided to omit 6 users with less than 10 months (300 days) of data to keep our analysis consistent. Another 6 survey respondents were excluded as they did not have any data uploaded into the cloud, likely due to user error. 1 participant gave conflicting answers in their survey that could not be reliably interpreted, so they were dropped from the analysis. This left us with 22 participants out of the original 35.

Users were separated into two categories depending on their survey response to the question: "Have you noticed any changes or alterations in your daily life since using the Oura ring?" Out of the 22 respondents, 7 reported having no lifestyle changes as a result of wearing the ring or declared changes that did not concern sleep. The remaining 15 declared changes in their sleep habits; some users mentioned that they were more mindful to maintain a consistent early bedtime while others said that they made an effort to have a sufficient amount of sleep each night (Table 1).

For the purpose of this study, we focused only on the differences between users' perceived changes in their sleep habits and the reality reflected in their data. To do this, we calculated the rolling weekly average of each user's daily sleep score and plotted it to determine whether there were any visible improvements in their overall sleep quality. As aforementioned, Oura's daily sleep score is a metric used to estimate how restful the user's sleep was, which is calculated through the tracking of several sleep contributors.

3.1   Participants Who Declared Changes to Their Sleep Habits

The 15 participants who declared changes in their sleep habits had either flat or downward trends in sleep quality as shown in their rolling average sleep scores (Fig. 2). Only 3 participants appear to have an upward trend, although the improvement is small. Some of these users also have significant gaps in their plots in which it was clear the ring was not worn. This was confirmed by looking into their non-wear time trends and verifying that the gaps matched periods of complete non-adherence to wearing the ring. One of the users also dropped the experiment in the first half of 2022. Regardless of whether users report a change in their frame of mind or an alteration in their tangible habits, their actual data does not reflect much improvement and may even show a decline in sleep quality over time.

3.2   Participants Who Did Not Declare Changes to Their Sleep Habits

Out of the 7 users who did not declare lifestyle changes related to sleep habits, 4 declared that they did not notice any changes or alterations in their daily life at all once they started wearing the Oura ring. The 3 users who did experience changes separate from sleep primarily reported improved attitudes towards fitness. There is very little visual difference between these users in terms of their rolling average sleep score trends: These users either have flat or downward trendlines, similar to those who declared changes in their sleep habits (Fig. 3). Both categories of users also have similar non-wear trends.

Although there does not appear to be a visual difference in sleep score trends between the user group who declared improvements in their sleep habits (Group 1) and the user group who did not declare any sleep-related lifestyle changes (Group 2), we decided to run a mixed effects logistic regression model to determine if there were any trends masked by the rolling averages of their sleep scores. Given that there are more users under Group 1 than Group 2, we chose a mixed-effects model as it is better suited to handle unbalanced data. The model looks at each user's sleep duration each day over the course of their participation while

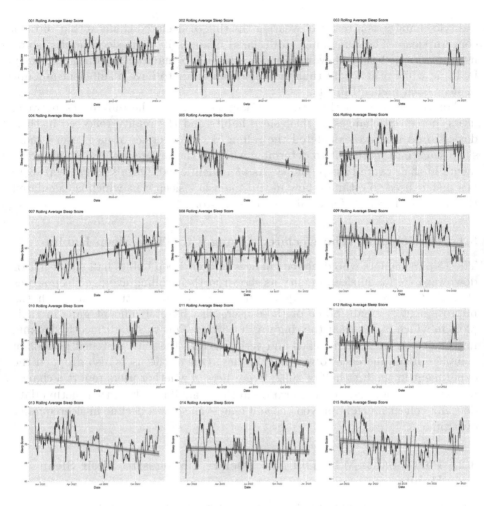

Fig. 2. Users who declared lifestyle changes related to sleep.

taking into consideration the day of the week and whether they declared changes in their sleeping habits. We wanted to determine whether the individual, the day of the week, or the duration of the person's sleep could predict which group they fell under.

Since users from Group 1 declared that they became more conscious of how much or how well they slept, we expected them to have a better amount of sleep versus the users from Group 2 who declared no changes in their lifestyle or in their sleep habits. We also expected the day of the week to influence the variation of people's sleep duration (presumably people sleep longer on the weekends). There was also a possibility that class (Group 1 vs. Group 2) and sleep duration were dependent on the individuals themselves. Thus, our mixed effects logistic regression model was fitted with total sleep duration as a continuous predictor,

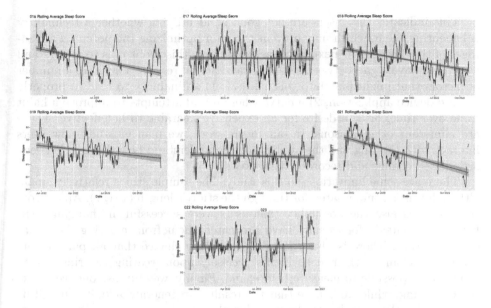

Fig. 3. Users who declared no lifestyle changes related to sleep.

weekday as a categorical predictor (Monday to Sunday), and a random intercept by user ID. The results showed that when it came to how much they slept on a regular basis, users who claimed that they had better sleep habits (Group 1) did not differ from users who claimed their sleep habits did not change (Group 2) (p-value = 0.953471). This could mean that users who declared changes in their sleep habits cannot accurately determine differences in their behavior and may only be experiencing a perception of improvement rather than actual change, or the changes that they did make are not impactful enough to reflect in their actual sleep data.

4 Discussion, Limitations, and Future Work

Many existing wearable devices and digital self-tracking tools provide the user with a blueprint of their quantified self but offer no additional insight on how they can properly utilize their data, leaving many users in the dark as to what they are meant to do next [4,5,9,11,12,15]. It would be desirable for designers and engineers of wearables if users who declare they are able to make improvements are actually able to make positive changes that are visible in data analysis. This would give validation to the applicability of their devices in the real world. In our year-long in-the-wild study, we do not see any differences between users who strongly declare positive sleep changes and those who do not. In fact, we see that many users who report positive sleep changes actually have data that suggests the opposite.

This indicates that users are not good at identifying whether a technology is benefiting them, which may prevent them for optimizing the potential advantages of the device. The next step towards solving this problem is to understand why users have a gap between self-belief and actual results. There are a number of factors that might play into this, such as: 1) an inability to read or properly use the device application, 2) a curve where initial attempts to improve a habit wane over time, or 3) a desire for an expensive wearable to be effective. There are numerous other reasons. In our future work, we plan to study how users interact with the ring and the applications to understand how this gap between articulated change and recorded data exists.

There are some limitations to this study. The sample size is relatively small, although this is compensated for through the study's length (1 year). Apart from this, there is also the possibility that users were successful in changing their habits but outside forces may have prevented them from creating data that exhibited that. There is also a small but unlikely chance that all participants drastically changed their sleep habits precisely upon wearing the ring, which would be impossible to measure beforehand. Finally, we only use one wearable, the Oura ring; while we believe that the results are generalizable, it can still be possible that they are due to the wearable alone.

5   Conclusion

In this work, we analyzed participants from a year-long in-the-wild study by looking at whether they declared positive changes to their sleep habits and whether this was visible in their sleep data collected by the Oura ring. We found that there was no positive correlation between improved sleep data and the declaration of the participant. This indicates that there is an inability for users of wearables to accurately assess the success of a habit change caused by the use of a device.

Acknowledgements. This work was supported in part by grants from JST Trilateral AI project, Learning Cyclotron (JPMJCR20G3), JSPS Kakenhi (20KK0235), and the Grand challenge of the Initiative for Life Design Innovation (iLDi).

References

1. Altini, M., Kinnunen, H.: The Promise of sleep: a multi-sensor approach for accurate sleep stage detection using the OURA ring. Sensors **21**(13), 4302 (2021). https://doi.org/10.3390/s21134302. number: 13 Publisher: Multidisciplinary Digital Publishing Institute
2. Attig, C., Franke, T.: Abandonment of personal quantification: a review and empirical study investigating reasons for wearable activity tracking attrition. Comput. Hum. Beh. **102**, 223–237 (2020). https://doi.org/10.1016/j.chb.2019.08.025

3. Choe, E.K., Lee, B., Zhu, H., Riche, N.H., Baur, D.: Understanding self-reflection: how people reflect on personal data through visual data exploration. In: Proceedings of the 11th EAI International Conference on Pervasive Computing Technologies for Healthcare, Barcelona Spain, May, pp. 173–182. ACM (2017). https://doi.org/10.1145/3154862.3154881

4. Choe, E.K., Lee, N.B., Lee, B., Pratt, W., Kientz, J.A.: Understanding quantified-selfers' practices in collecting and exploring personal data. In: Proceedings of the SIGCHI Conference on Human Factors in Computing Systems, Toronto Ontario Canada, April, pp. 1143–1152. ACM (2014). https://doi.org/10.1145/2556288.2557372

5. Epstein, D.A., Ping, A., Fogarty, J., Munson, S.A.: A lived informatics model of personal informatics. In: Proceedings of the 2015 ACM International Joint Conference on Pervasive and Ubiquitous Computing - UbiComp 2015, Osaka, Japan, pp. 731–742. ACM Press (2015). https://doi.org/10.1145/2750858.2804250

6. Garcia, J.J., de Bruyckere, H., Keyson, D.V., Romero, N.: Designing personal informatics for self-reflection and self-awareness: the case of children with attention deficit hyperactivity disorder. In: Augusto, J.C., Wichert, R., Collier, R., Keyson, D., Salah, A.A., Tan, A.-H. (eds.) AmI 2013. LNCS, vol. 8309, pp. 109–123. Springer, Cham (2013). https://doi.org/10.1007/978-3-319-03647-2_8

7. Gilmore, J.N.: Predicting Covid-19: wearable technology and the politics of solutionism. Cult. Stud. **35**(2–3), 382–391 (2021). https://doi.org/10.1080/09502386.2021.1898021

8. Grammel, L., Tory, M., Storey, M.: How information visualization novices construct visualizations. IEEE Trans. Visual Comput. Graphics **16**(6), 943–952 (2010). https://doi.org/10.1109/TVCG.2010.164

9. Huang, D., et al.: Personal visualization and personal visual analytics. IEEE Trans. Visual Comput. Graphics **21**(3), 420–433 (2015). https://doi.org/10.1109/TVCG.2014.2359887

10. Kefalidou, G., et al.: Enhancing self-reflection with wearable sensors. In: Proceedings of the 16th International Conference on Human-Computer Interaction with Mobile Devices & Services, Toronto ON Canada, September 2014, pp. 577–580. ACM (2014). https://doi.org/10.1145/2628363.2634257

11. Lazar, A., Koehler, C., Tanenbaum, J., Nguyen, D.H.: Why we use and abandon smart devices. In: Proceedings of the 2015 ACM International Joint Conference on Pervasive and Ubiquitous Computing - UbiComp 2015, Osaka, Japan, pp. 635–646. ACM Press (2015). https://doi.org/10.1145/2750858.2804288

12. Li, I., Dey, A., Forlizzi, J.: A stage-based model of personal informatics systems. In: Proceedings of the SIGCHI Conference on Human Factors in Computing Systems, Atlanta Georgia USA, April, pp. 557–566. ACM (2010). https://doi.org/10.1145/1753326.1753409

13. Malakhatka, E., Al Rahis, A., Osman, O., Lundqvist, P.: Monitoring and predicting occupant's sleep quality by using wearable device OURA Ring and smart building sensors data (living laboratory case study). Buildings **11**(10), 459 (2021). https://doi.org/10.3390/buildings11100459. number: 10 Publisher: Multidisciplinary Digital Publishing Institute

14. Marcengo, A., Rapp, A., Cena, F., Geymonat, M.: The falsified self: complexities in personal data collection. In: Antona, M., Stephanidis, C. (eds.) UAHCI 2016. LNCS, vol. 9737, pp. 351–358. Springer, Cham (2016). https://doi.org/10.1007/978-3-319-40250-5_34

15. Rooksby, J., Rost, M., Morrison, A., Chalmers, M.: Personal tracking as lived informatics. In: Proceedings of the SIGCHI Conference on Human Factors in Computing Systems, Toronto Ontario Canada, April 2014, pp. 1163–1172. ACM (2014). https://doi.org/10.1145/2556288.2557039
16. Sas, C., Dix, A.: Designing for reflection on experience. In: CHI 2009 Extended Abstracts on Human Factors in Computing Systems, Boston MA USA, April 2009, pp. 4741–4744. ACM (2009). https://doi.org/10.1145/1520340.1520730

Correction to: A Longitudinal Analysis of Real-World Self-report Data

Niels van Berkel, Sujay Shalawadi, Madeleine R. Evans, Aku Visuri,
and Simo Hosio

Correction to:
Chapter 34 in: J. Abdelnour Nocera et al. (Eds.):
Human-Computer Interaction – INTERACT 2023,
LNCS 14144, https://doi.org/10.1007/978-3-031-42286-7_34

In the originally published version of chapter 34, the label *'Anonymised Company'* was used during peer review and needs to be updated to 'Levell' in the published version. This has been corrected and a footnote has been updated.

The updated version of this chapter can be found at
https://doi.org/10.1007/978-3-031-42286-7_34

Author Index

Printed in the United States
by Baker & Taylor Publisher Services